THE MOJO COLLECTION

THE MOJO COLLECTION

The Ultimate Music Companion

Edited by Jim Irvin

First published in the UK in 2000 by MOJO Books, an imprint of Canongate Books
Ltd, 14 High Street, Edinburgh EH1 1TE

10 9 8 7 6 5 4 3 2 1

British Library Cataloguing-in-Publication Data
A catalogue record for this book is available upon request from the British Library.

ISBN 1 84195 067 X

Typeset in Perpetua and Gill Sans Condensed by
Palimpsest Book Production Limited,
Polmont, Stirlingshire

Printed and bound by Omnia Books Limited, Glasgow

Contents

We'd Love To Turn You On

An introduction to The MOJO Collection

To paraphrase Edwin Starr, "Music writing! Huh, good god! What is it good for?" If you can't resist a retort of "Absolutely *nuthin'*!" then perhaps you've come to the wrong book. But the regular MOJO reader, we trust, will have responded, "Actually, the best stuff makes me want to play music very loud." Which can make you feel very good. Therefore, words about music can actually improve your life. And there are now more than 600,000 of them in your hand.

We like to conduct MOJO each month like a giant "All back to ours" affair where, in various rooms, you can discover new music, old music, hot hits and cool cuts, with plenty of, "Heard this?" "Check out this bit . . .!" and "Did you ever hear this story about . . .?" going on. And it's that spirit we've aimed for in this book, a celebration of the finest examples of a great 20th century art form.

Like all collections, you'll find records here that you love, records you never play, records you've never heard, records that are widely held to be the finest of their kind and unfashionable records you take a guilty pleasure in. We realise we couldn't include every decent record ever released, but we hope to have represented every taste to some degree.

We've interpreted "popular music" in its broadest possible sense. You'll find albums in many genres – folk, funk, jazz, punk and so on – from the 1940s to the end of the 20th century, zillion-selling world-beaters to utterly obscure curiosities, hundreds of them written about in detail and many others recommended. However, it is an unashamedly biased selection, representing the collective enthusiasms of MOJO's contributors, undoubtedly favouring certain artists and strands of music over others, but our regular readers would expect nothing less. There's a lot of John Lennon and no Puff Daddy, but that's our thing. Over 65 writers have contributed, selecting records they love and finding out how they were done. Many entries include fresh interviews conducted especially for this book, others use material extracted from MOJO's extensive archives.

We have been rigid about one criterion. All these records were conceived as albums. We've insisted on work that made the most of the form – 40 minutes of music and 12 inches of card or, latterly, the more luxurious length but smaller canvas of the CD. In other words, we're celebrating the best use of the album format's wide possibilities rather than the tight pop nugget or the LP compiled from diverse sources. So you won't find any *Sun Sessions* or *Basement Tapes* as neither were originally intended to be albums, nor any Greatest Hits collections, however popular. We have not rated the albums or ranked them, instead they are presented chronologically so you can see how the album has developed as both an art form and a mirror of music history.

This may seem unfair to exponents of pure pop – the Motown clan, for example – artists whose ambitions or careers stretched no further than a few singles, or performers in genres like doo-wop or reggae which have centred themselves around single sides. Therefore, so no-one feels left out, we've gathered some of the best of this disqualified material in appendices at the back of the book covering easy listening and oddities, reggae and its nearest relatives, film soundtrack music and those compilations which scoop up significant developments in US and UK pop down the decades which may not have been best expressed on album, among them garage, country, punk and disco. Naturally, there are a few classic albums in each of these categories and they have been included in the main body of the book.

Doubtless we've left out some of your favourite records – we've certainly had to leave out some of ours, in some cases because they were further works by artists who were already represented (we've not included every Beatles, Dylan or Stones album, for example, just the very best) and we felt it fairer to make room for someone new. We hope to include all such albums, and many more, in future expanded editions, so, if you have any suggestions, corrections or additions please send them to us at the addresses below.

It has been an incredibly daunting task putting this book together and not – as you can probably imagine – one without fierce debate and disagreement, but it has also been tremendous fun and everyone involved in the editing process has rushed out and fallen in love with new music as a result. We hope you will too.

Jim Irvin
MOJO Magazine, August 2000

For suggestions and amendments, write to The MOJO Collection, c/o Canongate Books, 14 High Street, Edinburgh EH1 1TE, or look to the website http://www.canongate.net

What have we here?

The albums are arranged chronologically by release date. At the rear of the book are indexes by artist and album title. This is a celebration of a 20th century art-form – the pop album. We've selected hundreds of them from the very first vinyl pop album in 1946 to the biggest sellers of 1999 – and found out how they happened.

As well as the main text for each album, every entry of The MOJO Collection comprises the following information where available:

Artist

The album title
If an album is known by more than one name we've used that of the original issue.

Label
The label the album originally appeared on in the UK.

Producer

Recording information
Location and date recorded, if known.

Release date
Date first issued in the UK.

Chart peaks
Highest album chart placing in the UK and US.

Personnel
The key players and technicians. Abbreviations as follows:

ae = assistant engineer
ag = acoustic guitar
ar = arranger
b   = bass
bs = baritone sax
bv = backing vocals
c   = cello
d   = drums
db = double bass
e   = engineer
ep = electric piano
g   = guitar
hm = harmonica
k   = keyboards
m   = mixer
o   = organ
p   = piano
pc = percussion

ps = pedal steel guitar
rg = rhythm guitar
s   = saxophone
sg = steel guitar
syn = synthesiser
t   = trumpet
tb = trombone
ts = tenor sax
v   = vocals
va = viola
vn = violin

More esoteric instruments – zither, vibraphone, alpine horn etc. – are listed in full. When an album mentions particular keyboards – Hammond organ, Wurlitzer electric piano, VCS3 synth etc – these have also been included.

Track listing
Running order of the original UK release. Tracks issued as singles are marked (S).

Running time
Total time of the original album.

Current CD
The catalogue number of the most recent CD edition of the album. If no label is shown the original label applies. If the album has been reissued on a different label, that's here, plus the details of any bonus tracks, omissions or alterations.

Further listening
Other albums by the same artist that best complement this one, interesting solo albums or side-projects and, occasionally, albums by other artists that clearly influenced this record or were influenced by it.

Further reading
If there's a MOJO feature on the artist in question we've put the issue number here followed by the best biographies (whether or not they are still in print) and/or the most informative websites.

THE
Beginning

Frank Sinatra
The Voice of Frank Sinatra

The Voice Of The Century pioneers the vinyl pop LP.

In 1946 you could buy these eight songs on four heavy, perishable, 10-inch, shellac 78rpm discs packaged together in a binder to resemble a book. It was a format known in the trade as an album.

It sold like crazy, for this was the period when "Swoonatra" was cresting his huge first wave of popularity. At the beginning of the decade, the skinny "kid" from Hoboken, New Jersey had made a phenomenal impact upon leaving the Tommy Dorsey Orchestra to go solo. A well-orchestrated publicity campaign attracted pop's first posse of screaming school-age girls. By the time of these recordings he'd crossed into the affections of adults too and made inroads into a creditable film career with the hit movie Anchors Aweigh. Not surprisingly, when Columbia began releasing 10-inch microgroove long-playing records in early 1949, this was the first pop item to appear in the new format. The collection found Francis Albert Sinatra – aged 30 when these songs were sung – in a romantic mode, interpreting eight standards with the aid of his long-term arranger and conductor, Axel Stordahl, a string quartet, a rhythm section and the oboe of Mitch Miller. They were songs that Sinatra loved, in simple settings – like chamber music – that allowed the singer's innate tenderness with a lyric to shine (a ploy that Frank would revisit over the years, in particular on the 1956 *Close To You* sessions with The Hollywood String Quartet). It added up to what is, in effect, the first concept album by a pop performer, a collection of songs about a helpless heart. No matter if a lyric suggested that a girl cared for him, Frank remained the little boy lost, requiring someone to watch over him, not standing a ghost of a chance with the one he cared for most, and reflecting, by means of a few foolish things, on a past attachment gone wrong, the perpetual victim of unrequited love.

Sinatra would record most of these songs again in the '50s, when he made his reputation as 'Voice Of The Century' and when his instrument had the timbre of a wise cello, a little more worldly, but no less susceptible to hopeless affairs of the heart. But here, still a creamy viola, he delivered performances that were simply the state of the post-Crosby pop singing art; passionate but gentle, sexy but vulnerable. Little wonder that an

Record label:
Columbia

Produced
by Manny Sachs.

Recorded
in New York City; July 30 and December 7, 1945.

Released:
March 1946

Chart peaks:
None (UK) 1 (US)

Personnel:
Frank Sinatra (v) Axel Stordahl and his Orchestra

Track listing:
You Go To My Head; Someone To Watch Over Me; I Don't Know Why; These Foolish Things; Try A Little Tenderness; Ghost Of A Chance; Paradise; Why Shouldn't I

Running time:
22.35

Current CD:
CK 52868

Further listening:
Sing And Dance With Frank Sinatra (1950), the first album that Frank, with arranger George Siravo and producer Mitch Miller, shaped with a microgroove LP in mind. After that, take your pick from the wealth of mainly superb releases through Capitol and Reprise.

Further reading:
Sinatra – The Song Is You (Will Friedwald 1995) is the most detailed book on Sinatra's recording career; his daughter's Sinatra – An American Legend, (Nancy Sinatra, 1995) the most lavishly illustrated.

entire generation of adoring females experienced the simultaneous – and no doubt conflicting – arousal of their carnal and mothering instincts.

Housed in a fragile, plain, pink paper sleeve (now impossibly rare in good condition), *The Voice Of Frank Sinatra* subsequently appeared in a sturdier blue cardboard – again without any decoration – and a slightly later version picturing Frank in one of the floppy bow ties that his wife, Nancy, supposedly made for him. (The current CD edition comes packaged in a version of one of the early sleeves and contains an additional 17 tracks from the same period.) It was a modest start for a great 20th century artform, but fitting it should be by the only artist of the period who would still be hitting the charts – with *Duets II* – half a century later.

Peggy Lee
Black Coffee

Please welcome the fabulous Norma Deloris Egstrom!

Undoubtedly among the finest female singers to grace the world of popular music, Peggy Lee was vocally equipped to sing blues, jazz, Broadway standards or even cornball material, though she generally steered clear of the latter. She was also an accomplished songwriter; she fashioned the soundtrack for The Lady And The Tramp and picked up an Oscar nomination for her acting ability. All this and beauty too.

It was a long road to her debut album. Born Norma Jean Egstrom, she began as a teenage singer in 1936 with the Jack Wardlow Band, then joined Will Osborne (1940–41) before becoming part of vocal group The Four Of Us. Heard by King of Swing Benny Goodman, she became vocalist with his highly rated outfit, cutting her first records within days of taking the job and notching her first hit that same year with a cover of Duke Ellington's I Got It Bad And That Ain't Good. After several other hits with the Goodman outfit, she married the band's guitarist, Dave Barbour, whose own band featured on many of her initial solo recordings. Signed first to Capitol and then to Decca, Peg notched over 30 hit singles of varying quality (one was titled Bum, Bum, I Wonder Who I Am) between 1945 and 1953, when the opportunity arose to cut her first long-player.

It was released in ten-inch form with a mere eight tracks (four other songs, recorded at a Los Angeles session in April, 1956 were added when the record eventually appeared as a 12-inch). But with those original eight tracks the singer born Norma Deloris Egstrom established herself in the very top echelon, alongside Billie Holiday and Ella Fitzgerald. Though there was no outlet for her R&B talents, later manifest on such singles as The Comeback, *Black Coffee* allowed Peg the opportunity to swing effortlessly and phrase with dangerous abandon on such songs as I've Got You Under My Skin, faultlessly conjure a four-in-the-morning mood on the torchy title track, or interpret Johnny Mercer's superb lyric to When The World Was Young in such a manner that, to date, no one has yet managed to extract so much emotion from or bestow with such fragility.

Record label:
Decca

Producer:
unknown.

Recorded
in New York City; April 30, May 1 and 4, 1953.

Released:
1953

Chart peaks:
None (UK) None (US)

Personnel:
Peggy Lee (v); Pete Condoli (t); Jimmy Rowles (p); Wayne Bennett (b); Ed Shaughnessy (d)

Track listing:
Black Coffee; I've Got You Under My Skin; Easy Living; My Heart Belongs To Daddy (S); A Woman Alone With The Blues; I Didn't Know What Time It Was; When The World Was Young; Love Me Or Leave Me

Running time:
20.35

Current CD
MCLD 19363 adds: Sea Shells

Further listening:
The Man I Love, 1957 a bundle of string-laden ballads, recorded with an orchestra conducted by Frank Sinatra and containing a superlative The Folks That Live On The Hill.

Further reading:
Miss Peggy Lee (1990) an autobiography that fills many gaps without being entirely satisfactory; www.geocities.com/~peggyfan/home.html

Julie London
Julie Is Her Name

Intimate and sensual torch song motherlode.

"The girl with the come-hither voice," said Bill Balance in his sleevenotes – never mind that she was a married woman with two children. Her voice, a husky instrument that lingered on syllables like honey oozing off a spoon, was the sexiest entreaty American music could offer in 1955. Elvis may have been knocking on the door, but the torch singers of the '50s – Holiday, Lee, Vaughan, Fitzgerald – still held American men spellbound, and the statuesque Miss London – already with a modest movie career behind her – came to represent the genre.

She had already done plenty of work as a nightclub singer, encouraged by her pianist husband Bobby Troup, but Liberty was the only label interested in taking a chance on recording her. Troup insisted that she be recorded in the same setting as her live act – no orchestra, not even a piano, and just the bare strings of guitar and acoustic bass in support. Every song a ballad and nothing uptempo. Kessel (who also played on some of The Coasters' records from the same period) offers trim accompaniments that introduce just a lick of jazz, but nothing to disturb the besotted listener. The mood had to be 'round midnight', and even though there are 13 songs on the record, it barely exceeds half an hour in length. Troup's instincts were right. Released as a single, Cry Me A River was a major hit, and suddenly everyone *knew* that her name was Julie. The other songs are similarly lonesome, but here and there Julie flirts with a sort of blues feel, particularly on Easy Street. There is a little vibrato at the end of each line, just enough to make a strong man's legs go weak, and when she disappears with Gone With The Wind, it's as if someone has opened a window and she has just drifted off, a copper-haired phantom. Julie made many more albums for Liberty, and many of them were gorgeous, but this one still says it all.

Record label:
Liberty

Produced
by Bobby Troup.

Recorded:
1955.

Released:
December 1955

Chart peaks:
None (UK) 2 (US)

Personnel:
Julie London (v); Barney Kessel (g); Ray Leatherwood (b)

Track Listing:
Cry Me A River; I Should Care; I'm In The Mood For Love; I'm Glad There Is You; Can't Help Lovin' That Man; I Love You; Say It Isn't So; It Never Entered My Mind; Easy Street; 'S Wonderful; No Moon At All; Laura; Gone With The Wind

Running time:
31.11

Current CD:
VCS010

Further listening:
Julie Is Her Name Vol 2 (1956)

Further reading:
www.geocities.com/SunsetStrip/Lounge/8655/indexx.htm

The Four Freshmen

Four Freshmen And Five Trombones

Best album by vocal group that influenced The Beach Boys.

A four-piece vocal (and instrumental) group whose innovative harmonies completely changed the way such outfits sounded. Without them, there'd most likely have been no Beach Boys, no Jan And Dean. It could be argued that The Hi-Los were an even more inventive vocal group than the Freshmen, technically superior and, thanks to Clark Burrough's stratospheric flights of fancy, totally astounding to all raised on the traditional big-band harmony group sounds produced by artists like The Pied Pipers (with Tommy Dorsey) or Glenn Miller's Modernaires. But the Freshmen were warmer, somehow more human, able to reach a commercial market (something The Hi-Los were unable to do) without relinquishing their intricate way of things.

Voted Best Jazz Vocal Group of 1953, having earlier been dropped (and then reinstated) by Capitol – who initially failed to see the quartet's potential – they released their debut album, *Voices In Modern* the following year. But it was with *Four Freshmen And Five Trombones* that the breakthrough came. The format was hardly earth-shattering – just harmony interpretations of standards by such songwriters as Kern and Weill and lyricists who included Johnny Mercer, Ogden Nash and Oscar Hammerstein II, performed against a backdrop supplied by a team of Hollywood's top trombonists plus an equally stellar rhythm section. But the songs were sometimes delivered in surprising tempi, the traditionally romantic You Stepped Out Of A Dream virtually bursting out of its groove, Weill's Speak Low acquiring a Latin patina. And somehow, the album appealed to both those who tuned into the progressive jazz sounds of Stan Kenton and Woody Herman, and the family man who'd just cottoned onto hi-fi and wanted something spectacular but easy-on-the-ear.

When Brian Wilson heard the Freshmen, he became obsessed by their harmonies and contemporary arrangements. Claimed brother Carl: "Months at a time, days on end, he'd listen to Four Freshmen records." Later, the Beach Boys would even turn in an exact copy of the Freshmen's Graduation Day. No-one disputes that *Pet Sounds* started here.

Record label:
Capitol

Produced
by Dave Cavanagh and Pete Rugolo.

Recorded
at Capitol Studios, Hollywood; 1955.

Released:
February 1956

Chart peaks:
6 (UK) 6 (US)

Personnel:
Ross Barbour, Bob Flanigan, Ken Errair, Don Barbour (v); Frank Rosolino, Harry Betts Jr, Milt Bernhardt, Tommy Pederson, George Roberts (tb); Claude Williamson (p); Barney Kessel (g); Shelly Manne (d); Joe Mondragon (b)

Track listing:
Angel Eyes; Love Is Just Around The Corner; Mamselle; Speak Low; The Last Time I Saw Paris; Somebody Loves Me; You Stepped Out Of A Dream; I Remember You; Love; Love Is Here To Stay; You Made Me Love You; Guilty

Running time:
31.62

Current CD:
CCM0172 adds Four Freshmen And Five Trumpets

Further listening:
Tune in to The Hi-Io's Cherries And Other Delights (1994), a compilation of their radio appearances, to hear another exceptional array of harmonies and a sound that still resonates throughout contemporary vocal groups as Take 6.

Further reading:
American Singing Groups (Jay Warner, 1992)

Ella Fitzgerald
Sings The Cole Porter Songbook

Great American voice meets great American composer.

By 1955, Norman Granz, founder of Verve Records, had been trying to acquire Ella Fitzgerald as a recording artist for six years, though she'd been a valuable member of his touring jam-session-for-concertgoers – Jazz At The Philharmonic – since 1949. Her tenure at Decca under the canny A&R aegis of Milt Gabler had seen her juggle successful jukebox pop (My Happiness selling 500,000) with artistic successes (the 1950 and 1954 sessions with pianist Ellis Larkins) and a critical reputation that labelled her the First Lady Of Song (she also topped the Metronome and Downbeat polls for years). But Granz had sustained a campaign of public criticism about some of the fluff she was asked to record. "He used to have pieces in Downbeat saying how I was destroying her, giving her bad material," remembered Gabler.

By 1953 Granz was Ella's personal manager and announced a substantial Cole Porter songbook project for her. Recorded quickly with over thirty sides being cut in three sessions, there were "hardly any second takes," remembers pianist Paul Smith, "they were just sort of *ground* out." Clearly Granz was desperate for Ella to be associated with Porter's urbane blend of gently cynical romance (It's All Right With Me, Just One Of Those Things), sexy comedy (Too Darn Hot, Anything Goes) and elegant, witty sentiment (Ev'ry Time We Say Goodbye, From This Moment On). Ella's cool, clear delivery suited the material beautifully, although her personality was hardly the sort to overstate Porter's arch sophistication ("She is a simple person," judged massive fan and fellow jazz singer Mel Torme, "her approach to life is simple"), and the songs arrive in deceptively easy-going tones making for a subtle, rewarding listen.

The following few years saw Ella record songbooks of Rodgers And Hart, Duke Ellington and Irving Berlin, a five-album set of George Gershwin and sets of Kern and Mercer. Though some bemoaned the lack of jazz content in the series – and there remains critical dispute as to which songbook is the most artistically successful – *Cole Porter* was the most popular. "I don't actually like the man," said Mel Torme, "but I give Norman Granz great credit for saying to Ella, 'You are far more than a cult singer, you should be a national treasure,' and that's what he did for her."

Record Label:
Verve

Produced
by Norman Granz.

Recorded
in LA; February–March 1956.

Released:
Spring 1956

Chart peaks:
None (UK) 15 (US)

Personnel:
Ella Fitzgerald (v) with Buddy Bregman's Orchestra

Track Listing:
All Through The Night; Anything Goes; Miss Otis Regrets; Too Darn Hot; In The Still Of The Night; I Get A Kick Out Of You; Do I Love You; Always True To You Darling In My Fashion; Let's Do It; Just One Of Those Things; Ev'ry Time We Say Goodbye; Begin The Beguine; Get Out Of Town; I Am In Love; From This Moment On; I Love Paris; You Do Something To Me; Ridin' High; Easy To Love; It's All Right With Me; Why Can't You Behave; What Is This Thing Called Love; You're The Top; Love For Sale; It's Delovely; Night And Day; Ace In The Hole; So In Love; I've Got You Under My Skin; I Concentrate On You; Don't Fence Me In

Running time:
118.27

Current CD:
5372572

Further listening:
The following Songbooks are also indispensable: Sings The Rodgers And Hart Songbook (1956); Duke Ellington Songbook (1957); Irving Berlin Songbook (1958); Gershwin Songbook (1959)

Further reading:
Ella Fitzgerald (Stuart Nicholson, 1993)

Frank Sinatra

Songs For Swingin' Lovers

Sinatra's sophisticated cool peaks at the dawn of rock'n'roll.

When Capitol vice-president Alan Livingstone announced to their annual convention that he'd signed the down-and-out Sinatra (who had debt, depression and no career prospects), there was an audible groan. Livingstone: "My answer to them was, Look, I only know talent, and Frank is the best singer in the world." Though humble and grateful, Frank was having a hard time relinquishing his partnership with his '40s arranger Axel Stordahl. Livingstone was determined to put him together with burgeoning talent Nelson Riddle: "Nelson knew how to back up singers and make them sound great." Getting to know each other over a few sides, Sinatra was impressed with Riddle's 1953 treatment of World On A String, but upon hearing his polytonal ballad arranging told pianist Bill Miller, "Whew, we gotta be careful with him." Miller replied, "Hey, Frank, it's different, it's working."

By mid-'55 Sinatra was back on top (thanks to the movie *From Here To Eternity* and a series of confident albums) and Nelson was forging his distinctive heartbeat tempo, swing-band-plus-strings style that fitted the new Sinatra like a made-to-measure tux. Re-casting the repertoire of a previous generation in exhilarating new light and creating new standard songs in the process, *Songs For Swingin' Lovers* was the epitome of the rejuvenated, finger-poppin' Sinatra. Full of lyrical playfulness ("Stars fractured 'bama last night") and exuberant re-phrasing (his second chorus of It Happened In Monterey), this music had a vitality and sexiness that made women want to bed him and men want to be him, nowhere more so than in the legend that is the Riddle/Sinatra take on Cole Porter's I've Got You Under My Skin. A brooding, sensuous groove that builds into an explosive, sputtering trombone solo (played by Milt Bernhart over the wrong chords, balancing on a box to get closer to the mike) and pushes on with a hearty ardour before the detumescent coda, it's one of the most thrilling three and a half minutes in popular music.

While Riddle recognised it as a "cornerstone recording for both him and me", Neal Hefti, the great Basie arranger said "no one has come close to what Nelson achieved with Sinatra. . . God! That enthusiasm just keeps going on and on and on!"

Record Label:
Capitol

Produced
by Voyle Gilmore.

Recorded
at Capitol Studios, Hollywood; June 1955–January 1956.

Released:
June, 1956

Chart peak:
8 (UK) 2 (US)

Personnel:
Frank Sinatra (v); Nelson Riddle (a, oa); orchestra including Milt Bernhart (tb); Harry Edison, Conrad Gozzo (t); Harry Klee (flute); Mahlon Clark (clarinet)

Track Listing:
You Make Me Feel So Young; It Happened In Monterey; You're Getting To Be A Habit With Me; You Brought A New Kind Of Love To Me; Too Marvellous For Words; Old Devil Moon; Pennies From Heaven; Love Is Here To Stay; I've Got You Under My Skin; I Thought About You; We'll Be Together Again; Makin' Whoopee; Swingin' Down The Lane; Anything Goes; How About You?

Running time:
44.51

Current CD:
CDP-746570-2

Further listening:
Swing Easy (1954); A Swingin' Affair (1957)

Further reading:
Sinatra! The Song Is You: A Singer's Art (Will Friedwald, 1995)

Johnny Burnette And The Rock'n'Roll Trio

Johnny Burnette And The Rock'n'Roll Trio

Neglected classic from the birth of rock'n'roll.

Brothers Johnny and Dorsey Burnette and guitarist Paul Burlison had been cutting up the Memphis area for a good five years before they entered Owen Bradley's famed Nashville studio in July 1956. A few months previously, former schoolmate and work colleague Elvis Presley had hit Number 1 in both the album and singles charts. The Trio were choking on his exhaust. Over the next few days, however, they laid down a series of tracks that hold their own with a lot of The King's best.

The Trio had signed to Coral on the strength of a string of wins on The Ted Mack Amateur Show in New York. "One of the reasons we signed with Coral instead of Capitol," Burlison remembers, "was that they gave us a free hand on the material we wanted to record." Burlison brought a Tiny Bradshaw track, Train Kept A-Rollin', to the band's attention; but more importantly he told Bradley about an accident he'd recently had with his Fender Deluxe amplifier. "I dropped it between the band-room and stage one evening. That night I got this weird, fuzzed-up sound from it. After the gig I took the back off and found I'd knocked a tube loose." Bradley was wise enough to employ this primitive, ear-grabbing tone on both Train Kept A-Rollin' and Honey Hush, while Johnny B. let rip over the top with a backwoods, rockabilly shout that made Presley sound positively tame.

"I played a 1952 Esquire with a treble sound that could kill crab-grass," recalls Burlison, "but I listened to and played everything. In fact, Latin music is one of my favourites." And there, on the self-penned Lonesome Tears In My Eyes you hear his Hispanic stylings, while Johnny exercises the melodic control that would later serve him as a teen idol – garnering hits with Dreamin' and You're Sixteen. Unfortunately, fraternal rows and a lack of will on the record label's part meant that this 10-incher never got off the ground, and the group would founder only a year later. Nevertheless, Burlison is still revered as a sonic pioneer by players as important as Clapton, Mick Green and Jeff Beck; and many of the riotous numbers included here (Lonesome Train, All By Myself) are staples to this day for any self-respecting roots rock'n'rollers.

Record label:
Coral

Produced
by Owen Bradley.

Recorded
at Quonset Studio, 16th Avenue South, Nashville; July 2–5, 1956.

Released:
Autumn 1956

Chart peaks:
None (UK) None (US)

Personnel:
Johnny Burnette (v, g); Paul Burlison (g); Dorsey Burnette (b); Buddy Harman Jr (d); Owen Bradley (p); Anita Kerr Singers (bv)

Track listing:
Honey Hush; Lonesome Train (On A Lonesome Track) (S); Sweet Love On My Mind; Rock Billy Boogie; Lonesome Tears In My Eyes; All By Myself; The Train Kept A-Rollin' (S); Just Found Out; Your Baby Blue Eyes; Chains Of Love; I Love You So; Drinking Wine Spo-Dee-O-Dee, Drinking Wine

Running time:
26.27

Current CD:
BGO CD177 adds: Tear It Up; You're Undecided; Oh Baby Babe; Eager Beaver Baby; Touch Me; Midnight Train; If You Want It Enough; Blues Stay Away From Me; Shattered Dreams; My Love, You're a Stranger; Rock Therapy; Please Don't Leave Me

Further listening:
Burlison recently released an excellent album called, unsurprisingly, Train Kept A-Rollin' (1997) on which he is accompanied by members of The Band and Los Lobos among others.

Further reading:
www.angelfire.com/nj2/burnet/burnet2.html

Miles Davis
Birth Of The Cool

Young bop trumpeter and hip arrangers invent cool jazz.

In the late '40s, Miles Davis was the trumpeter in the Charlie Parker Quintet in New York. Although in awe of the bebop genius of Bird, Miles was uncomfortable being a lesser instrumental virtuoso than his boss; bop's default style was that of Dizzy Gillespie, Parker's former partner, who Miles idolised but whose attack, speed or range he couldn't get near. Also, he was tiring of the theme-solos-theme structure of much bop and his ears had been tuning into Gil Evans' adventurous, unorthodox arrangements for the Claude Thornhill Orchestra, Anthropology and Thriving From A Riff.

Evans was something of a mentor to a New York group of young modern musicians (including Gerry Mulligan, John Lewis and John Carisi) and when he approached Davis to be allowed to arrange his tune Donna Lee, Davis asked to see the charts and became a regular part of the circle who gathered at Gil's flat to theorise and experiment. Recognising the ideas of Evans and Mulligan as an ideal vehicle for him to "solo in the style that I was hearing" – a nine-piece band with modern harmonic voicing and light textures – Davis "cracked the whip" as Mulligan put it; he organised rehearsals, got a live engagement at the Royal Roost and crucially, got Capitol (not a company particularly disposed toward modern jazz) to record the band. Released as singles in 1949 and 1950 and finally gathered as an album in 1957 (when the sides were first named Birth Of The Cool), the eleven original instrumentals (plus one vocal) featured a seamless integration of the arranged and the spontaneous; warm, dense ensembles unusually underpinned by tuba and French horn open up into characterful, smoothly-phrased improvised solos by Davis and the 19-year-old altoist Lee Konitz. The miniature masterpieces include Mulligan's perky but luminous Venus De Milo, Crisis altered minor blues Israel and the mysterious harmonic pea-souper that is Evans's Moon Dreams.

Though the band existed for mere months, the recordings were immeasurably influential on orchestral jazz and the West Coast cool school movement, cerebral and (to some) anaemic music played mainly by white musicians that Davis was quick to distance himself from. This was the first of several times in the coming 30 years that Miles Davis projects would profoundly affect the development of jazz.

Record label:
Capitol

Produced
by Pete Rugolo.

Recorded
in New York; January–April 1949 and March 1950.

Released:
February 1957

Chart peaks:
None (UK) None (US)

Personnel:
Miles Davis (t, a); Kai Winding, J.J. Johnson, Mike Zwerin (tb); Junior Collins, Sandy Sielgelstein (french horn); Bill Barber (tba); Lee Konitz (as); Gerry Mulligan (bs, a); Al Haig (p); John Lewis (p, a); Joe Schulman, Nelson Boyd, Al McKibbon (b); Max Roach, Kenny Clarke (d); Kenny Hagood (v); Gil Evans (a)

Track Listing:
Move; Jeru; Moon Dreams; Venus De Milo; Budo; Deception; Godchild; Boplicity; Rocker; Israel; Rouge; Darn That Dream

Running time:
35.57

Current CD:
CDP7928622

Further listening:
Miles Ahead (1957); Porgy And Bess (1958); The Complete Birth Of The Cool (1998), inc Live Sessions: Birth Of The Cool Theme; Symphony Sid Announces The Band; Move; Why Do I Love You; Godchild; Symphony Sid Introduction; S'il Vous Plait; Moon Dreams; Budo (Hallucinations); Darn That Dream; Move; Moon Dreams; Budo (Hallucinations)

Further reading:
Miles – The Autobiography (Miles Davis and Quincy Troupe, 1989); Miles Davis (Ian Carr, 1999)

Nat 'King' Cole
Love Is The Thing

Gorgeous, moody and romantic in the extreme.

Nat 'King' Cole could be anything you wanted him to be – a vocal purveyor of pure pop able to apply his talents to the corniest material; a classy supper-club entertainer (known in his day as "the sepia Sinatra"); or even a poll-winning piano player able to jam with the best in jazz. He could deliver fine albums seemingly with the minimum of effort: swinging affairs, blues-hued wonders, country capers, lounge warmers filled with sly Latin licks, anything. But *Love Is The Thing* was the biggest of them all.

In October 1956, Nat was signed by NBC to host a TV show, the first black entertainer to have his own slot on a major network. Gordon Jenkins was brought in to provide the arrangements on Nat's first series and, despite problems with sponsors, it proved a winner with viewers, Nat's easy and relaxed style attracting a sizeable audience. When the time arrived for Cole to cut his next album, it made sense to continue the partnership with Jenkins, the creator of a distinctive string sound. The songs selected ranged from perhaps over-used standards such as Stardust and Ain't Misbehavin' through to the lovely When Sunny Gets Blue, previously a Johnny Mathis hit, and I Thought About Marie, a Jenkins original. There was also a link with Cole's past in When I Fall In Love, Where Can I Go Without You? and Love Letters, three songs penned by Victor Young, the composer responsible for Mona Lisa, one of Nat's most successful singles.

Love Is The Thing proved to be not only one of Cole's most moving albums – composer Hoagy Carmichael proclaimed Nat's version of Stardust the finest he'd ever heard – but also his best-selling LP, sitting at the peak of the US album charts for eight consecutive weeks. Among those who sat up and took notice was Capitol label-mate Frank Sinatra. He would turn to Jenkins to recreate the same mood on *Where Are You* and *No One Cares*, releases that followed in the path of *Love Is The Thing* but deliberately failed to offer the feeling of hope inherent in the Cole recording. An enormously influential record it, nevertheless, fails to gain a mention in Cole biographies.

Record label:
Capitol

Produced
by Lee Gillette.

Recorded
in Hollywood; December 19 and 28, 1956.

Released:
March 1957

Chart peaks:
None (UK) I (US)

Personnel:
Nat 'King' Cole (v); Gordon Jenkins And Orchestra

Track listing:
When I Fall In Love (S); Love Letters; Stardust; Stay As Sweet As You Are; Where Can I Go Without You?; Maybe It's Because I Love You; Ain't Misbehavin'; When Sunny Gets Blue; I Thought About Marie; At Last; It's All In The Game; Love Is The Thing

Running time:
35.47

Not currently available on CD

Further listening:
Where Did Everybody Go? (1963), a later Cole-Jenkins collaboration, is darker in tone, reflecting, perhaps, Nat's admiration for the Sinatra releases that followed in the path of his own.

Further reading:
Unforgettable: The Life And Mystique Of Nat 'King' Cole (Leslie Gourse, 1991).

Mose Allison
Back Country Suite

Debut album from a pianist / trumpeter / vocalist who would influence not only jazzmen but also The Who.

Mississippi born, Allison grew up in the bebop age and assimilated influences that ranged from blues and gospel through to the cool cabaret sounds of the Nat Cole Trio. A white boy raised in a largely black neighbourhood, he claims he absorbed a lot of blues from local jukeboxes. He played trumpet at high school, was a pianist in the army and later attended Louisiana State University. The last stint was to later cause him some embarrassment when a black magazine rang for an interview and asked if he was the first black student to graduate from LSU: "I think there's something you should know," began Mose.

He only needed one strike to make his mark and did so with *Back Country Suite*, an album that immediately established Mose as a musician who could be both down-home and city hip. The main thrust of the album is a series of vignettes, mainly instrumental, that depict his southern roots upbringing. Somehow Mose's amalgam of influences came together to produce a record that was totally original, and that would influence white blues practitioners throughout the '60s, The Who later pouncing on Mose's Young Man Blues and turning it into one of the highspots of *Live At Leeds*.

Though he's never made a poor record in his life, *Back Country Suite* remains Alison's most potent work, a record that provided the blueprint for what would become an extensive catalogue. "I regard a record as an expensive calling card. You have to have one in order to work," Mose once observed. *Back Country Suite* proved the ideal calling card and he's always found work easy to come by.

Record label:
Atlantic

Produced
by Rudy Van Gelder.

Recorded
in Hackensack, New Jersey; March 1957.

Released:
1957

Chart peaks:
None (UK) None (US)

Track listing:
Mose Allison (p, t, v); Taylor LaFargue (b); Frank Isola (d); Rudy Van Gelder (e)

Personnel:
New Ground; Train; Warm Night; Blues (Young Man); Saturday; Scamper; January; Promised Land; Spring Song; Highway 49; Blueberry Hill; You Won't Let Me Go; I Thought About You; One Room Country Shack; In Salah

Running time:
36.00

Current CD:
OJCCD0752

Further Listening:
Local Color (1958), a follow-up release that's virtually Back Country Suite part 2, and includes his highly personalised version of Parchman Farm.

Further Reading:
One Man's Blues (Patti Jones, 1998).

Nina Simone

Jazz As Played In An Exclusive Side Street Club

Neither, says the lady, jazz, nor her debut. Either way, it heralded a singular talent.

According to Nina, this was her second album. "The first album I ever made was a pirate that I never got paid for and knew nothing about." But *Jazz As Played In An Exclusive Side Street Club* — or *Little Girl Blue* as it is also known — which turned up in countless guises (and continues to do so) is the release that immediately established her as a unique performer, one who refused to be categorised — though record companies have repeatedly attempted to place Nina in 'file under' situations according to whichever trend is under scrutiny at the time.

Signed to Bethlehem, a jazz label, the singer-pianist born Eunice Waymon, found that her debut was initially sidelined into jazz racks. But a hit single, culled from the album, I Loves You Porgy, timed to coincide with the release of the film musical Porgy And Bess did provide her with a wider audience. Doubtless, those encountering the album for the first time experienced confusion. Certainly jazz pervaded several tracks, but Nina's instrumental version of Dizzy Gillespie's Good Bait proved as much Bach as bebop, while Duke Ellington might have faced difficulty recognising the intro to his Mood Indigo.

"I came to despise popular songs and I never played them for my own amusement," Nina claimed at the time. "Why should I when I could be playing Bach, Czeny or Liszt?" So things were hardly what they seemed on the track listing; even Little Girl Blue somehow mutated into Good King Wenceslas! But her late-night loner ballads — Don't Smoke In Bed and He Needs Me — are always moving, and Central Park Blues proves that she could provide a straightforward, heads-down, swinging instrumental if it took her fancy. In all probability, her now famous version of My Baby Just Cares For Me, with its rum-ti-tum rhythm and final lick nicked from Eddie Heywood's Begin The Beguine, was just Nina being perverse: "It was the last song we did and I spent the next three days playing Beethoven to get the recording session out of my system." Whatever she thought about it, it's an album that *still* reveals hidden facets.

Record label:
Bethlehem

Producer:
unknown.

Recorded
in New York City; 1957.

Released:
early 1958

Chart peaks:
None (UK) None (US)

Personnel:
Nina Simone (v, p); Jimmy Bond (b); Albert Heath (d)

Track listing:
Mood Indigo; Don't Smoke In Bed; He Needs Me; Little Girl Blue; Love Me Or Leave Me; My Baby Just Cares For Me; Good Bait; Plain Gold Ring; You'll Never Walk Alone; I Loves You Porgy (S); Central Park Blues

Running time:
45.73

Current CD:
CPCD8240-2 reissued by Charly as Lady Blue; adds concert album

Further listening:
Anthology: The Colpix Years (1996) a double-CD that features late '50s and '60s tracks taken from the diva's nine albums for the Colpix label.

Further reading:
I Put A Spell On You (Nina Simone with Stephen Cleary, 1991) an autobiography that, naturally enough, provides the Simone point-of-view.

The Crickets
The 'Chirping' Crickets

First album by one of the giants of modern popular music.

"Even around the seventh or eighth grade I knew he had it. Buddy just had that rock'n'roll charisma." A handful of years later school and band-mate Jerry Allison co-wrote The Crickets first hit, That'll Be The Day. Holly and Allison initially recorded the song for Decca under the auspices of legendary country producer Owen Bradley. However, this liaison didn't work out, and the boys headed to Norman Petty's tiny Clovis studio to try the song again. The punchy result was infinitely superior to the Nashville take, though Allison points out it was only a demo. "We intended to record it again a bit slicker, later. We liked the song, but didn't think that version would even be released, much less be successful." But Bob Thiele at Coral Records liked it just so and the track became a slow-burning hit.

The band carried on recording with Petty for several good reasons. "The studio had really good equipment, it was cheap – seems like our first demos cost $15 each – there was no time limit, Petty was a good engineer, and Vi Petty was a great lady who made everyone feel comfortable."

Over the next few months Petty consistently coaxed the best from Holly's idiosyncratic, quavering tones – part country, part blues, sometimes vulnerable, often boyishly confident. The tracks could then be released by Buddy as a solo artiste or as a member of The Crickets – a good way to double airplay and income. "The atmosphere around the studio was pretty laid back at first. The process changed a lot after we got the record deal. Then we'd do a song twenty times and it got to be like work. And after we went on the road Petty dubbed on the backing vocals, which were not particularly thrilling to us."

Interestingly, the band also recorded four of the album tracks, including the melancholic mid-tempo rocker Maybe Baby, while out on that road – Petty dragging his gear up to Oklahoma for the purpose. Allison still jibs at the "schmaltzy" backing vox which characterise The Crickets as opposed to the Holly material, and justifiably complains about dodgy song-writing attributions: "I co-wrote Not Fade Away, and I'm still bitching about the lack of a credit!" But the eerie, spartan, Bo Diddley vibe of that very number, the raucous pop-rockabilly of Oh Boy and the R&B spice of Chuck Willis's It's Too Late helped send Holly and his band right to the front of rock music's early leading pack.

Record label:
Coral

Produced
by Norman Petty.

Recorded
at Norman Petty Studios, Clovis, New Mexico; February–March and May–July 1957; Tinker Air Force Base, Oklahoma City, Oklahoma; September 27–28 1957.

Released:
March 1958

Chart peaks:
None (UK) None (US)

Personnel:
Buddy Holly (g, v); Niki Sullivan (g, b, v); Joe Mauldin (b); Jerry Allison (d); Larry Welborn (b); June Clark (bv); Gary and Ramona Tollett (bv); The Picks: John Pickering, Bill Pickering, Bob Lapham (bv)

Track listing:
Oh Boy (S); Not Fade Away; You've Got Love; Maybe Baby (S); It's Too Late; Tell Me How; That'll Be The Day (S); I'm Looking For Somebody To Love; An Empty Cup (And A Broken Date); Send Me Some Lovin'; Last Night; Rock Me Baby

Running time:
25.27

Current CD:
MCAD31182

Further listening:
Buddy Holly (1958); difficult to find 6-LP box set The Complete Buddy Holly (1979).

Further reading:
Remembering Buddy (John Goldrosen and John Beecher, 1987); http://homepage. ntlworld.com/buddyholly/holly

17

Billie Holiday
Lady In Satin

The life of jazz's greatest singer, laid desperately bare.

Billie loved the Ray Ellis string sound and played Ray's *Ellis In Wonderland* album continuously. After getting together, the duo began selecting the songs for the three-day session, Ellis later observing: "I didn't realise that the titles she was picking at the time were really the story of her life." Billie was in poor shape and was about to face a trial for drug possession. The once beautiful woman had become one of the living dead, haggard, stooping, with a voice that cracked and failed to hold notes. Producer Townsend, who'd earlier worked with Mahalia Jackson, admitted: "Billie was closer to the end than most stars, but she was Billie Holiday with a style and a voice like no other woman ever had."

Ray Ellis revealed that the sessions were nothing if not problematic. The singer would turn up completely stoned – in the case of The End Of A Love Affair she professed not to know the song at all. Eventually the backing track for the side had to be recorded without a vocal, Billie adding a top line at a later date. But the juxtaposition of sandpaper on satin worked marvellously well. Though the voice had to be constantly lubricated by tots of gin, and the imperfections were apparent to all, somehow the result was beauty of an inestimable kind as Billie poured pain over careworn classics like Glad To Be Unhappy and I Get Along Without You Very Well: pure emotion expressed by a voice that virtually disintegrates before your ears.

When the record was released, Holiday-lovers became locked in conflict. Many voiced the opinion that *Lady In Satin* should never have been released because it was tantamount to recording someone in their death-throes. Others, including one-time Holiday accompanist Jimmy Rowles, felt it was the singer's greatest achievement, the most revealing album ever made. She would make one more album, again with Ray Ellis. But it would be her last: by July 17, 1959 the legend born Eleanora Fagan was dead.

Record label:
Columbia

Produced
by Irv Townsend.

Recorded
at CBS Studios, New York; February 18–20, 1958.

Released:
Autumn 1958

Chart peaks:
None (UK) None (US)

Personnel:
Billie Holiday (v); with the Ray Ellis Orchestra

Track listing:
I'm A Fool To Want You; For Heaven's Sake; You Don't Know What Love Is; I Get Along Without You Very Well; For All We Know; Violets For Your Furs; You've Changed; It's Easy To Remember; But Beautiful; Glad To Be Unhappy; I'll Be Around; The End Of A Love Affair

Running time:
44.32

Current CD:
CK65144 adds four previously unissued bonus takes.

Further listening:
Billie's Greatest Hits (1998) – the best of the singer's US Decca recordings, songs that formed the basis for the Lady Sings The Blues soundtrack, except that these are the originals and far superior to Diana Ross's interpretations.

Further reading:
The Life And Times Of Billie Holiday (Donald Clarke, 1995), the most thoroughly researched Lady Day biography; www.cmgww.com/music/holiday/index.html

Mahalia Jackson
Live At Newport 1958

Maybe the most famous gospel album of all time.

It's said that when Mahalia Jackson began singing the jaunty spiritual Didn't It Rain during her Sunday morning slot at the '58 Newport Jazz Festival the soft summer drizzle suddenly stopped. We know from Mahalia's stage patter that it was actually still raining at the end of the concert, but it's testament to the truly unique spirit of her music that folks should insist some divine intervention took place. As her friend the Reverend Martin Luther King, Jr commented, a voice like hers came only "once in a millennium".

By 1958, Mahalia – then aged 46 – was a household name in America, following a string of crossover hits and a sensational performance on the Ed Sullivan Show two years earlier. Though she had made some recordings with Duke Ellington, she famously refused to sing pop or the blues, preferring to spread the word of the Lord through her beloved hymns and gospel music. She was far from a gospel 'snob', however; when musicologists from the Juilliard quizzed her about her extraordinary vocal technique in 1950, they discovered a woman who'd grown up listening to Enrico Caruso and blues queen Bessie Smith, as well as the maudlin jazz of New Orleans funeral marches and the religious music she heard in her father's church.

At 16, Mahalia, with $100 sewn into her underclothes, left the segregation and relentless poverty of New Orleans for the northern mecca of Chicago, where she'd heard that black and whites could sit together on the buses. Quickly recognised in her new church as an incredible talent, she was whisked away on gospel tours and to recording sessions, ever imploring the people around her to "make a joyful noise unto the Lord" and revel in the transcendental joy of religious singing. She also qualified as a beautician.

At Newport, Mahalia gave one of her finest ever performances, the rich, stirring rendition of An Evening Prayer kicking off a set of 19th century church music and 'modern' gospel innovations, all given a swinging jazz flavour by the backing of long-term accomplice Mildred Falls' piano, Lilton Mitchell's organ and Tom Bryant's bass. (In 1946, Mahalia had been one of the first gospel artists to use a Hammond organ on her records.) Three tracks – It Don't Cost Very Much, I'm Going To Live The Life I Sing About In My Song and Walk Over God's Heaven – were written by her favourite gospel composer, Thomas A. Dorsey, and her familiarity and identification with the material is clear in her mesmerising interpretations.

"I sing God's music because it makes me feel free," she once said. "It gives me hope. With the blues, when you finish, you still have the blues."

Record label:
Philips

Produced
by Cal Lampley.

Recorded
at Newport Jazz Festival; July 6, 1958.

Released:
November 1958

Chart peaks:
(UK) None; (US) None

Personnel:
Mahalia Jackson (v); Mildred Falls (p); Lilton Mitchell (o); Tom Bryant (b)

Track listing:
Introduction; An Evening Prayer; A City Called Heaven; It Don't Cost Very Much; He's Got The Whole World In His Hands; The Lord's Prayer

Running time:
17.19

Current CD:
Legacy CK53629 adds: I'm On My Way; Didn't It Rain; When The Saints Go Marching In; I'm Goin' To Live The Life I Sing About In My Song; Keep Your Hand On The Plow; Walk Over God's Heaven; Joshua Fit The Battle Of Jericho; Jesus Met The Woman At The Well; His Eye Is On The Sparrow

Further listening:
Home in on the classic Columbia years with Mahalia Jackson's Greatest Hits (1988)

Further reading:
Just Mahalia, Baby (Laurrain Goreau, 1984)

Frank Sinatra
Come Fly With Me

Sinatra's first and best collaboration with Billy May.

As heaven-made as the Nelson Riddle/Frank Sinatra partnership was, Frank was unwilling to be too closely identified with one arranger and turned to Billy May for his travelogue album *Come Fly With Me*, the first of his themed records that weren't to do with love, loss or swingin'. Working with May was likened by Sinatra to having a "bucket of cold water thrown in your face" so vibrant was the Fat Man's presence. May was already famous for his albums of exotic orchestral work featuring trademark slurping saxes and elaborate percussion and some of that colourful stuff was imported none-too-seriously onto tracks like Isle Of Capri and Brazil on which arranger and singer are clearly having a ball. However, May had a reputation as the most versatile arranger in Hollywood and the range of his work on this one album is proof enough. Autumn In New York and Moonlight In Vermont rank among the best Sinatra ballads ever, with their sighing-for-exotic-lands arrangements and Frank in hyperaware interpretative form while Come Fly With Me is art-swing of a very high order, from the take-off expectancy of the intro to the mysterious shimmer-in-the-clouds of the final string colour. May's favourite was the Victor Young waltz Around The World: "That's a beautiful tune, and Frank sang the shit out of it too. Boy! He's really a good singer."

But perhaps the most startling piece is the Rudyard Kipling-inspired On The Road To Mandalay. Banned from the UK issue of the album by Kipling's daughter ("How dare she?" bitched Sinatra at a 1958 concert, "of course, she drinks a little bit so we'll forgive her"), it has a bizarre ending ("And the dawn comes up like thunder!") that sounds like someone has prematurely lifted the needle. Originally, there was a gong followed by another half-chorus but saxist Skits Herbert recalled that "Billy just kind of waved his hands to signal 'Don't say anything.' And instead of going on, Frank put on his hat and threw his coat over his shoulder, like he does, and walked out of the studio! We all laughed like mad. That was the way they put it out."

Record Label:
Capitol

Produced
by Voyle Gilmore.

Recorded
at Capitol Studios, Hollywood; Autumn 1957.

Released:
November 1958

Chart peaks:
2 (UK) 1 (US)

Personnel:
Frank Sinatra (v); Billy May (a, conductor). Orchestra includes Alvin Stoller (d); Skits Herbert (clarinet, s).

Track Listing:
Come Fly With Me; Around The World; Isle Of Capri; Moonlight In Vermont; Autumn In New York; On The Road To Mandalay; Let's Get Away From It All; April In Paris; London By Night; Brazil; Blue Hawaii; It's Nice To Go Trav'ling

Running time:
38.46

Current CD:
CDP7484692

Further listening:
Follow-up Come Dance With Me (1959) was doubly driving and almost as good but Come Swing With Me (1961) was contractual obligation work of an artist keen to leave Capitol. Francis A And Edward K, the 1967 May-Ellington collaboration on Reprise, however, was majestic.

Further reading:
Sinatra! The Song Is You: A Singer's Art (Will Friedwald, 1995)

Frank Sinatra
Sings For Only The Lonely

The greatest of Sinatra's suicidal mood albums.

A s well as the classic mid-tempo good-time swingers Songs
For *Swingin' Lovers* (1955) and *A Swingin' Affair* (1956), in
the renaissance Capitol years Frank Sinatra had already produced
a classic torch album with arranger Nelson Riddle, *In The Wee
Small Hours* (1955), and had even dallied with arranger Gordon
Jenkins on the cloying deep gloom of *Where Are You?* (1957). But
neither quite prepared the listener for the devastating tragic-
romantic impact of *Only The Lonely*.

Set in sweepingly dramatic late-romantic/early-impres-
sionist orchestral textures, Sinatra the actor-singer is at his
absolute peak, in control of every technical and emotional
nuance, entirely involving, completely believable. Riddle,
regarding it as "the best vocal album I've ever done; because I
had time to work on the arrangements – a week!" excelled
himself with the beautiful intros alone. The Chopin-esque piano
of the title track, the whispering dissonances in the violins on It's
A Lonesome Old Town, the descending oboe line of Goodbye;
Riddle attributed the tone of his work to the recent death of his
daughter and imminent death of his mother – "if one can attach
events like that to music, perhaps Only The Lonely was the
result." Interestingly, though an astonishing arranger, Riddle was
known as a vague conductor and Frank apparently contrived to
have regular Sinatra concertmaster Felix Slatkin conduct the
tricky, tempoless numbers while Riddle was out of town.

The album featured two of Sinatra's favourite boozy loser
pieces, Angel Eyes and One For My Baby, one of which he
would always perform in concert as the saloon song segment
with just Bill Miller on piano accompaniment. He recorded Baby
like that (available on *The Capitol Years* 4CD set) but returned the
following day to cut it again with Riddle's discreet strings and
Gus Bovine's delicious *alto obligatio* to create a masterpiece, the
pinnacle – along with I've Got You Under My Skin from *Songs
For Swingin' Lovers* – of the Sinatra/Riddle partnership.

Sinatra recalled the session: "Word had somehow got
around, there were 60 or 70 people there, Capitol employees
and their friends, people off the street, anyone. We had kept this
song to the last track of the session. Dave Cavanaugh knew how
I sang it in the clubs and he switched out all the lights bar the
spot on me. The atmosphere in that studio was exactly like a
club. Dave said 'Roll 'em', there was one take and that was
that. The only time I've known it happen like that."

Record Label:
Capitol

Produced
by Dave Cavanaugh.

Recorded
at Capitol Studios, Hollywood; May–June
1958.

Released:
December 1958

Chart peaks:
5 (UK) 1 (US)

Personnel:
Frank Sinatra (v); Nelson Riddle (ac);
Felix Slatkin (c); orchestra included Al
Viola (g); Pete Condoli (t); Bill Miller (p);
Gus Bivona (as); Ray Sims (tb)

Track Listing:
Only The Lonely; Angel Eyes; What's New;
It's A Lonesome Old Town; Willow Weep
For Me; Goodbye; Blues In The Night;
Guess I'll Hang My Tears Out To Dry;
Ebb Tide; Spring Is Here; Gone with the
Wind; One For My Baby.

Running time:
54.35

Current CD:
CDP-7484471-2 adds Sleep Warm &
Where Or When.

Further listening:
In The Wee Small Hours (1955); Close To
You (1956)

Further reading:
Sinatra! The Song Is You: A Singer's Art
by Will Friedwald (1995)

Marty Robbins
Gunfighter Ballads And Trail Songs

The first successful C&W concept album.

G lendale, Arizona's Marty Robbins was already successful with smash hits such as Singing The Blues (1956) and A White Sport Coat (And A Pink Carnation) a year later, though nothing could have prepared him for the reaction an album full of Zane Gray/Louis L'Amour-like gunslinger tales would bring him. Marty's grandfather was 'Texas Bob' Heckle, a one-time Texas ranger who told his grandson spellbinding tales of the Old West. Robbins' grew up a Gene Autry fan, seldom if ever missing a movie by The Singing Cowboy, and had bit parts in two Hollywood horse operas.

When his theme from a Gary Cooper western, The Hanging Tree, climbed the charts in early 1959, it put Robbins in a position where he could lobby his label for an entire album of cowboy ditties. They agreed and Robbins compiled a list of his favourite Old West songs including the Sons Of The Pioneers' Cool Water, his friends the Glasers' Running Gun, three traditional cowboy ballads and four of his own songs. And what songs they were; Big Iron, which became a hit C&W single; The Master's Call, an almost Biblical tale of a cowpoke's redemption; In The Valley, and El Paso, the Number 1 pop hit which earned the first Grammy ever awarded to a country song and fast became Robbins' signature tune. A tale of a foolish young cowboy's love for a forbidden maiden, El Paso remains one of the greatest C&W songs, and has been covered by everyone from Johnny Cash to the Grateful Dead. Produced with a cinematic viewpoint by Englishman Don Law (who had recorded blues legend Robert Johnson a quarter of a century earlier) and propelled by Grady Martin's bittersweet Mexican guitar flourishes, it was the album's centrepiece, becoming one of the most played songs on country radio, propelling the album to platinum sales.

Robbins would have many more country – and crossover – hits in his career, and he would win a second Grammy a decade later, but nothing could eclipse the bright burning lights of this album just as nothing could stop that foolish cowboy from returning to his love at Rosa's Cantina in El Paso.

Record label:
Columbia

Produced
by Don Law.

Recorded
at Bradley Film and Recording, Nashville; April 7, 1959.

Released:
June 1959

Chart peaks:
(UK) 20; (US) 6

Personnel:
Marty Robbins (v, g); Thomas Grady Martin (g); Jack H Pruett (g); Bob L Moore (b); Louis Dunn (d); The Glaser Brothers (bv)

Track listing:
Big Iron (S); A Hundred And Sixty Acres; They're Hanging Me Tonight; Cool Water; Billy The Kid; Utah Carol; The Strawberry Roan; The Master's Call; Running Gun; El Paso (S); In The Valley; The Little Green Valley

Running time:
44.42

Current CD:
4952472 adds: The Hanging Tree (S); Saddle Tramp; El Paso (S)

Further listening:
Marty's Greatest Hits (1958) his first hits collection, released before Gunfighter Ballads And Trail Songs and containing all the early smashes.

Further reading:
The Encyclopedia Of Country Music (OUP, 1998)

Miles Davis
Kind Of Blue

Masterclass in modal improvisation. Whatever that is.

The band that arrived at Columbia's 30th Street Studio in NYC on March 2, 1959 to record the album that became known as *Kind Of Blue* were barely a band at all anymore. Coltrane had left Miles in '57, only to return again following a period with Thelonious Monk, but his confidence and conception had skyrocketed and he was on the verge of leaving again. Cannonball had said he would only stay a year and was ready to go too; Bill Evans had left months before but Davis was so struck by the pianist's limpid, shifting-sands harmonic style, he devised the album around it and recalled him for the sessions.

Davis had made it clear in a 1958 interview that he was on the verge of a major shift in his musical thinking. "The music has gotten thick," he said. "I think a movement in jazz is beginning away from the conventional string of chords and a return to emphasis on melodic rather than harmonic variation. There will be fewer chords but infinite possibilities as to what to do with them." Influenced by composer George Russell's theory of Lydian tonality, Davis produced simple, slow-moving harmonic frameworks – devised only hours previously – and indicated the scales/modes to be used for improvisation.

The resulting music was a uniquely beautiful triumph of content over form; seeing the sketches for the first time, each player surpassed himself to create line after inspired line of improvised melody. "Everything was a first take," remembered Miles in his autobiography, "which indicates the level everyone was playing on. It was beautiful."

Immensely popular and influential, *Kind Of Blue* is a rarity among great works of art; a fashionable masterpiece whose stature is virtually undisputed. Amazingly, Miles claimed to have not quite nailed what he was after, which was the sort of interplay between the dancers, drummers and the finger piano he had witnessed at a performance of the Ballet Africaine. "When I tell people that I missed what I was trying to do, getting the exact sound of that African finger piano up in that sound, they look at me like I'm crazy," he remembered. "I just missed." The main players went swiftly on to blaze further trails of their own – artistic (Coltrane, Evans), commercial (Adderley) and both (Davis) – but for many, the essence of what these remarkable jazz musicians had to offer as improvising instrumentalists is to be found on *Kind Of Blue*.

Record label:
CBS

Produced
by Irving Townsend.

Recorded
at Columbia 30th Street Studio, New York City; March 2 and April 22, 1959.

Released:
1959

Chart peaks:
None (UK) None (US)

Personnel:
Miles Davis (t); John Coltrane (ts); Julian 'Cannonball' Adderley (as); Bill Evans (p); Wynton Kelly (p); Paul Chambers (b); Jimmy Cobb (d)

Track listing:
So What; Freddie Freeloader; Blue In Green; All Blues; Flamenco Sketches

Running time:
45.37

Current CD:
MILLEN101 adds: Flamenco Sketches 2

Further listening:
Milestones (1958); '58 Sessions Featuring Stella By Starlight (1958)

Further reading:
Miles The Autobiography (Miles Davis and Quincy Troupe, 1989); Miles Davis (Ian Carr, 1999)

Charles Mingus
Ah Um

Brawny, belligerent and beautiful, the jazz composer's rootsy modern masterpiece.

One of the all time great jazz composers, Mingus quickly found that writing out parts for the players of his Jazz Workshop was not quite achieving the vibrant synthesis of composed and improvised material he was after. He took to directing musicians from the piano, demonstrating the parts, encouraging an adventuresome attitude. One sideman remembered: "You had to keep stretching yourself while you were with Mingus. He just wouldn't let you coast. Even in public he'd yell at you in the middle of a solo to stop playing just licks and get into *yourself*. He had more confidence in what we were capable of than we had."

Though by 1959 this titan of jazz creativity was already a colossus of modern bass playing and composition, Mingus always had a respectful ear for the roots of the music. He had grown up with church music – Duke Ellington's Orchestra was the first secular musical sound he heard – and had cut his teeth with the Dixieland-style bands of Kid Ory and Louis Armstrong. Earlier that year he had already recorded *Blues And Roots* for Atlantic, a modernist album drenched in raucous Afro-American musical tradition. He was in the same broad bag by May 1959 – when it was time to record what became *Ah Um* – but this time he had more explicit references in mind. *Ah Um*, for all its Mingussy flavour (double-time passages, riffs bouncing off one another, ragged ensembles and free-spirited improvised solos) can be seen as a tribute to his ancestors. Sometimes generic (the gospel of the pulse-racing Better Git It In Your Soul, the deep blues of Pussy Cat Dues), there are also character-specific pieces; Goodbye Pork Pie Hat salutes saxophonist Lester Young who had died two months earlier; the dense, multi-tempo Open Letter To Duke is a gorgeous pastiche of his idol Ellington; Bird Calls was the latest of his tributes to Charlie Parker; Jelly Roll is for the great jazz composer of the '20s, Jelly Roll Morton).

Its head in the present and its heart in the past, there's a richness of spirit and expressiveness that makes *Ah Um* one of those rare jazz albums that can reach beyond jazz heads into the wider listening world.

Record Label:
CBS

Produced
by Teo Macero.

Recorded
at 30th St Studio, NYC; May 5 and 12, 1959.

Released:
1959

Chart peak:
None (UK) None (US)

Personnel:
Charles Mingus (b); John Handy (as, clarinet); Booker Irvin (ts), Shafi Hadi (as, ts); Jimmy Knepper (tb); Horace Parlan (p); Dannie Richmond (d); Willie Dennis (t)

Track Listing:
Better Git It In Your Soul; Goodbye Pork Pie Hat; Boogie Stop Shuffle; Self-Portrait In Three Colors; Open Letter To Duke; Bird Calls; Fables Of Faubus; Pussy Cat Dues; Jelly Roll

Running time:
45:56

Current CD:
Legacy CK 65512 adds Pedal Point Blues, GG Train, & Girl Of My Dreams

Further listening:
Blues And Roots (1959); Black Saint And The Sinner Lady (1963)

Further reading:
Mingus: A Critical Biography (Brian Priestley, 1984); Beneath The Underdog (Charles Mingus, 1995)
www.mingusmingusmingus.com

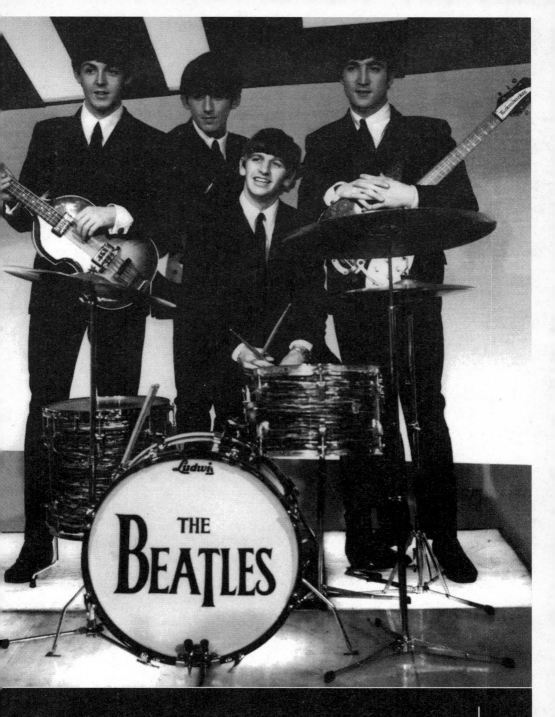

THE
1960s

Billy Fury
The Sound Of Fury

Driving debut from UK's only decent answer to Elvis, the man who had more hits in the '60s than The Beatles.

O nly a handful of early British rockers merit favourable comparison with their maverick American cousins. Cliff Richard, Lonnie Donegan and Johnny Kid may have had their moments, but only Billy Fury could really be considered the English Elvis. In April 1960, after a reasonably successful run of singles, Decca sent 20-year-old Fury into the studio to record a 10-inch long-player and, unusually for the times, the songs were all penned by Fury himself. (Impresario Larry Parnes had signed Ronald Wycherley [as was] at least partly on the strength of his compositional ability.) Producer Jack Good had assembled the customary crew of sheet-music reading jazz musicians for the session, but had added the rocking young guitarist Joe Brown to the line-up. Brown had backed Eddie Cochran and Gene Vincent on tour, and remembers Good's instructions vividly: "The record was Jack's take on the Sun Studio sound. He had even hired electric and stand-up bass players to double up to get Bill Black's big slapped bass sound. He asked Reg Guest (piano) to play like Floyd Cramer and told me to do my Scotty Moore. We did a run through of each number and then a take. Practically everything was done in one go."

The result is a powerful, varied set with loud echoes of Memphis 1954 – Since You've Been Gone mirrors the tempo-change tomfoolery of Elvis's Milk Cow Blues. Elsewhere Fury's sweet, edgy tenor is often the spit of Cochran's. There are also hints, however, of something new. The ballad You Don't Know exudes a peculiarly British sense of vulnerability – Fury's Liverpudlian vowels resonating through the sparse arrangement. As Brown attests, "Even though we knew we were copying the Yanks, of course we brought something of our own upbringing to it as well."

The Four Jays (hired to imitate The Jordanaires) were later managed by Brian Epstein and gained success as The Fourmost. A curiously shy star, Fury continued to have hits well into the '60s and was charming as the self-parodic Stormy Tempest in the film *That'll Be The Day*. Unfortunately, he was chronically ill throughout the '70s and died in 1983. But amongst his many achievements was an album, which marks the moment when British rock'n'roll grew up.

Record label:
Decca

Produced
by Jack Good.

Recorded
at Decca Studio 3, West Hampstead, London; January 8, 1960 and April 4, 1960.

Released:
May 1960

Chart peaks:
18 (UK) None (US)

Personnel:
Billy Fury (v); Joe Brown (g); Reg Guest (p); Bill Stark (acoustic bass); Alan Weighell (b); Andy White (d); The Four Jays (bv)

Track Listing:
That's Love (S/UK); My Advice; Phone Call; You Don't Know; Turn My Back On You; Don't Say It's Over; Since You've Been Gone; It's You I Need; Alright, Goodbye; Don't Leave Me This Way

Running time:
21.53

Current CD:
8206272 known as The Sound of Fury +10 adds: Gonna Type A Letter; Margo (Don't Go), Don't Knock Upon My Door, Time Has Come, Angel Face, The Last Kiss, My Christmas Prayer, Baby How I Cried, I Got Someone, & Don't Jump

Further listening:
Halfway To Paradise (1961); The One And Only (1983). Joe Brown continues to record; On A Day Like This (1999) is a fine recent album.

Further reading:
Hit Parade Heroes: British Beat Before The Beatles (Dave McLeer, 1993); Beat Merchants (Alan Clayson, 1997); Rock, You Sinners (fanzine dealing with pre-Beatles Brits, available from: 117 World's End Lane, Enfield, UK. EN2 7RG); www.billyfury.co.uk

Elvis Presley
Elvis Is Back!

The best rock'n'roll LP between Buddy Holly's death and the rise of The Beatles.

The omens were not good on March 20, 1960, when Presley, demob happy and shorn of sideburns, arrived for his first recording session since leaving the army. The Sun-era team of Elvis, Scotty and Bill was not an option. Scotty Moore had not spoken to Presley for two years but was willing to turn up, but Bill Black was pursuing a solo career. On the other hand, DJ Fontana, The Jordanaires and Floyd Cramer were still on board. The other musicians – most of whom were on the June 1958 date that was Elvis' most recent – were led to believe this was a Jim Reeves session. There was also a lot of business to be taken care of, not least a single (Stuck On You/Fame And Fortune) that had to be in the shops by the end of the week.

By 7am, that 45 plus four other tracks were in the can – Make Me Know It, the faintly biographical Soldier Boy, and two lascivious R&B songs, A Mess of Blues and It Feels So Right. With two weeks before the next date, Presley was whisked off to Miami for the Frank Sinatra TV Show. For the second recording date, April 3, Colonel Tom instructed that Elvis sing eight songs – all he was contractually obliged to give RCA for an LP – one of which was to be Are You Lonesome Tonight, a 1927 hit for Al Jolson, and his wife's favourite tune. By now Presley was back into his stride, with ideas that far outstripped his pre-draft capabilities. Fever featured just bass and two percussionists separated in the stereo mix; It's Now Or Never was mock-operatic, an adaptation of O Sole Mio; Like A Baby, Such A Night and Dirty, Dirty Feeling almost verged on the obscene. Recorded in the dark, Are You Lonesome Tonight was the ninth cut, although Elvis felt his voice wasn't suitable. The twelfth cut, Lowell Fulsom's bluesy Reconsider Baby, began as a jam and ended with everybody taking solos. By the time he left the studio, Stuck On You was Number 1 and Elvis had two weeks before starting work on GI Blues. A new beginning, but the end was already in sight.

Record Label:
RCA

Produced
by Steve Scholes and Chet Aktins.

Recorded
at RCA Studio B, Nashville; March–April 1960.

Release date:
July 1960 (UK); April 1960 (US)

Chart peaks:
1 (UK) 2 (US)

Personnel:
Elvis Presley (v, g); Scotty Moore (g); Bob Moore (b); Hank Garland (g, b); DJ Fontana (d); Buddy Harman (d); 'Boots' Randolph (s); Floyd Cramer (p); The Jordanaires (v); Bob Moore (e)

Track Listing:
Stuck On You (S); Fame And Fortune; Make Me Know It; Fever; The Girl Of My Best Friend (S); I Will Be Home Again; Dirty, Dirty Feeling; Thrill Of Your Love; Soldier Boy; Such A Night (S); It Feels So Right; Girl Next Door; Like A Baby; Reconsider Baby.

Running time:
31.29

Current CD:
07863677372 adds: Are You Lonesome Tonight (S); I Gotta Know (S), Mess Of Blues (S), & It's Now Or Never (S)

Further listening:
From Nashville To Memphis – The Essential '60s Masters Vol 1 (5 CD set)

Further reading:
Careless Love – The Unmaking Of Elvis Presley (Peter Guralnick, 1999)

Joan Baez
Joan Baez

As important as Dylan in popularising folk music in the '60s.

In 1960, Joan Baez (then 19) was exactly what the flat, dull and worthy folk scene needed. Unattractiveness was almost a mark of authenticity. That Joan was a striking, young raven-haired beauty with a sweet, pure voice certainly did not harm the prospects of her debut album.

She had been a huge hit at the Newport Festival in July the previous year, standing apart from a bill that included Bob Gibson (who invited her there), Pete Seeger, Odetta, Sonny Terry and Brownie McGhee. Unsurprisingly, *Joan Baez* was a folk revival landmark. No wonder Bob Dylan initially idolised her – his own rise would have been impossible without her. She turned a new younger generation onto folk music – kids who had no time for Pete Seeger singalongs and fresh-faced college boys singing Tom Dooley. It would have been enough if Joan Baez had simply given folk some sex appeal. Yet the content of her debut album also reflected what was happening on the campuses and in the coffee houses, and as one of the first folk soloists to achieve national (and later international) success, she brought the music into the mass market.

Joan Baez was recorded in a hotel ballroom in New York City and produced by Maynard Solomon, to whose label she signed – in preference to CBS – because Solomon was, like Joan, an idealist; he'd signed The Weavers, despite accusations that Pete Seeger was a Communist. She made her home at Vanguard for most of the decade, releasing a staggering 17 albums before a move to A&M. Despite her beautiful singing and the simple arrangements (she had to be persuaded to allow a second guitarist), the album may not be to current tastes; but at the time, its mixture of Carter Family songs (Wildwood Flower), the Negro spiritual All My Trials and a Spanish political song was quite captivating. The ballads – notably John Riley, Silver Dagger and Mary Hamilton – have lasted best.

In America, *Joan Baez* was an unlikely chart success. It eventually charted in the UK in July 1964, where she enjoyed a Top 10 single a year later with Phil Ochs' There But For Fortune.

Record label:
Vanguard

Produced
by Maynard Solomon.

Recorded
in New York City; autumn 1960.

Released:
October 1960

Chart peaks:
9 (UK) 15 (US)

Personnel:
Joan Baez (v, g); Fred Hellerman (second g)

Track listing:
Silver Dagger; East Virginia; Ten Thousand Miles; House Of The Rising Sun; All My Trials; Wildwood Flower; Donna Donna; John Riley; Rake And The Rambling Boy; Little Moses; Mary Hamilton; Henry Martin; El Preso Numero Nuevo

Running time:
37.30

Current CD:
VMD 2077-2

Further listening:
Farewell Angelina (1965)

Further reading:
www.baez.woz.org

Miles Davis
Sketches Of Spain

Trumpeter and arranger combine gloriously on timeless, impressionist orchestral jazz.

The Miles Davis/Gil Evans collaborations of the late '50s were era-defining statements of orchestral jazz that continue to inspire composers and arrangers of all persuasions.

Miles: "I loved working with Gil because he was so meticulous and creative, and I trusted his musical arrangements completely."

The Evans style – lugubrious, luminous brass, woodwind colours and modern shifting-sands harmony – was the ideal backdrop for the doleful splendour of Miles's horn and the music they made together spoke to an audience beyond jazz listeners. Indeed, some jazz lovers were openly sceptical about the balance between arrangement and spontaneity, though the reputation these days of the three albums they made between 1957 and 1960 is that of unassailable classics. It would have been a remarkable period for Davis with his sextet achievements alone (1958's *Milestones* and 1959's *Kind Of Blue*), but the artistic success of the *Birth Of The Cool* (1949/50) and the first full Evans collaboration *Miles Ahead* (1957), added to the commercial viability of their *Porgy And Bess* (1958), and assured Miles that "Gil and I were something special together musically."

When a friend played Miles Joaquin Rodrigo's guitar concerto, he excitedly shared it with Evans who ran with the Spanish idea, researching flamenco and the life of the Spanish gypsy, adapting Will O' The Wisp from Manuel de Falla's 1915 ballet El Amor Brujo and deriving Saeta from a religious Spanish march. Concept in place, the music proved elusive and difficult to play (Miles eventually instructed the ensembles to relax, creating a powerful raggedness). With awkward instrumental balances to record (several expensive sessions resulted in nothing being salvaged), it took fifteen 3-hour sessions and much editing to complete. The resulting record however, is perhaps the richest work that Davis and Evans had yet created; hypnotic percussive *ostinati*, drifting/hanging harmonic back-drops and Miles's floating, haunted meditations often on a single Spanish scale – music of ceremonial majesty.

There are resisters ("For the listener in search of jazz, there is mighty little of that commodity evident," observed the New York Times, "Inflated light music" maintains the respected Penguin Guide To Jazz On CD) but for generations of impartial listeners to come, *Sketches Of Spain* will continue to weave its spell.

Record Label:
CBS

Produced
by Teo Macero and Irving Townsend.

Recorded
at 30th St Studio, NYC; November 1959–March 1960.

Released:
1960

Chart peaks:
None (UK) None (US)

Personnel:
Miles Davis (t, flugelhorn); Gil Evans (a, oa); Ernie Royal, Bernie Glow, Louis Mucci, Taft Jordan (t); Dick Hixon, Frank Rehak (tu); Jimmy Buffington, John Barrows, Earl Chapin (french horn); Jimmy McAllister, Bill Barber (tuba); Al Block, Eddie Caine (flute); Romeo Penque (oboe); Harold Feldman (clarinet, oboe); Danny Bank (bass clarinet); Jack Knitzer (bassoon); Janet Putman (harp); Paul Chambers (bs); Jimmy Cobb (d); Elvin Jones (pc)

Track Listing:
Concierto De Aranjuez (Adagio); Will O' The Wisp; The Pan Piper; Saeta; Solea;

Running time:
41:24

Currently available CD:
Legacy CK 65142 adds: Song Of Our Country, Concierto De Aranjuez (Part One) & Concierto De Aranjuez (Part Two ending)

Further listening:
Miles Ahead (1957); Porgy And Bess (1958)

Further reading:
Miles The Autobiography (Miles Davis and Quincy Troupe, 1989); Miles Davis (Ian Carr, 1982)

Oliver Nelson
Blues And The Abstract Truth

Jazz philospher creates a bracing new blend of musical colours to inaugurate the 1960s.

Talking to Melody Maker in 1993, Donald Fagen explained why this record had exerted an influential fascination upon him. "[It's] a very popular jazz record, kind of mainstrem big band. Nelson had a West Coast sound, and the contrast between Eric Dolphy's solos and that slick, swinging rhythm section was very interesting to me."

It often seemed that the music of master arranger Oliver Nelson was in search of a seamless blend of Ellington's thought and Coltrane's emotion. *Blues And The Abstract Truth*, rightly regarded by Nelson as his high water mark, was where he made that blend sound like nobody but himself.

He loved to mix 'n' match styles – as one of the great jazz synthesizers, there was little he couldn't envelop in his warm embrace. "Classical music of the 19th century, and contemporary music of our own 20th century," Nelson wrote in the album notes, "brought about the need for adopting a different perspective in order to create music that was meaningful and vital. One device which has always been successful and vital in both classical music and in present-day jazz is to let the musical ideas determine the form and shape of a musical composition. In effect, that is what I have tried to do here."

The musical ideas encompassed jazz (traditional and modern), blues, spirituals, Broadway scoring and even country music and classical flourishes. The all-star band included stellar soloists Freddie Hubbard, Bill Evans, Eric Dolphy and Nelson himself. You'll find the more fiery Dolphy elsewhere; here his playing is relatively restrained. But Nelson, whose renown was mostly for his arranging chops, shows himself to be a gifted, deceptively relaxed soloist.

He'd been prepared for this eclectic work by early stints with Louis Jordan, Erskine Hawkins and Wild Bill Davis, a college education in music theory and composition, and a trial-by-fire as the house arranger at the Apollo Theatre. Following the success of this album, he eventually settled in LA, working primarily in film and TV scoring until a heart attack claimed him prematurely in 1975. Though his Hollywood work was of extremely high calibre, it tended to diminish the jazz profile he'd established in New York. But as long as we have *Blues And The Abstract Truth*, his stature as a jazz giant will be indisputable.

Record label:
Impulse

Produced
by Creed Taylor.

Recorded
at Van Gelder Studio, Englewood, New Jersey; February 23, 1961.

Released:
May 1961

Chart peaks:
None (UK) None (US)

Personnel:
Oliver Nelson (as, ts); Eric Dolphy (as, flute); Freddie Hubbard (t); George Barrow (bs); Bill Evans (p); Paul Chambers (b); Roy Haynes (d); Rudy Van Gelder (e)

Track listing:
Stolen Moments; Hoe-Down; Cascades; Yearnin'; Butch and Bitch; Teenies Blues

Running time:
36.43

Current CD:
IMP11542

Further listening:
Soul Battle (1960) – wonderful blowing session with Jimmy Forrest and King Curtis; More Blues And The Abstract Truth (1964)

Jimmy Smith
Back At The Chicken Shack

Hammond-led groove that spawned soul-jazz and became one of Blue Note's biggest sellers.

By 1960, Jimmy Smith had already recorded a phenomenal 19 albums for Blue Note. That same year he recorded four more – two of them (Midnight Special and Back At The Chicken Shack) from the same session at Van Gelder's Recording Studio in Englewood Cliffs, New Jersey. Produced by Alfred Lion, the latter set the precedent for every Hammond organ-led record since with its instantly infectious, gutsy groove featuring Smith's trademark walking basslines and right hand solos. (Mention should also be made of the striking sleeve by Francis Wolff: "Let's get some pictures with 'grease'," said Smith – hence the shot of him on a friend's farm, in natty attire, with dog Elsie and a rooster.)

A pianist from the age of nine, Smith gigged in jazz and R&B groups around his home in western Pennsylvania. Then came the switch to organ. "I saw Wild Bill [Davis] in 1953 and took up the Hammond on the spot. I taught myself. I kept it in a shed so no one knew I couldn't play it. I battled with that beast every single day." Two years later Smith played his first gig with the Hammond at Jimmy's Jazz Club in The Village, New York. "It was a challenge. Nobody had thought about taking the Hammond into jazz and those jazz fans didn't like it, no way. But I went nuts. I went crazy."

As for *Back At The Chicken Shack*: "I just went in there and played my guts out. There was a lot of respect going down between those guys in the studio. Stanley [Turrentine] and Kenny [Burrell] were downright funky. Donald [Bailey] kept the rhythm ticking over." Recorded on 2-track analogue tape, Smith composed two of the four tracks – Messy BS, a funky blues inspired by Charlie Parker's Confirmation, and the title track, an effortlessly cool and sassy down-home number. The Romberg/Hammerstein standard When I Grow Too Old To Dream spotlights Turrentine's almost vocal sax style. Turrentine's own Minor Chant, written for his *Look Out!* album, is 32 bars and seven-and-a-half minutes of minor key sauntering with Stanley wailing centre stage.

The following year Smith recorded another two records for Blue Note. Then in 1962 he signed to Verve, successfully experimenting with a full big band sound and earning his nickname, The Cat.

Record label:
Blue Note

Produced
by Alfred Lion.

Recorded
at Van Gelder's Recording Studio, Englewood Cliffs, New Jersey; April 25, 1960.

Released:
summer 1961

Chart peaks:
None (UK) None (US)

Personnel:
Jimmy Smith (o); Stanley Turrentine (ts); Kenny Burrell (g); Donald Bailey (d)

Track listing:
Back At The Chicken Shack; When I Grow Too Old To Dream; Minor Chant; Messy Bessie

Running time:
38.04

Current CD:
7464022 adds: On The Sunny Side Of The Street

Further listening:
The Cat (1964) – more swinging organ tunes but this time arranged and conducted by Lalo Schifrin; Monster (1965) – Oliver Nelson big band arrangements and organ-led takes on classic theme tunes.

Further reading:
www.bluenote.com

Bill Evans Trio
Sunday At The Village Vanguard

An innovative pianist finds his niche and makes jazz history.

The choice of pianist Bill Evans to replace Red Garland in the Miles Davis group in 1958 was not a universally popular one. For one thing, he didn't appear to swing as hard as Red, for another he was white. But Miles responded to Evans's sound – detailed touch, limpid harmonies, emotional scalar lines – which Miles described as "like crystal notes of sparkling water cascading down from some clear waterfall." As for his time playing, "Bill underplayed it," said Miles, "which for what I was doing now with the modal thing, I liked what Bill was doing better."

Bill, though thrilled to be in a band with Coltrane, Cannonball, Miles and Philly Joe Jones, was stung by the audience's indifference-bordering-hostility to his contributions – which, in a live setting, were the antithesis of his hard-blowing colleagues – and quit after seven months. He was recalled for the seminal Davis album *Kind Of Blue* – which Davis admitted was "planned" around Bill's playing – but was keen to form his own trio which he had very clear ideas about.

"I'm hoping the trio will grow in the direction of simultaneous improvisation," he had said, "if the bass player, for example, hears an idea that he wants to answer, why should he just keep playing a 4/4 background?" After a few false starts (he lost several potential collaborators due to poor treatment at a club supporting Benny Goodman), Bill ended up with responsive drummer Paul Motian and a remarkable young bassist, Scott LaFaro, who was willing and more than capable to fulfil Bill's vision of concurrent invention. "Ideas were rolling out on top of each other," Evans said of LaFaro, "it was like a bucking horse."

The trio made two fine studio albums: December 1959's *Portrait In Jazz* and February 1961's *Explorations*, but with the tapes rolling all day Sunday, 25 June 1961 at New York club the Village Vanguard ("a relatively painless way to extract an album from the usually foot-dragging pianist" said producer Orrin Keepnews), two and a half hours of glorious, symbiotic music was taped. It was a rich, delicate summation of the trio's matured conception of interplay. Ten days later, 25-year-old LaFaro was killed in a car crash.

Shattered at the loss, Bill Evans stopped playing the piano for months. The sessions – emerging over three albums of which *Sunday At The Village Vanguard* is the first – are generally regarded as Evans's finest and among the most important recordings in all of jazz.

Record Label:
Riverside

Produced
by Orrin Keepnews.

Recorded
live at The Village Vanguard, New York;
June 25, 1961.

Released:
September 1961

Chart peaks:
None (UK) None (US)

Personnel:
Bill Evans (p); Scott LaFaro (b); Paul Motian (d); Dave Jones (e)

Track Listing:
Gloria's Step; My Man's Gone Now; Solar; Alice In Wonderland; All Of You; Jade Visions

Running time:
40.11

Current CD:
OJC201402

Further listening:
Waltz For Debbie (1961); More From The Vanguard (1961)

Further reading:
How My Heart Sings (Peter Pettinger, 1998)

Ray Charles And Betty Carter

Ray Charles And Betty Carter

Masterly easy jazz vocal duets between the Genius Of Soul and Betty Bebop.

In the late '50s, Ray Charles was an R&B star with Atlantic records enjoying million-selling success with What'd I Say. ABC offered Charles better royalties, profit sharing, eventual ownership of his masters and, significantly, a production deal. Charles signed with them to the dismay of Atlantic. Given his own label to play with – Tangerine – Charles set about "trying to share something with his fellow man", as singer Jimmy Scott remembered. Scott himself got to record *Falling In Love Is Wonderful* ("the best record I ever made") under Ray's guidance but contractual difficulties prevented its release. No such problems for Ray's duet album with Betty Carter.

Carter was an uncompromisingly bold jazz singer whose inventive, musical way with a song had precluded wide appeal, but recommended to him by Miles Davis, Ray took her on tour and used his new entrepreneurial leverage to heighten her profile. The arranger Marty Paich was known for his super-hip, cool-school dektette work for Mel Torme but fashioned a more straightforward set of charts for the playful, romantic setting Charles had in mind. There were even the glutinous Jack Halloran Singers on a few of the cuts – much to the chagrin of some critics – but most of the resulting album bursts with relaxed, musicianly banter and sexual chemistry. Charles is growling and suggestive, Carter squirrelly and coy, and it remains one of the all-time great duet sets.

Baby It's Cold Outside was a massive hit and Charles went on to sustained popularity, starting with his huge-selling Hit The Road Jack. Carter enjoyed a degree of attention before temporarily retiring to bring up her family, re-emerging in the late '60s to build a reputation as the most fearsomely inventive singer in all of jazz, while admitting to "fond memories" of the easy listening album of duets with Brother Ray.

Record Label:
Atlantic

Produced
by Sid Feller.

Recorded
in Hollywood, California; June 1961.

Released:
1961

Chart peaks:
None (UK) None (US)

Personnel:
Ray Charles (p, v); Betty Carter (v); Jack Halloran Singers (bv); David 'Fathead' Newman (s); Marty Paich (a, oa)

Track Listening:
Ev'ry Time We Say Goodbye; You And I; Goodbye – We'll Be Together Again; People Will Say We're In Love; Cocktails For Two; Side By Side; Baby It's Cold Outside; Together; For All We Know; It Takes Two To Tango; Alone Together; Just You Just Me.

Running time:
67.17

Current CD:
5050042 adds Ray Charles's 1961 album Dedicated To You: Hardhearted Hannah; Nancy; Margie; Ruby; Rosetta; Stella By Starlight; Cherry; Josephine; Candy; Marie; Diane; Sweet Georgia Brown

Further listening:
Ray Charles: Modern Sounds In Country And Western (1962); An Audience With Betty Carter (1979)

Further reading:
Brother Ray (Ray Charles and David Ritz Da Capo, 1992); Ray Charles: Man and Music (Michael Lydon, 1999)

Charles Mingus

The Black Saint And The Sinner Lady

Some say it's the best jazz record ever made. Mingus thought it was folk music. Whatever it is, it's brilliant.

Charles Mingus decided in 1963 that henceforth his outfit would be known as the Charles Mingus New Folk Band. This rich, compelling work is closer to the metropolitan, symphonic jazz of Duke Ellington than anything a casual listener would recognise as folk music but, thinking about it, you can see his point – there's something very 'of the people' about this music, as sprawling, crowded and buzzy as a city, multi-faceted and teeming with life.

Superficially it has the sleazy, urban feel of an Elmer Bernstein film score; lots of conversational muted horns and slurring, *rubato* saxes, which, during recording, Mingus set in a V shape with the tenor at the fulcrum, furthest away from the mic. Such careful positioning gives the sound a theatrical sense of space – the brass interplay resembles dialogue. In this, though Mingus describes the music as a dance, it's more operatic. The use of overdubbing was unusual in jazz in the early '60s, but its employment here helps a modest-sized band sound busy and imposing.

Mingus, who'd spent some time as a patient in New York's Bellevue mental hospital, was never one for explaining himself rationally; his sleeve notes for the album were pell-mell. Starting to describe the action and then quickly digressing into a rant about critics, he asks the listener to "throw all other records of mine away except maybe one other". The track names weren't much help, and a review of the album by Mingus's psychiatrist tells us we're in the presence of mischief. Dr Edmund Pollock PhD, offers the following interpretation: "There are recurrent themes of loneliness, separateness and tearful depression, Mr Mingus cries of misunderstanding of self and people. Throughout he presents a brooding, moaning intensity about prejudice, hate and persecution." Cranky, stubborn and angry he may have been, but Mingus could not keep the intense pleasure that music brought him out of his work. Whatever the good doctor said, *The Black Saint And The Sinner Lady* drips with joy.

Record label:
Impulse

Produced
by Bob Thiele.

Recorded
in New York; January 20, 1963.

Released:
April 1963

Chart peaks:
None (UK) None (US)

Personnel:
Rolf Ericson, Richard Williams (t); Quentin Jackson (tb); Don Butterfield (tuba); Jerome Richardson (soprano sax, bs, flute); Dick Hafer (ts, flute); Charlie Mariano (as); Jaki Byard (p); Jay Berliner (g); Charles Mingus (b, p); Dannie Richmond (d)

Track listing:
Track A: Solo Dancer, Stop Look And Listen, Sinner Jim Whitney; Track B: Duet Solo Dancers, Hearts Beat And Shades In Physical Embraces; Track C: Group Dancers (Soul Fusion) Freewoman And Oh, This Freedom's Slave Cries; Mode D: Trio And Group Dancers, Stop! Look! And Sing Songs Of Revolutions!; Mode E: Single Solos And Group Dance, Saint And Sinner Join In Merriment On Battle Front; Mode F: Group And Solo Dance, Of Love, Pain And Passioned Revolt, Then Farewell, My Beloved, 'Til It's Freedom Day

Running time:
37.37

Current CD:
IMP11742

Further listening:
Mingus, Mingus, Mingus, Mingus, Mingus (1963); Astral Weeks (1964); Right Now! (1965)

Further reading:
Beneath The Underdog (Charles Mingus, 1971);
http://webusers.siba.fi/~eonttone/mingus/

James Brown
Live At The Apollo (Vol. 1)

A benchmark for thrilling soul performance, and the first of Brown's enormous selection of live albums.

Some people can't recognise a good thing when it falls in their lap. Syd Nathan, the label boss of King Records in Cincinnati, wasn't convinced by James Brown. "The worst piece of shit I've ever heard" he declared in 1955 upon hearing Please, Please, Please. Released to embarrass Ralph Bass, the A&R man who had brought Brown to Nathan's attention, Please, Please Please – that contradiction in terms, a hard-driving ballad – gave King a Number 6 R&B hit in 1956. The nine 'failures' that followed only confirmed Nathan in his doubts. He had big reservations, too, about Try Me, a song getting great reactions on tour, and released it spitefully, to prove Brown's instincts wrong. It soared to Number 1 in the US R&B charts (48 pop). Henceforward, Brown charted as the seasons changed, at least four singles a year on the R&B charts and as many on the Hot 100. By 1962 "Mr Dynamite" was the biggest live draw in the R&B market, his physically athletic and dramatic performances matched by impassioned ballads, relentless uptempo numbers and a tightly-drilled band. All this, suggested Brown and his manager, Ben Bart, should be caught live on tape. Still surprisingly indifferent to his star's power, Nathan's reply was, in effect, Over my dead body.

Undaunted, Brown put up $5,700 of his own money to record a show at Harlem's black music mecca, the Apollo. His season there began on October 18, 1962 and by the night of the 24th the band was in blistering form, delivering a finely-honed set of their hits to date with Brown blasting from one song to the next with scarcely a pause for breath. For his core black audience it provided a vivid souvenir of Mr Dynamite in his pomp – and for whites it was an ear-boggling introduction to a thrilling kind of performance rarely seen or heard. As Brown (then still only 29) sails through the first five tracks, varying the pace but not the emotional intensity, you'd swear you can hear the sweat spraying out of his pores. With *Live At The Apollo* James Brown became – and would remain for many years to come – The Hardest Working Man In Showbusiness.

Record label:
Polydor

Produced
by James Brown.

Recorded
at Apollo Theater, New York; October 24, 1962.

Released:
May 1963

Chart peaks:
None (UK) 2 (US)

Personnel:
James Brown (v); Bobby Byrd, Bobby Bennett and Baby Lloyd Stallworth (v); Lewis Hamilton (t, MD); Roscoe Patrick and Teddy Washington (t); Dickey Wells (tb); St. Clair Pinckney and Clifford MacMillan (ts); Al 'Briscoe' Clark (bs); Lucas 'Fats' Gonder (o); Les Buie (g); Hubert Perry (b); Clayton Fillyau (d)

Track listing:
I'll Go Crazy; Try Me; Think; I Don't Mind; Lost Someone; Please, Please, Please; You've Got The Power; I Found Someone; Why Do You Do Me Like You Do; I Want You So Bad; I Love You Yes I Do; Why Does Everything Happen To Me; Bewildered; Please Don't Go; Night Train

Running time:
31.36

Current CD:
843 479-2

Further listening:
Two more volumes of Live At The Apollo, the best being Volume III, Revolution Of The Mind (1971). Love Power Peace (1992), the JBs and Brown live at the Olympia in Paris in 1971, and Say It Live And Loud/Live In Dallas (1998), a coruscating performance from August 26, 1968.

Further reading:
James Brown: The Autobiography (1996); James Brown (Geoff Brown, 1996)

Sam Cooke
Night Beat

A pivotal moment in soul history.

The sixth note in the musical scale is owned by Sam Cooke. No one has done more for that note in the history of recorded vocal music. While his peers were over-using the flatted seventh and flatted third notes, Sam was smoothly pinning his style right on that pure sixth interval. All the rest just rented their notes; Sam owned his. Many decades after his untimely death, he still does.

Cooke rose from a church background, the heartthrob lead singer of gospel superstars The Soul Stirrers, where he built his dizzying, flawless, effortless style. His transition to pop caused his former soulmates to berate him for converting to "the Devil's music". Cooke became massively famous as a pop singer and made an unprecedented step over the US colour line. By 1963, with several hits under his belt, Cooke was anxious to show the more mature side of his artistry. Prior to *Night Beat*, his LPs were filled with singles and weary fillers. Sam wanted an album that didn't pander to the radio audience, one where he could express what he was moving towards as he grew older. He had no compunction about covering blues shouter Howlin' Wolf (Little Red Rooster) or big band belter Joe Turner (Shake, Rattle And Roll).

A crack studio band was assembled around his long-time associates Rene Hall and Clifford White. Studio freshmen Billy Preston on organ and Hal Blaine on drums still count these sessions as some of their most mesmerising. On the opening track, Sam duets with double bass player Cliff Hils while the rest of the band takes five. It stands as one of Cooke's greatest vocal legacies. Elsewhere, blues and semi-gospel gems are addressed with real feeling, the musical perfection breathtaking.

Cooke's goal was realised, and the album, out of print for decades, was re-released in 1997 to a legion of new fans.

Record label:
RCA Victor

Produced
by Hugo and Luigi.

Recorded
at RCA Victor Studios, Hollywood; February 22–23 and 25, 1963.

Released:
September 1963

Chart peaks:
None (UK) None (US)

Personnel:
Sam Cooke (v); Ed Hall, Hal Blaine (d); Rene Hall, Cliff White, Barney Kessell (g); Clifford Hils (b); Raymond Johnson (p); Billy Preston (o); Dave Hassinger (e)

Track listing:
Lost And Looking; Mean Old World; Nobody Knows The Trouble I've Seen; Please Don't Drive Me Away; I Lost Everything; Get Yourself Another Fool; Little Red Rooster; Laughin' And Clownin'; Trouble Blues; You Gotta Move; Fool's Paradise; Shake, Rattle And Roll

Running time:
37.35

Current CD:
ABKCO 1124-2

Further listening:
The only other album that approaches this intensity is Live At The Harlem Square Club (1963).

Further reading:
You Send Me: The Life And Times of Sam Cooke (Daniel Wolff, 1996), a Cinderella story with a Tupac ending.

Koerner, Ray And Glover
Blues, Rags And Hollers

Lo-fi early '60s blues from influential American stylists.

Back in 1963 Paul Nelson, the editor of folk magazine The Little Sandy Review had been approached by Ed Nunn, a hobby-recordist and independent record label owner, who was looking for a folk act to record. Nelson suggested Koerner, Ray And Glover and for 300 bucks they recorded an album for his Audiophile label (his previous best seller was an album with one whole side devoted to a thunderstorm). Ensconced in an old Women's Club for a ten-hour session fuelled by a little speed and some good burgers, the trio cut 40 songs in a variety of set-ups; a cappella, accompanied, duets, solo and all three together playing live. "It wasn't exactly a comfortable situation," recalls Tony Glover. "We were on the edge about recording and the producer wouldn't allow us our usual lubrication."

Further reduction left a 20-track set, of raw and rattling blues – still an unusual pursuit among young white boys. A limited edition of 300 copies were pressed, including their spirited versions of Leadbelly's Hangman, Robert Johnson's Dust My Broom and Blind Lemon Jefferson's One Kind Favor, interspersed with suitably raucous rallying calls of their own making. It sold out immediately.

Glover: "We figured that this would be our only album, so we wanted to get as many tunes on as possible. But the tracks went right up to the label and cut out on some people's players." When Elektra's Jac Holzman heard it he lost no time in signing the trio and buying out the rights to re-issue their debut. Elektra removed four songs per side (which are re-instated on the Red House CD re-issue) in order to enhance the sound quality and *Blues, Rags And Hollers* helped establish it as the hippest of labels.

"Some years later, Love were being courted by every label on the scene," Holzman remembered. "But Arthur Lee insisted on Elektra because it was the label that released Koerner, Ray and Glover. The same thing happened with Paul Butterfield and The Doors." John Lennon was a fan too. What had impressed them all was the intense passion that Koerner, Ray And Glover displayed for the material. People had never heard anything like it before.

As The Lovin' Spoonful's John Sebastian noted: "It was played much faster than the originals because it was done by three excitable young white guys."

Record label:
Elektra

Produced
by Paul Nelson with Koerner, Ray And Glover.

Recorded
at The Woman's Club, Milwaukee, Wisconsin; March 24, 1963.

Released:
November 1963

Chart peaks:
None (UK) None (US)

Personnel:
'Spider' John Koerner (v, g); Dave 'Snaker' Ray (v, hm, bottleneck guitar, 12-string); Tony 'Little Sun' Glover (v, hm)

Track listing:
Linin' Track; Ramblin' Blues; It's All Right; Hangman; Down To Louisianna; Creepy John; Bugger Burns; Sun's Wail; One Kind Favor; Go Down Ol' Hannah; Good Time Charlie; Banjo Thing; Stop That Thing; Snaker's Here; Low Down Rounder; Jimmy Bel

Running time:
41.41

Current CD:
RHR CD 76 adds Ted Mack Rag; Dust My Broom; Too Bad; Mumblin' Word

Further listening:
Lots More Blues Rags And Hollers (1964); Koerner and Glover's Spider Blues (1965); Koerner and Willie Murphy's Running, Jumping, Standing Still (1994)

Further reading:
Follow The Music (Jac Holzman, 2000); the sleevenotes to the Red House re-issue of Blues, Rags And Hollers

The Holy Modal Rounders
The Holy Modal Rounders

America's first truly underground group blend old-time banjo music, bluegrass and traditional folk with a unique vision.

The Greenwich Village folk scene of the early '60s attracted the ambitious and talented, the ambitious but *talentless*, the right-on, the put-upon and the just plain weird. The Holy Modal Rounders were as weird as it got. Stampfel and Weber were talented and accomplished players, who first met up in Greenwich Village in March 1963. In the original sleevenotes, Stampfel attempted to pin down the fruit of their union: "Steve calls it rockabilly and I call it progressive old-timey. No-one has ever played music like us before."

They kicked their music *out of* shape by playing every theatre, book store, street gathering, festival, coffee house and folk club around the Village prior to recording *The Holy Modal Rounders* on December 11, 1963, for the Prestige Folklore imprint. The other key folk labels of the day, Elektra and Vanguard, had also approached them; they went with Prestige's Paul Rothschild because he smoked dope.

Opening with Blues In The Bottle – an obscure 1930 recording later brought to the wider world courtesy of The Lovin' Spoonful, the album's tone is set: the Rounders' personalised lyrics veering close to the edge: "I don't need nobody sniffin glue." Hesitation Blues features the first recorded use of the word 'psychedelic'; it's one of three brilliant Charlie Poole songs on the album, all '20s period pieces transformed into a kind of lysergic folk. Almost every song comes loaded with drug references and scatological rhymes: the Rounders made up new words for all the material they covered, and sang in unconventionally blended voices; Weber's like early Dylan on helium and Stampfel's a nasal twang. Ultimately, *The Holy Modal Rounders* is tremendous fun.

That the band ever got to make an album is remarkable; that there was a second later that year smacks of complete madness on the part of their record label. But there's a wit, originality and sense of joy – and a prescient, subversive intent – that sets these two records apart from everything else in their day. Unsurprisingly, they soon teamed up with beat activists The Fugs (on whose first two albums they play), though they're probably still best known for 1968's Bird Song, featured in the movie Easy Rider. The band continued into the '70s with augmented line-ups that included Michael Hurley and playwright Sam Shephard as drummer at different times. But none of their subsequent work approaches the inspired mayhem on offer here.

Record label:
Prestige

Produced
by Paul Rothschild.

Recorded
in New York City; December 11, 1963 and January 17, 1964.

Released:
February 1964

Chart peaks:
None (UK) None (US)

Personnel:
Peter Stampfel (fiddle, banjo, v); Steve Weber (g, v)

Track listing:
Blues In The Bottle; Fiddler A Dram; The Cuckoo; Euphoria; Long John; Hesitation Blues; Hey, Hey Baby; Reuben's Train; Mister Spaceman; Moving Day; Better Things For You; Same Old Man; Hop High Ladies; Bound To Lose

Running time:
35.13

Current CD:
Big Beat CDWIKD 176 adds: Flop Eared Mule; Black Eyed Susie; Sail Away Ladies; Clinch Mountain Backstep; Fishing Blues; Statesboro' Blues; Jumko Partner; Mole In The Ground; Hot Corn Cold Corn; Down The Old Plank Road; Chevrolet Six; Crowley Waltz; Bully Of The Town; Sugar In The Ground; Soldier's Joy

Further listening:
Everything you need is on the CD above.

Further reading:
Follow The Music (Jac Holzman and Gavan Daws, 1997)

Davy Graham And Shirley Collins

Folk Roots, New Routes

A seemingly bizarre pairing of folk song's English rose and an inventive young guitar genius.

Graham was always one of the British folk scene's maverick characters. While he was instantly lumped in with the scene because he played an acoustic guitar and worked London's Soho club circuit — so fashionable in the early '60s — he was forever in search of a broader canvas. A compulsive traveller and an avid musical adventurer (perhaps because his father came from the Isle Of Skye and taught Gaelic and his mother hailed from Guyana) he was heavily into blues, modern jazz, Indian and Arabic music, playing it all on guitar while barely out of his teens.

It was Shirley Collins's former husband Austin John Marshall who suggested that his inventive interpretations of Indian ragas might provide an intriguing accompaniment for one of Shirley's traditional tunes, Pretty Saro. Graham, it transpired, was a big Collins fan (he also loved Robert Johnson, Charlie Parker, Mary Wells and Rimsky-Korsakov) and joined her on-stage at a concert at London's Mercury Theatre in July 1964. The audience may have been baffled, but the results were extraordinary enough for the pairing to dive into the studio at the first opportunity. Many purist British folkies were appalled, but after a 2,000 mile journey trekking through the southern states of America collecting blues, gospel, jazz and folk songs with Alan Lomax, Shirley's ears were nothing if not open to different musical styles, and she threw herself into the project with a relish that startled many.

The fusion, light years ahead of its time, didn't sell particularly well but was massively influential, opening the way for other inventive guitarists such as John Martyn. Even now, in a time when world music is only a high street store away, the other-worldly settings of traditional warhorses like Nottamun Town, Love Is Pleasin' and Reynardine still sound extraordinary.

Record label:
Topic

Produced
by Ray Horricks.

Recorded
at Decca Studios, London; January 1964.

Released:
March 1964

Chart peaks:
None (UK) None (US)

Personnel:
Shirley Collins (v, g, banjo); Davy Graham (g); Gus Dudgeon (e)

Track listing:
Nottamun Town; Proud Maisrie; The Cherry Tree Carol; Blue Monk; Hares On The Mountain; Reynardine; Pretty Saro; Rif Mountain; Jane Jane; Love Is Pleasin'; Boll Weevil Holler; Hori Horo; Bad Girl; Lord Greggory; Grooveyard; Dearest Dear

Running time:
44.16

Current CD:
Topic CD819

Further listening:
The Graham album Folk, Blues And Beyond (1964) took folk guitar deeper into alien worlds of modern jazz, blues, Indian and even Arabic music. Further examples can be heard on the excellent compilation Fire In The Soul (1970).

Further reading:
www.geocities.com/davygraham/

The Rolling Stones
The Rolling Stones

British beat moves up a gear; Jagger wanted to make this LP "the best ever by a British group".

The time manager Andrew Loog Oldham walked in on Keith Richards revising Buddy Holly's Not Fade Away was the day he knew his Stones could write as well as roll; the time he locked Mick and Keith in the kitchen and wouldn't let them out until they'd finished a song was the night that they realized it too. And the January 1964 sessions which produced the Stones' debut album told the world that they weren't going to be a blues band forever. Stylistically, of course, The Rolling Stones is little more than a verbatim recounting of the band's live set of the period – Bobby Troup, Bo Diddley, Chuck Berry, American soul and R&B. One dramatic Jagger/Richard ballad, Tell Me, joined a couple of pseudonymous efforts which disguised the team's own early bashfulness – the instrumental Now I've Got A Witness, dedicated to Phil Spector and Gene Pitney (and rewriting the stage staple Everybody Needs Somebody To Love) and Little By Little, co-starring both, and co-written with Spector. On paper, the album is the sound of British beat 1964, pure and simple. It was what was done with the beat that mattered, though. Engineer Bill Farley recalls, "When they arrived, no one had any thought about arrangements. They just busked it until they got the feeling of the number," and that is what made the Stones as musicians, and Oldham as producer, so special.

The Rolling Stones emerged with a freshness and vitality which belied the rigidity of its repertoire and the sterility of the studio. There was no overdubbing, no gimmickry, no prima donna virtuosity. They played, they taped, they jammed, they relaxed, and when it felt right to everyone, it was finished.

Making a record, Oldham confirms, is not a craft, it's an art. "It's not something you know, it's something you feel, in your heart, in your gut, in every fibre of your instinct." *The Rolling Stones* is all heart, gut and instinct.

Record Label:
Decca

Produced
by Andrew Loog Oldham.

Recorded
at Regent Sound Studio; January 1964.

Release date:
April 17, 1964

Chart peaks:
1 (UK) 11 (US)

Personnel:
Mick Jagger (v); Keith Richard (g); Brian Jones (g, v); Bill Wyman (b, v); Ian Stewart (k); Charlie Watts (d); Gene Pitney (p on Little By Little); Phil Spector (maracas on Little By Little)

Track Listing:
Route 66; I Just Want To Make Love To You; Honest I Do; Mona (UK only); Now I've Got A Witness; Little By Little; I'm A King Bee; Carol; Tell Me (S, US only); Can I Get A Witness; You Can Make It If You Try; Walking The Dog; Not Fade Away (S, US only)

Not available on CD
in original form, current CD replicates US release England's Newest Hitmakers: The Rolling Stones

Running time:
31.12 (US)

Current CD:
LK 4605

Further listening:
Rolling Stones #2 (1964); Boxed Set Singles 1963–69 (1980)

Further reading:
Stoned (Andrew Loog Oldham, 2000)

Dusty Springfield
A Girl Called Dusty

The debut album, recorded only months after the split of The Springfields.

Very few British pop albums from 1964 were built to last: pop was still a singles form, and long-players seemed like little more than a couple of hits and ten other tracks. Dusty Springfield's debut was an amazing exception, though it followed the already familiar path of including covers of contemporary hits. Springfield created an album that bore almost no resemblance to the style she'd found success with as one of The Springfields, who'd played their farewell concert only six months before this album's release. She had already had a solo hit with I Only Want To Be With You – the first record ever to be played on Top Of The Pops – which suggested that the folky sound of The Springfields had been traded in for a zippier pop beat. But *A Girl Called Dusty* went much further than that. Several of the tunes were covers of black pop hits (or soon-to-be hits) which Springfield refused to mellow out in the normal manner of white cover acts. Her spirited rush at The Supremes' When The Lovelight Starts Shining Thru His Eyes, for instance, was just as effective as the original. She sings both parts on the treatment of the Inez and Charlie Foxx hit Mockingbird without neutering the result. On You Don't Own Me (a success for Lesley Gore in the US), she comes close to sounding like a blues mama. In tracks like these, Dusty's reputation as Britain's great soul voice was born. But that famous misnomer – bolstered further by the later and probably over-rated *Dusty In Memphis* – conceals her greater talent, as a kind of ice queen of torch singing. The tracks which really stand out here are the Bacharach-David tunes: Twenty-Four Hours From Tulsa, Anyone Who Had A Heart, Wishin' And Hopin' and My Colouring Book, which approaches sheer desolation in feeling. Dusty was a great sufferer, and although even these songs would be surpassed by such monumental tearjerkers as I Close My Eyes And Count To Ten and All I See Is You, the record sows the seeds for her mastery of bathos. But that was some way off yet.

In 1964, this 25-year-old convent girl stared out from record racks and seemed an irresistible mix of country girl and pop diva.

Record Label:
Mercury

Produced
by John Franz.

Recorded:
1964.

Released:
April 1964

Chart peaks:
6 (UK) None (US)

Personnel:
Dusty Springfield (v); Ivor Raymonde (oa); The Breakaways (bv)

Track Listing:
Mama Said; You Don't Own Me; Do Re Mi; When The Lovelight Starts Shining Thru His Eyes; My Colouring Book; Mockingbird; Twenty Four Hours From Tulsa; Nothing; Anyone Who Had A Heart; Will You Love Me Tomorrow; Wishin' And Hopin'; Don't You Know

Running time:
56.33

Current CD:
534520-2 adds: I Only Want To Be With You (remix); He's Got Something; Every Day I Have To Cry; Can I Get A Witness; All Cried Out; I Wish I'd Never Loved You; Once Upon A Time; Summer Is Over

Further listening:
The Dusty Springfield Collection (1998)

Further reading:
www.dustyspringfield.nu

The Beatles
A Hard Day's Night

Rock'n'roll grows up as the Fabs write all of their third album.

By March 1964, The Beatles had changed pop music forever, setting standards of cross-generational appeal that remain a wonder to this day. They were also getting nods of musical approval from the establishment about their song writing and for their third album — also serving as the soundtrack to their first movie — they decided to go for an unheard-of option, an all-originals set. In the end, side one of the LP comprised songs from the film while side two contained other new songs. (In America, side two used George Martin instrumentals, the other tracks creeping out on other albums.) John Lennon, perturbed by a recent Beatles single A-side being nabbed by the Paul McCartney-penned Can't Buy Me Love, took full advantage of Paul being relatively distracted (by his romance with Jane Asher) to reassert his domination of the band by lead-composing or singing on ten of the thirteen resulting tracks.

Inevitably, given that the songs were written in the pressure bubble that was Beatlemania, the band — however spirited — occasionally sounded formulaic (Any Time At All, I Should Have Known Better, When I Get Home) but the best tracks were the pinnacle of what rock-era pop songwriting had yet achieved. Lennon's ballad If I Fell encapsulates what Carr and Tyler called the "excellence-through-innocence" that characterises the whole album while McCartney's And I Love Her was instantly seized upon by adult pop merchants as a new standard. "I consider it his first Yesterday," Lennon reflected much later.

There was the bluesy title track with its unforgettable opening chord (written specifically as a startling opening to the movie), exotic guitar textures courtesy of George's new Rickenbacker 12-string (which would have such an effect on West Coast Beatle-freak Roger McGuinn) and a pair of delicious compositions (Lennon's I'll Be Back — based on Del Shannon's Runaway — and McCartney's Things We Said Today) that wallow in minor/major ambivalence, signposts toward future sophistication. The Dick Lester-directed black-and-white biographical fantasy film was described by US critic Andrew Sarris as "the Citizen Kane of juke box movies" while elsewhere Lennon and McCartney were hailed as the greatest songwriters since Schubert.

Record Label:
Parlophone

Produced
by George Martin.

Recorded
at Abbey Road, London; January–June 1964

Released:
July 10, 1964

Chart peaks:
1 (UK) 1 (US)

Personnel:
John Lennon (v, g); Paul McCartney (v, b); George Harrison (v, g); Ringo Starr (d); George Martin (p)

Track Listing:
A Hard Day's Night; I Should Have Known Better; If I Fell; I'm Happy Just To Dance With You; And I Love Her; Tell Me Why; Can't Buy Me Love; Any Time At All; I'll Cry Instead; Things We Said Today; When I Get Home; You Can't Do That; I'll Be Back

Running time:
30.30

Current CD:
CDP7464372

Further listening:
With The Beatles (1963); Help! (1965)

Further reading:
Revolution In The Head (Ian Macdonald, 1998); The Beatles As Musicians (Walter Everett, 1999); The Beatles: An Illustrated Record (Roy Carr and Tony Tyler, 1975)

The Animals

The Animals

Provincial British R&B, as dirty and sweaty as the group's ill-fitting suits.

By 1964, the Merseybeat boom had fizzled out. Only The Beatles and The Searchers proved to have staying power. The new boom on the block was tough, rootsy R&B, propagated by a network of clubs across the UK. Newcastle's Club Au Go Go was an essential stop on any American bluesman's tour itinerary. However, when elder statesmen such as Sonny Boy Williamson II hit town, they ran the risk of being blown off-stage by the toughest outfit of the British blues boom. The Animals majored on the musicianship of Alan Price on piano and Vox Continental organ and the secret weapon of the raw impassioned vocals of Eric Burdon and their repertoire, drawn from the rougher end of Muddy Waters, Bo Diddley, John Lee Hooker, et al.

They were signed to EMI by producer Mickey Most, and debuted during three one-day sessions in January 1964. A second date in February and third in July provided the material for this album, the first three singles and their B-sides. The second of these was The House Of The Rising Sun, which, released in July, quickly topped the charts on both sides of the Atlantic.

For the album, The Animals essentially played their live set and that was it. Burdon gave out true bottled soul on Bury My Body and I'm Mad Again (one of three John Lee Hooker songs), while the unsung Hilton Valentine (the final member to join) provided a great growling guitar solo. Alan Price contributed rolling piano to Hooker standard, Dimples. ("He was always better on piano," says Burdon, "I hated the sound of that fucking Vox Continental, but it was the only practical thing to use for live dates.")

Thanks to *The Animals* and two other eponymous, largely R&B-influenced albums by British bands the same year – *The Kinks* and *The Rolling Stones* – this music would remain the dominant form in the clubs and charts until the end of 1965, with the rise of the mod bands, soul and an increasing air of experimentation.

1965 also saw Alan Price's departure, officially citing "fear of flying". Burdon himself blames Price's sole arrangement credit on the band's biggest hit as the real reason: "When Alan Price walked off with the publishing for House Of The Rising Sun, well, what does that amount to in terms of finances? It would have given everybody a sense of success and achievement if the money had been distributed equally. So the band was always split into factions."

Record Label:
Columbia

Produced
by Mickey Most.

Recorded
at EMI Studios, London; 1964

Released:
October 1964

Chart peaks:
6 (UK) 7 (US)

Personnel:
Eric Burdon (v); Alan Price (k); Hilton Valentine (g); Chas Chandler (b); John Steel (d)

Track listing:
Story Of Bo Diddley; Bury My Body; Dimples; I've Been Around; I'm In Love Again; The Girl Can't Help It; I'm Mad Again; She Said Yeah; The Right Time; Memphis; Boom Boom (S/US); Around And Around

Running time:
38.52

Current CD:
EMI 16137

Further listening:
The Complete Animals (1990)

Further Reading:
I Used To Be An Animal – But I'm All Right Now (Eric Burdon, 1992)

Eric Dolphy
Out To Lunch

Tour de force of articulate free jazz.

When Eric Dolphy first arrived in New York in the late
'50s with Chico Hamilton's West Coast group, AJ
Spellman noted that he "played nice – pretty and all". The same
writer noted that it was a different Dolphy who returned a year
later with Charles Mingus: "This one was wild and woolly,
played all kinds of unmentionable things you wouldn't say in
front of your mother."

Stylistically, Eric Dolphy was somewhere between the
slithery melodicism of Charlie Parker and the boundary-busting
disorder of Ornette Coleman, of whom Dolphy said, "He taught
me a direction." He had the energy and anarchy of a New Thing
player but there was an instrumental virtuosity, melodic intelligence and tonal refinement that somehow set him apart from
the centre of the avant-garde. Here, on his acknowledged
masterpiece, Dolphy is majestic on bass clarinet on Hat And
Beard (a witty nod to Monk in 9/4) and Something Sweet
Something Tender (a gorgeous, Mingus-like semi-abstract
reverie); lyrical and visceral by turns – sometimes within the
same phrase – but always thoughtful and engaging.

"I play notes that would not ordinarily be said to be in a
given key, but I hear them as 'proper'," Dolphy once explained.
"I don't think I 'leave the changes' as the expression goes; every
note I play has some reference to the chords of the piece."

While the chords on *Out To Lunch* are often not an issue
(the quintet go 'free' on several occasions), there is pulse and
rhythmic momentum throughout, though the rhythm section –
especially vibist Hutcherson – are employed as equal contributors rather than time and harmony keepers.

"Everyone's a leader on this session," commented
Dolphy, and how well they all lead; the lingering impression of
this challenging, often beautiful work is far from the dense,
cluttered argument that characterises much New Thing music,
but is rather one of aerated, witty conversation. Leaving
America soon after this date ("If you try and do anything
different in this country, people put you down for it"), Dolphy
died in Europe three months later of undiagnosed diabetes, aged
36. This tragedy, his musical boldness, and reputed personal
charm have elevated his standing to nothing short of jazz saint.

Record Label:
Blue Note

Produced
by Alfred Lion.

Recorded
at Van Gelder Studio, Englewood Cliffs,
New Jersey; February 25, 1964.

Released:
1964

Chart peaks:
None (UK) None (US)

Personnel:
Eric Dolphy (as, flute, bass clarinet);
Freddie Hubbard (t); Bobby Hutcherson
(vibes); Richard Davis (b); Anthony
Williams (d)

Track Listing:
Hat And Beard; Something Sweet,
Something Tender; Gazzelloni; Out To
Lunch; Straight Up And Down

Running time:
42.18

Current CD:
CDP7465242

Further listening:
Far Cry (1960); Conversations (1963)

Further reading:
Eric Dolphy (Vladimir Simosko, 1979),
http://farcry.neurobio.pitt.edu/Eric.html

John Coltrane
A Love Supreme

More than a jazz milestone, a landmark in music.

Few musicians have asked as much of music as John Coltrane. Fewer still have gotten as much out of it as Coltrane did with *A Love Supreme*. His musicians had only the sketchiest idea of what they would be recording that December day in 1964, but the tenor saxophone giant had been in preparation for years. After kicking a heroin habit in the late '50s, Coltrane's position as a fearless explorer of "new thing" jazz had been paralleled by a spiritual quest that embraced the wisdom of the Bible, Koran, Kaballah and other philosophical and mystical tracts.

"My goal is to live the truly religious life and express it in my music," Coltrane told Newsweek. "If you live it, when you play there's no problem because the music is just part of the whole thing. To be a musician is really something. It goes very, very deep. My music is the spiritual expression of what I am – my faith, my knowledge, my being ... When you begin to see the possibilities of music, you desire to do something really good for people, to help humanity free itself from its hang-ups. I think music can make the world better and, if I'm qualified, I want to do it. A musical language transcends words. I want to speak to their souls."

He did. From the gentle tenor invocation that opens this four-part suite, Coltrane is in command of something extraordinary – or perhaps *it* is commanding him. Neither as 'free' as the jazz he'd begin making the following year, nor as immediately accessible as *Giant Steps* or *My Favorite Things*, this music is distinguished by the spirit that moves through it. So complete was the moment that there is only one known instance of Coltrane attempting to play the piece live. (Another version of Acknowledgement, adding the sax of Archie Shepp and bassist Art Davis, was recorded the following day but is now lost.)

A Love Supreme is that rare thing: a work of exalted art that also touches the common consciousness. It was an immediate best-seller by jazz standards, indicating that there was a substantial audience for the new music. Certified gold in 1970, it has now sold more than a million copies.

Record label:
Impulse!

Produced
by Bob Thiele.

Recorded
at the Van Gelder Studio, Englewood Cliffs, New Jersey; December 9, 1964.

Released:
January 1965.

Chart peaks:
None (UK) None (US)

Personnel:
John Coltrane (ts); McCoy Tyner (p); Jimmy Garrison (b); Elvin Jones (d); Rudy Van Gelder (e)

Track listing:
Acknowledgement; Resolution; Persuance; Psalm

Running time:
33.03

Current CD:
IMP11552

Further listening:
Coltrane Live At Birdland (1963); Crescent (1964)

Further reading:
Ascension: John Coltrane and His Quest (Eric Nisenson, 1993); John Coltrane: His Life and Music (Lewis Porter, 1998)

The Beach Boys
The Beach Boys Today!

A teenage surf-band starts to grow-up strange.

Although no one could have known it when it was released, *The Beach Boys Today!* foreshadowed the end of the group's first era – the era of songs about cars, carefree love and surfing for which they remain most well known.

The first Beach Boys album of 1965 and their ninth studio album in three years (including a Christmas collection), *Today!* marked a critical point in Brian Wilson's development as a songwriter and producer. Perhaps as significantly, it was also when his lucidity was first brought into serious question.

Eager to better the artistic and commercial precedents set by The Beatles and Phil Spector, and increasingly insecure in his ability to do so, Wilson felt straitjacketed by the Boys' narrow – but winning – formula. His introduction to marijuana, and the bohemian community that supplied it to him, convinced him that the group's sound should expand as much as his mind if it was to remain relevant. Following an airborne breakdown en route to a Los Angeles live date on December 23, 1964, Wilson announced his retirement from the road to the horrified group, explaining that he would focus all of his creativity into the studio. "I told them I foresee a beautiful future for The Beach Boys, but the only way we could achieve it was if they did their job and I did mine," recalled Brian. "I felt I had no choice, I was run down mentally and emotionally."

Nothing looks amiss among the sweater-clad grinning boys beaming out from its cover, and the likes of Dance, Dance, Dance and Help Me, Ronda maintain the group's good-time reliability. Yet an air of delicate, desperate introspection bleeds from *Today*'s most beautiful songs (eight of the album's ten originals written by Brian alone), accentuated by complex orchestrations borne from Brian's new freedom. The album's entire second half, particularly, is regarded as the precursor to *Pet Sounds*' resolute, lush despair. Please Let Me Wonder (the first song Brian wrote stoned) and In The Back Of My Mind express love not as teenage paradise, but as a submission to paralysing vulnerability, the ultimate threat to childhood naiveté: "So happy at times that I break out in tears/In the back of my mind, I still have my fears." Even this side's cover version, The Students' doo-wop pearl I'm So Young, is equivocal. "I'm so young/ Can't marry no one."

Some of the group (can you guess who?) expressed concern over this break from custom, but to no avail. *The Beach Boys Today!* was the signpost to The Beach Boys' tomorrow.

Record label:
Capitol

Produced
by Brian Wilson.

Recorded
at Western Recording Studios and Gold Star Recording Studios, Hollywood; June 22, 1964, October 8 & 10, 1964, January 7, 19 1965

Released:
March 1965

Chart peaks:
13 (UK) 4 (US)

Personnel:
Mike Love (v, s); Carl Wilson (v, g, k); Alan Jardine (g, v); Brian Wilson (k, g, v); Dennis Wilson (v, d, k)

Track listing:
Do You Wanna Dance (S/US); Good To My Baby; Don't Hurt My Little Sister; When I Grow Up (To Be A Man); Help Me, Rhonda [LP Version] (S); Dance, Dance, Dance; Please Let Me Wonder; I'm So Young; Kiss Me Baby; She Knows Me Too Well; In The Back Of My Mind; Bull Session With 'Big Daddy'

Running time:
29.28

Current CD:
CI8296321

Further listening:
Pet Sounds (1966), Summer Days (And Summer Nights!!) (1965)

Further reading:
Heroes And Villains: The True Story Of The Beach Boys (Stephen Gaines, 1986); www.cabinessence.com; www.beach-boys.com

The Sonics
Here Are The Sonics

Before they made The Sonics they broke the mould.

T he secret behind the most visceral garage punk group of
the '60s? "We wanted people to gasp, we wanted people to
go 'oh my gawd!' And so that's how we approached it," reveals
drummer Bob Bennett. "We wanted to blow people off their
feet, not just with loudness, but with tightness, with music that
made you want to dance." Hence their debut single The Witch.
Originally intended as a simple dance number to rival The
Twist and The Mashed Potato, the song gradually mutated into
a raw, screaming horror show. On hearing the masters, the
band were devastated. "All I did was pound my drums and I
guess it just sounded like bashing when it was recorded," said
Bob, "I remember the engineers arguing. One guy says, 'That
doesn't even sound like drums,' and the other guy goes, 'Well
what am I gonna do – look at this guy'?"

The Witch became the biggest selling single in America's
Northwest and their record label Etiquette naturally demanded
an album. The only problem was songwriter and singer Gerry
Roslie's sloth. "I had to prod him," recalled Buck Ormsby,
Etiquette's A&R man who had discovered the group, "The
Sonics weren't great musicians, but they had this magic thing."

They eventually got it together at Audio Recording in
Seattle. Twelve cuts were recorded live onto two-track tape. Six
songs were covers, including a frenetic take on the Contours'
Do You Love Me and their ferocious reading of Little Richard's
Good Golly Miss Molly. Originals included Psycho, a deranged
maelstrom propelled along by pounding drums, the fearsome
Strychnine, which extols the virtues of guzzling poison and
features Rob Lind's raucous, wailing sax, and their supercharged
ode to a Ford Mustang, Boss Hoss.

What made The Sonics special was Gerry Roslie's
fiendish, manic vocals, which some likened to Little Richard. "I
always felt that somebody would have to come in and give him
a blood transfusion," engineer Kearney Barton said, "I thought
he was gonna tear his throat out – screaming from start to
finish – amazing!"

Though influencing just about every band that came out
of the North-west The Sonics were unable, despite their best
efforts to break out nationally. Instead, at the end of the '60s,
they broke up.

Record label:
Etiquette

Produced
as 'An Etiquette Production'.

Recorded:

Released:
March 1965

Chart peaks:
None (UK) None (US)

Personnel:
Gerry Roslie (v, p, o); Andy Parypa (b);
Larry Parypa (g); Rob Lind (s); Bob
Bennett (d)

Track listing:
The Witch (S/US); Do You Love Me; Roll
Over Beethoven; Boss Hoss; Dirty Robber;
Have Love Will Travel; Psycho (S/US);
Money; Walkin' The Dog; Night Time Is
The Right Time; Strychnine; Good Golly
Miss Molly

Running time:
29.20

Current CD:
CNW903 adds Keep A Knockin'; Don't
Believe In Christmas (S/US); Santa Claus;
The Village Idiot

Further listening:
second album and more of the same,
The Sonics Boom (1966)

Further reading:
http://surf.to/sonics

Bert Jansch
Bert Jansch

Possibly the very first British singer/songwriter album.

"People saw him as a rival to Bob Dylan," says Martin Carthy. "When his first album came out it really was a big day." Along with Carthy, Bert was one of the kings of the folk music castle in 1965. The 'folk boom' looked like exploding on a national level and offbeat singer-songwriters were converging on London for its all-nighter folk scene. With an astonishingly original sound, blending Broonzy's blues with Mingus's jazz, Scottish trad and a flavour of English guitar exoticist Davy Graham, Bert had drifted down from Edinburgh.

"[Singer] Anne Briggs took me firmly by the throat and said, 'Look, for God's sake you must do this record,'" says free-lance engineer Bill Leader. Bill had recorded Anne for trad label Topic, but there were no obvious outlets for the wayward Jansch. Not even owning a guitar, Bert recorded the album at Leader's flat on spec using a Revox and borrowed instruments. Anne was meanwhile lobbying Nat Joseph of Transatlantic, who finally agreed to a purchase of £100 and no royalties. It was the only option. "Perhaps if I'd sat on it for another six months," says Bill, "we might have done a better deal. But there comes a time when a record has to be released for an artist and if you miss that you bugger up his career."

Davy Graham's Angie, mischievously adopting Cannonball Adderley's Worksong as middle-eight, was the only cover – although Smokey River was essentially Jimmy Giuffre's Train And The River while Casbah had started life as Mingus's Better Get It In Your Soul. Mostly, though, these were intense, personal songs reflecting the lifestyle of its author, from his earliest composition Courting Blues through the swaggering imagery of Strolling Down The Highway – written in 1962 while hitch-hiking through France – to the more poignant reflections of Needle Of Death (the first anti-drugs song?) and Running From Home. Songs from the album were covered on record by Julie Felix, Marianne Faithful and Donovan while the moody cover shot of Bert with guitar in a bare flat completed the message that here was not only music to absorb but a way of life to acquire. "His work will touch youth with a force unknown to our present British artists," concluded Folk Scene. Another journal, Folk Music, nailed it: "It might be objected that this is not folk music, and of course it's not. But until our categories expand Bert must be included within folk in its broadest sense." Rightly or wrongly, he still is.

Record label:
Transatlantic

Produced
by Bill Leader.

Recorded
at 5 North Villas, Camden, London;
September 1964–January 1965.

Released:
April 16, 1965

Chart peaks:
None (UK) None (US)

Personnel:
Bert Jansch (v, g)

Track listing:
Strolling Down The Highway; Smokey River; Oh How Your Love Is Strong; I Have No Time; Finches; Rambling's Going To Be The Death Of Me; Veronica; Needle Of Death; Do You Hear Me Now?; Alice's Wonderland; Running, Running From Home; Courting Blues; Casbah; Dreams Of Love; Angie

Running time:
38.52

Current CD:
ESM CD407 adds It Don't Bother Me

Further listening:
Jack Orion (1966); Rosemary Lane (1971); When The Circus Comes To Town (1995)

Further reading:
MOJO 80; Dazzling Stranger: Bert Jansch And The British Folk And Blues Revival (Colin Harper, 2000)

Jerry Lee Lewis
Live At The Star Club, Hamburg

The Killer invents garage punk with a little help from the Nashville Teens.

When Jerry Lee Lewis crashed into Hamburg in April of 1964 he was a pill-fuelled anachronism, a brilliant '50s rocker staring out at an audience of bowl-haired boy-girl Beatles kids. At just 28 years old he looked like an old man out of time. The past six years had not been kind. On May 22, 1958, a 21-year-old Lewis had arrived in England for his first tour outside the US, with his 13-year-old wife *née* cousin Myra Gale, in tow. Lewis told the press she was 15. "Back home," Myra explained, "you can marry at 10." It put an effective halt on his career for the next 10 years.

From 1958 to 1968 Jerry Lee toured constantly on a strict diet – Biphetamin to take him up, placidyls to bring him down, whiskey to bridge the gap. His regular $10,000 per night fee was knocked down to $250. "I couldn't care less," said Lewis. "Life is too short to worry your brains over making a buck." Then, on Easter Sunday 1962 – while Jerry was coming down from another amphetamine-wild gig in Minneapolis – his three-year-old child, Stevie Allen, wandered out into the garden of his Memphis home and drowned in the mud-filled family swimming pool. God had found him out and punished him and the Jerry Lee who toured Britain and Europe for the next four years, the one you hear on this record, played like a man with the Holy Ghost in his soul and the devil on his tail.

This date had no rehearsals. The Star-Club's house-band, The Nashville Teens – a mythic whippet-thin Scouse wrecking crew and no-argument best live band in Britain – spent the gig either struggling to keep up with Lewis or storming ahead – locked into a teeth-grindingly tense race to the end of each song. From the cavernous howl of Mean Woman Blues through to a final ragged Whole Lotta Shakin' the rhythm section sound like they've been remixed by Tom and Ed Chemical while Pete Shannon and John Allen's screwed-up jags of guitar and Jerry Lee's demonic growls, wails, yelps and piano stabs are sweat-soaked punk pre-history. He carried on playing like this for the next three years – The Greatest Live Show On Earth. No contest, true, but it nearly killed him. Then, in 1968, recording *Another Time, Another Place* for Mercury, Jerry Lee Lewis found country, dispensed with the pills and the booze, and a whole other kind of star was born.

Record label:
Phillips

Produced
by Siggi Loch.

Recorded
at The Star Club, Reeperbahn, Hamburg, West Germany; April 5, 1964.

Released:
April 1965

Chart peaks:
None (UK) None (US)

Personnel:
Jerry Lee Lewis (v, p); The Nashville Teens: Pete Shannon (g); John Allen (g); Ray Phillips (b); John Hanken (d)

Track listing:
Mean Woman Blues; High School Confidential; Money (That's What I Want); Matchbox; What'd I Say (Part 1); What'd I Say (Part 2); Great Balls Of Fire; Good Golly, Miss Molly; Lewis' Boogie; Your Cheatin' Heart; Hound Dog; Long Tall Sally; Whole Lotta Shakin' Goin' On

Running time:
37.12

Current CD:
Spectrum 554 195-2

Further listening:
The Golden Hits Of Jerry Lee Lewis (1964); listen to Jerry Lee's proper touring band speed through the hits on The Greatest Live Show On Earth (1964); check out his country resurrection on Another Time, Another Place (1968)

Further reading:
Killer (Jerry Lee Lewis and Charles White, 1995); Hellfire (Nick Tosches, 1982)

Them

Them

Future superstar Van Morrison arrives with an influential slice of garage blues.

Any listener only familiar with the sophisticated sounds of the middle-aged Van Morrison would be shell-shocked hearing *Them*, on which the Belfast bluesman, then only 19 years old, sings with a ferocity that's still startling. The album is a British blues boom classic and yet under-appreciated; rumours are that it was actually made by sessionmen having sabotaged its – and the band's – reputation. Morrison has never publicly refuted the allegations, but his colleagues are adamant that like contemporaries The Kinks and The Who, session men – including Jimmy Page – were occasionally imposed upon them, only to fill out the sound of the core band, not the featured roles. And aural evidence supports this, for, frankly, the ramshackle excitement of the playing is surely the sound of a bunch of rowdies from the bars, clubs and dives of Belfast, rather than the sound of professional sessionmen.

Sometimes known as *The Angry Young Them* after the slogan emblazoned on the back of the sleeve, the album begins electrifyingly, with the rampaging Mystic Eyes, an instrumental until near the end, when Morrison improvises some enigmatic, fragmentary lyrics. "Van was always good at ad libbing," enthuses guitarist Billy Harrison. "He could just conjure words as he was performing. And no one in Britain could phrase like him." *Them* includes Gloria, previously the B-side of the band's debut hit, Baby Please Don't Go, which became a US hit for the Shadows Of Knight and a rock standard, covered by Hendrix, Patti Smith, the Grateful Dead and countless others. Morrison had been the last to join the original band ("We brought him in to play saxophone, but he knew more blues songs than me so he began to sing," recalls Harrison) but Them's personnel never stabilised, which further undermined the band's status.

"If management had supported, instead of exploited, Them could have been on a level with the Stones," sighs founder member Eric Wrixon. "We were more extreme and musically in advance of them." But it wasn't to be and, to many, Them are now regarded as only a trivial, early footnote in the history of Van the Man, the absurdity of which is obvious to anyone who has ever thrilled to the raw power that throbs from this extraordinary album.

Record label:
Deram

Produced
by Tommy Scott, Bert Berns and Dick Rowe.

Recorded
at Decca Studios, West End Lane and Regent Studios, Denmark Street; July, September–October 1964 and January 1965.

Released:
June 1965

Chart peaks:
None (UK) 54 (US)

Personnel:
Van Morrison (v, hm, s); Billy Harrison (g); Eric Wrixon, Jackie McAuley, Peter Bardens (k); Ronnie Millings (d); Pat McAuley (d, k); Alan Henderson (b)

Track listing:
Mystic Eyes (S); If You And I Could Be As Two; Little Girl; Just A Little Bit; I Gave My Love A Diamond; Gloria (S/US); You Just Can't Win; Go On Home Baby; Don't Look Back; I Like It Like That; I'm Gonna Dress In Black (S/US); Bright Lights Big City; My Little Baby; (Get Your Kicks On) Route 66

Running time:
39.13

Current CD:
ABR00102

Further listening:
Them Again (1966), the band's second album, on which Morrison is accompanied by an almost completely different line-up, which includes outstanding musicians like Ray Elliott, Jim Armstrong and John Wilson; The Story Of Them Featuring Van Morrison (1997) compiles virtually everything Morrison recorded with the band.

Further reading:
MOJO 50; Van Morrison: Inarticulate Speech Of The Heart (John Collis, 1996); www.harbour.sfu.ca/~hayward/van/van.html

B.B. King
Live At The Regal

Widely regarded as the greatest ever live blues album.

"The world's greatest blues singer, the King Of The Blues – B.B. King", is how he is introduced on this seminal live album. If anyone doubted that King deserved such an introduction before hearing this performance, no one could doubt it afterwards.

The Regal Theatre was one of the major stops on the chittlin' circuit and King often played several residencies there in a year. "I don't think I played any better than I've played before, but the feedback from the audience was good," he has said of this performance. He's not kidding: the crowd shriek, scream and holler throughout as King plays with a white-hot intensity, his own voice as impassioned as his guitar Lucille's on songs such as Every Day (I Have The Blues), Sweet Little Angel and You Upset Me Baby, some of which he'd been playing for a decade or more and was to continue to play into the 21st century. On the witty How Blue Can You Get, King declaims: "I gave you seven children / And now you want to give them back," punching out the lyrics with an anger that still shocks.

"Because I play it every night like for the first time. I never go note for note on the melody – I play what I'm feeling now, not what I felt yesterday."

King's guitar playing throughout is articulate and thrillingly emotive, with never a hint of grandstanding or cliché. "You don't play a note simply because you can find one," explains King. "You do it because it makes sense. To me, every note is important." Apart from the irresistible power of the music, the album is also notable for signalling the end of blues music as an exclusively black form. It's a fair bet that there wasn't a single white member of the Regal audience. Soon, however, King would be playing gigs at which a black face would be a rarity.

Record label:
Chess

Produced
by Johnny Pate.

Recorded
at The Regal Theatre, Chicago, Illinois;
November 21, 1964.

Released:
July 1965

Chart peaks:
None (UK) None (US)

Personnel:
B.B. King (g, v); other musicians
uncredited.

Track listing:
Every Day (I Have The Blues); Sweet
Little Angel; It's My Own Fault; How Blue
Can You Get; Please Love Me; You Upset
Me Baby; Worry, Worry; Woke Up This
Mornin'; You Done Lost Your Good Thing
Now; Help The Poor

Running time:
34.54

Current CD:
MCD11646

Further listening:
Another live album, Blues Is King (1967),
recorded in a Chicago nightclub; King Of
The Blues (1992) is a valuable 4-CD
compilation.

Further reading:
The Arrival Of B.B. King (Charles Sawyer,
1980), a comprehensive biography; Blues
All Around Me: The Autobiography of B.B.
King (1996)

Bob Dylan
Highway 61 Revisited

Dylan's experiments with rock backings reach full fruition.

Mostly written in Dylan's new 31-room mansion (which he sold within a year, preferring not to write in the same place twice), *Highway 61 Revisited* was the fulfilment of the musical vision he had first developed on the electric side of *Bringing It All Back Home*. Using a studio band based partly on the Butterfield Blues Band musicians who had backed him at his notorious 1965 Newport Folk Festival appearance, the results were streamlined, sardonic, surrealistic, and bulging with raw blues power.

"I can't tell you how disorganised it was," recalled Al Kooper of the sessions. "*Highway 61* has a very raw edge to it, because half the people involved were studio musicians and half weren't, so it's got that rough thing which Dylan loves." Kooper had hustled his way into proceedings by seizing the chance to contribute organ (an instrument he had never played before!) to Like A Rolling Stone, the first track recorded for the new album. Dylan liked the effect, and Kooper became a staple of his studio band, eventually serving as musical director for the following year's *Blonde On Blonde*.

Dylan's new material was a quantum leap beyond the folk and pop clichés of the time, offering new possibilities for the subject matter and vocabulary of both genres, from the damning personal put-downs of Like A Rolling Stone and Ballad Of A Thin Man to the cultural critiques of Tombstone Blues and Desolation Row. In these songs, his former protest style was transmuted into a surreal stream of imagery; the protests were still there, but had become more a matter of implication and inference than direct address, as Dylan responded to the literary influence of French Symbolist poet Arthur Rimbaud and beat novelist William Burroughs.

The record outraged or baffled as many of his old fans as it impressed (the English poet Philip Larkin, for instance, felt that Desolation Row had "an enchanting tune and mysterious, possibly half-baked words"), though Dylan himself – usually his own harshest critic – was in no doubt about what he had achieved. "I'm never gonna be able to make a record better than that one," he said at the time. "[It's] just too good. There's a lot of stuff on there that *I* would listen to!"

Record label:
CBS

Produced
by Tom Wilson and Bob Johnston.

Recorded
at Columbia Studios, New York;
June–August 1965.

Released:
August 1965

Chart peaks:
4 (UK) 3 (US)

Personnel:
Bob Dylan (v, g, k, hm); Mike Bloomfield (g); Charlie McCoy (g); Al Kooper (k); Paul Griffin (k); Russ Savakus (b); Harvey Brooks (b); Bobby Gregg (d); Sam Lay (d); Frank Owens (k, pc)

Track listing:
Like A Rolling Stone (S); Tombstone Blues; It Takes A Lot To Laugh, It Takes A Train To Cry; From A Buick 6; Ballad Of A Thin Man; Queen Jane Approximately; Highway 61 Revisited (S); Just Like Tom Thumb's Blues; Desolation Row

Running time:
51.40

Current CD:
4609532

Further listening:
The other core works of Dylan's electric period, Bringing It All Back Home (1965) and Blonde On Blonde (1966), form a triple pinnacle with Highway 61 Revisited.

Further reading:
My Back Pages: Classic Bob Dylan 1962-69 (Andy Gill, 1998); MOJO 60

Otis Redding
Otis Blue

The definitive Southern soul album.

I t is rare – and usually accidental – for a '60s soul album to sit well as an entity, as a cohesive statement by the singer about his art. But *Otis Blue*, Redding's third album, subtitled Otis Redding Sings Soul is exactly that. His customary *modus operandi* was to arrive at the studio with an album's worth of ideas, often worked out in collaboration with guitarist Steve Cropper, rehearse for a day or two and then cut the tracks fast. For *Otis Blue* he had only three originals. Respect, which he said took a day to write, 20 minutes to arrange and one take to record, the ballad I've Been Loving You Too Long, co-written with Jerry Butler, and Ole Man Trouble, the churning soul-blues driven by Cropper's guitar, which opens the album.

Redding started work on the album in April 1965, three months after the death of his great idol, Sam Cooke, hence the three cover versions (Shake, Wonderful World, A Change Is Gonna Come). Cooke purists demur as to the quality of these covers but they clearly illustrate Otis's ability to grab a song and in the context of the album, make it his alone. He covers the Smokey Robinson-penned Temptations' hit My Girl, William Bell's You Don't Miss Your Water, the Solomon Burke soul-gospel hit Down In The Valley and B. B. King's Rock Me Baby: a catholic trawl. But the most audacious cover version for his core black market was Satisfaction, the Rolling Stones' hit. For years white rock bands had usurped black hits. Here was a rare instance of a black artist turning the tables. Cropper suggested the song while Otis was out of the studio, the MGs and Memphis Horns worked up an arrangement. When Redding heard the song he didn't care for it but tried using "a lot of words different – I made them up."

"There were no planning sessions, we just went in and did it," the Memphis Horns' trumpeter, Wayne Jackson, recalled. "All the really great stuff at Stax was done quick, a big group effort. It would start with bones that somebody brought and the muscle and sinew and flesh and skin would be put on it and the monster would rise and live!" *Otis Blue* took just two days to record.

Record label:
Atlantic

Produced
by Jim Stewart.

Recorded
at Stax Studios, Memphis; April and July 1965.

Released:
September 15, 1965

Chart peaks:
6 (UK) 75 (US)

Personnel:
Booker T. Jones and Isaac Hayes (k); Steve Cropper (g); Donald 'Duck' Dunn (b); Al Jackson Jr (d); Earl Sims (bv); Wayne Jackson, Gene 'Bowlegs' Miller (t); Andrew Love (ts); Tom Dowd (e)

Track listing:
Ole Man Trouble; Respect; A Change Is Gonna Come; Down In The Valley; I've Been Loving You Too Long; Shake; My Girl; Wonderful World; Rock Me Baby; Satisfaction; You Don't Miss Your Water

Running time:
32.54

Current CD:
7567 80318-2

Further listening:
The comprehensive 4CD box sets Otis! The Definitive Otis Redding (1993) or Dock Of The Bay – The Definitive Collection

Further reading:
MOJO 49; Sweet Soul Music (Peter Guralnick, 1998); www.otisredding.com

Herb Alpert And The Tijuana Brass
Going Places

Fifth album from MOR kings, six weeks at Number 1.

In the mid-'60s, while the kids were in thrall to the Fabs and their guitar wielding, hair-shaking contemporaries, there was a parallel music market that catered for the less spicy tastes of their parents. Unassailably dominant in that market was the phenomenally successful Herb Alpert and his Tijuana Brass.

Twenty-five-year-old Los Angeles ex-actor and trumpeter, Alpert had been keen to find a distinctive sound on his instrument and in 1962, fooling around on a tape recorder in his garage with a tune written by friend Sol Lake called Twinkle Star, he noticed that the melody worked well played in Mexican-style thirds – the Mariachi sound of the Tijuana bull-fights Alpert occasionally frequented.

"I liked the Mariachi sound," said Alpert, "but it hadn't progressed much over the years and it seemed to me you could add an undercurrent of American sound, updating the bass-line and the guitars and timpani."

Forming a label with partner Jerry Moss – changing the title of Lake's tune to The Lonely Bull and naming the studio-creation (which soon became a real band) The Tijuana Brass – the ensuing single and album began a wave of popularity that saw The Tijuana Brass at their peak outselling the Beatles 2-to-1 and making A&M Records the most successful artist-owned label of all time.

Going Places was the fifth Tijuana Brass best-seller and typifies their exuberant, cheeky charm. Alpert's customised 'Ameriachi' style was by now so focused that the apparently incongruous, daringly juxtaposed material (Zorba The Greek, I'm Getting Sentimental Over You and The Third Man Theme on one album!) is vividly adapted, with the listener seduced into barely caring how these tunes originally sounded.

"It's a wild, happy sound, like the Mariachis," Alpert said, attempting to explain The Tijuana Brass's appeal. "It's good-natured and full of humour. It's not a protest and not a put-down. I think people were bugged with hearing music which had an undercurrent of unhappiness and anger, even sadism. But our music you can get with in a hurry, tap your feet and hum along." As The Tijuana Brass's popularity faded, Alpert, never a jazz player, continued making records in contemporary pop styles and on the back of A&M's success with The Carpenters, The Police and others, sold the label in 1990 to Polygram for $500 million.

Record Label:
A&M

Produced
by Jerry Moss.

Recorded
at Goldstar Studios, LA; 1965

Released:
September 1965

Chart peaks:
5 (UK) 1 (US)

Personnel:
Herb Alpert (t); Tonni Kalash (t); Julius Wechter (marimba/vibes); Bob Edmondson (tb); Pat Senatore (b); John Pisano (electric 12-string guitar); Lou Pagani (p); Nick Ceroli (d); Larry Levine (e)

Track Listing:
Tijuana Taxi; I'm Getting Sentimental Over You; More And More Amor; Spanish Flea; Mae; 3rd Man Theme; Walk, Don't Run; Felicia; And The Angels Sing; Cinco De Mayo; A Walk In The Black Forest; Zorba The Greek

Running time:
29.27

Current CD:
IMPT6402

Further listening:
The Lonely Bull (1963); Whipped Cream And Other Delights (1965)

Further reading:
http://members.aol.com/lanesong.HERBALPE.htm

Sun Ra
The Magic City

Pioneering big-band free jazz.

Following an apprenticeship as pianist and arranger for Fletcher Henderson's big band in the '40s, Sun Ra (*né* Herman Poole Blount) founded and led various line-ups of his own improvising big-band, Arkestra, until his death in May 1993, releasing literally hundreds of albums — mostly small editions in plain white (or hand-illustrated) covers on his own Saturn imprint — whose music ranged from manic swing and hard-bop outings to other-worldly solo synthesiser extravaganzas and bouts of collective improvisation.

Named after the promotional slogan of Ra's hometown Birmingham, Alabama, the 27-minute title-track of *The Magic City* is in the latter style, a breakthrough work contemporaneous with similar avant-garde explorations like Ornette Coleman's *Free Jazz* and John Coltrane's *Ascension*, but more fluid and obviously of a piece, the result of countless hours of development and rehearsal that enabled the Arkestra's musicians to play in each other's pockets even when they were navigating the most abstract sonic territory.

As producer Alton Abraham understood it, *The Magic City* was a city of fantasy, "a city without evil, a city of possibilities and beauty", whilst in a poem of the same title, Ra himself described it as "that city of all natural creation ... the magic of the Magi's thought".

The early parts find the mad-scientist whine of Ra's clavioline in cosmic dalliance with sprays of flute and piccolo over a bed of mournful bowed-bass, before bursting into volcanic new life as the horns take over, battling above the undergrowth of high-register wind parts. Also notable is the tape-delay effect (discovered by accident a few years earlier by Ra's recording engineer Thomas 'Bugs' Hunter, much to his boss's delight) that imposes its own semblance of order on one of the percussion parts.

The three pieces that make up the album's second side are further developments of the drum-choir style of his earlier *Nubians Of Plutonia*, with saxes trailing serpentine unison lines over complex polyrhythms of marimba, bongoes and tympani. Reissued several times by Ra's cottage industry through the late '60s, *The Magic City* eventually received its due acclaim when it formed part of an ambitious project which saw ABC/Impulse Records reissue ten Sun Ra albums in the early '70s.

Record label:
Saturn

Produced
by Alton Abraham.

Recorded
live at Olatunji's Loft, New York City;
April 1965.

Release date:
1965

Chart peaks:
None (UK) None (US)

Personnel:
Sun Ra (clavioline, p, bass marimba, tympani, electronic celeste, Sun Harp, dragon drum); John Gilmore (ts); Pat Patrick (bs, flute, tympani); Marshall Allen (as, flute, oboe, piccolo); Ronnie Boykins (b); Danny Davis (as, flute); Robert Cummings (bass clarinet); Harry Spencer (as); Walter Miller (t); Chris Capers (t); Teddy Nance (tb); Ali Hassan (tb); Jimmi Johnson (pc); Roger Blank (pc)

Track listing:
The Magic City; The Shadow World; Absract Eye; Abstract "I".

Running time:
45.10

Current CD:
Evidence ECD 22069-2

Further listening:
Other Planes Of There (1964), The Heliocentric Worlds Of Sun Ra, Vols 1 & 2 (1966, 1967)

Further reading:
Space Is The Place: The Life And Times Of Sun Ra (John F. Szwed, 1997)
www.holeworld.com/stellar.html

The Mamas And The Papas
If You Can Believe Your Eyes And Your Ears

The group who were the epitome of hippy become a commercial sensation musically, visually and commercially.

In his book Papa John, John Phillips described how he, Cass, Denny and Michelle auditioned for producer Lou Adler at Western Recording Studios in Hollywood while singing back-up vocals for Barry McGuire's This Precious Time. McGuire was an old pal from the group's Greenwich Village folk beginnings who was enjoying huge success with the protest pop of Eve Of Destruction. This was the summer of 1965 and the group was still using the name The New Journeymen. They sang California Dreamin' and Monday Monday for Adler, and he reputedly raved: "Wow, I can't believe my eyes and ears."

Within a month they were signed, had become The Mamas And The Papas and were back recording in the same studio. They looked and sounded like nothing else before or since. Along with The Byrds and The Lovin' Spoonful, also former folkies, The Mamas And The Papas were among the first American groups to present a challenge to the English Invasion: a year later, the whole California revival came along. By January 1966, California Dreamin' was all over the airwaves, anticipating the Summer of Love; Phillips also wrote that other Flower Power anthem, Scott McKenzie's San Francisco.

The Mamas And The Papas were the first public manifestation of hippiedom: their physical appearance, their flamboyant dress sense, and their moral stance anticipated the climate; outlandish rich kids living in Bel Air. All four of their albums are as strong as their debut, and each one maintained the high standard of John Phillips' songwriting. Cass usually pulled a favourite cover version out of her repertoire (Dedicated To The One I Love is, perhaps, the best known), but the crowning glory was the finest production that Los Angeles could offer, a clear and warm sound played by the same team of top flight session men on each record.

That The Mamas And The Papas' story ended in turmoil, strife, and eventually the death of Cass Elliot, after the group split in 1968 was almost inevitable given the love/hate tensions between them and an extraordinary drug intake. As is often the way, the sweetest music sprang from the darkest circumstances.

Record label:
RCA

Produced
by Lou Adler.

Recorded
at Western Recording Studios, Hollywood; late summer–autumn 1965.

Released:
January 1966

Chart peaks:
3 (UK) 1 (US)

Personnel:
John Phillips (v, g); Denny Doherty (v); Cass Elliot (v); Michelle Phillips (v)

Track listing:
Monday Monday (S); Straight Shooter; Got A Feelin'; I Call Your Name; Do You Wanna Dance; Go Where You Wanna Go (S); California Dreamin' (S); Spanish Harlem; Somebody Groovy; Hey Girl; You Baby; In Crowd

Running time:
34.58

Current CD:
MCAD-11739

Further listening:
Creeque Alley – The History Of The Mamas And The Papas (1991)

Further reading:
Papa John (John Phillips with Jim Jerome, 1987); www.psycho-jello.com/creeque

The Monks
Black Monk Time

Five GIs dressed as monks make garage rock in Germany. Strangely obscurity ensues.

Intentional squalling feedback rattles the control room windows as Polydor's genial producer struggles to protect Deutsche Gramophon's delicate equipment from the uber-beat onslaught of the Monks. The Velvet Underground will be bending VU needles in a couple of years time, egos bolstered by their art-world credentials. But now, in 1965, The Monks and their nihilist German mentors are forcing the issue in the rarefied atmosphere of the recording studio.

A year or so before, The Monks were a group of ex-GIs called The 5 Torquays, playing to Hamburg teens and US airbase personnel, until an alchemical reaction of boredom, experiment, and a pair of loopy existential visionaries called Walther and Karl brought about their miraculous transformation. Lovin' Spoonful bowlcuts and cuban heels give way to shaved tonsures, black shirts, and a bleakly realistic outlook. This was some of the hardest, most minimal and monochromatic rock'n'roll ever heard. Nobody in 1965 sang ferocious songs called things like I Hate You or Shut Up, stripped down to their fuzzed-up, screaming, percussive bones. Nowadays a lot of people do.

As bassist Eddie Shaw observes; "The Beastie Boys and Jello Biafra have said that our music had an effect on them. I really believe that music was evolving in this direction and we just stumbled across it early."

The album was never released by Polydor in the US; "They insisted we tone our music down ... or lose our contract" and The Monks disintegrated in a bitter flurry of impotent anger and disappointment. In retrospect, the album's unique appeal lies in the collision of naivety, rawness, and the utter pre-punk impossibility of its existence. Even its completely black cover-design, looking more Joy Division than Yellow Submarine, sounded a jarring note at the very dawn of flower-pop. They performed live shows with The Kinks, The Troggs and The Creation, but even these hardened outfits rarely got close to their live sound in the studio. Monk music – primal proto-punk, demented nursery rhymes – is all pounding drums, fuzztone bass, clattering electric banjo, gothic organ and histrionic vocals. As Shaw maintains, "Walther and Karl believed in having our music recorded as we played it. Studios, at that time, were not equipped to record our kind of music." They wouldn't be for some years to come.

Record label:
Polydor

Produced
by Jimmy Bowien.

Recorded
Polydor Studios, Koln, Germany; November 1965.

Released:
March 1966

Chart peaks:
None (UK) None (US)

Personnel:
Gary Burger (g, v); Larry Clark (o); Dave Day (banjo); Roger Johnston (d); Eddie Shaw (b)

Track listing:
Monk Time; Shut Up; Boys Are Boys And Girls Are Choice; Higgle-Dy Piggle-Dy; I Hate You; Oh, How To Do Now; Complication; We Do Wie Du; Drunken Maria; Love Came Tumblin' Down; Blast Off!; That's My Girl

Running time:
29.46

Currently unavailable on CD

Further listening:
Five Upstart Americans (1999) – sessions recorded before the album

Further reading:
Black Monk Time (Thomas Edward Shaw and Anita Klemke, 1994); www.the-monks.com

The Rolling Stones
Aftermath

The Stones take a quantum leap beyond recycled R&B.

U ntil *Aftermath*, the Stones were still largely thought of as
Brit-blues recyclers of US R&B modes, although Jagger &
Richards had already started to flex their compositional muscles
with successes like Satisfaction and 19th Nervous Breakdown,
the single which preceded the album's release. Featuring 14 of
their own songs, *Aftermath* laid down further markers for the
group's future ambitions, covering territory far removed from
their blues roots and employing a range of instrumentation only
equalled (in pop terms) when The Beatles released *Revolver* four
months later. Recorded towards the end of a gruelling American
tour, much of the material on *Aftermath* reflects the band's
frayed temperament in general and Mick Jagger's growing
hostility towards girlfriend Chrissie Shrimpton in particular.
Tracks such as Under My Thumb, Stupid Girl and Out Of Time
revealed a deep vein of misogyny that dogged the Stones' reputation for years, while the contemptuous tone of Mother's Little
Helper suggested an attitude towards drugs that was at best
ambivalent – OK if you were a rich rock star, but cause for
scorn if you were a hapless housewife.

"It was all a spin-off from our environment," Keith
Richards explained later. "Hotels and too many dumb chicks.
Not all dumb, by any means, but that's how one got. You got
really cut off."

There was widespread speculation, meanwhile, regarding
the inspiration for the song Lady Jane: their record label
claimed it was about Henry VIII's wife Jane Seymour, and Jagger
apparently allowed both Shrimpton and toff totty Lady Jane
Ormsby-Gore to believe it was about them. It turned out to be
derived from Lady Chatterley's Lover, being the gamekeeper's
term for his mistress's vagina. Though manager Andrew Loog
Oldham took the producer's credit, the album was effectively
recorded by Richards with the group's American engineer Dave
Hassinger. His job was not made any easier by Brian Jones'
unreliability, which left Keith having to play most of the guitar
parts by himself. Despite his growing drug and personality
problems, however, Jones' contributions were crucial to the
album's success. The band's most accomplished musician, he had
begun seeking out new and unusual instruments to add to their
sound: sitar on Mother's Little Helper, and marimba on Under
My Thumb and Out Of Time, while Lady Jane and Waiting

Record Label:
Decca

Produced
by Andrew Loog Oldham.

Recorded
at RCA Studios, Hollywood; December
1965.

Released:
April 1966

Chart peaks:
1 (UK) 2 (US)

Personnel:
Mick Jagger (v, p); Keith Richards (g, v);
Brian Jones (g, k, sitar, dulcimer,
marimba); Bill Wyman (b, pc); Charlie
Watts (d, pc); Ian Stewart (p); Jack
Nitzsche (k, pc); Dave Hassinger (e)

Track Listing:
Mother's Little Helper (S/US); Stupid Girl;
Lady Jane; Under My Thumb; Doncha
Bother Me; Goin' Home; Flight 505; High
And Dry; Out Of Time; It's Not Easy; I
Am Waiting; Take It Or Leave It; Think;
What To Do

Running time:
52.48

Current CD:
8444662 adds Paint It Black (S)

Further listening:
The next two studio albums, Between
The Buttons (1967) and Their Satanic
Majesties Request (1967), failed to deliver
on the promise of Aftermath, as the
Stones paddled up a psychedelic back-
water before regaining their bearings
with Beggar's Banquet (1968).

Further reading:
The Stones (Philip Norman, 1984); Keith
Richards – The Biography (Victor
Bockris, 1992).

featured the sound of a dulcimer that had been given to him by the folk singer Richard Farina.

"Brian would be down on his back, lying around the studio with his guitar strapped around him," Richards told biographer Victor Bockris. "Then suddenly, from nine hours of lying there, he'd just walk in and lay some beautiful things down on a track (piano, harpsichord), something that nobody'd even thought of." Released as *Aftermath* after their record company rejected the "blasphemous" original title *Could You Walk On The Water?*, the LP quickly topped the album chart in Britain, establishing them as a pop group with serious aspirations, though a savagely bowdlerised version lessened its impact in America.

The Beach Boys
Pet Sounds

In 1995, MOJO contributors voted it the 'Greatest Album Of All Time'.

Tony Asher thought it was a joke when someone at his ad agency told him Brian Wilson was on the phone, one day late in 1965. He'd played some songs for Wilson several months earlier, but since then had dumped songwriting for a more profitable gig as a copywriter. But Wilson couldn't have been more serious. He'd just heard The Beatles' *Rubber Soul* and decided he wanted to make a meaningful album of his own – without the aid of The Beach Boys' resident sun-and-fun lyricist Mike Love, who was on tour with the rest of the Boys.

Recent exposure to heavy doses of LSD-25 had also boosted Wilson's interest in mind-expanding music that would affect people on a deeper level. Wilson remembered Asher and felt that he was a writer who could give a voice to his musical introspection. He couldn't have been more right.

"It's fair to say that the general tenor of the lyrics was always his and the actual choice of words usually mine," Tony Asher told Nick Kent. "Brian was constantly looking for topics that kids could relate to. Even though he was dealing with the most advanced arrangements, he was incredibly conscious of this commercial thing, this absolute need to relate."

As the fluffiest of all Beach Boys' hits, Barbara Ann, was topping the British and American charts, Brian began tinkering with a song called Good, Good Vibrations and another called God Only Knows. When Mike 'Don't Fuck With The Formula' Love returned from Japan to lay down his vocal tracks, he pronounced it "Brian's ego music". It's true that I Know There's An Answer was originally called Hang On To Your Ego (until Love insisted the lyrics be changed, and Brian's chauffeur Terry Sachen obliged) but what Love hated most about *Pet Sounds* was its LSD influence. He later asserted that "some of the words were so totally offensive to me that I wouldn't even sing 'em". Actually, Brian didn't need many of Love's vocals, because he could do all the parts himself. When Brian wasn't singing, he was arranging the orchestra – which ranged up to 23 pieces – creating dense, lush arrangements that owed at least as much to Nelson Riddle as they did to Jack Nitzsche. Brian says today that he was also searching for a "live-band sound", a human element that helped give the album its intimacy, epitomised by Caroline, No – a haunting study of loss. Ironically, for a song that seems

Record label:
Capitol

Produced
by Brian Wilson.

Recorded
at Western, Sunset Sound, and Gold Star Studios, Los Angeles; July 1965 and November 1965–April 1966.

Released:
May 1966

Chart peaks:
2 (UK) 10 (US)

Personnel:
Brian Wilson (v); Carl Wilson (v); Mike Love (v); Bruce Johnston (v); Al Jardine (v); Dennis Wilson (v); Carol Kaye (b); Hal Blaine (d); Terry Melcher (v); Banana and Louie (dogbarking); Chuck Britz, Larry Levine, Ralph Balantin (e)

Track listing:
Wouldn't It Be Nice; You Still Believe In Me; That's Not Me; Don't Talk (Put Your Head On My Shoulder); I'm Waiting For The Day; Let's Go Away For A While; Sloop John B (S); God Only Knows (S); I Know There's An Answer; Here Today; I Just Wasn't Made For These Times; Pet Sounds; Caroline, No (S)

Running time:
36:24

Current CD:
5212412 adds: Hang On To Your Ego and features the album in both mono and stereo mixes.

Further listening:
Good Vibrations: 30 Years Of The Beach Boys (1993); 4CD box set Pet Sounds Sessions: Remastered (1997)

Further reading:
The Nearest Faraway Place (Timothy White, 1991); the liner notes for the CD

reissue are available at
www.beachboysfanclub.com/ps-liner.html

so personal, Caroline, No (released curiously as a Brian Wilson solo single) is said to have been inspired by three different people including Brian's high-school crush Carol Mountain. Yet, as Bruce Johnston has noted, on a deeper level it is about "Brian himself, and the death of a quality within him that was so vital, his innocence".

With the notable exception of Sloop John B (a hit single that Capitol stuck on the album against Wilson's wishes), every song on *Pet Sounds* evinced a spiritual tenderness that opened new doors in rock. "I thought of it as chapel rock," Wilson later explained, "commercial choir music." Unfortunately, it wasn't commercial enough for Capitol who rushed it out before Good Vibrations could be completed for inclusion and with at least one track (Let's Go Away For A While) left unintentionally instrumental. Even though it edged into the US Top Ten and made it to Number 2 in the UK (behind The Beatles' *Revolver*), just eight weeks after its release Capitol issued *Best Of The Beach Boys*. All the label's promotional efforts were diverted to this collection, which quickly went gold and stayed on the Billboard chart for 78 weeks. But *Pet Sounds* won the most souls. "I wanted to make an album that would stand up in ten years," Brian Wilson said. Make that thirty-four and counting.

John Mayall's Blues Breakers
Blues Breakers with Eric Clapton

The commercial breakthrough of British blues.

"I was arrogant, and I had an accelerator going," says Eric Clapton, explaining his dizzying ascent to star status in 1966. Eric Clapton quit The Yardbirds in March 1965; within a month, Mayall had sacked his guitarist Roger Dean, and persuaded Clapton to join up. Clapton describes Mayall as "a real father figure. I grew a hell of a lot in a short period of time with his help."

Mayall and producer Mike Vernon played Eric the latest records by Freddie King, Otis Rush and other Chicago greats. As well as copping their riffs, Clapton aimed for a similar density of sound. Seeing Freddie King photographed with a Gibson Les Paul, Clapton bought a second-hand Les Paul Sunburst and combined it with a newly-designed Marshall amp, to achieve a radically new sound; distorted, creamy and sustained: "I wanted some kind of thickness that would be a compilation of all the guitarists I'd heard, plus the sustain of a slide guitar," he remembers.

A June 1965 single, I'm Your Witchdoctor, demonstrated the band's raw power and helped Vernon persuade Decca to re-sign them. When they entered Decca's Studio 2 the following April they were all at their peak.

The songs included covers of Mose Allison, Little Walter, Ray Charles, some Mayall originals, and Robert Johnson's Rambling On My Mind – Clapton's vocal debut. "He was a little reticent about singing it," remembers Mayall, "but I had no doubts whatsoever."

There was one hurdle to clear. To achieve his sound, Clapton had to drive his Marshall amp to unprecedented volume levels. Freelance engineer (and future Elton John producer) Gus Dudgeon was staggered by his insistence on positioning the microphone – and refusing to turn down. Vernon let Clapton have his way. Mayall credits this as crucial: "Mike had the foresight not to mess with something that was happening live, to just get it down on tape, keeping all the spontaneity and feel."

Before the album ended its 17-week stay in the British charts, Eric Clapton had already left to form Cream. Mayall had the ideal replacement lined up in the shape of Peter Green. Neither party would ever look back.

Record label:
Decca

Produced
by Mike Vernon.

Recorded
at Decca Studio 2, London, April 1966.

Released:
July 1966

Chart peaks:
6 (UK) None (US)

Personnel:
John Mayall (v, g, hm); Eric Clapton (g, v); John McVie (b); Huey Flint (d); Gus Dudgeon (e)

Track listing:
All Your Love (S); Hideaway; Little Girl; Another Man; Double Crossing Time; What'd I Say; Key To Love; Parchman Farm (S); Have You Heard; Rambling On My Mind; Steppin' Out; It Ain't Right

Running time:
37.32

Current CD:
844827-2

Further listening:
A Hard Road (1967), with Peter Green shows band flourishing post-Clapton; Cream's Wheels Of Fire (1968) is Eric at his acid blues best.

Further reading:
MOJO 53; www.johnmayall.net

The Beatles
Revolver

The next great leap forwards for the Fab Four.

T he progression from the zesty "yeah, yeah, yeah" of 'She
Loves You to the mesmeric, acid-spiked Tomorrow Never
Knows took four Liverpool kids just 33 months. Drugs, Eastern
mysticism and fraternisation with their freakier peers (Dylan,
Stones, Byrds, Brian Wilson) have traditionally been seen as the
reason; yet one shouldn't underestimate the disorientating
effects of a pop megastardom without precedent and the heady
blend of fear and creative power that comes with it. *Rubber Soul*
had been reasonably straightforward but, suddenly, instead of
bashing down tightly-written songs within a few takes, The
Beatles fancied new working methods. For the first session of
their 1966 album, they oversaw a mad evening where engineers
wrestled with six mono tape machines simultaneously running
unwieldy loops of sound effects. Thus Lennon's 'recite the
Tibetan Book Of The Dead on LSD' opus, The Void, took shape.

This was 20-year-old, newly promoted engineer Geoff
Emerick's first session with The Beatles. "The group encouraged
us to break the rules," he recalls. "[They told me] that every
instrument should sound unlike itself: a piano shouldn't sound
like a piano, a guitar shouldn't sound like a guitar, hence putting
things through a Leslie speaker, and so on. When we were doing
the horns on Got To Get You Into My Life we tried putting the
mikes right into the bells of the trombones – treating mikes like
camera lenses, in a way – and that hadn't been done before. I
started moving the mike closer to the bass drum too. I was
reprimanded for that, because, according to the technical staff
[at Abbey Road], the air pressure from the drum would destroy
the mikes! I got a special letter saying I could do it, but only on
Beatles sessions."

John encouraged radical treatments on his voice. Paul
experimented with his new Brennel tape recorder, George
began mastering the sitar (and was awarded his first opening
album cut with the punchy Taxman) and, on Tomorrow Never
Knows (as The Void was renamed), Ringo's kit was split between
two channels and fed into a limiter to achieve the famous 'back-
ward' rush that propels the track. Every song came complete
with some curious sonic innovation.

"I know for a fact that, from the day *Revolver* came out,
it changed the way everyone else made records," says Emerick.
"No one had ever heard anything like that before. Everyone

Record label:
Parlophone

Produced
by George Martin.

Recorded
at EMI Studios, Abbey Road, London;
April 6–June 21, 1966.

Released:
August 5, 1966 (UK); August 8, 1966
(US)

Chart peaks:
I (UK) I (US)

Personnel:
John Lennon (rg, o, v); Paul McCartney
(b, ag, v); George Harrison (g, v); Ringo
Starr (d, v); Geoff Emerick (e); John
Gilbert, Sidney Sax, John Sharpe, Jurgen
Hesse (vn on Eleanor Rigby); Stephen
Shingles, John Underwood (va); Derek
Simpson, Norman Jones (c); Amil Bhagwa
(tabla on Love You To); Anyana Deva
Angadi (sitar); Eddie Thornton, Ian
Hamer, Les Condon (t on Got To Get
You Into My Life); Alan Branscombe,
Peter Coe (ts); Brian Jones, Marianne
Faithfull, Patti Harrison, Mal Evans, Neil
Aspinall, Terry Condon, John Skinner (v
on Yellow Submarine)

Track listing:
Taxman; Eleanor Rigby (S); I'm Only
Sleeping; Love You To; Here, There And
Everywhere; Yellow Submarine (S); She
Said She Said; Good Day Sunshine; And
Your Bird Can Sing; For No One; Dr
Robert; I Want To Tell You; Got To Get
You Into My Life; Tomorrow Never Knows
(Initial US edition omitted I'm Only
Sleeping, Doctor Robert, And Your Bird
Can Sing which had been included on
US album, Yesterday ... And Today)

Running time:
34.59

Current CD:
CDP 7 46441 2

Further listening:
Material from this period can be heard in development on Anthology 2.

Further reading:
MOJO 1, 24, 26, 35, 71; The Complete Beatles Chronicle (Mark Lewisohn, 2000); Revolution In The Head (Ian McDonald, 1995)

knew how we were doing those things; word would get round. But they could never quite get those sounds because they weren't using the same band!"

"It was a good point for us," agrees Paul McCartney. "It depends what you want from an album, but if you really look at it bluntly, most people just want good songs. There's a lot of good songs on *Revolver*. In fact, they're all good."

The Association
And Then ... Along Comes

Classy, harmony pop, and one of the most-played songs of all time.

I f ever a group were sabotaged by their image, it was surely
The Association. For on the sleeve of their classic 1966 debut,
the sextet are pictured shamelessly togged out in matching
three-piece suits, shirts and ties and proudly polished leather
shoes. Naturally, all self-respecting rock fans dismissed them —
a colossal shame, for the album is a delightful lite-psychedelic
gem by one of rock's great harmony bands, produced with
dazzling wit and flair by Curt Boettcher, with finger cymbals,
electronic sound effects and crazily inspired harmonies that dart
insanely in and around the lead vocals.

Boettcher, who died in 1987, did not remember the
band fondly. "They were never able to handle their own
success," he told Zigzag. "It really changed them as people."
Despite the gushing sleeve notes improbably claiming that Terry
Kirkman played 23 instruments, Boettcher also revealed that the
music on the album was played by sessionmen. This fact isn't
disputed, with Bluechel admitting to Goldmine that "all those
tracks were recorded by studio musicians". Kirkman adds: "We
had the same guys who played for The Beach Boys", although
Alexander does assert that he played on all the sessions.

The album's most famous track is Along Comes Mary,
credited to Tandyn Almer, although Boettcher always maintained
he co-wrote the song. The song was rumoured to refer to marijuana, although the lyrics are impenetrable. Eight of the album's
12 songs were written by band members, the best of which is
Kirkman's Cherish: one of the era's most beautiful love songs
and an American Number 1 single, displaying the complex and
striking multi-part harmonies typical of the band. Unfortunately,
its success marked the end of their relationship with Boettcher.

"They informed me during the fourth week of Cherish
being at the top that they no longer required my services and
were going to produce themselves," recalled Boettcher bitterly.
It was a catastrophic miscalculation by the band, who never
sounded so enchanting again.

At the last count, Cherish had been played on US radio
over four million times.

Record label:
Warner Brothers

Produced
by Curt Boettcher.

Recorded
at GSP Studios (aka Gary Paxton's
garage) and Columbia Studios, Hollywood;
June 1966.

Released:
August 1966

Chart peaks:
None (UK) 5 (US)

Personnel:
Gary Alexander (v, g); Terry Kirkman (v,
woodwind, reeds); Russ Giguere (v, g, pc);
Brian Cole (v, b); Ted Bluechel (v, d);
Jim Yester (v, g, k); Gary Paxton (e);
Pete Romano (e). The above musicians
were mainly replaced by sessionmen
including Mike Deasy (g); Ben Benay (g);
Hal Blaine (d)

Track listing:
Enter The Young; Your Own Love; Don't
Blame It On Me; Blistered; I'll Be Your
Man; Along Comes Mary (S); Cherish (S);
Standing Still; Message Of Our Love;
Round Again; Remember; Changes

Running time:
31.24

Current CD:
WPCR-10074

Further listening:
Third album, Insight Out (1967), contains
the classics Never My Love and Windy;
Waterbeds In Trinidad! (1972), is
outstanding.

Further reading:
http://theassociation.hypermart.net/

David Blue
David Blue

Unexpectedly caustic debut from former Dylan affiliate.

Hanging around with Bob Dylan in the early '60s can't have done much for your confidence. Aspiring folkie David S Cohen (later Blue) was part of the Bob in-crowd that included Eric Anderson, Dave Van Ronk, Phil Ochs and Tom Paxton. According to Anthony Scaduto's book Bob Dylan, he even strummed the chords while Bob pencilled in the lyrics for Blowin' In The Wind.

While Bob rallied the masses, Paxton and Ochs signed to Elektra and by 1965 Jac Holzman's label also had designs on a whole host of other regulars from the Greenwich Village scene. As David S Cohen, Blue's first recordings appeared on The Singer-Songwriter Project alongside tracks by Richard Farina, Patrick Sky and Bruce Murdoch and, within a year he was in the studio recording this self-titled album. It should have all been so easy. But it wasn't. For whatever reason, David Blue left David S Cohen's folky innocence in the closet. Instead, his debut became a strange mutation of influences – musical, social and otherwise. Dylan's *Highway 61 Revisited* had changed all the rules about electricity, while Love had just signed to Elektra and their first two albums bookended Blue's, changing the expectations of the label as the scene matured. Blue took up the challenge but to no avail.

Released alongside Tim Buckley's self-titled debut, this terrific album went on the missing list. At the time its phased guitars, swirling organ, quasi-classical motifs and jazz-paced breaks were part and parcel of a music scene that was encouraging experiment. But lyrically, Blue added yet another dimension, presenting a grubby insight into Village life. Indeed, the album rolls around the floors of bedsit Greenwich examining its inhabitants, like a Super-8 movie shot against a sub-psychedelic backdrop. Its failure signalled Blue's departure from the label and his slow decline into moody, morbid introversion. Certainly there's a sense of foreboding amid the cool and smoky jazz inflections. You kind of know it's all going to end in tears.

Record label:
Elektra

Produced
by Arthur Gorson

Recorded:
New York, 1966

Releases:
August 1966

Chart peaks:
None (UK) None (US)

Personnel:
Paul Harris (p, o, celeste); Harvey Brooks (b); David Blue (v, g); Monte Young (g); Herbert Lovelle; Buddy Salzman (d)

Track listing:
The Gasman Won't Buy Your Love; About My Love; So Easy She Goes By; If Your Monkey Can't Get It; Midnight Through The Morning; It Ain't The Rain That Sweeps The Highway Clean; Arcade Love Machine; Grand Hotel; Justine; I'd Like To Know; The Street; It Tastes Like Candy.

Running time:
41:57

Currently unavailable on CD

Further listening:
From his eponymous debut, David Blue became bleaker and more circumspect. The eventual follow-up These 23 Days In September (1968) is well worth locating as is Stories (1972) and Nice Baby And The Angel (1973), none of which are available on CD.

Further reading:
Follow The Music (Jac Holzman and Gavan Dawes, 1997); Bob Dylan (Anthony Scaduto, 1998)

Bob Dylan
Blonde On Blonde

*Translucent poetic imagery and steaming Chicago blues —
the single most convincing case for Dylan's genius.*

F ollowing some largely unsuccessful sessions in New York
(from which only One Of Us Must Know, featuring Band
members Rick Danko and Richard Manuel, eventually made the
album), Dylan took producer Bob Johnston's advice and
recorded the rest of *Blonde On Blonde* in Nashville, taking along
only guitarist Robbie Robertson and organist Al Kooper to
augment a crew of Tennessee's top session players. Used to
recording three tracks in a typical three-hour session, the
Nashville cats were surprised to find themselves left to their
own devices for hours on end while Dylan finished writing the
songs, whereupon Al Kooper — serving as musical director —
would translate his ideas for the band.

"We would come in an hour late," explains Kooper, "and
I would go in and teach the first song to the band. Then he
[Dylan] would arrive, and the band would be ready to play."
Compared to the more abrasive manner of New York players,
the Nashville crew took everything in their stride as Dylan
searched for what he called "that thin, wild, mercury sound", a
more refined blend of the guitars/piano/organ/bass/drums/
harmonica set-up that had proved so effective on *Highway 61
Revisited*.

"Nobody bitched or complained or rolled their eyes,"
recalls Kooper. "Their temperaments were fabulous — they were
the most calm, at-ease guys I'd ever worked with." They weren't
even fazed when Dylan requested a marching band to play on
Rainy Day Women #12 & 35, assuring him that if he was after a
more ramshackle sound, they could "play pretty dumb if we put
our minds to it". With a local friend, Wayne Butler, drafted in to
play trombone, and Charlie McCoy playing bass and trumpet
simultaneously, the track was cut in 20 minutes — so quickly
that Robbie Robertson, who had nipped out to buy cigarettes,
missed the session completely.

The album's string of love songs was generally found to
be less esoteric than the texts of *Highway 61 Revisited*, though
the dense, allusive imagery of Visions Of Johanna and Stuck
Inside Of Mobile With The Memphis Blues Again, in particular,
exercised the explicatory facilities of fans as much as anything in
Dylan's oeuvre. At the time he considered the album's third
epic, Sad Eyed Lady Of The Lowlands — amazingly, cut in one

Record label:
CBS

Produced
by Bob Johnston.

Recorded
at Columbia Studios, New York; January
1966; Columbia Music Row Studios,
Nashville, Tennessee; February–March 1966.

Released:
August 1966

Chart peaks:
3 (UK) 9 (US)

Personnel:
Bob Dylan (v, g, k, hm); Robbie
Robertson (g); Wayne Moss (g); Jerry
Kennedy (g); Charlie McCoy (g, hm, t); Al
Kooper (k); Hargus 'Pig' Robbins (k);
Richard Manuel (k); Joe South (b); Henry
Strzelecki (b); Rick Danko (b); Kenny
Buttrey (d); Bobby Gregg (d); Wayne
Butler (tb)

Track listing:
Rainy Day Women #12 & 35 (S);
Pledging My Time; Visions Of Johanna;
One Of Us Must Know (Sooner Or Later)
(S); I Want You (S); Stuck Inside Of
Mobile With The Memphis Blues Again;
Leopard-Skin Pill-Box Hat (S); Just Like A
Woman (S); Most Likely You Go Your Way
(And I'll Go Mine); Temporary Like
Achilles; Absolutely Sweet Marie; 4th Time
Around; Obviously Five Believers; Sad
Eyed Lady Of The Lowlands

Running time:
72.30

Current CD:
CD22130

Further listening:
The other core works of Dylan's electric
period, Bringing It All Back Home (1965)
and Highway 61 Revisited (1965).

Further reading:
My Back Pages: Classic Bob Dylan
1962–1969 (Andy Gill, 1998)

perfect 11-minute take – "the best song I've ever written", and it was accordingly given the accolade of an entire side to itself, the first time that had occurred on a 'pop' record. Despite the album's hefty price-tag (it was rock's first double album), it sold well, being immediately recognised as a landmark work, a reputation it has rightly sustained ever since. "It's an amazing record, like taking two cultures and smashing them together with a huge explosion," reckons Al Kooper. "Dylan was the quintessential New York hipster – what was *he* doing in Nashville? But you take those two elements, pour them into a test-tube, and it just exploded."

The Byrds
Fifth Dimension

Splicing Dylan, jazz and quantum physics. And why not.

T he Byrds faced some formidable obstacles during the
recording of their third album. Their recent groundbreaking single Eight Miles High had been banned because of
alleged drugs references in the title and, worse still, its
composer, Gene Clark, had flown the nest. Clark had provided
the key in-house songs on the first two albums prompting critics
to wonder whether the Byrds could survive his loss. A policy
decision to avoid relying on Bob Dylan as a song source meant
that their troubles were doubled. The obvious answer lay with
McGuinn and Crosby, who were forced to mature as singer-
songwriters in order to fill the gap. McGuinn looked back to his
folk roots and emerged with some tastefully orchestrated takes
on Wild Mountain Thyme and John Riley. Crosby, eager to
pursue the jazz direction pioneered on Eight Miles High,
included the moody What's Happening?!?! and spacey I See You.
The presence of Eight Miles High ensured that the album
secured chart honours but McGuinn's hopes for a big hit with
the title track 5D were scuppered as a result of further drugs
allegations.

At the time of the record's release showbiz bible *Variety*
featured the ominous headline: "Pop Music's Moral Crisis: Dope
Tunes Fan DJ's Ire". As McGuinn ruefully observed: "I was
talking about something philosophical and very light and airy
with that song, and everyone took it down … they took it down
to drugs. They said it was a dope song and that I was on LSD,
and it wasn't any of that, in fact. I was dealing with Einstein's
theory of relativity, the fourth dimension being time and the
fifth dimension not being specified so it's open, channel five, the
next step. I saw it to be a timelessness, a sort of void in space
where time has no meaning. All I did was perceive something
that was there."

Record Label:
Columbia

Produced
by Allen Stanton.

Recorded
at CBS, Hollywood; January, April and
May 1966.

Released:
September 22, 1966 (UK); July 18, 1966
(US)

Chart peaks:
27 (UK) 24 (US)

Personnel:
Jim McGuinn (g, v); David Crosby (g, v);
Michael Clarke (d); Chris Hillman (b); Ray
Gerhardt (e)

Track Listing:
5D (Fifth Dimension) (S); Wild Mountain
Thyme; Mr Spaceman (S); I See You;
What's Happening?!?!; I Come And Stand
At Every Door; Eight Miles High (S); Hey
Joe; Captain Soul; John Riley; 2-4-2 Fox
Trot.

Running time:
28:34

Current CD:
Legacy 483707 2 adds: Why; I Know My
Rider; Psychodrama City; Eight Miles High
(RCA studio version); Why (RCA studio
version); John Riley (instrumental)

Further listening:
Younger Than Yesterday (1967); The
Notorious Byrd Brothers (1968)

Further reading:
MOJO 41; The Byrds: Timeless Flight
Revisited (Johnny Rogan, 1997).

The Kinks
Face To Face

Ray Davies's satirical gaze — here turned on himself — finds its first full expression in album format.

Once the more important business of selecting their next hit single had been completed, The Kinks usually booked some studio time and rushed through a threadbare selection of uninspired material. By 1966, the pop aristocracy, inevitably led by The Beatles, was starting to use the album format for artistic expression, Ray Davies decided it was time to grasp the nettle and dazzle with 14 of his own compositions. A full year before *Sgt Pepper* he was planning an alluring montage in which tracks would be connected by sound effects. Davies's musical ambitions coincided with a dramatic turn in his life. Over the previous year, he had split with manager Larry Page and music publisher Eddie Kassner. A debilitating court battle lay ahead and Ray's nerves were frazzled. In the meantime, The Kinks had been banned in America and were fighting among themselves. Like Brian Wilson across the water, Davies was battling personal demons and simultaneously trying to push his group into fresh musical areas.

"I was a zombie," he admits. "I'd been on the go from when we first made it until then, and I was completely out of my mind. I went to sleep and woke up a week later with a moustache. I don't know what happened to me. I'd run into the West End with my money stuffed in my socks, I'd tried to punch my press agent, I was chased down Denmark Street by the police, hustled into a taxi by a psychiatrist, and driven off somewhere."

With Davies succumbing to a nervous breakdown, The Kinks had to complete a short European tour using a ringer. Meanwhile, Ray rested at home and composed this remarkable series of songs, many of which articulated his ambivalent feelings about wealth, fame and class. His pining for his sister, who'd emigrated just before The Kinks' formation, is behind Rosy Won't You Please Come Home. By contrast, the singalong Sunny Afternoon seems to centre around the life of a disillusioned young pop star with aristocratic pretentions; a memorable summer Number 1 single, it nestled comfortably here alongside other tales of nouveau riche overreaching — Most Exclusive Residence For Sale and House In The Country, the latter inspiring Blur's Number 1 single Country House thirty years on.

Record Label:
PYE

Produced
by Raymond Douglas Davies.

Recorded
at Pye Studios, London; October 1965 and April–June 1966.

Released:
October 1966

Chart peaks:
12 (UK) 135 (US)

Personnel:
Ray Davies (g, v); Dave Davies (g, bv), Mick Avory (d); Pete Quaife (b, bv)

Track Listing:
Party Line; Rosie Won't You Please Come Home; Dandy (S,US only); Too Much On My Mind; Session Man; Rainy Day In June; A House In The Country; Holiday In Waikiki; Most Exclusive Residence For Sale; Fancy; Little Miss Queen Of Darkness; You're Looking Fine; Sunny Afternoon (S); I'll Remember.

Current CD adds:
I'm Not Like Everybody Else; Dead End Street (S); Big Black Smoke; Mister Pleasant; This Is Where I Belong; Mr Reporter; Little Women

Running time:
59.44

Current CD:
ESM CD 4797

Further listening:
Something Else By The Kinks (1967); Arthur Or The Decline And Fall Of The British Empire (1969)

Further reading:
The Kinks: The Sound And The Fury (Johnny Rogan, 1984); The Kinks: The Official Biography (Jon Savage, 1984)

The Butterfield Blues Band
East-West

US blues rock pioneers. At the crossroads, but headed for the upper stratosphere.

In some ways The Butterfield Blues Band's second album didn't measure up to their electrifying debut, an unprecedented blues-rock blast from start to finish and as close as we're likely to get to a hot night in a bar on Chicago's South Side in 1964. *East-West* was more stylistically scattered, reflecting in part a piecemeal recording schedule necessitated by the tour demands of a hot underground following. But its enduring strength is its diversity, a reflection of a pop world looking to flex its new-found creative muscles.

East-West is known first and foremost for its two "long songs". The Butterfield crew's instrumental workouts on Nat Adderly's Work Song (7:53) and Mike Bloomfield's titanic title jam (13:10) featured the expanded canvas and solo virtuosity previously associated with jazz. Rock did a lot of growing up with these two songs. "*East-West* was such a radical departure, melodically, structurally and chordally from the rock and roll modes and licks at that time," Bloomfield explained to Tom Yates. "It was a long, long series of solos using scales that just had not been played by rock'n'roll guitar players. But believe me, I knew that they were not my scales. They were things I'd heard on John Coltrane records. I'd been listening to a lot of Ravi Shankar and guys who played modal music. These two tunes really broke a lot of ground for other guitar players. I think Carlos Santana still plays that way."

There are a couple of undistinguished blues fillers, almost as if the band was losing interest in the simple structures, but their versions of Robert Johnson's Walkin' Blues, Allen Toussaint's Get Out Of My Life Woman and Mike Nesmith's Mary Mary are all top drawer. And despite the epic performances, Mike Bloomfield's best demonstration of guitar wizardry may be the intro to I Got A Mind To Give Up Living, where he goes from a moan of despair to a howl of pain and then tears, all in the space of 42 seconds.

The Butterfield Band's take on virtuosity was markedly different from most of what it inspired. Bloomfield was the first real guitar hero of the 1960s, but he was part of a group that could soar with him. (Butterfield himself could match him solo for solo on harp.) Later, blues-rock bands became just rhythm sections there to keep the beat while some kid with no life experience would "jam the blues" past the threshold of annoyance. Therefore, we should revere the Butterfield Blues Band's version of blues rock, not blame them for the idiot children it spawned.

Record label:
Elektra

Produced
by Paul A. Rothchild, Mark Abramson and Barry Friedman.

Recorded
in NY and LA; spring–summer 1966.

Released:
December 1966

Chart peaks:
None (UK) 65 (US)

Personnel:
Paul Butterfield (v, hm); Mike Bloomfield (g); Elvin Bishop (g); Mike Naftalin (p); Jerome Arnold (b); Billy Davenport (d)

Track listing:
Walkin' Blues; Get Out Of My Life, Woman; I Got A Mind To Give Up Living; All These Blues; Work Song; Mary Mary; Two Trains Running; Never Say No; East-West

Running time:
44:55

Currently unavailable on CD

Further listening:
The Paul Butterfield Anthology (1998) (2-CD retrospective)

Further reading:
Mike Bloomfield (Ed Ward 1982)

Duke Ellington
Far East Suite

Jazz composer giant still hitting the heights 40-odd years into his career.

It's hard to overstate Duke Ellington's stature as a 20th century musician. Honoured by world leaders, respected by 'legit' cats and revered by jazz musicians of all styles and generations – Miles Davis once famously suggested that "all musicians should get down on their knees and thank Duke." His 2000-plus pieces of lovingly, compellingly crafted Negro Music (Ellington preferred the term to 'jazz') composed between 1923 and 1973, ranged from solo piano miniatures through art songs, pop novelties, tone parallels (his own term) and sprawling suites for jazz orchestra and choir, all characterised with discernible Ellingtonian wit, density and intelligence.

What makes his output doubly miraculous is that he kept an orchestra on the road his whole professional life. Financed by his own songwriting royalties, it was his travelling composer's workshop, enabling him to try things out as soon as he had written them. Rarely doing anything other than sleeping, eating, fornicating (he was a confessed "sexual intercourse freak"), performing, writing and travelling, he would compose on trains or at recording sessions and often rehearse after performances into the morning in an amazing sustained feat of unreasonable dedication. "It's our hobby," he would say, smiling.

Inspired by "that big, wonderful and beautiful world" the band visited the Middle East and Japan in 1963–64. Ellington and his friend and co-composer Billy Strayhorn fashioned first the four-movement Impressions Of The Far East, developing it into the nine-movement Far East Suite which ranks among their greatest achievements. Densely colourful and vividly exotic, it is at the same time archetypal Ellington with blues forms, impressionistic swing and characterful jazz solos, taking care not to over-utilise ethnic musical material. Ellington explained that other musicians had already copied the rhythms and scales of these places and he preferred to absorb the essence of an influence and "let it roll around, undergo a chemical change and then seep out on paper in a form that will suit the musicians who are going to play it." Those mighty players included tenorist Paul Gonsalves, serpentine and voluptuous on Tourist Point Of View, clarinetist

Record Label:
RCA Bluebird

Produced
by Brad McCuen.

Recorded
at RCA Victor, Studio A; December 19–21, 1966.

Released:
1967

Chart peaks:
None (UK) None (US)

Personnel:
Cootie Williams; William "Cat" Anderson; Herbie Jones; Mercer Ellington (t); Lawrence Brown, Charles "Chuck" Connors, Buster Cooper (tb); Johnny Hodges (as); Russell Procope (as, clarinet); Paul Gonsalves (ts); Jimmy Hamilton (clarinet, ts); Harry Carney (bs); Duke Ellington (p); John Lamb (b); Rufus Jones (d)

Track Listing:
Tourist Point Of View; Bluebird Of Dehli (Minah); Isfahan; Depk; Mount Harissa; Blue Pepper (Far East Of The Blues); Agra; Amad; Ad Lib On Nippon

Running time:
43.51

Currently available CD:
RCA 66552-2

Further listening:
Such Sweet Thunder (1957); Ella Fitzgerald Sings The Duke Ellington Songbook (1957); New Orleans Suite (1970)

Further reading:
Beyond Category: The Life And Genius Of Duke Ellington (John Edward Hasse, 1993); Duke Ellington Reader (Mark Tucker, 1993)

Jimmy Hamilton fleet and playful on Blue Bird Of Delhi, and altoist Johnny Hodges magnificently sensual on Isfahan (where Ellington observed "all was poetry"), an unspeakably beautiful piece which must take its place within the top hour of all Ellingtonia. Strayhorn died months after the recording and though Ellington continued to produce rigorous work, the loss of his intimate musical confidant since 1941 signified the end of an era.

Bobby Darin
If I Were A Carpenter

Former teen idol reinvents himself for the third time with a Tim Hardin song.

D arin had one of rock'n'roll's most unfathomable careers. Listen to the records he made across a career cut short at the age of only 37 (he died of a heart attack in December 1973) and you have almost no clues to the man's identity. There are undoubted classic moments; his own Dream Lover (1959) is one of the era's classic teen ballads. But just a year later he was the finger-clicking swinger behind Mack The Knife.

There's some doubt, of course, that *If I Were A Carpenter* was truly Darin's own brainchild. The album's producers Charles Koppelman and Don Rubin brought the songs to the table, seven of which were by either Tim Hardin or John Sebastian, both of whom they also represented. Yet Darin was no stranger to folk or even folk rock. As early as 1963 he'd recorded the folk-based *Earthy* and *Golden Folk Hits*; James Burton, Jim McGuinn, Fred Neil and Phil Ochs allegedly attended the sessions. Darin was also the first to perform Dylan songs at Las Vegas around this time (a dubious honour, perhaps). But whatever the motives, *If I Were A Carpenter* and the similar *Inside Out*, which followed a few months later, are stylistic triumphs.

Darin recorded If I Were A Carpenter as a single in August 1966. Hardin's own released version would not appear for over a year, but his arrangement is clearly what Darin's treatment was based upon. Hardin complained bitterly that Darin had completely copied his phrasing. Susan Moore (Hardin's wife), later recalled: "Tim and I were out driving when it came on the radio. I thought it was him, it was so close. The brakes screeched. The door slammed. And Tim was stomping on the side of the road, screaming and swearing." Would Hardin's own version have met with the same success? Somehow it's doubtful.

There's further irony that Tim Hardin's only US chart hit (Number 50 in 1969) was Simple Song Of Freedom — penned by Bobby Darin. But 1967 was the last year that Bobby Darin himself was to grace the charts.

Record label:
Atlantic

Produced
by Charles Koppelman and Don Rubin.

Recorded
at Gold Star Studio, Los Angeles; August 15, November 31 and October 1, 1966.

Released:
January 1967

Chart peaks:
None (UK) 142 (US)

Personnel:
Bobby Darin (v); no other musicians credited

Track listing:
If I Were A Carpenter(S); Reason To Believe; Sittin' Here Lovin' You(S); Misty Roses; Until It's Time For You To Go; For Baby; The Girl That Stood Beside Me(S); Red Balloon; Amy; Don't Make Promises; Day Dream

Running time:
26.03

Current CD:
DIAB864 adds Inside Out

Further listening:
The 4-CD As Long As I'm Singing: The Bobby Darin Collection (1998)

Further reading:
www.bobbydarin.net

The Doors
The Doors

A great mess of an artist, Jim Morrison, captured in all his wild majesty.

The Doors is a touchstone of rock history, wherein Jim Morrison and friends tunnel through the collective subconscious; in the late '60s it seemed very much to speak for the times, but it has transcended period and generation.

Morrison was the narcissistic stuff of rock legend. Shortly after graduating from the Theatre Arts department at UCLA in 1964, he met the classically trained keyboard player Ray Manzarek. In July the following year they got together with Robby Krieger and John Densmore – the drummer had shared a Transcendental Meditation class with Manzarek. Significantly, they took their name from Aldous Huxley's *The Doors Of Perception*, an account of a mescaline trip. They clicked immediately: Manzarek's alternately jittery and flowing organ identified a sound punctuated by Krieger's blues riffs, jazzy runs, and Spanish finger-picking, and Densmore's fluid sensitivity to the overarching personality of the frontman. Morrison was magnetic: wild, handsome and possessed of a rich baritone. When producer Paul Rothchild (who also recorded Paul Butterfield Blues Band, Janis Joplin and Love) saw The Doors live during a six-month residency at the Whisky A-Go-Go, Los Angeles, in July, 1966, he was so impressed by their presence that, according to his engineer Bruce Botnick, he at once proposed making a studio album as an "aural documentary" of their live set.

Remarkably, that is what he achieved with *The Doors*, capturing iconic songs propelled by an awe-inspiring sense of drama. Break On Through bounds in on Densmore's double-time bossa nova cymbal ride, Manzarek's charging organ bassline and Krieger's unison guitar; Morrison delivers his sermon with an evangelist's certain fervour. The American Number 1 single Light My Fire, a Krieger composition, rolls in on a majestic Manzarek organ line, stretches out on keyboard and guitar solos, but always returns to Morrison's sonorous vocal and the addictive chorus.

But, of course, there were problems inherent in Morrison's temperament, fuelled by his artistic wrestling bouts with the nature of order and chaos. His most extreme exploration occurred during the final session – appropriately, while working on The End. Comprehensively wrecked, the

Record label:
Elektra

Produced
by Paul Rothchild.

Recorded
at Sunset Sound Recorders, Los Angeles; September 1966.

Released:
January 1967

Chart peaks:
None (UK) 2 (US)

Personnel:
Jim Morrison (v); Ray Manzarek (o, p); Robby Krieger (g); John Densmore (d); Larry Knechtel (b); Bruce Botnick (e)

Track listing:
Break On Through (S/US); Soul Kitchen; The Crystal Ship; Twentieth Century Fox; Alabama Song (Whisky Bar) (S); Light My Fire (S); Back Door Man; I Looked At You; End of the Night; Take It As It Comes; The End

Running time:
43.25

Current CD:
7559740072

Further listening:
The Doors Box Set (1997); Waiting For The Sun (1968); LA Woman (1971)

Further reading:
Break On Through: The Life and Death of Jim Morrison (James Riordan and Jerry Prochnicky, 1991); No One Here Gets Out Alive (Jerry Hopkins and Danny Sugerman, 1981); www.thedoors.com

singer wound up lying on the floor mumbling the words to his Oedipal nightmare, "Fuck the mother, kill the father." Then, suddenly animated, he rose and threw a TV at the control room window. Sent home by Rothchild like a naughty schoolkid, he returned in the middle of the night, broke in, peeled off his clothes, yanked a fire extinguisher from the wall and drenched the studio. Alerted, Rothchild came back and persuaded the naked, foam-flecked Morrison to leave once more, advising the studio owner to charge the damage to Elektra; next day the band nailed the track in two takes. Morrison lived for only another five years.

The Lovin' Spoonful
Hums Of The Lovin' Spoonful

Much-loved '60s hitmakers' finest album, packed with classic songs by John Sebastian.

N owadays the Spoonful's chief songwriter, singer and all-round supremo John Sebastian plays in a jugband. And if he survives a gig without being constantly heckled to play Spoonful songs, he is prone to remarking, "Thank you for letting me outgrow my 20s". But if ever a songwriter had no reason to feel embarrassed by his early work it is surely Sebastian. He always wrote with a wit and care for language exceptional in rock, and with The Lovin' Spoonful he created jubilant music in a distinctive style influenced by rock'n'roll, country, blues and folk.

His admirers included Clive James, who, in 1972, argued that, "Randy Newman is the only man who has outstripped his brilliant lyric technique". The Los Angeles Times described Sebastian as "one of the very select group of song-writers, including also John Lennon, Ray Davies and Brian Wilson, for which the term genius doesn't seem just a publi-cist's wild notion."

Listen, for example, to Nashville Cats, in which Sebastian declares, gloriously ungrammatically: "There's 1352 guitar pickers in Nashville and anyone who unpacks his guitar can play twice as better than I will!" His lyrics were nonchalantly fun-filled and quirky and irresistibly amusing. Consider Darlin' Companion, later covered by Johnny Cash, a virtuosic masterclass in rhyme, half-rhyme and assonance, or Summer In The City, a perfect evocation of New York, which Sebastian co-wrote with his brother Mark and bassist Steve Boone.

"It was a collaboration and the extra strength came out of that," asserts Sebastian of his most famous song. "We were putting out singles that sounded different all the time," he adds, a claim fully justified by this album's four diverse US hits, Summer In The City, the truly lovely and evocative Rain On The Roof, Nashville Cats and Full Measure.

Record label:
Kama Sutra

Produced
by Eric Jacobsen.

Recorded
at Columbia Studios, New York; 1966.

Released:
January 1967

Chart peaks:
None (UK) 14 (US)

Personnel:
John Sebastian (g, v, hm); Zal Yanovsky (g, banjo, v); Steve Boone (b, k, v); Joe Butler (d, v); Roy Hallee (e)

Track listing:
Sittin' Here Lovin' You; Bes' Friends; Voodoo In My Basement; Darlin' Companion; Henry Thomas; Full Measure (S/US); Rain On The Roof (S); Coconut Grove; Nashville Cats (S); 4 Eyes; Summer In The City (S)

Running time:
27.24

Currently unavailable on CD,
though many of the tracks are available on compilations.

Further listening:
All four of the Sebastian-era non-film soundtrack Spoonful albums are worth buying, but Daydream (1966) probably runs Hums closest. The Very Best Of (1996) is a good budget-priced compila-tion.

Further reading:
www.lovinspoonful.com

Fred Neil

Fred Neil

Recluse comes out of hiding long enough to leave indelible footprint in the sands of pop history.

Recording Fred Neil was a bitch. Though blessed with a remarkable rich baritone – and the author of simple but affecting blues-stained folksongs – the reclusive singer/songwriter was notoriously studio-shy, and a reluctant participant once coaxed there. Elektra producer Paul Rothchild had managed to squeeze two albums out of him, the excellent *Tear Down The Walls* (with Vince Martin, 1964) and the exceptional *Bleecker And Macdougal* (1965). But when plans for a third Elektra album to be cut in Nashville fell through, producer Nik Venet signed him to Capitol in LA.

Venet had known Neil since their intersecting Brill Building experiences in the late '50s, and had a pretty good idea how to approach this difficult proposition. "I've recorded Fred Neil but we didn't make records," the late producer told Goldmine's Simon Wordsworth. "I guess I should be commended for what I didn't do. Because in this case it was keeping everything out of the way of the music. In fact, I used three engineers and recorded directly to stereo. None of those songs are remixed; everything you hear on the albums I did with Fred are as they happened in the studio. What you hear there is all Fred Neil. There were no arrangements; no one rehearsed."

It was the East Coast folkie meeting the electric West Coast mob that Venet had used with Linda Ronstadt And The Stone Poneys. With the guitar of Neil familiar Peter Childs to act as a bridge, the pairing meshed. Fred was in superb, rumbling voice, and had what most would come to consider his best collection of songs, yet it remained difficult to pull them out of him.

"Getting Fred to even let you in on what songs he was going to record was damn near impossible," says then-manager Herb Cohen. "We went in and started putting down whatever songs he had. That was the way it was. We might have known a couple of titles ahead of time. We certainly *didn't* know Everybody's Talkin', because he didn't know it. We needed another song, and he said he might have one more. Matter of fact, I think he completed it in the toilet of the Capitol Records Studio. As you can tell by the lyric, all he wanted to do was finish the album and go back to Florida."

Record label:
Capitol

Produced
by Nik Venet.

Recorded
at Capitol Studios, Hollywood; autumn 1966.

Released:
January 1967

Chart peaks:
None (UK) None (US)

Personnel:
James E Bond (b); John T Forsha (g); Peter Childs (g); Al Wilson (hm); Billy Mundi; Cyrus Faryar (g, bouzouki); Rusty Faryar (finger cymbals); UFO (bv); Fred Neil (v, g); John Kraus (e); Pete Abbot (e)

Track listing:
The Dolphins; I've Got A Secret (Didn't We Shake Sugaree); That's The Bag I'm In; Everybody's Talkin'; Everything Happens; Sweet Cocaine; Green Rocky Road; Cynicrustpetefredjohn Raga

Running time:
38.27

Current CD:
The Many Sides Of Fred Neil compiles Fred Neil, Sessions and The Other Side Of This Life

Further listening:
Bleecker And Macdougal (1964); The Many Sides Of Fred Neil (1998), a 2-CD compilation including a batch of rare early cuts and unreleased stuff.

Further reading:
Mojo 75 (February 2000); feature by Simon Wordsworth in Goldmine 411 (1996) (see www.krause.com/records/gm/)

Though it originally fared little better than his Elektra albums, *Fred Neil* captures an elusive artist at the peak of his powers. It contains his two best-loved songs (Everybody's Talkin' and The Dolphins), his loveliest blues rewrites (Shake Sugaree and Faretheewell) and original blues lyrics (That's The Bag I'm In). Even the eight minute 'raga' filler feels like it belongs. By the time of the album's release, Neil had retreated to his Coconut Grove Sanctuary, from which he'd ventured forth only under duress. When Harry Nilsson's cover of Everybody's Talkin' was used as the theme for the Academy Award-winning 1969 film *Midnight Cowboy*, the duress factor, and Fred's stubbornness both went through the roof. Though he'd attempt further, and mostly unsatisfying, recording, his closest brush with fame effectively ended his public life. Everybody's Talkin' would go on to become one of the most performed songs of all time (over five million performances!); the thing that drove him away for good was also what provided him his means of escape.

The Left Banke

Walk Away Renee / Pretty Ballerina

Fey New York band combine pop with chamber music.

'Baroque-rock' this was the label attached to a young band who emerged in 1966 with a new sound on a Top 5 debut single. The Left Banke came together around keyboard player Michael Brown while he was working at the tiny Manhattan recording studio owned by his father, the arranger and producer Harry Lookofsky. The only trained musician in the group, Brown was just 16 when he wrote Walk Away Renee.

Inspired by his unrequited adoration of Renee Fladen, Tom Finn's girlfriend, the lyrical mixture of heartfelt yearning and salvaged pride displayed an astonishing maturity. As Brown later recalled: "It's not a love song about possession – it's about loving someone enough to set them free." The song's production was equally striking (amazing for 1965, when it was done): Lookofsky's unorthodox arrangement kept the guitars low in the mix, the string quartet allowed Martin's distinctive voice and Brown's mellifluous harpsichord to shine.

Defying the custom of its time, the subsequent album was far more than just a vehicle for the group's hits (follow-up single Pretty Ballerina, also inspired by Fladen and arguably even more beautiful had reached number 15 in the US charts), composed entirely of originals, were driven for the most part by Brown's old-master keyboards. Barterers And Their Wives was, perhaps, the most literally baroque, but the songs also encompassed slow ballads (the aching Shadows Breaking Over My Head), country (What Do You Know) and brash fuzz guitar (Lazy Day).

With a raft of catchy, if rather melancholy, pop tunes, 'English-style' long hair and a look that critic Lillian Roxon described as "almost too pretty for rock", The Left Banke looked destined for greatness. But the album, recorded piecemeal over a year, was released too late to capitalise on their early success and Brown, disillusioned with touring, left to form a rival outfit under the same name. When both Left Bankes released singles simultaneously, writs began to fly and radio stations quickly shunned the band. Subsequent recordings, including an enchanting second LP, produced diminishing returns and by 1969 the band had dispersed to other projects.

Record label:
Smash/Phillips

Produced
by Harry Lookofsky, Steve and Bill Jerome.

Recorded
at World United Studios, New York; December 1965, January, March and November 1966; Mercury Studios, New York; January 1967.

Released:
February 1967

Chart peaks:
None (UK) 67 (US)

Personnel:
Michael Brown (k, v); Steve Martin (v); Jeff Winfield (g); Tom Finn (v, b); George Cameron (v, g, d); Warren David (d); George Hirsch (g); Hugh McCracken (g); Rick Brand (g)

Track listing:
Pretty Ballerina (S); She May Call You Up Tonight (S); Barterers And Their Wives (S); I've Got Something On My Mind (S); Let Go Of You Girl; Evening Gown; Walk Away Renee (S); What Do You Know; Shadows Breaking Over My Head; I Haven't Got The Nerve (S); Lazy Day (S)

Running time:
28.50

Current CD:
Mercury 848 095-2.

Further listening:
Their work is collected on the CD There's Gonna Be A Storm: The Complete Recordings 1966–1969 (1992).

Further reading:
http://users.aol.com/bocad/leftbank.htm

Aretha Franklin

I Never Loved A Man The Way I Loved You

Breakthrough of a soul legend.

At 24 years old, Aretha Franklin could've been forgiven for thinking she had seen it all already. Daughter of a famous gospel preacher, already a mother and wife, a professional singer for some years and a much experienced performer, she had already rubbed shoulders with the greats from Sam Cooke and Ray Charles to boxer Joe Louis and more. After her deal with Columbia Records expired, Jerry Wexler wasted no time signing her to Atlantic in November 1966.

The soul music scene was rapidly growing with Wilson Pickett, Sam And Dave, Otis Redding, Carla Thomas and the more urbane Motown acts already achieving great chart success. But Wexler knew he had something special. Aretha's first six weeks with Atlantic were spent choosing the proper material. On January 24, 1967 Wexler, Franklin and her then husband Ted White flew to a tiny country airstrip outside of Florence, Alabama and drove over to Muscle Shoals. There Chips Moman had assembled what is now rightly considered a legendary band, but it was a legendary band with no black faces; Wexler had specifically asked for an *integrated* band. With Aretha on piano they cut I Never Loved A Man – Dan Penn: "Less than two hours and it was in the can and it was a killer, no doubt about it. That morning we knew a star had been born."

However, a drinking contest had begun between White and one of the horn section, degenerating into an ugly, name-calling argument, and work on the second song, Do Right Woman-Do Right Man, ground to an abrupt halt. Wexler pulled the plug and with White (who doubled as Aretha's manager) refusing to step foot in Alabama again, the sessions were rescheduled for New York City, where they were eventually completed in February.

"Of the hundreds of sessions I have participated in," Spooner Oldham recalls today, "I can honestly say those first few times with Aretha Franklin were simply and magically unforgettable."

Record label:
Atlantic

Produced
by Jerry Wexler.

Recorded
at Muscle Shoals Studios, Alabama; January 24, 1967 and Atlantic Studios, New York; February 8 and 14–16.

Released:
March 10, 1967

Chart peaks:
36 (UK) 2 (US)

Personnel:
Aretha Franklin (v, p); Spooner Oldham (k); Jimmy Johnson (g); Chips Moman (g); Tommy Cogbill (b); Roger Hawkins (d); Gene Chrisman (d); Melvin Lastie (cornet, t); Ken Laxton (t); Ernie Royal (t); David Hood (tb); Charlie Chalmers (ts); King Curtis (ts); Joe Arnold (ts); Willie Bridges (bs); Carolyn Franklin, Erma Franklin; Cissy Houston (bv); Tom Dowd (e); Arif Mardin (e)

Track listing:
Respect (S); Drown In My Own Tears; I Never Loved A Man (The Way I Loved You) (S); Soul Serenade; Don't Let Me Lose This Dream; Baby Baby Baby (S); Dr Feelgood (Love Is A Serious Business); Good Times; Do Right Woman-Do Right Man; Save Me; A Change Is Gonna Come

Running time:
41.26

Current CD:
8122719342 adds: Respect; I Never Loved A Man (The Way I Love You) (2); Do Right Woman-Do Right Man (2)

Further listening:
Lady Soul (1968).

Further reading:
Sweet Soul Music: R&B And The Southern Dream Of Freedom (Peter Guralnick,

The Velvet Underground
Velvet Underground And Nico

New York's brutally realistic, genre-spawning riposte to the West Coast dream of psychedelia.

Now acknowledged as one of the most influential albums of all time, The Velvet Underground's 1967 debut barely limped into the Billboard chart at 197, then disappeared. New York's avant-garde art overlord Andy Warhol financed it, securing three days in Cameo-Parkway studios, Broadway, for $2,500. In return, the Velvets were obliged to use Warhol's latest 'superstar', Nico, as their vocalist, and to credit Warhol, who rarely visited the studio, as producer.

"The studio was still under construction," remembers Velvets' viola player John Cale. "The floorboards were up, the walls were out." Understandably, this did nothing to mitigate their open hostility to Nico. "We'd hear her go off-key or hit the wrong pitch. We would sit there and snigger." Nico's worst trial was I'll Be Your Mirror, which her relentless tormentors forced her to sing endlessly until she broke down in tears.

According to drummer Mo Tucker, time restrictions meant that most tracks were recorded live, virtually no over-dubs and engineering limitations forcing the band to play unusually quietly. "Heroin is such a good song," says Tucker, "but it's a pile of garbage on the record. The guys couldn't have their amps up loud in the studio, so I couldn't hear anything."

Once the album was complete, the band began hawking it around. "We took it to Ahmet Ertegun (at Atlantic) and he said, 'No drug songs.'" remembered the late Sterling Morrison. "We took it to Elektra and they said, 'No violas.'"

They finally scored a deal with Dylan's producer Tom Wilson, who arranged for its release on Verve. But, like Warhol, Wilson's primary interest was Nico. He made Reed write another song for her, which he would produce and release as a single. Reed delivered Sunday Morning but, once in the studio, insisted on singing it himself. By the time the album hit the streets, Verve had lost interest and was concentrating instead on marketing another recent signing, The Mothers of Invention. Yet, despite the album's tortuous genesis, its patchy sound and the limited playing ability of its creators, for the few who did discover *The Velvet Underground And Nico*, it was like that first glimpse of a Fellini movie after a lifetime of Disney. In Lou Reed's songs, tenderness and

Record Label:
Verve

Produced
by Andy Warhol and Tom Wilson.

Recorded
at Cameo-Parkway, New York, and T.T.G., Hollywood; April 1966.

Chart peaks:
None (UK) 197 (US)

Released:
March 15, 1967

Personnel:
Lou Reed (g, v); Nico (v); John Cale (va, k, b); Sterling Morrison (g, b); Maureen Tucker (pc)

Track Listing:
Sunday Morning (S); I'm Waiting For The Man; Femme Fatale; Venus In Fur; Run Run Run; All Tomorrow's Parties; Heroin; There She Goes Again; I'll Be Your Mirror; The Black Angel's Death Song; European Son

Running time:
48.26

Current CD:
5312502

Further listening:
For the vicious side, White Light/White Heat (1968). For tuneful stuff, The Velvet Underground (1969)

Further reading:
Up-Tight — The Velvet Underground Story (Victor Bockris and Gerard Malanga,1983); What's Welsh For Zen (John Cale, 1999); www.velvetunderground.com

violence were overpowering, the drugs were dangerous, and the music could scar you for life. The Record Mirror scribe who wrote, "It's solid and by no means freaky," was presumably one hell of a weird dude.

Merle Haggard And The Strangers

I'm A Lonesome Fugitive

All hail the first New Traditionalist.

Many country singers sang about a fantasy. Not Flossie Haggard's boy, who began running away from home when a young teen and who knew divorce, alcohol, railroads, even life behind bars. When people asked why he got himself into so much trouble, he'd tell them he just wanted to experience the kind of life he heard about in Jimmie Rodgers songs. Haggard was a New Traditionalist 20 years ahead of his time – and he sang about the classic country topics with authority and a tender, understanding grace.

Although he had had some success on his friend Fuzzy Owens's small Talley Records, it seemed like every song he released would be covered by a more established singer who would get the bigger hit. Fortunately, Capitol's country producer and A&R man Ken Nelson saw the pattern and called Owen in 1965 saying, "Why don't y'all cut out this baloney and get up here and let's take care of this thing." Which they did, signing to the label. Three albums later, Haggard's popularity was rising but he had still not made his mark in the eyes of the country music public. On the advice of a local agent he travelled to Liz Anderson's house to hear some songs she had written. Sitting down at a battered old pump organ, she performed the song that would become this album's title track.

Haggard was stunned as he listened. He felt the song defined him perfectly, outlining a persona he could quite comfortably colour in. His version of her song made Number 1 in the country singles charts – one of three hit singles he scored in 1966. Meanwhile, as demand for an album increased, Haggard set to writing (or, more precisely, dictating, or scribbling on used paper bags) some of the best material of his career – including classic honky tonk lament Drink Up And Be Somebody and the haunting Life In Prison, later covered by Gram Parsons on The Byrds' *Sweetheart Of The Rodeo* – augmenting them with a cover of Jimmie Rodgers's My Rough And Rowdy Ways. Haggard would go on to have better selling albums but he would never again be quite as raw and authentic.

Record label:
Capitol

Produced
by Ken Nelson.

Recorded
in Nashville; August 1–3, November 16 and December 16, 1966

Released:
March 1967

Chart peaks:
None (UK) None (US)

Personnel:
Merle Haggard (v, g); James Burton (g, dobro); Glen Campbell (bv, g); Lewis Talley (g); Shorty Mullins (g); Billy Mize (g, bv); Jerry Ward (b); Bonnie Owens (bv); Glenn D. Hardin (p); Ralph Mooney (ps); James Beck Gordon (d)

Track listing:
I'm A Lonesome Fugitive (S/US); All Of Me Belongs To You; House Of Memories; Life In Prison; Whatever Happened To Me; Drink Up And Be Somebody; Someone Told My Story (S/US); If You Want To Be My Woman; Mary's Mine; Skid Row; My Rough And Rowdy Ways; Mixed Up Mess Of A Heart

Running time:
31.16

Current CD:
CTS5547 adds: Mama Tried; Green Green Grass Of Home; Little Ole Wine Drinker Me; In The Good Old Days; I Could Have Gone Right; I'll Always Know; Sunny Side Of Life; Teach Me To Forget; Folsom Prison Blues; Run 'Em Off; You'll Never Love Me Now; Too Many Bridges To Cross Over

Further listening:
Branded Man (1967);

Further reading:
My House Of Memories: For The Record (Merle Haggard with Tom Carter, 1999)

The Mothers Of Invention
Freak Out

Rock music's first double album takes in blues, R&B, doo-wop, rock, surrealist satire and La Monte Young.

When Frank Zappa gathered up his motley collection of bar band oddballs, LBJ "great society" rejects and bona fide freaks, and landed himself a major label record contract he alerted the world to the new American underground. *Freak Out* was a landmark that arguably has never been surpassed in scope and ambition. MGM hardly knew what they were getting.

"The first track we laid down was Any Way The Wind Blows," said Zappa. "The second was Who Are The Brain Police? I could see [producer] Tom Wilson on the phone through the control room window calling the head office in New York saying, Well you're not going to believe this."

Who Are The Brain Police? is one of the scariest songs ever to emerge from the rock psyche, a Kafka-esque vision of contemporary America where personal identity and individuality are erased. In context, it offers a nightmarish counterpoint to the more overt political polemic of Hungry Freaks Daddy and Trouble Every Day (the latter originally titled The Watts Riot Song). Although much of the music was played by the Mothers, Zappa was shrewd enough to augment *Freak Out* with the cream of LA's session musicians (credited as The Mothers Auxiliary). Go Cry On Somebody Else's Shoulder; You Didn't Try To Call Me; Any Way The Wind Blows; I'm Not Satisfied; How Could I Be Such A Fool — all later re-recorded for *Cruising With Ruben And The Jets* — are given full orchestral treatments and reveal Zappa's formidable talent as an arranger. Sure, the Mothers looked like Hell's Angels who'd come for your daughter, but there was also a good chance they'd take her home to play her Stravinsky and Charles Ives. Subsequently, Zappa tended to apportion his musical iconoclasm to specific albums: savage satire (*We're Only In It For The Money*); classical motifs and musique concrete (*Lumpy Gravy*) and doo wop (*Cruising With Ruben And The Jets*). Only the equally impressive *Uncle Meat* casts its net as wide as does this audacious debut.

Record Label:
Verve

Produced
by Tom Wilson.

Recorded
at Sunset Highland Studios of T.T.G. Inc.

Released:
March 1967 (UK); August 1966 (US)

Chart peaks:
None (UK) None (US)

Personnel:
Frank Zappa (g); Ray Collins (v); Jim Black (d); Roy Estrada (b); Elliot Ingber (g); various unknown LA sessioniers

Track Listing:
Hungry Freaks Daddy; I Ain't Got No Heart; Who Are The Brain Police?; Go Cry On Somebody Else's Shoulder; Motherly Love; How Could I Be Such A Fool; Wowie Zowie; You Didn't Try To Call Me; Any Way The Wind Blows; I'm Not Satisfied; You're Probably Wondering Why I'm Here; Trouble Every Day; Help I'm A Rock; It Can't Happen Here; The Return Of The Son Of Monster Magnet

Running time:
60.31

Current CD:
RCD 10501

Further listening:
Uncle Meat (1969); Mystery Disc (Rykodisc RCD 10580)

Further reading:
Waiting For The Sun (Barney Hoskyns, 1996); Frank Zappa In His Own Words (1993); The Negative Dialectics Of Poodle Play (Ben Watson, 1996)

Jimi Hendrix Experience

Are You Experienced?

Landmark debut from rock's original wild axe-man.

*A*re You Experienced? is best experienced in mono. With rock's involvement with stereo still confined to spacey panning and scattering vocals around either speaker – and period psychedelia only adding to the confusion – even the best realised record was a plague of distracting gimmickry. In mono, however, the full majesty of Hendrix's vision shatters the speakers, proof that this boy didn't need technology to make him ricochet round the room. He was doing it quite successfully, already – as engineer Eddie Kramer remembers. "He would come up with some kind of crazy sound, I would catch it on tape, then try and twist it around and make it even sillier." The freakish Third Stone From The Sun and the title track are the epics which paint Hendrix's future in screaming colours, but the title track is the brightest of the bite-sized rockers – Foxy Lady, Manic Depression, Fire – tracks whose success, Kramer insists, came down to manager/producer Chandler. "If you look at the first record, most of the tracks are three-and-a-half, four minutes long, and that was Chas's influence. He came from that whole pop vibe, keeping it to three and a half minutes, which was a bit frustrating for Jimi. But I think it was a good thing because it kept the improvising very intense and very compact."

It was this intensity which ensured the album's immortality. Dave Marsh has called *Are You Experienced?* "the greatest, most influential debut album ever released." Keith Altham described Hendrix as "a new dimension in electrical guitar music ... a one man assault upon the nerve cells." But Noel Redding laughs at the much-vaunted perfection of the album. "There's mistakes on the Experience albums ... I remember, I'd call over to Chas, 'Hey, I hit a wrong note,' and he'd go 'Don't worry, no one will fucking notice,' in that wonderful Geordie accent of his. Then Hendrix used to drop a couple of notes here or there, or miss a slight lyric, and Chas would say 'Don't worry, mate.' It was great, we paid a lot of attention to what we were doing, but it was the feel we were after, more than technical perfection." And that is what they got. An album which feels great and sounds just fine. Especially in mono.

Record Label:
Track

Produced
by Chas Chandler.

Recorded
at De Lane Lea, London; January–March 1967; Olympic Studios, London; February–April 1967.

Released:
May 12, 1967 (UK); August 23, 1967 (US)

Chart peaks:
2 (UK) 5 (US)

Personnel:
Jimi Hendrix (v, g); Noel Redding (b, v); Mitch Mitchell (d)

Track Listing:
Foxy Lady (S, US only); Manic Depression; Red House (UK only); Hey Joe (US only) (S); Can You See Me? (UK only); Love Or Confusion; I Don't Live Today; May This Be Love; Wind Cries Mary (US only) (S, UK only); Fire; Third Stone From The Sun; Remember (UK only); Purple Haze (S, US only); Are You Experienced?

Current CD adds:
Stone Free; 51st Anniversary; Highway Chile

Running time:
38.38 (US version)

Current CD:
MCD11608

Further listening:
Axis Bold As Love (1967); Electric Ladyland (1968)

Further reading:
Are You Experienced? (Noel Redding and Carol Appleby, 1990)

Tim Hardin
Tim Hardin 2

Second album by the errant young singer-songwriter, many of whose songs have become standards.

Susan Yardley was a young actress making a name for herself in the TV series The Young Marrieds when she first met Tim Hardin in Los Angeles. Hardin, already a hardened drug addict, had a bad record with women and may have had dishonourable intentions towards Susan, if the lyrics to The Lady Came From Baltimore are anything to go by. Instead he fell deeply and irrevocably in love with the actress – real name Susan Morss – who became his wife and inspired virtually all the songs that flooded out of him and formed the basis of *Tim Hardin 2*.

He set up a studio in his house and recorded a series of songs of poignant wonder which detail not only his intense love for Susan, but also the paranoia and neuroses that smothered him. Red Balloon is an anguished song about drugs; Black Sheep Boy confronts his sense of failure and alienation; Tribute To Hank Williams has him identifying strongly with the tragic, too-fast-to-live legend of the country icon. If I Were A Carpenter poetically relates his inferiority complex over his marriage to the well-connected Susan Morss, renamed as Susan Moore by Hardin for artistic purposes. If I Were A Carpenter went on to become his most celebrated song, a hit for Bobby Darin, Four Tops and many others. Not that it impressed Hardin, still unsuccessfully fighting his habit. It's said that when he first heard Bobby Darin's cover of Carpenter in the car, he screamed the car to a halt, jumped out and stamped on the ground in a rage.

There were no happy endings for Tim Hardin or Susan Moore. He eventually died of an OD, 13 years after the release of *Tim Hardin 2*. He had a long, difficult struggle with his own numerous demons, which included a terror of live performance, low self-esteem, constant writer's block, the emotional roller coaster of his on-off marriage and various attempts to escape the clutches of the drugs that ultimately killed him.

Record label:
Verve

Produced
by Charles Koppelman and Don Rubin

Recorded
at Hardin's home studio, Los Angeles; winter 1967.

Released:
May 1967

Chart peaks:
None (UK) None (US)

Personnel:
Tim Hardin (v, g, p); Artie Butler (strings); Felix Pappalardi (b); Sticks Evans (d); Phil Krauss (vibes)

Track listing:
If I Were A Carpenter; Red Balloon; Black Sheep Boy; Lady Came From Baltimore; Baby Close Its Eyes; You Upset The Grace Of Living When You Lie; Speak Like A Child; See Where You Are And Get Out; It's Hard To Believe In Love For Long; Tribute To Hank Williams.

Running time:
28.30

Current CD:
REP7030WP adds: Tim Hardin

Further listening:
Suite For Susan Moore And Damion (1969) is a disturbing confessional in song and poetry of a man whose life is falling apart. Of his later albums Nine (1973) is probably the best, though his magical songwriting had deserted him, he proved himself a sensual soul-blues singer.

Further reading:
www.mathie.demon.co.uk/th/index.html

The Beatles

Sgt. Pepper's Lonely Heart's Club Band

The most famous rock album of all time.

While recording Sgt Pepper, Paul McCartney read an allegation that The Beatles had "dried up", so quiet were they from *Revolver* (August 1966) through the winter and spring of 1967. (Apart, that is, from releasing one of the greatest singles of all time, the double-A-sided Penny Lane/Strawberry Fields Forever.) But he knew exactly what The Beatles had up their sleeves.

"I was sitting rubbing my hands, saying, You just wait!" he remembers. His arrogance is intriguing: The Beatles could not have known what the public's reaction to *Sgt Pepper* would be. It may have baffled the bulk of their fans, so great was its scale and ambition. But over the 129 days it took to record, the Fabs were following their noses, and no-one was going to tell them what could or couldn't be achieved. Their favourite expression in the studio at this time was "There's no such word as 'can't'."

The first song recorded (Strawberry Fields Forever) was quickly deemed too plain and a new, orchestral arrangement ordered. The next three songs recorded were When I'm Sixty Four, Penny Lane and A Day In The Life, a gauge of how different this record was intended to be from its predecessors. Their ambitions even stretched to plans for a TV special following the recording. (In the end only one session was filmed, the orchestra playing on A Day In The Life and it has received scant airing since.) *Sgt Pepper* reeks of confidence and the desire to set new standards. It was a whole creation (and the first Beatles album to have the same sequence in Britain and America). McCartney – whose vision glued the project together – was especially daring, challenging Lennon to come up with sparkle to match. A Day In The Life was composed by them both, and the nods and winks that passed between the two as they put lyric onto paper belies the common misconception that they were worlds apart by this time. George Martin was urged to concoct brass, woodwind and orchestral parts, future Gary Glitter mastermind Mike Leander was commissioned to supply a string arrangement for She's Leaving Home and the engineers were encouraged to stretch Abbey Road's rather modest technology to its limits.

Record label:
Parlophone

Produced
by George Martin.

Recorded
at Studio Two, Abbey Road, London and Regent Sound Studio, Tottenham Court Road, London; December 6, 1966–April 21, 1967.

Released:
June 1, 1967

Chart peaks:
1 (UK) 1 (US)

Personnel:
Paul McCartney (b, k, v); John Lennon (g, k, v); George Harrison (g, sitar, v); Ringo Starr (d, pc, v); Geoff Emerick, Richard Lush, Phil McDonald, Keith Slaughter (e)

Track listing:
Sgt. Pepper's Lonely Hearts Club Band/With A Little Help From My Friends (S/released 1978); Lucy In the Sky With Diamonds; Getting Better; Fixing A Hole; She's Leaving Home; Being For The Benefit Of Mr. Kite; Within You Without You; When I'm Sixty Four; Lovely Rita; Good Morning Good Morning; Sgt. Pepper's Lonely Hearts Club Band (Reprise); A Day In The Life

Running time:
39.50 or, on vinyl, infinite

Current CD:
CDP 7 46442 2

Further listening:
Hear Pepper develop on Anthology II (1996)

Further reading:
MOJO 1, 24, 26, 35, 71; The Complete Beatles Chronicle (Mark Lewisohn, 1996); Revolution In The Head (Ian McDonald, 1995)

What they all came up with is arguably the reason for this book's existence, for it energised the album form, providing a high watermark for anyone with the chance to record 40 minutes of music and decorate twelve square inches of card. It may not be the best album ever made – it's not even the best Beatles album ever made – and in retrospect there's a lot that's gimmicky about it. It wasn't the first 'grown-up' rock album, the first to use an orchestra, the first themed album or the first psychedelic album, but it *was* by The Beatles, and consequently it became the first of these to be noticed by the wider public and to mark the moment where pop music simultaneously reflected and defined the times. When the final E major triad cluster (played on three pianos and multitracked four times) struck, it sounded a death-knell for pop's callow youth.

Donovan
Sunshine Superman

Donovan, at his peak, shakes off the junior plastic Dylan tag. Nobody shouts Judas.

History has been unkind to Donovan Philip Leitch. Dismissed first as a Dylan imitator and then as a cosmic buffoon, he was nevertheless a bit of a trailblazer: the first pop star to be busted for drugs (jumping naked onto a policeman's back while high on LSD) and one of the first British solo stars to top the US charts – with the title track of this album.

His rise to fame was unusually swift. Born in Glasgow, raised in Hatfield, at 18 he was already a seasoned itinerant musician when discovered playing in a St Albans folk club by songwriter Geoff Stevens. A deal was quickly struck with Southern Music. "I was a big fan of Buddy Holly," declares Donovan. "Southern published Buddy, so I felt right at home there. I walked in and they said, 'What shall we do with this young man with a guitar? Perhaps he can be a Bob Dylan for Europe.'"

Stevens suggested covering Gale Garnett's American hit We'll Sing In The Sunshine. But the teenaged troubadour wanted to record a poem he'd just set to music, Catch The Wind. Stevens alerted Bob Bickford, a scout for Ready Steady Go!, and the unsigned singer was booked for the show in February 1965. "Two nights on from sleeping on somebody's floor I was on national television!" Donovan wore a denim Breton fisherman's cap, sat on a stool and made up a song in a Woody Guthrie style, Talking Pop Star Blues, which poked fun at the current acts in the charts. The show was flooded with positive mail and Donovan was quickly booked for the following week.

Catch The Wind was swiftly leased to Pye and the single first aired on his third Ready Steady Go! appearance. By the end of March the song was at Number 4 and the teen magazines were full of advertisements for "The Donovan Cap". An American scout caught Ready Steady Go! and booked him for a slot on Shindig, still only weeks after that support slot in St Albans. Catch The Wind made 23 in the US. A few singles later, he signed up with hit-maker Mickie Most and at the end of 1965 they cut Sunshine Superman and aired it on the short-lived UK TV show A Whole Scene Going. However, legal problems held its release over until September 1966, when its mildly trippy, upbeat blues sound chimed perfectly with the

Record label:
Pye

Produced
by Mickie Most.

Recorded
in Hollywood and London; 1965 (title track) and summer 1966.

Released:
June 1967 (UK); September 1966 (US)

Chart peaks:
(UK) 25 ; (US) 11

Personnel:
Donovan (v,g); Eric Ford (g); Jimmy Page (g); Bobby Rae (b); Spike Healey (b); Shaun Phillips (sitar); Bobby Orr (d); Fast Eddie Hoh (d); Tony Carr (pc); John Cameron (k, a); Harold McNair (f); Danny Thompson (db)

Track listing:
Sunshine Superman; Legend Of A Girl Child Linda; The Observation; Guinevere; Celeste; Writer In The Sun; Season Of The Witch; Hampstead Incident; Sand Of Foam; Young Girl Blues; Three Kingfishers; Bert's Blues.

Running time:
49.00 (UK) 41.22 (US)

Current CD:
Beat Goes On BGOCD68. US version also available: Sunshine Superman; Legend Of A Girl Child Linda; Three Kingfishers; Ferris Wheel; Bert's Blues; Season Of The Witch; The Trip; Guinevere; The Fat Angel; Celeste. Epic SLD 23562

Further listening:
Mellow Yellow (1967); A Gift From A Flower To A Garden (1967); Barabajagal (1969)

Further reading:
www.sabotage.demon.co.uk/donovan

emergent hippy movement and the single sailed to Number 1 in the US and Number 2 in Britian.

This marvellous album – a record whose musical ambition was certainly ahead of its time – was, in fact, released late in the UK and compiled from two American releases *Sunshine Superman* and *Mellow Yellow*. Pye omitted three of the American version's most psychedelic tracks – The Trip (later released on the flip of the Sunshine Superman single), The Fat Angel (a tribute to Cass Elliot which namechecks Jefferson Airplane and was later covered by the band) and Ferris Wheel.

Whichever edition you hear, however, the album offers a daring musical blend of jazz, folk, rock, raga and Arabic influences, while lyrically exploring a combination of Celtic and Anglo-Saxon mythology, wry social satire and beat poetry. Unmistakably acid-tinged in places, there are cautionary moments too, particularly on the superb, elliptical rocker Season Of The Witch (with its 'beatniks out to make it rich'). *Sunshine Superman* caught Donovan at the crossroads, wary of pop stardom and protest ("I just want to *please*") and trying on the multi-coloured mantle of a hippy Celtic bard for size. He wore it well.

The Monkees
Headquarters

TV's phoney-rockers prove they can make their own music.

The success of The Monkees, whose origins dated back to a September 1965 *Variety* ad for four "spirited" boys, had surpassed their corporate creators' dreams. While The Monkees' public image was of a self-contained group, record mogul Don Kirshner, who chose their songs and oversaw their records, made no effort to hide his role in their fame. In January 1967, when their second album, *More Of The Monkees*, hit the stores, the group was on tour. As Peter Tork later recalled: "In Cleveland, we went across the street and bought the first copy of our record that we'd seen. The back liner notes were Don Kirshner congratulating all his boys for the wonderful work they'd done, and, oh, yes, this record is by The Monkees."

Thus began a rebellion by the prefab four, which climaxed in a legendary run-in with Kirshner at a Beverly Hills hotel, where Michael Nesmith reportedly put his fist through a wall. Nesmith proceeded to spill to *TV Guide*, "The music on our records has nothing to do with us. It's totally dishonest, tell the world we're synthetic, because, dammit, we are!" At the insistence of the TV show producers, Kirshner relaxed control and the group chose its own producer, Turtles bassist Chip Douglas (real name: Douglas Farthing Hatlelid), formerly of the Modern Folk Quartet. As the group-penned liner notes to *Headquarters* explained, a tad defensively: "We aren't the only musicians on this album, but the occasional extra bass or horn player played under our direction, so that this is all ours."

Opener, Nesmith's You Told Me, makes it clear that *Headquarters* is indeed the work of a self-contained group, sounding closer to a garage band than the polished combos that cut The Monkees' previous records. The group's exhilaration at being let loose is obvious. The prevailing influence is folk-rock, especially on Nesmith's three compositions (it was rumoured for years that The Byrds played on his sparkling You Just May Be The One). Yet the album's most notorious track is, stylistically, all-but uncategorisable.

The Monkees' US label, Colgems, didn't deem any of *Headquarters* worthy of single release, but UK label, RCA, heard a song it thought perfect for the British market: Dolenz's absurdist rant Randy Scouse Git. (Dolenz had picked up the title watching 'Til Death Do Us Part while romancing British wife Samantha.) There was, however, the small problem of the title.

Record label:
RCA

Produced
by Douglas Farthing Hatlelid, aka Chip Douglas.

Recorded
at RCA Victor Studios, Hollywood; February–April 1967.

Released:
June 1967

Chart peaks:
1 (UK) 2 (US)

Personnel:
Mike Nesmith (g, ps, o, v); Davy Jones (pc, v); Micky Dolenz (d, g, v); Peter Tork (k, 12-string guitar, b, banjo, v); Vince DaRosa (French horn); Fred Seykora (c); Chip Douglas (b)

Track listing:
You Told Me; I'll Spend My Life With You; Forget That Girl; Band 6; You Just May Be The One; Shades Of Gray; I Can't Get Her Off My Mind; For Pete's Sake; Mr. Webster; Sunny Girlfriend; Zilch; No Time; Early Morning Blues And Greens; Randy Scouse Git (S/UK — released as Alternate Title)

Running time:
28.56

Current CD:
450997662 adds: Girl I Knew Somewhere; All Of Your Toys; Nine Times Blue; Jericho; Peter Gunn's Gun; Pillow Time

Further listening:
The Monkees (1966); More Of The Monkees (1967); Pisces, Aquarius, Capricorn And Jones (1967)

Further reading:
Monkees sessionography site: www. geocities.com/SunsetStrip/Towers/3152.

An RCA rep wrote to The Monkees' US office, "You are no doubt aware that many English expressions have a totally different meaning in America and vice versa, and in this case it is a question of the versa being vice. To give you a perfectly straightforward translation of the title, you are referring to someone as being an 'oversexed illegitimate son of a prostitute from Liverpool'." Hence The Monkees' second-biggest UK hit was known as Alternate Title.

Small Faces

Small Faces

The Small Faces' second album proper took a subtle, organic approach to psychedelia.

Following their split with Decca and manager Don Arden at the end of 1966, the Small Faces signed to Immediate, an independent label run in a libertine spirit wholly in keeping with proprietor Andrew Oldham's day-job as The Rolling Stones' manager. With virtually unlimited access to Olympic's new 8-track facility, the Small Faces – under the auspices of virtuoso engineer Glyn Johns – began to experience a creative awakening akin to The Beatles' in '65, experimenting with multi-tracking and other studio trickery, while expanding their minds with copious acid and 'gear'.

The outcome was a rich, inventive and wonderfully cheery brew of folk, psychedelia, music hall, swing, soul and psychedelia, with a strong English baroque twist – McLagan often swapping his trademark Hammond for harpsichord. Congas, celeste and Mellotrons also enriched the sound, with brass (on the calypso-flavoured Eddie's Dreaming) courtesy of Georgie Fame's horn section.

"We really were ahead of our time," says Kenny Jones. "We were fortunate that we had Glyn Johns; he was in our opinion the best engineer in Britain. He got us some amazing sounds and he encouraged us to be experimental."

The contrast with the group's first album on Decca (confusingly also titled *Small Faces*) – a nervy but one-dimensional R&B outing – is abundantly clear. Complementing Steve Marriott's legendary lungs, Ronnie Lane sings on five tracks, while McLagan tackles his own utterly charming Up The Wooden Hills To Bedfordshire. Though *Small Faces* spawned no singles, and was soon eclipsed by the stellar success of their Summer Of Love Number 1, Itchycoo Park, it arguably captured better than any other contemporary British album the excitement, optimism and sheer fun of like-minded spirits journeying together through the acid era.

Record label:
Immediate

Produced
by Steve Marriott and Ronnie Lane.

Recorded
at Olympic Studios, London; 1967.

Released:
June 1967

Chart peaks:
12 (UK) None (US)

Personnel:
Steve Marriott (g, v); Ronnie Lane (b, v); Ian McLagan (k, v); Kenny Jones (d); Glyn Johns (e)

Track listing:
(Tell Me) Have You Ever Seen Me; Something I Want To Tell You; Feeling Lonely; Happy Boys Happy; Things Are Going To Get Better; My Way Of Giving; Green Circles; Become Like You; Get Yourself Together; All Our Yesterdays; Talk To You; Show Me The Way; Up The Wooden Hills To Bedfordshire; Eddie's Dreaming

Running time:
28.26

Current CD:
ESMCD476 adds: Here Come The Nice; Itchycoo Park; I'm Only Dreaming; Tin Soldier; I Feel Much Better

Further listening:
Ogden's Nut Gone Flake (1968); posthumous compilation, The Autumn Stone (1969)

Further reading:
MOJO 12A; All The Rage: A Riotous Romp Through Rock'N'Roll History (Ian McLagan, 1998)

Albert King
Born Under A Bad Sign

Breakthrough album for an unorthodox blues giant.

K ing – a left-hander who finger-picked an upside-down, right-handed Flying V – was into his '40s with only a couple of R&B hits to his name when he signed to Stax. Admittedly, he already had a smokin' reputation, but the Stax house band were to help him reach his true soul-blues potential.

After a trio of unsuccessful singles, two studio stints in mid-'67 provided the bulk of an album which was to exert massive influence on other guitarists, and at the same time launch King as a darling of the white college and stadium circuit. Wayne Jackson, who played trumpet on these and literally hundreds of other hit-making sessions for the label: "Albert was the sweetest man you could imagine: a man of the Old South. He used to call me his whistle-tooter. It was a very happy studio. Steve Cropper and Al Jackson ran the recordings. Jim Stewart [company boss] wasn't a producer – Al knew all the chords and lyrics better than anyone. He would stop things if they were going wrong. Albert's guitar was always out of tune with everything else, but he was such a strong man he would just bend those notes back in! The band kept things simple because we were all young guys learning together. We didn't know how to play it any better!"

The 10-bar-blues smoulder of the title track opens proceedings ("Sometimes the funk got so thick you could spread it on bread and eat it"), and the bad-ass syncopations of Crosscut Saw keep the heat on. The jump-shuffle of Kansas City is a welcome throwback, and his rendition of The Very Thought Of You proves that King could sing. But ultimately the guitar's the thing. The stinging, howling, weeping solo on Personal Manager is, simply, one of the greatest ever: King may have played from a relatively small stock of phrases but he made every one of them count.

The following year, on the back of the album's artistic success, King opened for Hendrix at San Francisco's Fillmore. As a teenager Hendrix had worshipped King. He never stopped, even recording Born Under A Bad Sign in 1969.

Record label:
Stax

No producer credited.

Recorded
at Stax Studios, McLemore Avenue, Memphis, Tennessee; March 3, September 3 and November 2, 1966; May 17 and June 9, 1967.

Released:
July 1967

Chart peaks:
None (UK) None, (US)

Personnel:
Albert King (g, v); Steve Cropper (g); Booker T. Jones (p); Isaac Hayes (p); Donald 'Duck' Dunn (b); Al Jackson Jr (d); Wayne Jackson (t); Andrew Love (s, flute); Joe Arnold (s); Jim Stewart (supervision)

Track listing:
Born Under A Bad Sign (S); Crosscut Saw (S); Kansas City; Oh Pretty Woman (S/US); Down Don't Bother Me; The Hunter; I Almost Lost My Mind; Personal Manager; Laundromat Blues (S/US); As The Years Go Passing By; The Very Thought Of You

Running time:
34.41

Current CD:
SCD 723 – 2

Further listening:
Live Wire/Blues Power (1968), live recordings from the Fillmore shows mentioned above; Ultimate Collection (1983), a 2-CD round-up.

Further reading:
Soulsville, USA: The Story Of Stax Records (Rob Bowman, New York); www.blueflamecafe.com/Albert_King.html

The West Coast Pop Art Experimental Band
Part One

Drug-free psych made to satisfy the lusts of an eccentric millionaire.

If ever an album demonstrated the haphazard way in which much psychedelic music of the late '60s was recorded, *Part One* must surely be it. After going to see their heroes, The Yardbirds, play at a hip Hollywood party, teenage hopefuls Michael Lloyd and the Harris brothers found themselves locked into a Faustian pact with the host, eccentric millionaire Bob Markley. The deal? He would promote their band and buy expensive equipment if they let him bang a tambourine on stage. According to Lloyd, music was the last thing on Markley's mind: "He had seen the incredible amount of girls that thought rock and roll was really cool and that was his only motivation."

Coining the ludicrously cumbersome name, Markley used his society contacts to secure the group a three-LP deal with Reprise, but once in the studio his younger bandmates soon began to tire of their patron's increasing dominance. As Shaun recalls: "The part that was frustrating was that he had no musical aptitude of any kind and so what he was trying to do to be different and innovative ended up sounding contrived. It was an embarrassment."

Well, time can tell a different story. Recorded without the influence of drink or drugs, it is precisely the palpable tensions within the band – and the unexpected juxtapositions within the music – which make *Part One* so extraordinary. Alongside passionate, harmonic pop songs like Transparent Day and the cover of PF Sloan's Here's Where You Belong, lurk the hard-edged, distorted weirdness of Leiyla, Zappa's Help I'm A Rock and 1906. The latter, with Markley eerily reciting his lyrics, attempts to convey a dog's premonition of the San Francisco earthquake: "See the frightened foxes/See the hunchback in the park/He's blind and can't run for cover/I don't feel well."

Another of Bob's Tinseltown friends, Baker Knight (who had written for Elvis and Ricky Nelson) composed two of the album's highlights: a beautifully sparse arrangement of Shifting Sands and If You Want This Love. As Danny recalls, the latter was transformed by a driving time signature: "When Baker Knight first heard the playback he didn't know what to make of

Record label:
Reprise

Produced
by Bob Markley and Jimmy Bowen.

Recorded
at United Western Recording Studios, Los Angeles; late 1966.

Released:
July 1967

Chart peaks:
None (UK) None (US)

Personnel:
Bob Markley (v, p); Shaun Harris (v, b); Danny Harris (v, g); Michael Lloyd (v, g); Ron Morgan (g); Hal Blaine or Jim Gordon (d)

Track listing:
Shifting Sands (S); I Won't Hurt You; 1906 (S); Help I'm A Rock; Will You Walk With Me; Transparent Day; Leiyla; Here's Where You Belong; If You Want This Love; 'Scuse Me Miss Rose; High Coin

Running time:
30.36

Not currently available on CD

Further listening:
A Child's Guide To Good And Evil (1968); A Group (1970) Bob Markley 'solo' LP which reunited the original members.

Further reading:
http://users.bart.nl/~cvdlely/wcpaeb.html

it and said: 'Hey! I thought this was a country song!'" These were balanced in turn by the delicate dreamy songs I Won't Hurt You (backed with a heartbeat) and the acoustic, post-apocalyptic Will You Walk With Me, complete with string quartet and celeste; the album closed with an energetic reading of Van Dyke Parks's High Coin. The group would go on to record another four albums, each as individual as the last, but none would quite capture the sound of their first Reprise LP – the sound of teenage dreams diverted.

The Electric Prunes
Underground

Dissolution around the corner, dark psychedelic visionaries — briefly — reach flashover.

Like many musicians of their time The Electric Prunes were not masters of their own destiny. The three albums they recorded in a mere nine months during 1967 tell a cautionary tale of what happens when a gifted band are subjected to the whims of an equally talented producer and brilliant, but erratic, songwriters. Although their debut album *I Had Too Much To Dream Last Night* contained material equally as powerful as the classic single from which it spawned its title, it had been marred by ill-judged gimmicks. By the time of the third LP, *Mass In F Minor*, the band would effectively be reduced to session musicians languishing under the weight of composer David Axelrod's quasi-religious visions. Between these two extremes, *Underground* comes closest to expressing the unique spirit of a group who will long be regarded as one of the finest exponents of psychedelic pop.

The stunning sleeve shows the Prunes charging out of the cover, a forlorn face looming above them — an image whose mystery and energy are reflected in opening cut The Great Banana Hoax. With pounding drums and a pulsing rhythm as irresistible as The Byrds' Eight Miles High, at its centre is one of the group's defining moments: a plaintive organ note rises from the maelstrom and seamlessly gives way to Williams' biting guitar solo.

Aided by producer Dave Hassinger, they created a collage of effects without swamping each individual contribution, and conjured an atmosphere of haunting melodrama. Lowe's vocals wavered between soft innocence and sneering malice while the band shifted between the soft, sparse arrangements of tracks like I and the electrical charge of Hideaway. Antique Doll and Children Of Rain explore dark corners of childhood and themes of emotional isolation. In the hyperactive Dr Do-Good, Lowe's demented cartoon voice was juxtaposed with a riot of distorted guitar; but the real treat comes at the album's climax where raw punk and eastern-tinged psychedelia blend perfectly in Long Day's Flight.

Sadly, however, the Prunes were running out of juice. The album sold poorly. They produced only one more single before losing control of both their name and their future.

Record label:
Reprise

Produced
by Dave Hassinger.

Recorded
at the American Recording Company, North Hollywood, California; mid-1967.

Released:
August 1967

Chart peaks:
None (UK) 172 (US)

Personnel:
James Lowe (v, autoharp, hm); Mark Tulin (b, o, p); Ken Williams (g, effects); James 'Weasel' Spangola, Mike Gannon (v, g); Preston Ritter, Michael 'Quint' Weakley (d); Richie Podolor, Bill Cooper (e)

Track listing:
The Great Banana Hoax (S); Children Of Rain; Wind-Up Toys (S); Antique Doll; It's Not Fair; I Happen To Love You; Dr Do-Good (S); I; Hideaway (S); Big City; Capt. Glory; Long Day's Flight (S)

Running time:
34.43

Current CD:
CCM133

Further listening:
I Had Too Much To Dream Last Night (1967)

Further reading:
www.electricprunes.com/

Etta James
Tell Mama

The toughest female soul voice of the '60s gets the full Muscle Shoals treatment.

Etta James began singing at the age of five, as little Jamesetta Hawkins belting out gospel at Los Angeles' St Paul Baptist Church. Discovered and re-christened by LA band leader Johnny Otis, the 16-year-old Etta James had her first hit in 1955 with Roll With Me Henry. For the next five years James' life was one of constant touring and full immersion in a rough on-the-road life – sex, drugs and real mean men. A voice of sweet'n'lowdown power, like a born-bad angel, James signed to Leonard Chess's Chess Records in 1960 and the hits soon followed: At Last, Something Got A Hold Of Me and Stop The Wedding. By 1967 she was a full-time soul star with painted-on cat eyes, tight cup dresses, a pistol in her purse, and a full-time heroin habit – "Working to get high, stay high, live high and, if the stuff was strong enough, die high."

James sang the life she lived. Leonard Chess was convinced that the only woman who did it like Etta was Aretha Franklin. So, after Jerry Wexler put Aretha in Rick Hall's Fame Studios in 1967 to cut the R&B heartache classic *I Never Loved a Man The Way I Love You*, Chess decided to do the same with Etta. The first track James cut with the Muscle Shoals team was I'd Rather Go Blind, a song ripped from the heart about loving someone so much that you "just don't want to be free." James knew all about that. At the time she was seeing a guy called Billy Foster. Sometimes they fought so hard that Etta would end up sticking Billy with a kitchen knife. Etta says *she* wrote I'd Rather Go Blind. The songwriting credit went to Billy Foster. James sang about Security as she saw it slipping through her fingers. "The same rope that pulls you up/sure can hang you," she hollers on The Same Rope.

What she ended up with was an album of pure pain and suffering, and drum-tight soul. Just don't expect Etta to love it in the same way. "They rant and rave about *Tell Mama*," says James, "how I sang the shit out of it. I wish I could agree. I don't like being cast in the role of the Great Earth Mother, the gal you come to for comfort and easy sex. Nothing was easy then. My career was building up but my life was falling apart."

Record label:
Chess

Produced
by Rick Hall.

Recorded
at Fame Studios, Muscle Shoals, Alabama; early 1967.

Released:
August 1967

Chart peaks:
None (UK) None (US)

Personnel:
Etta James (v); Albert Lowe Jr (g); Jimmy Ray Johnson (g); David Hood (b); Roger Dawkins (d); Dewey Oldham (p); Carl Banks (o); Gene 'Bowlegs' Miller (t); Charles Chalmers, Aaron Varnell, Floyd Newman (s); George Davis (p)

Track listing:
Tell Mama (S); I'd Rather Go Blind (S); Watch Dog; The Love Of My Man (S); I'm Gonna Take What He's Got; The Same Rope; Security (S); Steal Away; My Mother In Law; Don't Lose Your Good Thing; It Hurts Me So Much; Just A Little Bit

Running time:
30.10

Currently unavailable on CD.

Further listening:
live album Etta James Rocks The House (1964); Etta James Sings Funk (1970); Chess Masters (1983)

Further reading:
Rage To Survive (Etta James and David Ritz, 1998)

Pink Floyd
The Piper At The Gates Of Dawn

London's underground goes overground with a mix of playpen pop and grown-up acid rock.

"*The Piper At The Gates Of Dawn* was Syd," declares Roger Waters, "and Syd was a genius." Having built up a keen underground club following, Pink Floyd went overgrown early in 1967. Despite their reputation, two singles – Arnold Layne and See Emily Play – were disarmingly melodic and surprisingly successful. However, the Floyd always saw themselves as an albums band. Some critics, notably Pete Townshend (who said the LP was "fucking awful"), doubted whether their live performances would work in the studio, but history proved them wrong: *Piper* virtually defines British psychedelia. It was completed in just 16 sessions at EMI's Abbey Road Studios over four months, several of those purely for overdubs. It was long enough, though, for the group to push in two seemingly irrec-oncilable musical directions, a division that in retrospect clearly mirrored Barrett's increasingly fractured mental state. Extended pieces born of onstage jamming (Astronomy Domini; Interstellar Overdrive; POW R To H; Take Up Thy Stethoscope And Walk), sat oddly alongside Barrett's nursery-rhyme fantasies (Matilda Mother; The Gnome; Bike; Scarecrow), a dichotomy emphasised by further contradictions (electric/acoustic; cosmic/rural; blissful/fearful; adult/child). Holding these extremes together inevitably led to conflicts, not least because EMI staff Norman Smith was keen to impress with his first production job. "Working with Syd was sheer hell and there are no pleasant memories," he said later, citing Barrett's unpre-dictability and unwillingness to play songs (or even parts) the same way twice. Incredibly, despite Barrett's habit of handling the mixing controls as if he were painting a canvas, Smith turned in a remarkable job, capturing both dimensions of the band's work without sacrificing the edginess or the childlike innocence. "Gadzooks, it's foot-tapping stuff," wrote a puzzled Nick Jones in Melody Maker. "'Avant garde', I think it's called." It wasn't the last time the Floyd would baffle the critics, but with Barrett barely able to function within weeks of the album's release, it was a rather less extraordinary Floyd that re-emerged without him.

Record Label:
EMI Columbia

Produced
by Norman Smith.

Recorded
at Abbey Road Studios, London; March 15–July 5, 1967.

Released:
August 1967

Chart peaks:
6 (UK) None (US)

Personnel:
Syd Barrett (g, v); Roger Waters (b, v); Richard Wright (o, p); Nick Mason (d); Peter Brown (e)

Track Listing:
Astronomy Domine; Lucifer Sam; Matilda Mother; Flaming (S, US only); Pow R To H; Take Up Thy Stethoscope And Walk; Interstellar Overdrive; The Gnome; Chapter 24; Scarecrow; Bike

Running time:
41.57 (stereo); 42.13 (mono)

Current CD:
E21S31261 (stereo edition); 7243 8 59857 2 0 (mono edition box set). The mono mix was the one the band oversaw and is, in many respects, superior to the stereo master.

Further listening:
Relics (1971); the spectre of Syd Barrett looms large over Piper follow-up, A Saucerful Of Secrets (1968). Pink Floyd/1967 – The First Three Singles (1997)

Further reading:
MOJO 20, 31; Syd Barrett And The Pink Floyd (Julian Palacios, 1998) ourworld.compuserve.com/homepages/ PFArchives/pfa.htm

Jefferson Airplane
Surrealistic Pillow

San Francisco's psychedelic secrets get their first airing.

Coffee-bar folkies energised by the British Invasion and The Byrds, Bob Dylan and Beat texts, free love and LSD, Jefferson Airplane were the mid-60s San Francisco scene's first fledglings. After headlining a series of druggy dances in autumn 1965, they secured a major deal with RCA and released a mild-mannered folk-rock album (*Takes Off*) in August 1966.

"We were unhappy with the results," remembered Paul Kantner, so he invited The Grateful Dead's Jerry Garcia along to the sessions for the follow-up, as a peacemaker between the band, whose working methods were increasingly rooted in improvisation, and the production team. More crucial still, was the arrival of singer Grace Slick, an ex-model who'd cut her teeth with Bay Area combo The Great Society. Slick brought a steely beauty, a scat singing style and, said Kantner, "an early punk attitude"; not to mention two breathtaking songs, Somebody To Love and White Rabbit, on which the album's reputation is largely based. Also in tow was new drummer Spencer Dryden (replacing the errant Skip Spence), whose free-flowing style liberated the rhythm section. Remarkably, sessions for *Pillow* began just two weeks after Slick's stage debut, yet her contribution was instantly felt. "A quantum leap" is how Jorma Kaukonen describes the record, though a surfeit of love songs, vogueish reverb and acoustic instruments tends to belie the album's acid reputation.

Writing in *Esquire*, Robert Christgau described it as "amplified Peter, Paul & Mary", and "competent, original folk-rock" at best; but to Garcia's ears it sounded "as surrealistic as a pillow". White Rabbit, with its "feed your head" pay-off, may have been an obvious paean to acid, inspired by Ravel's Bolero and Alice In Wonderland, but much of the album's countercultural clout was understated. A wistful "Too many days are left unstoned" (D.C.B.A.-25), sung in harmony over a gentle folk-rock backing, was more typical. White Rabbit aside, the moments of amplified abandon were reserved for each side's opening cuts, the Diddleyesque She Has Funny Cars, and 3/5 Of A Mile In 10 Seconds, with its memorable Balin rage, "Do away with people laughing at my hair". The singer's tear-stained vocals on Today and Comin' Back To Me sat uneasily beside the group's wayward image, but *Surrealistic Pillow* would have been far less enigmatic without him.

Record Label:
RCA

Produced
by Rick Jarrard.

Recorded
at RCA Studios, Hollywood; October 31–November 22, 1966.

Released:
September 1967

Chart peaks:
None (UK) 3 (US)

Personnel:
Grace Slick (v, p, k, recorder); Paul Kantner (g, v); Jorma Kaukonen (g, v); Jack Casady (b, g); Spencer Dryden (d); Marty Balin (v, g); Jerry Garcia (g, musical and spiritual adviser); Dave Hassinger (e)

Track Listing:
She Has Funny Cars; Somebody To Love (S); My Best Friend; Today; Comin' Back To Me; 3/5 Of A Mile In 10 Seconds; D.C.B.A.-25; How Do You Feel; Embryonic Journey; White Rabbit (S); Plastic Fantastic Lover

Running time:
34.26

Current CD:
PCD13766

Further listening:
After Bathing At Baxter's (1967)

Further reading:
Jefferson Airplane And The San Francisco Sound (Ralph J Gleason, 1969)
www.discographynet.com/airplane/airplane.html

The Thirteenth Floor Elevators
Easter Everywhere

Alleged to get you high even when you're straight.

The Thirteenth Floor Elevators were the first band to describe or advertise their music as psychedelic, beating The Grateful Dead by two weeks. "I come out of Buddy Holly and then ran straight into Bob Dylan who then ran outta me," Roky Erickson said in 1996, "I was as Texas as I ever was, like a full dead creature could be." Which is about as articulate and succinct a statement about the Elevators as one could hope for today.

Producer Lelan Rodgers was a record business veteran — like famous brother Kenny — when he discovered the band playing in Houston. Signed to his optimistically named International Artists label, they hit Number 55 in the USA with Roky's You're Gonna Miss Me. Rodgers was convinced he had hit makers on his hands but jug player/chief lyricist/resident Owsley-type Tommy Hall kept the band pioneering psychedelia and they never troubled the charts again, becoming Lone Star state legends instead.

Hall, his wife Clementine, virtuoso guitarist Stacy Sutherland (more responsible for the style of those Fillmore West acid guitar solos than Jorma Kaukonen or Jerry Garcia) and Erickson wrote songs whose lyrics were laced with a stoned mysticism. Coupled with their hypnotic music, the lyrics were supposedly enough to give the listener the answer they were searching for, as well as provide him or her with a real high. Ya dig? Rodgers deliberately underpromoted the band because, he claimed, he wanted their growing mystique (they caused the authorities in Texas as much worry as the Sex Pistols would in the UK) to snowball. Which meant outside Texas relatively few heard the West Coast/Gulf Coast power of Slip Inside This House or Nobody To Love, the sweet folkish balladry of I Had To Tell You or Sutherland's stunning guitar leads or Erickson's manic vocals (he had one of the most earnest singing styles in pop).

By the end of these sessions they were already too far gone (Erickson would take acid over 300 times) and the authorities were waiting to pounce. The band began a slow dissolution. Yet ask any Texas musician over 40 about them and they'll tell you: the Elevators weren't mere prophets, they were Kings.

Record label:
International Artists

Produced
by Lelan Rodgers.

Recorded
in Houston; late spring 1967.

Released:
September 1967

Chart peaks:
None (UK) None (US)

Personnel:
Roky Erickson (v, g); Tommy Hall (jug, v); Dan Galindo (b); Stacy Sutherland (g); Danny Thomas (d)

Track listing:
Slip Inside This House (S/US); Slide Machine; She Lives (In A Time Of Her Own) (S/US); Nobody To Love; Baby Blue (S/US); Earthquake; Dust; Levitation (S/US); I Had To Tell You; Pictures (Leave Your Body Behind)

Running time:
43.15

Current CD:
CDGR 111 adds: Gettin' There; What's Your Movie?; Ever Since I Stole The Blues; Was; Gettin' Paid Waltz; My Backyard; Certified Senior Citizen; This Ain't Me; You Can't Push People Around; Earth Wants Me

Further listening:
The Psychedelic Sounds Of (1966), their first album.

Further reading:
There are several good Thirteenth Floor Elevators websites, try ex-Elevator Danny Thomas' http://www.geocities.com/ucdnlo/or a lengthy mass interview with several ex-members at http://web.wt.net/~duane/13thfloo.html

Bonzo Dog Doo-Dah Band
Gorilla

Debut from Britain's best comic-rock troupe.

The Bonzos tumbled out of the heady, early '60s art-school scene, an ever-changing troupe of eccentrics who delighted the college crowd with a riot of exploding wardrobes, archaic instruments, pre-war novelty songs and jazz-age pop. In 1966 they decided to get a bit more serious. Recalls Neil Innes, "The New Vaudeville Band had a hit with Winchester Cathedral, but as they were a studio creation we were asked to be the band. Bob Kerr was the only one who went. But Viv and I realised we had to write our own material. *Gorilla* is us in the throes of becoming modern."

Some of those songs from the '20s and '30s (Jollity Farm, Mickey's Son And Daughter) found their way onto the album, but now any idiom was fair game. Look Out, There's A Monster Coming is a calypsoed comment on personal vanity, the brassy Big Shot lampoons *film noir* gumshoes, while the quite brilliant The Intro And The Outro starts with the jazz tradition of introducing the band and, as Innes notes, takes it to absurd levels. "That was a collective effort. Amazingly enough it was done on four-track. We had a very good engineer – his name escapes me – who just kept bouncing things down." Lines such as "And looking very relaxed, Adolf Hitler on vibes" and "The Count Basie Orchestra on triangle", ooze comic greatness. Innes – later to write the songs for the superb Rutles mock-umentary – contributed a dollop or two of Fabs-derived fare. "*Sergeant Pepper* had just been released, and of course it was a great influence. We were actually driving to Liverpool when the idea for Equestrian Statue came to me. I was reading Jean Paul Sartre in the van, as you do, and there was some tosh about whether a lamp-post exists in the same way a human does so I thought, why not a statue.

"The whole recording process was very spontaneous. We never really discussed what we were doing. We just had a shared sense of community. We all had problems with our shirts." *Gorilla*, with patronage from The Beatles (the Bonzos performed Death Cab For Cutie in Magical Mystery Tour), established them as acerbic court jesters to the burgeoning rock business; an essential role they performed admirably, in various guises, on into the '70s.

Record Label:
Liberty

Produced
by Gerry Bron.

Recorded
at Regent Sound, Abbey Road and Landsdowne studios, London; May–July 1967.

Released:
October 1967

Chart peaks:
None (UK) None (US)

Personnel:
Viv Stanshall (v, brass, ukelele); Neil Innes (v, g, k); Roger Ruskin Spear (brass, xylophone, bells); 'Legs' Larry Smith (d, tuba, tap-dancing); Sam Spoons (b, p); Vernon Dudley Bohay-Nowell (b, brass, banjo); Rodney Slater (brass, wind)

Track Listing:
Cool Britannia; Equestrian Statue (S); Jollity Farm; I Left My Heart In San Francisco; Look Out There's A Monster Coming; Jazz, Delicious Hot,Disgusting Cold; Death Cab For Cutie; Narcissus; The Intro And The Outro; Mickey's Son And Daughter; Big Shot; Music For The Head Ballet; Piggy Bank Love; I'm Bored; The Sound Of Music

Running time:
34.38

Current CD:
BGOCD82

Further listening:
The Doughnut In Granny's Greenhouse (1968); Keynsham (1969)

Further reading:
MOJO 18, 67;
www.cam.anglia.ac.uk/~systimk/music/bonzos/index.html

Country Joe And The Fish

Electric Music For The Mind And Body

Pioneers of psychedelic-protest mix acid and satire.

*E*lectric Music For The Mind And Body certainly sounds like an 11-song panegyric for LSD but, unusually for 1967, it also acknowledged the real world of Vietnam-era politics. That was largely due to activist/frontman Country Joe McDonald, who'd formed the group in 1965 to play jugband protest songs to Berkeley University beatniks. One, I-Feel-Like-I'm-Fixin'-To-Die-Rag, later became the counter-culture's key anti-war anthem, eclipsing the band's psychedelic reputation in the process.

A druggy mid-1966 EP, *Rag Baby*, enjoyed considerable success in and around San Francisco and later that year the Fish were signed to Vanguard.

"In many ways, *Electric Music* is fairly unrepresentative of what the band actually sounded like in concert," says Barry Melton. "When we played live, the amps had a typical over-driven sound that was much more rock'n'roll-ish. But (engineer) Bob DeSousa insisted we turn the amps down very low so that he could maintain separation between the instruments and balance them." The result was far more polished and rehearsed than the Fish had intended, but in spring 1967, *Electric Music* – dressed in one of the era's more evocative sleeves – was still way ahead of the competition. Taut, psyche-delicised R&B (Flying High, Love) and waltz-time craziness (Porpoise Mouth, The Masked Marauder), were complemented by some extraordinary acid-rock excursions (Bass Strings, Section 43 and Grace), where Melton's highly-strung guitar, Cohen's asthmatic Farfisa and Joe's stoner vocals detonated over dreamlike, mock-Eastern rhythms. There was satire here too (Superbird, Flying High), but essentially *Electric Music* was about the politics of mind-altering drugs.

"It's hard to say who was right in the end," says the guitarist. "Bob may have come up with a more artistic recording, and cleaned us up enough to be commercial. But maybe we were cleaned up so much that we never had the smash success with our records that we had on stage." That said, *Electric Music* was a consistent seller throughout the Summer Of Love, and remains one of the few truly successful US psyche-delic albums.

Record label:
Vanguard

Produced
by Samuel Charters.

Recorded
at Sierra Sound Laboratories, California;
January–February 1967.

Released:
October 1967

Chart peaks:
None (UK) 39 (US)

Personnel:
Joe McDonald (v, g, hm, tambourine);
Barry Melton (v, g); David Cohen (g, o);
Bruce Barthol (b, hm); Chicken Hirsch
(d); Bob DeSousa (e)

Track Listing:
Flying High; Not So Sweet Martha
Lorraine; Death Sound Blues; Happiness Is
A Porpoise Mouth; Section 43; Superbird;
Sad And Lonely Times; Love; Bass Strings;
The Masked Marauder; Grace

Running time:
44.15

Current CD:
VAN792444

Further listening:
Try I-Feel-Like-I'm-Fixin'-To-Die (1967) for
more of the same, albeit with a little
more bad-trip darkness.

Further reading:
www.well.com/user/cjfish/

The Hollies
Butterfly

As close as they came to a classic.

B y September 1967, the Indian Summer of Love was in full Technicolor bloom. If *Sgt Pepper* psychedelia's excesses had become public property, The Hollies – in particular Graham Nash – wanted in.

Butterfly, their fourth album of entirely self-penned songs in only two years (credited to the nucleus of Hicks/Clarke/Nash), represented all that was good and bad about British psychedelia. Although a typically well-crafted Hollies record, and blessed with their immaculate three-part harmonies, it features all the trademarks of its time – fairy tale lyrics (Pegasus), stuff about being "high as the sky" (Elevated Observations), full orchestral arrangements (Away Away Away) and, inevitably, Eastern instrumentation (Maker). High points include Nash's intricate Dear Eloise and Butterfly itself, in spite of its "lemonade lakes" and "candy floss snow" (a lower point is Clarke's embarrassing tale of two rag and bone men, Charlie And Fred). It is also largely Graham Nash's record: he sings most of the leads and his wistful, winsome qualities prevail.

In the US the album was known as *Dear Eloise/King Midas In Reverse* and included Nash's King Midas In Reverse, arguably The Hollies' finest recorded moment but a relative flop as a single and left off the UK edition. It had been released against the advice of the group's long-standing producer Ron Richards, who argued that it was too complex for Hollies fans. He was proved right.

Nash, however, wanted to reach beyond the limits of the band's fanbase. He met David Crosby while attending a Mamas And Papas recording session in LA at the end of 1967, and the seeds of a new collaboration were sewn. A follow-up to *Butterfly* was underway by March 1968 but was soon scrapped. Two new Nash songs (Marrakesh Express and Lady Of The Island) were not even attempted. For the rest of the year Nash's relationship with the band was increasingly strained. The appeal of the seaside cabaret circuit and a mooted album of Dylan covers led him to leave the band on December 8, whereupon he went straight into rehearsals with Crosby and Stephen Stills. Meantime, *The Hollies' Greatest*, their only Number 1 album, was still enjoying a 22-week run in the Top 10.

Record label:
Columbia

Produced
by Ron Richards.

Recorded
EMI Studios, London; September 1967.

Released:
October 1967

Chart peaks:
None (UK) None (US)

Personnel:
Allan Clarke (v, g); Tony Hicks (g); Graham Nash (v, rg); Bernie Calvert (b, k); Bobby Elliott (d)

Track listing:
Dear Eloise; Away Away Away; Maker; Pegasus; Would You Believe; Wishyouawish; Postcard; Charlie And Fred; Try It; Elevated Observations; Step Inside; Butterfly

Running time:
31.25

Current CD:
4997712

Further listening:
The Special Collection 3-CD box set (1997)

Further reading:
www.cae.wisc.edu/~gansler/hollies/hollies.htm

Frank Sinatra
Francis Albert Sinatra and Antonio Carlos Jobim

The Voice Of The Century's last consistently great vocal performance.

S inatra came relatively late to the bossa boom. The bewitching melodies of Brazilian composer Antonio Carlos Jobim and sensual slow-motion samba rhythms of the bossa nova had been common adult pop currency since Stan Getz, Joao and Astrud Gilberto had popularised them in 1962–63, but Sinatra had been trying different approaches to find a commercial foothold in "Beatleland", as he had it. There was the country rock of half of *Sinatra 65* and the Ray Charles-ish blues pop of the single That's Life that followed the commercial jackpot of Strangers In The Night. All this kept the blue-eyed one on the radio but the albums were lousy, either unsatisfying mish mashes (*Sinatra 65*, *That's Life*), or openly contemptuous of the material (*Strangers In The Night*). But by immersing himself in the bossa nova and programming seven of Jobim's elegant compositions along with three standards done Jobim-style (the closest he got to recording a songbook album, he didn't consider that the English lyrics were sufficiently good at the time to make it an all-Jobim set), Sinatra fashioned one of his most majestic recorded achievements.

With by far the gentlest singing of his career, Sinatra's tender-strong voice is a wonder, respectfully piping through the Brazilian's graceful, economic tunes, as if to acknowledge the greatness of this new generation of standards. Sinatra said "I haven't sang this soft since I had laryngitis"— it's the polar opposite approach of his bluesy snarling on That's Life.

Like a more minimalist version of Jobim's Verve recordings – arranger Claus Ogerman and Jobim's 'personal drummer' Dom Um Romao were key figures of those sessions – Sinatra kept urging Ogerman to remove elements of the arrangement until the air played its part. A magical ingredient was Jobim himself, picking at his gut guitar and murmuring a Portuguese counterpoint on four of the tracks, less a duet partner than a wise composerly appendage. Jobim described Sinatra as "Mount Everest for a songwriter" while Frank rated "Tone" (as he called him) "one of the most talented musicians I have ever met"; the album they made together outdid the praise they had for each other and is probably the last essential Sinatra record. An attempt to follow it up two years later was compromised by palpably lower grade performances and flip side rock-ballad programming.

Record label:
Reprise

Produced
by Sonny Burke.

Recorded
in Hollywood, LA; 1967

Released:
October, 1967

Chart peaks:
28 (UK) 19 (US)

Personnel:
Frank Sinatra (v); Antonio Carlos Jobim (g, v); Claus Ogerman (a, conductor); orchestra including Dick Noel (tb); Dom Um Romao (d)

Track Listing:
The Girl From Ipanema; Dindi; Change Partners; Quiet Nights Of Quiet Stars; Meditation; If You Never Come To Me; How Insensitive; I Concentrate On You; Baubles Bangles And Beads; Once I Loved

Running time:
27.47

Current CD:
Reprise FS1021-2

Further listening:
Sinatra and Company (1969)

Further reading:
Sinatra! The Song Is You: A Singer's Art (Will Friedwald, 1995)
www.repriserec.com/sinatra/index.html

Tim Buckley
Goodbye And Hello

Landmark in the shift from folk to singer/songwriting music.

Recorded in June 1967, the month the Beatles released *Sgt. Pepper*, Tim Buckley's second album is drenched in the musical freedom of that mythologized time. "We saw ourselves sailing along in the direction that Bob Dylan was taking lyrics and that The Beatles were taking instrumentation," says poet Larry Beckett, Buckley's old school friend, then creative collaborator and co-writer of half the songs on *Goodbye And Hello*. "That is, toward making rock'n'roll into art songs, where they're so beautifully made that they're meant to last in the culture."

According to producer Jerry Yester, "When Buckley and Beckett came to me, the only idea they had was that the album would be free of restraint or commercial consideration. There was to be no compromising on the songs or how they were presented. Working with Tim was a stretch. When someone says you can do anything you want, it's a little intimidating at first, and then it's totally exciting."

Though *Goodbye And Hello* feels like an orchestrated album, in fact only the ambitious title track was orchestrally sweetened. The album's broad spectrum of sound is suggested through the flexibility of relatively few instruments and Buckley's most diverse collection of songs: the topical folk-rock of No Man Can Find The War; a blistering dialogue with drug dependency in Pleasant Street; the cathartic I Never Asked To Be Your Mountain (addressed in part to his ex-wife Mary and son Jeffrey Scott). The tender, lamenting Once I Was ("Soon there'll come another/to tell you I was just a lie") is a cousin of Fred Neil's Dolphins (which Tim performed regularly); Morning Glory ("write me a song about a hobo" was the singer's entire instruction to his lyricist) became Buckley's most covered song, and closes the album with a brief, exquisite wave of choral harmony.

What holds *Goodbye And Hello* together, and animates its occasionally bombastic conceits, is a string of vocal performances of staggering authority for a young man not yet twenty one. The musical freedom trumpeted so clearly here was something Tim would insist on for the rest of his career, to the dismay of those who hoped he'd linger a little longer at some of the stops along the way.

Record label:
Elektra

Produced
by Jerry Yester.

Recorded
at TTG Studios, and mixed by Bruce Botnick at Sunset Sound, Los Angeles; June 1967.

Released:
November 1967

Chart peaks:
None (UK) 171 (US)

Personnel:
Tim Buckley (v, g, sg, kalimba, vibes); Lee Underwood (lead g); Brian Hartzler (g); John Forsha (g); Jimmy Bond (b); Jim Fielder (b); Eddie Hoh (d); Carter CC Collins (pc, congas); Dave Guard (kalimba, tambourine); Don Randi (p, hamonium, harpsichord); Jerry Yester (o, p, harmonium); Henry Diltz (hm)

Track listing:
No Man Can Find The War; Carnival Song; Pleasant Street; Hallucinations; I Never Asked To Be Your Mountain; Once I Was (S/UK); Phantasmagoria In Two; Knight-Errant; Goodbye And Hello; Morning Glory (S)

Running time:
42.53

Current CD:
740282

Further listening:
Happy Sad (1969) — jazz/folk lullabies; Blue Afternoon (1970) — his most focused songwriting; Starsailor (1972) — wild avant-jazz and Song To The Siren; Greetings From LA — soul-inspired and drenched in sweat; Dream Letter — Live In London 1968 (1990)

Further reading:
MOJO 20; Dream Brother (David Browne, 2000); www.timbuckley.com

Buffalo Springfield
Buffalo Springfield Again

Landmark album recorded in the brief space between inventing West Coast rock and falling apart.

" A great group," said Neil Young. "Everybody was a fucking genius at what they did – but we just didn't get it on record."Not that they gave it much of a go; by this, their second album, the band was practically in pieces. For such a short-lived outfit, Buffalo Springfield would have a huge influence: much of the '70s West Coast rock movement, from the Eagles on down, could trace its ancestry back to the stormy combo founded when Young, his folk-singing career in Canada going nowhere, jumped the border in a hearse with his friend Bruce Palmer and headed for Los Angeles in search of old acquaintance Stephen Stills.

Buffalo Springfield – named after the steamroller tearing up the road outside their house – found themselves in quick succession endorsed by The Byrds, made house-band at the Whisky A Go Go and given a major label deal. Just as quickly, its members were busy falling out. Even during the recording of their eponymous debut there were arguments over whose songs would be included. It gave them their first hit single – the Stills-penned Sunset Strip protest song For What It's Worth – and was critically acclaimed, big things were expected of the follow-up.

Tracks were recorded in New York and Los Angeles – several under the supervision of label boss Ahmet Ertegun – for an album to be called *Stampede*. But the record was abandoned amid squabbles over songs, arrangements and band leadership (the latter role increasingly nabbed by Stills, who had been to military school as a kid). Outside pressures didn't help: Bruce Palmer had been arrested on a dope charge and deported to Canada. Ken Koblun, Young's old friend from The Squires, came down to help out but went back to Canada when the tense atmosphere became too much. A summer single was released – two new songs, Steve's Bluebird backed with Neil's Mr Soul. Stills on one side, Young on the other, just as they were in reality – they were rarely in the studio at the same time, and Young was torn between quitting the band (which he did twice, over their decisions to appear on Johnny Carson's mainstream Tonight Show and at the Monterey Pop Festival) and asking to rejoin. Differences aside, the music they were coming up with in the rescheduled sessions (some of it reworked *Stampede* material) was often superb.

Record label:
Atco

Produced
by Ahmet Ertegun and Buffalo Springfield.

Recorded
at Sunset Sound, Gold Star, Los Angeles; June–September 1967.

Released:
November 1967

Chart peaks:
None (UK) 44 (US)

Personnel:
Neil Young (v, g); Stephen Stills (v, g); Richie Furay (v, g); Bruce Palmer, Jim Fielder, Bobby West (b); Dewey Martin (d); Don Randi (p); Jack Nitzsche (electric piano, a); Jim Messina, Ross Meyering, Bruce Botnick, William Brittan, Bill Lazarus (e)

Track listing:
Mr Soul; A Child's Claim To Fame; Everydays; Expecting To Fly; Bluebird; Hung Upside Down; Sad Memory; Good Time Boy; Rock And Roll Woman; Broken Arrow

Running time:
33.56

Current CD:
756790391-2

Further listening:
Buffalo Springfield (1967)

Further reading:
The Story Of Buffalo Springfield: For What It's Worth (John Einarson and Richie Furay, 1997)

"We were just really discovering a lot of new things and experimenting," said Young, who'd been working on arrangements with his friend, Phil Spector sidekick Jack Nitzsche, on songs like Broken Arrow and Expecting To Fly (reportedly inspired by Young's acid experiences). Other highlights included Stills' Rock 'n' Roll Woman and Bluebird (its extended instrumental jam, cut off the original album, was reinstated on the later anthology). In May 1968 – barely four months after the second album's release – the band broke up. A third album appeared posthumously.

Stills joined the equally unstable Crosby Stills & Nash. Richie Furay and engineer Jim Messina formed Poco. Young, who went solo, still waxes nostalgic about his old band.

"The music that we played was really good," he says, even though he considers all their albums "failures". Live, on-stage, they would "get so into the groove of the thing, that's all we really cared about, but when we got into the studio, the groove just wasn't the same, and we couldn't figure out why. This was the major frustration. It fucked me up so much. Buffalo Springfield should have been recorded live from the very beginning."

Country Joe And The Fish
I-Feel-Like-I'm-Fixin'-To-Die

San Francisco scenesters second, an essential acid rock milestone.

"Gimme an F ... Gimme an I ... Gimme an S ... Gimme an H ... What's that spell? FISH! What's that spell? FISH!" Country Joe's second album begins, bizarrely, in a stoned, subversive, demented parody of high school cheerleaders. But they actually had their roots in the traditional US jugband and folk scenes, before developing their sound to become the Bay Area's foremost psychedelic adventurers, dizzyingly blending acid rock, satire, revolutionary politics and mischief.

The rollicking title song, a satirical, anti-war masterpiece, was written as America's involvement in Vietnam deepened disastrously. "Be the first one on your block to have your boy come home in a box," is typical of the lyrics, sung to a disconcertingly jaunty tune while the band cheerily chant, "Psychedelic, psychedelic!" in the background. The song remains McDonald's personal favourite.

"It's affected so many people's lives and it's affected history. I don't know if I can claim writing it because it just popped out of my head one day, but I'm most proud of facilitating that."

Janis is a tender love song for McDonald's former girlfriend Janis Joplin, while unlisted between Thought Dream and Thursday, is The Acid Commercial, a jolly jingle advertising lysergic pursuits: "If you're tired or a bit rundown/Can't seem to get your feet off the ground/Maybe you ought to try a little bit of LSD!"

The outrageousness of The Acid Commercial still startles. "The Establishment weren't paying attention to what we were doing so we were able to do anything we wanted," reasons McDonald. "We were the best ever psychedelic band."

They certainly took their role as acid pioneers seriously. "I've taken LSD 300 times," boasted guitarist Barry Melton in 1968. In a truly hallucinatory twist the same Melton, in another life, was in 1985 named by the San Francisco Bar Association as Outstanding Lawyer In Public Service."

Record label:
Vanguard

Produced
by Samuel Charters.

Recorded
at Vanguard Records' 23rd Street Studio, New York City; June–September 1967.

Released:
November 1967

Chart peaks:
None (UK) 67 (US)

Personnel:
Joe McDonald (v, g, o); Barry Melton (g, v, kazoo); David Cohen (o, calliope, harpsichord, g, v); Bruce Barthol (bs, hm, v); Chicken Hirsh (d); Ed Friedner (e)

Track listing:
The Fish Cheer And I-Feel-Like-I'm-Fixin'-To-Die Rag; Who Am I (S/US); Pat's Song; Rock Coast Blues; Magoo; Janis (S/US); Thought Dream; Thursday; Eastern Jam; Colors For Susan

Running time:
45.03

Current CD:
VMD 79266-2

Further listening:
Electric Music For The Mind And Body (1967), the band's debut, which McDonald has proudly described as "the best psychedelic rock record ever made by anybody in the world".

Further reading:
www.countryjoe.com. Apart from being excellently informative, McDonald's website gives you the chance to be the first on your block to buy a Gimme An F... condom!

Cream
Disraeli Gears

The great virtuoso excess starts here.

On March 25, 1967, Cream arrived in New York for their first trip to America, performing I Feel Free and I'm So Glad five times a day for 10 days on Murray The K's pop show. With three days left on their visas, they went into Atlantic Studios to record their follow-up album to *Fresh Cream*.

Released in December 1966, *Fresh Cream* was a relatively straight-ahead homage to Eric Clapton's blues influences, covering the songs of Robert Johnson, Skip James and Muddy Waters. But *Disraeli Gears* was a very different proposition for three reasons. The first was the flowering of the Bruce/Brown co-writing partnership. Nearly half the album is credited to them, including enduring Cream classics such as Sunshine Of Your Love and Tales Of Brave Ulysses. Of the former, Jack Bruce recalls: "Pete and I had been up all night trying to write stuff and getting nowhere. I started playing this riff. Pete was looking out the window and said, 'It's getting near dawn, and lights closed their tired eyes ...'"

In addition, in Felix Pappalardi they found a producer who understood Cream in a way their manager and producer of *Fresh Cream*, Robert Stigwood, never would. Pappalardi's tasteful production and Tom Dowd's sensitive engineering brought Clapton's new Hendrix-inspired tone and effects to the fore. Pappalardi was also an excellent musician and writer himself, credited along with his wife Gail Collins with Strange Brew and World Of Pain (a tragically ironic title, as Collins was to shoot her husband dead in 1983).

Finally, there was the influence of LSD. Songs like She Was Like A Bearded Rainbow (SWLABR) weren't conceived on cups of tea. During a conversation about racing bikes, instead of saying "derailleur gears", roadie Mick Turner said something else. It became the title of Cream's landmark excursion into a sometimes whimsical interpretation of psychedelic blues, gift-wrapped in an equally famous riot of day-glo colour by Martin Sharp encapsulating its acid-drenched mood. Right album, right place, right time.

Disraeli Gears broke the band in the States, with Sunshine Of Your Love (its war dance rhythm suggested to Ginger Baker by Tom Dowd) becoming Atlantic's biggest selling single. The album reveals Cream at their most cohesive: from then on, the pressure of touring, resentments over writing royalties and the resurgence of animosities between Bruce and Baker led to their inevitable break-up just a year after this album's release.

Record label:
Reaction

Produced
by Felix Pappalardi.

Recorded
at Atlantic Studios, New York; May 8–19, 1967.

Released:
November 1967

Chart peaks:
5 (UK) 4 (US)

Personnel:
Eric Clapton (g, v); Ginger Baker (d); Jack Bruce (b, v); Tom Dowd (e)

Track listing:
Strange Brew (S); Sunshine Of Your Love; World Of Pain; Dance The Night Away; Blue Condition; Tales of Brave Ulysses (S); SWLABR; We're Going Wrong; Outside Woman Blues; Take It Back; Mother's Lament.

Running time:
31.00

Current CD:
Polydor 5318112

Further listening:
Fresh Cream (1966); Wheels Of Fire (1968); Goodbye (1969); or the whole shebang on Those Were The Days (1997).

Further reading:
Strange Brew (Chris Welch, 1988); Lost In The Blues (Harry Shapiro, 1992); Edge Of Darkness (Chris Sandford, 1994); www.whereseric.com and www.thecream.net

Kaleidoscope
Tangerine Dream

One of the very few genuine British psychedelic albums.

The clever money in early '67 was on a pioneering bunch of groups whose trade was neither R&B or hit parade pop, but something altogether odder, more visual, quite new. Pink Floyd, The Soft Machine and Kaleidoscope hogged the column inches but the latter — the ones with the nimblest melodies — were destined for a long run of near-misses.

Originally The Sidekicks, a beat group from Harrow, they became The Key in 1965 and, on signing to Fontana in late 1966, Kaleidoscope. As their line-up had remained constant, their debut 45 (Flight From Ashiya c/w Holidaymaker) sounded supertight. Replete with Pumer's nerve-jangling guitar line and exquisite vocal interplay, Flight was played to death by the pirates and, though not a hit, encouraged Fontana enough to proceed with the album.

Opening with plucked harp and ferocious drums, the self-titled signature tune sets the scene for *Tangerine Dream*. Like The Bee Gees or The Kinks, Peter Daltrey's songs are vignettes; pilots on their final flights, elderly watch repairers (prescient of Mark Wirtz's Teenage Opera), Dickensian murder scenes. Everywhere there are beautiful drones courtesy of Pumer, fine high harmonies. All is crisp. Ultimately there is Dive Into Yesterday — five minutes of ebbing and flowing, atonal scraped guitar and a dive-bombing Duane Eddy hookline — and The Sky Children which maintains beautiful fairytale imagery with an astonishingly simple and hypnotic arrangement for a full nine minutes.

"Their songs are the best since The Beatles," said that pop oracle The Daily Sketch. Radio One offered them session after session. Kenny Everett called them "incredible". *Tangerine Dream* exuded summertime optimism, but it was sadly misplaced. Three more albums followed (two as Fairfield Parlour, the last not obtaining a release until the '90s) but a place deep in the heart of psych fanatics is all Kaleidoscope earned after such a promising start.

Record label:
Fontana

Produced
by Dick Leahy and Jack Baverstock.

Recorded
at Stanhope Place Studios, London; mid-1967.

Released:
November 1967

Chart peaks:
None (UK) None (US)

Personnel:
Peter Daltrey (v, k); Eddie Pumer (g); Steve Clark (b); Danny Bridgman (d); John Cameron (oa); John Paul Jones (b); Clem Cattini (d); Dave Voyde (e)

Track listing:
Kaleidoscope; Please Excuse My Face; Dive Into Yesterday; Mr Small The Watch Repairer Man; Flight From Ashiya; The Murder Of Lewis Tollani; (Further Reflections) In The Room Of Percussion; Dear Nellie Goodrich; Holidaymaker; A Lesson Perhaps; The Sky Children

Running time:
36.20

Currently unavailable on CD
though most of its tracks appear on Dive Into Yesterday: A Kaleidoscope Anthology

Further listening:
as Fairfield Parlour, From Home To Home (1970)

Further reading:
http://hem.passagen.se/chla1014/Reviews.html

Moody Blues
Days Of Future Passed

Birmingham beat group turn into lush art-rockers.

When the Moody Blues recorded *Days Of Future Passed*, in October 1967, most of the record-buying public thought that the group's day had indeed passed. Their original lead singer, Denny Laine, was gone, and despite the addition of new members Justin Hayward and John Lodge, they hadn't managed a hit in over two years. Their label, Deram (a Decca subsidiary), was losing patience and had assigned staff producer Tony Clark to oversee the Moody Blues' recordings after Laine's departure, with a mandate to create hit singles that would recoup the group's £5,000 advance.

After two singles missed the charts entirely, the label gave the group an album project – of a sort. They were to make a demonstration record of the label's new 'Deramic Stereo' process to show the potential it held for rock and classical music. Specifically, they were to create a rock version of Dvorak's New World Symphony, augmented by Peter Knight's orchestrations. It is unclear if the group ever really intended to create the album Deram wanted. They requested one week of 'lockout time' at the label's studios so they could have them for 24 hours a day instead of just the usual morning sessions. Then they convinced Knight to allow them to record the stage act that they had been working on for the past year, a song cycle chronicling a day in the life of an Everyman called Moody Blue. (Yes, they beat a certain song cycle about Mr Pink Floyd by about 12 years.) They also sought to replicate the feel of what Hayward later called "the first concept album" – not *Sgt. Pepper* or, in fact, the work of a band, but a studio concoction – *The Zodiac* by Cosmic Sounds.

"That was the birth of that sound, the tinkling bells and weird effects," Hayward explained. "It was our oracle. It was a simple concept – 12 songs based on the signs of the zodiac."

The sessions were, according to Hayward, "a bit frantic. As soon as we had recorded each track, we rushed a copy over to Peter and he wrote a link for the orchestra and recorded it. When both parts had been taped, we went back to the studios and mixed everything." The group debuted the album at a party for Decca's brass. According to Lodge, some of the label's staff didn't know what to make of it. "When it finished, initially, stunned silence reigned. The singles head didn't like it, neither did the managing director, who said, 'You can't dance to it. You

Record label:
Deram

Produced
by Tony Clarke and Michael Dacre-Barclay.

Recorded
at Decca Studios, West Hampstead; October 1967.

Released:
November 11, 1967

Chart peaks:
27 (UK) 3 (US)

Personnel:
Justin Hayward (g, v); John Lodge, (b, v); Michael Pinder (k, mellotron, v); Ray Thomas (hm, flute, v); Graeme Edge (d, pc); Hugh Mendl (executive producer). With the London Festival Orchestra; Peter Knight (conductor)

Track listing:
The Day Begins; Dawn: Dawn Is A Feeling; The Morning: Another Morning; Lunch Break: Peak Hour; The Afternoon: Forever Afternoon (Tuesday?); (Evening) Time To Get Away; Evening: The Sun Set; Twilight Time; The Night: Nights In White Satin

Running time:
41.47

Current CD:
Universal/Decca 8200062

Further listening:
The Moody Blues maintained a consistently high level of artistry through 1972's Seventh Sojourn.

Further reading:
www.frisk.org/rgs/mb.html

can't play this at a party.'" Others were mystified over who would buy it. In the end, the label's desire to make back its investment won out, and what had once been intended as a promotional item was instead made an official release. Although Tuesday Afternoon was a reasonably-sized US hit, *Days Of Future Passed* is forever identified with Nights in White Satin. The wistful ballad made Number 19 in the UK in 1967 and became a surprise US smash five years later when it was rediscovered by a Seattle DJ. It subsequently hit Number 9 in the UK too. Hayward, while proud of the song's lyrical depth, would later confess that its inspiration was surprisingly prosaic: "Somebody had actually given me some white satin sheets. They were totally useless, especially if you've a decent growth of beard like I have. Dreadful things, satin sheets."

Jimi Hendrix Experience

Axis Bold As Love

Hendrix gets trippier.

G iven that he had to hit the UK for his talents to be appreciated, Jimi Hendrix relied heavily on English boffins;
British Marshall and Sound City amps were an integral part of
his sound, and when he felt the need to customise his electronic
armoury, he called on Roger Meyer, a London electronics guru
who modified Jimi's fuzzboxes and wah wahs, and invented
entirely new effects pedals for him.

George Chkiantz, an employee at London's Olympic
Studio, was another crucial influence: "George was a tape op
who would hang around in the maintenance department,"
remembered Jimi's producer and co-manager, Chas Chandler.
"He was very hung up on sound, and would work out new
ways to bastardise the equipment." This spirit of experiment
pervaded Jimi's second album, recorded on the run between
live engagements. Material, such as opener EXP, with its then-
fashionable UFO references, sound dated in hindsight, despite
the still-thrilling guitar exploration. The ostensibly simple songs
that would prove more durable, notably Little Wing, which
opened with a gorgeously simple guitar intro, heavily influenced by Curtis Mayfield. Castles Made Of Sand also employed
subtle soul guitar styles; indeed for many guitarists Hendrix's
fluent use of guitar voicings, sliding 4ths and other techniques
make *Axis Bold As Love* the album that most rewards constant
listening.

Bassist Noel Redding points out that the album's finest
moments see the band working at the limits of their powers:
"On the last track, Bold As Love, there's one point where we're
playing three different rhythms at the same time. Most of those
things were worked out in the studio."

Ironically, given the intense work that had gone into the
rushed recording, Jimi ended up losing the master reel for half
of the album – possibly on purpose, because he was unhappy
with the sound. Chandler and engineer Eddie Kramer heroically
remixed the entire side in one night, with the exception of If 6
Was 9. The two couldn't match their lost, first mix, "But in the

Record label:
Track

Produced
by Chas Chandler.

Recorded
mainly at Olympic Studios, London;
May–October 1967.

Released:
December 1, 1967

Chart peaks:
5 (UK) 3 (US)

Personnel:
Jimi Hendrix (v, g); Noel Redding (b, bv);
Mitch Mitchell (d)

Track listing:
EXP; Up From The Skies; Spanish Castle
Magic; Wait Until Tomorrow; Ain't No
Telling; Little Wing; If 6 Was 9; You Got
Me Floatin'; Castles Made Of Sand; She's
So Fine; One Rainy Wish; Little Miss
Lover; Bold As Love

Running time:
39.35

Current CD:
MCD11601

Further listening:
The Jimi Hendrix Experience, (2000)
contains fascinating out-takes from the
Axis sessions.

Further reading:
MOJO 23, 50, 72; Electric Gypsy (Harry
Shapiro and Caesar Glebbeek, 1991);
www.jimi-hendrix.com

end we found that Noel had taken a copy on $7\frac{1}{2}$ ips to play at home on his domestic machine," remembered Chandler. "His machine had chewed the tape up, so we had to iron it flat. Then we mastered from that copy."

Jefferson Airplane
After Bathing At Baxter's

A defiant statement of the possibilities of acid-rock.

The surprise success of *Surrealistic Pillow* and its two singles had transformed Jefferson Airplane into a Top 10 act. *After Bathing At Baxter's*, its title a euphemism for psychedelic drug-taking, hastily reaffirmed their underground credentials. Uprooted from their communal home in Haight-Ashbury, the band rented a mansion in the Hollywood Hills, complete with pool and underground bowling alley, where they held "parties, strange parties, and then weird parties". With rookie producer Al Schmitt manning the mixing-desk, the high-jinx continued in the studio.

"We took over the soundboard," remembered Kantner. "We had motorcycles in the studio, nitrous oxide tanks, marijuana everywhere. Smoke rose out of the boards with Jack's bass parts overloading. (We) experimented with every button."

"The material was being written as we were in the studio," remembered Grace Slick. Few bands had hitherto enjoyed such freedom. At the time, Marty Balin, the band's erstwhile leader and frontman, described *Baxter's* as "a whole new and different thing for the group". With Slick and Kantner emerging as the group's leading writers, and instrumentalists Kaukonen and Casady hellbent on undermining pop song convention, it also marked the end of his influence, Balin by now reduced to one writer's co-credit and a single lead vocal.

Baxter's was single-mindedly dedicated to the pursuit of high art via hallucinogenics. Songs were grouped together as 'suites', the mix was unprecedentedly 'open', with the instrumental balance often throwing strange sounds to the fore, and the range of the material was huge. At its extremes were a silly stoned sound collage (A Small Package Of Value Will Come To You, Shortly) and an inspired power-trio jam (Spare Chaynge). Central to the album were Kantner's robust, harmony-drenched anthems (The Ballad Of You And Me And Pooneil; Wild Tyme; Watch Her Ride; Won't You Try). Meanwhile, Slick's rejoyce (a sharp-witted anti-war lament inspired by Joyce's Ulysses) and Two Heads were the album's brilliant, baffling, idiosyncratic wild cards. "It was sort of a progress report on how things were going," concluded Kantner.

Record label:
RCA

Produced
by Al Schmitt.

Recorded
at RCA Studios, Hollywood; June–October 1967.

Released:
December 1967

Chart peaks:
None (UK) 17 (US)

Personnel:
Grace Slick (v, k, recorder); Paul Kantner (g, v); Marty Balin (v, tambourine); Jorma Kaukonen (g); Jack Casady (s); Spencer Dryden (d, v); Richie Schmitt (e)

Track Listing:
Streetmasse: i. The Ballad Of You and Me and Pooneil; ii. A Small Package Of Value Will Come To You, Shortly; iii. Young Girl Sunday Blues. The War Is Over: i. Martha; ii. Wild Tyme. Hymn To An Older Generation: i. The Last Wall Of The Castle; ii. rejoyce. How Suite It Is: i. Watch Her Ride; ii. Spare Chaynge. Shizoforest Love Suite: i. Two Heads; ii. Won't You Try/Saturday Afternoon

Running time:
43.55

Current CD:
0786366798-2

Further listening:
Surrealistic Pillow (1967); Crown Of Creation (1968) replaces '67's heady vibe with more apocalyptic visions.

Further reading:
Jefferson Airplane And The San Francisco Sound (Ralph J Gleason, 1969)
www.discographynet.com/airplane/airplane.html

Traffic
Mr Fantasy

Pastoral debut from the crushed velvet heart of hippie England.

By autumn 1966 Steve Winwood had outgrown his role as teenage prodigy with the Spencer Davis Group and become a restless 20-year-old keenly aware of the new mood sweeping through pop. That summer the Davis band had scored major hits with Keep On Running and Gimme Some Loving, but Winwood was tired of being the star of a group bearing another's name. Even as their *Autumn 66* album appeared, Winwood was jamming around his home town of Birmingham with younger, more adventurous spirits, among them the three future members of Traffic.

In February 1967 Winwood officially quit the Spencer Davis Group and swapped Birmingham for the Berkshire village of Aston Tirrold, where Island supremo Chris Blackwell had found him a cottage to rent. Blackwell, with whom Winwood had managerial ties, saw Winwood as a future mainstay of his label as it grew a rock roster from its reggae roots.

Winwood occupied the cottage alone, but there were numerous visitations from the band, and the blend of bucolic Berkshire and the intoxications of the Summer Of Love proved creatively invigorating. So began the myth of 'getting it together in the country', a notion that has trapped numerous bands into stoned, fruitless escapism (The Stone Roses' *Second Coming* is but one case in point). The cover of *Mr Fantasy* shows the group gathered in the candle-lit cottage. Rural tranquillity does pervade a portion of the record, though Berkshire Poppies is little more than an update of cockney music hall (various Small Faces are present on it).

Produced with striking clarity by Jimmy Miller, the record soared on Winwood's soulful voice and inventive keyboard and guitar playing. Behind the balmy moods of Coloured Rain and Heaven Is In Your Mind lay much bickering over whether the pastel psychedelia of Dave Mason's Utterly Simple was fit to sit alongside mournful Winwood creations like No Face No Name No Number. The schism between Mason and the others was there in the pair of singles that preceded the album's release at the close of '67, Paper Sun and Hole In My Shoe (both included on the US edition), the latter a sitar and patchouli confection from Mason which Winwood recorded only under pressure. Time has certainly been kinder to the questing spirit of the title track than Mason's surrealist escapades, yet *Mr Fantasy* would be a less endearing encapsulation of its era without them.

Record label:
Island

Produced
by Jimmy Miller.

Recorded
at Olympic Sound Studios; April 1967.

Released:
December 1967

Chart peaks:
8 (UK) 17 (US)

Personnel:
Steve Winwood (o, g, b, p, harpsichord, pc, v); Dave Mason (g, Mellotron, sitar, tambura, shakkai, b, v); Chris Wood (flute, s, o, v); Jim Capaldi (d, pc, v); Eddie Kramer (e)

Track listing:
Heaven Is In Your Mind; Berkshire Poppies, House For Everyone, No Face No Name No Number; Dear Mr Fantasy; Dealer; Utterly Simple; Coloured Rain; Hope I Never Find Me There; Giving To You

Running time:
34.30

Current CD:
IMCD 264 adds: Paper Sun (S); Hole In My Shoe (S); Smiling Phases; We're A Fade You Missed This and the whole of the American edition of the album.

Further listening:
Traffic (1968)

Further reading:
Back In the High Life: A Biography of Steve Winwood (Alan Clayson, 19??); www.stevewinwood.com

Captain Beefheart And His Magic Band
Safe As Milk

Howlin' Wolf projected into the future. Extraordinary debut from one of rock's premier league eccentrics.

Perhaps impressed by the way in which Captain Beefheart's early singles Diddy Wah Diddy (a Bo Diddley cover) and Moonchild had paralleled contemporary blues-boom developments in Britain, A&M co-owner Jerry Moss was sufficiently encouraged to commission an album from the Los Angeles-based band. Upon hearing the demos, however, he refused to release the album on the grounds that it was too negative, and that songs like Electricity were not safe for his daughter to listen to. With their A&M contract finished, the first Magic Band broke up, leaving Beefheart free to sign with Buddah Records, (recently reactivated as "Buddha") where Bob Krasnow set to work polishing the songs that A&M had refused.

Deciding he needed help with the songwriting, Beefheart reworked seven of the songs with bassist Herb Bermann – chosen because, as a professional songwriter already, he might lend a little more credence to the Captain's compositions in the eyes of the second Magic Band. This new aggregation retained guitarist Alex St Clair Snouffer and bassist Jerry Handley from the previous line-up, alongside two new players who would add distinctive elements to the band's sound: idiosyncratic drummer John "Drumbo" French, and 16-year-old slide-guitar virtuoso Ry Cooder, whose curling lines set the desert-dry tone of the album's opener Sure 'Nuff 'N Yes I Do, a modernised take on Muddy Waters' classic Rollin' And Tumblin' riff. This and a cover of Robert Pete Williams' Grown So Ugly provided the clearest connection with the Captain's blues roots, though already there were signs of Beefheart's burgeoning sonic ambitions, notably in the presence of the theremin in Electricity and Autumn's Child, and the addition of Milt Holland's log-drum and marimba to the grungey Dropout Boogie. Horns and backing vocals, meanwhile, brought an authentic Southern soul feel to Call On Me.

Though later albums would head for much weirder territory, the basic elements of the Magic Band sound were already in place on *Safe As Milk*: the rumbustious, jerky polyrhythms; the spindly, interlocking guitar lines; the abrupt

Record label:
Buddah

Produced
by Bob Krasnow and Richard Perry.

Recorded
at RCA Studios and Sunset Studios, Hollywood, Los Angeles; April 1967.

Released:
February 1968

Chart peaks:
None (UK) None (US)

Personnel:
Don Van Vliet (v, hm, theremin, bass marimba); Alex St Clair Snouffer (g); Ry Cooder (g, b); Jerry Handley (b); Herb Bermann (b); John 'Drumbo' French (d); Milt Holland (pc); Taj Mahal (pc); Russ Titelman (g); Hank Cicalo, Gary Marker (e)

Track listing:
Sure 'Nuff 'N Yes I Do; Zig Zag Wanderer; Call On Me; Dropout Boogie; I'm Glad; Electricity; Yellow Brick Road (S); Abba Zabba (S); Plastic Factory (S); Where There's Woman (S); Grown So Ugly; Autumn's Child

Running time:
34.25

Current CD:
74321691752 adds: Safe As Milk; On Tomorrow; Big Black Baby Shoes; Flower Pot; Dirty Blue Gene; Trust Us; Korn Ring Finger

Further listening:
The challenging Trout Mask Replica (1969) takes the Captain's unique musical vision into avant-garde jazz territory, while Clear Spot (1972) captures him at his most accessible and commercially adapted.

Further reading:
Captain Beefheart (Mike Barnes, 2000); Captain Beefheart – The Man And His Music (C.D. Webb, 1989); Lunar Notes: Zoot Horn Rollo's Captain Beefheart Experience (Bill Harkleroad 1998)
www.beefheart.com

changes in tempo; Beefheart's raw blues-harp; and most of all, Beefheart's voice, a fearsome multi-octave instrument capable of swooping mid-line from a high-pitched squawk to a subterranean bass growl. According to engineer Hank Cicalo, it was Beefheart's vocals that were responsible for destroying a $1200 Telefunken microphone – a feat he later repeated on The Woody Woodberry TV Show. Though the album caused few ripples on its American release, it became one of the most ubiquitous artefacts of UK hippiedom thanks to British DJ John Peel's assiduous championing.

Leonard Cohen
The Songs Of Leonard Cohen

Definitive harbinger of bedsit melancholia.

Having made his reputation as a poet and novelist through the late '50s and '60s, Canadian songwriter Leonard Cohen originally intended to go to Nashville to become a country singer, but had been, as he put it, "hijacked" by New York, where he lived for a while in the mid-'60s at the notorious bohemian domicile, The Chelsea Hotel. His plan was to "make a record, make some money, and go back to writing books", although he found the ordeal of performance particularly gruelling to begin with.

Signed by legendary Columbia A&R man John Hammond after Judy Collins had featured his song Suzanne on her *In My Life* album, Cohen made an immediate impression with this debut album, whose sombre sepia cover hinted at the sometimes unflinching nature of the contents. Already well into his 30s by the time of its release, Cohen's work boasted a maturity and emotional intensity denied to the more youthful singer-songwriters that had appeared in Bob Dylan's wake. The album's songs dealt with personal issues, mostly this legendary ladies' man's relationships with women – particularly Norwegian girlfriend Marianne Jensen, whom he met during his time on the Greek island of Hydra, where he had spent much of the preceding decade (she's in the rear sleeve photo of his second album *Songs From A Room*). Both So Long Marianne and Hey That's No Way To Say Goodbye were responses to their gradually failing relationship, while Suzanne celebrated his subsequent partnership with Suzanne Elrod, who would bear Cohen's children Adam Nathan and Lorca Sarah.

Sung in his characteristic lugubrious baritone over rippling waves of fingerstyle acoustic guitar, Cohen's songs possessed a brooding intimacy which proved surprisingly erotic: *Songs Of Leonard Cohen* remains, along with Tim Buckley's *Happy Sad* and Tim Hardin's first two albums, one of the masterpieces of boudoir-folk-rock. At the time, however, critics like the Village Voice's Richard Goldstein castigated him for being a "Visceral Romantic ... who suffers gloriously in every couplet", crystallising a notion of Cohen as gloomily self-indulgent that would take years of wry drollerie to dispel.

Record label:
Columbia

Produced
by John Simon.

Recorded
at Columbia Records Studio E, New York;
1967.

Released:
February 1968

Chart peaks:
13 (UK) 83 (US)

Personnel:
Leonard Cohen (v, g)

Track listing:
Suzanne (S); Master Song; Winter Lady;
The Stranger Song; Sisters Of Mercy; So
Long Marianne (S); Hey That's No Way
To Say Goodbye; Stories Of The Street;
Teachers; One Of Us Cannot Be Wrong

Running time:
41.14

Current CD:
4686002

Further listening:
His debut's immediate successors Songs
From A Room (1969) and Songs Of Love
And Hate (1971) continued Cohen's soul-
mining in similar manner. Later albums
are less reliable, but 1988's superb I'm
Your Man is one of rock's more notable
comeback successes.

Further reading:
Leonard Cohen – A Life In Art (Ira
Nadel, 1994) www.leonardcohenfiles.com

Fleetwood Mac
Peter Green's Fleetwood Mac

Young Brit-blues master Green in excelsis. Not much to do with the Californian edition of Fleetwood Mac.

In the summer of 1967, Peter Green was wondering where to go next after leaving John Mayall's Bluesbreakers. He half thought about going to Chicago and hanging with the true blues guys. Then again, Mayall's producer, Mike Vernon, was starting a new label, Blue Horizon. Green wondered whether there might be a role for him as house guitarist, like Buddy Guy was for Chess. Vernon, however, keen to sign Green, encouraged him to form a band. By the autumn, Fleetwood Mac had come together and embarked on a hectic schedule of dates which left time only for sporadic recording. Vernon says the whole process was protracted, spread over five months with the end result being "a series of short stories rather than a novel".

Disenchanted with John Mayall's lurch towards jazz, Green wanted to record a no-nonsense 12-bar blues album. He provided the B.B. King stylings, Jeremy Spencer did a mean Elmore James and the whole thing was locked down by the Fleetwood and McVie rhythm engine. But they all had a very casual approach, didn't really believe the band would come to much, and were just out to have a good time. This did their recordings no harm, contributing to the louche, loose-limbed bounce of Shake Your Moneymaker and No Place To Go, which proved beyond all expectation that a British blues band could swing.

But their laid-back ways often drove Vernon to distraction. Spencer repeatedly sang all the wrong words to Hellhound On My Trail, and then, as the producer tried to get My Heart Beats Like A Hammer under way, the band subjected him to a barrage of raucous guitar intros until he rapped schoolmaster-like on the talk-back microphone to bring the urchins to order. The FM Blue Horizon box-set version of the album (see below) carries the full gamut of cock-ups Vernon had to put up with before he could patiently craft a final take.

Despite all the misdemeanours along the way, the "dog and dustbin" album – Chicago south side by way of the back streets of Battersea – proved a massive seller and an abiding testament to the stomping blues glory of swinging '60s London.

Record label:
Blue Horizon

Produced
by Mike Vernon.

Recorded
at CBS and Decca studios, London;
November–December 1967.

Released:
February 1968

Chart peaks:
4 (UK) 198 (US)

Personnel:
Peter Green (g, v, hm); Jeremy Spencer (g, v); John McVie (b); Bob Brunning (b); Mick Fleetwood (d); Mike Ross (e)

Track listing:
My Heart Beat Like A Hammer; Merry Go Round; Long Grey Mare; Hellhound On My Trail; Shake Your Moneymaker; Looking For Somebody; No Place To Go; My Baby's Good To Me; I Loved Another Woman; Cold Black Night; The World Keep On Turning; Got To Move

Running time:
34.20

Current CD:
4773582

Further listening:
Fleetwood Mac: The Complete Blue Horizon Sessions 1967–1969 (1999), comprising the first album, Mr Wonderful (1968); Pious Bird Of Good Omen (1969); Blues Jam at Chess and Original Fleetwood Mac (1971). The whole collection is full of alternate takes, false starts, studio talk and previously unissued material plus excellent notes by Mike Vernon.

Further reading:
Peter Green: The Biography (Martin Celmins, 1998) gives the most detail on the early days of Fleetwood Mac;
www.fleetwoodmac.net

Love

Forever Changes

An unclassifiable trove of bittersweet pop.

A psychedelic masterpiece with neither lengthy jams nor studio wizardry; folk-rock with scant hint of protest or sweet harmonies: *Forever Changes* is an enigma wrapped in a web of contradictions – which hasn't harmed its impeccable cult credentials one bit. Starting life as a British Invasion-fixated bunch of Byrds acolytes, Love's primary weapon was Arthur Lee, a precocious songwriter reared on The Beatles, Beethoven and James Brown. "It was my name, my band, my music," Lee said, "and my music forever changes." It did, and rapidly, too. Besides Lee's dominating presence; Love's multi-racial mix juxtaposed Latin flavours with Lee's quirky R&B and Maclean's gentle folk-pop.

After releasing two albums (*Love* and *Da Capo*) in quick succession, the band retreated to Bela Lugosi's old mansion in the Hollywood hills, known as 'The Castle'. While they virtually fell apart, the acrimony magnified by paranoia-inducing quantities of heroin and acid, Love's Elektra rivals The Doors were succeeding fast. "The way I wrote music then was according to my lifestyle and environment," Lee later recalled. That certainly helps explain the disturbed, claustrophobic feel which undermines the album's deceptively blissful demeanour.

It was recorded in just seven sessions, over a period of four months. Neil Young produced the first day's work (The Daily Planet, Andmoreagain), with Phil Spector's 'Wrecking Crew' (Hal Blaine, Billy Strange and Carol Kaye) providing backing. After some tearful complaints, Young and the session players were banished and the band reclaimed the songs the following day by overdubbing new parts. David Angel's elegant string arrangements, so vital to the album's dreamlike charm, were added late in September at the end of the recordings. After Lee and Maclean grudgingly approved them, the results were mixed in a gruelling 17-hour session: "No coffee, a few cigarettes and a lot of cocaine", recalled Ken Forssi. Out of chaos came, according to Elektra at the time, "a vast study in moods". Maclean's Old Man and Alone Again Or were almost unbearably plaintive, but it was the nagging expressions of a seething irascibility (the contradictory voices on The Red Telephone, the spontaneous guitar duels on A House Is Not A Motel and Live And Let Live, Lee's alienated visions and sardonic delivery) that fortify the album's eggshell melodies with tough, impervious centres.

Record Label:
Elektra

Produced
by Arthur Lee and Bruce Botnick.

Recorded
at Sunset Sound Recorders, Los Angeles; June 9, 10 and 12; August 11–12; September 10 and 25, 1967.

Released:
February 1968 (UK); November 1967 (US)

Chart peaks:
24 (UK) 154 (US)

Personnel:
Arthur Lee (g, v); Bryan Maclean (g, v); John Echols (g); Ken Forssi (b); Michael Stuart (pc); David Angel (a); Hal Blaine (d); Billy Strange (g); Carol Kaye (b)

Track Listing:
Alone Again Or (S); A House Is Not A Motel; Andmoreagain (S); The Daily Planet; Old Man; The Red Telephone; Maybe The People Would Be The Times Or Between Clark And Hilldale; Live And Let Live; The Good Humor Man He Sees Everything Like This; Bummer In The Summer; You Set The Scene

Running time:
42.58

Current CD:
7559-60656-2

Further listening:
Da Capo for signs of incipient greatness, Love Story for the bigger picture.

Further reading:
MOJO 43; Try fanzine The Castle, edited by David P Housden, information on 01945 870065. The Delta Sweete Bobbie Gentry

Nirvana

The Story Of Simon Simonpath

Sumptuous soft-psych classic from the original UK Nirvana.

The brainchild of songwriters Patrick Campbell-Lyons and Alex Spyropoulos, Nirvana was originally conceived as a group but devolved into a duo by the time they signed to Chris Blackwell's Island Records.

"Blackwell said, 'You'll have to have an album' because he wasn't interested in singles as such," Lyons remembers. "It just evolved. We went back to a flat in Shepherd's Bush and used to work long days and long nights completing songs. This character Simon came out of the song Wings Of Love which also inspired the sleeve artwork." A lonely kid, living in a sixth dimensional city, is obsessed with the idea of sprouting wings and flying. After reaching the stars, he encounters an extra-terrestrial centaur and is taken to Nirvana where he meets and ultimately weds the impossibly beautiful mermaid creature Magdelena.

They dubbed their creation, "a science fiction pantomime". "To describe it as a concept album seems naff to me now," Lyons cautions. "We saw it as a musical pantomime for grown-ups with a slightly druggy undertone to it. I don't know if we really knew what psychedelia meant but we had our own feeling about it. Many people were living psychedelic lives in those days."

The musical backdrop was an oddly eclectic mix emphasising the schizophrenic divide between pop and rock in 1967. As ambitious songwriters, Lyons and Spyropoulos had one foot in Denmark Street's Tin Pan Alley but were also aspiring towards more adventurous studio experiments.

The album included upbeat singalongs like We Can Help You, the catchy Wings Of Love and even a bizarre trad jazz item, 1999. It says much for the interest in the album that these songs were covered by acts as diverse as Alan Bown, Herman's Hermits and Kenny Ball, respectively. The key track on the work was undoubtedly Pentecost Hotel, one of the finest pieces of orchestral pop ever released. "It really encapsulated the whole concept of the album," Lyons notes. "It was a journey somewhere out there. There was a lot of poetic licence in the whole concept. Maybe that's what makes it attractive, its naïveté, which is missing in a lot of things today."

Record label:
Island

Produced
by Chris Blackwell.

Recorded
at Pye Studios 1 and 2; early 1967.

Released:
February 1968

Chart peaks:
None (UK) None (US)

Personnel:
Patrick Campbell-Lyons (g, v); Alex Spyropoulos (k); Herbie Flowers (b); Frank Riccotti (g); Alan Parker (g); Alan Hawkes (k); Michael Coe (french horn); Sylvia Schuster (c); Barry Morgan (d); Clem Cattini (d); Sue & Sunny, Madeleine Bell, Lesley Duncan (bv); Brian Humphries (e); Syd Dale (a, oa)

Track listing:
Wings Of Love; Lonely Boy; We Can Help You; Satellite Jockey; In The Courtyard Of The Stars; You're Just The One; Pentecost Hotel (S); I Never Found A Love Like This; Take This Hand; 1999

Running time:
25.35

Current CD:
EDCD 465

Further listening:
All Of Us (1968)

Further reading:
Rainbow Chaser (Patrick Campbell-Lyons: unpublished manuscript extracted in liner notes to Nirvana's All Of Us)

Bobbie Gentry
The Delta Sweete

Her great lost concept album.

"A perfect set of ivories, coffee-coloured eyes, a warm sensual face ... no-one would ever dream of throwing *her* off a bridge." So surmised Gordon Coxhill in his 1969 NME interview with Bobbie Gentry. In the two years since Ode To Billie Joe she'd had little in the way of a hit and journalists were apt to dismiss her as just another pretty face. Born Roberta Streeter in Chickasaw County, Mississippi, Gentry was, in fact, a self-taught musician who'd graduated from the Los Angeles Conservatory of Music, writing by day and spending her evenings as a Las Vegas chorus girl where she was discovered by Capitol A&R man Kelly Gordon.

"Kelly came into my office one night so choked he could hardly talk." remembers fellow A&R man David Axelrod. "He said, 'We've got a demo and I know it's real good.' It was Ode To Billie Joe. I said, 'This is terrific, what's the problem?' He said, 'General manager of A&R turned it down.' The guy who owned the song was Larry Shane, one of the biggest independent publishers. I dialled him and said 'What do you want for this?' He said 'Ten thousand dollars.' I said 'Done.' I hung up. Happy. Went over the general manager's head. Her stuff was too good *not* to hear."

Her second album, however, was roundly ignored. A concept album about white southern life in which all intros and outros are underscored by sad strings, each track flowing into the next, *The Delta Sweete* was a work of great emotional power. It ranged from the fractured Mississippi funk of Okolona River Bottom Band to Courtyard, the sparsely arranged tale of an imprisoned woman, and her most beautiful, tragic composition.

"No-one bought it but I didn't lose sleep over it," Gentry told NME, "I've never tried to pre-judge public taste."

After *The Delta Sweete* Gentry appears to have had difficulty deciding on a career path. Following a number of saccharine chart hits with Glen Campbell (Let it Be Me, All I Have To Do Is Dream), she returned with the hard country soul of *Fancy*, recorded with Rick Hall at Muscle Shoals. An astute businesswoman, by 1970 she also owned considerable property in California and had a large financial interest in the Phoenix Suns baseball team. She dropped out of the public eye altogether in 1976.

Record label:
Capitol

Produced:
by Kelly Gordon

Recorded:
winter 1967

Release date:
March 1968

Chart peaks:
None (UK) None (US:)

Personnel:
Bobbie Gentry (g, v); Jimmie Haskell and Shorty Rogers (a); other musicians not known.

Track listing:
Okolona River Bottom Band (S); Big Boss Man; Reunion; Parchman Farm; Mornin' Glory; Sermon; Tobacco Road; Penduli Pendulum; Jessye' Lisabeth; Refractions; Louisiana Man; Courtyard

Running time:
33.44

Currently unavailable on CD

Further listening:
Fancy (1970); Touch Em With Love (Capitol, 1969)

Further reading:
Not much. http://www.folkmusic.org/ is the perfect search engine for seeking out Gentry info.

The Incredible String Band

The Hangman's Beautiful Daughter

Celtic minstrels record their psychedelic masterpiece and copyright the concept of "getting it together in the country".

Fired by the success of their second album *The 5,000 Spirits*, Heron and Williamson repaired to a Chelsea studio to construct the album that would seal their reputation forever. With them they brought exotic instruments from a road-trip to Morocco and a collection of incandescent tunes requiring, for the most part, a single roll of the tape and a touch of embroidery.

"This was the first time multi-tracking was possible," Williamson remembers, "though it was still done in a pretty slapdash, anarchic, have-a-go kind of way. The whole album was recorded in a few days. We didn't even stay for the mixes. The basic tracks were mostly one take, live vocal and guitar, and then the other instruments were put on top. Mercy I Cry City was pretty much live, with me playing two whistles and drums all at the same time. Waltz Of The New Moon had a harp player on it, and we had Dolly Simpson's flute organ on Water Song, but otherwise it was just us overdubbing the other parts." Williamson's contributions were written in a disused railway carriage in the garden of his friend Mary Stewart's house near Glasgow. It's Stewart's children who appear in the *Hangman's* hugely influential cover picture, an image (taken on Christmas Day '67) that so perfectly captured the album's mystic appeal and sent kindred spirits scurrying for the hills in search of a rural retreat. There was instant critical acclaim, along with loud endorsements from Mick Jagger, John Lennon, Robert Plant and Jimmy Page.

"A very pleasant surprise," says Williamson, "but I felt it was something special even while we were making it. The whole of London had this fantastic atmosphere at the time, particularly Chelsea. A wonderful feeling of optimism after the 1950s, a tremendous flowering of the notion that the war was actually over and that life and love could be obtained. Hence the name of the album – The Hangman being the death in the war and The Beautiful Daughter being the coming age. Look at that misty gleam in our eyes on the cover: we were standing back and looking in amazement at what was going on!"

Record label:
Elektra

Produced
by Joe Boyd.

Recorded
at Sound Techniques Studios, London; December 1967.

Released:
March 1968

Chart peaks:
5 (UK) None (US)

Personnel:
Robin Williamson (v, g, gimbri, whistle, pc, pan pipe, p, oud, mandolin, Jews harp, chahanai, water harp, hm); Mike Heron (v, s, Hammond organ, g, dulcimer, harpsichord); Dolly Collins (flute, organ, harpsichord); Davis Snell (harp); Licorice McKechnie (v, finger-cymbals)

Track listing:
Koeeoaddi There; The Minotaur's Song; Witches Hat; A Very Cellular Song; Mercy I Cry City; Waltz Of The New Moon; The Water Song; There Is A Green Crown; Swift As The Wind; Nightfall

Running time:
49.55

Current CD:
7559-60835-2

Further listening:
Wee Tam And The Big Huge (1968); The 5,000 Spirits (1967); Liquid Acrobat As Regards The Air (1970)

Further reading:
MOJO 81

Tom Rush
The Circle Game

Pivotal bedsit folk album that — though largely built around covers — helped herald the arrival of the singer/songwriter.

Exactly when folk singers became known as 'singer/song-writers' is hard to pinpoint, but this 1968 song cycle is certainly a milestone in that journey. *The Circle Game* was among folk rock's first fully orchestrated albums, recorded at roughly the same time as Phil Ochs' *Pleasures Of The Harbor* and Love's *Forever Changes* (though both beat it to the street by a couple of months). As a true concept album, it bettered the framing devices of *Sgt. Pepper* and *The Who Sell Out*; it also just happened to introduce the world to the work of no less than three singer/songwriter icons: James Taylor, Jackson Browne, and Joni Mitchell.

The seed was planted when Cambridge folk star Rush met the unknown Mitchell in a Detroit coffee house, and she taught him her song Urge For Going. A tape of Rush's moving six-minute demo of the song was played on Boston Top 40 powerhouse WBZ in the spring of 1967, where it became the radio station's most requested song for the next six months. Urge For Going would obviously be a centrepiece of his next album, but Mitchell's contribution didn't end there. "I got a package in the mail from Joni," Rush recalls. "It was a tape she'd made in her apartment, wonderful songs like Tin Angel and Moon In The Mirror. A the end she did this little spoken disclaimer: 'Gee, here's a song I just finished. I'm not sure if it's any good, but here it is.' That was The Circle Game."

Rush had always been an open-minded folkie – his previous album had featured a side of Al Kooper electric arrangements – and he conceived this record as an orchestrated song cycle that would trace the arc of a relationship from hello to goodbye; side one would be the upside, side two the down. Mitchell's tape had given him a title song (though The Circle Game was originally written for her old Toronto friend Neil Young), and a place to start in Tin Angel ("In a Bleecker Street café/She found someone to love today"). The narrative was fleshed out with songs from unknowns Taylor (Something In The Way She Moves and Sunshine Sunshine) and Browne (Shadow Dream Song), both still in their teens. And though Tom Rush was known primarily as an interpreter, the two songs that cap *The Circle Game* were his own: the melancholy instrumental Rockport Sunday running into supreme break-up song No Regrets, which The Walker Brothers would spin into gold six years later.

Record label:
Elektra

Produced
by Arthur Gorson.

Recorded
at Century Sound, New York and Sunset Sound, Los Angeles; autumn 1967.

Released:
March 1968

Chart peaks:
None (UK) 68 (US)

Personnel:
Tom Rush (v, ag); Bruce Langhorne (g); Hugh McCracken (g); Don Thomas (g); Eric Gale (g); Jonathan Raskin (classical guitar, b); Joe Mack (b); Bob Bushnell (b); Paul Harris (k, oa, a); Herbie Lovelle (d); Bernard Purdie (d); Richie Ritz (d); Joe Grimm (s); Buddy Lucas (s); Brooks Arthur, Bruce Botnick (e)

Track listing:
Tin Angel; Something In The Way She Moves; Urge For Going (S/US); Sunshine Sunshine; The Glory Of Love; Shadow Dream Song; The Circle Game; So Long; Rockport Sunday; No Regrets (S/UK)

Running time:
38.36

Current CD:
740182

Further listening:
Take A Little Walk With Me (1966); The Very Best Of Tom Rush: No Regrets 1962–1999 (1999)

Further reading:
Baby Let Me Follow You Down: The Story of the Cambridge Folk Years (Eric von Schmidt and Jim Rooney, 1979); www.tomrush.com

The United States Of America

The United States Of America

The electronic rock revolution starts here.

A short-lived collective of experimental musicians, The United States Of America created one of the first successful marriages of electronic music and pop. Leader Joseph Byrd was a pivotal figure of "serious" modern music in the mid-'60s as a composer, conductor and producer. He moved to Los Angeles in 1967 to study at UCLA, but promptly got together with four other avant-gardiste students, started the band, tuned up and dropped out.

Every instrument they played was in some way treated through distorted amplifiers, ring modulators and other devices. Craig Woodson pioneered electronic drums, Gordon Marron played an electronically adapted violin. But what distinguished them was their distinctive sense of pop featuring the twisted lyrical intelligence of Dorothy Moskowitz.

Given its title, their only album had to aim high and it did. The opening track parodied *Sgt. Pepper's Lonely Hearts Club Band* with The American Metaphysical Circus which is loosely based on Being For The Benefit Of Mr Kite. The American Way Of Love observed homosexual prostitutes on New York's 42nd Street, while radio favourite I Won't Leave My Wooden Wife For You, Sugar adeptly sent up the straight suburban family cut off from the world in their "split-level house with a wonderful view" (this track became their best known via inclusion on CBS's key compilation/sampler album *The Rock Machine Turns You On*).

If some of *The United States Of America*'s enthusiastic phasing, echo and channel-swapping date-stamps it, it endures nonetheless through solid merit – musical verve and imagination, the melodic appeal of the trippy The Garden Of Earthly Delights and gentler pieces Love Song For The Dead Ché and Cloud Song. Thirty years on, Moskowitz, who moved on to Country Joe's All Star Band before becoming a music teacher, commented on the web: "I have no regrets about the electronic excess under which my voice was buried. It was part of the aesthetic and I was the one who insisted on singing through a ring modulator."

Byrd later worked with Phil Ochs and a relatively unimpressive band called The Field Hippies (1969) and also produced Ry Cooder's *Jazz* (1978).

Record label:
CBS

Produced
by Dave Rubinson.

Recorded
at CBS studios, autumn 1967.

Released:
March 1968

Chart peaks:
None (UK) 181 (US)

Personnel:
Joseph Byrd (electronic music, electric harpsichord, o, calliope, p); Dorothy Moskowitz (v); Gordon Marron (electric violin, ring modulator); Rand Forbes (bs); Craig Woodson (electric drums, pc)

Track listing:
The American Metaphysical Circus; Hard Coming Love; Cloud Song; The Garden Of Earthly Delights; I Won't Leave My Wooden Wife For You, Sugar; Where Is Yesterday; Coming Down; Love Song For The Dead Che; Stranded In Time; The American Way Of Love

Running time:
37.07

Current CD:
Edsel EDCD 541

Further listening:
There's not much out there that relates to this one-off delight, though Joseph Byrd did cut his own electronic LP of Christmas music, Xmas Yet To Come (1980).

Further reading:
www.freakemporioum.co.uk

The Byrds
The Notorious Byrd Brothers

Recorded amid group turmoil this unexpectedly emerged as their most gentle and reflective work.

T he Byrds were at the peak of their artistic powers in 1967 and following the celebrated *Younger Than Yesterday* looked likely to climb new heights as a creative force. Unfortunately, they were also being eaten away from within. The rivalry between McGuinn and Crosby over leadership and direction continued to fester, most notably at the crucial Monterey festival where David Crosby played the counter-culture king, advocating LSD use and telling the world that the Kennedy assassination was a hushed-up conspiracy. To top it all, he appeared onstage with the Buffalo Springfield. "They were very upset when he played with them," manager Jim Dickson recalled. "There was a big dilemma. David seemed as if he was intent on destroying the group. I'm sure he didn't see it that way. It was compulsive behaviour."

In August, The Byrds commenced work on their new album, but friction in the studio threatened to overwhelm them. Apart from the bickering between McGuinn and Crosby, there was an ongoing battle with drummer Michael Clarke who responded to David Crosby's condescension with the priceless, "What do you know, man? You're not a musician." More problems ensued when McGuinn and Hillman rejected Crosby's *ménage á trois* ballad Triad as tasteless. He rebelled by declining to play on the Goffin & King number Goin' Back. With emotions running high, McGuinn and Hillman drove over to Crosby's house and told him he was fired. Gene Clark was recalled, but only lasted three weeks and contributed nothing to the album. By the end of the sessions, Michael Clarke had joined the ranks of ex-Byrds.

The final product should have been a disjointed mess but instead was breathtaking – evocative songs made otherworldly by Gary Usher's innovative use of phasing, reversed tapes, string sections and synthesizers. The Byrds survived destabilizing line-up changes during this period and would go on to record six more albums, but they would never again find the magic or mystery unveiled during this time of unprecedented internecine strife.

Record label:
Columbia

Produced
by Gary Usher.

Recorded
at CBS, Hollywood, August–December 1967.

Released:
April, 12 1968

Chart peaks:
12 (UK) 47 (US)

Personnel:
Roger McGuinn (g, v, syn); David Crosby (g, v); Michael Clarke (d); Chris Hillman (b); Roy Halee (e); Don Thompson (ae)

Track listing:
Artificial Energy; Goin' Back; Natural Harmony; Draft Morning; Wasn't Born To Follow; Get To You; Change Is Now; Old John Robertson; Tribal Gathering; Dolphin's Smile; Space Odyssey

Running time:
28.30

Current CD:
Legacy 4867512 adds: Moog Raga; Bound To Fall; Triad; Goin' Back; Draft Morning; Universal Mind Decoder

Further listening:
Younger Than Yesterday (1967)

Further reading:
MOJO 41; The Byrds: Timeless Flight Revisited (Johnny Rogan, 1997)

The Zombies
Odessey And Oracle

Gorgeous album, overlooked in UK, since acknowledged as a key example of British psychedelia.

St Albans, Hertfordshire was not renowned as the birthplace of pop gods. And after the unsensational ascent of The Zombies that hadn't changed. They were hardly the stuff of teenage fantasy and carried no aroma of danger or wild innovation. But beneath the tidy suits, nice jumpers and thick spectacles beat the hearts of five terrific musicians, more-than-merely-gifted writers who – in She's Not There and Time Of The Season – created two of the decade's most evocative and enduring hits – and perhaps deserved a greater share of contemporary acclaim.

They were almost classic one-hit wonders; the beautiful and timeless She's Not There proving impossible to follow. It hit around the world and provided them with plenty of experience on the road, but further singles performed poorly and their debut album was a disappointing, but typical, ragbag of blues covers and low-wattage originals. After more than two years of touring, these smart boys had become disillusioned with the amount of hard slog and the lack of hard cash, and were close to giving up. But chief writers Rod Argent and Chris White had a few ideas about ditching their old formula and making a proper album, and they took their plan to CBS Records. CBS liked it.

On June 1, 1967, the attention of the entire rock world was fixed upon the release of The Beatles' *Sgt Pepper's Lonely Hearts Club Band*, or so they say. The entire rock world *except*, that is, for five former beatsters holed up at Abbey Road, commencing the recording of *their* psychedelic masterpiece. At The Beatles' behest, the studio technicians had jerryrigged various 4-track recording machines so the group would have more tracks to work with; when The Zombies walked in to start recording, engineers Geoff Emerick and Phil MacDonald were busily disconnecting those same machines. Paul Atkinson later recalled, "We said, 'What are you doing? Plug those back in again.' And they said, 'No, no, please. We've had six months of this. It's been driving us crazy. We want to unplug all this stuff and get back to recording normally.'"

The group had a budget of £2,000, which, even then, didn't buy much time at Abbey Road. As a result, *Odessey And Oracle* (the title was misspelt by the sleeve designer) was a

Record label:
CBS

Produced
by Rod Argent and Chris White.

Recorded
at Abbey Road and Olympic Studios, London; June 1967.

Released:
April 19, 1968

Chart peaks:
None (UK) 95 (US)

Personnel:
Rod Argent (p, o, Mellotron, bv); Chris White (b, bv); Colin Blunstone (v); Paul Atkinson (bv, g); Hugh Grundy (bv, d)

Track listing:
Care Of Cell 44; A Rose For Emily; Maybe After He's Gone; Beechwood Park; Brief Candles; Hung Up On A Dream; Changes; I Want Her She Wants Me; This Will Be Our Year; Butcher's Tale (Western Front 1914); Friends Of Mine; Time Of The Season

Running time:
33.04

Current CD:
Ace CDWIKD 181 adds: A Rose For Emily (2); Time Of The Season (2); Prison Song

Further listening:
The all-killer/no-filler 4-CD box set Zombie Heaven (1997)

Further reading:
Alec Palao's fine liner notes to Zombie Heaven; also check out the Zombies Fan Page, members.aol.com/bocad/zom.htm

tightly arranged album that utilised their engineers' skills to the full. Songs such as Care Of Cell 44 showcase a dense and creamy mixture of choirboy-cum-Beach Boy harmonies and hook-studded, baroque melodies, with lead singer Colin Blunstone at the top of his game. Despite cutting corners by using a mellotron instead of orchestra and flute, The Zombies still wound up having to spend £200 of their own money to pay for a stereo mixdown.

The record came out to almost universal indifference – this was a band whose big hit was three years behind them, after all. A disheartened Paul Atkinson quit the band and Rod Argent took it as the final sign: "We may as well split then."

Within weeks, the angelic-voiced Blunstone was working at an insurance company. Meanwhile, CBS recording artist and A&R man Al Kooper, who'd heard the album in Britain, persuaded his label to issue it stateside. Several extracted singles flopped before DJs unexpectedly picked up on Time Of The Season. In the spring of 1969 the song soared to Number 3 in the American charts. Nevertheless, Rod Argent resisted pressure from CBS to reform the band and The Zombies curious career, bookended by two huge hits, was finally laid to rest.

Johnny Cash
Johnny Cash At Folsom Prison

Cash's big-time comeback, after five years of declining sales and battles with pills and the law.

By 1968, Johnny Cash was a tired old C&W performer who seemed all washed up. Languishing on the Columbia label, he hadn't had a real hit in years and faced a middle age of playing two-bit roadhouses for declining audiences and diminishing returns. A live album might be his only salvation.

Cash had been held behind bars a number of times, and Columbia bosses agreed with him that an album recorded in one of the prisons where he'd done time might revive his moribund career. Cash chose Folsom Prison as the venue: he had several times enthralled inmate audiences there with his honest blue collar life stories and sympathetic banter. Cash returned to Folsom with high hopes, a full mobile recording crew and his future wife June Carter.

His music was the same as it always had been. Kicking off with his old Sun hit Folsom Prison Blues and following his usual formula of performing equal parts Cash originals and folk/country covers, he had the inmates of Folsom in the palm of his hand as his formidable storytelling abilities rose to the occasion. Lyrics about poverty, cocaine and whiskey abuse, about endless days of coalmining and the horror of life behind bars are stock-in-trade American folklore to Cash's many fans, but of course resonated even more strongly to the inmates he sang for on that chilly January evening.

Cash remains justifiably proud of this recording, which not only re-ignited his career in the States but signalled a turnaround in his previously chaotic private life: "(You) listen closely to this album and you hear the clanging of doors, the shrill of the whistle, the shouts of the men — even laughter from men who had forgotten how to laugh. There's some stuff here I'm proud of."

Record label:
CBS

Produced
by Bob Johnston.

Recorded
live at Folsom Prison, California; January 13, 1968.

Released:
April 1968

Chart peaks:
8 (UK) 13 (US)

Personnel:
Johnny Cash (v, g); June Carter (v); Carter Family (v); Marshall Grant (b); W.S. Holland (d); Carl Perkins (g); Luther Perkins (g); The Statler Brothers (v)

Track listing:
Folsom Prison Blues (S); Busted; Dark As The Dungeon; I Still Miss Someone; Cocaine Blues; 25 Minutes To Go; Orange Blossom Special; The Long Black Veil; Send A Picture Of Mother; The Wall; Dirty Old Egg-Suckin' Dog; Flushed From The Bathroom Of Your Heart; Joe Bean; Jackson (S); Give My Love To Rose; I Got Stripes; The Legend Of John Henry's Hammer; Green Green Grass Of Home; Greystone Chapel

Running time:
55.49

Current CD:
SNY659522

Further listening:
Johnny Cash At San Quentin (1969); American Recordings (1994)

Further reading:
The New Johnny Cash (Charles Paul Conn, 1973); Johnny Cash: The Autobiography (Johnny Cash with Patrick Carr, 1998)

Flat Earth Society

Waleeco

Teenage prodigies create Willy Wonka-style curio.

For some bands obscurity seems almost inevitable: for the Flat Earth Society it was assured. When the Boston-based F.B. Washburn Candy Company decided to promote their tasty new Waleeco candy bar by holding a competition amongst local groups to write a radio jingle, the prize they offered the winning band was the chance to cut an album. After submitting the chosen song, the Flat Earth Society, a group of talented teenagers from Lynn, Massachusetts, assembled at Fleetwood Studios. With no previous recording experience they found that they had only rehearsed enough songs for half the album and so the rest had to be written on the spot. Time was at a premium and the studio facilities were crude, but with considerable ingenuity the results were remarkable. Paul Carter recalls that in order to give his bass more definition he had to place his amplifier in the studio's bathroom: in Feelin' Much Better, a phasing effect was achieved by spraying an aerosol can into a bucket!

The band were heavily influenced by Jefferson Airplane and, of course, The Beatles, but also by folk music, which comes to the fore on When You're There and Prelude For The Town Monk. There's a beautiful electric piano rendition of Midnight Hour – the only non-original track – but it is on the second side that the group, forced to improvise, really show their talents; the atmospheric Dark Street Downtown; Portrait in Grey is an extended instrumental with haunting recorder playing; Satori, the album's mysterious, psychedelic climax, a wash of backwards piano spiked with sitar-like guitar. As the hype on the back cover put it: "Their bag is that they're in no particular bag at all."

Unfortunately, anyone who wished to hear the album was required to send off $1.50 together with six Waleeco wrappers. Few bothered and, with little else in the way of promotion, the record was destined to become a land-fill. Happily, now it's reissued on CD, everyone can hear it, without rotting any teeth.

Record label:
Fleetwood

Produced
by Quinn & Johnson, Inc. and Charlie Dreyer.

Recorded
at Fleetwood Studios, Revere, Massachusetts

Released:
April 1968

Chart peaks:
None (UK) None (US)

Personnel:
Jack Kerivan (p, o, v); Phil Dubuque (g, recorder, v); Rick Doyle (g, pc, v); Curt Girard (d); Paul Carter (b, v)

Track listing:
Feelin' Much Better; Midnight Hour; I'm So Happy; When You're There; Four And Twenty Miles; Prelude For The Town Monk; Shadows; Dark Street Downtown; Portrait In Grey; In My Window; Satori

Running time:
32.16

Current CD:
Arf-Arf AA-042

Further listening:
There's nothing at all, unfortunately. But the Arf-Arf label has lots of similar curiosities in its catalogue.

Magic Sam
West Side Soul

The record that announced a new generation of American electric blues.

In the early 1960s, no fresh African-Americans were breaking out from the Chicago blues bars, and it seemed that the music might one day become a museum piece until a young entrepreneur named Robert Koester began a talent hunt for his small label. He found it. Samuel Maghett was young yet already an experienced performer, easy on the eye, a gentleman in his dealings, charismatic, an incredible guitarist with his own style, a dramatic singer and the author of some bruising blues songs. Sam had already recorded for Cobra in 1957, Chief in 1960–61 and Crash in 1966 when Delmark signed him, but this time around he was promised a free hand. Thus, on a sticky summer's day, he entered a small Chicago studio to make blues history.

Sam knew to appeal to the young Caucasian college fan just discovering blues music as well as to his regular crowd: the album had to hang together musically, had to be of one piece like a rock album. Maghett lived on Chicago's West Side where he and his cohorts were much more ready to embrace music beyond the blues – rock'n'roll, soul and Latin – than his contemporaries on the South Side, the Chess Records crowd who were blues purists. It was this distinction that gave the album its uptempo drive and its title.

Sam's staccato lead guitar (he played with his fingers and thumb, forcefully plucking the strings) pushed through a Fender amp with reverb on full was a new sound in blues, and after *West Side Soul*'s release Sam briefly toured with The Grateful Dead, wowing Jerry Garcia when his Stratocaster was heard through a state-of-the-art PA system.

"Looking Good, his show-stopping boogie, blew guitar players' minds," remembers ex-manager Denny Bruce. "Ry Cooder came to my house to meet Sam and learn a few finger-picking tricks from him. Sam never showed him. He never got his due as a singer but his Mama Mama Talk To Your Daughter and Sweet Home Chicago are role models for so many out there."

Alas, it was not to last. After two years of growing fame, Magic Sam Maghett called to his wife one morning complaining of heartburn. It was a cardiac arrest, and within minutes Sam was dead. He was 32.

Record label:
Delmark

Produced
by Robert G. Koester

Recorded
at Sound Studios, Chicago; July 12 and October 25, 1967.

Released:
April 1968

Chart peaks:
None (UK) None (US)

Personnel:
Magic Sam Maghett (v, g); Mighty Joe Young (g); Stockholm Slim (p); Earnest Johnson (b); Odie Payne (d); Odie Payne III (d); Mack Thompson (b)

Track listing:
That's All I Need; I Need You So Bad; I Feel So Good (I Wanna Boogie); All Of Your Love; I Don't Want No Woman; Sweet Home Chicago; I Found A New Love; Every Night And Every Day; Lookin' Good; My Love Will Never Die; Mama Mama Talk To Your Daughter

Running time:
45.52

Current CD:
DD-615 adds: I Don't Want No Woman (alternate take)

Further listening:
follow-up Black Magic (1969); Easy Baby (1990), a collection of his early sides reissued by Charly.

Further reading:
Living Blues magazine, issues 125 (January–February 1996) and 127 (May–June 1996); www.laze.net/magicsam

Billy Nicholls
Would You Believe

Long-lost harmony-laden psych-pop rarity.

Immediate Records' head, Rolling Stones manager Andrew Loog Oldham was bowled over by the precocious talent of the 17-year-old singer/songwriter, who had been recommended to him by no less a person than George Harrison.

As Nicholls puts it, getting signed was a teenage dream; "Getting paid £20 a week, with my own room full of Revoxes, Mellotrons, and the Stones' guitars." Between writing songs for the album Oldham produced for Del Shannon, *Home And Away* (not released at the time, though tracks eventually turned up on various collections), and doing uncredited vocals on the Small Faces' classic *Ogden's Nut Gone Flake*, Nicholls got to make his own single, Would You Believe. Initially produced by Steve Marriott and Ronnie Lane, but an overambitious Oldham overlaid it with an orchestra, killing its commercial chances. (One wag called it "the most overproduced single of the '60s".)

While the ensuing *Would You Believe* album was comparatively modest, it fell foul of Immediate chaotic management and was left in the can, save for a few promo copies that became highly prized among collectors, some selling for over £1,000. Its reputation was enhanced by the knowledge that its credits included a veritable Who's Who of British late-'60s rockers: the Small Faces, John Paul Jones, Nicky Hopkins, Caleb Quaye, the great session guitarist Big Jim Sullivan, and Humble Pie drummer Jerry Shirley. Songs like the vibrant Girl From New York testify to what a great time Nicholls must have been having in the studio.

In 1998, Nicholls, by then a successful songwriter and musical director for The Who (and father to Morgan Nicholls of Senseless Things and Morgan), took pity on those lacking a large disposable income and made *Would You Believe* available to the masses for the first time, on his own Southwest label. It is greatly to his credit that the result was not a collective sigh of disappointment, as can be the case when long-hyped rarities are finally brought to light, but rather unanimous shouts of praise from critics and fans of song-oriented '60s pop.

Record label:
Immediate

Produced
by Steve Marriott, Ronnie Lane, and Andrew Loog Oldham.

Recorded
at Olympic Studios, Barnes, and IBC Studios, London; late 1967–early 1968.

Released:
April 1968

Chart peaks:
None (UK) None (US)

Personnel:
Billy Nicholls (ag, v, bv); Steve Marriott (g, bv); Ronnie Lane (b); Ian MacLagan (o); Kenny Jones (d); Big Jim Sullivan (g, ag); Caleb Quaye (p); Nicky Hopkins (k); John Paul Jones (b); Joe Moreti (g); Denny Gerrard (bv); Barry Husband (bv); Jerry Shirley (d); Arthur Greenslade, John Paul Jones, Denny Gerrard (oa)

Track listing:
Would You Believe; Come Again; Life Is Short; Feeling Easy; Daytime Girl; Daytime Girl Coda; London Social Degree; Portobello Road; Question Mark; Being Happy; Girl From New York; It Brings Me Down

Running time:
33.33

Current CD:
Sequel NENCD414 adds: Would You Believe (alternative take); Daytime Girl (alternative take)

Further listening:
Love Songs (1974); lone, self-titled album by a group that included Nicholls, White Horse (1976), both available on Nicholls's Southwest label.

Further reading:
www.nicholls.co.uk

Simon & Garfunkel
Bookends

Massively successful breakthrough album for former folkies.

*B*ookends was the fourth album from Simon & Garfunkel, but the first to reach a mass audience. Side One comprised a song-suite tracing the journey from birth to death – all original Simon compositions, aside from Voices Of Old People, drawn by Garfunkel from taped interviews with OAPs, which is the only jarring note in an otherwise seamless sweep.

Save The Life Of My Child reflects the raucous paranoia of America as the Vietnam war tore the nation apart, and parents everywhere scratched their heads and asked "What's become of the children?" It was also one of the first pop songs to use a synthesiser, and probably the first to use a sample – Simon & Garfunkel themselves can be heard singing Sounds Of Silence way down in the mix. America is timeless – a weary, disaffected odyssey – and its pristine production, blank-verse narrative and timely state-of-the-nation reflections, ensure that it sounds as fresh in the 21st century as it did in 1968. Overs is a bleak catalogue of marital breakdown, while the concluding Old Friends finds Simon reflecting: "How terribly strange to be 70" – not a sentiment shared, or cared-about, by many of his contemporaries at the time.

Never one to be rushed by a deadline, Simon didn't have enough new songs to complete *Bookends*, so the second side was padded out with previously released singles. Fakin' It was a dope-induced contemplation of an earlier life; Hazy Shade Of Winter had been a pounding, atmospheric single in 1967; while At The Zoo was an engaging, if none-too-subtle parable – human society symbolised by animals – but all matched Simon & Garfunkel's exacting standards. The two new songs were the quirky Punky's Dilemma – which director Mike Nichols rejected for *The Graduate* – and the song about that film's mature femme fatale, Mrs Robinson.

Simon & Garfunkel only had complete control of three of the five albums they recorded together, and in many ways *Bookends* stands as their finest moment. The duo stood in charge of the production and overall sound, and were eager to leave the formulas of pop-production and willing to experiment, which may help to explain the album's timeless quality. It was to be two years before there was another Simon & Garfunkel album, the all-conquering but, by comparison to *Bookends* a little sterile *Bridge Over Troubled Water*.

Record label:
CBS

Produced
by Paul Simon, Art Garfunkel, Roy Halee, Bob Johnson and John Simon.

Recorded
October 1967–February 1968.

Released:
April 1968

Chart peaks:
1 (UK) 1 (US)

Personnel:
Paul Simon (g, v); Art Garfunkel (v)

Track listing:
Bookends Theme; Save The Life Of My Child; America; Overs; Voices Of Old People; Old Friends; Bookends Theme; Fakin' It (S); Punky's Dilemma; Mrs Robinson (S); A Hazy Shade Of Winter (S); At The Zoo (S)

Running time:
29.45

Current CD:
Columbia CD 63101 P

Further listening:
Old Friends, Simon & Garfunkel box set (1997)

Further reading:
The Complete Guide To The Music Of Simon & Garfunkel (Chris Charlesworth, 1997); The Boy In The Bubble: The Paul Simon Story (Patrick Humphries, 1988); http://members.xoom.com/pspages/

Harper's Bizarre
The Secret Life Of . . .

A much underrated vocal group, smooth but perverse.

Marshmallow rock, soft and ultra-sweet. Maybe they shouldn't have added up to anything much – they didn't even boast a strong line in harmonies. But Harper's Bizarre possessed an indefinable something that set them apart from most other groups of the period.

Certainly everyone worthwhile at Warners thought so. Randy Newman pitched in to help them; so too did heavy-hitters Nick De Caro, Bob Thompson, Van Dyke Parks and Leon Russell. In their easy-on-the-ear way, Harper's Bizarre were ahead of the game, adventurous. They'd started out as The Tikis, a Santa Cruz band. Then, during 1966, they settled down as five-piece Harper's Bizarre (guitarist Eddie James having gone AWOL). They were still a young outfit – Scoppettone was 21 and Templeman 22 when they cut their debut album *Feelin' Groovy*, which gave them an immediate hit with a fizzy version of Simon and Garfunkel's 59th Street Bridge Song.

That first album set the mould. It included new songs from Parks and Newman, plus Happy Talk (from South Pacific) and, even dottier, a less-than-two-minutes-long rendition of Prokofiev's Peter And The Wolf. *Anything Goes* (1967) proved similarly diverse – Chattanooga Choo Choo, along with Van Dyke Parks' much-heralded High Coin. The stage was set for *The Secret Life*. This time around, the song selection was woven into a kind of Walter Mitty-ish dream sequence. Set against a recurring backdrop provided by Burton Lane and Yip Harburg's wistful Look To The Rainbow, the foursome sang of riding with cowboys, the battle of New Orleans, of building a stairway to paradise and other exploits that were hardly workaday and not exactly brimming with the radical spirit of '68.

The ultimate in melodic escapism, the album did little for the group's career and, in the wake of *Harper's Bizarre 4* (1970) – which featured contributions from Ry Cooder and Jack Nitzche – the group split, Templeton moving on to become an A&R mainman and significant producer at WEA. In 1976 the original line-up, minus Templeton, regrouped for a fifth album, *As Time Goes By*. But though some of the old idiosyncrasies remained – a theme from the New World Symphony rubbed shoulders with Back In The Saddle Again – the group's distinctive sound had, somewhere along the way, evaporated.

Record label:
Warner Brothers

Produced
by Lenny Waronker.

Recorded
in Hollywood; early 1968.

Released:
May 1968

Chart peaks:
None (UK) None, (US)

Personnel:
Dick Yount (b, v); John Peterson (d, v); Ted Templeman (g, t, v); Dick Scoppettone (g, v); Gloria Jones, Carolyn Willis, Sherlie Matthews (v, gospel choir)

Track listing:
Look To The Rainbow; Battle Of New Orleans; When I Was A Cowboy; Interlude; Sentimental Journey; Las Manitas; Bye Bye Bye/ Vine Street; Me Japanese Boy; Interlude; I'll Build A Stairway To Paradise; Green Apple Tree; Sit Down You're Rocking The Boat; Interlude; I Love You Mama; Funny How Love Can Be; Mad; Look To The Rainbow; The Drifter; Reprise

Running time:
33.52

Not currently available on CD

Further listening:
Feelin' Groovy: The Best Of Harper's Bizarre (1997), the only music by the group available in the UK, includes the magical Witchi-Tai-To.

Further reading:
There's next to nothing available, although the 16-page booklet enclosed with the above CD contains an informative interview with Lenny Waronker.

Iron Butterfly
In-A-Gadda-Da-Vida

Herein the Iliad and Odyssey of heavy metal jamming.

Technically speaking, there was no Iron Butterfly on the night the band christened the glorified riff that would become its biggest hit and ticket to immortality. The band had already made one album, *Heavy*, but because of disputes between its producers and Atlantic and between members of the band, Iron Butterfly were no longer airborne. While the two remaining members, keyboardist Doug Ingle and drummer Ron Bushy, looked for new members, things grew so dire that Bushy was actually hawking pizza at a Sunset Strip nightclub. One night, upon returning to the apartment he shared with Ingle, Bushy found his roommate in a state of delirium. Not only had he been up for nearly two days, he had consumed almost a gallon of Red Mountain wine and possessed all the verbal dexterity of a caveman. He told Bushy he'd been writing a new song. Bushy could not make out the words, so he wrote them down phonetically: In-A-Gadda-Da-Vida. Only later did he learn that Ingle had been mumbling, "in the Garden of Eden".

Of course there is more to the song than its weird title. A classically trained keyboardist, Ingle needed constant reminders not to play bass with his left hand. Bass player Lee Dorman took one of those superfluous lines and simplified it to make what is arguably the most primal riff in all of rock. Though the other (surprisingly poppy) tunes on *In-A-Gadda-Da-Vida* were recorded in Hollywood, the famed 17-minute opus was recorded on Long Island, while the band took a break from touring with Jefferson Airplane.

When they turned up at Ultra-Sonic Studios, producer Jim Hilton had not yet driven out from New York City. To save time, studio owner Bones Howe asked if there was a song they could play to set volume levels. "We said, 'We have this really long song that we want to record and throughout it we have solos where each instrument is featured,'" says Dorman. Perfect. Off they went with what the band assumed was a sound check. For some reason, the engineers rolled tape, and they got virtually the entire song in one take. Though Atlantic first baulked at releasing the heavy epic (it had to be edited down to 2.52 for radio play), the label finally gave in and must be glad they did. The album sold 4 million copies in the US alone; until Led Zeppelin came along it was Atlantic's top seller.

Record label:
Atco

Produced
by Jim Hilton.

Recorded
at Gold Star Studios, Hollywood, California and Ultra-Sonic Studios, Hempstead, LI; spring 1968.

Released:
June 14, 1968.

Chart peaks:
None (UK) 4 (US)

Personnel:
Doug Ingle (k, v); Ron Bushy (d); Lee Dorman (b, v); Erik Brann (g, v)

Track listing:
Most Anything You Want; Flowers And Beads; My Mirage; Termination; Are You Happy; In-A-Gadda-Da-Vida

Running time:
36.00

Current CD:
7567903922

Further listening:
Rhino's deluxe re-release, Iron Butterfly: In-A-Gadda-Da-Vida (1996) includes three versions of the song — the original epic, the single and a live version — plus all original album tracks.

Further reading:
The Iron Butterfly website is at www.ironbutterfly.com

Os Mutantes
Os Mutantes

Eccentric Brazilian trio invent Psouth American Psych.

T he explosion of invention in mid-60s pop was startling
enough to anyone listening on the Anglo-American axis.
Imagine how it must have sounded in a place where music
followed rigid traditional guidelines and "pop" was the province
of fife and drum bands. When a particularly insane Brazilian
rock trio called Os Mutantes (The Mutants) unveiled a mischievous, wayward hybrid of Pepper Beatles, Piper Floyd and
Disraeli Cream having a bossa-nova jam – at a popular Brazilian
music festival in September 1967, no one was too surprised
when the crowd started booing and throwing things, or when
the use of electric guitars was subsequently banned at the
festival.

Originally from São Paolo, Os Mutantes became the
adopted rock band of the Tropicalia movement, a group of
artists from Bahia state who brought together music, pop art
and concrete poetry to good-humouredly undermine conservative tradition and irritate the ruling military regime, taking
pleasure in sending-up Brazilian sacred cows or appearing on TV
in plastic trousers for a dada freak-out. Eccentric singer and
percussionist Rita Lee, her loopy husband Arnaldo Baptista and
his brother Sergio, all still in their teens, were guaranteed to
delight or offend as required. A third Baptista brother remained
off-stage building guitars for Sergio and creating fearsome
musical devices out of electric sewing machines. There were also
contributions from Tropicalia's pet orchestrator, the gifted
Rogério Duprat.

This, the team's debut album was a lovely antic party in
Portuguese, featuring wild versions of their contemporaries'
songs. Tropicalia colleagues Caetano Veloso, Gilberto Gil and
Jorge Ben were all present, as was a cover of The Mamas and
Papas' Once Was A Time I Thought (translated into Portuguese
by the Baptistas' dad, a noted Brazilian poet) and an alkaline
guitar sound which seared its way across Veloso's languid blues
for the modern era, Baby.

Inspired by *Sgt Pepper* to experiment in the studio, their
more peculiar inventions included using aerosol sprays in place
of cymbals and serving a meal in the vocal booth and recording
the prandial proceedings. One might assume that they were
familiar with psychedelic drugs. In fact, the Baptista brothers
were naturally bizarre enough not to need any chemical assis-

Record label:
Polydor

Produced
by Manuel Barenbeim.

Recorded
at Philips Studios, Brasil; 1967–1968.

Released:
June 1968

Chart peaks:
None (UK) None (US)

Personnel:
Rita Lee (v, pc, flute); Arnaldo Baptista
(b, v); Sergio Dias Baptista (g); Rogerio
Duprat (oa)

Track listing:
Panis Et Circencis; A Minha Menina; O
Relogio; Adeus Maria Fulo; Baby; Senhor
F; Bat Macumba; Le Premier Bonheur Du
Jour; Trem Fantasma; Tempo No Tempo;
Ave Genghis Khan

Running time:
36.01

Current CD:
Omplatten FJORD001

Further listening:
Mutantes (1969); A Divina Comedia Ou
Ando Meio Desligado (1970); Technicolor
(1970) recently released collection of
highlights re-recorded in English, never
issued at the time. Jardim Eléctrico
(1971); Arnaldo Baptista's solo album
tribute to his lost love, Rita (1974);
Everything Is Possible: The Best Of Os
Mutantes (1999)

Further reading:
www.slipcue.com/music/brazil/mutantes.html

tance, and didn't sample acid until they visited London in 1970.

Their crazy dream went sour in 1972 when Rita and Arnaldo split after a studio quarrel and she began a successful solo career. Relations between the two factions have been intensely awkward ever since. The brothers' subsequent albums went into the realms of prog-rock and Arnaldo descended into something akin to Brazil's answer to Syd Barret. But at their peak they were producing some of the '60s most vital music – in any language.

Small Faces
Ogdens' Nut Gone Flake

Mods go prog on loveably nutty concept album in circular tobacco-tin sleeve.

1968 had started out bumpily for the Small Faces, first with organist Ian McLagan getting nicked for drug possession at Heathrow Airport and then a gruelling visit to Australia with The Who, which saw both groups herded around at gun-point after an ill-tempered slanging match with the tabloid press. A second album for Andrew Oldham's Immediate Records was due in the summer, and work on it had been slow so, around Easter time Oldham dispatched the band on a barging holiday up the Thames to replenish their creative juices and, more importantly, finish the new songs.

With dogs, girlfriends and guitars in tow, the group journeyed lazily from Henley to Maidenhead, pleasantly stoned on a mixture of LSD, booze and hash. In between visits to riverside pubs and several nautical disasters, a 'concept' for their new record was hatched, relating to the mystical *rite de passage* of a psychedelic chap called Happiness Stan and his quest to find where the moon went when it waned.

Soon their new Sony cassette machine was full of ideas for songs like The Hungry Intruder, The Journey and Happydaystoytown, whose baroque, bombastic melodies and tragi-comic lyrics had strong echoes of the music hall of their native East End, as well reflecting the growing obsession with Victoriana that had followed in the wake of *Sgt. Pepper*.

Throughout May, the band refined the tracks at Olympic Studios, fleshing them out with harpsichord, Mellotron and brass, under the watchful eye of legendary engineer Glyn Johns. "The idea was to let the group's imagination run wild," remembers Andrew Oldham. "It was like, You wanna go off and live on a barge for a month? Fine. You wanna spend months in the studio doing this record? Great. The most important thing was creating something new and exciting."

The band originally asked Spike Milligan to script and narrate the links between the Happiness Stan tracks on Side Two, but he was unavailable so Stanley Unwin was drafted in instead. Famed for his jumbled, surreal manner of speaking, he had the band in fits of laughter with his barmy version of their '60s rock speak: "What's bin your hang up, man? Blow your cool, man."

Already in the bag were a handful of rockier songs that

Record label:
Immediate

Produced
by Steve Marriott and Ronnie Lane

Recorded
at Olympic, Pye, Trident, spring 1968

Release date:
June 1968

Chart peaks:
1 (UK) None (US)

Personnel:
Steve Marriott (g,v), Ronnie Lane (b,v), Ian McLagan (k,v), Kenny Jones (d), Stanley Unwin (narration). Glyn Johns (e)

Track listing:
Ogdens' Nut Gone Flake; Afterglow (Of Your Love) (S); Long Agos And Worlds Apart; Rene; Son Of A Baker; Lazy Sunday (S); Happiness Stan; Rollin' Over; The Hungry Intruder; The Journey; Mad John; Happydaystoytown

Running time:
38.31

Current CD:
Castle ORRLP001 adds Tin Soldier

Further listening:
their first Immediate album, Small Faces (1967), is a must-have and is currently available with extra tracks, while Autumn Stone (1969) mops up late-era rarities and hits.

Further reading:
McLagan's autobiography All The Rage (Sidgwick & Jackson) and Quite Naturally: A Day-By-Day Guide by Keith Badman and Terry Rawlings (Complete Music Publications).

eventually filled the first side, including the steely drive of Song Of A Baker (sung by Ronnie), the Foxy Lady-ish Rollin' Over – all throat-shredding Marriott vocals and heavy guitar – and Lazy Sunday, the Cockney sing-along which the band grew to regret after it was released as a single, thus further pigeonholing them as a novelty knees-up band. Ironically, the album's crowning glory would probably have met the same fate; the brilliant, musical hall-inspired Rene was a delightfully raucous, rinky-dink romp about a dockside prostitute with illegitimate kids "of many shapes and colours", who nightly could be found "groping with a stoker from the coast of Kuala Lumpur".

On its release in June 1968, in the first ever circular album sleeve with artwork inspired by a tin of ready-rubbed tobacco, *Ogdens* shot straight to Number 1. The experience both established the band as a major commercial force in the serious 'rock' market, and sowed the seeds of its destruction, the group feeling they could never better it (they split in March 1969, having failed to produce a follow-up). In *Ogdens*, though, they had undoubtedly produced one of the freshest and most unusual albums of the late '60s, with a joyous spirit few bands have ever matched since.

The Beach Boys
Friends

"I haven't talked to anyone who's discovered Friends," says Beach Boy Bruce Johnston. "They think it's a TV show."

*F*riends remains, perhaps, The Beach Boys' most misunderstood and underrated album. Upon its release in the early summer of 1968, it was thought to confirm the once mighty group's swift decline into commercial and cultural irrelevancy. Its American chart peak of 126 was profoundly lower than any of its 18 predecessors.

Friends is a polar opposite to the lushly orchestrated, hyper-emotional density of Pet Sounds. Friends also signifies the moment at which much of the group's remaining fanbase abandoned any hope that Brian Wilson would deliver a true successor to his 1966 masterwork. Spare, calm and "full of air", says Johnston, Friends was the result of the group's deliberate attempt to make "a really subtle album that wasn't concerned with radio". Indeed, the album's dozen shockingly brief tracks (five are under two minutes) rarely last long enough to anchor their delicate hooks before swiftly fading out. Only its lovely, waltz-time title track charted (and was, incidentally, the band's lowest charting single in six years).

It could be argued that virtually anything The Beach Boys might have released during the musical, cultural and political upheavals of 1968 would have failed. "The Beach Boys were just unfashionably unhip," admits Johnston. "*Friends* came out just after Hendrix and Cream. The whole country had discovered drugs, discovered words, discovered Marshall amplifiers, and here comes this feather floating through a wall of noise." Given distance and hindsight, however, Friends is a uniquely rewarding Beach Boys album that, excepting Pet Sounds, is the group's most sonically and thematically unified. Its 26 weightless minutes make up possibly the sweetest album ever to be filed under rock.

Significantly, Friends also marked the songwriting debut of drummer Dennis, whose beautifully fragile Be Still and Little Bird are highlights, signalling his development into a songwriter of major emotional reach. Friends has won many admirers since its initial humiliating launch. In his 1991 autobiography, Brian himself called it "my favourite Beach Boys album".

Record label:
Capitol

Produced
by The Beach Boys.

Recorded
at Brian Wilson's home studio, Bel Air, California; I.D. Sound Los Angeles; February–April 1968.

Released:
July 1968

Chart peaks:
6 (UK) 126 (US)

Personnel:
Mike Love (v, s); Carl Wilson (v, g, k); Alan Jardine (g, v); Brian Wilson (k, g, v); Dennis Wilson (v, d, k)

Track listing:
Meant For You; Friends; Wake The World; Be Here In The Morning; When A Man Needs A Woman; Passing By; Anna Lee, The Healer; Little Bird; Be Still; Busy Doin' Nothin'; Diamond Head; Transcendental Meditation

Running time:
25.58

Current CD:
CDP7936972 adds 20/20

Further listening:
20/20 (1969); Sunflower (1970)

Further reading:
The Nearest Faraway Place (Timothy White, 1996); www.hollywoodandvine.com/beachboys

Dr John, The Night Tripper

Gris-Gris

The record that transformed session player Mac Rebennack into post-hippie psychedelic voodoo king Dr John.

Mac Rebennack had no intention of singing on this brooding underground classic; New Orleans belter Ronnie Barron had been designated for the job. But with Barron unavailable – "his manager thought it was a bad career move" – the man who had worked as a session keyboardist and guitar player (until a gunshot wound put paid to the picking) on albums by Professor Longhair, Joe Tex and Frankie Ford, morphed into his alter ego – mystical, menacing growler Dr John, The Night Tripper, a character he had learned about in the '50s from voodoo artist Prince LaLa.

"I said, Oh, I'll just do it," recalls the Doctor. "I figured it would be a one-off thing. I was thinking this is probably going to only sell four records in New Orleans."

Rebennack was familiar with the mystery and magic of Crescent City – his nightmarish 1965 *Zu Zu Man* borrowed liberally from the voodoo chants and incantations that were as prevalent as incense smoke in the tawdry French Quarter. But *Gris Gris* went further, grafting voodoo's dark, esoteric heart to a hypnotic groove with funky blues, sparse, repetitive minor chord melodies, funereal keyboards and Afro-Cuban syncopation shot through with feral noises, gibberish and metaphysical threats and boasts, creating an unwholesome witchy brew of sorcery and chicanery that fascinates as much as it disturbs.

"One thing I always did was believe. I used to play for gigs for the Gris-Gris church. I dug the music, and that's what I was trying to capture." Using left-over time at Gold Star from a Sonny and Cher session, Dr John and his fellow refugees did their best to turn the legendary studio into a voodoo church – to the consternation of the staff. "I remember Hugh Masekela was cutting next door to us – he was doing his first record, too – and the engineers at Gold Star were nervous. They were used to Phil Spector and Sonny Bono and people like that coming in, and they saw my crew and next door they saw Hugh's crew and these guys didn't look like your regulation studio-looking kind of guys, and we were burning candles and incense to get into the mood and everything. But I got a kick out of that."

Centrepiece Walk On Gilded Splinters – a song since covered by artists as diverse as Humble Pie, Allman Brothers, Paul Weller, and Marsha Hunt and sampled by PM Dawn and

Record label:
Atlantic

Produced
by Harold Battiste.

Recorded
at Gold Star Studio, Los Angeles, California; autumn 1967.

Released:
July 1968

Chart peaks:
None (UK) None (US)

Personnel:
Max Rebennack, (v, g, o); Steve Mann (g); Alvin 'Shine' Robinson (g, v); Ernest McLean (g); Harold Battiste (bs, clarinet); Ron Johnson (b); David West (b); Richard 'Didimus' Washington (d, pc); John Boudreaux (d); Dave Dixon (v, pc); Jessie Hill (v); Shirley Goodman (v); Tami Lynn (v); Joanie Jones (v); Sonny Raye (v); Ronnie Barron (v, o); Morris Bachamin (ts); Plas Johnson (s)

Track listing:
Gris-Gris Gumbo Ya Ya; Danse Kalinda Ba Boom; Mama Roux (US/S); Danse Fambeaux; Croker Courtbullion; Jump Sturdy (US/S); I Walk On Gilded Splinters

Running time:
33.32

Current CD:
CCM 131-1 R2 7508

Further listening:
Babylon (1969); Gumbo (1972); Dr John Plays Mac Rebennack (1982); Anutha Zone (1998)

Further reading:
Under A Hoodoo Moon: The Life of the Night Tripper (Mac Rebennack with Jack Rummel, 1994) www.drjohn.com

Beck — was based on a traditional voodoo church song. "It's supposed to be 'Splendors' but I turned it into 'Splinters'," said the Doctor. "I just thought splinters sounded better and I always pictured splinters when I sung it." And the ambling, subliminal title cut wormed its way into the nascent waves of American FM radio where it became a late night staple, catching the cresting wave of psychedelia and hippiedom. More than three decades on, the album retains its extraordinary power to cast a spell.

J.K. & Co.
Suddenly One Summer

Dreamy psychedelia from Canada! Now a cult classic.

One of those treasured items record collectors occasionally stumble across and pick up merely because they find the cover to be interestingly tacky, *Suddenly One Summer* has proven to be a jewel of a record, albeit a mystifying one. Canadian in origin, and issued in the US on White Whale Records – a label with a bizarrely eclectic artist roster that included The Turtles, Nino Tempo And April Stevens, and British under-achievers John's Children – the record is a whooshing, floating trip.

As its cover credits only three humans to speak of – and anonymously named ones at that – one is left to ponder whether J.K. & Co was in fact a band or a psychedelic predecessor of the Alan Parsons Project. In some ways it indeed seems a producer's record: opening vocal track Fly boasts a drum sound lifted straight off The Beatles' A Day In The Life; a sitar can be heard on The Magical Fingers Of Minerva; Little Children features the inevitable sound effect of children at play and actually breaks into a few bars of Frere Jacques; and, most appropriately, album closer Dead includes the voice of a clergyman invoking burial rites, and – nice touch, this – the sound of someone shovelling actual dirt.

But what holds *Suddenly One Summer* together throughout is the voice and song of one Jay Kaye, who has crafted a rather special song cycle. From its whirling beginning – in which Kaye in lazy reverie sings, "If you want to fly . . ." – through the troubled lyrics of Nobody ("My happiness is a needle/I will escape for another day"), which recalls Love's Signed D.C. – to the cheery sound of that gravedigger's shovel, there's a story of some sort being told here.

Consider this one of those late '60s psychedelic concept albums – Ford Theatre's *Trilogy For The Masses* and Mandrake Memorial's *Puzzle* are two others – that in their ambition to tell some sort of life parable emerge with an oddly open-ended suite that can be interpreted in any manner the listener finds appropriate. In the end, the big question is less the matter of J.K.'s identity and more the motivation of the people who made the record – not to mention the expectations of the label that decided to release it. Stranger still is how Fly manages to antici-pate Radiohead's OK Computer, a mere 30 years beforehand. What goes around . . .

Record label:
White Whale

Produced
by RH Spurgin.

Recorded
at Vancouver Recording, Canada, dates unknown.

Released:
July 1968

Chart peaks:
None (UK) None (US)

Personnel:
Jay Kaye; (all instruments, v); RW Buckley (a)

Track listing:
Break Of Dawn; Fly; Little Children; Christine; Speed; Crystal Ball; Nobody; O.D; Land Of Sensations & Delights; The Times; Magical Fingers Of Minerva; Dead

Running time:
33.03

Currently unavailable
on legitimate CD, though bootlegs exist.

Further listening:
Ford Theatre, Trilogy For The Masses (1968); Mandrake Memorial, Puzzle (1970)

Further reading:
You just read it!

The Millennium
Begin

Ambitious, avant-garde, but accessible West Coast genius from a legendary cult figure

The Millennium were the brainchild of LA-based producer Curt Boettcher (1943–1987), whose work on The Association's 1966 debut album had yielded the hits Along Comes Mary and Cherish. Seeing himself as an auteur in the Phil Spector mould, Boettcher sought a broad canvas for his outpouring of ideas. His production partner was Keith Olsen, a whiz-kid engineer who quit his gig as bass player in the Music Machine to follow Boettcher's lead. (Olsen would later become a hit producer himself for Fleetwood Mac, The Grateful Dead, and others.)

Armed with a concept and a partner, all Boettcher needed was an angel. He found one in the form of Brian Wilson's former writing partner, Gary Usher. A staff producer at Columbia, Usher first learned of Boettcher in 1966, when he heard strange sounds wafting down the hall at Studio Three West. As Usher (who died in 1990) later recalled, he was not the only one who was impressed; "Brian Wilson said, 'What is *that*?'" It was Boettcher doing a single with future Millennium member Lee Mallory. "That record stunned Brian. He's doing little surfer music, and here comes this kid who is light years ahead of him. I had never seen Brian turn white. All he could talk about for a week was that song and that kid. Brian sensed that that was where it was at, that's where it was going."

In early 1967, Usher heard Boettcher's music again, when Boettcher was in the Ballroom, which also included future Millennium member Sandy Salisbury. Through Usher, Boettcher and Olsen got a Columbia production contract which enabled them to follow their muse.

Although The Millennium was conceived as a studio group, its line-up was solid. In addition to Mallory, Salisbury, and Boettcher, it included former Music Machine members Ron Edgar and Doug Rhodes, newcomer Joey Stec, and future Crabby Appleton leader Michael Fennelly.

Begin was recorded on two jerryrigged 8-track machines, making it only the second album to use 16-track technology. (Simon And Garfunkel's *Bookends* was the first.) The sound is dense; Boettcher's philosophy could be summed up as, 'Sixteen tracks and every one of them has to be filled!' At the same time, it escapes being a Wall of Mush; in fact, it sounds

Record label:
Columbia

Produced
by Curt Boettcher and Keith Olsen.

Recorded
at Columbia Studios, Los Angeles; early 1967 to mid 1968.

Released:
July 1968

Chart peaks:
None (UK) None (US)

Personnel:
Curt Boettcher (v, g); Lee Mallory (v, g); Doug Rhodes (b, tuba, p, o, harpsichord, v); Ron Edgar (d, pc, v); Michael Fennelly (v, g); Joey Stec (v, g); Sandy Salisbury (v); Michelle O'Malley (v); Red Rhodes (ps); Mike Deasy (g); Toxie French (d); Jerry Scheff (b); Pat Shanahan (d) Paulinho DaCosta (pc)

Track listing:
Prelude; To Claudia On Thursday; I Just Want To Be Your Friend; 5am; I'm With You; The Island; Sing To Me; It's You; Some Sunny Day; It Won't Always Be The Same; The Know It All; Karmic Dream Sequence #1; There Is Nothing More To Say; Anthem (Begin)

Running time:
43.15

Current CD:
Rev-Ola CREV052 adds: Just About The Same; Blight

Further listening:
The album made by Curt Boettcher and various Millenium personnel as Sagittarius, Present Tense (1968); the first release of material by the band pre-Millennium, as The Ballroom, Preparing For The Millennium (1998)

Further reading:
www.geocities.com/Hollywood/3218 (The
Millennium Home Page)

strikingly modern, rendering the West Coast vocal-harmony
sound of the time with a lush intricacy. The songs are as strong
as the production, too: Fennelly-Stec composition It's You
presages '70s power pop, while Boettcher's The Island sparkles
like beach glass in the sun. It's no surprise that the album is a
favourite of contemporary pop confectioners such as Belle And
Sebastian, Saint Etienne, and The High Llamas. Even in 1968,
when *Begin* died a commercial death, there were people who
knew that it pointed towards the sound of the next millennium.
And then, there were also those who didn't want to know. "I
sent Brian [Wilson] a copy of The Millennium album," Usher
recalled. "Freaked him out. He never called me back."

The Band
Music From Big Pink

Astonishing debut from Dylan's backing band, a soulful throwback completely against the grain of the times.

Following a gruelling period backing Bob Dylan on his 1966 world tour, the musicians later christened "The Band" by Capitol Records (in preference to the more controversial "Crackers") re-grouped at their Woodstock hideaway Big Pink, where the informal sessions that resulted in Dylan's *Basement Tapes* also gave rise to the material that made up their own debut album. Recorded with the imaginative young producer John Simon at sessions in New York and Los Angeles, these songs favoured the wisdom and values of a shared tradition over the transitory upheavals of the youth movement.

"The songs were more like buried treasure from American lore than new songs by contemporary artists," claims John Simon. "They were playing out of what I called their 'Appalachian scale', a pentatonic, five-note scale like the black keys on the piano. That was the palette from which those melodies came."

Lyrically, the band's main songwriter Robbie Robertson had clearly learnt much from his time with Dylan, whose hand was initially believed by many to be behind the mythopoeic single The Weight. Dylan did, however, collaborate with Rick Danko and Richard Manuel on This Wheel's On Fire and Tears Of Rage respectively (as well as providing the surreal-naïve cover painting), while The Band's version of his I Shall Be Released became the definitive version of this modern liberation anthem.

"The music was the sum of all the experiences we'd shared for the past ten years, distilled through the quieter vibe of our lives in the country," believes Levon Helm. Yet for all its traditional virtues, the album featured several innovatory musical strategies, notably from inventive organist Garth Hudson.

The album kick-started the "country-rock" trend – a term they hated – and was an immediate critical success. Reviewers in *Time*, *Life* and *Rolling Stone* acclaimed it as a work which presciently articulated contemporary doubts and uncertainties about the direction of American "progress", while musicians such as George Harrison and Eric Clapton also garlanded it with praise. Appropriately enough, it is one of the few recordings from its era whose power remains immune to the passage of time.

Record Label:
Capitol

Produced
by John Simon.

Recorded
at A&R Studios, New York; Capitol Studios, Los Angeles; January–March 1968.

Release date:
August 1968

Chart peaks:
25 (UK) 30 (US)

Personnel:
Jaime Robbie Robertson (g, v); Rick Danko (b, v); Richard Manuel (k, v); Garth Hudson (k, s); Levon Helm (d, v); John Simon (horns); Shelly Yakus (e); Rex Updegraft (e)

Track Listing:
Tears Of Rage; To Kingdom Come; In A Station; Caledonia Mission; The Weight (S); We Can Talk; Long Black Veil; Chest Fever; Lonesome Suzie; This Wheel's On Fire; I Shall Be Released

Running time:
42.03

Current CD:
CDP 7 46069 2

Further listening:
Follow-up The Band (1969) is, if anything, even better. Stage Fright (1970), Northern Lights – Southern Cross (1975) and live triple Rock Of Ages (1972) are the best of their other albums. Robbie Robertson, Rick Danko and Levon Helm each subsequently released several solo albums.

Further reading:
Across The Great Divide (Barney Hoskyns, 1993); This Wheel's On Fire: Levon Helm And The Story Of The Band (Levon Helm with Stephen Davis, 1993); http://theband.hiof.no/

Blue Cheer

Outsideinside

Second album by San Francisco lysergic hard rock outfit who sowed the seeds of punk and grunge.

Blue Cheer's fearsome reputation as one of the founding fathers of the metal genre is largely due to the ferocity of their bombastic *Vincebus Eruptum* debut. A fine example of cro-magnon hard rock, it featured a deranged re-working of Eddie Cochran's Summertime Blues along with a similarly crazed cover of Mose Allison's Parchment Farm. While *Vincebus* can be seen as reflecting the growing sense of social unrest and violence fuelled by the escalation of the Vietnam conflict, it also happens to sound one-dimensional when placed alongside Blue Cheer's second effort, *Outsideinside*.

The album's intriguing title is down to the fact that the threesome of Dickie Peterson, Leigh Stevens (as he's credited on the sleeve, despite spelling his surname Stephens) and Paul Whaley elected to record half of the album outdoors. Rock mythology suggests that this occured after the band's use of excessive volume caused too much damage to assorted studios.

The result adds a melodic edge to Blue Cheer's patented sonic assault. Tracks like Sun Cycle and Gypsy Ball, for instance, both bear testimony to Jimi Hendrix's influence on the trio, the latter nodding in the direction of The Wind Cries Mary and making the most of the newfound joys of stereo panning.

High-octane tracks like Come And Get It point the way forward for the likes of the MC5, Just A Little Bit boasts a similar feel to Hendrix's re-working of Fire, while the fantasti-cally titled Magnolia Caboose Babyfinger is an instrumental piece of proto-grunge which Mudhoney would later cover. Elsewhere, Blue Cheer attempt to emulate the success of their Summertime Blues cover by turning their hand to a version of the Stones's (I Can't Get No) Satisfaction, delivering it at double the speed. Album closer Babylon is a further slice of funky, cowbell-banging hard rock.

Virtually ignored on its release (most UK publications didn't even bother to review the album), *Outsideinside* just about managed to sneak into the Billboard 100 in the US. A remark-able dip in form when you consider that *Vincebus...* managed to peak at Number 11 less than 12 months earlier.

Outsideinside remains a criminally under-rated second effort from a band whose legacy is substantial but who have yet to receive the credit for embarking on what Leigh Stevens describes as "a violent and frightening trip".

Record label:
Mercury

Produced
by Abe 'Voco' Kesh.

Recorded outside
at Gate 5, Sausalito, and Muir Beach, California; Pier 57 (Department Of Marine And Aviation), New York City; studio sessions recorded at Pacific Recorders, San Mateo, California; A&R Studios, Olmstead Studios and The Record Plant, New York City; early 1968.

Released:
August 1968

Chart peaks:
None (UK) 90 (US)

Personnel:
Dickie Peterson (b, v); Leigh Stevens (g, v); Paul Whaley (d, v); Ralph Burns Kellogg (k); Eric Albronda (v); Eddie Kramer, Hank McGill, Jay Snyder, Tony May (e)

Track listing:
Feathers From Your Tree (S); Sun Cycle (S); Just A Little Bit; Gypsy Ball; Come And Get It; (I Can't Get No) Satisfaction; The Hunter; Magnolia Caboose Babyfinger; Babylon

Running time:
33.10

Current CD:
Line AK012

Further listening:
Vincebus Eruptum (1968); New! Improved! (1969)

Further reading:
the official Blue Cheer site at: http://bp.bpcwsb.com/inet.files/fo01.htm#bl uecheer15 The site offers a fantastic set of images as well as links to the indi-vidual sites run by band members, including the ever-active Dickie Peterson.

Nilsson
Aerial Ballet

The Beatles' favourite songwriter and group.

"I always thought," mused Harry Nilsson, "I was a street cat who could pass for someone who went to college." *Aerial Ballet*, his second album, perfectly showcases his unique, utterly charming blend of earthiness and airiness. In an era bloated with confessional songwriters, Nilsson was a contradiction. His lyrics often seemed extraordinarily intimate, yet he bristled when fans attempted to read too much meaning into them. He was accommodating enough to explain the album's title — Nilsson's Aerial Ballet was a name his grandparents used for their trapeze act. However, when asked the meaning of one of his songs, he was likely to give an answer like the one he gave Hugh Hefner on TV's Playboy After Dark. Hef had inquired as to the inspiration behind *Aerial Ballet*'s Good Old Desk. With a straight face, Nilsson replied that the song's meaning was in its initials: G.O.D.; "I bullshitted him," Harry admitted later. "I thought it was funny. Nobody else thought it was funny!"

Shortly before the release of *Aerial Ballet*, Nilsson's career received the kind of boost most performers can only dream of. Derek Taylor, The Beatles' close friend and former press agent, had given the group a copy of Nilsson's first album, *Pandemonium Shadow Show*. At an Apple press conference, when asked to name their favourite singer, The Beatles said "Nilsson". Asked about their favourite group, they gave the same reply. Nilsson subsequently met the Fabs during a trip to England, where he played Lennon *Aerial Ballet*. Lennon especially liked Mr. Richland's Favorite Song (named after record promoter Tony Richland). Recalling those times with Lennon, Nilsson told Rolling Stone, "I really fell in love with him. I knew he was all those things you wanted somebody to be."

Although it was largely Nilsson's songwriting that impressed The Beatles, it was *Aerial Ballet*'s lone non-original that would catapult him to fame. According to legend, it was the inexhaustible Taylor who turned director John Schlesinger on to Nilsson's version of Fred Neil's Everybody's Talkin', which had an unsuccessful run as a single on *Aerial Ballet*'s release. When it emerged in August 1969 as a single from the film's soundtrack, it became an international smash. Everybody's Talkin' won Nilsson his first Grammy: Best Contemporary Vocal Performance, Male.

Record label:
RCA

Produced
by Rick Jarrard.

Recorded
at RCA Victor's Music Center of the World, Los Angeles; late 1967–early 1968.

Released:
August 1968

Chart peaks:
None (UK) None (US)

Personnel:
Harry Nilsson (v); Larry Knechtel (b, p); Lyle Ritz (b); Al Casey (g); Dennis Budimir (g); Michael Melvoin (harpsichord, o, p). With orchestra; George Tipton (a)

Track listing:
Good Old Desk; Don't Leave Me; Mr Richland's Favorite Song; Little Cowboy; Together; Everybody's Talkin'; I Said Goodbye To Me; Little Cowboy (reprise); Mr. Tinker; One; The Wailing Of The Willow; Bath

Running time:
25.15

Current CD:
74321 757422 2CD set includes Pandemonium Shadow Show and Aerial Pandemonium Ballet, the 1971 remixed compilation of the two albums.

Further listening:
Nilsson said that his albums came in trilogies. Aerial Ballet could be said to be the middle of a trilogy that began with his debut, Pandemonium Shadow Show (1967), and ended with Harry (1969), both highly recommended.

Further reading:
www.jadebox.com/nilsson

David Ackles

David Ackles

A former toilet-factory security guard taps into the American heartland on classic debut.

Born into a showbiz family, at the age of four David Ackles was half of a song-and-dance act with his sister, and in his early teens was a Hollywood B-movie child actor. Contracted to Elektra purely as a songwriter in the late '60s, label boss Jac Holzman soon realised that compositions as idiosyncratic as The Road To Cairo, about a man immobilised by fear, or His Name Is Andrew, detailing the pain of lost faith, would best be served if Ackles sang them himself. Partnered with his old school-friend David Anderle as producer, he set to work recording and orchestrating his poignant story-songs.

"We had to make that album twice to get what I wanted," explained Ackles later. The second attempt came when Ackles was introduced to Rhinoceros, another recent Elektra signing. "We sat around and I played the songs and they filled in, and we just had such a good time. We knew that was the right thing to do."

The album offered the intelligence and imagery of Leonard Cohen without the self-pity, as it stumbled along on Ackles' curious piano rhythms, augmented with Michael Fonfara's whistling organ and Doug Hastings' empathetic guitar filigrees. These collaborative arrangements tended towards stagey structures, as if written for some half-realised off-Broadway musical, ideal for tracks like Down River, an ingeniously plotted, semi-autobiographical, one-sided conversation with a sting in its tail. Ackles later recalled the sessions as "an easy-going, friendly affair", but the atmosphere was shot through with the singer's world-weary aching and loneliness. On release, *Rolling Stone* complimented his voice but reckoned his melodies were "almost no melodies at all" while the nearest *Record Mirror* got to a positive comment was "a plaintive sort of collection". After four unsuccessful albums, Ackles became variously a lecturer, TV scriptwriter and scorer of ballets. As if he was becoming a character in one of his own songs, various accidents left him with an all-but crippled arm and a steel hip before he had his first encounter with cancer. Tracked down in 1994, Ackles said, "I'm really enjoying my life, which will no doubt come as a shock to fans of my first two albums, in whose angst they swim." On March 2, 1999, David Ackles died of lung cancer, leaving a legacy of four of the most beautiful but rarely heard albums of his era.

Record Label:
Elektra

Produced
by David Anderle and Russ Miller.

Recording
location unknown.

Released:
September 3, 1968

Chart peaks:
None (UK) None (US)

Running time:
37.54

Personnel:
David Ackles (p, v); Michael Fonfara (o); Danny Weis (g); Douglas Hastings (g); Jerry Penrod (b); John Keliehor (pc)

Track Listing:
The Road To Cairo (S); When Love Is Gone; Sonny Come Home; Blue Ribbons; What A Happy Day; Down River (S); Laissez-Faire (S); Lotus Man; His Name Is Andrew; Be My Friend

Currently unavailable on CD

Further listening:
American Gothic (1972)

Further reading:
MOJO 57;
http://www.mathie.demon.co.uk/da/

The Byrds
Sweetheart Of The Rodeo

The Byrds unintentionally kickstart the country rock boom of the early '70s.

Streamlined to a trio at the start of 1968, The Byrds were reduced to playing small club dates and support slots. "We really needed somebody," Roger McGuinn recalls. Three months later, he was auditioning for a jazz keyboard player and improbably chose Gram Parsons. It rapidly transpired that Parsons knew nothing about jazz but was a promising country singer and songwriter. A Harvard dropout with a Southern background that would not have been out of place in the tortured pages of a Tennessee Williams play, Parsons was thrusting and ambitious enough to replace the recently fired David Crosby as The Byrds' resident troublemaker. After allying himself with fellow country enthusiast Chris Hillman, Parsons successfully deflected McGuinn from pursuing his dream concept of a double album chronicling the history of 20th century music. McGuinn had intended to tackle traditional country, move on to folk, R&B and rock, then conclude the work with some snatches of jazz and synthesizer experimentation. Once Parsons arrived, they never got beyond the country.

"Chris, Gram and producer Gary Usher just didn't want to go along with the electronic music idea, so I was outvoted," McGuinn explains. The Byrds certainly played the country angle to perfection. First they cut their hair, then moved to Nashville and even risked their lives playing before a staunch redneck audience at the Grand Ole Opry. The new line-up appeared at the Royal Albert Hall in July and sounded highly accomplished with a neat combination of country-style material and Byrds classics. The future looked bright but on the day they were due to set forth on a controversial tour of South Africa, Parsons quit.

The following month, his four months as a Byrd was validated with the release of this groundbreaking and innovative album. At a time when rock was in danger of suffocation by the overblown excesses of hard rock and stale psychedelia *Sweetheart* offered a sense of place and respect for tradition. Like Dylan's *John Wesley Harding* and The Band's *Music From Big Pink*, it evoked an America before the fall, articulated most vividly in Parsons' Hickory Wind and the Woody Guthrie classic Pretty Boy Floyd. The sales were disappointing – hardly surprising considering Gram was now gone – but in challenging their audience, The Byrds had shown a courage that was commendable.

Record label:
Columbia

Produced
by Gary Usher.

Recorded
in Nashville; March–April 1968.

Released:
September 27, 1968

Chart peaks:
27 (UK) 24 (UK)

Personnel:
Roger McGuinn (g, v, banjo); Kevin Kelley (d); Chris Hillman (b, v, mandolin); Gram Parsons (g, v); Earl P. Ball (p); Jon Corneal (d); Lloyd Green (sg); John Hartford (banjo, g); Roy M. Huskey (b); Jaydee Maness (sg); Clarence J. White (g); Roy Halee (e); Charlie Bragg (e)

Track listing:
You Ain't Going Nowhere (S); I Am A Pilgrim (S); The Christian Life; You Don't Miss Your Water; You're Still On My Mind; Pretty Boy Floyd; Hickory Wind; One Hundred Years From Now; Blue Canadian Rockies; Life In Prison; Nothing Was Delivered

Running time
58.55

Current CD:
Legacy 4867522 adds: You Got A Reputation; Lazy Days; Pretty Polly; The Christian Life (rehearsal); Life In Prison (rehearsal); You're Still On My Mind (rehearsal); One Hundred Years From Now (rehearsal); All I Have Is Memories

Further listening:
Younger Than Yesterday (1967); The Notorious Byrd Brothers (1968)

Further reading:
MOJO 41; The Byrds: Timeless Flight Revisited (Johnny Rogan, 1997).

The Jeff Beck Group
Truth

A great band built on shifting sand, export the blues back to America.

Jeff Beck always meant more in America than on his home turf, and though it had little impact in the UK, *Truth* (released in the US as a Jeff Beck solo album), has a reputation in America as a seminal '60s heavy rock album that laid the foundations for what would become heavy metal. The band – comprised of Beck, Rod Stewart, Ron Wood and Mickey Waller – gained notoriety through their clever reworking of blues, embellished with Beck's visionary guitar, his fondness for electronic effects, and his pioneering use of distortion and feedback. The Wood/Waller rhythm section, taut and gutsy yet spartan enough to leave ample space for Beck's embellishments, also contributed mightily to the sound. The Jeff Beck Group sounded lighter and more fluid than any other British blues contenders, with a dramatic element other bands didn't possess – Rod Stewart's gritty and resolute singing, trading guitar and vocal lines – which would become the blueprint for hard rock bands in years to come.

According to Beck, the practice began as a lark. "We did that because it was fun. We used to make up stuff at the spur of the moment, and if it was a bit rough around the edges it would be great, because the next night it wouldn't be rough around the edges," Beck explains. But the band's dynamics – both musically and politically – often seemed to be underpinned by the interplay of grace *and* attack. At the time, Rod Stewart would complain that fans and even record company executives would come up to him, slap him on the back, and say, "Great show, Jeff!" – automatically assuming that the band was named after the singer. Beck remembers it a little differently. "No, we were getting on pretty well then. The fact was that they all began to see the method in my madness when they heard the playbacks, and that I was prepared to put my own money into getting really good players, like John Paul Jones. On Ol' Man River we used John Paul, Nicky Hopkins and Moonie on timpani."

Though *Truth* occupies an important place in the evolution of rock, Beck had a few reservations. "We had a great sound," he remembers, "but nobody had written any songs. Rod wrote folk songs then, which wouldn't have worked out for us, so he suggested we do [The Yardbirds'] Shapes Of Things." The band also did a version of the Willie Dixon's seductive classic

Record label:
Columbia

Recorded
at Abbey Road Studios, London; May 14–16 and May 25, 1968.

Produced
by Mickie Most and Jeff Beck.

Released:
September 28, 1968

Chart peaks:
None (UK) 15 (US)

Personnel:
Jeff Beck (g, b); Rod Stewart (v); Ron Wood (b, g); Nicky Hopkins (k, p); Keith Moon (d); Aynsley Dunbar (d); Mickey Waller (d); Ken Scott (e)

Track listing:
Shape Of Things; Let Me Love You; Morning Dew; You Shook Me; Ol' Man River; Greensleeves; Rock My Plimsoul; Beck's Bolero; Blues De Luxe; I Ain't Superstitious

Running time:
40.26

Currently unavailable on CD

Further listening:
Beckology, the 3-disc, 55-track set released in 1998 spanning Beck's entire career includes three unreleased tracks and a 64-page booklet encased in a guitar-shaped box.

Further Reading:
In Session With Jeff Beck: Guitar-Tab Book and CD (1997)

You Shook Me. Unknown to Beck at the time, former bandmate Jimmy Page's new outfit Led Zeppelin would also record the song for their own debut album; but to Beck's delight, theirs was released the next year.

"I took that as a compliment, because that album was already second-hand. And we both did You Shook Me in a slightly different style. It was a flattering thing, but the flattery went out the window when they began to be known for it and we weren't." While not the closest of friends, Beck did allow that Stewart was behind the album's title: "Whenever Rod and I used to go on-stage, he'd say, 'Shall we tell them the truth tonight?' It was a great thing to say. It was his way of saying, 'Are we going to pull out every bit of emotion we can?' When we were on speaking terms, we used to use that as a measuring stick, that we gave them the truth tonight. And so I said, 'Why don't we call the album that?' He went misty-eyed on me. There was a good vibe about the whole record."

Whistler, Chaucer, Detroit And Greenhill

The Unwritten Works Of Geoffrey, Etc.

Showcase of the sophisticated scene in Ft. Worth, Texas.

Anyone picking up this nondescript 1968 Uni Records album expecting to glean any information about the performers within were confronted with period liner notes reading: "I predict Benjamin Whistler, Geoffrey Chaucer, Nathan Detroit and Phillip Greenhill will be the next big thing, and I'm sure after you dig this album you'll agree they have what it takes to be just that."

Anyone reading the songwriting credits, though, would note that producer Joseph Burnett — soon known as T-Bone — penned four of the album's 11 tracks, and that the real names of the mysterious 'next big thing' were nowhere to be seen. In fact, WCD&G were not a band, but a loosely based, non-performing group of musicians "just learning to use the studio, really," says T-Bone Burnett today. With Houston's John Carrick the only non-Ft. Worth homeboy, Burnett, David Bullock, Scott Fraser, Phil White, and Eddie Lively were just making it up as they went along.

"We were hanging out recording stuff down in the basement of this radio station in Ft Worth. We did the Legendary Stardust Cowboy at that time, then we recorded a bunch of tunes — mostly staying up all night taking a lot of speed or something, staying up for five days at a time making music. And that group of tunes somehow ended up being a record. And I don't know how that name came about."

The music from those non-stop recording sessions is surprisingly coherent rock'n'roll that comes from all directions and provided this "group" with the same sort of varied sound that made bands like Buffalo Springfield and Moby Grape so worthy. With notably different singing and writing styles, the lingering impression was of vast untapped talent waiting to come to further fruition on follow-up or solo albums yet unmade. Much of this crew would end up recording a memorable, Byrdsy classic for Epic as Space Opera in 1973, then disappear.

"I was by far the least talented of all these people," says Burnett, "and — this just shows you that life is tricky — I think it's funny that that I've managed to stay doing it all these years."

Record label:
Uni

Produced
by Joseph Burnett.

Recorded
at Sound City Studios, Forth Worth, Texas and United Audio Studio, Santa Ana, California.

Released:
September 1968.

Chart peaks:
None (UK) None (US)

Personnel:
David Bullock; Scott Fraser; John Carrick; Phil White; Eddie Lively; T-Bone Burnett; George J Fernandez (m, special effects)

Track listing:
The Viper (What John Rance Had To Tell); Day Of Childhood; Upon Waking From The Nap; Live 'Til I Die; Street In Paris; As Pure As The Freshly Driven Snow; Tribute To Sundance; House Of Collection; Just Me And Her; On Lusty Gentlemen; Ready To Move

Running time:
28.12

Currently unavailable on CD

Further listening:
J Henry Burnett, The B-52 Band And The Fabulous Skylarks (1972); Space Opera (1973)

Jimi Hendrix Experience
Electric Ladyland

Mould-busting double disc set, notorious in UK for its gratuitous naked lady-lined gatefold.

"We call our music Electric Church Music," said Hendrix. "It's like a religion to us. Some ladies are like the church to us too. Some groupies know more about music than the guys. People call them groupies but I prefer the term 'electric ladies'. My whole *Electric Ladyland* album is about them." Physically, eight months and the Atlantic Ocean divided the first and last sessions for *Electric Ladyland*; spiritually, a lifetime sundered the set. The soft soul of the title track was only the first of the surprises in store, as Hendrix pulled away from the visceral sex-rock of his first two albums and began daubing from the broader, expressionist palette of subsequent experience. The sessions could have produced two great single albums. But blended together, they were heart-stopping. Wild experimentation blurred into solid rocking grooves. All Along The Watchtower not only reinvented Dylan's original for the audience, it reinvented it for Dylan as well – he subsequently performed the song as a *de facto* Hendrix cover. The two Voodoo Chiles offer first, a funkadelic jam with Winwood and Cassidy; then a screaming guitar exorcism (based around Cream's Sunshine Of Your Love riff, played backwards); and Burning Of The Midnight Lamp is spectral moodiness grafted to a mid-period Stones' arrangement.

Yet bassist Redding recalls, "The stuff we did in America, apart from Midnight Lamp, didn't work as well. I'd say we all preferred working in London. While we were at Olympic, the Stones were next door. We used to go and hang out, have a smoke, all that stuff, and it was a good atmosphere. If Chas wanted to do a bit of mixing, he'd go 'alright lads, go down the pub,' and we'd troop off. It was very relaxed. Whereas American studios were always so clinical. It wasn't such a good environment to be working in."

Chandler's withdrawal from the sessions, sick of constantly rowing with Hendrix, only exacerbated the discontent. Indeed, says Redding, "By the time we recorded Little Miss Strange (on April 20/21), the band had already broken up." They would carry on gigging for another year, but only because their work schedule was already mapped out that far in advance.

Record label:
Track

Produced
by Jimi Hendrix (and Chas Chandler)

Recorded
at Olympic, London; December 20, 1967–January 28, 1968; Record Plant, New York; April 18–August 27, 1968.

Released:
October 25, 1968 (UK)

Chart peaks:
6 (UK) 1 (US)

Personnel:
Jimi Hendrix (g, v); Noel Redding (b, v); Mitch Mitchell (d); Rainy Day; Still Raining: Mike Finnigan (o); Freddie Smith (horn); Larry Faucette (congas); Buddy Miles (d); Stevie Winwood (o on Voodoo Chile); Jack Cassidy (b); Al Kooper (p)

Track listing:
... And The Gods Made Love; Have You Ever Been (To Electric Ladyland); Crosstown Traffic (S); Voodoo Chile; Little Miss Strange; Long Hot Summer Night; Come On (Let The Good Times Roll); Gypsy Eyes; Burning Of The Midnight Lamp (S, UK only); Rainy Day Dream Away; 1983 ... (A Merman I Should Turn To Be); Moon Turn The Tides ... Gently Gently Away; Still Raining, Still Dreaming; House Burning Down; All Along The Watchtower (S); Voodoo Child (Slight Return) (S, UK only)

Running time:
75.29

Current CD:
MCD 11600

Further listening:
Experience Hendrix: The Best Of (1997)

Further reading:
Are You Experienced? (Noel Redding and Carol Appleby 1990); www.jimihendrix.com

Pentangle
Sweet Child

The UK's folk-rock supergroup make their definitive work.

Including two celebrated solo recording artists in Jansch and Renbourn, and a second-to-none rhythm section drafted in from previous spells with Alexis Korner and Duffy Power's Nucleus, the Pentangle were a supergroup from day one – and uniquely so in fusing together individuals and repertoire from both the folk and jazz/blues scenes of the day.

The group existed initially as a spare-time concern, playing almost exclusively at their own Sunday night club at the Horseshoe Hotel in Tottenham Court Road throughout 1967. At the start of that year Bert Jansch had filled a series of thousand-seater city halls on his own and many people, record label included, viewed his commitment to developing the group project bewildering.

It could indeed have been a disaster. There were a number of blown opportunities and false starts in trying to move beyond the Horseshoe before the arrival of New York publicist Jo Lustig, who became the group's manager in early 1968. He immediately oversaw the release of a first album, *The Pentangle*, secured substantial print, radio and TV coverage, and curtailed all group and solo live appearances, invariably in small clubs, to allow for their relaunch as a concert hall act – a scam that worked perfectly.

The Festival Hall concert on June 29 was thus widely anticipated and, as Melody Maker's review concluded, 'Will go down on record as a great success and a highlight in the group's career'. This was literally correct: the show was recorded for this, the second album, and featured an extraordinarily wide-ranging repertoire, utilising the quintet's virtuosic membership in a whole range of solo, duo, trio, quartet and full band combinations. Never again would the balance between them be so perfect or the interplay so fresh and dynamic. Traditional and contemporary folk songs shared space with modern jazz covers, medieval dance pieces, blues, and group originals closer to the folkish end of the rock underground than the whimsical style of their perceived rivals, the Incredible String Band.

The live half of the set includes most of the concert bar first-album material (pointless to issue at the time), a couple of solo tracks and a failed crack at Sweet Child – a complex piece which was subsequently done full justice for the equally eclectic studio half. Conversely, Haitian Fight Song was tried in the studio but the live version retained. The group reached a commercial peak with the UK No 5 LP *Basket Of Light* the following year, but creatively and critically *Sweet Child* was the apogee.

Record label:
Transatlantic

Produced
by Shel Talmy.

Recorded
at the Royal Festival Hall; June 29, 1968; and IBC Studios, London; September, 1968.

Released:
November 1, 1968

Chart peaks:
None (UK) None (US)

Personnel:
Jacqui McShee (v); Bert Jansch (v, g); John Renbourn (v, g); Danny Thompson (db); Terry Cox (v, d, glockenspiel); Damon Lyon-Shaw (e)

Track listing:
Live: Market Song; No More My Lord; Turn Your Money Green; Haitian Fight Song; A Woman Like You; Goodbye Pork-Pie Hat; Three Dances: i. Brentzel Gay; ii. La Rotta; iii. The Earle Of Salisbury; Watch The Stars; So Early In The Spring; No Exit; The Time Has Come; Bruton Town Studio: Sweet Child; I Loved A Lass; Three Part Thing; Sovay; In Time; In Your Mind; I've Got A Feeling; The Trees They Do Grow High; Moondog; Hole In The Coal

Running time:
84.48

Current CD:
ESMCD354

Further listening:
Basket Of Light (1969); Reflection (1971)

Further reading:
Dazzling Stranger: Bert Jansch And The British Folk And Blues Revival (Colin Harper, 2000)

The Beatles

The Beatles

The White Album.

Following a particularly relaxing and fertile meditation break in India, The Beatles presented over 30 songs for consideration for the follow-up to Sgt. Pepper, deciding to record as many as possible for a double.

The normal state of Beatles sessions was soon disrupted by the presence of Lennon's constant companion, avant-garde artist Yoko Ono. "Once I found *the* woman, the boys became of no interest whatsoever," Lennon would explain later. "The old gang of mine was over the moment I met her." It was the first time anyone had been allowed access to the band's inner working process and McCartney, Harrison and Starr were naturally thrown by both Lennon's distraction and Yoko's vocal opinions on their music. Things were further aggravated by Lennon's extreme mood swings, caused by his recently acquired heroin habit. Tired of the tension, long-time engineer Geoff Emerick quit. Equally sick of the atmosphere (and disheartened by McCartney's drumming instructions), Ringo walked out for two weeks. McCartney pragmatically (and skilfully) took over on drums for a few tracks and later took to recording on his own in an adjacent studio, which Lennon later confessed to being stung by: "I can't speak for George but I was always hurt when Paul knocked something off without involving us." But then, McCartney had felt equally excluded by Lennon and Yoko contriving the nine-minute sound collage Revolution 9 without him.

With the breakdown of both communication and the old team spirit, the tormented sessions actually produced a rich, amazing record encompassing an incredibly wide stylistic range. From the compellingly visceral (Helter Skelter, Yer Blues, Birthday) to the comically whimsical (Honey Pie, Goodnight, Martha My Dear); from the obscured confessional (Julia, Everybody's Got Something To Hide) to political commentary (Revolution, Blackbird), the whole is rated by some as the pinnacle of The Beatles' genius, by others as disappointingly indulgent.

Producer George Martin famously tried to persuade the band to trim the fat and make it a "really super" single album, starting a debate that continues to this day. McCartney's having none of it: "Come on, it's The Beatles' White Album."

Record Label:
Apple

Produced
by George Martin.

Recorded
at Abbey Road, London; June–October 1968.

Released:
November, 22 1968

Chart peaks:
1 (UK) 1 (US)

Personnel:
John Lennon (v, g, p, o); Paul McCartney (v, b, p, g, d); George Harrison (v, g); Ringo Starr (d); George Martin (p); Chris Thomas (harpsichord); Eric Clapton (g)

Track Listening:
Back in the USSR.; Dear Prudence; Glass Onion; Ob-La-Di, Ob-La-Da; Wild Honey Pie; The Continuing Story Of Bungalow Bill; While My Guitar Gently Weeps; Happiness Is A Warm Gun; Martha My Dear; I'm So Tired; Blackbird; Piggies; Rocky Raccoon; Don't Pass Me By; Why Don't We Do It In The Road?; I Will; Julia; Birthday; Yer Blues; Mother Nature's Son; Everybody's Got Something to Hide Except Me And My Monkey; Sexy Sadie; Helter Skelter; Long, Long, Long; Revolution 1; Honey Pie; Savoy Truffle; Cry Baby Cry; Revolution 9; Good Night

Running time:
93.15

Current CD:
CDS 7 46443 8

Further listening:
Let It Be (1970); Anthology 3 (1997)

Further reading:
www.getback.org/bwhite.html

The Kinks

The Kinks Are The Village Green Preservation Society

Chart success on the wane, Ray Davies conceives one of the quintessentially English pop albums.

T rue to its title, *Village Green Preservation Society* eschewed the wide-eyed psychedelia and studio experiment of its contemporaries. Which may be why it was grossly overlooked at the time. Instead, it focused on the wistful, sharp social commentary of Davies's writing and it's the fulcrum on which his deserved reputation as a songsmith pivots.

While Davies's peers on *Village Green* are not from the rock and pop world, neither are they – despite the claims of many a pop historian – the kitchen sink dramatists of the early '60s. If anything, Davies alludes to the short stories of Harold Nicholson, the Bloomsbury essays (rather than novels) of E.M. Forster, George Orwell's Coming Up For Air, and the mundane urbanity of Philip Larkin. What Davies seemed to crave was certainty and stability, the bastion of the familiar. The title track speaks of saving everything from "strawberry jam to variety, china cups and virginity", but Picture Book anticipates the bleaker Shangri-La (from *Arthur*) and Last Of The Steam Powered Trains hints at something darker and more direction-less.

The album contains at least two bona fide classics (three if you include the subsequent hit single Days, withdrawn from the original LP but restored to the CD). Do You Remember Walter updates David Watts, the hero-emulation of schooldays replaced by sentiments that seesaw between fondness and regret and a sad denouement in which the narrator talks himself out of a reunion, realising that memories are all that he and Walter have. People Take Pictures Of Each Other, with its weary refrain "Don't show me no more please" offers a cameo of human beings validating a transitory existence and also serves as a metaphorical postscript for the swinging '60s. Musically, the band complement Davies's lyrical concerns majestically, illustrating a similar disregard for contemporary musical fashion, and Nicky Hopkins provides wonderfully ornate touches on celeste and harpsichord throughout. Not a phased guitar in sight.

Record Label:
PYE

Produced
by Ray Davies.

Recorded
at Pye Studios; February 1967–August 1968.

Released:
Original 12 track stereo version released and withdrawn September 1968. Revised 15 track mono album released November 1968.

Chart peaks:
None (UK) None (US)

Personnel:
Ray Davies (v, g, k); Dave Davies (v, g); Pete Quaife (b, v); Mick Avory (d); Nicky Hopkins (k); Rasa Davies (v); Alan Mckenzie, Brian Humphries (e)

Track Listing:
15 track mono album: The Village Green Preservation Society; Do You Remember Walter; Picture Book; Johnny Thunder; Last Of The Steam Powered Trains; Big Sky; Sitting By The Riverside; Animal Farm; Village Green; Starstruck; Phenomenal Cat; All My Friends Were There; Wicked Annabella; Monica; People Take Pictures Of Each Other. 12 track stereo album: The Village Green Preservation Society; Do You Remember Walter; Picture Book; Johnny Thunder; Monica; Days; Village Green; Mr Songbird; Wicked Annabella; Starstruck; Phenomenal Cat; People Take Pictures Of Each Other

Running time:
36.15

Current CD:
Essential ESM CD 481

Further listening:
Arthur Or The Decline And Fall Of The British Empire (1969)

Further reading:
Kinks: The Official Biography (Jon Savage, 1984); X Ray (Ray Davies, 1994)

The Smoke
The Smoke

Forgotten American psych-pop in thrall to The Beatles and dedicated to Stuart Sutcliffe.

Michael Lloyd was a precocious 12-year-old when he first decided to be in a band. It was 1962 and he was swimming with a friend. "We were far out from the shore and we heard music coming from the beach. It sounded great. So we paddled in and there were these local guys playing Ventures songs – they were very good – and that started us thinking. We've got to have a band!"

A couple of bands later, Lloyd started at the Hollywood Professional School. where he met Shaun and Danny Harris. Together they formed The West Coast Pop Art Experimental Band and made an album in Michael's bedroom. (He left before they signed to Reprise.) Still only 17, he was next handed a number of projects by young executive Mike Curb, under names such as The Laughing Wind and The Rubber Band and for Epic Records he produced a group of fresh-faced teenagers called October Country. Although it flopped, that album gave him a taste of what he could achieve with good studio facilities at his disposal and he persuaded Curb to give him some studio time. Thus was born The Smoke.

Michael poured all he had learnt into the album, he produced, arranged, sang lead vocals and played bass and keyboards while Stan Ayeroff, who co-wrote three of the songs, handled guitar and Steve Baim played drums. The record opens with the organ-driven Cowboys and Indians, echoing Brian Wilson's Heroes and Villains. There are overt Beatles references throughout, too. The chorus of Lucy In the Sky With Diamonds is quoted in the fade to Fogbound and its influence is clear in Gold Is The Colour of Thought.

"I didn't really think of what I was doing as psychedelic," says the undoubtedly clean-cut Lloyd. "There may have been drug references in Beatles songs, but in my naive way it just seemed to be some brilliant creative thing they were doing."

Despite a wide release, nothing ever happened with the album. Curb subsequently appointed Lloyd Vice-President of MGM, where he finally achieved commercial success as a producer and composer, with The Osmonds, Lou Rawls and Debbie Boone (he produced You Light Up My Life) and the multi-million selling soundtrack to Dirty Dancing. But this non-moneyspinning nugget from his psych-pop roots is still one of his favourites.

Record label:
Tower

Produced
by Michael Lloyd

Recorded
at Hollywood Boulevard Studios, LA, summer 1968.

Released:
November 1968

Chart peaks:
None (UK) None (US)

Personnel:
Michael Lloyd (v, k, g, b, horn and string ar), Stan Ayeroff (g), Steve Baim (d).

Track listing:
Cowboys And Indians; Looking Thru The Mirror; Self-Analysis, Gold Is The Colour Of Thought, Hobbit Symphony; Daisy-Intermission; Fogbound; Song Thru Perception; Philosophy; Umbrella; Ritual Gypsy Music Opus 1; October Country, Odyssey.

Currently unavailable on CD

Further listening:
October Country (1967). In a similar vein, try The Millennium Begin.

Further reading:
The West Coast Pop Art Experimental Band Story by Tim Forster, published in Ptolomeic Terrascope magazine, 1999.

The Beau Brummels
Bradley's Barn

Psychedelic San Franciscan pop outfit turns up in Nashville. With creamy results.

The Beau Brummels had spent the early '60s interpreting the British invasion from the safety of their San Francisco home. Impressed by the Fabs and The Searchers, they'd hit on an angular version of beat music which songwriter Ron Elliott perfected for the deep, country-toned voice of singer Sal Valentino. Their early records on the Autumn label (some produced by hip young house producer Sylvester Stewart AKA Sly Stone) were state-of-the-art pop-rock and they enjoyed several American hits, but Autumn crumbled in 1966 and members of the band started to peel off.

Moving to Warners they cut *Beau Brummels '66* and then in 1967 hit on a folk vein which they mined for the moderately successful, but quite exquisite album *Triangle*. Their Warners contract demanded another album forthwith, and the last remaining original members, Valentino and Elliott, decided to decamp to Nashville to come up with the goods. It was to prove a real culture shock for them. "To be sure, Dylan and Ian And Sylvia had recorded there, sleeve note compiler Stan Cronyn pointed out. But this was The Beau Brummels who flew down to meet the younger Nashville musicians on common ground."

"We arrived in a Chrysler and all the Nashville guys had Cadillacs," recalled Sal. Musical differences were also on the cards when they sat down with the local musicians and unveiled their songs. "It was a 180 degree shift from what Nashville was about."

The venue for the showdown was, of course, Bradley's Barn and the resultant collection, although not the style-shattering opus the press and public at the time were led to believe, is an exceptional example of roomy country playing which envelops Valentino's rich, resonant voice. Cronyn's notes conclude that "In Bradley's Barn a pop album was created in a hush!" and indeed the far-reaching effects of this mild-mannered country rock can't be under-rated. *Bradley's Barn* is as much about the ambience of its setting, as anything else. In that, it's a quiet classic.

Record label:
Warner Brothers

Produced
by Lenny Waronker.

Recorded
at Bradley's Barn, Wilson County, Tennessee; 1968.

Released:
1968

Chart peaks:
None (UK) None (US)

Personnel:
Sal Valentino (v); Ron Elliott (g); Jerry Reed (g); Wayne Moss (g); Harold Bradley (g); Billy Sanford (g); Norbert Putnum (b); David Briggs (k); Kenny Buttrey (d)

Track listing:
Turn Around; An Added Attraction; Deep Water; Long Walk Down To Misery (S); Little Bird; Cherokee Girl (S); I'm A Sleeper; The Loneliest Man In Town; Love Can Fall A Long Way Down; Jessica; Bless You California

Running time:
31.50

Not currently available,
though it has been reissued on CD but is currently deleted.

Further listening:
The Brummels' Triangle (1967) is well worth casting back over and there's a good Rhino retrospective Best Of The Beau Brummels (1981) if you want to scan their whole career from Mersey to flower power and beyond.

Further reading:
www.geocities.com/brummel_beau/

The MC5
Kick Out The Jams

Bucking tradition, these Motor City rock revolutionaries released a live album as their debut.

Detroit's MC5 fuelled their vision of revolution by grafting it onto high-octane garage rock, using their guitars as assault weapons against a lethargic status quo. Under the guiding hand of poet and activist John Sinclair, The MC5 created the soundtrack for the nascent White Panther Party, promulgating the incendiary ethos of "Rock'n'roll, dope and fucking in the streets".

Over the years, the leftist politics may have become quaint, but *Kick Out The Jams* remains a fine blast of serrated rock rage. In addition to polemics, the "5" established their own religion, Zenta, and it was on the Zenta New Year in1968 – Halloween weekend – that the band planned to record their debut record at Detroit's Grande ballroom, where they'd been gigging weekly for two years, opening up for better known bands. In fact, the band dubbed their album after a phrase they used to heckle the star attractions.

"More often than not, the bands were really tired,' explains guitarist Wayne Kramer. "They'd come from San Francisco and play all this kind of electric folk music. I mean they were wimpy, they had no passion, they were posers, slackers, and we were young and aggressive fellows and so we used to harass them. We'd scream at them from the wings, 'Kick out the jams or get off the stage.' Or, 'Get down, brother or get the fuck out!'"

MC5 were offering up a gritty, cacophonous rock show, complete with atonal industrial din of the Detroit factories and unapologetic distortion that was best experienced live, so it was not a surprise that they chose to debut with a live album.

"We really worked hard at perfecting a performance that on a bad night would be great and on a good night would be unbelievable," remembers Kramer. "The MC5 were a mercurial band. All of a sudden this was "the" night, we were making "the" record, the posters were up, the fans were there and the recording truck was in from California, and the record company was there, and it was a lot of pressure for us to be under. In fact it rattled us. I hear it every time I listen to the record." Though he admits it's not the band's best work, Kramer acknowledges, " Our power is concentrated in that record in a way that you can't deny. *Kick Out The Jams* is a powerful statement of a time."

Record label:
Elektra

Produced
by Jac Holzman and Bruce Botnick.

Recorded
at the Grande Ballroom, Detroit, Michigan; October 30 and 31, 1968.

Released:
February 1969

Chart peaks:
None (UK) 30 (US)

Personnel:
Rob Tyner (v); Fred 'Sonic' Smith (g, v); Wayne Kramer (g, v); Dennis Thompson (d, v); Michael Davis (b); Bruce Botnick (e)

Track listing:
Ramblin' Rose; Kick Out The Jams; Come Together; Rocket Reducer No. 62 (Rama Lama Fa); Borderline; Motor City Is Burning; I Want You Right Now; Starship

Running time:
36.17

Current CD:
AMCY2563

Further listening:
High Time (1971) – the band's final studio album was a return to their rough and tumble roots, after the more sanitized "commercial" sounds of 1970's Back In The USA; Babes In Arms (1973) rarities and never released tracks; The Big Bang Beat: The Best Of The MC5 (2000) a well-chosen collection of the 5's grittiest tracks and free jazz masterworks.

Further reading:
MOJO 27;
http://ourworld.compuserve.com/home-pages/rauk/mc-5.htm

Silver Apples
Contact

Second album from pioneers of loops and ambience. Now active again after belated recognition.

In 1967, Simeon Coxe III began to spice up the performances of his conventional rock band by adding electronic effects. "One of my best buds then was a serious composer called Harold Rodgers. He had an old Second World War oscillator. He used to get loaded on vodka and try to play along with Beethoven, Bartok, etc. One day I put on a Stones record and played along. I was hooked!"

The band quickly became a duo, based around Simeon's rapidly multiplying and interlinked battery of audio-generators and Danny Taylor's massive, carefully tuned drum kit. Their 1968 debut introduced the maverick coupling, but *Contact* marks the apotheosis of their sound. "The first album was a recording studio project, whereas *Contact* was recorded during and after a three-month tour and my pipes were road-toughened," says Coxe. It's a harder record than their debut — titles such as A Pox On You and the harsh, edgy wailings of Cox's electrickery speak volumes.

"I was fortunate enough to know Hendrix [Danny Taylor had drummed with Jimi's Blue Flames]. We traded gear and talked about new sound distortions. He called me Mr Apple and I called him Mr Experience." The influence is apparent on the bucking, electro-ballistics of You're Not Foolin' Me and Gypsy Love, while Taylor's urgent, human-drum-machine beats provide the perfect underpinning. Coxe: "By 1969 a lot of the hippy dream had faded. I'm not sure the world had become dystopian, but I was sure feeling the darker side." This finds a perfect expression in the dissonant flower-power anthem I Have Known Love, a perfectly curdled pop song. And if things didn't sound weird enough, Simeon — who was raised in the Tennessee mountains — found time to play banjo on Ruby and Confusion, to create a sort of techno-bluegrass.

Unfortunately, Kapp had no money to promote *Contact*, and Silver Apples went into cold storage for almost 25 years. "At the time," Coxe notes ruefully, "electronics as a musical concept had not yet been embraced by musicians and fans as something that could stand on its own, other than in universities and laboratories. We embraced that concept."

Record label:
Kapp

Produced
by Silver Apples, co-produced by Barry Bryant.

Recorded
at Universal Studios, Los Angeles and Apostolic Studios, New York; late 1968.

Release date:
February 1969

Chart peaks:
None (UK) None (US)

Personnel:
Simeon Coxe III (oscillators [often known as 'The Simeon'], banjo, v); Danny Taylor (pc, v); Jack Hunt (e)

Track listing:
You And I (S); Water; Ruby; Gypsy Love; You're Not Foolin' Me; I Have Known Love; A Pox On You; Confusion; Fantasies

Running time:
40.21

Current CD:
MCD 11680 adds Silver Apples: Oscillations; Seagreen Serenades; Lovefingers; Program; Velvet Cave; Whirly-Bird; Dust; Dancing Gods; Misty Mountain

Further listening:
Long-lost third album The Garden (1970) is now available; two recent albums, Beacon (1997) and Decatur (1998). See also the collaborations The Alchemysts And Simeon (2000) and A Lake Of Teardrops (1998, with Sonic Boom from Spaceman 3).

Further reading:
long interview with Simeon in Ptolemaic Terrascope 22, February 1997 (www.terrascope.org); www.silverapples.com

Bee Gees
Odessa

Red velvet-covered double which almost killed them.

Beautifully sung, delicately orchestrated and filled with highly individual songs about lost love, electric light and sinking ships, *Odessa* was the culmination of a burst of creativity which almost destroyed the Bee Gees before the '70s had begun. Returning to the UK from Australia in early 1967 the Gibb brothers followed their breakthrough New York Mining Disaster 1941 with a further six hit singles and three highly-successful albums in just sixteen months. It was hardly surprising that by the time they re-entered the studio in 1968 some strain was beginning to show. While working titles such as *Masterpeace* and *American Opera* might suggest some grand artistic design, Barry Gibb recalls that the real motivation came from manager Robert Stigwood: "I think it was basically a financial deal. If we do a double album everyone makes more money – except the group. So we were doing something that we weren't motivated to do and it became full of all this stuff that didn't necessarily blow me away."

Yet the finished work justified Stigwood's faith in his young protegés. Opening with a dramatic swirl of strings, acoustic guitar and cello and the line "14th of February 1899, the British ship Veronica was lost without a sign," the dense, melancholy title track set the tone. Bill Shepherd's sympathetic orchestration, which went far beyond mere sweetening – three of the tracks were instrumental – allowed the melodies to shine and in Sound Of Love and the Eleanor Rigby-influenced Melody Fair the Bee Gees produced two of their finest ballads. Less predictably, there were also nods towards American country-rock: Marley Purt Drive was a deliciously languid number complete with electric piano, slide guitar and banjo.

Unfortunately, discord arising over the choice of the album's single precipitated Robin's departure to pursue a solo career: it would be another eighteen months before all three brothers were reunited on one record. Yet *Odessa* remains one of the Bee Gees finest albums, a work of extraordinary depth of feeling and a fitting end to an important chapter in their career. With little nostalgia, Barry suggests the key to its success: "Maybe it's because there was so much trouble and strife going on at the time. I think there's probably a little bit of that in every song."

Record label:
Polydor

Produced
by Robert Stigwood and the Bee Gees.

Recorded
in New York, August–December 1968; De Lane Lea and IBC Studios, London; early 1968.

Released:
March 1969

Chart peaks:
10 (UK) 20 (US)

Personnel:
Barry Gibb (v, g); Robin Gibb (v, o); Maurice Gibb (v, b, p, g); Colin Petersen (d); Paul Buckmaster (c); Bill Shepherd (MD); P Wade, E Sharp, A Barber (e)

Track listing:
Odessa (City On The Black Sea); You'll Never See My Face Again; Black Diamond; Marley Purt Drive; Edison; Melody Fair; Suddenly; Whisper Whisper; Lamplight (S); Sound Of Love; Give Your Best; Seven Seas Symphony; With All Nations (International Anthem); I Laugh In Your Face; Never Say Never Again; First Of May (S); The British Opera

Running time:
64.22

Current CD:
825 451-2 omits: With All Nations

Further listening:
Horizontal (1968); Idea (1968)

Further reading:
www.tales-of-the-brothers-gibb.co.uk

Quicksilver Messenger Service
Happy Trails

Hippies get heavy, live and loud.

Anyone who has ever sneered at drippy, wimpish hippies should have their attention forcibly drawn to *Happy Trails*, on which Quicksilver play with a visceral, crunching power that is the absolute antithesis of drippiness or wimpiness.

As acid rock adventurers Quicksilver were peers of the Grateful Dead and Jefferson Airplane, but, unlike those bands, their roots weren't in the folk, bluegrass or jugband scenes. The band's John Cippolina, raunchiest of the great '60s psychedelic guitarists, has explained: "I cut my teeth in blues and hard rock. My biggest influence was Link Wray . . . the grandfather of punk. I heard that sound and thought, 'God, you can swear without using four letter words!'"

Much of the album comprises various live tapes from the Fillmores East and West, spliced together. "We were always better live," Cipollina later told Zigzag magazine. "We found the [studio] atmosphere a little strange when we cut our first album and we decided to cut the follow-up live in a familiar setting and with a familiar audience, so we could really cook and let ourselves go."

The album's highlight is an improvisation, comprising the whole of the first side of the original album, on Bo Diddley's Who Do You Love, an exuberant deconstruction and exploration of the song's every nuance, described by critic Greil Marcus as "One of the best rock'n'roll recordings to emerge from San Francisco [and] some of the finest hard rock ever recorded."

Throughout the track, Cipollina's distinctive, quivering, vibrato-heavy playing, with its surprising hint of flamenco, is massively exciting, while one section of the performance features the Fillmore audience exchanging yelps and howls with the band, an interlude that Marcus describes as "a beautiful example of the kind of communication rock'n'roll is all about." With the exception of the title track, a brief and amusingly straightfaced rendition of the corny old Roy Rogers ditty, Side Two also comprises one, extended piece of music, the most thrilling element of which is Calvary, recorded live in the studio and described by Cipollina as "our interpretation of the Crucifixion: it starts with the condemnation, goes through the journey to the cross and ends with the angels coming." Full of ideas these hippies, huh?

Record label:
Capitol

No producer credited.

Recorded
at Fillmore East and West; Calvary recorded live at Golden State Recorders, San Francisco; November 19, 1968.

Released:
March 1969

Chart peaks:
None (UK) 27 (US)

Personnel:
John Cipollina (g); Gary Duncan (g, v); David Freiberg (b, v); Greg Elmore (d, v)

Track listing:
Who Do You Love Suite: Who Do You Love [Part 1] (S/US); When You Love; Where You Love; How You Love; Which You Love; Who Do You Love [Part 2]; Mona; Maiden Of The Cancer Moon; Calvary; Happy Trails

Running time:
50.18

Current CD:
Beat Goes On BGOCD151

Further listening:
The band's previous album, their self-titled debut (1968), is also worth hearing, as is Anthology (1973), which compiles 1968–1971 tracks.

Further reading:
www.penncen.com/quicksilver

Flying Burrito Brothers
The Gilded Palace Of Sin

Gram Parsons' finest work: fusing soul, country and R&B in one package.

When the Byrds teetered on the brink of collapse at the end of 1968, founding member Chris Hillman decided to join erstwhile member Gram Parsons in a new venture – the Flying Burrito Brothers. 'Country rock' was still a neologism at the time they pushed forward with this groundbreaking record. Holed up in a house together, Parsons and Hillman wrote some of the best songs of their lives.

"When I was living with Parsons I woke up one day and said, This old town's filled with sin, it'll swallow you in," Hillman remembers. "Gram then finished the second part. As far as lyrics and melody went, we shared it all the way."

Parsons spoke of his vision of 'Cosmic American Music' fusing soul, R&B and traditional country alongside a distinctive rock beat. Image was also a part of the equation. Inspired by the Stones, Parsons took to wearing make-up and on the cover of the album the group were dressed in garish, floral suits adorned with cannabis leaves, the creation of the famous Nashville tailor Nudie.

The music was both inspired and confrontational, brazenly mixing steel guitars and mandolins with advanced studio effects, phasing and synthesized brass. It was a potent concoction. The compositions were righteous assaults on LA life, with riveting tales of groupies (Christine's Tune), drug abuse (Juanita), draft evasion (My Uncle) and lost innocence (Hippie Boy). Parsons' vocals displayed a remarkable range of emotion, sometimes forthright, occasionally vulnerable and, most famously, cracking with emotion on the heart-rending Hot Burrito #1, which Elvis Costello later revived using the less impressive title I'm Your Toy. Parsons' finest work was featured on this album but only the cognoscenti were listening. Lost in the gap between the country and rock markets the Burritos never received the acclaim they deserved. It was left to successors like the Eagles to reap the benefits of their pioneering work.

Record label:
Asylum

Produced
by The Burritos, Larry Marks and Henry Lewy.

Recorded
at A&M Studios, Los Angeles; February 1969.

Released:
April 21, 1969

Chart peaks:
None (UK) 164 (US)

Personnel:
Gram Parsons (g, v); Chris Hillman (g, v, mandolin); Chris Ethridge (b, p); Sneeky Pete Kleinow (sg); Jon Corneal (d); Eddie Hoh (d); Sam Goldstein (d); Popeye Phillips (d); Henry Lewy (e)

Track listing:
Christine's Tune; Sin City; Do Right Woman; Dark End Of The Street; My Uncle; Wheels; Juanita; Hot Burrito # 1; Hot Burrito # 2; Do You Know How It Feels; Hippie Boy

Running time:
37.33

Current CD:
Edsel EDCD 191

Further listening:
Burrito Deluxe (1970); Gram Parsons, GP (1973) and Grievous Angel (1974)

Further reading:
MOJO 41; The Byrds: Timeless Flight Revisited (Johnny Rogan, 1997)

Tommy James And The Shondells
Cellophane Symphony

Bubblegum pin-up becomes psychedelic pop composer.

A child prodigy at 13, Tommy James spent the early '60s fusing garage rock with bubblegum pop. A second incarnation of his group The Shondells charted with I Think We're Alone Now in 1967 and Mony, Mony in 1968 before the psychedelic bug bit and the album and single Crimson And Clover introduced a new phase for the group. Still with songwriting partner Richie Cordell, James moved into new, less formulated territory. Influenced by *Sgt Pepper*, the group changed garb and paid lip service to musical fashion while retaining their pert pop sound. However, by the end of 1968 James had seized full control of proceedings and *Cellophane Symphony* became his most ambitious project yet.

The opening title track was a nine-minute-plus instrumental, some way from the three-minute slices of pop he was renowned for, sounding more like an atmospheric Pink Floyd outtake complete with Farfisa organ. The mood generally is one of irreverence: plenty of tongue-in-cheek wordplay and even, at one point, a John Wayne impersonation, before side one closes with the vaudevillian Papa Rolled His Own. In the spirit of Zappa's *We're Only In It For The Money*, *Cellophane Symphony* climaxes with James's very own attack on the establishment, On Behalf Of The Management And Staff, a spoof party singalong where James is presented with a gold watch for services rendered. The mood takes an even more bizarre twist when James starts squealing "It doesn't work, it doesn't work/the watch doesn't even work/I hate you." Perhaps it was a refutation of the futility of playing the pop game. Whatever, James is seen seated in an empty auditorium on the reverse of the original UK version of the album with an expression that seems to be asking "What the hell was all that about?"

Record Label:
Roulette

Produced
by Tommy James.

Recorded
in New York City, summer 1968–January 1969.

Released:
April 1969

Chart peaks:
None (UK) None (US)

Personnel:
Tommy James (v, g); Eddie Gray (g); Ronnie Rossman (k); Mike Vale (b); Pete Lucia (d)

Track Listing:
Cellophane Symphony; Makin' Good Time; Evergreen; Sweet Cherry Wine (S); Papa Rolled His Own; Changes; Loved One; I Know Who I Am; The Love Of A Woman; On Behalf Of The Entire Staff And Management.

Running time:
41.55

Current CD:
NEMCD647 (with Crimson And Clover)

Further listening:
Crimson And Clover (1968) is well worth tracking back to and it's available on one CD with Cellophane Symphony. Of course, the early singles are ace.

Further reading:
www.tommyjames.com

Dusty Springfield
Dusty In Memphis

Landmark white-soul session that almost didn't happen.

They may have sent Dusty South, but the South had to meet her halfway. When this beautiful album first appeared, the general feeling among record buyers was that barge-poles just weren't long enough. But they were in good company: Dusty loathed it too. She confessed to MOJO 20 that it took over a year before she could bear to play the record at all.

Atlantic's idea had been a great one. Send Dusty down South with Jerry Wexler, just as they'd done with Aretha Franklin. After all, despite the West Hampstead background, the blonde bouffant and the history of pneumatic Euro-pop melo-drama, here was a soulful vocalist whose subtlety was combined with impressive firepower. But, whether it was fear, fastidious-ness or just cussedness, Dusty took an age to agree on material – though the eventual selections were impeccable, with Randy Newman, Goffin/King and Bacharach/David to the fore – and sessions in Muscle Shoals had to be cancelled.

Once actually in Memphis, Dusty's painstaking way of working was at odds with Wexler's, and she froze. Tension filled the air (as did a flying ashtray, at one point) in the absence of Dusty's vocals. In fact she didn't sing until she'd left Memphis, cutting the final vocals in Atlantic's New York studios. Despite all the problems, the music was gorgeous. Clipped and slinky Memphis funk complements the easy-going material with great sophistication. Son Of A Preacher Man became the key track, but even more seductive were Breakfast In Bed and Just A Little Lovin'. Even in Wexler's exalted company it is Springfield's intuitive feel for each song's emotional possibilities that remains the record's ultimate virtue.

Record label:
Philips

Produced
by Jerry Wexler, Tom Dowd and Arif Mardin.

Recorded
at American Studios, Memphis; September 1968. Vocals overdubbed at Atlantic Studios, New York City.

Released:
April 1969

Chart peaks:
None (UK) 99 (US)

Personnel:
Bobby Wood (p); Bobby Emmons (o); Reggie Young (g); Gene Chrisman (d); Tommy Cogbill (b); The Sweet Inspirations (bv); Ed Kollis (e)

Track listing:
Just A Little Lovin'; So Much Love; Son Of A Preacher Man (S); I Don't Want To Hear It Anymore; Don't Forget About Me; Breakfast In Bed; Just One Smile; The Windmills Of Your Mind; In The Land Of Make Believe; No Easy Way Down; I Can't Make It Alone

Running time:
33.36

Current CD:
5286872-2 adds: Willie And Laura Mae Jones; That Old Sweet Roll (Hi-De-Ho); What Do You Do When Love Dies

Further listening:
A Girl Called Dusty (1964); Everything's Coming Up Dusty (1965)

Further reading:
MOJO 20; Dusty (Lucy O'Brien, 1997); www.simonbell.com/Dustydevotedly.html

The Youngbloods
Elephant Mountain

New York quartet go West to make sprawling Sgt. Pepper-*inspired masterpiece.*

In 1967, two years before a television ad promoting brother-hood turned it into a national smash, The Youngbloods' Get Together had been a regional hit on the West Coast. Excited by its success, the New York City-based quartet headed west, settling in bucolic Inverness, California, 30 miles up the coast from San Francisco. The dominant feature of the landscape was Black Mountain, which resembled an elephant's back, so when it came time to name the ambitious album they seemed to have been working on for ever (two years, in fact), The Youngbloods did not hesitate: it was *Elephant Mountain*.

"Recording actually began in New York," says Lowell Levinger, who played just about every instrument on it except bass and drums, and also wrote arrangements. "When we were all living out here, we would fly down to LA for two or three weeks at a time to work on it. We'd stay at the Tropicana Hotel and go to the studio every night." The commute cost them their second guitar player, Jerry Corbitt.

"Just about when we first began flying down to Los Angeles, Jerry developed an aversion to flying," says Levinger. "Then he developed an aversion to a lot of other things." The Youngbloods' sound was always distinguished by the soft, airy tenor of founder Jesse Colin Young "the Golden Throat", as Levinger calls him. But they were actually one of the more eclectic, adventuresome bands of their time, with a repertoire of styles ranging from folk and upbeat country to jazz, blues and even ragtime. Inspired by the ambitiousness of *Sgt Pepper* and their own live shows, which often sprawled over three hours, the band conceived *Elephant Mountain* as an organic whole. Its 13 tracks flow into one another with the help of short instrumental segues and studio banter.

"We used to do a lot of improvising in the studio with the tape running," says Levinger. "Joe spent a lot of time going through those tapes and finding good snippets." One amusing snippet is Turn It Over: an obsolete 12 seconds since no one needs to be reminded to turn a record over in the CD age. The album's centrepiece is Darkness, Darkness, a minor-key meditation on the seductiveness of oblivion. "Producing that song took forever," says Levinger. "I played the echo on Jesse's voice the same as I would any other musical instrument." Levinger's raw, intense guitar solo is just one high point of this beautiful, ambitious record.

Record label:
RCA

Produced
by Charles E. Daniels with Bob Cullen and The Youngbloods.

Recorded
at RCA Studios, New York City; RCA's Music Center of the World, Hollywood; autumn 1967–winter 1968.

Released:
April 1969

Chart peaks:
None (UK) 113 (US)

Personnel:
Jesse Colin Young (v, b); Lowell Levinger, aka 'Banana' (g, ps, p, k, o, harpsichord, v); Joe Bauer (d, pc); David Lindley (fiddle); Victor Feldman (vibes); Plas Johnson (s); Joe Clayton (t); Richie Schmidt, Hank Cicalo, Mickey Crofford (e)

Track listing:
Darkness, Darkness (S/US); Smug; On Sir Francis Drake; Sunlight; Double Sunlight; Beautiful; Turn It Over; Rain Song; Trillium; Quicksand; Black Mountain Breakdown; Sham; Ride the Wind

Running time:
39.51

Current CD:
EDCD 276

Further listening:
The Youngbloods contains the band's two biggest hits, Get Together and Grizzly Bear, while Best Of The Youngbloods is a good introduction despite being a little thin at 10 tracks.

Further reading:
Jesse Colin Young raises coffee in Kona, Hawaii. The web page for his business — www.jessecolinyoung.com — also has some music information.

The Who
Tommy

Huge double concept-album, the first rock opera, spawning a movie, an orchestral spin-off and a stage musical.

Early in 1968, Pete Townshend had emerged from an encounter with Indian mystic Meher Baba with a growing sense of frustration at the limitations of rock in general, and The Who in particular, he announced to the NME that on their next record he wanted The Who to "preach", a notion he'd first approached in an aborted song called You've Gotta Have Faith In Something Bigger Than Yourselves. However, he recognised that Roger Daltrey might not look convincing singing that one, so he went back to work on their fourth album – provisionally titled *Who's For Tennis* – and started coming at the idea from a different direction.

Townshend had often been musically ambitious. A Quick One was an unprecedented nine-minute song cycle, *The Who Sell Out* packaged itself as a pirate radio show devoted to the band. But that was primitive stuff compared to the scope of what he eventually unveiled: *Tommy* – the seemingly bizarre idea of a thematic double album telling how a deaf, dumb and blind boy found salvation in his genius on a pinball machine and became the leader of a reclusive religious cult. It still sounds mad, but in an age when rock heroes were taking on the persona of prophets, *Tommy* was both credible and captivating, orchestral links lending gravitas to The Who's characteristically colourful pulsating rock which swung from the proto-prog grandeur of Amazing Journey to the music hall jauntiness of Tommy's Holiday Camp and the searing rock of Acid Queen.

"I wanted the story of *Tommy* to have several levels, a rock singles level and a bigger concept level," Pete wrote later. "I wanted it to appeal as a fairy story to young kids and also be intellectually entertaining. And I wanted it have a spiritual message too."

Not everyone bought it. "It's sick!" denounced horrified Radio 1 DJ Tony Blackburn and plenty of critics shared his view.

"*Tommy* wasn't as big a success as people now imagine," says Roger Daltrey, "not when it was released anyway. It wasn't particularly big at all – it was only after we'd flogged it on the road for three years and played Woodstock and things like that it got back in the charts. Then it stayed in the charts for a year and took on a life of its own."

Record label:
Track

Produced
by Kit Lambert.

Recorded
at IBC Studios, London; October 1968–March 1969.

Released:
May 23, 1969

Chart peaks:
2 (UK) 4 (US)

Personnel:
Roger Daltrey (v, hm); Pete Townshend (v, g, k); Keith Moon (v, d); John Entwistle (v, b, k); Damon Lyon-Shaw (e); Chris Stamp (executive producer)

Track listing:
Overture/It's A Boy; 1921 (You Didn't Hear It); Amazing Journey; Sparks; Eyesight To The Blind (The Hawker); Christmas; Cousin Kevin; Acid Queen; Underture; Do You Think It's Alright?; Fiddle About; Pinball Wizard; There's A Doctor I've Found; Go To The Mirror Boy; Tommy Can You Hear Me?; Smash The Mirror; Sensation; Miracle Cure; Sally Simpson; I'm Free; Welcome Tommy's Holiday Camp; We're Not Gonna Take It

Running time:
74.00

Current CD:
8411212

Further listening:
The Who's other classic rock opera, Quadrophenia (1973)

Further reading:
A good place to start might be The Who In Print: An Annotated Bibliography, 1965 Through 1990 (Stephen Wolter and Karen Kimber, 1992); www.thewho.net

Richie Havens
Richard P. Havens 1983

Double folk apocalypse from the Woodstock Freedom man.

It's been said about a lot of albums recorded between 1967 and 1971, but what *were* they on when they made this?

Thanks to that landmark performance at 1969's Woodstock Festival – hollering "Freedom!", hammering away at a battered acoustic guitar – and such albums as 1967's *Mixed Bag* and 1971's *The Great Blind Degree*, the common perception of Richie Havens is of a rough-edged folk shouter dealing in ten-cent peace 'n' love. His background *was* a folk one, growing up in the Bedford-Stuyvesant district of New York, hanging out with street-corner harmony groups and watching the legendary Dino Valente and Fred Neil harmonise at The Cafe Wha? He studied the songs of Neil, Hardin and Gene Michaels and perfected his trademark open tuning technique (playing all six strings and using his thumb to make different chords at every fret stop). However, his first two albums for Jerry Schoenbaum's MGM offshoot, Verve Folkways pushed that 'folk' definition to the limits. It was a new label with free reign and on *Mixed Bag* and 1968's *Something Else Again* producer John Court told Havens to try everything.

"He said we should avoid songs of any one type" says Havens. "He told me I could sing opera if I wanted." It all made for a distinctive combination of Village folk, New York pop and a rumpled psychedelia which sold over a million copies. Richie became a valuable commodity and MGM gave him the freedom to set up his own Stormy Forest production company and make the *Richard P Havens 1983* double album.

It was a stunning, labyrinthine achievement – combining the fractured hippie visions of Leonard Cohen, Donovan, The Beatles and Dylan with such cryptic Havens folk puzzles as Indian Rope Man and Just Above My Hobby Horses's Head.

"The year was 1969," he explains. "The title *1983* was based on the idea that I thought we were already in the world created in George Orwell's 1984, which warned about the dangers of a monolithic society. My album said there was still time brother, but not much..."

After Woodstock, Richie Havens was set for life, securing a $650,000 deal with MGM that included his own office on the 20th floor. Apocalyptic urgency went out of the window. He would make other great records but nothing ever approached the bewitching insanity of this one.

Record label:
Verve Forecast

Produced
by Richie Havens and Mark Roth

Recorded
at RKO Sound Studios, New York City, early 1969

Released:
May 1969

Chart peaks:
None (UK) 80 (US)

Personnel:
Richie Havens (v, g), Arnie Moore, Carol Hunter, Brad Campbell and Stephen Stills (b), Skip Prokop and Don MacDonald (d), Weldon Myrick (sg), Paul Williams (g), Jeremy Steig (flute), Colin Walcott (sitar), Paul Harris (p), Warren Bernhardt (k), John Ord (p, o), Carter C.C. Collins (congas)

Track listing:
Stop Pulling And Pushing Me; For Haven's Sake; Strawberry Fields Forever; What More Can I Say, John; I Pity The Poor Immigrant; Lady Madonna; Priests; Indian Rope Man; Cautiously; Just Above My Hobby Horse's Head; She's Leaving Home; Putting Out The Vibration And Hoping It Comes Home; The Parable Of Ramon; With A Little Help From My Friends; Wear Your Love Like Heaven; Run Shaker Life; Do You Feel Good?

Running time:
69.37

Currently unavailable on CD

Further listening:
Mixed Bag (1967); Alarm Clock (1971)

Further reading:
They Can't Hide Us Anymore (Richie Havens and Steve Davidowitz, 1999)

Neil Young
Everybody Knows This Is Nowhere

First electric album with Crazy Horse blueprinted the guitar-driven sound that would later inspire grunge.

Neil Young was in search of something new. Freed from the burning intensity of Buffalo Springfield he had signed to Reprise as a solo artist and issued a lavishly arranged, predominantly acoustic album which gained solid reviews but sold poorly. His voice had been buried in the mix which briefly caused him to disown the album. Now, he was determined to start afresh. His new direction owed much to a debilitating bout of flu which had rendered him helpless but simultaneously unleashed his imagination. High with fever, he'd written three songs – Cinnamon Girl; Cowgirl In The Sand; Down By The River. The lyrics were understandably vague and dreamy and the chords simple yet arresting. In his mind, Young began to hear a hypnotic beat that cried for electric instrumentation. He could have assembled a crack team of LA session players but instead he chose a bar band that he knew from the Springfield days. The Rockets had made one album for White Whale but weren't exactly setting Hollywood alight. "He took the rhythm section, which was me, Billy Talbot and Danny Whitten," drummer Ralph Molina recalls. "It evolved into Crazy Horse. We hadn't played many shows as the Rockets anyway."

Crazy Horse was one of Young's most inspired moves. They provided him with the same excitement he remembered from the heyday of Buffalo Springfield, albeit without the mind games and rivalry that characterised his dealings with the fiery Stephen Stills. Although the partnership would drift at various points in his career, Young would always return to Crazy Horse in search of renewal. This album proved one of the best electric guitar albums of its era and established Young's reputation as a player of great passion and unrestrained intensity.

"I still think that us being with Neil was fate," Molina concludes. "We were just four guys. That Crazy Horse sound came from all four of us. Neil wouldn't have found that sound with anybody else. That was the way we played – with raw emotion."

Record Label:
Reprise

Produced
by David Briggs and Neil Young.

Recorded
in Los Angeles; March 1969.

Released:
May 1969

Chart peaks:
None (UK) 34 (US)

Personnel:
Neil Young (g, v); Danny Whitten (g, bv); Ralph Molina (d, bv); Billy Talbot (b, bv); Robin Lane (v); Bobby Notkoff (vn)

Track Listing:
Cinnamon Girl (S/US); Everybody Knows This Is Nowhere (S/US); Round And Round; Down By The River (S); The Losing End; Running Dry (Requiem For The Rockets); Cowgirl In The Sand

Running time:
40.32

Current CD:
87599272422

Further listening:
Tonight's The Night (1975); Zuma (1976); Rust Never Sleeps (1979); Arc/Weld (1991)

Further reading:
MOJO 10, 25, 44; Neil Young: Here We Are In The Years (Johnny Rogan, 1982); http://hyperrust.org

Euphoria
A Gift From Euphoria

Two musical nomads take psychedelic rock, bluegrass and orchestral ballads into lasting obscurity.

From the cover of their only album, Wesley Watt and Bill Lincoln stare out moodily like an odd couple in an old master, beneath them a pseudo-biblical text ending: "For I am the music, the instrument of God". Well, the music certainly moves in mysterious ways.

Little is known about Euphoria, but how they secured a deal with Capitol allowing them to record this ambitious album is perhaps the greatest puzzle of all. The culmination of a musical journey between California and Texas, Nashville and London — encountering such disparate bands as the Thirteenth Floor Elevators, Love and the Bee Gees — *A Gift from Euphoria* is a work of startling diversity and eccentric charm. After the lushly orchestrated opening, which is sung partly in French, a crash of tympani heralds the first of a series of sudden, disorientating transitions, as Lisa surrenders to the Stone River Hill Song — a slice of banjo bluegrass and bar-room piano.

The album's defining moment follows with the exhortation: "Jesus knew life is changing/So take my hand/To change this land/*Change it!*" whereupon the band burst raucously into Did You Get The Letter and any remaining preconceptions are swept away in a blaze of distorted guitar. The remainder is a roller-coaster ride of laid-back psychedelia (Through a Window), unabashed country (I'll Be Home To You), atmospheric sound effects (Young Miss Pflugg) and whispered voices over delicate harpsichord (Lady Bedford). The crowning moment is the achingly beautiful Sunshine Woman: "Ice cream palace in your eyes/Paper horses racing by", which heralds a subtle, splendid climax of strings, French horns and female chorus. With its quintessentially English references to chips and tea, it is tempting to suggest that Docker's Son was one of the tracks recorded in London. It was here that Euphoria may have crossed paths with the Bee Gees (given "special thanks" on the inside cover) who, in the same year, brought an unexpected Nashville influence to their double album, *Odessa*. Benefiting from Nik Venet's sympathetic production, *A Gift From Euphoria* exemplifies the bravado and folly of an era that was rapidly approaching its close. It must have cost a small fortune to record, yet its scope was probably too ambitious for most people to comprehend. The present whereabouts of Watt and Lincoln are unknown.

Record label:
Capitol

Produced
by Hamilton Wesley Watt Jr, William D Lincoln, Nik Venet (credited as 'Nikolas Venetoulis').

Recorded
in Hollywood, Nashville and London; 1968.

Released:
spring 1969

Chart peaks:
None (UK) None (US)

Personnel:
Hamilton Wesley Watt Jr (v, g); William D Lincoln (v, g); Irwin Webb (oa)

Track listing:
Lisa; Stone River Hill Song; Did You Get The Letter; Through A Window; Young Miss Pflugg; Lady Bedford; Suicide On The Hillside Sunday Morning After Tea; Sweet Fanny Adams; I'll Be Home To You; Sunshine Woman; Hollyville Train; Docker's Son; Something For The Milkman; Too Young To Know; World

Running time:
43.05

Current CD:
SEE CD 465

Further listening:
There's nothing else. But the Bee Gees' Odessa has a similar spirit.

Burt Bacharach
Make It Easy On Yourself

Having conquered the Brill Building, Broadway and movies, Burt becomes a reluctant pop star.

As a composer, producer and arranger of hits by Dionne Warwick, Dusty Springfield, Cilla Black, Tom Jones, Herb Alpert and scores of other eminent '60s popsters, it was only a matter of time before Burt Bacharach stepped into the spotlight himself. Especially given his twinkling good looks and soft-spoken charisma. But he insists he had to be coaxed into his star turn.

"I was very insecure about singing," he says. "It's one thing to do it in a live performance on stage. It's like yesterday's newspaper. It's forgotten. It wasn't so good, okay. But when you go onto tape, it's there forever. I try to sing the songs not as a singer, but just interpreting it as a composer and interpreting a great lyric that Hal [David] wrote."

On his second solo LP, he surrounds his voice (the liner notes called it a "rumpled, earnest baritone") with all the energetic components of what became known as the "Bacharach Sound" – honey-dipped flugelhorns, bossa-nova sidesticks, breezy flutes, molto fortissimo strings and cooing female voices – and interprets hits such as I'll Never Fall In Love Again, Promises, Promises and Make It Easy On Yourself.

"I didn't want to make the songs the same way as they'd been done," Bacharach says, "so I'd split vocals and instrumentals and try to make it interesting to me, and hopefully interesting to the listener. 'For me, it's about the peaks and valleys of where a record can take you. You can tell a story and be able to be explosive one minute then get quiet as kind of a satisfying resolution."

His co-producer and engineer Phil Ramone recalls how the dynamics originated from Burt himself: "The whole room would come to life with his conducting – the way he would look over at the drummer and with just the flick of his finger, things could happen. Once the groove was happening in the room, forget it, there was nothing like it. And everything, including the strings, responded to the kind of body movement that Burt had. He brings an incredible amount of life to the studio. He's probably one of the most amazing musicians in the world."

Record label:
A&M

Produced:
by Burt Bacharach and Phil Ramone.

Recorded:
at A&M Studio, New York; 1968.

Released:
June 1969

Chart peaks:
None (UK) 51 (US)

Personnel:
Burt Bacharach (v, a, oa); Phil Ramone (e); with orchestra

Track listing:
Promises, Promises; I'll Never Fall In Love Again; Knowing When To Leave; Any Day Now; Wanting Things; Whoever You Are I Love You; Make It Easy On Yourself; Do You Know The Way To San Jose; Pacific Coast Highway (S); She's Gone Away; This Guy's In Love With You

Running time:
35.32

Current CD:
Universal 394188

Further listening:
The Look Of Love: The Burt Bacharach Collection (1998)

Further reading:
MOJO 28;
http://studentweb.tulane.edu/~mark/bacharach.html

Creedence Clearwater Revival
Bayou Country

Second album from San Francisco's own Southern boys.

In 1964, the Californian, Berkeley-based jazz label Fantasy decided the time had come to cash in on the beat craze and auditioned local instrumental group Tommy Fogerty and the Blue Velvets. Encouraged by A&R man Hy Weiss to sound more British, they became The Visions and then The Golliwogs, releasing singles on the label's Scorpio subsidiary without much success. Then in 1966, key personnel John Fogerty and Doug Clifford were drafted. 18 months later, Fogerty returned home determined to quit trying to sound British and do something a little truer to his roots.

"Rock'n'roll is Southern," he says today, "and that's why I'm Southern. Because what I learned from was Southern. I rest my case." And there are few Southern rock tracks greater than the joyful, folksy chug of Proud Mary, with its utopian vision of Mississippi river life, the kind of song that sounds as if it has always been there. Freshly discharged from the army, Fogerty wrote the song as an expression of his overwhelming sense of freedom.

The group's new style needed a new name and The Golliwogs became Creedence Clearwater Revival. A cover version of Dale Hawkins' Suzie-Q attracted attention as a welcome antidote to the pretensions of acid rock and the sterility of bubblegum pop, and Fantasy switched them to the parent label. John Fogerty has since maintained that he steered the group every inch of the way from that moment on. "This stuff is hardly rocket science," says bassist Stu Cook, rebutting such claims. "It's not as if we had two-and-a-half brain cells and needed a guiding light to lead us through the key of E. We'd been together 10 years already. We learned how to play together. The Proud Mary bassline is mine for a start – I could go on." Cook in no way impugns Fogerty's composing skills or vision, often describing him as a "genius", but adds that he's learned to "beware of geniuses".

"*Bayou Country* is my favourite Creedence album because we had played those songs live and because we were still a band," continues Cook. "We still had an input at the mix, welcomed or not. Hank McGill got a great sound from my Rickenbacker on tape and it survived all sabotage attempts!"

Record label:
Fantasy

Produced
by John Fogerty.

Recorded
at RCA Studios, Hollywood

Released:
June 1969

Chart peaks:
None (UK) 7 (US)

Personnel:
John Fogerty (g, v); Tom Fogerty (g); Stu Cook (b); Doug 'Cosmo' Clifford (d); Hank McGill (e)

Track listing:
Born On The Bayou; Bootleg; Graveyard Train; Good Golly Miss Molly; Penthouse; Proud Mary (S); Keep On Chooglin'

Running time:
34.07

Current CD:
FCD24 8387-2

Further listening:
Green River (1969); Willy And The Poor Boys (1970); Cosmo's Factory(1970): The Blue Ridge Rangers: Blue Ridge Rangers (1973), essentially a John Fogerty solo album of Country covers, lovingly rendered.

Further reading:
Bad Moon Rising: The Unofficial Story Of Creedence Clearwater Revival (Hank Bordowitz, 1998); Up Around The Bend: The Oral History Of Creedence Clearwater Revival (Craig Werner, 1998); www.jyu.fi/~petkasi/ccr-jcf

The album is bookended by the two tracks that opened and closed the band's sets at clubs such as Deno's and Carlo's: Born On The Bayou is a rocking, funky thing that announces Fogerty's long-running obsession with Southern pop, while Keep On Chooglin' is a rumbling, good-time salute to blue-collar pleasures. Vocally, Fogerty is superb throughout. His wonderfully rugged rendition of Little Richard's Good Golly Miss Molly tips a nod to one mentor and the hypnotic Graveyard Train does the same to bluesman Howlin' Wolf. *Bayou Country* represents the start of CCR's golden period – doing much to establish their unique coalition of fans, ranging from hippies to grown-up bobby-soxers and truck-drivin' men.

Crosby, Stills And Nash
Crosby, Stills And Nash

One moment of harmony beget a roller-coaster career.

Disillusioned by the commerciality of his work with The Hollies, and increasingly beguiled by the burgeoning underground music scene in the States, Graham Nash was spending more and more time with ex-Byrd David Crosby and former Buffalo Springfield kingpin Stephen Stills. The three were already united by a love of dope and good music, when they discovered the flawless compatibility of their voices. Crosby and Stills were working out one of the latter's compositions, You Don't Have To Cry, when, as an experiment, Nash added an irresistible third harmony.

"It was," Stills reflected, "one of those moments."

Crosby, Stills & Nash were, on paper, an unbeatable combination, and much was riding on their debut album. They began rehearsing together at Notting's Hill's Moscow Road in late 1968, with The Beatles' Blackbird as an early vocal try-out, and all three brought their best material to the sessions. Nash, who had been chafing at what he saw as The Hollies' musical conservatism, supplied the drug-infused Marrakesh Express and Pre-Road Downs; Crosby contributed the beguiling Guinevere and timely Long Time Gone; but it was Stills who felt he had most to prove, and his were the lengthy opening (Suite: Judy Blue Eyes) and closer (49 Bye-Byes), as well as the inimitable Helplessly Hoping – the one song on the album that indicated the trio's potential for true greatness.

Harmonically intricate and musically potent, the album was more than just a calling card for Messrs Crosby, Stills & Nash; it was an album very much of its time, an Us vs Them broadside across the Hippie-Straight divide. The album spoke directly to the millions of young people who, while disillusioned by a society they saw as without values and despairing of inequality, were also terrified of getting drafted to fight in the war that was raging in Vietnam. Besides the knowing drug innuendoes and heavy emphasis on "ladies", there was Stills' Spanish coda to Suite: Judy Blue Eyes – a plea to President Nixon to let US citizens visit Cuba.

Short of a fourth member for touring, Neil Young, Stills' old sparring partner from Buffalo Springfield was recruited, and within three months of this album's release, Crosby, Stills, Nash & Young were playing at Woodstock – it was only their second gig, but the world had got its first supergroup.

Record label:
Atlantic

Produced
by Crosby, Stills and Nash.

Recorded
at Wally Heider's Studio III, Los Angeles

Released:
June 1969

Chart peaks:
25 (UK) 6 (US)

Personnel:
8David Crosby (v, rg); Stephen Stills (g, b, o, v); Graham Nash (v); Dallas Taylor (d); Bill Halverston (e)

Track listing:
Suite: Judy Blue Eyes (S); Marrakesh Express (S); Guinevere; You Don't Have To Cry; Pre-Road Downs; Wooden Ships; Lady Of The Island; Helplessly Hoping; Long Time Gone; 49 Bye-Byes

Running time:
40.57

Current CD:
WEA 7567-82651-2

Further listening:
The Best Of Crosby Stills And Nash box set (1991)

Further reading:
The Complete Guide To The Music Of Crosby, Stills, Nash And Young (Johnny Rogan, 1998); Crosby, Stills, Nash And Young: The Visual Documentary (Johnny Rogan, 1996);
www.crosbystillsnash.com

Judy Henske & Jerry Yester
Farewell Aldebaran

The definitive space-blues-Arthurian-bubblegum album.

Signed to Frank Zappa former Lovin' Spoonful member Jerry Yester and his singer/songwriter wife Judy Henske, created a forgotten classic. Its ten songs range from surreal rock (Snowblind) and spoof bubblegum (Horses On A Stick) to Arthurian folk rock (Three Ravens) and, on the title track, full blown avant-garde composition, owing more to Stockhausen or Sun Ra than the pop psych of the Spoonful.

The couple got together in 1962 when Henske was in vogue as a pop singer with a distinctive, lusty voice and Yester was her accompanist. Jerry then joined the Modern Folk Quartet and Judy signed to Elektra where she made several albums with Herb Cohen as producer, scoring a hit with High Flying Bird (later recorded by Jefferson Airplane). When Jerry was invited to join The Lovin' Spoonful the couple moved to New York and started writing together. When the Spoonful finally split, Cohen suggested they move back to California and record for Straight.

With help from Jerry's Spoonful comrade Zal Yanovsky, began to graft musical flesh onto the songs they'd written. Powerful opening track Snowblind, was a testament to the skills of this experienced line-up.

"We wrote the song kind of as we did it," reveals Yester. "I was playing rhythm guitar, Zal was playing lead, Judy was singing and Larry Beckett [ex Tim Buckley] was playing drums. The whole thing just took shape in an hour." Another stellar moment is the closing, title track, which leaves pop and rock trajectories to enter another musical orbit.

"I loved the idea of a huge asteroid burning up in our atmosphere and telling its story," says Jerry. Creating the apocalyptic voice of this imagined invader involved some unusual techniques. "For the voice of the asteroid, we put Judy's voice through a series of ring modulators, took all the actual tone out and just made it all overtones."

Despite some rave critical response, *Farewell Aldebaran* crashed to earth. Henske and Yester went on to form the short-lived Rosebud until their marriage collapsed and they went their separate ways.

Record label:
Straight

Produced
by Jerry Yester and Zal Yanovsky.

Recorded
Feb–March 1969.

Released:
June 1969

Chart peaks:
None (UK) None (US)

Personnel:
Judy Henske (v); Jerry Yester (k, Moog, g, banjo, zither); Zal Yanovsky (g, b); Ry Cooder (rhythm mandolin); David Lindley (bowed banjo); Solomon Feldthouse (dulcimer); Toxey French (d); Larry Beckett (d); Jerry Scheff (b); Joe Osborn (b); Dick Rosmini (g)

Track listing:
Snowblind; Horses On A Stick; Lullaby; St. Nicholas Hall; Three Ravens; Raider; One More Time; Rapture; Charity; Farewell Aldebaran

Running time:
33.48

Currently unavailable on CD

Further listening:
Judy Henske's solo LPs, High Flyin' Bird (1963) and Little Bit Of Sunshine (1965)

Further reading:
www.seorf.ohiou.edu/~xx103/bio.html

Kaleidoscope (US)
Incredible

Apogee of these undervalued American avatars of acid-rock comes with Middle-Eastern spice.

Jimmy Page once described the American band called Kaleidoscope as, "My favourite band of all time, my ideal band. Absolutely brilliant"; the influential critic Robert Shelton, who crucially boosted Dylan's early career, enthusiastically called them "super-eclectic"; and pioneering FM disc jockey Tom Donahue hailed them as, "one of the best groups in the country". And much good did such acclaim do the band, for *Incredible*, like the other three albums they released during their original career (they reformed in the late '70s), sold negligibly. And yet in their adventurousness and their eclecticism, Kaleidoscope were an archetypal '60s band, creators of cutting edge acid-rock and trailblazers of world and fusion musics, who by rights should now be regarded as legends.

"We wanted to experiment with a music which could combine various other musical areas with rock . . . to see if we could come up with something new and interesting," asserts guitarist David Lindley.

And *Incredible*, their third album, triumphantly demonstrates how they achieved their ambition, for the music sweeps up rock, blues, country, folk, cajun and Near and Middle Eastern musics, all linked by an unmistakeably psychedelic consciousness. Timid souls should however be warned that this is not the whimsical, cutesy psychedelia of the "Let's all go and blow our minds down in Toytown" variety. Much of the album is possessed by a unnerving strangeness. Cuckoo, for example, the band's reinvention of a traditional folk song, is permeated with a sense of evil, singer Feldthouse chillingly snarling the line, "Let's make love now," an invitation that never sounded less enticing. Or consider Petite Fleur, which ends with a sinister cackle. Or the near 12-minute Seven-Ate Suite, where the cymbals sound like knives being sharpened, assorted exotic instruments solo eerily, and suddenly, after more than five intense minutes, Feldthouse starts wailing in tongues.

"He's singing Turkish obscenities," explains Lindley, more prosaicly. "We didn't want to be a conventional band."

Record label:
Epic

Produced
by Jackie Mills.

Recorded
1969.

Released:
June 1969

Chart peaks:
None (UK) None (US)

Personnel:
David Lindley (g, vn, banjo, v); Solomon Feldthouse (g, o, clarinet, caz, jumbus, v); Templeton Parcely (vn, o, v); Stuart A Brotman (b, v); Paul Lagos (d, v); Max Buda (hm); Bob Breault (e)

Track listing:
Lie To Me; Let The Good Love Flow; Tempe Arizona aka Killing Floor (S/US only); Petite Fleur; Banjo; Cuckoo; Seven-Ate Sweet

Running time:
30.58

Current CD:
Edsel EDCD 533

Further listening:
Side Trips (1967) and A Beacon From Mars (1968) have the same killer combination of acid rock and fearless eclecticism. Do not confuse them with the British psych-pop band of the same name — as record shops often do.

Further reading:
very little exists except the booklets that accompany the CD reissues.

Jeff Beck
Beck-Ola

Career high-point for mercurial guitar genius.

In retrospect, *Beck-Ola* is clearly the soundtrack of a band in the midst of disintegration. By 1969, The Jeff Beck Group was barely intact. The seeds of discontent had been sown after the release of *Truth*, when other band members complained that their credits were too small. To ensure his visibility this time, vocalist Rod Stewart insisted that the credits for *Beck-Ola* read: "Rod Stewart, vocalist extraordinaire".

On *Beck-Ola*, Beck's guitar is more combative and flinty than the sinuous sounds of *Truth*, but that is perhaps because the band members were constantly at odds. Prior to the band's second tour of America in February 1969, Beck had fired and rehired Ron Wood twice and, having shown drummer Mickey Waller the door, replaced him with Sounds Incorporated stickman Tony Newman. Only Rod Stewart seemed beyond Beck's compulsive changes. During the band's second US tour, Beck collapsed after a concert in Minneapolis and cancelled the rest of the dates, hastening home to make another record.

"The world was ready for the Jeff Beck Group in a way much bigger than I had imagined," he says. "I suddenly realised I had to go home and do something about it. So in four days, we nailed together *Beck-Ola*. The whole damn album was pretty much dreamt up on the spot. It was made in desperation to get product out. We just got vicious on it, because we were all in bad moods, and it came out quite wild."

In the brief liner notes, Beck became an apologist for the material: "Today, with all the hard competition in the music business, it's almost impossible to come up with anything totally original. So we haven't. However, this album was made with the accent on heavy music."

To drive the point home, the former art student chose a Magritte print of an oversized green apple for the album cover. "The painting had something heavy and weighty about it. Ron Wood and I were looking through this book of Magritte, and I said, 'Let's just open the book at random and see what happens'."

Beck sees *Beck-Ola* today as "a good reference point for where serious metal started. It may not be up to scratch sound-wise, but the riffs, the notes, the whole attitude was vicious."

Record label:
Columbia

Produced
by Mickie Most.

Recorded
at Kingsway Recorders, London; May 1969.

Released:
July 1969

Chart peaks:
39 (UK) 15 (US)

Personnel:
Jeff Beck (g, b); Rod Stewart (v); Ron Wood (b, g); Tony Newman (d); Nicky Hopkins (k, p); Martin Birch (e)

Track listing:
All Shook Up; Spanish Boots; Girl From Mill Valley; Jailhouse Rock; Plynth (Water Down The Drain) (S/withdrawn); Hangman's Knee; Rice Pudding

Running time:
30.29

Current CD:
TOCP6318

Further listening:
Truth (1968), the band's sparkling debut; Blow By Blow(1975), an all-instrumental effort where Beck teamed up with Beatles producer George Martin; Beckology 3-CD box set.

Further reading:
www.epicrecords.com/jeffbeck

Fairport Convention
Unhalfbricking

The record that sowed the seeds of British folk-rock

In its long, chequered history, Top Of The Pops has screened many bizarre TV moments. Few, perhaps, quite as mad as the sight in 1969 of Fairport Convention performing the Bob Dylan song If You Gotta Go, Go Now – Cajun style. Richard Thompson on accordion, Ashley Hutchings playing double bass with a French loaf, Dave Mattacks on washboard the song leapt to the dizzy heights of Number 21 in the British charts, their only hit. "We were," mused Hutchings, "very impetuous in those days, very sparky. There was certainly a feeling of experimentation, great energy then."

Unhalfbricking played a crucial role in the Fairport story, marking the arrival of Dave Swarbrick on fiddle and the first hint of their epochal step into serious folk music territory. It was also the album they'd just finished when drummer Martin Lamble was killed on the M1 in May, '69 as roadie Harvey Branham drove their transit van near Scratchwood Services on the way back from a gig in Birmingham. The band were still in shock when the album was compiled by Boyd and released, and they almost split completely. Eventually they opted to regroup with Swarbrick as a full time member and Dave Mattacks as drummer. (It was this line-up that cut *Liege & Lief*.)

Unhalfbricking stands as a folk rock benchmark; Thompson believes it's better than its more celebrated successor. While there was a real sense of fun about the Cajun influence of Million Dollar Bash, Cajun Woman and If You Gotta Go (which they translated into French), Thompson weighed in with a dramatic composition which provided a signpost to his songwriting future, Genesis Hall, and singer Sandy Denny contributed her greatest song, Who Knows Where The Time Goes? But most profound of all was their epic arrangement of A Sailor's Life. "Sandy used to sing Scots ballads in the bus or dressing room, and that's really what got them intrigued by British traditional music," explains producer and manager Joe Boyd. "She specifically played them A Sailor's Life, which she used to do in the clubs. I went to see them in Bristol and heard them do it for the first time and it was wonderful. How do you put a rock'n'roll attitude to a traditional ballad? There it is."

Record label:
Island

Produced by
Joe Boyd and Simon Nicol.

Recorded
at Olympic Studios, London; March–April 1969.

Released:
July 1969

Chart peaks:
12 (UK) None (US)

Personnel:
Dave Swarbrick (fiddle, mandolin, v); Sandy Denny (v, g); Richard Thompson (v, g); Marc Ellington (v); Ashley Hutchings (b, v); Trevor Lucas (g, pc, triangle, v); Simon Nicol (v, g); Martin Lamble (d, vn); Ian Matthews (v); Marc Wellington (v); John Wood (e)

Track listing:
Genesis Hall; Si Tu Dois Partir (S); Autopsy; A Sailor's Life; Cajun Woman; Who Knows Where The Time Goes?; Percy's Song; Million Dollar Bash

Running time:
35.42

Current CD:
IMCD61

Further listening:
What We Did On Our Holidays (1968); Liege & Lief (1969); Sandy Denny: The North Star Grassman And The Ravens (1970). Hear an alternative take of A Sailor's Life on Watching The Dark, a 3-CD retrospective of Richard Thompson. Other favoured Fairport albums are Full House and Rising For The Moon.

Further reading:
MOJO 9, 55; Meet On The Ledge: Fairport Convention, The Classic Years (Patrick Humphries, 1997)

Procol Harum
A Salty Dog

Procol Harum remain a greatly undervalued band, and this was undoubtedly their finest hour.

For most people, the story of Procol Harum began, and ended, with Whiter Shade Of Pale. After that one era-defining single, the band simply skipped the light fandango right out of the frame. But that, as with so many rock'n'roll clichés, is only half the picture. Procol Harum actually went on to record a further ten albums, and this, their third, is generally regarded among fans as their best.

A Salty Dog was their fourth single, released in June 1969 – a swirling, Gothic epic, drenched in salt spray, it was progressive rock at its very best, Procol Harum *in excelsis*. The subsequent album built on the band's strengths – Trower's guitar flowed freely (he was yet to be subsumed by his Hendrix infatuation); Brooker had rarely sung better; Fisher's production was '69 rock in Cinerama; and Barrie Wilson's thunderous drumming (he was Jimmy Page's original choice for the Led Zeppelin drumstool) underpinned the whole album. As well as the title track, the music was ambitious on Matthew Fisher's epic Pilgrim's Progress and Wreck Of The Hesperus. They got all heavy on The Devil Came From Kansas, folkie on Milk Of Human Kindness, and slipped into a Latin rumba groove on Boredom; while All This And More took Procol Harum into a stratospheric place all of its own.

The 1999 reissue added the single's B-side – the robust Long Gone Geek – which found Procol trying to sound like the Small Faces; some out-takes; and a real gem, in the shape of the only existing take of McGregor.

In its day, *A Salty Dog* received respectful reviews, and helped cement Procol's position as critics' favourites – particularly in America where they toured pretty much non-stop during the late 60s; but increasing apathy at home led to their split in 1977. Posthumously, Procol Harum began to receive the respect they had always deserved. Latterly, A Salty Dog has been covered by Marc Almond and, ahem, Sarah Brightman; while Pete Townshend and Brian May have testified to Procol's influence on The Who and Queen. Unfortunately, in the aftermath of *A Salty Dog*, the band let slip the one gig that could really have lifted them up another notch: by declining to appear at a rock festival in upstate New York – reputedly because the Trower family had already booked their summer holidays – Procol Harum missed out on Woodstock.

Record label:
Regal Zonophone

Produced
by Matthew Fisher.

Recorded
at Abbey Road, London; January–February 1969.

Released:
July 1969

Chart peaks:
27 (UK) 32 (US)

Personnel:
Gary Brooker (p, v, hm, celeste, recorder); Matthew Fisher (o, g, marimba, recorder); Dave Knights (b); Barrie Wilson (d, pc); Robin Trower (g, tambourine); Kellogs (bosun's whistle); Ken Scott; Ian Stuart, Henry Lewy (e)

Track listing:
A Salty Dog (S/UK); The Milk Of Human Kindness; Too Much Between Us; The Devil Came From Kansas (S/US); Boredom; Juicy John Pink; Wreck Of The Hesperus; All This And More; Crucifiction Lane; Pilgrim's Progress

Running time:
43.07

Current CD:
WESM534 adds Long Gone Geek; All This And More (Alt take); The Milk Of Human Kindness (Alt take); Pilgrim's Progress (Alt take) McGregor; Still There'll Be More

Further listening:
Procol Harum: 30th Anniversary Collection (1997). For the excellent later incarnation of the band seek out the mighty Grand Hotel (1973), a real forgotten gem.

Further reading:
Procol Harum: Beyond The Pale (Claes Johansen, 2000); www.procolharum.com

Jethro Tull
Stand Up

Featured a pop-up likeness of the group in the gatefold.
Sadly, a marketing wheeze that never caught on.

There was a time when Jethro Tull were kings of the British rock underground. Hard to imagine, perhaps, given the perception of many that they're purveyors of music-hall buffoonery in monstrously unfashionable clothing, but they came second only to The Beatles in the Melody Maker poll of 1969, streets ahead of more conventionally swaggering rock behemoths like Led Zeppelin or The Who. Having worked their way up by constant gigging and a reputation founded largely on Ian Anderson's uniquely charismatic and eccentric stage persona (shabby raincoat, hair, flute, standing on one leg), Tull would enjoy a good two or three years as rock aristocracy before slipping gently down to a more sustainable level. As Anderson was quick to realise, being "top of the second division" has its advantages, not least in longevity. Thirty years later the Tull brand would still be shifting a dependable half-million worldwide units per annum.

Though America would always prefer *Aqualung* (1971) and *Thick As A Brick* (1972), for the Brits the flute-dominated *Stand Up* is the fondest memory – a triumph of youthful imagination, drive, wit and naïveté with just a little dash of melancholy, where later there would be cleverness, cod-pieces and concepts.

"When we did *Stand Up*," Anderson recently recalled, "I thought, Hey, we're on our second album – there could be a third! That's about as far as I saw it going. I can remember writing the material for it and really struggling for ideas. If you get one, firstly it's a relief and secondly, if it's a good one then you're jumping up and down. That excitement was there then and it's still there now. Mind you, it would be difficult for me to write Jeffrey Goes To Leicester Square now. It would seem a bit silly."

As on Tull's debut, the influences were "black American blues, which it all started with when I was 16 years old and, from growing up in Scotland, Scottish folk music, as well as the English folk heritage which I started getting aware of later. I don't think you could call it folk rock, although it's one of the many terms that have been applied to it. I can only say we're sort of a rock band, but with a lot of different influences."

Record label:
Island

Produced
by Terry Ellis and Ian Anderson.

Recorded
at Morgan Studio, London; April 1969.

Released:
August 1, 1969

Chart peaks:
(UK) 1, (US) 20

Personnel:
Ian Anderson (v, g, flute, k, mandolin, balalaika, hm); Martin Barre (g, flute); Glen Cornick (b); Clive Bunker (d, pc); Andy Johns (e)

Track listing:
A New Day Yesterday; Jeffrey Goes To Leicester Square; Bouree; Back To The Family; Look Into The Sun; Nothing Is Easy; Fat Man; We Used To Know; Reasons For Waiting; For A Thousand Mothers

Running time:
38.18

Current CD:
CDP3210422

Further listening:
Aqualung (1971); LP/singles compilation, Living In The Past (1972)

Further reading:
Flying Colours: The Jethro Tull Reference Manual (Greg Russo, 2000) From Elvis In Memphis Elvis Presley

Elvis Presley
From Elvis In Memphis

Hot from his TV comeback, the King exorcises the frustration of his wasted years in Hollywood

Elvis's output in the '60s is unfairly maligned: whenever Presley was inspired, the results were phenomenal: *Elvis Is Back!*, the TV special, two religious albums – *His Hand In Mine* (1960) and *How Great Thou Art* (1967) – and a handful of great flop singles; but all anybody remembers are the movies. When the 34-year-old singer arrived at 827 Thomas Street, Memphis, he knew he was as good as washed-up. Chips Moman wanted the kudos of producing The King; Memphis Horn Wayne Jackson was fairly enthusiastic, "it wasn't like doing Neil Diamond," he admitted; but others were more concerned about the lack of decent material – publishers no longer needed Presley to sing their songs and take a cut. After a heated fight over Suspicious Minds (never part of any album), which Moman owned, Presley broke rank – get the songs, to hell with the percentages. Then the sessions began.

From the hoarse, autobiographical howl – "I had to leave town for a little while" – that opened Wearin' That Loved On Look, it was obvious Elvis was for real. The band, the hottest in the States in '69, fused gospel, soul and rock perfectly – though country was beyond their reach (particularly obvious on It Keeps Right On A-Hurtin'). In nine days, 20 tracks were completed; 14 more were recorded in February. Everybody knew the songs were the business, but would they sell? Deciding to keep the best track until they'd tested the water, RCA stuck out In The Ghetto. It was his first Top 10 hit since Crying In The Chapel; *From Elvis In Memphis* – "unequivocally the equal of anything he has ever done", according to Rolling Stone – recorded a respectable 13 in the US charts, then Suspicious Minds propelled him back to the top, the first time he'd been there in America since Good Luck Charm.

By this time, he'd returned to live performance, at the International Hotel in Las Vegas. A live album was welded to a second selection from Memphis: the studio set is disappointing, but the Vegas disc is essential, especially a seven-minute run at Suspicious Minds. For two more years, Presley was on top of his game again, creating a mature brand of rock that crossed the generation gap.

Record label:
RCA

Produced
by Lincoln 'Chips' Moman.

Recorded
at American Studios, Memphis;
January–February 1969.

Released:
August 1969

Chart peaks:
1 (UK) 13 (US)

Personnel:
Elvis Presley (v, g, p); Reggie Young (g);
Mike Leech (b); Gene Chrisman (d);
Bobby Emmons (o); Tommy Cogbill (b);
Bobby Wood (p); The Memphis Horns
(brass); Ed Hollis (hm); Al Pachuki (e)

Track listing:
Wearin' That Loved On Look; Only The
Strong Survive; I'll Hold You In My Heart
(Till I Can Hold You In My Arms); Long
Black Limousine; It Keeps Right On A-
Hurtin'; I'm Movin' On; Power Of My
Love; Gentle On My Mind; After Loving
You; True Love Travels On A Gravel
Road; Any Day Now; In The Ghetto (S)

Running time:
36.51

Current CD:
ND 90548

Further listening:
5-CD box-set, From Nashville To Memphis
(2000); The '68 Comeback Special – the
entire TV show (1992); Elvis In Person
(At The International Hotel) (1970);
Suspicious Minds (1999) – the whole
session plus outtakes.

Further reading:
MOJO 63; Careless Love: The Unmaking
Of Elvis Presley (Peter Guralnick, 1998)

Fleetwood Mac
Then Play On

The last and greatest recording of the Mac's first phase.

By the time Fleetwood Mac came to record *Then Play On*, they'd scored hit singles with the languid Albatross and the heartbreakingly beautiful Man Of The World, giving notice that their blue horizons were ever broadening. Danny Kirwan was now on board: his songwriting skills and his folk leanings edged an increasingly detached Jeremy Spencer further to the margins and emphasised the new directions the band were taking.

Sessions began in April 1969 with two Kirwan songs, Coming Your Way and Although The Sun Is Shining. Engineer Martin Birch recalled how he would work individually with Green and Kirwan; "Peter would come in and show me the feel and structure, lay down the basic track and when we were happy with the drums, the bass and two guitars, the others would disappear and I would work on his song until it was completely recorded . . . Then I would do the same with one of Danny's songs and it would alternate like that until the album was done."

While great music emerged, this way of working was indicative that the band was in the early throes of fragmenting. There were disputes over Oh Well, with Fleetwood and McVie almost convincing Peter not to release this magnificent work as a single.(neither was the song on the original UK version of the album).

Producing the album themselves was a mistake, according to Green. "We should have had a producer, then it might have sold better . . . we weren't completely aware of what the producer's job was."

In hindsight, you can also hear it in the songs. Green has often noted that Show-Biz Blues, "says it all about why I left Fleetwood Mac". Musically, it was a homage to Bukka White's percussive slide guitar, but "Now tell me anybody, do you really give a damn for me" is the cry of a band leader in the spotlight and under pressure. Even now, 30 years after the event, Peter Green complains, "They could have helped me more, but they just stayed in the background." Perhaps even more chilling was the spectral Closing My Eyes, Green's stark and plaintive cry for religious redemption. (His disturbed state would be further explored on his final Mac single, the majestic Green Manalishi where Green is stalked by a malevolent demon.)

Then Play On delivered symphonic, elegiac rock, so far

Record label:
Reprise

Produced
by Fleetwood Mac.

Recorded
in London; April 1969.

Released:
September 9, 1969

Chart peaks:
6 (UK) 109 (US)

Personnel:
Peter Green (g, v, hm); Jeremy Spencer (p); Danny Kirwan (g, v); John McVie (b); Mick Fleetwood (d); Martin Birch (e)

Track listing:
Coming Your Way; Closing My Eyes; Show-Biz Blues; My Dream; Underway; Oh Well (S); Although The Sun Is Shining; Rattlesnake Shake (S/US); Searching For Madge; Fighting For Madge; When You Say; Like Crying; Before The Beginning

Running time:
54.16

Current CD:
927448-2

Further listening:
The Vaudeville Years Of Fleetwood Mac 1968-1970 (1998). A spiffing two CD set which contains unreleased and extended versions of tracks on Then Play On plus unissued versions of Man of World and Green Manalishi.

Further reading:
Peter Green: The Founder Of Fleetwood Mac (Martin Clemens, 1998); My 25 Years In Fleetwood Mac (Mick Fleetwood, 1992); www.fleetwoodmac.net/penguin

removed from the rough hewn white-blooze of only 18 months previous. Whatever his state of mind at the time, Green was rightly proud of the album upon completion and remains so. "I love it, every minute of it. It is very clear to me because it's like our thoughts and feelings. There is nothing I feel I could have done better."

A Californian aesthetic was already looming – the wave-washed beaches and rolling highways suggested by Danny and Peter's wistful guitar sounds and Mick Fleetwood 's tyres-on-the road thump. Americans loved it. One can only wonder what Fleetwood Mac might have achieved had Peter stayed and created a fourth album. Oh well . . .

The Beatles
Abbey Road

Glorious almost-swan-song for the ultimate pop group.

The Beatles were falling apart in 1969. The January Get Back sessions (temporarily shelved but later Spectorised and released as *Let It Be* in May 1970) had been even more miserable than those for the White Album, John Lennon appeared more interested in promoting himself and Yoko as avant-garde peacenik performance artists than his old band, and a dispute over who should take control of The Beatles' finances saw the group that had represented such an explosion of artistic and spiritual possibilities in the '60s ending the decade as bitter, feuding businessmen. Even their remarkable producer, the normally unruffled George Martin had stayed away from the Get Back sessions: "I thought, oh gosh, I don't want to be a part of this anymore." So, he was surprised to be asked by Paul to produce a Beatles record "like we used to" but agreed on the condition that he be allowed to produce a polished studio album, which is exactly what he did. With excellent group performances, slick programming and high production values (it's the best *sounding* Beatles album) giving the impression of a unified whole, in fact the sessions were as disparate as ever, the band personally uncomfortable with each other, rarely attending the overdubbing sessions of each other's songs.

"On Come Together I would have liked to sing harmony with John," McCartney said later, "but I was too embarrassed to ask him." Paul wanted the songs linked together while John wanted each song separate, preferably with all of his on one side; the compromise of separate songs on side one and a medley taking up much of side two was reached. Although Lennon would later talk of he and Paul "cutting each other down to size to fit into some kind of format" as the main artistic reason why The Beatles could no longer continue as a group, it's also the reason why *Abbey Road* is such a success. Excesses are mostly curbed, strengths are emphasised. This, combined with Harrison's two offerings – for the first time, comparable to Lennon's and McCartney's (Frank Sinatra sang Something throughout the '70s, famously calling it "the greatest love song of the last fifty years") – make *Abbey Road* a heart-breakingly fitting epitaph. Get a certain kind of music fan of a certain age in a certain mood and he'll tell you that pop music was all downhill from here.

Record label:
Apple

Produced
by George Martin.

Recorded
at Abbey Road; February–August 1969.

Released:
September, 26 1969

Chart peaks:
1 (UK) 1 (US)

Personnel:
John Lennon (v, g, p, o); Paul McCartney (v, b, p, g, d); George Harrison (v, g, syn); Ringo Starr (d); Billy Preston (o)

Track Listing:
Come Together; Something; Maxwell's Silver Hammer; Oh! Darling; Octopus's Garden; I Want You (She's So Heavy); Here Comes The Sun; Because; You Never Give Me Your Money; Sun King; Mean Mr Mustard; Polythene Pam; She Came In Through The Bathroom Window; Golden Slumbers; Carry That Weight; The End; Her Majesty

Running time:
47.26

Currently available CD:
CDP 7 46446 2

Further listening:
Let It Be (1970); Anthology 3 (1997)

Further reading:
Revolution In The Head (Ian Macdonald, 1998); Many Years From Now (Barry Miles, 1997); The Beatles As Musicians (Walter Everett, 1999)

Jack Bruce
Songs For A Tailor

Ex-member of world's biggest band boldly follows his muse into the realms of jazz-rock.

Only a rock superstar at the peak of his power, as Bruce was after the success of Cream, could have taken a record like *Songs For A Tailor* into the charts, for the music on the album is uncompromising, uncommercial, contemporary jazz fusion. Bruce recruited some of Britain's most creative young jazz musicians, all of whom play scintillatingly, with techniques light years ahead of the average rock musician. The songs were all co-written by Bruce and lyricist Pete Brown.

"My songs are usually written using the piano and the music tends to come first," explains Bruce. "It's a question of getting into Jack's mind," offers Brown. "Some of the songs took an awfully long time – The Clearout and Weird Of Hermiston took two and a half years before we got what we wanted."

One of the album's most acclaimed songs is the cryptic Theme From An Imaginary Western.

"The words were about the Graham Bond band," clarifies Brown, referring to one of Bruce's early outfits. "I saw them as a mob of cowboys and pioneers. I was always amazed at the camaraderie between the early groups but now and then you'd get explosive situations between them, just like in the Westerns."

There is no title song, the album title being a dedication to clothing designer Jeannie Franklyn, who died in the Fairport Convention van crash.

"The day she was killed I got a letter from her which said all the little things she always used to say, like, 'Sing some high notes for me,'" recalls Bruce.

Colosseum drummer Jon Hiseman, who plays on the album, still enthuses about it. "It was the best album I ever made. Jack was a genius: he plays the best bass in the world, he's a magnificent singer and he writes wonderful music. But I think the reason he never was a major star after Cream was Pete Brown's lyrics are too obscure for a popular audience." Bruce seems unconcerned. "I've never wanted extreme commercial success. Cream was an accidental thing that was such a huge success I don't have to worry about money, so I've been able to concentrate on what I want to do."

Record label:
Polydor

Produced
by Felix Pappalardi.

Recorded
at De Lane Lea, London; April–June 1969.

Released:
September 1969

Chart peaks:
6 (UK) 55 (US)

Personnel:
Jack Bruce (v, p, b, o, c, g); Harry Beckett (t); Henry Lowther (t); Dick Heckstall-Smith, Art Themen (s); Chris Spedding (g); Jon Hiseman (d); John Marshall (d); Felix Pappalardi (v, pc, g); John Mumford (tb); L'Angelo Misterioso (g); Andrew Johns (e)

Track listing:
Never Tell Your Mother She's Out Of Tune; Theme For An Imaginary Western; Tickets To Water Falls; Weird Of Hermiston; Rope Ladder To The Moon; The Ministry Of Bag; He The Richmond; Boston Ball Game, 1969; To Isengard; The Clearout

Running time:
31.47

Current CD:
835 242-2

Further listening:
Of the three jazz-influenced albums Bruce released after Cream, his own favourite is Harmony Row (1971), "I just sat down at the piano, with a joint, and there it was," he declared.

Further reading:
MOJO 18; www.jackbruce.com

Chicago Transit Authority

Chicago Transit Authority

A benchmark for brass and guitar-fuelled jazz-rock.

At the tail end of the '60s rock big-band Chicago Transit Authority were peers and label mates with Santana, Janis Joplin, and Sly And The Family Stone. The band had honed their craft playing up to six sets a night on the bar band circuit. Based in Chicago and its suburbs, they had begun as Big Thing, changing their name to Chicago Transit Authority in May, 1967. In August they were spotted by manager James William Guercio, who was producing local Top 40 band The Buckinghams and would cut the breakthrough second album by Blood Sweat And Tears. Robert Lamm did most of the writing and Jim Pankow most of the arranging on their debut album, but Guercio played a crucial role, imposing tightness and economy.

For all the indulgence soon to be associated with rock LPs – not least Chicago's – their first album was recorded in just two weeks. It contains some great musical moments: the *Forever Changes*-style latin brass coda at the end of Beginnings, Kath's guitar sustain as he comes in after the lengthy percussion break in I'm A Man – his guitar runs are exemplary throughout when he's augmenting, not soloing. Then there's the "The whole world is watching" chant recorded from the demonstration at the 1968 Democratic Convention in Chicago. No band that learned its chops at the same time as Mayor Daly's law enforcers were cracking heads could have emerged from that bloody environment without comment – a great McLuhanesque soundbite from the days when it really did look like the revolution might be televised.

It hasn't all worn so well. Kath and Lamm's mannered rock growls and Cetera's wavery upper register do, in truth, grate a bit over the four sides. Strange to consider that their harmonies sounded sublime at the time. In essence that's Chicago. A greater-than-the-sum-of-their-parts outfit who, in their early days at least, soared majestically. Their second album was equally inspired, but dedicating it 'to the revolution' whilst being promoted with the big bucks of the CBS rock machine merely aroused the ire of the rock press and the band's early critical acclaim rapidly wilted. Bludgeoning a fresh and inventive formula to death by issuing three consecutive double albums, and a live quadruple, in the space of two years didn't help matters either – so remember them this way.

Record Label:
Columbia

Produced
by James William Guercio.

Recorded
at CBS studios, New York

Released:
September 1969

Chart peaks:
9 (UK) 17 (US)

Personnel:
Peter Cetera (v); Terry Kath (g, v); Robert Lamm (k, v); James Pankow (tb); Daniel Seraphine (d); Walter Parazaider (woodwind; v) Lee Loughnane (t, v); Fred Catero (e)

Track Listing:
Introduction; Does Anybody Really Know What Time It Is?; Beginnings; Questions 67 And 68; Listen; Poem 58; Free Form Guitar; South California Purples; I'm A Man; Prologue August 29, 1968; Someday August 29, 1968; Liberation

Running time:
77.43

Current CD:
CRD3001

Further listening:
Chicago II

Further reading:
'Chicago At Carnegie Hall', from Psycotic Reactions And Carburetor Dung (Lester Bangs, 1988)

The Stooges
The Stooges

Debut from Michigan misfits, regarded by most as the world's punk pioneers

R ock music distilled down to its barest essentials, *The Stooges* still sounds fresher and more contemporary than most of the punk, alternative, glam and thrash-metal material it allegedly spawned in the ensuing decades. Fittingly, its recording was a perfect combination of planning and serendipity. Signed by Elektra as a kind of adjunct to leading Detroit band the MC5, The Stooges hit New York intent on capturing their live set, which comprised around four songs: "We had I Wanna Be Your Dog, 1969 and No Fun, along with We Will Fall," says guitarist Ron Asheton. "[Label boss Jac] Holzman goes, 'You got any more songs?' and we said, 'Oh yeah.' So we sat down in the Chelsea Hotel, came up with Little Doll, Real Cool Time and Not Right, we rehearsed it one time and did it all the next day, one take for each tune."

The Stooges' simplistic, gonzoid sound did not derive from mere stupidity; the minimal lyrics, mostly taken from Stooge in-house slang, were meant to echo the stripped down couplets of the bluesmen Iggy had heard in Chicago. The slow pace at which the band attack the songs adds a monumental, menacing under-tone: "The tempos were a little slow because we were all constantly on pot," says Iggy. "When there was an audience the tempos would come up because we were shitting our collective little pants. But without the audience the dope took over!"

The day after their writing stint, The Stooges stacked up their Marshalls in the Hit Factory: "We stick our Marshalls on 10 and start doing our thing, and Cale's shouting 'No no no, you can't play this loud!'" says Asheton. "This was the only way we knew how to play, because the sound of the instruments, the power, was the catalyst to drive us on. So we went on strike. They couldn't believe it, we went into the sound booth, sat down and started smoking hash." Producer John Cale engineered a compromise, the band turned down one notch to 9, and the songs were recorded with minimal decorum. Iggy claims that Cale's "bizarre art mix" of the album was dumped after the singer staged a tantrum in Jac Holzman's office; Iggy supervised the mix heard on the final version. Released to widespread indifference outside the band's Detroit stronghold, *The Stooges* scraped into the lower reaches of the American charts, and was deleted just a couple of years before every aspiring British punk guitarist started learning the iconic riffs to No Fun, 1969, and I Wanna Be Your Dog.

Record label:
Elektra

Produced
by John Cale.

Recorded
at Jerry Ragavoy's R&B Studio (later the Record Plant), New York; June 19–21 1969.

Released:
September 1969

Chart peaks:
None (UK) 106 (US)

Personnel:
Iggy Stooge (v); Ron Asheton (g); Scott Asheton (d); Dave Alexander (b)

Track listing:
1969; I Wanna Be Your Dog (S); We Will Fall; No Fun; Real Cool Time; Ann; Not Right; Little Doll

Running time:
34.24

Current CD:
EKS 47051

Further listening:
Fun House (1970) takes the basic blueprint one step further.

Further reading:
MOJO 29; www.rawiguana.com

Van Morrison
Astral Weeks

*Van's first official solo album went beyond blues rock to a
magical place many have tried to revisit since.*

Released from his contract with Bert Berns's Bang Records,
Van was free at last to explore his musical vision. With a
handful of songs written in Belfast and Boston, he went into
Century Sound Studios on Manhattan's West 52nd Street and
created a recording of such breathtaking originality that it
sounded like a career pinnacle rather than a beginning.

He'd told his new managers Lewis Merenstein and Robert
Schwaid that he was aiming for a "jazz feel". So jazz buff Schwaid
recruited a quartet of crack New York sessionmen that included
his bassist friend Richard Davis and drummer Connie Kay from
The Modern Jazz Quartet. The only member of Van's then-
current band was flautist John Payne. Shortly after Van's 23rd
birthday, on the September 25 session, from 7–11pm they
recorded Cyprus Avenue, Madame George, Beside You and Astral
Weeks, with Van isolated in a vocal booth and apparently lost in
his own thoughts. Three weeks later the same musicians returned
to record Sweet Thing, Ballerina, Young Lovers Do and Slim Slow
Slider. String overdubs and the harpsichord on Cyprus Avenue
were added by arranger Larry Fallon during mixing sessions; even
where they sound like an afterthought, they add an unexpected
texture to the basic tracks' jazz lilt, heightening the eerie,
nostalgic mood that makes *Astral Weeks* so enduringly fascinating.

Guitarist Jay Berliner hadn't heard of Van Morrison
before the September 25 session and wasn't to hear the album
until the late '70s when younger friends pointed out to him that
he had contributed to a classic. "In those days I was so busy that
I had no idea what I was playing on," recalls Berliner. "I played
classical guitar [which] was very unusual in that context. We
were used to playing to charts, but Van just played us the songs
on his guitar and then told us to go ahead and play exactly what
we felt." Although the finished tracks were essentially live takes,
both Schwaid and John Payne remember the material being
much longer during recording. "About five minutes of improvisational sax playing was cut from Slim Slow Slider," says Payne.
"I was just jamming with Van and Richard Davis. It was incredible stuff. It made me sick that they cut it out." (Tapes of the
jams were given to Warner Brothers by Schwaid in the '70s but
have never featured on any reissues.)

Although production was credited to Lewis Merenstein,

Record label:
Warner Brothers

Produced
by Lewis Merenstein.

Recorded
at Century Sound Studios, New York City;
September 25 and October 15, 1968.

Released:
September 1969

Chart peaks:
None (UK) None (US)

Personnel:
Van Morrison (v, g); Jay Berliner (ag);
Richard Davis (b); Connie Kay (d); John
Payne (flute, soprano s); Warren Smith Jr
(pc, vibraphone); Larry Fallon (oa); Brooks
Arthur (e)

Track listing:
Astral Weeks; Beside You; Sweet Thing;
Cyprus Avenue; Young Lovers Do; Madame
George; Ballerina; Slim Slow Slider

Running time:
47.14

Current CD:
7599271762

Further listening:
Tupelo Honey (1971); St. Dominic's
Preview (1972); Veedon Fleece (1974)

Further reading:
Van Morrison: Too Late To Stop Now
(Steve Turner 1993); Celtic Crossroads:
The Art Of Van Morrison (Alan Clayson
and Brian Hinton, 1997); Van Morrison
(John Collis, 1998)

Robert Schwaid and engineer Brooks Arthur (who owned Century Sound Studios), all played an important part in the sound. "In all fairness to Van, he was the one who was directing the taping," admits Schwaid. "Lew and I were in the control room but Van was the real producer." No one involved in the sessions can boast that they knew they were making a masterpiece. "I thought it was a great record at the time," says Schwaid, "but initially it was a failure. I don't think we did 20,000 copies. It wasn't until years later that people started to come up to me and tell me that their lives had been changed by *Astral Weeks*."

King Crimson
In The Court Of The Crimson King

A bunch of unknown British jazz-rock virtuosos and their pet wordsmith define prog rock with their ambitious debut.

This intense brew of classical melodies, jazz and hard rock, matched with fantastical lyrics – and housed in an intriguing, lurid sleeve – created the template for progressive rock. All the more remarkable, then, that the music was created in a week by four practically unknown musicians and a lyricist who had worked together for only six months.

Michael Giles and Robert Fripp had briefly been together in a band called Brain and moved in a folky direction as a trio, Giles, Giles & Fripp (with Michael's brother Peter), cutting one poor-selling album *The Cheerful Insanity Of . . .*, and a single which featured former Army bandsman Ian McDonald as a guest. Greg Lake, a schoolfriend of Fripp's and former member of The Gods, joined, Peter Giles left and the new quartet scored a management deal, a John Peel session and a three-month residency at the Marquee Club in London under the name King Crimson. Pete Sinfield, an associate of McDonald's, was recruited as a roadie and lyricist. They began work on the album shortly after appearing in front of 600,000 people at The Rolling Stones free concert in Hyde Park.

Because of Robert Fripp's subsequent takeover of the group, *In The Court Of The Crimson King* is often wrongly assumed to be largely his record. But it was a collective effort. A session with Moody Blues producer Tony Clark fell apart and the band quickly concluded they could work better by themselves. Ian McDonald, who wrote much of the music, recalls: "We recorded it in eight days, very quickly. There was no argument about anything. We just knew if an idea was usable and if it wasn't there was no fighting." They employed whatever came to hand in the studio: all the keys on an ancient pipe organ were jammed down to create the wheezy industrial noises that open the record. A Mellotron was used for the grandiose backdrop to the title track. McDonald grabbed a set of vibes for Illusion, the last segment of Moonchild. This meandering trilogy – which Fripp now admits should probably have been edited – was improvised when they realised they'd used all their original material but were reluctant to record a cover version.

Record Label:
Island

Produced
by King Crimson.

Recorded
at Wessex Sound Studios, London; July 1969.

Released:
October, 10 1969

Chart peaks:
5 (UK) 28 (US)

Personnel:
Robert Fripp (g); Ian McDonald (reeds, woodwind, vibes, k, v, Mellotron); Greg Lake (b, v); Michael Giles (d, pc, v); Peter Sinfield (words, illumination)

Track Listing:
21st Century Schizoid Man (S) (including Mirrors); I Talk To The Wind; Epitaph (including March For No Reason; Tomorrow And Tomorrow); Moonchild (including The Dream; The Illusion); The Court Of The Crimson King (S) (including The Return Of The Fire Witch; The Dance Of The Puppets)

Running time:
43.54

Current CD:
EGCD1

Further listening:
Fripp and Sinfield taped the rest of the line-up's material on In The Wake Of Poseidon (1970). Cirkus (1999) is a good two CD round-up of 30 years of Crimson.

Further reading:
MOJO 73; Robert Fripp (Eric Tamm, 1990); www.elephant-talk.com; www.discipline.co.uk

The album was released to wide acclaim, not least for the new standards of musicianship it set. Pete Townshend of The Who declared it "an uncanny masterpiece". But some pundits (and anyone who liked to dance) were suspicious; critic Lester Bangs condemned it as an unholy mix of "myth, mystification and Mellotrons". Nonetheless, the album quickly climbed the charts. But within four months the line-up had fallen apart, exhausted by touring and the pressure of sudden success. Says Fripp, who still leads a version of King Crimson today, "Some of the musical vocabulary may seem dated now, but there's still something remarkable there waiting for listeners."

Frank Zappa
Hot Rats

Instrumental, jam-heavy fusion masterpiece.

T he arrival of *Uncle Meat* in the spring of 1969 made
Zappa's frustrations abundantly clear: his love of satire
and talent for outrage were clearly denying him recognition as
a composer. Its comparative simplicity, downplayed lyrics and a
sleeve note advertising the joys of something called "overdubbing", set the stage for its immortal successor six months later.
The almost entirely instrumental *Hot Rats* was the perfect
Zappa release for those intrigued by his music but bored – or
possibly repulsed – by his wit and somewhat twisted worldview. It remains his biggest seller in the UK where its cover –
GTO stalwart Christine Frka in an abandoned swimming-pool
– so perfectly captured the progressive mood of the period.
Lured by the possibilities of its 16-track desk, Zappa repaired
to Sunset Sound and installed the most accomplished collection of West Coast veterans that money could buy – Paul
Humphrey had drummed with Wes Montgomery and Lee
Konitz, bassist Max Bennett was a Hollywood studio legend
who'd worked with Quincy Jones and Peggy Lee, Sugarcane
Harris had pioneered R&B hits in the late '50s as part of the
duo Don & Dewey. Together they cut a series of superbly
drilled compositions combining a fiercely hip (and uniquely
American) technical proficiency and a peerless ability to
improvise, much of its ornate embroidery the result of Zappa
and Underwood's jazz and classical influences.

"It was extremely interesting because the music was
interesting," Underwood reflects. It took two months of
relentless multi-tracking to perfect, with many of
Underwood's original parts eventually erased by the composer.
"*Hot Rats* was more about overdubbing than anything else,"
Zappa remembered. It also made much of that sonic device du
jour, the wah-wah pedal, of which Zappa was the absolute
master. The only vocal on the entire album – the growling
blues delivery of Willie The Pimp – was supplied by fellow
art-rock alchemist and former schoolfriend Captain Beefheart.
The lyrics coming from an interview conducted by Zappa with
a New York-based groupie called Annie. "It was kind of a turn
from the way the (earlier) band had been," Underwood
remembers. "It was a chance just to use a few studio musicians
and try other routines out."

Record label:
Reprise

Produced
by Frank Zappa.

Recorded
at Sunset Sound Studio, Los Angeles;
August–September 1969.

Released:
October 10, 1969

Chart peaks:
9 (UK) 173 (US)

Personnel:
Frank Zappa (g, octave b, pc); Ian
Underwood (p, organus maximus, flute,
clarinet, s); Captain Beefheart (v on
Willie The Pimp); Don 'Sugarcane' Harris,
Jean Luc Ponty (vn); Max Bennett,
Shuggy Otis (b); John Guerin, Paul
Humphrey, Ron Selico (d); Cliff Goldstein,
Jack Hunt, Dick Kunc (e)

Track Listing:
Peaches En Regalia; Willie The Pimp; Son
Of Mr Green Genes; Little Umbrellas; The
Gumbo Variations; It Must Be A Camel

Running time:
47.17

Current CD:
Ryko RCD 10508

Further listening:
Uncle Meat (1969); Mystery Disc (1998)

Further reading:
MOJO 4; Waiting For The Sun (Barney
Hoskyns, 1996); Frank Zappa In His Own
Words (1993); The Negative Dialectics Of
Poodle Play (Ben Watson, 1996); The
Complete Guide To The Music Of Frank
Zappa (Ben Watson, 1998 Oar Alexander
Spence

Alexander Spence
Oar

Among the most enigmatic solo albums in all of pop music.

The man who walked into Columbia studios in Nashville in December 1968 to make *Oar* was a man with a troubled history. Alexander "Skip" Spence had fallen out of Moby Grape in New York earlier that year, soon after the release of *Wow*, their excessive (but mostly superb) second album. He did not have a good time in the Big Apple; the large quantities of psychedelic drugs Spence consumed took their toll on the man. Following a violent studio incident in July 1968 in which he went after his fellow Grapesters with an axe – truly, rock criticism of the harshest sort – Spence was arrested and eventually committed to New York's Bellevue Hospital for six months. When he emerged, Columbia – amazingly – gave him the opportunity to record again and bankrolled the Nashville sessions that would comprise *Oar*. And what very weird sessions they were.

Among *Oar*'s major claims to fame is its status as one of the very first true solo, multi-tracked rock recordings. Spence indeed played and sang every note on the album – guitar, bass, drums and unforgettably intimate vocals included – in a series of sessions that in fact took several days, despite the album's back-cover claim of a one-day affair. Still, the looseness of the songs, the haphazard rhythms and fade-in/fade-out guitar overdubs, made that claim believable, which only added to the album's mystique. Then again, there were the songs themselves. One could easily imagine him making them up while staring at the walls of the mental hospital he had just spent a half-year in.

"I remember him," says Mike Figlio, the Columbia engineer most intimately involved in the making of the record. "He was kind of a way-out cat, creative, knew what he wanted. He just did one instrument at a time, just kept building it – and once we got it all down as far as instruments, he and I sat in the studio and decided how we wanted to mix it and how we wanted to make it sound."

"I think it's genius," Moby Grape guitarist Jerry Miller now says of *Oar*. But at the time, Columbia Records didn't agree – which might be a major reason the album sold minimally and was (despite favourable reviews) quickly deleted. "I think they humoured him. Not that they didn't promote it – but I don't know how they could've ever thought it was mainstream enough to *do* anything with."

Record label:
CBS

Produced
by Alexander Spence.

Recorded
at Columbia Studios, Nashville, Tennessee; December 16, 1968.

Released:
October 1969

Chart peaks:
None (UK) None (US)

Track listing:
Alexander Spence (all instruments); Charlie Bradley, Mike Figlio, Don Meehan (e)

Track listing:
Little Hands; Cripple Creek; Diana; Margaret-Tiger Rug; Weighted Down; War In Peace; Broken Heart; All Come To Meet Her; Books Of Moses; Dixie Peach Promenade; Lawrence Of Euphoria; Grey; Afro

Running time:
60.39

Current CD:
SC 11075 adds: This Time He Has Come; It's The Best Thing For You; Keep Everything Under Your Hat; Furry Heroine (Halo Of Gold); Givin' Up Things; If I'm Good; You Know; Doodle; Fountain; I Think You And I

Further listening:
Moby Grape, Moby Grape (1967); Oar tribute album, More Oar (1999)

Further reading:
The official Moby Grape website www.realgrape.com Puzzle The Mandrake Memorial

The Mandrake Memorial
Puzzle

Psychedelic delight from Philadelphia.

A stunning set upon its 1969 arrival — both because of its gorgeous packaging (Escher graphic, Milton Glaser design) and the even more beautiful music within — *Puzzle* is unlike any album you've likely heard. The final LP by this highly regarded Philadelphia-based band, it smoothly blends slightly trippy, ballad-laced rock with full orchestration and chorale and seduces with every listen. With vague lyrics that pop in and out of focus intermittently, including such snippets as "my dolphin friend and I", and the recurring reality check Just A Blur, one is left with the impression that the LSD has unexpectedly, suddenly, just kicked in.

Actually the second attempt at making the same album — the first, much more acoustic version had been recorded in the UK months earlier with producer Shel Talmy but didn't work out — *Puzzle* is notably juiced by the participation of onetime Melanie producer Frangipane.

"He was actually the guy who wanted to add all the orchestral things," notes Mandrake's guitarist and prescient electronics whiz, Craig Anderton. "He saw us play live a couple of times, and he always felt that we were pushing for something grander and bigger in our onstage thing, which we always were. For three people, we made a lot of noise."

Conspicuously impressed was famed classical conductor Seiji Ozawa — so much so that his quote calling *Puzzle* a musical masterpiece appeared in several ads Poppy Records took out in the pop press at the time.

"Actually, there's a terrible story about that," says Anderton. "We were supposed to do a promotional appearance with him, and I had come down with this horrible, horrible flu, and so had our bass player — so the only person who got to meet him was the drummer. I had to call up and cancel, which was just horrible because I really wanted to meet this guy — you know, Seiji Ozawa, *wow*. And I think he was kind of offended that only one of us showed up. But I didn't want to be responsible for reading in the paper 'Seiji Ozawa cancels concert tour owing to flu.' It was kind of unfortunate."

The band would follow-up the album with a final single, a relatively unnecessary cover of Thunderclap Newman's Something In The Air. One listen to *Puzzle*, and you'll suspect something was indeed.

Record label:
Poppy

Produced
by Ronald Frangipane.

Recorded
at Century Sound Recording Studios, New York; 1969.

Released:
autumn 1969

Chart peaks:
None (UK) None (US)

Personnel:
Kevin Lally (d); Randy Monaco (b, v); Craig Anderton (g); Brooks Arthur (e)

Track listing:
Earthfriend Prelude; Earthfriend; Just A Blur (Version 1); Hiding; Just A Blur (Version 2); Tadpole; Kyrie; Ocean's Daughter; Volcano Prelude; Volcano; Whisper Play; Bucket Of Air; Children's Prayer; Puzzle; Just A Blur (Version 3)

Running time:
47.30

Current CD:
Collectables MMCD 013 adds Something In The Air

Further listening:
Mandrake Memorial (1968); Medium (1969)

Further reading:
M.C. Escher: His Life And Complete Graphic Work (Harry N Abrams, 1992)

The Grateful Dead
Live/Dead

The Dead at their improvisational best.

In the autumn of 1969, having spent eight months in the studio recording *Aoxomoxoa*, The Grateful Dead were deep in debt to Warner Bros. No one was so stoned or unrealistic as to believe that the highly experimental *Aoxomoxoa* was going to recoup all that money, so someone had a bright idea: put out a live album, easily culled from the many shows the band was playing in the Bay Area. Not only would such an album finally showcase the band at its spacey, jamming best, it would be incredibly cheap to make.

The Dead took a state-of-the-art 16-track recorder to gigs at the Avalon and Carousel ballrooms, and from those shows came *Live/Dead*, a double album that, according to Lenny Kaye's review in Rolling Stone, "explains why the Dead are one of the best performing bands in America, why their music touches on ground that most other groups don't even know exists." The album kicks off with a great version of Dark Star, 23 minutes of jazzy jamming. "They'd usually only play Dark Star if they were pretty high," said Caroline 'Mountain Girl' Garcia. Not just high: this is music from deepest space, as if someone had recorded the sound of a star exploding then slowed it down to its dreamy, pulsing elements. The song's great appeal was that no one – neither audience nor band – knew where it was headed.

"People loved it for the mystery of it," said manager Rock Scully. Robert Hunter's first lyrics for the Dead speak volumes about where the band was coming from at the end of the '60s: "Shall we go, you and I while we can?/Through the transitive nightfall of diamonds." While clearly this was music for altered states, the band were always quick to point out that pulling it off required plenty of rehearsal time. Phil Lesh's The Eleven, named for its highly unusual 11/4 time signature, was based on the rhythmic calisthenics the band performed during practice, in which part of the band played 11 beats while the rest played 33 or even 66. "It was really designed to be a rhythm trip," said Lesh. "It wasn't designed to be a song."

The Dead were genuinely experimental, following each other down strange paths and hoping they'd find their way back, as on the frenzied storm of noise that is Feedback. "It was like somebody tossing a bloody chicken into a school of pirhanas," marvelled Mickey Hart. "For a few minutes you'd be out on the edge with the roaring animal all around you, and it was always an open question whether it was going to go back into its cage or not."

Record label:
Warner Bros

Produced
by The Grateful Dead, Bob Matthews and Betty Cantor.

Recorded
at Avalon and Carousel ballrooms, San Franciso; summer of 1969.

Released:
November 10, 1969

Chart peaks:
None (UK) 64 (US)

Personnel:
Jerry Garcia (g, v); Bob Weir (g, v); Phil Lesh (b, v); Mickey Hart (pc); Bill Kreutzmann (pc); Pigpen, aka Ron McKernan (o, congas, v); Tom Constanten (k)

Track listing:
Dark Star; Saint Stephen; The Eleven; Turn On Your Lovelight; Death Don't Have No Mercy; Feedback; And We Bid You Tonight

Running time:
73.05

Current CD:
7599271812

Further listening:
Anthem of the Sun (1968); the two-CD Fillmore East: 2/11/69 (1997); or the five-CD So Many Roads (1965–95) (1999).

Further reading:
There are almost literally more books, fanzines and websites than you can count. The American Book Of The Dead: The Definitive Grateful Dead Encyclopedia (Oliver Trager, 1997) is a start. Also, Dead to the Core: An Almanack Of The Grateful Dead (Eric Wybenga, 1994) and Garcia, by the editors of Rolling Stone (1999). A website with good discography is at www.discographynet.com/dead/dead.html

Kevin Ayers
Joy Of A Toy

Urbane ex-Soft Machine chap goes to Majorca and pens a slice of classic 'anglodelica'.

Taking its name from a track on Soft Machine One, which in turn had been taken from an Ornette Coleman composition, *Joy Of A Toy* evocatively captured its performer before he was burdened with the trappings of cultdom or the requirements of trying to be a pop star. Although he'd retreated to Majorca to write the songs for this album only the singalong title track, The Clarietta Rag, and Oleh Oleh Bandu Bandong convey any sense of carefree sunny climes (and the latter was mainly a legacy of Ayers' colonial upbringing in Malaya, at that). In fact *Joy Of A To* is an unmistakably English, at times (as on the sombre Town Feeling) resolutely urban record full of drizzly streets and hungover memories of last night's party.

Song For Insane Times, a bittersweet freeze frame full of astute cameos, perfectly captures the post-Summer Of Love spirit of ennui, disillusion and detachment that was abroad in the late-'60s. Both lyrically and musically it would have sat easily on Soft Machine Two had Ayers stayed with the band he helped form. (Incidentally, the voice captured in a snatch of studio dialogue at the beginning of Song For Insane Times, for a long time rumoured to be Syd Barrett, is in fact Robert Wyatt.) Lady Rachel, a mainstay of Ayers' live set, was written for his daughter. Girl On A Swing shimmers like heat haze on a summer's day with some beautifully delicate piano played by arranger David Bedford (soon to join Ayers' band The Whole World). Stop This Train (Again Doing It) was, like Why Are We Sleeping? on Soft Machine One, inspired by the teachings of Gurdjieff, the mystic and philosopher who has also inspired the music of Robert Fripp, Kate Bush, and Keith Jarrett, among others.

"Gurdjieff's teachings were the lightening bolts that formulated my later ideas," Ayers told MOJO. "You develop a fairly comfortable little story and then slip something startling in as if nothing had happened." *Joy Of A Toy* is full of such moments. As the man once said, "Banana".

Record label:
Harvest

Produced
by Peter Jenner.

Recorded
at EMI Studios, London; 1969

Released:
November 1969

Chart peaks:
None (UK) None (US)

Personnel:
Kevin Ayers (g, v); Robert Wyatt (d); Mike Ratledge (k); Hugh Hopper (b); Rob Tait (d); David Bedford (k, p); Peter Mew (e); Sean Murphy (e); Ian Knight (e)

Track listing:
Joy Of A Toy; Town Feeling; Clarretta Rag; Girl On A Swing; Song For Insane Times; Stop This Train (Again Doing It); Eleanor's Cake (Which Ate Her); Lady Rachel; Oleh Oleh Bandu Bandong; All This Crazy Gift Of Time

Running time:
41.30

Current CD:
Beat Goes On BGOCD 78

Further listening:
Whatevershebringswesing (1970)

Further reading:
Why Are We Sleeping fanzine; www.users.globalnet.co.uk/~marwak/

Captain Beefheart And His Magic Band

Trout Mask Replica

The most radical-sounding record of the 1960s.

In 1968, a revamped Magic Band moved into a rented house in Woodland Hills, near Los Angeles, and set about rehearsing the music for *Trout Mask Replica*. *Safe As Milk* and the full-blown acid rock of *Strictly Personal* had made the group's reputation, but now signed to Frank Zappa's new Straight label, Beefheart – aka Don Van Vliet – was about to make his art statement. To avoid any confusion arising from his musical instructions and whistled lines, he set about composing on the piano. Technically, he couldn't really play the instrument, but at this point he had confidence to spare.

Beefheart had put the brakes on his voracious consumption of LSD but was convinced the house was built on a native American burial ground, and claimed he talked to the spirits. Meanwhile the group spent six months in grinding poverty learning John (Drumbo) French's transcriptions of Don's piano outpourings – which were often overlaid in different keys and metres; a feat of superhuman dedication. Beefheart had given all the musicians new names and was becoming increasingly tyrannical. Problems like noise complaints from the neighbours were minor compared to elongated 'brainwashing' sessions, fist fights breaking out in the fractious atmosphere, and the group getting arrested during a shoplifting spree. By spring 1969 they were ready to make a 'field recording' in the house with Dick Kunc – a near neighbour, occasional house guest, and regular engineer on Zappa's music – bringing over his portable two-track Uher reel-to-reel.

"They were certainly well rehearsed. I seem to recall it was pretty much controlled chaos, with Don very much in command," he says. After a few tracks had been recorded, Beefheart insisted they use a proper studio, and they decamped to Whitney, in nearby Glendale. Although Kunc was "ready for anything" he admits that "as a neophyte to that galaxy of music at the time, I wondered how to tell the difference between good and not-so-good performances."

The album was recorded at breakneck speed and emerged as a massive scrapbook of free jazz, blues, rock and surreal poetry. Lester Bangs waxed rhapsodic in Rolling Stone, while others found it incomprehensible. In Britain, largely

Record label:
Straight/Reprise

Produced
by Frank Zappa.

Recorded
at Whitney Studios, Glendale, California and Ensenada Drive, Woodland Hills, California; March–April 1969.

Released:
November 1969

Chart peaks:
21 (UK) None (US)

Personnel:
Zoot Horn Rollo (g, flute); Antennae Jimmy Semens (g); Captain Beefheart (bass clarinet, ts, soprano sax, simran horn, musette, v); The Mascara Snake (bass clarinet, v); Rockette Morton (b, narration); Drumbo (d); Doug Moon (g); Dick Kunc (e)

Track listing:
Frownland; The Dust Blows Forward 'N The Dust Blows Back; Dachau Blues; Ella Guru; Hair Pie: Bake 1; Moonlight On Vermont; Pachuco Cadaver (S/France); Bills Corpse; Sweet Sweet Bulbs; Neon Meate Dream Of A Octafish; China Pig; My Human Gets Me Blues; Dali's Car; Hair Pie: Bake 2; Pena; Well; When Big Joan Sets Up; Fallin' Ditch; Sugar 'N Spikes; Ant Man Bee; Orange Claw Hammer; Wild Life; She's Too Much For My Mirror; Hobo Chang Ba; The Blimp (mousetrapreplica); Steal Softly Thru Snow; Old Fart At Play; Veteran's Day Poppy

Running time:
79.08

Current CD:
7599271962

Further listening:
Hear the original Trout Mask 'house recordings' on the Grow Fins box set

(1999), and how the style evolved on Lick My Decals Off, Baby (1970), Beefheart's favourite among his own albums.

Further reading:
MOJO 2; *Lunar Notes: Zoot Horn Rollo's Captain Beefheart Experience* (Bill Harkleroad, 1998); www.beefheart.com

thanks to the patronage of John Peel's Top Gear, *Trout Mask Replica* almost broke into the top twenty and remains surprisingly popular for such an extreme record. In an HMV poll of customers' favourite albums in 1998, it ambled in at number 42, one place above Bowie's *Hunky Dory*.

Creedence Clearwater Revival

Green River

Third album from archetypal roots-rockers. Internal schisms forming.

Green River was CCR's second album of 1969 and John Fogerty, their driven front-man, assumed even more power during its making – banning the rest of the band from the studio during the mix. Drummer Doug Clifford remembers: "It was like, 'Turn in your key'. It was a lock-out. We were allowed back in for 10 minutes to do the 'wah doo days' on The Night Time Is The Right Time!"

"I just refused to let them be there because it was so disruptive," explains Fogerty. "It was a go-around I had with Tom for the whole three years we were Creedence. He kept saying, 'My part's not loud enough.' The truth is, I would write the song, and then the producer in me would take over and write the arrangement, and I would show everyone *exactly* how it went." Clifford recollects things differently. "The good news was that I was the only drummer in the band, and he was less stringent with me than with the other guys. All the groovy little things I put in got to stay." Such as the spine-tingling high-hat work at the end of the Mephistophelean swamp-rock of Sinister Purpose? "That was pure instinct; it was just a natural process."

The tension between the players is also manifest in the subject matter of several tracks. The titles shout for themselves – Commotion, Tombstone Shadow, Bad Moon Rising.

"If there wasn't a demon there John would invent one," bassist Stu Cook reckons, "which was great when he was writing!" And in the writing Green River is almost faultless. From the churning, nostalgic Country R&B of the title track to the Sun-era rockabilly bounce of Cross-Tie Walker, Fogerty assimilated his influences perfectly and the band did him proud.

"The circumstances weren't exactly pleasant," muses Clifford, "but we did a job. We laid down the basic tracks in two days or so, and then waited to hear the record!"

"Some of the initial playback tapes sounded better than the final product," remembers Stu Cook, "but I suppose it was partly our fault for letting him get away with it." Despite these problems, the album represents the pinnacle of Creedence's achievement, and thus one of the high-points of late '60s American Rock. Fogerty agrees. "My favourite album is Green River. That's the soul of where I live musically, the closest to what's in my heart."

Record label:
Fantasy

Produced
by John Fogerty.

Recorded
at Wally Heider Studio, San Francisco

Released:
December 1969

Chart peaks:
20 (UK) 1 (US)

Personnel:
John Fogerty (v, g); Tom Fogerty (g, bv); Stu Cook (b, bv); Doug Clifford (d); Russ Gary (e)

Track listing:
Green River (S); Commotion; Tombstone Shadow; Wrote A Song For Everyone; Bad Moon Rising (S); Lodi; Cross-Tie Walker; Sinister Purpose; The Night Time Is The Right Time

Running time:
29.20

Current CD:
FCD24 8393-2

Further listening:
Bayou Country (1969); Willy And The Poor Boys (1970); Cosmo's Factory (1970); The Blue Ridge Rangers: Blue Ridge Rangers (1973), essentially a John Fogerty solo album of country covers, lovingly rendered.

Further reading:
Bad Moon Rising: The Unofficial Story Of Creedence Clearwater Revival (Hank Bordowitz, 1998); Up Around The Bend: The Oral History Of Creedence Clearwater Revival (Craig Werner, 1998); www.jyu.fi/~petkasi/ccr-jcf

Fairport Convention
Liege And Lief

The first British electric folk album.

"The thing is," said Dave Swarbrick in that informal, matey way he has of cutting right to the chase, "if you're singing about a bloke having his head chopped off or a girl screwing her brother and having a baby and the brother cutting her guts open, stamping on the baby and killing his sister, that's a fantastic story by anybody's standards. Working with a storyline like that with acoustic instruments wouldn't be half as potent as saying the same things electrically."

Applying rock arrangements to traditional ballads which so outraged folk purists when Fairport first tried it. It was bass player Ashley Hutchings, the Fairport member with the least folk credentials, who pushed hardest for the unequivocal move into traditional song, courting Sandy Denny and Dave Swarbrick for the band and driving even them to distraction with his obsessive fascination with the potential of folk song. It still didn't sway everyone. Despite the contributions of Sandy and Swarb the folk world still regarded them as chancers, while rock fans frowned in confusion at their move away from more commercial West Coast roots. Rolling Stone dismissed the album as "boring".

Even Richard Thompson later conceded that he felt it was artificial and contrived, yet *Liege And Lief* left an indelible mark on both the folk and rock worlds, providing a reference point for Steeleye Span, the Albion Band and many others to follow. The recording sessions were stormy, and rifts over the controversial new direction went so deep the group was in tatters even before the album was released. Hutchings and Denny, both quit in the wake of quarrels in the studio. Denny had already had her fill singing ballads in folk clubs and was more interested in writing her own material. Hutchings was concerned his dream wouldn't materialise with Fairport, especially with Thompson also keen to develop his own writing, and he resolved to form Steeleye Span with musicians more entrenched in the folk world. So *Liege And Lief*'s often thrilling amalgam of ancient and modern was both a beginning and an end.

Record label:
Island

Produced
by Joe Boyd.

Recorded
at Sound Techniques, London; June-July 1969.

Released:
December, 1969.

Chart peaks:
17 (UK) None (US)

Personnel:
Dave Swarbrick (v, mandolin, v, va); Sandy Denny (v, g); Richard Thompson (g); Ashley Hutchings (g, b, v); Simon Nicol (g, v); Dave Mattacks (d); John Wood (e)

Track listing:
Come All Ye; Reynardine; Matty Groves; Farewell Farewell; The Deserter; The Lark In The Morning; Tam Lin; Crazy Man Michael

Running time:
36.33

Current CD:
IMCD60

Further listening:
For a similar excursion into folk-rock check out Unhalfbricking (1969), or Fotheringay, the band formed by Sandy Denny following her departure.

Further reading:
Meet On The Ledge: A History Of Fairport Convention (Patrick Humphries, 1997)

THE
1970s

Simon & Garfunkel
Bridge Over Troubled Water

A generation-defining, multi-platinum farewell to the '60s.

By the time Simon & Garfunkel came to make *Bridge Over Troubled Water*, they were drifting apart. Art was preoccupied with his acting career and, consequently, Paul felt he was no longer pulling his weight.

"It was a tough album to make," Garfunkel has admitted, "but tough is one of the words that leads to great results." That it still stands as their definitive statement is a measure of Simon's tendency to shine brightest in adversity.

According to Simon, "I knew the minute I wrote, 'Like a bridge over troubled water I will lay me down,' that I had a very clear image. The whole verse was set up to hit that melody line. With certain songs you just know it." Even so, he remembers the original demo as "a much less grandiose thing than the record. In fact, it wasn't grandiose at all. It was a humble, little gospel hymn song with two verses and a simple guitar behind it." Embellished with a Spector-ish production and a staggering arrangement, it has since made its presence felt in virtually every poll of best-ever singles.

The Boxer emerges as another astonishing achievement and, in some ways, a more satisfying song than Bridge, with its rippling guitar soaring into the 'lie-la-lie' hook (written because Simon couldn't think of any words) set against Roy Halee's brilliantly engineered percussion effects (the signature explosive snare crack was recorded in an echoing CBS stairwell, one night when the building had been vacated), rising towards the haunting, primitive, synthesiser solo, climaxing with celestial strings and synth-bass drones before fading finally into Simon's lonesome acoustic picking.

Fellow musicians were blown away. "It's a great record," declared Sandy Denny, "fantastically produced." Some critics, however, were less perceptive. "Their music has gotten stale," opined Rolling Stone's Gregg Mitchell. "Everything they play, someone else has played before." Joe Public disagreed. On February 21, 1970, the album entered the UK chart at Number 1, a position it held for a staggering 35 weeks topping both UK and US charts. Ironically, just as the duo had split before their first hit Sounds Of Silence in 1965, by the time Bridge Over Troubled Water scooped six Grammys, on March 16, 1971, Paul Simon was a solo artist.

Record Label:
CBS

Produced
by Paul Simon, Arthur Garfunkel and Roy Halee.

Recorded
in New York and Los Angeles; June 13, 1968–November 19, 1969.

Chart peaks:
1 (UK) 1 (US)

Released:
January 26, 1970

Personnel:
Paul Simon (g, v); Art Garfunkel (v); Larry Knechtel (k); Fred Carter Jr (g); Hal Blaine (d); Joe Osborn (b); Jimmy Haskell, Ernie Freeman (oa)

Track Listing:
Bridge Over Troubled Water (S); El Condor Pasa (If I Could) (S); Cecilia (S); Keep The Customer Satisfied; So Long, Frank Lloyd Wright; The Boxer; Baby Driver; The Only Living Boy In New York; Why Don't You Write Me; Bye Bye Love; Song For The Asking

Running time:
837.26

Current CD:
Columbia 4624882

Further listening:
Any hits compilation, or their second greatest album, Parsley, Sage, Rosemary & Thyme (1966)

Further reading:
MOJO 50; Simon And Garfunkel: The Definitive Biography (Victoria Kingston, 1997); freespace.virgin.net/r.kent/ has links leading to several excellent S&G sites.

The Band
The Band

The definitive Americana classic.

A consistently high scorer in polls of the greatest albums of all time– especially amongst fellow musicians – The Band's second album had the peculiar quality of sounding as if it had existed for decades, the very first time you heard it. This impression was partly due to the richly-textured arrangements, which employed mandolin, fiddle, accordion and various arcane wind instruments alongside the group's basic instrumentation; partly to the distinctive vocal harmonies, whose soulful bluegrass intervals contravened the smooth West Coast close-harmony style of the times; and partly to the evocative lyrics, which seemed to traverse the entire course of American history in a dozen songs, relating events through the voices of ordinary working-class folk at work, rest, play and war.

Relocating to Los Angeles in February 1969 to record the songs they had been developing since their debut *Music From Big Pink*, the group rented Sammy Davis Jr's house in the Hollywood Hills, living in the various suites and converting the pool-house into a studio. When Capitol Records were a month late installing the recording equipment, the band used what Richard Manuel called "them high-school fat-girl diet pills" to help them meet the tight schedule, though they still had to finish three songs back in New York. Levon Helm found a set of drums with wooden rims in a Hollywood pawnshop – "old-fashioned instruments, but they read well on the microphones" – which added their own distinctive flavour to the album, and Garth Hudson was as diligent as ever in his search for the appropriate sound, frequently staying late "sweetening" the tracks with extra layers of horns, keyboards, "whatever was needed to make that music sing".

Flashy solos were a rarity, each instrumental part being sublimated to a song's overall feel. They made an even bigger break with the era's virtuosic tendencies by swapping instruments around amongst themselves and making a virtue of their limitations. Rag Mama Rag – a Top 20 UK hit in 1970 – featured the drummer playing mandolin, the pianist playing drums, the bassist playing fiddle, the organist playing piano, and co-producer John Simon playing tuba (for the first time in his life!). Rarely has an album been greeted with quite as much acclaim as *The Band*, as critics marvelled at its musical depth and range of styles, with the Village Voice claiming it was "beyond anything in rock except some of The Beatles' best work."

Record label:
Capitol

Produced
by The Band and John Simon.

Recorded
at Sammy Davis Jr's pool house, Sunset Plaza Drive, Los Angeles; February–April 1969; and The Hit Factory, New York; April 1969.

Released:
January 1970

Chart peaks:
25 (UK) 9 (US)

Personnel:
Garth Hudson (k, s, acc, slide trombone); Richard Manuel (v, k, d, s, mouth harp); Levon Helm (v, d, g, mandolin); Rick Danko (vn, b, v, tb); Jaime Robbie Robertson (g, e); John Simon (tuba, k, high school and peck horns, e); Joe Zagarino (e)

Track listing:
Across The Great Divide; Rag Mama Rag (S/UK); The Night They Drove Old Dixie Down; When You Awake; Up On Cripple Creek (S); Whispering Pines; Jemima Surrender; Rockin' Chair; Look Out Cleveland; Jawbone; The Unfaithful Servant; King Harvest (Has Surely Come)

Running time:
43.58

Current CD:
CDP 746493 2

Further listening:
The Band's debut Music From Big Pink (1968) remains a classic; of their other albums, Stage Fright (1970), Northern Lights – Southern Cross (1975) and the live triple-album Rock Of Ages (1972) are all worth investigating.

Further reading:
Across The Great Divide (Barney Hoskyns, 1993); This Wheel's On Fire (Levon Helm with Stephen Davis, 1993)

Syd Barrett
The Madcap Laughs

*Pink Floyd's usurped frontman makes his first solo album.
Somehow.*

Listening to *The Madcap Laughs* is like watching a man fooling around on a cliff-edge. Evidence of Barrett's original musical genius and exquisite painterly lyricism ("Pussy willow that smiled on this leaf") is shaded by evidence of his impending mental collapse ("My head touched the ground/I was half the way down"). This makes for some distinctly uneasy, at times voyeuristic, listening.

The album was painstakingly put together in three stages. Floyd manager Peter Jenner produced the first sessions between May and July 1968, which were largely fruitless. Silas Lang, Swan Lee and Lanky weren't pursued further, Clowns And Jugglers became Octopus, a wonderfully off-kilter attempt to emulate Green Grow The Rushes O. Syd frittered away the next few months, occasionally turning up unannounced backstage at Top Of The Pops, where he liked to hang out. Finally Harvest's head Malcolm Jones appointed himself producer in April 1969 and drafted in Soft Machine to help out on No Good Trying, but Syd was beginning to lose his grip. "Every time he played a tune through, the bars before the chord change were different," says Soft Machine's keyboard player Mike Ratledge. "You had to watch his hands. It was the only way you could follow what was going on."

Exasperated, Jones asked Dave Gilmour and Roger Waters to help out in June 1969. They finished the album in a matter of days. The haste of those sessions is exemplified by the sequence of She Took A Long Cold, Look, Feel and If Its In You which include Syd's audibly agitated studio chatter and wildly out-of-tune first takes. But glimpses of the Barrett genius linger in Late Night, with its gossamer-light slide guitar and tender lyric, the brooding menace of Dark Globe, the starkly beautiful adaptation of James Joyce's poem Golden Hair, Octopus and No Good Trying. Syd was upbeat upon its release, promoting the album with interviews and a session for John Peel's Top Gear, before going into the studio with Gilmour to record a follow-up, *Barrett,* which was even more chaotic. In his 1973 NME appraisal, The Cracked Ballad Of Syd Barrett, journalist Nick Kent accurately called these thirteen songs, "exercises in distance". They make up a strange, poignant album, so tangential it refuses to yield up its inner logic.

Record label:
Harvest

Produced
by David Gilmour, Roger Waters and Malcolm Jones.

Recorded
at Abbey Road Studios, May 1968 – June 1969

Released:
January 1970

Chart peaks:
40 (UK) None (US)

Personnel:
Syd Barrett (g, v); Willie Wilson (b); Jerry Shirley (d); Hugh Hopper (b); Robert Wyatt (d); Mike Ratledge (k); Jeff Jarratt, Pete Mew, Mike Sheady, Phil Mcdonald (e)

Track listing:
Terrapin; No Good Trying; Love You; No Man's Land; Dark Globe; Here I Go; Octopus (S); Golden Hair; Long Gone; She Took A Long Cold Look; Feel; If It's In You; Late Night

Running time:
39.00

Current CD:
CDGO 2053

Further listening:
The even more hard-won follow-up Barrett (1970); the subsequent collection of outtakes and fragments, Opel. Both form part of Crazy Diamond boxed set.

Further reading:
MOJO 34; The Dark Stuff: Selected Writings On Rock Music 1972–1993 (Nick Kent, 1995)

Miles Davis
Bitches Brew

Davis's first full-blown excursion into jazz-rock.

While Miles Davis had already broached the idea of jazz melding into rock with *In A Silent Way*, *Bitches Brew* was the real thing. It doesn't sound like other rock music, but it stood a country mile away from the post-bop and soul-jazz which Davis's contemporaries had been creating as their response to rock's take-over. Miles liked the style and the energy of rock, but he couldn't entertain any dumbing-down in his own music. So he sought players like McLaughlin, the young British bassist Dave Holland, and Chick Corea; spirits fresh enough to inject something new into his own outlook, but virtuosos in their own right. The previous record had been put together with a lot of post-production work, but for this set, Davis simply took his men into the studio for three days and set them off.

"It was just like one of them old-time jam sessions we used to have up at Minton's back in the old bebop days," enthused the leader. "Everybody was excited when we all left there each day." Teo Macero's main job was simply to let the tapes run and call the tunes.

The result was an album of six tracks, two of them breaking the 20-minute barrier, and all of them (bar the brief John McLaughlin) by turns spacey, frenetic, ferocious and even whimsically funky (Miles Runs The Voodoo Down). It sounds like a recipe for commercial disaster, but an audience that had grown used to the trance-like jamming of The Grateful Dead ate it up and put Miles in the charts. These were early days for recording this kind of thing, and although Columbia have since released an extensively cleaned-up set – *The Complete Bitches Brew Sessions* – much of it still sounds almost primitive, with its wayward guitar tone and clanking electric keyboards. Davis himself, though, always cuts through; the most modern sound on the record.

Not everyone saw *Brew* as an epiphany: many long-time Davis admirers were scathing in their condemnation. Perhaps the best summary was the sympathetic one offered some years later by Jack Bruce: "Miles wants to be Jimi Hendrix, but he can't work it out on trumpet".

Record label:
CBS

Produced
by Teo Macero.

Recorded
in New York City, August, 1969.

Released:
July 1970

Chart peaks:
71 (UK) 35 (US)

Personnel:
Miles Davis (t); Wayne Shorter (s); Bennie Maupin (bass clarinet); Chick Corea, Larry Young, Joe Zawinul (p); John Mclaughlin (g); Harvey Brooks, Dave Holland (b); Jack DeJohnette, Charles Alias, Lenny White (d); Jim Riley (pc)

Track listing:
Pharoah's Dance; Bitches Brew; Spanish Key; John McLaughlin; Miles Runs The Voodoo Down; Sanctuary

Running time:
93.57

Current CD:
C2K65774, adds: Feio

Further listening:
Jack Johnson (1970); Live-Evil (1970); On The Corner (1972)

Further reading:
The Penguin Guide To Jazz On CD (1999)

Little Milton
If Walls Could Talk

Highpoint of this giant of soul blues.

John Lee Hooker has described Little Milton Campbell as "One of the finest blues singers and guitar players there ever was", but unlike his great contemporary B.B. King, Milton has failed to achieve significant crossover success. And yet for nearly 50 years he has been one of the most powerful and emotive performers in American blues, his talents at least recognised by Greg Allman, for one, who has declared, "Milton has been one of the biggest influences on my life. B.B. King and Little Milton are tied for first in my book. But when it comes to power, Little Milton has the edge over everybody."

If Walls Could Talk splendidly showcases Milton's prowess, with magnificent soulful singing, excellent songs, impressive ensemble work and glorious horn arrangements. One of the best moments is Your Precious Love, a touching declaration of the redeeming power of love, with Milton humbly acknowledging, "Your love has made me a better man."

"When I got into what music was all about I discovered I catered for women in my songs," he explains. "I sing about the goodness women have done for me, how important the woman is to me and how much I love her. I know if I draw twenty women, I'm going to draw forty men, see?"

Another powerfully emotive performance is Let's Get Together, on which Milton implores his ex for a second chance, alleging of her new lover that, "He's treating you twice as bad as I used to!"

For all these riches, Milton's distinctive playing is heard sparingly on the album. "Les Paul influenced me with that little plucking thing. I took that same sound, added my own feel and transformed it into a blues thing." Milton is philosophical about his failure to cross over. "I'm not a superstar and I don't know if I want to be. I want to be free to go where I want, and not worry about being kidnapped and every time I go to bed somebody got to pull my clothes off and tuck me in. Or I go to the bathroom and they're there with some toilet paper to wipe my butt. I'm doing OK and I love what I do and I'll be doing it till I die."

Record label:
Chess

Produced
by Calvin Carter.

Recorded
in Chicago; spring 1969 and 15–16 October 1969.

Released:
January 1970

Chart peaks:
None (UK) None (US)

Personnel:
Little Milton (v, g); Gene Barge (oa); Donny Hathaway (p); David Purple (e)

Track listing:
If Walls Could Talk; Baby, I Love You (S/US); Let's Get Together (S); Things I Used To Do; Kansas City; Poor Man's Song; Blues Get Off My Shoulder; I Play Dirty (S/US); Good To Me As I Am To You; Your Precious Love; I Don't Know

Running time:
32.21

Currently unavailable on CD

Further listening:
Raise A Little Sand and We're Gonna Make It compile tracks from the '50s and '60s respectively. Since the mid-'80s Milton has released a number of terrific, soul-drenched albums on Malaco.

Further reading:

The MC5
Back In The USA

The band's taut, foot-to-the-floor second LP; a precursor to punk adrift in a climate of hippy rock.

The MC5 had much to live up to with their second album, and almost as much to live down. '69's *Kick Out The Jams* had been one of the most electrifying debuts of 1969. But their rabble-rousing had got them kicked off Elektra, and their White Panther rhetoric got them branded a "revolutionary hype". Typical was a savaging in Rolling Stone at the hands of first-time contributor Lester Bangs, which wrote them off as a musically regressive joke. (Bangs later recanted, but the tone of the back-lash had been set.) "I wanted to make a note-perfect record," guitarist Wayne Kramer states. "I was still stinging from Lester Bangs' remarks, and wanted to answer the criticism that we used excessive volume to hide the fact that we couldn't play. I knew what bullshit that was, and we wanted people to know that we were the best band in the world. The guitars are gonna be in tune, the tempos are gonna be right on. No excuses for nothing."

Initial sessions in June with first-time producer Jon Landau were unproductive. When Landau returned to Detroit a month later, the change was astonishing. They'd worked out physically as if they were a sports team, jogging and eating a high protein diet, and had rehearsed relentlessly. "There was discipline and a return to basics," said late singer Rob Tyner. "We got back to the kind of straight-ahead band we'd been in the early days. We focused our energy. We tried to make it sound like – whoosh! – it was racing right past you. Total velocity. Our souls got psychedelicized there for a while, so it felt good to be back in the pocket."

Bookended by Little Richard and Chuck Berry, *Back In The USA* is an affirmation of the root values of rock'n'roll. Most songs stay well south of the three minute mark, the solos are sharp and to the point. Throughout, the guitars of Kramer and Fred 'Sonic' Smith are so perfectly meshed that they often sound like a single instrument (though there may not be a single track where the five members all played together). Despite some of their most overtly political material (American Ruse and Human Being Lawnmower) and the creative emergence of Smith (Tonight and Shakin' Street), the radical revamping of their sound bewildered their Detroit constituency, and failed to connect with a national audience more interested in rock operas and drum solos.

Record label:
Atlantic

Produced
by Jon Landau.

Recorded
at GM Studios, Detroit; July–September 1969.

Released:
January 1970

Chart peaks:
None (UK) 137 (US)

Personnel:
Rob Tyner (v); Wayne Kramer (g, b); Fred 'Sonic' Smith (g); Michael Davis (b); Dennis Thompson (d); with Danny Jordan (p); Jim Bruzzese (e)

Track listing:
Tutti Frutti; Tonight (S/US only); Teenage Lust; Let Me Try; Looking At You; High School; Call Me Animal; The American Ruse; Shakin' Street (S/US); The Human Being Lawnmower; Back In The USA

Running time:
28.30

Current CD:
8122710332

Further listening:
The Big Bang! Best Of The MC5 (2000)

Further reading:
MOJO 27; www.futurenowfilms.com/

Laura Nyro
New York Tendaberry

The second in a classic trilogy from a highly individual singer and songwriter.

At once a reclusive and an almost overpoweringly frank artist, Nyro records are a strange legacy of a talent that never quite found its best expression. She is often still more remembered for her failures: the disastrous appearance at Monterey in 1967, where she was booed offstage, or the feeble *Mother's Spiritual*, her last studio album.

"She was born 150 years too late," opined Robert Christgau, dismissive of her romantic tendencies. But here was a singer-songwriter who aspired to a sophisticated, metropolitan pop-soul at a time when most of her peers preferred gentrified folk. Her third record, *New York Tendaberry*, was the centrepiece of what came to be seen as a three-part cycle – *Eli And The 13th Confession* and *Christmas And The Beads Of Sweat* came either side. Common to all three is the feeling that they pivoted around Nyro singing by herself at the piano: there are rhythm sections and strings and brass which break in from time to time, but these are more like framing devices for the rise and fall of Nyro's voice, swelling into an ecstatic high passage on Captain For Dark Mornings and falling away into a whisper in the next few bars.

All her music has a stop-start feel to it, something which she only surrendered when in her most facile pop-tune mood (and some would say that's what she should have stuck to, on the basis of such three-minute glories as Wedding Bell Blues and Stoney End). At its most eccentric, as on the murderous Tom Cat Goodbye, she sounds like she's making a *grand guignol* opera. But the texture of the record, engineered by Roy Halee, soundtracks a great, dangerous city in darkness: it actually *feels* like New York at night. There is a heart-stopping moment in Gibson Street, where the horns blare in over the gorgeous harmonies, and the music seems to be soaring past skyscrapers. Beyond its setting, *New York Tendaberry* is also a treatise on damned love, and one that suggests disturbing depths. Among countless chilling lines are these: "I wish my baby were forbidden/I wish my world be struck by sleet/I wish to keep my mirror hidden/To hide the eyes that looked on Gibson Street".

Record label:
Columbia

Produced
by Laura Nyro and Roy Halee.

Recorded
in New York; 1969.

Released:
January 1970

Chart peaks:
None (UK) 32 (US)

Personnel:
Laura Nyro (p, v); Roy Halee (e)

Track listing:
You Don't Love Me When I Cry; Captain For Dark Mornings; Tom Cat Goodbye; Mercy On Broadway; Save The Country; Gibson Street; Time And Love; The Man Who Sends Me Home; Sweet Lovin' Baby; Captain Saint Lucifer; New York Tendaberry

Running time:
46.22

Current CD:
XUSK019737

Further listening:
Christmas & The Beads Of Sweat (1970); Gonna Take A Miracle (1971)

Further reading:
www.LauraNyro.net; www.lauranyro.com

Van Morrison
Moondance

For the follow-up to the legendary Astral Weeks, *Van changed direction, and not for the last time.*

Much as he might dislike it now, Brown Eyed Girl was the song that saved Van Morrison's skin. In New York following the split of Them, Morrison let producer Bert Berns lead him to the pop charts. When the song was a hit in 1967, Warner Bros signed Morrison, and the result was the 1968 album which is regularly voted among the best ever made. But *Astral Weeks* had yet to be cemented into the rock pantheon when Van came to record *Moondance*.

    Astral Weeks was a mesmerising song suite – an acoustic journey – in which Morrison, in exile in America, recalled his distant home-town of Belfast. During 1969 Morrison had moved to an artistic hamlet in upstate New York but, following the famous festival, Woodstock had become in Van's words "a joke". While he was there though, Van – like so many of his peers – had become mesmerised by The Band. By the beginning of the new decade, The Band had long moved on from simply being Bob Dylan's backing group, and were fashioning their own brand of rural rock'n'roll: gritty and lived-in, it was a sound which Van Morrison found particularly enticing. The over-riding sound of *Astral Weeks* had been acoustic, with its feet in folk and jazz; *Moondance* is brass-based, harder-edged, rooted in jazz and R&B. While *Astral Weeks* meandered, *Moondance* had a more disciplined song structure, with only Brand New Day edging over the five minute mark. The original album's first side was as strong as any in rock's 15 year history. And It Stoned Me and Into The Mystic are enchanting, inscrutable souvenirs of the era; Crazy Love and Caravan display Morrison's peerless blue-eyed soul; while the title track, which had begun life as "a saxophone solo", would go on to become one of Van's best-loved songs.

    The other outstanding song on *Moondance*, the anthemic Brand New Day, was inspired by Morrison hearing The Band's version of Dylan's I Shall Be Released on a Boston radio station.

    Upon its release, Rolling Stone called *Moondance* "an album of musical invention and lyrical confidence". It gave Van Morrison his solo chart debut. Following the dispiriting split of Them, the unrepresentative Brown Eyed Girl and the unsuccessful *Astral Weeks*, the man was on his way.

Record label:
Warner Brothers

Produced
by Van Morrison.

Recorded
at Century Recording, New York; 1969

Released:
February 1970

Chart peaks:
32 (UK) 29 (US)

Personnel:
Van Morrison (g, pc); Jack Schrorer (s); Collin Tillton (s, flute); Jeff Labes (k); John Platania (g); John Klingberg (b); Garry Malabar (d); Guy Masson (d); Emily Houston, Judy Clay & Jackie Verdell (bv); Tony May, Elliot Schierer, Shelly Yakus, Steve Friedberg, Neil Schwartz (e)

Track listing:
And It Stoned Me; Moondance; Crazy Love; Caravan; Into The Mystic; Come Running (S); These Dreams Of You; Brand New Day; Everyone; Glad Tidings

Running time:
39.17

Current CD:
7599-27326-2

Further Listening:
The Best of Van Morrison (1990); The Philosopher's Stone (1998)

Further Reading:
It's Too Late To Stop Now (Steve Turner, 1993); Wavelength, The Unofficial Van Morrison Magazine, PO Box 80, Winsford, Cheshire, CW7 4ES, UK
www.wavelengthltd.co.uk;
www.harbour.sfu.ca/~hayward/van

Black Sabbath

Black Sabbath

The smelting house of Heavy Metal.

The sound of the industrial factory floor fed through an amp and turned up to 11, *Black Sabbath* lays more claim than any record before or since to having invented heavy metal. Its occult imagery, slow, menacing songs and murky, Sensurround production made to be played at previously unheard-of volume, were to have a widespread, lasting influence.

With a grass-roots following amassed by solid touring, Sabbath comprised four working class men from Birmingham who had played together in various blues- and jazz-rock combos with names like Earth and Polka Tulk before bassist Butler's interest in Dennis Wheatley novels and the band's discovery of a '30s horror film gave them both a winning name and a gimmick. They were sent into the studio with producer Rodger Bain and a £600 budget from Phillips' new progressive rock label Vertigo.

"We were given just two days to record," said Tony Iommi. "In those days we didn't know if two days was a long time or short", so they finished it in a day.

Said Ozzy Osbourne, "We were just kids. We were coming out with a new thing and we knew fuck all about recording, so we just went in and played it innocently and it was really raw and earthy. It sounded like a live record without the audience.

Aggressive, ponderous, dripping black-country doom and gloom from the opening track, *Black Sabbath* was one of the final nails in the coffin of hippy rock – or would have been but for the quasi-psychedelic noodlings into which Sabbath occasionally launched during the long instrumental jams. Mostly, though, it was basic and unfussy: Ozzy Osbourne's piercing, cheerless but affecting vocals, Butler's rumbling bass, Ward's aggressive drums and Iommi's much-imitated guitar.

"A lot of the songs had an aggressive mood, Satanic if you like, but that was the way we felt," said Iommi, "so that was the way we played." The record attracted immediate attention, the band's supposedly satanic stance won them some controversy. They were even interviewed on Radio 4's Today programme. If it was intended to scare off the kids it, naturally, had the opposite effect. The album was an instant Top 10 hit, and was followed just six months later with the equally-enduring *Paranoid*.

Record label:
Vertigo

Produced
by Rodger Bain with Geezer Butler and Tony Iommi.

Recorded
at Trident Studios; February 1970.

Released:
April 1970

Chart peaks:
8 (UK) 23 (US)

Personnel:
Ozzy Osbourne (v); Tony Iommi (g); Terry 'Geezer' Butler (b); Bill Ward (d); Barry Sheffield, Bill Freesh, Lee DeCarlo, Tom Allom (e)

Track listing:
Black Sabbath; The Wizard; Behind The Wall Of Sleep; N.I.B; Evil Woman Don't Play Your Games With Me (S/UK); Sleeping Village; Warning

Running time:
30.16

Current CD:
Essential/Castle ESMCD301 adds: Wicked World

Further listening:
Paranoid (1970); Sabbath Bloody Sabbath (1973); 3CD box set The Ozzy Osbourne Years (1991)

Further reading:
Wheels Of Confusion: The Story Of Black Sabbath (Steven Rosen, 1996); www.black-sabbath.com

The Who

Live At Leeds

What the rock opera pioneers really sounded like. One of rock's live milestones.

1970 was a heady time for The Who. They'd been performing their celebrated rock opera *Tommy* in front of classical music critics and European royalty in opera houses, and the talk was of maturation of rock music, deepening of insight and extension of form. All this for a band who in live performance also represented the pinnacle of freeform rock. The inspired lunacy of Keith Moon's whirlwind percussion style, the huge-sounding, restlessly exploratory basslines of John Entwistle and the chopping, plangent power-chording of Pete Townshend's guitar could turn Mose Allison's Young Man Blues – originally a two minute aside on his rural-cool *Back Country Suite* (1957) – into an electrifying one-chord work-out of immense power and dynamic control. They were a unique live band and they knew it.

Entwistle: "When we go on stage we all try and upstage one another. We play full tilt from the very start. Then at the end of the set we have to pull something extra out of the bag as a climax. It's as simple as that."

So a live album would serve both as a handy stop-gap before the next Big Idea and present another side to The Who. With Pete Townshend unable to face listening through the hours of material recorded on a US tour – he instructed the tapes to be destroyed on a bonfire to foil bootleggers – the Pye mobile was enlisted to record the Leeds University Valentine's Day set. The musical chemistry of the band could be volatile; if Moon wasn't on top form, they could sound like they were limping from one sloppy drum fill to the next – but this day Moon was crisp and alert and the band responded accordingly, delivering a boiling set.

Recorded with great immediacy by Jon Astley and packaged like a bootleg, the original *Live At Leeds* featured a pair of old singles, a couple of rock'n'roll covers, the remarkable Young Man Blues and the legendary 14 minute 45 seconds of My Generation which incorporated Tommy themes, blues hollering, glorious finger-picking, slap-back guitar interludes and a range of tensions and climaxes that leaves the listener breathless. Influential on many up-and-coming volume-heavy combos, *Live At Leeds* still has the edge on other fine live Who recordings of the period, standing proud as a landmark live rock album. Though the CD issue more than doubles the original playing time, the real magic remains most vivid on the originally released tracks.

Record label:
Track

Produced
by Jon Astley.

Recorded
at Leeds University, England; February 14 1970.

Released:
May 1970

Chart peaks:
3 (UK) 4 (US)

Personnel:
Roger Daltrey (v, hm); Pete Townshend (g, v); John Entwistle (b, v); Keith Moon (d)

Track listing:
Young Man Blues; Substitute; Summertime Blues; Shakin' All Over; My Generation; Magic Bus.

Running time:
37.10

Current CD:
Polydor 527 169-2 adds: Heaven And Hell; I Can't Explain; Fortune Teller; Tattoo; Happy Jack; I'm A Boy; A Quick One, While He's Away; Amazing Journey/Sparks

Further listening:
Live At The Isle Of White (1970); Woodstock (1969); The Kids Are Alright (1978)

Further reading:
Hope I Die Before I Get Old (Dave Marsh, 1995); Maximum R&B (Richard Barnes, 1996)

Free

Fire And Water

Young, British R&B band craft song that echoes round the
world for 30 years. Fortunately, it's on their best album.

At the height of the British blues boom, on April 19 1968
four boys, aged 15-18, got together in a London pub for
their first rehearsal. From disparate backgrounds – Paul Kossoff's
father a famous actor, Paul Rodgers's an unknown Teesside ship-
yard worker – but all steeped in R&B, they clicked, wrote at
least four songs that night, and hit the road for six-gigs-a-week.
With Kossoff a follicle-shivering guitarist, Rodgers a hard yet
mellifluous singer, Andy Fraser a remarkably original, melodic
bass player, and Kirke the adamantine drummer required to keep
these young guns firing in the same direction, Free built a strong
live reputation. Even so, their first two albums, *Tons Of Sobs* and
Free sold only 20,000 apiece. But then, in autumn 1969, after a
rare bad gig, according to Kirke, "In the dressing-room I said,
We've got to have a song people can dance to!, and Andy and
Paul Rodgers started bopping around, going, All right now, all
right now." Free had the song that changed their lives.

All Right Now accentuated their gradual shift of
emphasis from blues to soul stylings – for instance, Fraser and
Rodgers deliberately wrote Fire And Water with Wilson Pickett
in mind and, to prove their point, in 1971 he covered it. The
first six tracks of the album are dark, sparse and powerful. Then
comes the explosive relief of All Right Now. "We were *allowed*
to be happy!" enthuses Kirke. "We all picked up maracas and
tambourines and sang back-ups together. Then Andy and me got
down on our hands and knees and hammered the bass pedals on
the Hammond organ with our fists."

They recorded quickly, but only on the odd day when
they didn't have a gig. Then, confusingly, a row with Blackwell
led to two mixes of the album being released and marketed ever
since – plus a conflict over the single edit of All Right Now
which Free objected to on purist grounds. But, in UK and
America, the charts endorsed Blackwell's view. At every gig
they were mobbed. By girls!

Yet, inconceivably, the following May Free broke up –
exhausted, disappointed with follow-up album *Highway*'s abysmal
sales, and rather disgusted with the pop reputation All Right
Now brought them. They did reunite and had more hits before
their final separation and Kossoff's sorry decline into drug-
induced death at 25. But All Right Now and *Fire And Water* left
one glorious summer to remember them by.

Record label:
Island

Produced
by Free.

Recorded
at Trident Studios, Island Studios, London,
January–April 1970.

Released:
June 26, 1970

Chart peaks:
2 (UK) 17 (US)

Personnel:
Paul Rodgers (v, g); Paul Kossoff (g);
Andy Fraser (b); Simon Kirke (d); Roy
Thomas Baker (e)

Track listing:
Fire And Water; Oh I Wept; Remember;
Heavy Load; Mr Big; Don't Say You Love
Me; All Right Now (S)

Running time:
35.33

Current CD:
IMCD 80 842 556 (the UK CD comes
from Chris Blackwell's remix of the
album, originally released on the second
pressing of the vinyl album; the US CD
retains some of Free's original mixes as
released on the first vinyl pressing in
UK – the difference is most evident on
the title track)

Further listening:
Free (1969) – earlier, more R&B Free
(with the famous "girl full of stars"
cover)

Further reading:
MOJO 54; Heavy Load (2000);
www.allrightnow.com

Deep Purple

Deep Purple In Rock

The UK's proto-heavy metal scene spawns a monster.

"Quite simply," says bassist Roger Glover, "there was nothing to lose." Deep Purple were already on a hiding to nothing; they'd had a taste of fame in the US with Hush, but the departure of original vocalist Rod Evans and bassist Nick Simper meant that the line-up convening to record the band's fourth album was almost completely unknown. Right at the start, guitarist Blackmore told his bandmates, "If it's not dramatic or exciting, it has no place on this album," and the band took him at his word.

"If I had to pick one image which sums up *In Rock*," Glover says, "it would be the VU meters on the consoles bent hard over to the right." It *is* a deafening record – the opening Speed King, co-opting a clutch of Gillan's favourite rock-'n'rollers, sees to that. But it also contains one of their most powerful numbers, the anti-war tract Child In Time, rewritten from It's A Beautiful Day's Bombay Calling, but taken to a new dimension by Gillan's near-supernatural screams. Indeed, with sessions squeezed in between gigs, one can almost trace the band's evolution, from proto-prog tinged sellers of psych to classically tinted merchants of mayhem as the album progresses – Flight Of The Rat even exploded out of an extemporised romp through Flight Of The Bumblebee.

Though the album would soon be established as Purple's first classic, not everyone in the band was immediately keen on it. Glover concludes, "We were on a train going up to Scotland for a gig. We'd just come out of the studio the previous night, and I said, Ah, it's not as good as it could have been if we'd been more together, and Jon Lord turned round, gave me a sharp look . . . he was much more of a senior member in those days . . . and he says 'Roger, you're wrong.' And that stopped me in my tracks. Then he said, 'If it could have been better, it would have been better. It is what it is and that's it. So shut the fuck up.'" Consider yourself told.

Record label:
Harvest

Produced
by Deep Purple.

Recorded
at IBC, London; De Lane Lea, London; Abbey Road, London; October 14, 1969–April 13, 1970.

Release date:
June 1970

Chart peaks:
4 (UK) None (US)

Personnel:
Ian Gillan (v); Ritchie Blackmore (g); Roger Glover (b); Jon Lord (k); Ian Paice (d); Andy Knight, Martin Birch, Philip McDonald (e)

Track listing:
Speed King; Bloodsucker; Child In Time; Flight Of The Rat; Into The Fire; Living Wreck; Hard Lovin' Man

Running time:
43.17

Current CD:
7243 8 34019 2 5 Anniversary Edition adds Black Night (S); Speed King (piano version); Cry Free (Roger Glover remix); Jam Stew; Flight Of The Rat (Roger Glover remix); Speed King (Roger Glover remix); Black Night (unedited Roger Glover remix)

Further listening:
Fireball (1971); Machine Head (1972)

Further reading:
Child In Time (Ian Gillan with David Cohen, 1994) www.deep-purple.com

John Phillips
John, The Wolfking of LA

Papa goes solo.

Sometimes an artist can totally undervalue his own work. Such is surely the case with John Phillips, who, after The Mamas And The Papas disbanded, recorded this wonderful solo album – which he clearly loathes.

"I never had the front man's ego and that LP proved it," he wrote dismissively in his autobiography. "I sounded seriously depressed. The songs were fine, the backup vocalists and musicians were fine, but the lead singer seemed groggy. That work sounded lethargic." Well, what to Phillips seems like lethargy is perceived by the album's admirers as being soothing and attractively restrained; and the vocals which Phillips thought groggy, seem warm and intimate. Certainly the music has nothing of the sunny sparkle of The Mamas And The Papas and there are few moments where anyone breaks sweat, but the music is exquisitely crafted.

"Do it to me, James," Phillips instructs James Burton on Mississippi and sure enough, Burton does it to him, and to us, with a wonderful dobro solo, while the piano of Larry Knechtel and the steel guitars of Buddy Emmons and Red Rhodes, are also scintillating throughout the record.

Drummer Hal Blaine remembers it fondly. "John was a fine musician, always a gentleman. There are no studio credits because the studio was an attic. John had bought the Jeanette MacDonald estate in Bel Air, which was like a fairyland, and in this beautiful attic he built the most magnificent studio in the world. There was magnificent woodwork throughout this home and one secret panel. When you touched the secret button this door opened and you entered the secret world of John Phillips." The songs are wonderfully appealing but undeniably less commercial than those Phillips had written for The Mamas And The Papas, and their meanings are elusive, although they often seem to be describing Phillips' debauched, rich hippie lifestyle. However the album flopped and within a year or two Phillips' life began to spiral out of control. He was convicted of trafficking in narcotics in 1981, and spent a considerable amount of time in rehabilitation. Finally, in 1989, he resurrected The Mamas And The Papas as a touring attraction, though he was the only original member.

And the house? Well, that, as it happens, was flogged, studio and all, to Sly Stone, who famously recorded *There's A Riot Going On* in it.

Record label:
Stateside

Produced
by Lou Adler.

Recorded
at 783 Bel Air Road; 1969–70.

Released:
June 1970

Chart peaks:
None (UK) None (US)

Personnel:
John Phillips (v, g, hm); Hal Blaine (d); Larry Knechtel (p); Joe Osborne (b); David Cohen (g); Dr Hord (g); Darlene Love, Jean King, Fanita James (bv); James Burton (g, dobro); Buddy Emmons, Red Rhodes (sg); Gordon Terry (fiddle); Chuck Britz (e)

Track listing:
April Anne; Topanga Canyon; Malibu People; Someone's Sleeping; Drum; Captain; Let It Bleed, Genevieve; Down The Beach; Mississippi (S); Holland Tunnel

Running time:
32.42

Current CD:
Edsel EDCD372

Further listening:
addictions to heroin, barbiturates and alcohol sapped Phillips' creativity and he recorded little of note after Wolfking. But The Mamas And The Papas' best, such as If You Can Believe Your Eyes And Ears (1966) are always worth hearing.

Further reading:
Papa John: An Autobiography (John Phillips with Jim Jerome, 1986) is a grim rock'n'roll horror story. Sadly there is much more on Phillips' addictions than on his music.

Soft Machine
Third

London underground mavericks journey into jazz-rock.

The Soft Machine's early career was plagued by personal acrimony, musical differences and record company apathy. Consequently, the UK underground's second sons (behind Pink Floyd) only got round to recording their debut in 1968 while touring the States with Jimi Hendrix. Before the second album Kevin Ayers left and was replaced by Hugh Hopper, Wyatt and Ratledge had stopped speaking to each other.

Volume Two maintained the psych-pop vision, fortified with Hopper's fuzz bass and Ratledge's increasingly sophisticated, jazz-inflected compositions. After supporting Hendrix and Traffic at the Albert Hall early in 1969, the trio on Wyatt's suggestion, briefly experimented with a four-piece brass section. "This hastened the demise of our commitment to songs," says Hopper, "because the brass tended to play Robert's vocal parts."

By the time work began on *Third*, in spring 1970, the group had advanced considerably. "We weren't consciously playing jazz-rock," Hopper insists. "It was more a case of not wanting to sound like other bands; we certainly didn't want a guitarist." Rock was now a dirty word. "We'd got into that John Coltrane Quartet sound, mainly modal things, rather than the tricky bebop timings."

Third, a double album consisting of just four side-long pieces, was daringly ambitious, turned around the band's fortunes, and even prompted an appearance at that year's Proms. Yet the intra-band tensions remained.

"We worked round it by each looking after different chunks of the record," maintains Hopper. "If we hadn't had done that, we might never have finished it." The bassist's extraordinary Facelift, a live/studio concoction of assault-style keyboards, Zappa-like riffs and squealing tape loops was in marked contrast to Ratledge's smoother contributions. Most idiosyncratic was Wyatt's Moon In June, a hugely affecting, largely solo piece that features what's probably the longest coda in rock and – gulp – vocals. A little over a year later Wyatt was fired. "I loved playing their music, and I admired them enormously," he claims, "but one day I got a phone call from the organist and I was out."

Record label:
CBS

Produced
by Soft Machine.

Recorded
at IBC Studios, London; spring 1970. Facelift recorded live at Fairfield Hall, Croydon; January 4, 1970 and Mothers Club, Birmingham; January 11, 1970.

Released:
June 1970

Chart peaks:
18 (UK) None (US)

Personnel:
Mike Ratledge (o, p); Hugh Hopper (b); Robert Wyatt (d, v); Elton Dean (s, saxello); Rab Spall (vn); Lyn Dobson (flute, s); Nick Evans (trombone); Jimmy Hastings (flute, b, clarinet); Andy White (e); Bob Woolford (e)

Track listing:
Facelift; Slightly All The Time; Moon In June; Out-Bloody-Rageous

Running time:
75.19

Current CD:
Legacy XUSK0230339

Further listening:
Fourth (1971) refines the sound; The Peel Sessions (1990) includes contemporaneous reworkings of Third material.

Further reading:
MOJO 64; Wrong Movements: A Robert Wyatt History (Mike King, 1994)

Traffic
John Barleycorn Must Die

Pop band's curious folk-soul experiment.

By 1970 Steve Winwood was barely out of his teens, yet he had already seen service in The Spencer Davis Group, Traffic and Blind Faith. The world was waiting for the solo album – and there are tantalising tales of just what remains in Island's vaults from those sessions, including a rumoured 20 minute version of Dylan's Visions Of Johanna. In the event, what began life as Winwood's solo debut – to be called *Mad Shadows* and produced by Guy Stevens – became instead Traffic's third studio album.

True to both his talent and the spirit of the times, Winwood started out playing every instrument himself; and two tracks – Stranger To Himself and Every Mother's Son – were recorded with Stevens. But Winwood wanted more musicians, and it was only a matter of time before old band-mates Capaldi and Wood were recruited and Traffic were back. Thanks to his lustrous pedigree, it was inevitably Winwood on whom all eyes focused – and *John Barleycorn Must Die* was a remarkable showcase.

But this was Winwood the former member of Blind Faith at work, not a return to Traffic's former guise as a pop group, and he allowed the six songs to meander, kicking off with the instrumental Glad, before finding a groove on Freedom Rider and the haunting Stranger To Himself. But, for many, the highlight of the album was its title track – following on from Fairport Convention's pioneering *Liege & Lief* the previous December, in Traffic's hands this centuries-old traditional folk song seemed to confirm a strong folk-rock fusion for the new decade. To promote the album, Traffic toured America where they had enjoyed a loyal following from the beginning and – again true to the spirit of the times – an in-concert album was recorded. Sadly though, *Live-November 70* never saw the light of day – although two tracks from the album do appear as bonus tracks here. Traffic were always a band who promised more than they actually delivered. But, from the complexity and confusion that characterised the band at the end of the '60s, they did at least summon up the stamina to record this magnificent album, before spiralling downhill during the '70s.

Record label:
Island

Produced
by Chris Blackwell, Steve Winwood and Guy Stevens.

Recorded
at Island and Olympic Studios, London; 1969.

Released:
July 1970

Chart peaks:
5 (UK) 11 (US)

Personnel:
Steve Winwood (k, g, v); Jim Capaldi (d, bv); Chris Wood (s, flute); Andy Johns, Brian Humphries (e)

Track listing:
Glad; Freedom Rider; Empty Pages (S/US); Stranger To Himself; John Barleycorn Must Die; Every Mother's Son

Running time:
34.38

Current CD:
IMCD266 adds: I Just Want To Know; Sittin' Here Thinkin' Of My Love; Who Knows What Tomorrow May Bring (Live); Glad (Live)

Further listening:
Heaven Is In Your Mind: An Introduction To Traffic (1998)

Further reading:
Keep On Running: The Steve Winwood Story (Chris Welch, 1989);
www.stevewinwood.com
www.azstarnet.com/~bobbieg/winwood.htm

The Carpenters
Close To You

The unfashionably sunny brother-sister duo truly arrives,
platinum sales result.

For their second album, A&M honcho Herb Alpert advised
The Carpenters to cover (They Long To Be) Close To You, an
obscure 1963 album track written by Bacharach & David for
Dionne Warwick. "Dionne's had a straight eighths feel. I was the
first one to put it into a slow shuffle, and then the bit at the
end was mine," Richard Carpenter says. "We cut two early
versions of Close To You, one where Karen tried to sing it like
Nilsson. Herb hated it. The third time was a charm. We brought
in Hal Blaine. As fine a drummer as Karen was, she couldn't lay
into them the way – and I'm going to sound like a chauvinist
pig – a man can. Everyone was excited as hell about the song.
Even the people around A&M who didn't much care for us
were pushing open the door to the studio, saying, 'What is that?
We've never heard anything like it.' Herbie was ecstatic. He
played it over the phone for Burt. Burt was ecstatic. Herb asked
me, 'What do you think it's going to do?' and I said, 'It's either
going to be Number 1 or a complete stiff.'

"So we've got six songs complete, then out comes Close
To You. You could tell within a week that it was going Top 5.
That's when the phone rang and it was, 'Get your album done!'.
All of a sudden we had no time."

Thirty years later, Richard still marvels at his sister's
poise under pressure. "Karen didn't need to warm up. She
didn't give a damn what time of day it was. She didn't need a
special headphone mix. They took her right into the board. She
was a marvel. Everything about her – the phrasing, the timbre,
the diction." The only sore spot for Richard remains the cheesy
cover photo. "We protested but were told, 'Learn to live with
it.' I learned to live with it in that I haven't committed suicide!
It's good to know that we're still so popular that the album is in
release 30 years later – but there it is around the world, as we
speak, with that awful, *awful* cover. That was the whole beginning of that image thing that so many writers have gone on
about – where you were in camps when it came to The
Carpenters. That cover started the whole thing."

Record label:
A&M

Produced
by Jack Daugherty.

Recorded
at A&M Studios, Los Angeles; January–May
1970.

Released:
August 19, 1970

Chart peaks:
23 (UK) 2 (US)

Personnel:
Karen Carpenter (v, d); Richard Carpenter
(k, v, o); Hal Blaine (d); Joe Osborn (b);
Danny Woodhams (b); Jim Horn, Bob
Messenger, Doug Strawn (woodwind); Ray
Gerhardt, Dick Bogert (e)

Track listing:
We've Only Just Begun (S); Love Is
Surrender; Maybe It's You; Reason To
Believe; Help; (They Long To Be) Close To
You (S); Baby It's You; I'll Never Fall In
Love Again; Crescent Noon; Mr Guder; I
Kept On Loving You; Another Song

Running time:
38.35

Current CD:
3931842

Further listening:
A Song For You (1972)

Further reading:
MOJO 29; The Carpenters: The Untold
Story (Ray Coleman, 1994)

The Moody Blues
A Question Of Balance

The finest hour of the forgotten emperors of portentous pop.

W hen The Moody Blues entered the studio to record what became their fourth album, they had no finished songs.

"It was a deliberate intention to get back to something that was very playable on stage – almost a live recording," says Justin Hayward.

Ray Thomas adds, "We found that with *Children's Children*, it was one thing putting layer upon layer on tape but, at the end of the day, even with the Mellotron, there was only five of us and some tracks literally couldn't be reproduced on stage. So we arranged *A Question Of Balance* so the songs were easier for us, because it's very hard to promote your album if you can't play it live."

For five weeks, the band jammed, developed ideas and committed hours of music to tape. "The sharing was fabulous," recalls John Lodge, "because when any one of us had written something, we'd put it on the table and say this is my song. But as soon as we'd played it for everyone in the band, it became a Moody Blues song, and you sort of relinquished ownership in a spiritual way. Everyone had suggestions and that's what you wanted to happen."

Though they saw it as a back to basics, their penchant for heady lyrics still came through, from the war protest of Question (a song Hayward stitched together from two unfinished fragments the night before it was recorded) to the invitations to self-discovery on Dawning Is The Day and The Balance.

"We were still very young, in our early 20s," says Lodge, "so I think *Question Of Balance* was us questioning who we were again. Also, were we doing the right things? This is where the album came from, trying to get a perspective, a balance on our own lives – as people, as human beings and as very successful musicians, with all that brings. By reflecting on who we were, we were able to make *A Question Of Balance*, which then everyone else could relate to. Because whatever level you're at, there is always a question of balance of everything."

Record label:
Threshold

Produced
by Tony Clarke.

Recorded
at Decca Studios, London; spring 1970.

Released:
August 1970

Chart peaks:
1 (UK) 3 (US)

Personnel:
Justin Hayward (g, v); John Lodge (b, v); Ray Thomas (flute, v); Graeme Edge (d, v); Mike Pinder (k, v); Derek Varnals (e)

Track listing:
Question (S); How Is It (We Are Here); And The Tide Rushes In; Don't You Feel Small; Tortoise And The Hare; It's Up To You; Minstrel's Song; Dawning Is The Day; Melancholy Man; The Balance

Running time:
38.32

Current CD:
Universal 844771-2

Further listening:
Days Of Future Passed (1967); On The Threshold Of A Dream (1969)

Further reading:
index of Moody Blues sites at www.frisk.org/mbindex/pages/

Black Sabbath
Paranoid

It defined them, and heavy metal, for all time.

Y ou don't hear the riff so much as feel it, like a distant mudslide slowly moving your way or the last few seconds before the bus hits the school gates, when everything seems to slow down and a second lasts for ever. And then the voice cuts in with "generals gathered in their masses . . ." and it doesn't even matter that the next rhyme is "masses" too because, one minute and three seconds into the opening War Pigs, you're not looking to Sabbath for subtlety or art. You're looking for them to rip the top of your head off, and you know they're going to do it.

Following on from their eponymous debut, *Paranoid* not only gave Black Sabbath a chart-topping album, but the title track came close to topping the singles chart too. They never followed it up, but, as journalist Andrew Wiener remarked two years later, if they had "they could have established themselves as the biggest singles band since the Stones. Think of that – Sabbath on Top Of The Pops, month after month, churning out their Awful Warnings. How could Gary Glitter hope to follow that?"

That's how big Sabbath were – and how potent their Satanic imagery was. Chief lyricist Geezer Butler disagrees. "Even at the beginning, when everyone was calling us devil worshippers, I didn't think we had a Satanic image. I was brought up an incredibly strict Catholic, and though I'd been taught about God and Jesus no one ever went into what the Devil was all about. So when I was 16 or 17, I went about trying to find out. And because I wrote most of Black Sabbath's lyrics, some of that ended up in the songs. It was a dark name, Black Sabbath, but the songs were *never* advocating Satanism. It was warning against evil."

Indeed, ol' Beelzebub doesn't get a mention on *Paranoid*. Rather, the album is pure science fiction and, from the drifting oddity of Planet Caravan and the robotic apocalypse of Electric Funeral, to the future conflict wickedness of War Pigs and the tragedy of Iron Man, *Paranoid* has more in common with Asimov. The difference was, Isaac's Armageddon always took place in space. Sabbath's was an earthbound experience. And it started with the riff.

Record label:
Vertigo

Produced
by Roger Bain.

Recorded
at Regent Sound, Island Studios; July 1970.

Released:
September 1970

Chart peaks:
1 (UK) 12 (US)

Personnel:
Ozzy Osbourne (v); Tony Iommi (g); Terry 'Geezer' Butler (b); Bill Ward (d)

Track listing:
War Pigs; Paranoid (S); Planet Caravan; Iron Man (S/US); Electric Funeral; Hand Of Doom; Rat Salad; Fairies Wear Boots

Running time:
42.09

Current CD:
ESMCD 302

Further listening:
Black Sabbath (1970), Master Of Reality (1971) and try and find the quadro-phonic mix of Paranoid, for a brain-peeling remix of War Pigs.

Further reading:
Wheels Of Confusion (Steven Rosen, 1998); www.black-sabbath.com

Santana

Abraxas

Santana take in jazz alongside staple Latino-blues-rock. The first world-music crossover success?

By the time the '60s drew to a close, Santana had built up a reputation as an awesome live outfit whose brand of fiery Latin-streaked blues-rock was guaranteed to get audiences on their feet. Much of their early set, however, was made up of covers they had adapted to their own jamming needs — such as a version of Chim Chim Cheree done in the style of Coltrane's My Favourite Things (!) — and by the time they came to record the follow-up to their Top 5 debut album, they realised they needed to develop more of their own material.

"Bill Graham made us aware that we needed songs to get on the radio," says Carlos Santana. "But it wasn't until *Abraxas* that we started hearing our own babies. For me, one of the first ones was Samba Pa Ti, where I just heard a voice singing. Once we learned how to do that, it gave us confidence to find our own place." Accordingly, all bar two of the album's nine tracks were penned by band members, though ironically it would be the two covers that would bring the band their biggest single hits.

Dissatisfied with the sound of their debut, the group brought in as co-producer the veteran jazz engineer Fred Catero, whose skills proved invaluable in balancing the new range of musical flavours Santana were bringing into their sound: the result was a giant step on from their debut. Incident At Neshabur prefigures the group's subsequent move towards jazz, while their core Latin-blues style reached a new level of sophistication with a gorgeous version of Fleetwood Mac's Black Magic Woman, transformed into an elegant samba and served with a side-order of Hungarian jazz guitarist Gabor Szabo's Gypsy Queen. The album's other big hit was an infectious version of Tito Puente's Oye Como Va, which Carlos Santana believed would strike a universal chord.

"I thought, this is a song like Louie Louie or Guantanamera," he said, "a song that when you play it, people are going to get up and dance, and that's it". *Abraxas* remains Santana's most accomplished record, a landmark release which spent over a year on the UK charts and eventually went quadruple platinum, cementing the band's position as one of the most vibrant, fertile units of the era, and bearing out Rolling Stone reviewer Jim Nash's contention that Santana "...might do for Latin music what Chuck Berry did for the blues."

Record label:
CBS

Produced by
Fred Catero and Santana.

Recorded
at Wally Heider Studios, San Francisco; June–July 1970; Pacific Recording, San Mateo; May 1970.

Released:
October 1970

Chart peaks:
7 (UK) 1 (US)

Personnel:
Carlos Santana (g, v); Gregg Rolie (k, v); Dave Brown (b, e); Mike Shrieve (d); Jose Areas (timbales, conga); Mike Carabello (conga); John Fiore (e)

Track listing:
Singing Winds, Crying Beasts; Black Magic Woman/Gypsy Queen (S); Oye Como Va (S); Incident At Neshabur; Se A Cabo; Mother's Daughter; Samba Pa Ti (S); Hope You're Feeling Better (S); El Nicoya

Running time:
51.13

Current CD:
489543 2 adds tracks recorded live at Royal Albert Hall, April 4, 1970: Se A Cabo; Toussaint L'Ouverture; Black Magic Woman/Gypsy Queen

Further listening:
Eponymous first (1969) and third (1970) albums depict early development. By fourth album Caravanserai (1972) they've drifted deeper into jazz-rock. 2-CD compilation Viva Santana! (1988) and 1999 comeback Supernatural are worthy efforts too, while Carlos Santana/John McLaughlin collaboration Love Devotion Surrender (1970) showcases guitarist's more out-there jazz explorations.

Further reading:
MOJO 70; www.santana.com

Lindisfarne
Nicely Out Of Tune

*Geordie folk-rockers arrive with a debut of charismatic,
rough-hewn magic.*

In the late '60s, songwriter and mental nurse Alan Hull was
having trouble relating to the trend in heavy rock on the north
eastern club scene so he played his songs at folk clubs, eventually
starting his own in 1969 at the Rex Hotel, Whitley Bay. His interests at the time revolved around madness ("In that mental hospital
I met about three extraordinary poets and they were locked up in
that place just because they saw too much and it scared me a
little bit"), Buddhism ("Buddhism proper, nothing flash like Zen")
and Edgar Allen Poe's Tales Of Mystery And Imagination. His
material – like the dream-inspired Lady Eleanor ("I wrote it
almost in a trance") – reflected those interests, but, faced with
folk club audiences, he found himself inclined to write lighter,
more communal fair like We Can Swing Together, a song about an
erroneous drug bust at a Newcastle party.

One of the bands that played at his club were a bunch of
blues-cum-folk musicians looking for a direction, called Brethren.
Hull heard them "doing exactly the same things as I was" and
mutually impressed, they joined forces. "The first time it really
happened we played Lady Eleanor – we'd just arranged it and I've
never had such a tremendous feeling. There were only about a
hundred people there but they were friends and it really
happened. And afterwards I came off feeling great and Ray Laidlaw
came up and said, 'Heeeey, Alan' with a big smile on his face, 'I
think we've got it.' And I knew what he meant." Lady Eleanor was
a magical, otherworldly number with misty acoustic guitar and
haunting harmonies, but in the end it was Ray Jackson's earthy
harmonica playing (Jackson would do a whole spot of drinker-
pleasing tunes including Blaydon Races and Z-Cars) that convinced
Tony-Stratton Smith to sign them to Charisma. Changing their
name to Lindisfarne (Brethren had already been nabbed by a US
band) their debut album was an endearingly ragged reflection of
their live style, combining knees-up (Jackhammer Blues) with
plaintive introspection (Scarecrow Song) and droning folk-rock
(Turn A Deaf Ear, Things We Should Have Said).

Amid talk of Hull being "one of the finest songwriters
this country has produced since the emergence of the patriarchs
Lennon and McCartney" (Roy Carr, NME), their best-selling
follow-up *Fog On The Tyne* established Lindisfarne as one of the
most popular bands in the UK. For many, though, the band's
charm is best heard on their debut.

Record label:
Charisma

Produced
by John Anthony.

Recorded
at Trident Studios, Soho; 10–14, August,
1970.

Released:
November 1, 1970

Chart peaks:
8 (UK) None (US)

Personnel:
Alan Hull (v, g); Ray Jackson (v, hm,
mandolin); Si Cowe (g); Rod Clements
(bs, vn); Ray Laidlaw (d)

Track listing:
Lady Eleanor; Road To Kingdom Come;
Winter Song; Turn A Deaf Ear; Clear
White Light Part 2; We Can Swing
Together; Alan In The River With Flowers;
Down; Things I Should Have Said;
Jackhammer Blues; Scarecrow Song.

Running time:
53.00

Currently available CD:
CASCD1025 adds: Knacker's Yard Blues;
Nothing But The Marvellous Is Beautiful.

Further listening:
Fog On The Tyne (1971); Dingly Dell
(1972)

Further reading:
The Official History Of Lindisfarne
(1998); www.lindisfarne.de

Spirit

The 12 Dreams Of Dr Sardonicus

A surreal trip, potent as purest California Sunshine.

Measured in sales, Los Angeles' psychedelic pioneers Spirit never meant much. And, even compared to the minor chart placings of their previous albums, *Dr Sardonicus* was the low watermark, stalling well outside the US Top 50. Still, the departure of Spirit's first producer/mentor Lou Adler, prompted guitarist Randy California to stroll up Topango Canyon and seek neighbour Neil Young's advice, one spring morning in 1970. When Young recommended his own producer, David Briggs, California proceeded to Briggs' house, at the bottom of the canyon, and introduced himself. In Randy's assessment, Briggs transformed Spirit from a great band into a transcendently great band.

"David became a sixth member – guided us to our very best studio performances – this album could not have happened without David." Indeed, *Dr Sardonicus* is the nickname the band bestowed on the studio mixing desk. Sardonicus' songs ranged across the concerns of the era – racism, ecology, war, pornography – but the weighty topics never edged out catchy hooks and an astonishing assortment of mind-tickling new noises. Taught by Hendrix, Randy California's guitar work varied from proto-metal on Nothin' To Hide to delicate finger-picking on Why Can't I Be Free, and the unlikely juxtaposition of his coruscating licks with Cassidy's meaty big-band drumming and John Locke's jazzy keyboards, further added to this kaleidoscopic sonic palette. But to achieve all this, California assumed control, and other members felt sidelined. Vocalist Jay Ferguson recalls how

"The fights we were having were so bitter and people were threatening to quit all the time," vocalist Jay Ferguson recalls. In California's version, Ferguson plotted to betray Spirit by forming a new band, Jo Jo Gunne, with bassist Mark Andes. "Jay and Mark were sneaking off rehearsing and not telling anybody, and so a lot of the mixing and finishing up for *Sardonicus* was just left with me and David." On release, Nick Tosches of Rolling Stone had reservations but still rated it "a blockbuster", while Record Mirror's Lon Goddard reckoned "Spirit have excelled themselves – beautifully blown and precisely picked." One month later, the original Spirit line-up played its last ever concert, on New Year's Eve at the Fillmore East. Once again, the work of birthing a classic album had torn a band apart.

Record label:
Epic

Produced
by David Briggs.

Recorded
at Sound City Studios, Los Angeles;
April–September 1970.

Chart peaks:
None (UK) 63 (US)

Released:
November 25, 1970

Running time:
39.13

Personnel:
Randy California (g, v); Ed Cassidy (d);
Jay Ferguson (v, pc); John Locke (k);
Mark Andes (b)

Track listing:
Prelude – Nothin' To Hide; Nature's Way;
Animal Zoo; Love Has Found A Way; Why
Can't I Be Free; Mr Skin; Space Child;
When I Touch You; Street Worm; Life Has
Just Begun; Morning Will Come; Soldier

Current CD:
Epic 476603 2

Further listening:
The double CD Time Circle (1991)
compiles Spirit's early high points, while
the sprawling Spirit Of '76 (1977) is a
flawed masterwork.

Further reading:
Hot Wacks, special edition, Issue 16, June
1978; http://www.lls.se/~johanb/spirit/

Family

Anyway

Turning point from prog rock to unlikely pop stardom for early '70s style-straddlers.

Family were not obvious pop stars. Hailing from Leicester, this unkempt, beardy bunch inhabited a curious musical backwater all their own and became a staple on the college rock circuit. Their sound centred around the gritty, almost operatic vibrato of stick-thin vocalist Roger Chapman. It was an odd, warbling voice which could sour milk, but Chapman (a man with LOVE and HATE tattooed on his knuckles) could also provide a richly emotive foil for the intricate guitar and tricky arrangements of Charlie Whitney and the instrumental adventures of their band.

Family's first recordings had dabbled in psychedelia – 1967's truly oddball single, Scene Through The Eye Of A Lens – then added jazz, neo-classical and folk influences to form a unique but quite serious brand of rock for boys. Family's thoughtful sound eventually came to the fore in August 1970, when a three track EP, Strange Band, took them to Number 11 in the singles chart. Startled by commercial success, the group hurriedly shelved plans to make their fourth album a double live affair, and released *Anyway* instead. On paper it was a dangerous half-way house – their heavier live sound showcased on four songs and their intended future path on four studio takes. It could have easily alienated all-comers but, instead, it sounded audaciously eclectic, littered with violin figures, tinkling piano and the roar of a band on stage. Family had become pin-sharp through incessant touring and the studio songs were full of innovation. "Because Olympic was used for film music there would always be tons of gear waiting to be collected the next day," recalls multi-instrumentalist Poli Palmer. "So in the middle of the night, you'd have a good look through, pull out bits of percussion or a harpsichord and have a go."

The result was housed in a suitably unusual sleeve, with a Leonardo Da Vinci illustration printed in gold upon a textured plastic bag, which apart from its eccentricity, did little to prepare the listener for Family life within. Family songs functioned as playlets; there was always something gritty and resolutely English about them. They really don't make records like this any more.

No one followed in Family's footsteps.

Record label:
Reprise

Produced
by Family for Bradgate Bush Ltd.

Recorded:
Tracks 1–5 recorded live at Fairfield Hall, Croydon; tracks 6–11 recorded at Olympic Studios, London.

Released:
November 1970

Chart peaks:
7 (UK) None (US)

Personnel:
Charlie Whitney (g, b); Roger Chapman (v); Rob Townsend (d, p); John Weider (v, b); Poli Palmer (p, pc, vibes, d, f)

Track listing:
Good News – Bad News; Willow Tree; Holding The Compass; Strange Band (S); Part Of The Load; Anyway; Normans; Lives And Ladies. Current CD adds: Today (S); Song For Lots; Today (edit)

Running time:
52.40 (includes extra tracks)

Current CD:
Essential ESMCD615

Further listening:
The three previous Family albums, Music In A Doll's House (1968); Entertainment (1969) and A Song For Me (1970) are all excellent, and Anthology: Best Of (2000) is a very useful 2CD collection.

Further reading:
MOJO 33

Carole King
Tapestry

Brill Building contract songwriter makes successful transition to solo artist, and sells 10 million albums in two years.

Superficially, with *Tapestry*, King seemed to be coat-tailing contemporaries like Joni Mitchell or Laura Nyro. In fact she had been a working songwriter, and occasional artist, for a decade, composing over 100 Top 40 hits with lyricist Gerry Goffin, eight of which reached Number 1. As the '60s ended, however, King had to change her *modus operandi*. The success of Dylan and The Beatles, she explained, meant that "the need for outside writers was less. The only way to get my songs heard was to sing them myself." Most of *Tapestry*'s songs were done as demos, intended for other artists, but as her producer Lou Adler noted, "When she was writing for other people, Carole was, in effect, impersonating somewhat the sound and feel of an artist's hit." To become a singer-songwriter, she had to find her own identity, and Adler knew how to help. "I had a definite theme in mind, to have that lean, almost demo-type sound, with a basic rhythm section and Carole on piano, playing lots of her figures."

Partly because King's friend James Taylor was recording *Mud Slide Slim And The Blue Horizon* nearby, he provided another valued presence on *Tapestry*, contributing ideas, backing vocals and guitar. Although It's Too Late gave King her only US Number 1 single, the core of *Tapestry* is probably You've Got A Friend, which King says, "was as close to pure inspiration as I've ever experienced. The song wrote itself. It was written by something outside of myself, through me." Unfortunately, she couldn't release it as a single, because Taylor got there first.

"*Tapestry* maybe cost $15,000, but I doubt it was that much," says Adler. "I remember the first ad, Honesty Is Back." The timing was perfect. The simple veracities of King's lyrics and her understated performances came as soothing balm to listeners who, for the past five years had been subjected to the excesses of psychedelia and prog. Indeed, asked why it became such a huge success, King has said, "Right time and the right place." Even so, it's hard to disagree with Jon Landau of Rolling Stone whose review called it "an album of surpassing personal intimacy and musical accomplishment, and a work infused with a sense of artistic purpose." On June 19, 1971, it hit Number 1 in Billboard, and stayed put for 15 weeks, ultimately spending 302 weeks in the chart – the longest-charting album by any female solo artist. At the Grammys, she collected Best Album, Best Song, Best Record and Best Female Vocalist.

Record Label:
Ode

Produced
by Lou Adler.

Recorded
at A&M Studios, Hollywood; January 4–15, 1971.

Chart peaks:
4 (UK) 1 (US)

Released:
November 1970

Personnel:
Carole King (k, v); James Taylor (g, v); Danny "Kootch" Kortchmar (g); Charles Larkey (b); Jim Gordon (d); Ralph Shuckett (k); Curtis Amy (s, flute); Perry Steinberg (b); Terry King (c); Barry Socher (vn); Joni Mitchell (bv); Merry Clayton (bv); Julia Tillman (bv); David Campbell (oa)

Track Listing:
I Feel The Earth Move; So Far Away (S); It's Too Late (S); Home Again; Beautiful; Way Over Yonder; You've Got A Friend; Where You Lead; Will You Love Me Tomorrow; Smackwater Jack; Tapestry; (You Make Me Feel Like) A Natural Woman

Running time:
43.30

Current CD:
Sony Legacy 4931802, adds: Out In The Cold; Smackwater Jack (live)

Further listening:
The Ode Collection 1968–1976 contains all of Tapestry, plus the best of King's other work, while The Goffin & King Songbook collects versions of her Brill Building hits.

Further reading:
members.home.net/caroleking/

James Taylor
Sweet Baby James

*Sophomore disc by the unassuming bard of bedsitterland
that begat the singer-songwriter movement.*

Shy, retiring James Taylor was only 22 when *Sweet Baby James*
broke. He had recorded an album in London in 1968 for The
Beatles' Apple label, but it was only back in Los Angeles, with
former Apple executive Peter Asher as manager, that he hit paydirt. "The album was made fast, back when music was still my
hobby," said Taylor. But although the album was barely half an
hour long, he still had a job finishing it. The last – and longest –
track, Suite For 20G, was made up of several unfinished songs
pieced together and named "somewhat cynically" after the fact
that "we were getting twenty grand for delivering the album."

The title track is a poignant narrative of a young cowboy
alone on the range, thinking about "women and glasses of beer",
while the album's best-known song, the captivating Fire And
Rain, is a tragic recollection of a girlfriend's suicide, couched in
accessibly poetic lyrics. "Other than Fire And Rain, much of the
record is very whimsical, very un-self-important, and not taken
very seriously," Taylor reflects, "which is probably why it still
comes off fresh. After *Sweet Baby James* things changed, and I
became professional, which meant a loss of innocence and a
shift of motivation."

Peter Asher handled the clean, crisp production; Carole
King helped out on piano (just prior to recording her own landmark *Tapestry*) and Taylor's teenage friend Danny Kortchmar
(they had been together in the band The Flying Machine, which
features in Fire And Rain's lyrics) played guitar. "I joke that I
knew James before he was sensitive," chuckles Kortchmar, "but
the truth is that James is the archetypal singer-songwriter – *the*
mould. He's a guitar virtuoso who subverted folk forms with a
lot of major 7ths and higher inversion chords and he mixed
influences like Stephen Foster, Pete Seeger, Aaron Copland,
Lightnin' Hopkins and The Beatles, so they disappeared into the
James Taylor stew. His songs sound like blues, like Christmas
carols and like a church choir too, yet it all essentially comes
only from him."

Sweet Baby James's loose-limbed charm and Taylor's easy
way with a song – not to mention the to-die-for cheekbones –
would quickly make him a college pin-up, a Time magazine
cover-boy and a reluctant superstar.

Record label:
Warner Brothers

Produced
by Peter Asher.

Recorded
at Sunset Sound, Los Angeles; December
1969.

Released:
November 1970

Chart peaks:
7 (UK) 3 (US)

Personnel:
James Taylor (g); Danny Kootch (g);
Carole King (p); Russ Kunkel (d); Randy
Meisner (b); Bobby West (b); John London
(b); Red Rhodes (ps); Chris Darrow (vn);
Jack Bielan (a); Bill Lazerus (e)

Track listing:
Sweet Baby James; Lo And Behold; Sunny
Skies; Steamroller; Country Road (S/US);
Oh Susannah; Fire And Rain (S); Blossom;
Anywhere Like Heaven; Oh Baby, Don't
You Loose Your Lip On Me; Suite For
20G.

Running time:
31.53

Current CD:
7599-27183-2

Further Listening:
(Live) (1993)

Further Reading:
MOJO 46; www.james-taylor.com

John Lennon
John Lennon/Plastic Ono Band

He kicks the '60s into touch and invents angst-rock.

Exorcising one's torment through rock music was still a relatively new idea when John Lennon made his first proper solo album. There had always been the blues, of course, but the transatlantic white rock aristocracy had tended to avoid all but the most oblique soul-baring. Lennon had occasionally made an exception – cf Help! and Yer Blues – but *John Lennon/Plastic Ono Band* saw him reaching new heights of confessional honesty.

The reason lay in his and Yoko's trip to America on April 23, 1970. They flew to Los Angeles to begin a course of Dr Arthur Janov's 'primal scream' therapy; but the stay, meant to last well over a year, was cut short by the US immigration authorities on August 1. John and Yoko duly returned to their Tittenhurst Park mansion, and Lennon began writing a new batch of songs. They dealt explicitly with Janov's treatment, and found Lennon attempting to clear out his psyche in preparation for a new phase of life. Thus, he dealt with the loss of his mother (in Mother and the mini-song My Mummy's Dead), the delusions of hippydom (I Found Out), and the roots of his own inner dislocation in the British class system (Working Class Hero). Most spectacular of all was God, his scattershot rejection of religion, Dylan, Elvis and life as a Beatle.

The group he used was deliberately tiny – indeed, on Mother and God, there is little more than piano, bass, drums and vocals – and though the involvement of Phil Spector might have suggested a detour into polish and embellishment, Lennon ensured that he attended only the last three days of the sessions, employing him as a mixer rather than an old-style producer. "We never gave him his head," said Lennon. "But we used his amazing ear for pop music and sound without it becoming *Spector*."

"They said it was simplistic and self-indulgent," said Lennon in 1980. "Now, self-indulgent means you talk about yourself, right? If we'd have used pseudonyms and called it *Tommy, The Rock Opera* or *Ziggy Stardust*, or sung in the third person, it might have been more acceptable. But we prefer to not wear make-up."

Record label:
Apple

Produced
by John Lennon, Yoko Ono and Phil Spector.

Recorded
at Abbey Road, London; September 26–October 5, 1969.

Released:
December 11, 1970

Chart peaks:
11 (UK) 6 (US)

Personnel:
John Lennon (v, g, p); Klaus Voorman (b); Ringo Starr (d); Billy Preston (p); Phil Spector (p); Phil McDonald, Richard Lush, John Leckie (e)

Track listing:
Mother (S); Hold On; I Found Out; Working Class Hero; Isolation; Remember; Love; Well Well Well; Look At Me; God; My Mummy's Dead

Running time:
39.48

Current CD:
Parlophone CDFA3310

Further listening:
The John Lennon Anthology (1998)

Further reading:
We All Shine On (Paul Du Noyer, 1999); The Lives Of John Lennon (Albert Goldman, 1989)

James Brown
Sex Machine

The refining of bass-heavy funk, and definitive evidence of the rapid evolution of Brown's music.

"Recorded live at home in Augusta Georgia with his bad self" claimed the sleeve. Actually, only tracks 6–14 were cut in concert. And there were two different bands. The second half of *Sex Machine* captures the Fred Wesley-Maceo Parker band recorded live and at its peak in Augusta, Georgia in 1969, shortly before a dispute over money led them to walk out/be sacked. Tracks 1–5 and 8 were studio-recorded with audience brouhaha dubbed afterwards. On four of these, Brown uses the youthful vigour and enthusiasm of his new rhythm section to recast old material. Bassist Bootsy Collins, authoritative beyond his years (hear him fly on Give It Up Or Turn It A Loose), his elder brother guitarist Catfish Collins and long-serving drummers Jabo Starks and Clyde Stubblefield are at the eye of this particular storm, with Brown audibly enthused by their propulsive drive. He revisits the title track (its older version was a hit single at the time), and reins in the horn section, making it an adjunct of the rhythm section, a process heard more obviously on another of the remakes, the brief I Got The Feelin'.

The second track, Brother Rapp, was cut with the older, more-seasoned troupe and melodically makes more use of the horns, while the guitars of Nolen and Kellum have richer, thicker tones. Brown veterans also drive the genuine in-concert recordings and they are in exceptional form. The horn players even get solos! I Don't Want Nobody bounces along on the beat, and the punishing pace of Licking Stick makes it little wonder these guys pulled fines for mistakes. When, in Man's Man's Man's World – which, incidentally, is a terrific example of his rapport with his audience – Brown says "Give the band a hand for being so together," you can't quite work out if he's fining them in code or not; when he quietly admonishes, "Don't play so much jazz," you know they're in trouble. Still, they sound great to these ears. Two superb bands for the price of one and a 36-year-old musical revolutionary marching forward with a different drum ringing in his ears. It's soul history in the making.

Record label:
Polydor

Produced
by James Brown.

Recorded
at King Studios, Cincinnati, Ohio; July 23 and October 14, 1969; Bell Auditorium, Augusta, Georgia; October 1, 1969 and Miami, Florida; June 12, 1969.

Released:
December 1970

Chart peaks:
None (UK) 29 (US)

Personnel:
James Brown (v, k); Clayton 'Chicken' Gunnels, Darryl 'Hasaan' Jamison, Richard 'Kush' Griffith, Joseph Davis (t); Maceo Parker (ts, o, MC); St. Clair Pinckney (ts, bs); Robert 'Chopper' McCullough, Eldee Williams (ts); Alfred 'Pee Wee' Ellis (as); Fred Wesley (tb); Bobby Byrd (o, v); Phelps 'Catfish' Collins, Jimmy Nolen, Alphonso 'Country' Kellum, Kenny Poole (g); William 'Bootsy' Collins, 'Sweet' Charles Sherrell (b); John 'Jabo' Starks, Clyde Stubblefield, Melvin Parker (d)

Track listing:
Get Up I Feel Like Being A Sex Machine; Brother Rapp (Part I & Part II); Bewildered; I Got The Feelin'; Give It Up Or Turn It A Loose; I Don't Want Nobody To Give Me Nothing (Open Up The Door And I'll Get It Myself); Licking Stick; Lowdown Popcorn; Spinning Wheel; If I Ruled The World; There Was A Time; It's A Man's Man's World; Please, Please, Please; I Can't Stand Myself (When You Touch Me); Mother Popcorn

Running time:
65.00

Current CD:
517 984-2

Further listening:
There It Is (1972)

Further reading:
James Brown: The Autobiography (1996)

Derek And The Dominos

Layla And Other Assorted Love Songs

A flop when first released: now widely regarded as the height of Clapton's achievement.

During 1969–1970, Eric Clapton had at least one monkey on his back; like both Hendrix and Peter Green, he was tired of being regarded as a guitar hero. He sought refuge with white soul singers Delaney and Bonnie, revelling in their laid back style and rootsy authenticity. By May 1970, their musicians had become Eric's, while he in turn had become Derek, a half-joking, half-serious attempt to become anonymous again.

August saw the band camped out at the Criteria Studios in Miami trying to turn bits of songs and half-formed ideas into an album. *Layla* came together through endless jamming; "We really didn't know what we were going to do," says Bobby Whitlock. "Tom and the engineers' job was just to make sure they hit those faders as soon as we started playing. That fade in on Key To The Highway was the only time they missed."

Among the new songs was the surging and lyrical title track, Eric's cry of unrequited love for George Harrison's wife Patti. Clapton and Whitlock formed a fertile writing and vocal partnership, but the ante soared with the arrival of Duane Allman who took the music to another place. The musicians themselves were already there, thanks to copious amounts of drugs. Though ultimately highly destructive, there seems little doubt that the chemicals played an important part in the magic of the Dominos. Eric has never played any less; the gorgeous runs, fills and solos were present, but it was all so much more measured and restrained. It was a unique situation which could never be repeated; the closeness of the musicians interlocking with each other on several levels, the womb-like environment of Criteria, the sympathetic production of Tom Dowd, the freedom and space to create.

As engineer Karl Richardson put it, "We knew it was phenomenal. You couldn't not know that the music flying out of Studio B was phenomenal. You'd have to be deaf." But this was not the view of the music-buying public; the initial critical and commercial failure of the album when first released just added to the problems piling up for the band both as a group and as individuals. Indeed, if Eric originally entered the project to take it easy, he ended up making things infinitely harder for himself,

Record label:
Polydor

Produced
by Tom Dowd.

Recorded
at Criteria Studios, Miami;
August–September 1970.

Released:
December 1970

Chart peaks:
None (UK) 16 (US)

Personnel:
Eric Clapton (g, v); Duane Allman (g); Bobby Whitlock (p, o, v); Carl Radle (b, pc); Jim Gordon (d, pc, p); Ron Albert, Chuck Kirkpatrick, Howie Albert, Karl Richardson, Mac Emmerman (e)

Track listing:
I Looked Away; Bell Bottom Blues (S/US); Keep On Growing; Nobody Knows You When You Are Down And Out; I Am Yours; Anyday; Key To The Highway; Tell The Truth; Why Does Love Got To Be So Sad (S/UK); Have You Ever Loved A Woman; Little Wing; It's Too Late; Layla (S); Thorn Tree In The Garden

Running time:
77.09

Current CD:
Polydor 5318202

Further listening:
3 CD 20th Anniversary box set Derek and the Dominos: the Layla Sessions (1990) comprising not only the album, but also all the alternative version, long jams plus the tracks from the abortive second album.

Further reading:
Midnight Riders: The Story Of The Allman Brothers Band (Scott Freeman, 1995); www.whereseric.com

becoming addicted to heroin.

After tours of Britain and America, including a string of dates in small UK clubs, the Dominos broke up in acrimony after only a year, in May 1971, during an attempt to record a follow-up to *Layla* in London. Drugs and madness did for them all in one way or another. Whitlock survives but Allman and Radle are both dead, Jim Gordon is serving a life sentence for murdering his mother. Derek eventually became Eric again – not just a cult guitar hero, but a musician and songwriter of international repute – though at some cost.

The Grateful Dead
American Beauty

Minimalist rootsy opus from mellowing masters of the elongated jam.

Having visited their country roots on *Workingman's Dead* earlier in the year, The Grateful Dead delved even deeper with *American Beauty*. The heady days of psychedelia and guiltless freedom had swiftly passed and their search for a context in the subsequent months of political unrest and Vietnam war protest, not to mention a slew of drug busts, led them to flee to the country, where they explored folkloric melody, subdued storytelling and three-part harmony. The latter was a direct influence of Crosby Stills & Nash, whose first album they'd paid homage to on *Workingman's Dead*, but who, in the subsequent months, they actually visited at work on *Deja Vu*. Seeing how CS&N recorded vocals — all three around a 360° mic plus an identical overdub mixed at three-quarters of the level — really turned the Dead's heads.

"It amazed them," recalled Graham Nash in MOJO 67. "They'd been used to doing individual voices. [That's why] *Workingman's Dead* didn't sound anywhere near *American Beauty* vocally. Whatever they'd learned from us they put into good practice." FM radio noticed and began to give the album's great ballads, Box Of Rain and Ripple, unexpected support, which in turn won the Dead new fans. The key was simplicity. The songs were extracted from fruitful back-porch jams (Jerry Garcia and lyricist Robert Hunter were sharing a house by this time) that not only spawned this album but also a Garcia side project, The New Riders Of The Purple Sage. Among the many friends invited along to these pick-a-thons was mandolin player Dave Grisman: "The original recordings were built out of endless sessions where Jerry and I would play off against each other, with the rest of the New Riders crew sitting in too. The end result was a far more stripped down version of what we were doing."

In fact, it's the paring-down and editing of the material that was the making of *American Beauty*. At times, it is utterly bare, just the harmonies of Garcia, Weir and Lesh melding into a kind of gothic choir. And, in places it's truly moving, too, as in the beautiful melodies of Sugar Magnolia and Friend Of The Devil, the sound of America shaking itself awake to a challenging new decade. And if that weren't enough definitive Dead, there's also the more prosaic Truckin', their road-jockey's anthem that quickly became part of their legend, mainly because it included their most memorable line: "What a long, strange trip it's been."

Record label:
Warner Brothers

Produced
by The Grateful Dead.

Recorded
at Wally Heider Studios, San Francisco; autumn 1969.

Released:
December 1970

Chart peaks:
None (UK) None (US)

Personnel:
Jerry Garcia (v, g, ps, p); Bob Weir (rg); Ron 'Pigpen' McKernan (v, hm); Phil Lesh (b, g, p, v); Bill Kreutzman (d); Mickey Hart (pc); David Nelson (g); David Grisman (mandolin); Dave Torbert (b); Howard Wales (o, p); Ned Lagin (p)

Track listing:
Box Of Rain; Friend Of The Devil; Sugar Magnolia; Operator; Candyman; Ripple; Brokedown Palace; Till The Morning Comes; Attics Of My Life; Truckin' (S/US)

Running time:
42.28

Current CD:
7599271902

Further listening:
Workingman's Dead (1970) was composed in the same period. "I think of those as being really one record, in a way," said Jerry Garcia. Hear also the closely related New Riders Of The Purple Sage's self-titled first album (1971).

Further reading:
for a comprehensive Grateful Dead bibliography, try www.sfmuseum.org/hist1/deadbib.html

George Harrison
All Things Must Pass

A chart-topping triple set that sounds better and better as time goes by.

W hen promo copies of Paul's solo album, *McCartney* were sent out in April 1970, the press release inadvertently tipped off the tabloids that The Beatles were finished. Paul had grumbled on many occasions about strained relationships within the group, so he didn't expect to be the one who broke the news and took the blame.

It was a messy finish that didn't seem conclusive. As months went by, though, it began to dawn on the public that their favourite pop group really had gone for good. Suddenly, George – of all people – came to the rescue with a bountiful triple boxed set accompanied by the first solo Beatle US Number 1 single, My Sweet Lord (not released in the UK until January). A bumper Christmas treat with a little religion thrown in – perfect. George certainly announced his arrival as a solo artist in grand style.

"I've always looked at *All Things Must Pass* like someone who's had constipation for years and then finally they get diarrhoea," he explained helpfully to Billboard's Craig Rosen. Indeed, he'd acquired a backlog of material while with The Beatles and one or two of the songs had been, by necessity, road-tested elsewhere. My Sweet Lord and All Things (Must) Pass appeared on Billy Preston's Apple album, *Encouraging Words*. Tapes also exist of George demoing songs with engineer Phil Macdonald, including titles like Everybody, Nobody; Window, Window; Cosmic Empire; Mother Divine and Tell Me What Has Happened To You, none of which made it onto this record. George was clearly enjoying a creative burst.

On May 1, 1970 he'd jammed with Bob Dylan during sessions for the *New Morning* album, played slide guitar on Bob's version of If Not For You and written I'd Have You Anytime with him. By late May, George was ready to record his own album and backing tracks were laid at Abbey Road with an all-star cast of heavy session friends, including an uncredited Eric Clapton audible on many tracks, and Phil Spector joining George at the controls. Overdubbing was done at Trident Studios and Abbey Road from June and mixes were completed in New York.

The third disc – Apple Jam, featuring Harrison, Clapton, Billy Preston, Bobby Keys and Klaus Voormann – included an impromptu 30th birthday greeting to John Lennon,

Record label:
Apple

Produced
by George Harrison and Phil Spector.

Recorded
at Abbey Road and Trident Studios, London.

Released:
December 1970

Chart peaks:
4 (UK) I (US)

Personnel:
George Harrison (g, v); Eric Clapton (g); Dave Mason (g); Pete Ham, Tom Evans (rg); Ringo Starr, Jim Gordon, Alan White (d, pc); Klaus Voormann, Carl Radle (b); Gary Wright, Bobby Whitlock, Billy Preston, Gary Brooker (k); Bobby Keys (ts); Jim Price (t); Pete Drake (psg); Mal Evans (tea, sympathy, tambourine); John Burnham (oa); Ken Scott, Phil Macdonald (e)

Track listing:
I'd Have You Anytime; My Sweet Lord; Wah-Wah; Isn't It A Pity (Version One); What Is Life; If Not For You; Behind That Locked Door; Let it Down; Run Of The Mill; Beware Of Darkness; Apple Scruffs; Ball Of Sir Frankie Crisp (Let It Roll); Awaiting On You All; All Things Must Pass; I Dig Love; Art Of Dying; Isn't It A Pity (Version Two); Hear Me Lord; Out Of The Blue; It's Johnny's Birthday; Plug Me In; I Remember Jeep; Thanks For The Pepperoni

Running time:
105.11

Current CD:
EMI CDS 7 46688 8

Further listening:
Extra Texture (1975), specifically the single You.

Further reading:
The Beatles After The Break-Up
1970–2000 (1999)

It's Johnny's Birthday, sung to the tune of Congratulations. This "free gift" inevitably hiked the price of the album and now spoils its overall mood on CD. It is perhaps the unwieldy (and costly) nature of the whole package that has prevented *All Things Must Pass* from being more popular down the years. The two main albums are superb, the best George ever produced, concise and filler-free. Spector's warm, pillowy sound provides an epic grace and an engaging habitat; George's sense of freedom is audible and many of the songs outshine his contributions to Beatles albums. This music's at least the equal of Lennon's more lauded solo work. Curiously, John was rather cool about the album upon release ("I wouldn't play that kind of music at home"), but used it as a template for his own *Imagine* a year later.

Talking of which, try playing Imagine The Beatles Had Stayed Together. Gather all the Beatles solo material released in the year after the split and see if you can compile what might have been The Beatles' album for 1971. You'll find when it comes to selecting George's contributions you'll be spoilt for choice.

The Stooges
Fun House

*Stooges sophomore album anticipated the dense metallic
sound of punk, goth and industrial music.*

The plan behind *Fun House* was simple. It was to be a faithful
reproduction, in sequence, of The Stooges' live set. First,
however, the band needed a sympathetic producer. Elektra boss
Jac Holzman selected one-time Kingsman Don Gallucci. Gallucci
went to see the band and turned down the job: "I said, 'Jac, it's
a performance band, it's got a lot of vitality and energy, but
there is nothing musical here.'" Holzman, relishing the creative
tension, told Gallucci he was doing the job anyway. His confidence was repaid; realising the importance of retaining the
band's live energy, Gallucci, aided by the staid but inspired
British enginer Brian Ross-Myring, stripped Holzman's elegant
studio of all its carpeting and sound baffling and had the band
set up as if playing live; lead singer Iggy roamed the floor with a
basic hand mic.

Fortunately, the band already had everything nailed
before recording commenced. As Iggy puts it, "It had a unity
and a reality before we ever got on the studio. I knew exactly
what I wanted it to be." New Stooge Steve Mackay, recruited
shortly before the session, concurs: "Iggy's already got *Fun House*
written in his head and knows there's gonna be sax on it, so he
invites me for a coffee and already knows he wants to take me
to Los Angeles to record." Mackay's saxophone fitted in
perfectly with The Stooges' stripped-down ethos, distilled from
a musical diet of James Brown, Hendrix, and Harry Partch.

By now, Ron Asheton's guitar playing had progressed
from the charming primitivism of the band's debut, to something much more powerful and concise: "There is not one solo
that is overdubbed; the only thing I went back and overdubbed
was little picking pieces, rhythms here and there."

The results were unique in musical history, an aggressive
rock band packing in high-density musical ideas, captured with
the natural freedom of a jazz recording. Iggy describes it as
"Osterberg's fifth symphony". The rest of the world, however,
was unmoved. Lester Bangs' epic Creem review, run over two
weeks, didn't prevent the album sinking without trace. Its most
immediate consequence for The Stooges would be a collective
heroin habit, acquired in LA's low-spots.

Record label:
Elektra

Produced
by Don Gallucci.

Recorded
at Elektra Sound Recorders, Los Angeles;
May 11–24, 1970.

Released:
December 1970

Chart peaks:
None (UK) None (US)

Personnel:
Iggy Pop (v); Dave Alexander (b); Ron
Asheton (g); Scott Asheton (d); Steve
Mackay (ts); Brian Ross-Myring (e)

Track listing:
Down On The Street (S); Loose; TV Eye;
Dirt; I Feel Alright; Fun House; LA Blues

Running time:
36.28

Current CD:
7559-60669-2

Further listening:
Funhouse Sessions (2000) a 6-CD box
set containing session out-takes.

Further reading:
MOJO 29; www.rawiguana.com

Emitt Rhodes
Emitt Rhodes

The best LP that Paul McCartney never made.

P oor Emitt Rhodes was as ill-fated in business as he was
blessed with musical talent. He had two golden opportunities, both of which began promisingly and ended in
disappointment. Rhodes' first proper band The Merry Go
Round secured an A&M deal in 1967 and released a first single
Live that was a huge regional hit and made it to Number 63
nationally. Packed off to make an album, Rhodes discovered a
talent for inventiveness in the studio and got the bug; the band
disintegrated and he became a one-man studio-bound band
instead.

Purchasing a 'washing machine type four track' he shut
himself away in his parents' garage., recording a good half of the
material on *Emitt Rhodes* there before doing a deal with Dunhill.
The album was completed with the mix-down assistance of
Keith Olsen (who would later produce Fleetwood Mac) and
Curt Boettcher, already something of a soft-pop legend for his
work with The Association, Millennium and Sagittarius.

Things began like a dream. A single, Fresh As A Daisy,
ascended the charts and the album reached as high as 29 by the
beginning of 1971. Then the music business corrupted it all.
Firstly A&M cobbled together a spoiler album *The American
Dream* which ate into sales of *Emitt Rhodes* and then Dunhill
suspended him for not delivering a second album on time. His
career started to disintegrate and the whole affair left a bitter
taste. Yet *Emitt Rhodes* is a true delight and far more than a mere
footnote in pop history. At least the equal of other Beatles
inspired records by Badfinger or Todd Rundgren. Rhodes took
classic Beatles motifs and made them his own: *Abbey Road* guitar,
McCartney upper register bass lines, and the familiar call and
response harmonies of Hello Goodbye. And it anticipates each
wave of Fabs-obsessed powerpop that followed, from The
Raspberries to Jellyfish to Matthew Sweet.

Neither of his two final Dunhill albums quite measured
up, *Mirror* in 1971 and the prophetic *Farewell to Paradise* in 1973.
By the '80s, in his own words, he was washed up, putting his
decline down to "demos, debauchery and drugs". All in all, a
tragedy, made more poignant by the wide-eyed exuberance of
this lovely record.

Record label:
Dunhill

Produced
by Emitt Rhodes and Harvey Bruce.

Recorded
at Homes Studios, Hawthorne, California.

Released:
winter 1970

Chart peaks:
None (UK) 29 (US)

Personnel:
Emitt Rhodes (all instruments, v, e)

Track listing:
With My Face On The Floor; Somebody
Made For Me; She's Such A Beauty; Long
Time No See; Lullaby; Fresh As A Daisy;
Live Till You Die; Promises I've Made; You
Take The Dark Out Of The Night; You
Should Be Ashamed; Ever Find Yourself
Running; You Must Have

Running time:
32.05

Current CD:
Edsel EDCD569

Further listening:

Further reading:
Power Pop: Conversations With The
Powerpop Elite (Ken Sharp and Doug
Sulp, 1997)

Fela Kuti
Fela's London Scene

Funky music, sho' nuff turns Africa on.

As the 1960s turned into an angrier, uglier decade, Nigeria's Fela Kuti hit top gear, taking the funk and politics of America's Black Panthers and offering it back to its homeland. In 1969, Fela and his band, the Koola Lobitos, arrived in Los Angeles, where Sandra Isidore, a black activist (and later a member of the Hummingbirds) introduced him to Black Power. His eyes opened, he renamed the band The Nigeria 70 and dreamt up Afrobeat. They scraped together enough money to record – *The '69 Los Angeles Session*, an uneven collection of soul and funk pastiches – then headed home.

Back in Lagos, the speed of development of Afrobeat was startling, with live shows and regular singles increasing his fan base, fleshing out the politics and breathing life into the music. His record company decided to support a visit to London, where Fela had been a student at the Royal College of Music in 1958. This time, he was feted as a star of Africa: living in a luxury hotel and recording at Abbey Road. He also had A-list celebrity pals – Ginger Baker had made friends with Kuti in Lagos in 1969, and was on hand to help the band acclimatise to Britain. Keeping their hand in, Nigeria 70 gigs were scheduled around London, but the real action was taking place in the studio.

J'Ehin J'Ehin attacks fools (people who "eat their own teeth"); Buy Africa is a nationalistic anthem encouraging pan–Africanism; and the centrepiece, the 13-minute Egbe Mi O (recorded live with Baker) uses dancing as metaphor, warning the overindulgent that "all your underwear drop". Fela's development was not complete – he would soon use pidgin English rather than Yoruba, to increase his audience – but the musical blueprint was there.

Almost immediately, he changed the band's name again – to Africa 70 – and started getting heavy. EMI refused to release his next LP, the two-song *Why Black Man Dey Suffer*, but Fela was on a roll, with a torrent of singles and albums that would grow increasingly political. In 1977, the army retaliated, attacking his home, fracturing his skull and murdering his mother. But the band played on.

Record label:
Barclay

Produced
by Fela Kuti.

Recorded
at Abbey Road Studios, London; 1970.

Released:
1970

Chart peaks:
None (UK) None (US)

Personnel:
Fela Kuti (v, k, s); Ginger Baker (d); Tony Allen (d); Igo Chico (s); Lekan Animashaun (s); Tony Njoku (t); Tutu Sorunmu (g)

Track listing:
J'Ehin J'Ehin; Egbe Mi O; Who're You; Buy Africa; Fight To Finish

Running time:
43.24

Current CD:
STERNS3007 adds: Shakara Oloje; Lady

Further listening:
Open And Close (1971); He Miss Road (1974); Expensive Shit (1975); Confusion (1975); The Best Best Of: Black President (1999)

Further reading:
Fela: The Life And Times Of An African Musical Icon (Micheal E Veal, 2000)

Essra Mohawk
Primordial Lovers

Second album by former Frank Zappa protégé; rave reviews, no sales, cult legend.

In a parallel world, Essra Mohawk's name would be so familiar no one would confuse it with an unfortunate hairstyle. But in this world, she remains a largely overlooked figure, famous more for her associations with an almost laughably impressive number of significant '60s pop music icons than her ability as a record maker. Had more people believed what they read about *Primordial Lovers* – the five-star review in Downbeat, or Rolling Stone's lauding it as "one of the best 25 albums ever made" – that likely wouldn't be the case.

Discovered in the mid-'60s by producer Shadow Morton and introduced to the pop world as Sandy Hurvitz via a debut album bearing Frank Zappa's picture on its cover – 1969's *Sandy's Album Is Here At Last* – Mohawk spent a brief period with the Mothers Of Invention before being offered a deal by Reprise Records' Mo Ostin. *Primordial Lovers* would be the eventual result, but not before she married the album's producer Frazier Mohawk, whose name can be found on Nico's *The Marble Index* as well. ("Of course his real name was Barry Friedman," she'd later note, "but Danny Kortchmar gave Barry the choice of Frazier Mohawk or Gabriel Roughweather. I think it's fortunate for me that he chose Frazier Mohawk.")

With its impressive cast of backing musicians, including members of San Francisco's Jerry Hahn Brotherhood and Tim Buckley's longtime guitarist Lee Underwood, the LP is firstly a sonic marvel, providing Mohawk's songs a beautiful setting she'd never capture again. And as for the songs themselves – an intimate collection of one-to-one lyrics addressed to a lover (presumably primordial) – they are magnificently, almost erotically, sung. When the raves came – and there were many – nobody listened. Was it a lack of promotion? Was it merely a question of cover art?

"They came up with a mostly black album," Mohawk recalls, "which does not draw light, does not draw eyes. And my idea was to have one set of bodies across the front and back – instead of the Rorschach effect that you have – and that would've been mostly white. And then superimposed over that a sunset and the earth – so it would be heaven and earth, primordial lovers. The horizon would be made by the meeting of the bodies." But back in black, it stayed in the rack.

Record label:
Reprise

Produced
by Frazier Mohawk.

Recorded
at Elektra Sound Recorders, Los Angeles and Pacific High Recording Co., San Francisco; 1969.

Released:
1970

Chart peaks:
None (UK) None (US)

Personnel:
Essra Mohawk (k, v); Doug Hastings (g); Jerry Hahn (g); Lee Underwood (g); Mel Graves (b); Jerry Penrod (b); Dalls Taylor (d); George Marsh (d); Phil Sawyer, Brian Ross-Myring (e)

Track listing:
I Am The Breeze; Spiral; I'll Give It To You Anyway; I Have Been Here Before; Looking Forward To The Dawn; Thunder In The Morning; Lion On The Wing; It's Up To Me; It's Been A Beautiful Day

Running time:
41.46

Currently unavailable on CD

Further listening:
Essra Mohawk (1975); Essra (1977)

Further reading:
When The Music Mattered (Bruce Pollock, 1984); www.rockersusa.com/EssraMohawk/

Yoko Ono
Yoko Ono / Plastic Ono Band

Companion set to Lennon's solo debut that could have been recorded tomorrow.

John Lennon was once asked to explain why people didn't understand Yoko: "She is a woman and she's Japanese – it's as simple as that." He neglected to mention that she was also a former member of Fluxus, the '60s art movement dedicated to ridiculing the establishment, and to blurring the distinction between art and life. She had inspired Lennon to do likewise, but with much public recrimination. By 1970, the lives of the "two gurus in drag" had indeed become inseparable from their work, just as Lennon's separation from The Beatles had finally become public knowledge. The wranglings over the group's demise left deep scars; The Primal Scream author Arthur Janov was called on to help the pair confront their pain using a radical healing therapy based on catharsis. Lennon responded in singer-songwriterly fashion by recording the most revealing songs of his career; Ono opted to recreate the treatment's howling exorcisms on this extraordinary album which only really began to make sense after punk. (Appropriately, Lennon had dubbed it "1980s music".) But the decision to release both records on the same day, and in matching sleeves, didn't exactly help Yoko's cause. "Yoko is as important to me as Paul and Dylan rolled into one," Lennon insisted. Cynics assumed he was either joking or, more likely, hopelessly in love.

The real folly was in mistaking dazzling originality for gimmickry; as far back as 1961, Yoko envisaged "a 'New Music', a fusion of avant-garde jazz rock and East and West". Earlier collaborations with Lennon – *Two Virgins*, *Life With The Lions*, *Wedding* Album – may have been prankish excursions into the pair's private world, and gave little hint of what to expect on this improvised, exhilarating solo debut, made all the more remarkable for its swift execution: "Yes, it was recorded in one afternoon, and we mixed it that evening," Ono confirms.

The Starr/Voormann rhythm section used on Lennon's album remained but the transformation, particularly on the uptempo cuts (Why; Touch Me), was breathtaking. Lennon's abrasive guitar playing wouldn't have disgraced PiL's Metal Box, while the insistent rhythms evoke Can or early '70s Miles Davis. Elsewhere (Greenfield Morning; Paper Shoes), Yoko utilised tape loops and layers of heavily reverbed vocals reminiscent of mid-'70s dub. Lennon compared her to Spector. And the Stones and Townshend. And no, he wasn't joking.

Record label:
Apple

Produced
by John and Yoko.

Recorded
at Abbey Road Studios, London; one day in October 1970, except AOS, recorded in rehearsal for Albert Hall show; February 1968.

Released:
January 1971

Chart peaks:
11 (UK) None (US)

Personnel:
Yoko Ono (v); John Lennon (g); Ringo Starr (d); Klaus Voormann (b); Ornette Coleman (t on AOS); Edward Blackwell (d on AOS); Charles Haden (b on AOS); Phil MacDonald, John Leckie, Andy Stevens, 'Eddie' (e)

Track listing:
Why; Why Not; Greenfield Morning I Pushed An Empty Baby Carriage All Over The City; AOS; Touch Me; Paper Shoes. CD bonus tracks: Open Your Box; Something More Abstract; The South Wind

Running time:
40.37

Current CD:
Apple 10414

Further listening:
Fly (1971) is marginally more subdued than its predecessor but, being a 2-LP set, has more room to roam.

Further reading:
www.yoko.com

Serge Gainsbourg
Histoire De Melody Nelson

French master of outrage crafts mould-breaking suite for rock band and orchestra. Nobody notices.

It was while Jane Birkin – her acting career blossoming – was in the South of France making a film (the not-quite-classic Mustard Goes Up My Nose) that Gainsbourg started work on his masterpiece. Its plot revolves around a middle-aged Frenchman running into a teenage redhead cyclist in his Rolls Royce. He and the "délicieuse enfant" Melody fall in love and go off to a hotel for sex (the sound effects in L'Hotel Particulier feature Jane, being tickled by her brother Andrew). But she soon becomes homesick – for Sunderland! – and flies back home. The plane crashes, the distraught narrator becomes a crazed obsessive.

"When I first met him he had given me a nice little leather-covered book called Chansons D'Aujourdhui," recalls Jane, "and in it he wrote: 'To Jane Mallory' – my maiden name – 'for whom I shall write the story of Melody Nelson. Je T'Aime,' and on the next page he wrote 'Moi non plus'. Therefore he had already got the idea in 1968 when he met me to write about a girl who came, like my father did, from the North of England – which is why she's going back to Sunderland."

Gainsbourg originally planned the music as the score for a TV special which was never shot. The recordings took place in Philips' London studios with a 50-piece orchestra and a large choir, plus a basic rock rhythm section of guitars, bass and drums. There's also one bar of piano during L'Hotel Particulier. "As for the never-ending ending, we'd never heard anything like it," recalls Birkin. "We were ecstatic about the album. My brother was so enthusiastic that he got a demo and ran to every English disc jockey he knew to have it played. He was absolutely convinced it was going to be an overnight hit. But no-one wanted to play it. Even in France it wasn't a hit – although it's a gold record now, and for most people that and *Cabbage Head* are their favourites."

Discerning French critics hailed its seven tracks, two of them nearly eight minutes long, as "the first true symphonic poem of the pop age"; "One of my favourite albums," said Françoise Hardy. "Musically completely new, extremely refined, and utterly, inimitably original."

It *was* incredibly unusual for its time and it still sounds thoroughly modern. "There's an ambition, a conceptual depth to

Record label:
Philips

Produced
by Jean-Claude Desmarty.

Recorded
at Philips Studios, Marble Arch, London;
1970.

Released:
March 1971

Chart peaks:
None (UK) None (US)

Personnel:
Serge Gainsbourg (v); Jane Birkin (v);
JC Vannier (oa); Jean-Claude Charvier (e);
Rémy Aucharles (ae)

Track listing:
Melody; Ballade De Melody Nelson; Valse De Melody; Ah! Melody; L'Hotel Particulieur; En Melody; Cargo Culte

Running time:
28.02

Current CD:
532 073-2

Further listening:
L'Homme A Tete De Chou (1976)

Further reading:
Serge Gainsbourg: View From The Exterior (Alan Clayson, 1996);
www.francevision.com/nsltr/vf14/gains.htm;
www.geocities.com/Paris/Musee/1489/
gainsbourg/serge.html

Melody Nelson that's incredibly hard to pull off but which he does completely," says contemporary fan, Beck Hanson. "One of the best marriages of rock band and orchestra that I've ever heard. It's a very cool record, and the dynamic of it is genius – there's this band that's completely rocking on this almost acid tangent, but they're buried in the mix with him whispering on top, and he's the loudest thing on it."

Jane, four months pregnant with daughter Charlotte Gainsbourg, was photographed for the cover. "He wanted Melody to have red hair, so they bunged a wig on my head and put on a lot of freckles. I'm holding my monkey – which I buried with Serge because he always wanted it, so it will keep him safe now."

Elvis Presley

Elvis Country (I'm 10,000 Years Old)

His last truly great album.

The first half of 1970 had been kind of a drag for Elvis. There'd been the Vegas rehearsals and karate lessons to occupy his mind but there was a whole bunch of dead time as well. With no big movie or TV special to lose weight for it was easy to just sit around, gobbling pills, scarfing burgers, shooting stuff, getting bored. Even the live shows, as evidenced on the *On Stage – February 1970* album weren't really doing it. Then, when the time came to do another album, Elvis just didn't want to go back to Memphis. Despite the success of the recordings at American Studios, Elvis felt that producer Chips Moman hadn't accorded him enough respect. Instead he went back to his official producer Felton Jarvis in Nashville. Ever since first working with Elvis in 1966, Felton had wanted to assemble a band who could really keep up with the King. The original Muscle Shoals rhythm section, wrestled from Rick Hall's studio, Elvis' new band were as sharp as anything. They were also frightened to death. As bassist Norbert Puttnam tells it "I was scared, staring at my reflection and saying 'Dear God, don't let me be the one to screw up the session...don't let me be the first guy to ruin it . . .'"

Elvis was thoroughly inspired by the new band. He insisted that they group around him, watch his moves, shifting gears at the slightest sign. They worked well, cutting seven masters on the first night and another 12 over the next couple of nights with Elvis constantly open to suggestion, taking each song by the scruff of the neck, singing ahead of the beat, attacking tracks like Whole Lotta Shakin' for all he was worth. Over five nights the band cut 35 masters. The true broken heart of the album can be found in such deep gospel ballads as Tomorrow Never Comes, Funny (How Time Slips Away) and I Really Don't Want to Know, tracks invested with a soul power lost to Elvis for the previous 15 years. Passionate, wild, dynamic, *Elvis Country* sounds like it's tapped straight from the true soul of that once and future King. He'd never sing like this again.

After those five days, Elvis returned to Memphis to prepare for more Vegas shows. In no time he was back on a diet of burgers. The only way was down.

Record label:
RCA

Produced
by Felton Jarvis

Recorded
at RCA's Nashville Studios, June 4–8, 1970

Released:
March 1971

Chart peaks:
6 (UK) 12 (US)

Personnel:
Elvis Presley (v); James Burton (g); Charlie McCoy (g, b, d, hm); Chip Young (g); David Briggs (k); Jerry Carrigan (d); Norbert Puttnam (b); the Jordonaires (v); The Imperials Quartet (v); Don Tweedy (ar); Cam Mullins (ar); Bergen White (ar)

Track listing:
Snowbird; Tomorrow Never Comes; Little Cabin On The Hill; Whole Lotta Shakin' Goin' On; Funny How Time Slips Away; I Really Don't Want To Know; There Goe My Everything; It's Your Baby, You Rock It; The Fool; Faded Love; I Washed My Hands In Muddy Water; Make The World Go Away

Running time:
38.54

Current CD:
74321 146922

Further listening:
From Elvis In Memphis (RCA 1969)

Further reading:
Careless Love: The Unmaking Of Elvis Presley – (Peter Guralnick 1999). Indispensable.

Anne Briggs
Anne Briggs

Belated debut from singer who exiled herself to obscurity.

"To hear the elusive Anne Briggs on her first solo album is an opportunity not to be missed," opined the Melody Maker. Already by 1971 a mythical figure in British folk, Anne had existed on the fringes of the commercial recording world – with a handful of a cappella releases between 1963–66 – as a singer of magical beauty and pursuer of a truly alternative, nomadic lifestyle. Mostly travelling in Ireland, her five-year silence had been tantalisingly broken in August 1969 by a BBC radio session for John Peel. This subsequent album captured Anne at the point where her confidence in songwriting and in using accompaniment was perfectly balanced with her mostly dark traditional repertoire. A moody silhouette of the loping young lass and her faithful hound adorned the cover while eight traditional songs – as stunning as any previous work – and two originals were featured. The most extraordinary piece, Living By The Water, had been written on bouzouki during a period of solitude on Bull Island, off western Ireland.

"Very profound time that," says Anne of this lonely episode. "Focuses the mind wonderfully on priorities. I've always felt totally at one with the natural environment – the landscape, the wildlife. What is. It's only people that make life difficult."

Along with Go Your Way, co-written with Bert Jansch in 1965, it typifies a strain of nature-driven writing that remains a hallmark of her work. Anne's boyfriend of the time, Johnny Moynihan, in between stints with Sweeney's Men and Planxty, cameos on Willy O'Winsbury.

The album would be a virtual source book for the Fairport generation. Indeed, Sandy Denny recorded The Pond And The Stream in 1970 in awe of Anne – free to come and go while peers like herself, Bert Jansch and others were tied to the commercial treadmill. "I assumed they were all having a great time," says Anne, "making a great deal of money and travelling all over the world. There was me, happy to wander around. Sandy made her choice and I made mine."

Anne disappeared from music in 1973, surfacing sporadically for a few gigs and a duet with Bert Jansch in the BBC film *Acoustic Routes*. Her aborted final album appeared in 1997.

Record label:
Topic

Produced
by A L Lloyd.

Recorded
in London, probably City Of London Recording Studios; late 1970.

Released:
April 1971

Chart peaks:
None (UK) None (US)

Personnel:
Anne Briggs (v, g, bouzouki); Johnny Moynihan (bouzouki)

Track listing:
Blackwater Side; The Snow It Melts The Soonest; Willie O'Winsbury; Go Your Way; Thorneymoor Woods; The Cuckoo; Reynardine; Young Tambling; Living By The Water; Ma Bonny Lad

Running time:
41.53

Current CD:
TSCD 504 reissued as Anne Briggs: A Collection adds: Recruited Collier; Doffin Mistress; She Moves Through The Fair; Let No Man Steal Your Thyme; Lowlands; My Bonny Boy; Polly Vaughan; Rosemary Lane Gathering Rushes In The Month Of May; Whirly Whorl; Stonecutter Boy; Martinmas Time

Further listening:
The Time Has Come (1971); Sing A Song For You (1973)

Further reading:
MOJO 52; Colin Harper's sleevenote to Anne Briggs: A Collection (1999)

Caravan
In The Land Of Grey And Pink

The quintessential Canterbury album.

Caravan started life on Decca, but they were a progressive lot, and in 1971 the classically-slanted label decided the band's third album would be a better bet for new offshoot Deram. Bands worked quickly in those days: it was only a few months after they'd released their second set, *If I Could Do It All Over Again, I'd Do It All Over You*. David Hitchcock made his debut as the group's producer, but otherwise it was the same line-up as before, with British jazzman Jimmy Hastings – older brother to guitarist Pye – guesting on sax, flute and piccolo.

The key members of Caravan in this period, however, were the Sinclair cousins. Richard had been in the original line-up of The Wilde Flowers, the semi-legendary early '60s group which never released a record but spawned the idea of a "Canterbury" movement in English rock, since out of it came Kevin Ayers and the Whole World, Soft Machine, Gong and Caravan. Canterbury isn't much different to any other provincial cathedral town, but the music associated with the name came to possess a particularity which Caravan embodied perhaps better than any other group. Light, slightly wayward vocals; whimsical lyrics; long, vaguely jazz-inflected solos played over a driving but not overpowering rock pulse; and the indefinable sense of something poised between an English meadow and outer space. Richard Sinclair's Home Counties voice and Dave Sinclair's energetically meandering fuzztone organ and piano solos dominate this record, which most Caravanners still hold up as their finest hour.

Golf Girl, with an uncredited trombonist echoing the melody line, is as sweet-natured as English rock would ever be, but the centre is Nine Feet Underground, which runs almost 23 minutes and took up side two of the album. A seamless integration of a string of themes, this oddly mournful but spirited suite is a timeless memento of Canterbury's legacy. As time went on, "we spent less time getting stoned and playing music together", as Richard Sinclair ruefully remembered, "and Caravan became more and more like an orthodox touring band, turning out pleasant but uneventful records.

Record label:
Deram

Produced
by David Hitchcock.

Recorded
at AIR and Decca Studios, London;
November 1970–January 1971.

Released:
April 1971

Chart peaks:
None (UK) None (US)

Personnel:
Richard Sinclair (b, g, v); Pye Hastings (g, v); Dave Sinclair (o, p, mellotron, v); Richard Coughlan (d); Jimmy Hastings (f, ts, piccolo); David Grinsted (cannon, bell wind)

Track listing:
Golf Girl; Winter Wine; Love To Love You; In the Land Of Grey And Pink; Nine Feet Underground: i. Nigel Blows a Tune; ii. Love's a Friend; iii. Make It 76; iv. Dance of the Seven Paper Hankies; v. Hold Grandad By The Nose; vi. Honest I Did!; vii. Disassociation; viii. 100% Proof

Running time:
43.18

Current CD:
820520-2

Further listening:
Waterloo Lily (1972)

Further reading:
perso.club-internet.fr/calyx/cantdisco/C.html

David Crosby
If I Could Only Remember My Name

With CSN&Y at their commercial zenith, Crosby cuts controversial experimental mood piece.

Record label:
Atlantic

Produced
by David Crosby.

Recorded
at Wally Heiders, San Francisco, California; autumn 1970.

Released:
April 24, 1971 (UK); March 8, 1971 (US)

Chart peaks:
12 (UK) 12 (US)

Personnel:
David Crosby (g, v); Jerry Garcia (g, b,v); Phil Lesh (b); Mickey Hart (d); Bill Kreutzmann (tambourine); Jorma Kaukonen (g); Joni Mitchell (v); Neil Young (g, v); Laura Allan (autoharp); Greg Rollie (p); Michael Shrieve (d); Jack Casady (b); Paul Kantner (b, v); David Freiberg (b, v); Grace Slick (b, v); Graham Nash (b, v); Stephen Barncard (e); Ellen Burke (e)

Track listing:
Music Is Love (S, US only); Cowboy Movie; Tamalpais High (At About 3); Laughing; What Are Their Names; Traction In The Rain; Song With No Words (Tree With No Leaves); Orleans; I'd Swear There Was Somebody Here

Running time:
37.54

Current CD:
7567814152

Further listening:
Crosby, Stills & Nash (1969); Deja Vu (1970)

Further reading:
MOJO 62; Crosby, Stills, Nash And Young: The Visual Documentary (Johnny Rogan, 1996)

The sense of community in the rock world was still strong in the wake of Woodstock and few typified its ideals more than David Crosby. A firm believer in the dictum 'Peace, Love and Music', he saw his first solo album as a gathering of the tribes and invited the cream of the West Coast community to join him for a musical love-in. On paper it looked like another case of hippie superstar indulgence but the results were both unexpected and extraordinary: a striking and experimental mood piece. Neil Young produced an expressive guitar solo on the conspiratorial What Are Their Names and Jerry Garcia excelled himself on the CSN&Y allegory Cowboy Movie; Joni Mitchell added a wonderful vocal flourish on Laughing, while various Dead and Jefferson Airplane personnel brought further depth to the arrangements. Crosby masterminded the entire proceedings and his underlying melancholy cut through the stoned beatitude. Prior to the recording his girlfriend Christine Hinton had been killed in a car accident leaving the singer distraught.

"Crosby went to see her body and he's never been the same since," Graham Nash confided. The album closed on an eerie note with the disturbing I'd Swear There Was Somebody Here, a Gregorian-styled requiem to his lost love. "I was in the studio and I felt like she was there," Crosby remembers. "I was singing and just started feeling she was there, which hadn't happened before and hasn't happened since." Engineer Stephen Barncard was astounded by the results. "I've rarely seen anything that intense," he recalls. "It just happened. I witnessed the creation of the song in real time and recorded it as we went along. It was probably the most remarkable event in my entire life." Critical reaction was divided at the time of the album's release. Both Rolling Stone and Melody Maker were particularly harsh in their assessments but the album still went gold. In the UK, Melody Maker was bombarded with letters and phone calls railing against Richard Williams's negative review. It was one of biggest public backlashes against a reviewer in the long history of the music paper.

The Flamin' Groovies

Teenage Head

Fashion-disdaining San Francisco rock'n'rollers third, and most influential album.

The Flamin' Groovies were in a spot. It seemed like they were always in a spot, but this time fate was really having a laugh. Their guitarist Tim Lynch was fighting the draft – at a time when the draft meant Vietnam – and their other guitarist Cyril Jordan and vocalist Roy Loney were increasingly in conflict – *Teenage Head* would be the singer's last album with the band. And although the band had one of the world's great rock-'n'roll producers on board for *Teenage Head*, they'd employed him to *play piano*, giving the production job to a writer and talented magician who, although indisputably a music-lover, was not a musician at all.

If that wasn't enough, although they had signed to Kama Sutra the previous year and made one of the best albums of their career (*Flamingo*), other San Francisco bands continued to look down on them, and promoter Bill Graham was still reluctant to book them. In end-of-the-'60s San Francisco the Groovies stuck out like a sore thumb, playing short, catchy, greasy, garage rock'n'roll in an era dominated by the complex, freak-outery of Jefferson Airplane and the Dead.

Galvanised by seeing the MC5 kick out the jams in Detroit one night on a trip to the Midwest they abandoned their jug band influences and decided to crank up to 11 – which is exactly what can be heard on this session.

Arguably, the blueprint for *Teenage Head* is The Rolling Stones' *Sticky Fingers*. Yet while Yesterday's Numbers is certainly Stonesy and Whiskey Women recalls John Lennon, Evil Hearted Ada sounds like an unreleased Elvis Sun side. As for the title track, Jordan's own description – "the Mothers Of Invention doing Led Zeppelin" – is spot on, although like everything else on this album it sounds more like the Groovies, putting pedal to the metal and unapologetically side-swiping the hippie zeitgeist. *Teenage Head*, once again shunned by West Coasters, was a favourite among hip New Yorkers and a cult hit in Europe – indeed, when Loney left for a solo career the mark II band decamped to Europe for several years, hooking up with fan Dave Edmunds before releasing their next album *Shake Some Action* some five years later. *Teenage Head* stands as a barometer of contemporary hip and a signpost on the way to punk.

Record label:
Big Beat

Produced
by Richard Robinson.

Recorded
at Bell Sound Studio, New York City;
January 1971.

Released:
May 1971

Chart peaks:
None (UK) None (US)

Personnel:
Cyril Jordan (g, v); Roy Loney (v); Danny Mihm (d); George Alexander (b); Tim Lynch (g); Jim Dickinson (p); Jeff Hanna, Jim Fadden, Jimmy Ibbotsen (bv)

Track listing:
High Flying Baby; City Lights; Have You Seen My Baby?; Yesterday's Numbers; Teenage Head; 32-20; Evil Hearted Ada; Doctor Boogie; Whisky Woman

Running time:
47.38

Current CD:
74321716902 adds: Shakin' All Over; That'll Be The Day; Louie Louie; Walkin' The Dog; Scratch My Back; Carol; Going Out Theme

Further listening:
Flamingo (1970); Shake Some Action (1976)

Further reading:
Issues 3, 4 and 6 of Greg Shaw's late, great fanzine Who Put The Bomp?

Bert Jansch
Rosemary Lane

Released at the height of electric folk-rock in Britain, Bert's stripped-down masterpiece was criminally ignored.

Although immersed in the frantic international touring of the Pentangle era, the making of *Rosemary Lane* was, for Bert, a throwback to more carefree times. It was recorded simply, on portable equipment, by his first producer Bill Leader over the course of periodic visits to his rustic home. "We'd set the gear up and then we'd go for a pint, discuss it, and if I felt like recording we did it," says Bert. "The songs were just wherever my head was at the time. I was losing interest in the band, wishing for other things to do."

Fuelled by a sense of longing for times past, *Rosemary Lane* was romantic, pastoral and daringly stark. The dearth of tangible contemporary references – save for a glimpse of America, a place he now loathed, and the undateable nature of Bert's instrumental technique – he produced a work of timeless quality. With his unmistakably rough-hewn voice displaying a new poise and clarity, the material here – traditional songs, baroque vignettes and a clutch of singer-songwriter originals – was accompanied by an open invitation to the mind's eye. And the view was breathtaking. When Bert sings on the traditional English title track one hears something straight from a fireside storyteller in some indeterminate place and time. The same is true of Reynardine: the accompaniment a masterful distillation of Bert's guitar vocabulary.

"The thing with Jansch is that you cannot compare him with anyone else, you can only draw the comparison between the man as he was and the man as he is today," wrote Jerry Gilbert in Sounds, establishing a truism that still stands. Jansch's solo career was effectively on hold during the Pentangle era and bar one solitary concert at the Festival Hall in June 1971, with guests Anne Briggs and Clive Palmer (who had both influenced *Rosemary Lane*'s content), there were no opportunities to air this material onstage. Only a few tracks have re-entered his repertoire since, although stunning versions of Rosemary Lane and Reynardine were performed, by request, for the Channel 4 documentary Dream Weaver. It remains his greatest work.

Record label:
Transatlantic

Produced
by Bill Leader.

Recorded
at Bert's home in Ticehurst, Sussex; June 1970–January 1971.

Released:
May 1971

Chart peaks:
None (UK) None (US)

Personnel:
Bert Jansch (v, g)

Track listing:
Tell Me What Is True Love?; Rosemary Lane; M'Lady Nancy; A Dream, A Dream, A Dream; Alman; Wayward Child; Nobody's Bar; Reynardine; Silly Woman; Peregrinations; Sylvie; Sarabanda; Bird Song

Running time:
37.40

Currently unavailable on CD

Further listening:
When The Circus Comes To Town (1995)

Further reading:
MOJO 80; Dazzling Stranger: Bert Jansch And The British Folk And Blues Revival (Colin Harper, 2000)

Paul And Linda McCartney

Ram

Bruised ex-Beatle comes out of hiding with his new missus.

R*am*, his second post-Beatles album, was the midpoint in McCartney's nervous re-integration with the outside world. *McCartney* had been a determinedly upbeat DIY construction, assembled in his remote Scottish hideaway. The third, Wings' *Wildlife*, would find him nostalgically touring the UK with a minibus and the security of another band around him. But the autumn of 1970 found McCartney renting a New York hotel suite and a block of time at Manhattan's A&R Studios, and signing up session drummer Denny Seiwell (who later joined Wings) and guitarist Dave Spinoza (who turned the chance down). Locked in the control room for hours on end working up the basic compositions, he was acutely aware of his need for another sounding-board.

"Obviously I was used to having a collaborator and I felt the pinch after John," McCartney reflects today. "I was used to writing solo stuff too, of course, but some of them I'd get a bit stuck on – like I would with John – and Linda would change some of the words, alter a little piece here and there, write a line or two, give me ideas. It was just me and her in the studio most of the time, there together all day, so it would have been churlish not to credit her really." Paul's publisher, Lew Grade, who refused to believe that Linda – who wasn't part of their deal – had collaborated on the songs and threatened to sue, wasn't the only one to give the project a cool reception; but, apparently unfazed, McCartney opted to mine this whimsical seam for most of his solo career. And the public seemed to approve; the decidedly odd Uncle Albert/Admiral Halsey even topped the US singles chart.

Arriving in the middle of the very public John/Paul spat, *Ram* was scrutinized for Lennon references – and didn't disappoint (the photo of the copulating beetles on the back cover was also subject to some imaginative interpretation). Monkberry Moon Delight descends gloriously into primal scream pastiche; Too Many People ("Too many people preaching practices"), he now admits, "was about John and Yoko telling people what to do. I thought, Bollocks to that." The couple even expressed their ire in the backing vocals, 'piece of cake' rendered as "piss off cake". "Just mad!" Paul chuckles. "You had to get your feelings out one way or another."

Record label:
Apple

Produced
by Paul and Linda McCartney.

Recorded
at A&R Studios, New York;
October–November 1970 and
February–March 1971.

Released:
May 1971

Chart peaks:
1 (UK) 2 (US)

Personnel:
Paul McCartney (g, bs, v); Linda McCartney (k, pc, v); Denny Seiwell (d); Hugh McCracken (g); Dave Spinoza (g)

Track listing:
Too Many People; 3 Legs; Ram On; Dear Boy; Uncle Albert – Admiral Halsey (S); Smile Away; Heart Of The Country; Monkberry Moon Delight; Eat At Home; Long-Haired Lady; Ram On; The Back Seat Of My Car (S)

Running time:
50.51

Not currently available on CD

Further listening:
McCartney (1970); Band On The Run (1973)

Further reading:
Many Years From Now (Barry Miles, 1998)

The Rolling Stones
Sticky Fingers

The centrepiece of the great Stones triptych found them at their most rootsy and American.

Recorded in a period when the Stones were beset by financial problems, contemplating tax exile, and experiencing an ever-widening palette of influences, *Sticky Fingers* turned out to be one of the band's most consistent works. The reason lay back in 1966, when Keith Richards started a new educational regime: "I started getting into different blues tunings, Fred McDowell, 12-string and slide. Then I met Ry Cooder in '68, when he was hanging around with Taj Mahal and Jesse Ed Davis. And Clarence White was around too. You'd just pick stuff up."

Those new influences made their debut on 1969's Honky Tonk Women single; by 1970, Richards was still pushing forward the boundaries of the 'Open G' tuning he had learned from Cooder. As he puts it, "It restricts you so much, five strings, three notes, two fingers . . . one asshole! And there's something about being restricted that opens up the possibilities."

Richards' delving into Americana was complemented by the band's two-day stay at Muscle Shoals, Alabama to record Brown Sugar, Wild Horses and You Gotta Move (the other songs were mainly recorded at Mick Jagger's home, Stargroves). Appropriately, given the surroundings, Keith's new trademark tuning suggested country music, but as album opener Brown Sugar demonstrated, it was a vehicle to take the Stones somewhere entirely new. The song's basic two-chord rock'n'roll strut obviously derived from Chuck Berry, but the sudden swerve eight bars in (as Keith modulates from G to an utterly unexpected E flat) show the Stones suddenly liberated by Richards' self-imposed restrictions.

Wild Horses, probably the Stones' tenderest, most perfectly-formed ballad, demonstrated the other extreme of the possibilities thrown up by Keith's new style. It has been incorrectly claimed that The Flying Burrito Brothers' own version, released in May 1970, was a crucial influence, but the Stones had already laid down their basic track in December 1969. In any case, the chordal structure fits so snugly within the limits of Richards' tuning that the melody must be his alone, for as Richards points out, "Gram taught me a lot, but he was strictly a standard tunings guy."

Perhaps it was appropriate that the Stones chose such a cultural melting pot as the site of their most audacious grab-bag

Record label:
Rolling Stones Records

Produced
by Jimmy Miller

Recorded
at Muscle Shoals Sound Studios Alabama; Rolling Stones Mobile, Stargroves Newbury; Olympic Studios, London, December 1969–May 1970.

Release date:
May 1971

Chart peaks:
1 (UK) 1 (US)

Personnel:
Mick Jagger (v); Bill Wyman (b); Charlie Watts (d); Keith Richards (g); Mick Taylor (g); Bobby Keyes (s); Ian Stewart Nicky Hopkins (p); Ry Cooder (sg)

Track listing:
Brown Sugar; Sway; Wild Horses; Can't You Hear Me Knocking; You Gotta Move; Bitch; I Got the Blues; Sister Morphine; Dead Flowers; Moonlight Mile

Running time:
46.27

Current CD:

Further listening:
Let It Bleed (1969) spans a similar mix of styles to its successor; Ry Cooder's Into The Purple Valley (Reprise 1972) shows Keith's one-time guitar guru constructing his own parallel version of Americana.

Further reading:
Blown Away: The Rolling Stones & The Death Of The Sixties (AE Hotchner, 1990)

of styles to date. Yet their touch remained sure; although the purist country of Dead Flowers was tempered with British irony, the chicken-lickin' Southern soul of Bitch and the North Mississippi blues of You Gotta Move were played essentially straight, yet given a ramshackle authenticity by the Stones' loose-limbed style. Andy Warhol's sleeve design featured the zippered crotch of Factory face Joe Dallessandro – whose torso would later crop up on the cover of The Smiths' debut album

Ironically, given that the world's stadiums were beckoning, *Sticky Fingers* would prove the Stones' mastery of small-scale, minority music. A rousing critical reception preceded its ascent to the top of the UK charts on May 8 1971; a couple of weeks later it topped the charts in the US, demonstrating that, in a brand new decade, the Stones sounded anything but dated. Once again they had managed the enviable feat of selling America's culture back to its country of origin.

Bridget St John

Songs For The Gentle Man

Exquisitely arranged folk album by unheralded contemporary of John Martyn and Nick Drake.

Responsible for the very first album on John Peel and Clive Selwood's quirky Dandelion label, folk singer Bridget St. John was a unique talent that, in her understated way, occupied the same creative space as her better known male contemporaries (and friends) John Martyn, Nick Drake and Michael Chapman. That album, *Ask Me No Questions*, was a bare-bones production that introduced to the world a quiet, thought-provoking singer/songwriter with a deep voice not unlike an on-key Nico; part of its minimalist charm was the simple fact that it was recorded in 10 consecutive hours at CBS Studios.

"I don't know if that was the time I was given, but that's the time it took," says St. John today, now in New York, a resident there since 1976. "That was my first ever thing in the recording studio, so I wouldn't have known how to do anything differently. John Peel was producing it, and he really just made it sound like I *was* at that time, and that was a very honest recording."

But by no means was its follow-up, *Songs For The Gentle Man*, dishonest on any level. A simply gorgeous album, the 1971 disc paired Bridget with producer/arranger Ron Geesin, whose work with Pink Floyd (*Atom Heart Mother*) and Roger Waters (*Music From The Body*) had brought him significant critical success. Unrestrained and inventive, Geesin provided the gentle singer a context that was extremely alluring.

"I did a lot of work with Ron on that," she says. "I remember going to his house, where he had his own studio and we did a lot of preparation there." Filled with cellos, violas, flutes, bassoons, a "celestial organ" and St. John's own guitar and harmonium, *Gentle Man* is a quiet jewel of a record that sounds surprisingly contemporary 30 years on.

A final Dandelion album would come, then a brief move to Chrysalis for *Jumble Queen* in 1974, but in 1976, Bridget departed for New York to be with boyfriend Gordon Edwards of American band Stuff (who once backed Fred Neil) and has lived there since. One is tempted to say "in obscurity", but every one of her albums has been reissued on CD since (though as we went to press they were currently out of print). "It absolutely amazes me," she says. "My boyfriend is Gordon from Stuff, and I think of them as a massive band – and yet Warner Brothers has never re-released their albums over here. It's incredible to me."

Record label:
Dandelion

Produced by
Ron Geesin.

Recorded
at Sound Techniques Ltd., London.

Released:
May 1971.

Chart peaks:
None (UK) None (US)

Track listing:
Bridget St. John (v, g, hm); Ron Geesin (g, oa); Rick Sanders (g); Jerry Boys (e)

Track listing:
A Day A Way; City-Crazy; Early-Morning Song; Back To Stay; Seagull-Sunday; If You'd Been There; Song For The Laird Of Connaught Hall – Part Two; Making Losing Better; The Lady And The Gentle Man; Downderry Daze; The Pebble And The Man; It Seems Very Strange

Running time:
38.21

Currently unavailable on CD

Further listening:
Ask Me No Questions (1969); Thank You For . . . (1972)

Loudon Wainwright III
Loudon Wainwright III

Debut by Canadian folk-singing specialist in social commentary and wry observation.

Record label:
Atlantic

Produced
by Milton Kramer and Loudon Wainwright III.

Recorded
at Media Sound, A&R Studios, and Atlantic Recording Studios, New York.

Released:
May 1971

Chart peaks:
None (UK) None (US)

Personnel:
Loudon Wainwright III (g, v)

Track listing:
School Days; Hospital Lady; Ode To Pittsburgh: Glad To See You've Got Religion; Uptown; Black Uncle Remus; Four Is A Magic Number; I Don't Care; Central Square Song; Movies Are A Mother To Me; Bruno's Place

Running time:
38.02

Not currently available on CD, bar a Rhino Handmade limited edition, available via the internet, which adds Album II, and Drinking Song.

Further listening:
Album II (1971) featuring Motel Blues is essential, while Album III (1973) and Attempted Moustache (1974) are both worthy of investigation.

Further reading:
http://lwiii.com/

B ack in 1971, Loudon Wainwright III came to the UK to support the release of his debut album. He played BBC2's American-oriented rock show The Old Grey Whistle Test. He also opened for The Everly Brothers at the Albert Hall, where he was bottled off by Teddy Boys; undoubtedly, the wit and wisdom of this clever singer/songwriter from North Carolina went way above their quiffs. Previously, Wainwright had honed his act on the live circuit where he'd gained a reputation as a "new Bob Dylan", and as the '60s came to a close he signed to Atlantic and produced this stark and moving album. Almost 30 years on it still sounds pointed and pertinent, even if Wainwright himself is long since tired of the set.

"I'm fed up of the generation of people who are hung up on those early records," he said back in the '80s. "People want you to stay the way they were in 1971 because it just so happens they were 20 then, were having fun and weren't divorced yet, so they say, 'Ah man, that first album, that's the best album.'" According to Wainwright, "some of those songs like School Days and Central Square Song are great, but others like Black Uncle Remus and I Don't Care are very marginal."

Certainly subsequent albums have songs that rank alongside the likes of School Days, Glad To See You've Got Religion and Four Is A Magic Number, but it's the uneasy minor chords, and this virginal introduction to Loudon's distinctive singing style that makes the album special. In 1971 this album had all the social realism that was needed for people looking for something to believe in after the frivolity of the '60s. Songs such as the rite-of-teenage-passage School Days linked the angst of the post-hippy era with another, presumably survivable, period of confusion and loss.

Fan and friend Pete Fallon, in his sleevenotes on a recent Rhino limited reissue, concludes: "He should be better known. He should be richer and more famous. He should be a legend. The best of these songs, they've lasted already. And they will last."

Link Wray
Link Wray

Guitar godfather takes acoustic guitars and dobros on a journey up country.

In 1958 Link Wray changed the face of electric guitar playing with his ominous, power-chord driven instrumental, Rumble – a track which persuaded Pete Townshend, among others, to take up the instrument. Wray continued to record in-yer-face guitar rockers for smaller and smaller labels, until the late '60s found him in semi-retirement on the family farm. Link's brother, who had played with him in various bands over the years, moved his three track recorder into one room and a chicken coop was coverted into a studio. Thus, The Shack – perhaps the most basic arrangement ever to record a major label release – came into being.

In a contemporary interview Link outlined the problems: "The two rooms were never connected so we still have to yell back and forth, 'Is it running Ray?' every time we want to start." At this time producer Steve Verocca saw Wray performing in a local club. "I was overwhelmed. Here was a man singing out his soul. I asked him about recording an album, and I suggested we do it at The Shack. I believe The Shack has a soul. You can hear people burping on the record, and that's great. It's real."

The music produced at The Shack is a beautiful but raggedy quilt sewn from blues, country, soul, folk and patterns from a deeper past – Wray is after all half Shawnee Indian. This last element is most evident in the anything-to-hand percussion which rattles the bones of songs such as Fire And Brimstone: a title which also contributes to the album's rich gospel atmosphere. (The seemingly infinite backing vocals on Take Me Home Jesus and the fuzz-guitared, revivalist vim of God Out West would make the Devil testify.) But Link has always been as much about the dark side; and his version of Willie Dixon's Tail Dragger is a throwback to his earlier, leathered-up incarnation. Other groups, notably The Band, have explored similar territory, but even they cannot match the backwoods glory that Wray's tortured, reedy vocals summon up. Polydor's executives heard the magic, but after releasing this bare-arsed masterpiece put Wray into a studio with Jerry Garcia et al. The result, *Be What You Want To Be*, isn't a bad album, but for authentic roots-rock, head to The Shack.

Record label:
Polydor

Produced
by Steve Verroca and Ray Vernon in association with Bob Feldman.

Recorded
at Wray's Shack Three Track, Accokeek, Maryland; October 1970.

Released:
May 1971

Chart peaks:
None (UK) None (US)

Personnel:
Link Wray (v, g, b, dobro); Billy Hodges (k, v); Bobby Howard (mandolin, k); Doug Wray (d, pc, v); Steve Verocca (d, pc, v)

Track listing:
La De Da; Ice People; Take Me Home Jesus; Black River Swamp; Rise And Fall Of Jimmy Stokes; Fallin' Rain; Fire And Brimstone; God Out West Crowbar; Juke Box Mama; Tail Dragger

Running time:
43.52

Currently unavailable on CD.

Further listening:
Guitar Preacher: The Polydor Years (1995) includes all of Link Wray as well a plethora of tracks from the other albums Wray recorded for the label; there's an excellent accompanying booklet by Colin Escott. Rocking '50s and '60s guitar instrumentals available on Norton's fine Missing Links series.

Michael Hurley And Pals
Armchair Boogie

*Second album from the folk troubadour, the ultimate
outsider.*

The term maverick might have been invented for
Pennsylvania-born, Ohio-based Hurley, an American one-
off whose devoted cult following includes many musicians half
his age. While his music borrows from Depression-era folk,
blues, country, railroad songs, swing, ragtime, even '50s doo
wop, the songs' subject matter makes them unique. Hurley's
1965 debut *First Songs* — recorded by American musicologist
Fred Ramsey Jr for the Folkways label — was, despite some
pretty unconventional moments, a tense and earnest record. By
follow-up *Armchair Boogie*, some six years later, Hurley had loos-
ened up a little — almost to the point of falling apart. By now
he had found a more sympathetic home — The Youngbloods'
label Raccoon — although even *they* baulked at releasing songs
with titles like Your Monkey Pissed In My Beer And Your Dick Is
Hanging Out Of Your Pants. Mainstream acceptance was never
one of Hurley's considerations, and it was this indifference
rather than a lack of songs that brought about the long gap
between the first and second albums.

"I don't normally intend to write songs," he once said.
"I always seem to happen upon them or they happen upon me.
There was never a time when I experimented with putting out
my music in any way other than I felt it."

Armchair Boogie was recorded in Hurley's house with
Jesse Colin Young handling the production, which mostly
required rolling the tapes then switching them off. "It just saun-
ters along in the buff," is how Hurley's sleevenote writer
described it. "It recalls a time when quaintness was one of
American regional music's most valuable elements."

The record also marked the first appearance of Hurley's
cartoon paintings of Boone and Jocko, a pair of Bohemian
wolves. They have graced the sleeve of every subsequent Hurley
album, a singular link to his world of sentiment and sorrow, the
real and the surreal.

Record label:
Raccoon

Produced
by Jesse Colin Young.

Recorded
at Hurley House, Brookline, Massachusetts;
May–June 1970.

Released:
spring 1971

Chart peaks:
None (UK) None (US)

Personnel:
Michael Hurley (v, g); Maggie Hurley (bv,
tambourine); Robin Remailly (fiddle,
mandolin); Michael Kane (cornet, b); Jeff
Myer (d); Earthquake (hm); Scott
Lawrence (p); Jesse Young (b)

Track listing:
The Werewolf; Grand Canyon Line; English
Noblemen; Be Kind To Me; Troubled
Waters; Red Ravagers Reel; Sweedeedee;
Open Up; Jocko's Lament; Light Green
Fellow; Get The Best Of Me; Biscuit
Roller; When The Swallows Come Back To
Capistrano; Penguins

Running time:
41.35

Currently unavailable on CD

Further listening:
Long Journey (1976)

Further reading:
www.snock.com

Bill Withers
Just As I Am

Recorded while he was still working in a factory making toilet seats for jet planes.

Though Let It Be was the Beatles song Bill Withers chose to cover on his debut album, a better theme for his late-blooming career might have been The Long and Winding Road. Born in tiny Slab Fork, West Virginia, Withers spent nine years in the US Navy then worked at a number of factory jobs before finally launching his music career in his mid-30s. Indeed, when he began making *Just As I Am* in 1970, he was still working at the Lockheed factory in Los Angeles, manufacturing toilet seats and airstairs for 747 jets. The cover photo, which shows him in dungarees, carrying a lunch bucket, was shot during his lunch hour at the plant. Withers was laid off in the course of making the album but, as he coyly puts it, "As things turned out, I didn't have to go back." Ain't No Sunshine went to number 3 and won the Grammy for Best R&B Song, though that too was something of a surprise since the intended single was Harlem, with Ain't No Sunshine as its B-side. "Folks on the radio flipped it, and began playing the B-side, which is meant to be a throw-away, right?" says Withers. "That shows you how good people are at predicting."

Bill had been using his own money to make demos since 1967, but had gotten nowhere. It was Ray Jackson of the Watts 103rd Street Rhythm Band who started things moving for Withers. Jackson passed one of those demo tapes on to Forrest Hamilton, son of jazz drummer Chico Hamilton, who in turn passed it on to Clarence Avent of Sussex Records, who liked what he heard. Originally Jackson was going to produce the album, but when touring commitments made that impossible, Avent introduced Withers to Booker T. Jones, of the MGs.

It is hard to imagine that Jackson – or anyone else for that matter – could have done a better job than Jones of creating such perfect settings for Withers's warm voice, which manages to convey endurance while perching right on the edge of breaking. The music was unmistakably R'n'B, but Jones's use of acoustic guitars and strings gave it a whiff of gospelly country right out of Slab Fork. Nowhere was that more true than on Grandma's Hands, Withers' tribute to the woman who raised him and his five brothers and sisters after his father died when Withers was very young.

For the early sessions, Jones used the MGs, with

Record label:
Sussex

Produced
by Booker T. Jones.

Recorded
at Sunset Sound Recorders and Wally Heider Recording Studio, Hollywood, California; throughout 1970.

Released:
June 1971

Chart peaks:
None (UK) 39 (US)

Personnel:
Bill Withers (v,g); Booker T. Jones (k,g); Stephen Stills (g); Donald 'Duck' Dunn (b); Chris Ethridge (b); Al Jackson (d); Jim Keltner (d); Bobbie Hall Porter (pc)

Track listing:
Harlem (S); Ain't No Sunshine (S); Grandma's Hands; Sweet Wanomi; Everybody's Talkin'; Do It Good; Hope She'll Be Happier; Let It Be; I'm Her Daddy; In My Heart; Moanin And Groanin; Better Off Dead

Running time:
35.39

Currently unavailable on CD

Further listening:
Still Bill (1972) contained the evergreen Lean On Me. Written while at Lockheed, the song was, according to Withers, a song of gratitude for all the support he'd received from his co-workers.

Further reading:
The Billboard Book Of Soul (1992)

Stephen Stills subbing for Steve Cropper. But Sussex Records ran out of money, halting recording for six months, and when work resumed, Dunn and Jackson had been replaced by Chris Ethridge and Jim Keltner. The relaxed atmosphere Jones encouraged in the studio also helped relax Withers.

"Graham Nash, who was a fun guy because he was drinking then, was hanging out," recalls Withers. "When I'd get frustrated Graham would sit in front of me and offer encouragement. All these people who had established careers were going out of their way to help me. It was reassuring, because hearing yourself played back for the first time can be a sobering moment."

The Beach Boys
Surf's Up

A career-saver and the boys' best post-Brian achievement.

R ecent years had delivered a series of body blows to The
Beach Boys and by 1970 they were reeling. The psychological fragility of their creative core, Brian Wilson, had left them
struggling to find a voice in the acid-rock era. To make matters
worse, an ex-hanger-on and Dennis Wilson collaborator –
Charles Manson – had been revealed as head of a cult that had
perpetrated the Sharon Tate murder; singer Mike Love became
temporarily deranged, spending time in a clinic; their last
album, *Sunflower* (1970) – a gorgeous, elegantly mature set –
had been their worst selling record ever.

Jack Rieley, an "aspiring broadcast journalist", gained
their confidence with positive ideas about career and artistic
direction and with a couple of boosts – including a triumphant
appearance with The Grateful Dead at the counter culture
temple, the Fillmore East – they set about recording an album
to be called *Landlocked*. Al Jardine pursued his penchant for folk
with Rieley-inspired social concern and eco-overtones, Bruce
Johnson had his finest Beach Boys moment with the intelligent
nostalgia of Disney Girls, Carl Wilson and Rieley co-wrote two
magnificent pieces of spiritual yearning (Feel Flows and Long
Promised Road): the boys were finding their feet. Brother
Brian's offering – 'Til I Die, a personal, sensitive piece
reflecting his untethered state of mind – was coolly received
("What a fucking downer", Brian recalled Mike Love saying). He
also co-wrote with Rieley a bizarre little song (Day In The Life
Of A Tree) which Jack was allowed to croakily sing.

"I was tricked into that," Rieley told MOJO in 1995. "It
was going to be sung by Brian. I went over to produce the
vocal, guide him through it. He said "Jack, I just don't get it.
You gotta explain to me how I'm going to sing this," and went
up into the control room. I put on the cans and sang it a half-a-
dozen times to show how it went. He came out roaring with
laughter saying, "It's done! The vocal's done!" I thought it was
just a quick joke of Brian's but it turned up on the record. It
was a long-term joke. For a brief moment I felt flattered, but it
wasn't what I intended for the song. There's one argument that
it does indeed sound like a dying tree!"

Still short of material, the band once more unearthed a
remnant of Brian's aborted 1967 masterpiece-that-never-was
Smile (elsewhere they had revived Cabinessence and Our

Record label:
Brother/Reprise

Produced
by the Beach Boys.

Recorded
at Brother Studio, Santa Monica; 1970.

Release date:
July 25, 1971

Chart peaks:
15 (UK) 29 (US)

Personnel:
Carl Wilson (g, v); Alan Jardine (g, v);
Dennis Wilson (d, v); Mike Love (v);
Bruce Johnson (k, v); Brian Wilson (k, v);
Jack Rieley (v)

Track listing:
Don't Go Near The Water; Long Promised
Road; Take A Load Off Your Feet; Disney
Girls (1957); Student Demonstration Time;
Feel Flows; Lookin' At Tomorrow (A
Welfare Song); A Day In The Life Of A
Tree; 'Til I Die; Surf's Up

Running time:
32.46

Current CD:
ZK46951

Further listening:
Sunflower (1970); Holland (1973)

Further reading:
Heroes And Villains (Steven Gaines, 1986);
The Nearest Faraway Place (Timothy
White, 1994); Wouldn't It Be Nice (Brian
Wilson with Todd Gold, 1991)
www.beachboys.com

Prayer), the mysterious and deeply beautiful Surf's Up, building the track around Brian's piano and voice performance on a 1967 Leonard Bernstein TV special. Initially opposed to the idea ("I was superstitious about the *Smile* material"), Brian attempted a new vocal but Carl finally delivered the mellifluous lead. Constructed without Brian's input, the by-now title track was a masterpiece showing – along with the other successes of *Surf's Up* – that with or without Brian, The Beach Boys were big boys now. Rieley's curious inspirational influence on the band became tainted; his homosexuality didn't go down well, he was eventually revealed as a serial liar and having moved the group to Holland, refused to return with them, whereupon he was sacked. But by then, with *Surf's Up* achieving healthy sales, the group had been re-established.

The Allman Brothers Band
At Fillmore East

It made them national stars and launched the Southern rock movement.

Veteran producer Tom Dowd was sitting in a mobile production truck outside Fillmore East taping the first of four weekend shows from which the classic album *The Allman Brothers Band at Fillmore East* would be taken. Dowd knew the band well, having already worked with them on the album that would become *Eat A Peach*. With one eye on the stage video monitor and one on his set list, Dowd was cuing the engineers through a set that showed the band at their bluesy, blistering peak.

"Everything is sweet as a nut," says Dowd, "when one of the engineers says, 'What track do I put the horns on?'" Dowd, knowing there should be no horns, told him precisely where he could stick those horns. "The guy says, 'No, look.' I look at the monitor and I see two horns and a harp coming on. I heard them play like, two bars, I jumped off the chair, ran through the backstage door and grabbed Duane. I screamed, 'Don't ever, *ever* put them on stage with your band as long as you live!' I was livid. These horn players were wasted. That was the norm for the day, fine. But they were out of tune and not even playing the right parts." Dowd made a key decision. "For the rest of the night I made sure we had rough mixes of every song," he says. "After the last set I went backstage and said, 'I want you to come uptown to go over what you did.'"

So at three o'clock in the morning Dowd and the band raced uptown to Atlantic Studios on West 60th Street. "We're sitting there listening and they're saying stuff like, 'Don't use that,' or 'Well, we don't have to do that again. That's as well as we can play it.'" They cringed on hearing the horns, but kept Thom Doucette's harmonica.

Some call *Fillmore* the finest live album ever made. Certainly it launched the band from regional to national fame, showcasing the brilliant interplay between Duane Allman and Dicky Betts on guitar. When Duane died in a motorcycle crash seven months after the Fillmore shows and bass player Berry Oakley followed in 1972, *At the Fillmore East* acquired a terrible poignancy.

Record label:
Capricorn

Produced
by Tom Dowd.

Recorded
at Fillmore East, New York City; March 12–13, 1971.

Released:
July 1971

Chart peaks:
None (UK) 13 (US)

Personnel:
Duane Allman (g); Gregg Allman (v, o, p); Dickey Betts (g); Berry Oakley (b); Jai Johanny Johanson (d, congas, timbales); Butch Trucks (d, tympani); Thom Doucette (hm)

Track listing:
Statesboro Blues; Done Somebody Wrong; Stormy Monday; You Don't Love Me; Hot 'Lanta; In Memory of Elizabeth Reed; Whipping Post

Running time:
78.38

Current CD:
823 273-2

Further listening:
Eat A Peach (1972), with three tracks taken from the Fillmore shows, and The Fillmore Concerts (1992), a 2-CD collection remastered by Tom Dowd, who says it features better takes than the original.

Further reading:
Midnight Riders: The Story of the Allman Brothers Band, (Scott Freeman and Michael Pietsch, 1996); www.allmanbrothersband.com

The Move
Message From The Country

Heavy, genre-busting pop music bearing the seeds of the Electric Light Orchestra.

*M*essage From The Country was created under some duress. The Move made it, essentially, to keep their record labels happy. In the UK, Harvest had signed Roy Wood and Jeff Lynne's new idea for a 'serious' band The Electric Light Orchestra, whose concept, the pair leaked to the press, was to pick up from where The Beatles' I Am The Walrus left off and integrate classical instrumentation into rock'n'roll. All well and good, but when Harvest realised that Wood and Lynne intended to take their own sweet time making the first ELO album, they tried to talk them into making a Move album to keep their name alive. At the same time, US label Capitol insisted that they were *committed* for one more Move album, following which the label would *then* decide if it wished to release the Electric Light Orchestra's debut.

Perhaps it was a certain Dunkirk spirit that resulted in *Message From The Country* having more humour than any of the group's other works. There are several out-and-out parodies – the Johnny Cash-style Ben Crawley Steel Company; the Elvis rip Don't Mess Me Up; the megaphonic My Marge. Even many of the 'straight' numbers – It Wasn't My Idea To Dance; Until Your Mama's Gone – are done in an ironic style that prompted Rolling Stone to compare the group favourably to the Bonzo Dog Band, adding that *Message From The Country* "ranks right up there with Procol Harum's *Broken Barricades* as a prime contender for 1971's best album". What takes *Message From The Country* out of jokey territory is Wood and Lynne's eagerness to experiment. On the two most irony-free cuts – the haunting title track and the delicate No Time – the band created a gorgeous, ethereal sound more felt than heard, while on the melodramatic It Wasn't My Idea To Dance, Wood's ranging cello calls up dark, forboding, atonal notes worthy of a Bernard Hermann soundtrack. It was the kind of experimentation that they would bring to fruition later that same year on ELO's eponymous debut.

Record label:
Harvest

Produced
by Roy Wood and Jeff Lynne.

Recorded
early 1971, location unavailable.

Released:
July 1971

Chart peaks:
None (UK) None (US)

Personnel:
Roy Wood (g, v); Rick Price (b); Bev Bevan (d); Jeff Lynne (v, k, g)

Track listing:
It Wasn't My Idea to Dance; The Minister; Message from the Country; The Words of Aaron; Ben Crawley Steel Company; Until Your Mama's Gone; No Time; Ella James; Don't Mess Me Up; My Marge

Running time:
38.28

Currently unavailable on CD

Further listening:
Movements (1997), a three-CD set, compiles practically all the Move's pre-Message recordings.

Joni Mitchell
Blue

Spare. Tender. Moving. Perfect.

Joni Mitchell, singer, poet and devout smoker, regards herself first and foremost as a painter. She maintains that had her training at Calgary Art College in Canada been stimulating enough, she'd never have drifted towards music. Claiming she first picked up a ukulele "with the intention of accompanying dirty drinking songs at weiner roasts", she found she could make pin money by singing in coffeehouses while at college in the early '60s. A visit to the Mariposa Folk Festival in 1964 alerted her to the Yorkville folk scene in Toronto and she decided to stay there, marrying singer Chuck Mitchell in 1965. They toured as a duo while Joni's original songs found favour with American singers Tom Rush and Judy Collins. When the marriage fell apart in 1967, Joni planned to settle in New York and paint. However, making her rent on the folk scene once again, she was spotted by manager Elliot Roberts, who introduced her to David Crosby. The two singers became lovers and Crosby "pretended to produce" her first album with engineer Henry Lewy, who stayed with Joni for 13 albums. *Blue*, her fourth, consolidated her reputation as queen of the Californian singer-songwriters. Aptly, this suite of solitude found her almost entirely alone. "Only Henry and I were in there," she recalls. The closed-set atmosphere reflected the extent to which she was baring her soul on the 10 songs she had chosen. From the naked desire of All I Want to the more scornful The Last Time I Saw Richard, *Blue* offered self-examination, vulnerability and a sharp, railing cynicism still pretty new to rock.

"I perceived a lot of hate in my heart," Mitchell has said of the mood behind *Blue*, adding that the album is "probably the purest emotional record I will ever make." Throughout the sessions she felt defenceless to the point of hallucination: "Everything became transparent . . . I was so thin-skinned, just nerve endings." Loneliness, grief and infatuation were just three themes of an album which has become a sacred text of nostalgic introspection and a source of almost healing power.

"I have felt that it was perhaps my role on occasion," says Joni, "to pass on anything I learned that was helpful to me on the route to fulfilment or a happy life." It's the honesty and unmediated emotion of *Blue* that still resonate with anyone who has ever lost sleep over lost love.

Record label:
Reprise

Produced
by Joni Mitchell (uncredited)

Recorded
at A&M studios, Los Angeles; spring 1971.

Released:
August 1971

Chart peaks:
3 (UK) 15 (US)

Personnel:
Joni Mitchell (g, p, dulcimer, v); James Taylor (g); Stephen Stills (b); "Sneaky" Pete Kleinow (psg); Russ Kunkel (d); Henry Lewy (e)

Track listing:
All I Want; My Old Man; Little Green; Carey; Blue; California; This Flight Tonight; River; A Case Of You; The Last Time I Saw Richard

Running time:
36.16

Current CD:
7599271992

Further listening:
Follow-up For the Roses (1972) was less intimate, but full of good songs. After the excellent Court And Spark (1973), Mitchell turned to a more oblique, cerebral mode, fruitfully explored on the superb Hissing Of Summer Lawns (1975), and to jazz for Hejira (1976) and the largely overlooked Mingus (1977).

Further reading:
www.jonimitchell.com

The Who
Who's Next

A classic album snatched from the ashes of a conceptual Tower Of Babel.

"I thought it was a huge technical magnum opus," says Pete Townshend of The Who's aborted *Lifehouse* project. "It was an extraordinary moment of visionary imagination from me, and it seemed to have been wasted."

Lifehouse was a brave attempt to go one better than *Tommy*, via the creation of an integrated movie and album. But it was hampered by one key problem: the inability of its author to explain exactly what it was all about. The songs were composed in the winter of 1970–71, as Townshend worked in his home studio in Twickenham, making unprecedented use of synthesisers. The new compositions were bound up with a story involving a society in which individuals are dependent on a government-controlled "grid" for their entertainment, until a group of "savages" who've been keeping rock'n'roll alive in the woods turn up to battle with the forces of evil. There was a spiritual dimension too – songs were often infused with the beatific insights Townshend derived from his guru, Meher Baba, the likes of Pure And Easy and Song Is Over certainly drip with the stuff of enlightenment.

In February 1971, The Who began a series of shows at the Young Vic Theatre in South London, aimed at road-testing the new material and putting some of Townshend's new theories (particularly those about the audience/performer relationship) into practice. Meanwhile, attempting to tie up a movie script, a stage show and a song cycle simultaneously, Townshend was tumbling into a nervous breakdown.

"People thought I was raving mad," Pete recalled. "Until, constantly trying to tell this, I thought, really simple story to people in a number of different ways – film producer, record producer, theatre director, and so on, in a language each would understand – I actually did start to go completely mad."

Finally, manager/producer Kit Lambert persuaded Pete to just try recording some songs. He and the band took up residence at New York's Record Plant in March 1971. The sessions, some of which included work with Cream and Mountain producer Felix Pappalardi, produced some good raw material. But Townshend was still having trouble letting go of *Lifehouse* and, going through "a prim phase", was appalled that Lambert was using heroin. Keith Moon, meanwhile, was all but

Record label:
Polydor

Produced
by The Who and Glyn Johns.

Recorded
at Olympic Studios, Barnes; The Record Plant, New York; 1971.

Released:
August 1971

Chart peaks:
1 (UK) 4 (US)

Personnel:
Roger Daltrey (v); John Entwistle (b, brass, v, p); Pete Townshend (g, VCS3 organ, ARP syn,v, p); Nicky Hopkins (p); Dave Arbus (vn); Glyn Johns (e)

Track listing:
Baba O'Riley; Bargain; Love Ain't For Keeping; My Wife; The Song Is Over; Getting In Tune; Going Mobile; Behind Blue Eyes (S/US); Won't Get Fooled Again (S)

Running time:
43.27

Current CD:
527 760-2 adds: Pure And Easy; Baby Don't You Do it; Naked Eye; Water; Too Much Of Anything; I Don't Even Know Myself; Behind Blue Eyes (original version)

Further listening:
The Lifehouse Chronicles (1999), Pete Townshend's boxed set of the development of Lifehouse

Further reading:
MOJO 32, 82; Before I Get Old: The Story Of The Who (Dave Marsh, 1983); www.thewho.net

uncontrollable. Exhausted Townshend finally agreed to let Glyn Johns who'd be angling to work on the record have a go at salvaging the sessions. In the early summer, they began work at Mick Jagger's country house, Stargroves. They then moved to Olympic in Barnes where Johns had recorded much of his work with the Stones. By this time well-rehearsed (there had even been a few *Lifehouse* try-out gigs), the songs practically flew onto tape, six complete within a week. Such was the group's bafflement about what exactly to do with the material that they simply handed Johns the tapes and instructed him to come up with a single album. *Who's Next* was the result: an expansive, consummately-realised album that contains at least two milestones within rock music's progress: Won't Get Fooled Again and Baba O'Riley. Still, Townshend – who finally realised *Lifehouse* as a radio play and box set in 1999 – considered the album a partial failure.

"It has tremendous merits, and it sounds fantastic, but it could have been the musical 2001," he says. "That's why on the cover, we're pissing over the obelisk. The band didn't get it, but that was the idea."

Beaver and Krause
Gandharva

Synthesiser pioneers employ the acoustics of a San Francisco cathedral for cultish ambient jazz suite.

The unique nature of this "score for a non-existent film" reflects the diverse backgrounds of its creators: Paul Beaver was a jazz organist who met Bernie Krause through a shared interest in electronic music; Krause had performed with the Weavers folk group and produced for Motown. Together they became pioneers of the Moog synthesiser, working with The Doors, The Byrds, The Rolling Stones and George Harrison, among others. Krause was also interested in the sounds of the natural world and the pair's previous record, *In A Wild Sanctuary*, is claimed to be the first to use environmental sounds as a central part of the composition. "*Gandharva* was an attempt to continue in that vein," says Krause, "but we wanted to explore our own music – to take the chaos of rock'n'roll on the opening track and bring it down to a more spiritual level on side two." The music finally fades into long, pure notes that echo slowly around the walls of Grace Cathedral – the "sound" of the building itself. Side one features clattering blues-rock, a gospel choir plus synthesiser and vocal experiments. But it is for side two, recorded in the cathedral with its seven-second sound decay, that the disc is remembered.

"It's an unbelievable cavern," explains Krause. "It allowed you to use the whole space as an instrument, which was our intent."

In this slow, contemplative music Gerry Mulligan and Bud Shank star on saxophones with Krause playing Moog and Beaver at the cathedral organ. The record was the first to be recorded live in quadraphonic sound and the musicians were encouraged to wander among the four sets of mics. *Gandharva* was premiered at a San Francisco film theatre using sound equipment lent by the Grateful Dead and distributed in stereo and three competing quad formats (ever wonder why the system failed?). Paul Beaver died in 1975, but Krause has forged a career in bioacoustics and soundscaping.

"I couldn't tell you what the music is on *Gandharva*," he says. "It was categorised all over the place; it was pop, it was jazz. I don't like to be too specific. It just was what it was."

Record label:
Warner Bros

Produced
by Beaver and Krause.

Recorded
at various studios in Los Angeles and Grace Cathedral San Francisco; January–February 1971.

Released:
September 1971

Chart peaks:
None (UK) None (US)

Personnel:
Paul Beaver (Moog, o); Bernard Krause (Moog); Mike Bloomfield, Ronnie Montrose, Rik Elswit, Howard Roberts (g); Gerry Mulligan (sax); Bud Shank (s, flute); Lee Charlton, George Marsh (pc); Gail Laughton (harp); Clydie King, Patrice Holloway, the Beaver and Krause choir (v)

Track listing:
Soft; White; Saga Of The Blue Beaver; Nine Moons In Alaska; Walkin'; Walkin' By The River; Gandharva; By Your Grace; Good Places; Short Film For David; Bright Shadows. US CD also includes In A Wild Sanctuary (1970)

Running time:
34.36

Current CD:
Warner Bros. 456632

Further listening:
In A Wild Sanctuary (1970). Try also Paul Horn, Inside (1968), a flautist explores the astonishing acoustics of the Taj Mahal. One of the first, and best, "New Age" ambient recordings.

Further reading:
www.wildsanctuary.com

Funkadelic
Maggot Brain

Eco-friendly funkateers marry psychedelic rock to a whacked-out soul groove.

Funkadelic's previous two records – their self-titled debut and its follow-up *Free Your Mind And Your Ass Will Follow* – saw funk as the road to redemption and transcendental experience. *Maggot Brain* was no exception. With a screaming black woman's head rising out of the earth on the album sleeve, liner notes that quoted the teachings of the Process Church Of Final Judgement and eerie, foreboding lyrics that informed the listener: "I have tasted the maggots in the mind of the universe/And I was not offended/For I knew I had to rise above it all/Or drown in my own shit!", their third album was a frighteningly frazzled trip.

Fourteen years on from his innocent beginnings as singer in doo wop group The Parliaments, George Clinton was on a mission centred around LSD-inspired liberation and black consciousness and pride. Fusing the R&B of James Brown, Sly Stone and Curtis Mayfield with trippy acid-rock riffs, Funkadelic confounded both critics and listeners, despite reaching Number 14 in the US R&B chart.

"Back then people said, 'You just can't do that sorta thing on a record, George,'" explains Clinton. "And I was sayin' right back, 'You bet yo' ass I can.'"

Little is remembered about the actual recording sessions that gave birth to *Maggot Brain*. Clinton admits the album was produced while he was on acid. "I just got in there and turned the knobs," Clinton said. "It was such a vibe. I didn't know any better – you can only do that stuff when you don't know any better." Despite Clinton's unusual approach to producing, *Maggot Brain* successfully mixed politically charged comment (You And Your Folks, Me And My Folks tackled racism, Wars Of Armageddon dealt with the horrors of Vietnam) with gospel music (Can You Get To That) and cosmic funk rock stomps (Super Stupid).

But the finest moment has to be the haunting, transcendental title track. Rumour has it that Clinton had discovered his brother's decomposed body lying in a Chicago apartment with a cracked skull – hence the Maggot Brain – and he locked guitarist Eddie Hazel alone in the studio with the brief to "play like your mother just died". Hazel did just that producing an anguished, fragile, nine-minute guitar solo that rivalled Hendrix and was a world away from Funkadelic's next project, the more conventional funk sound of *America Eats Its Young*.

Record label:
Westbound

Produced
by George Clinton.

Recorded
at Universal Studios, Detroit; late 1970–early 1971.

Released:
September 1971

Chart peaks:
None (UK) 108 (US)

Personnel:
George Clinton (v); Eddie Hazel (g); Tawl Ross (g, v); Bernie Worrell (k, v); Billy 'Bass' Nelson (b); Tiki Fullwood (d); Clarence 'Fuzzy' Haskins (v, d); Ray Davis, Rose Williams, Pat Lewis, Diane Lewis, Grady Thomas, Calvin Simon, Gary Schider (v); McKinley Jackson (tb); Eddie Bongo (bongos); James Wesley Jackson (Jew's Harp)

Track listing:
Maggot Brain; Can You Get To That; Hit It And Quit It; You And Your Folks, Me And My Folks; Super Stupid; Back In Our Minds; Wars Of Armageddon

Running time:
36.58

Current CD:
CDSEWM002

Further listening:
Funkadelic (first album, spaced-out psychedelic funk 1970)

Further reading:
Funk (Rickey Vincent, 1996), For The Record: George Clinton And P-Funk (Dave Marsh, 1998); www.gnofn.org/~1nation

Marvin Gaye
What's Going On

The last great Motown record from Detroit and their first overtly political soul album.

W hen arranger and conductor David Van DePitte was assigned to a Marvin Gaye album he was surprised to find that he was alone in his enthusiasm for the project. All the other producers offered their condolences. "They'd all found him to be a pain in the fanny," he says. He'd soon find out why.

What's Going On, the song, had been written by Renaldo 'Obie' Benson of The Four Tops with lyricist Al Cleveland. The Four Tops wouldn't do it and an attempt to sell it to Joan Baez had failed, so Benson offered it to Gaye. Marvin, now fancying himself as a producer, tried to give it to unsung Motown band The Originals, but Benson offered him a share of the publishing if Marvin cut it himself. "We measured him for the suit and he tailored it," Benson told MOJO 64. "He fine-tuned the tune and added spice to the lyrics." To cut the song Marvin assembled a large band of percussionists and his buddies from the Detroit Lions football team to provide a party atmosphere, then got everybody stoned.

"My first thought was that it was never gonna fly," says Van DePitte of these sessions. "Then after we both got into a 'to hell with the company' mode, whatever happened, happened."

Berry Gordy was appalled by the results, and was mad at Motown president Barney Ales when What's Going On was mooted as a single, reportedly calling it the worst record he'd ever heard. Apparently he wasn't alone, employee Harry Balk, an early fan of the track, says his only ally at Motown was Stevie Wonder, others said the mix was "like two radio stations playing at once". "Put it out or I walk," Gaye demanded. The single sold 100,000 in its first day and Motown was forced to run with whatever Marvin wanted for the resultant album.

That's when Van DePitte's headaches began. Marvin hadn't finished any songs and kept missing sessions, and when he did show, work was inconclusive and slow. It was only when Gordy bet him a substantial sum that he couldn't finish it in 30 days, that Marvin was energised to complete the album. He worked on songs with Benson, Cleveland and veteran Motown switchboard operator Jamie Nyx, who supplied lyrics to Inner City Blues. The rhythm tracks were recorded and edited into one long piece over which the string, brass and vocal overdubs were laid.

Record label:
Tamla Motown

Produced
by Marvin Gaye.

Recorded
at Motown Studios and Golden Studios, Detroit; June–July 1970 and March 1971.

Released:
September 1971

Chart peaks:
None (UK) 6 (US)

Personnel:
Marvin Gaye (p, v); Eli Fontaine (as); Bill Moore (ts); Joe Messina, Robert White, Earl Van Dyke (g); Bob Babbit, James Jamerson (bs); Chet Forest (d); Jack Ashford (pc); Eddie Brown (bongos); Earl De Rouen (congas); Jack Brockensha (vibes); David Van DePitte (oa); Ken Sands, Steve Smith (e)

Track listing:
What's Going On (S); What's Happening Brother; Flyin' High (In The Friendly Sky); Save The Children (S); God Is Love; Mercy Mercy Me (The Ecology) (S); Right On; Wholly Holy; Inner City Blues (Make Me Wanna Holler) (S)

Running time:
35.30

Current CD:
5308832

Further listening:
Marvin's orchestral tour-de-force was the Trouble Man soundtrack (1973). The politics of sex were explored on Let's Get It On (1973), explored even further on I Want You (1976) and followed, perhaps inevitably, by the politics of divorce on Here, My Dear (1979).

Further reading:
MOJO 64; Troubleman (Steve Turner, 1999); Divided Soul (David Ritz, 1991)

Meanwhile, Marvin refined his new approach to the vocals, having chanced upon his trademark dual-vocal style after hearing two separate takes being played back at once. "I'd been studying the microphone for years," he said, "and I realised what I'd been doing wrong. I'd been singing too loud. One night, listening to a record by Lester Young it came to me. Relax, just relax." Apparently, Marvin's patent relaxation techniques included hours of masturbating before attempting a vocal take.

The album was mixed in LA (while Marvin shot a small part in a biker movie, Chrome And Hot Leather) and rush-released to great acclaim weeks later. Listeners were fascinated by the lush, spacious and supple arrangements, the mellow weave of Marvin's vocal tracks and the socially-aware sentiments of the lyrics. For once there was no mention of sex on a Marvin Gaye album.

It was intriguing that the Motown staffers had been wary of this new sound. *What's Going On* signalled great changes in the label's music. The happy-go-lucky Motown sound was doomed. By the following year, Berry Gordy had taken Motown to LA to become just another Californian record company. The unique spirit of Hitsville was left behind.

John Lennon
Imagine

Lennon's greatest solo success, produced amid domestic harmony before he and Yoko fled the UK for ever.

The primal screaming *John Lennon/Plastic Ono Band* had alienated critics and fans alike. *Imagine* – released exactly a month after John and Yoko took up permanent residence in the US – proved to be Lennon's greatest solo commercial and critical success, causing his controversial chronicler Albert Goldman to note sourly: "Which doesn't speak well of the tastes of the public or reviewers." *Imagine* was a product of the genial atmosphere in which it was recorded in late spring 1971. This is evident from the good-humoured film shot during the sessions at Lennon's Ascot mansion, Tittenhurst Park, as well as the personal accounts of those involved. "It was great," recalls drummer Alan White. "We'd all sit around the long table in the kitchen with the builders building around us. John had that sound in his head. He wanted Phil Spector to do it and he loved everything that was turning out, so he was very happy."

Contributions from such long-term associates as George Harrison and Klaus Voorman, as well as Joey Molland and Tom Evans from the Apple-signed Badfinger and Mike Pinder from beat rivals The Searchers, further lent to the harmonious feel. Not that all is sweetness and light. Lurking beneath the "chocolate-coated" surface, the same dark themes festered: self-disgust (Crippled Inside, Jealous Guy), hatred (How Do You Sleep?) and paranoia (Gimme Some Truth). Even the idealistic title track had a dark side.

"It's Working Class Hero with sugar on for conservatives like yourself," Lennon spat at McCartney, so roundly and famously lambasted on How Do You Sleep? "The only thing you done was Yesterday," sang Lennon, who would later withdraw the attack. "It's like Dylan says, often these things are really about yourself," he muttered.

"He couldn't help but show himself in all facets of his character," says Yoko Ono. "I think that was very sweet about him, the fact that he was so honest. Gimme Some Truth is what he was expecting from people too, but he was also expecting it from himself, obviously. He was showing himself as he was and I like that about him."

According to Yoko, the aim was to achieve broad appeal by sugaring the pill. "He wanted Imagine to be a song that would circulate in a larger world," she says. "He was very, very

Record label:
Apple

Produced
by John Lennon and Yoko Ono with Phil Spector.

Recorded
at Ascot Sound Studios; late spring 1971.

Released:
October 3, 1971

Chart peaks:
1 (UK) 1 (US)

Personnel:
John Lennon (v, g, p, mouth organ, whistling); Klaus Voorman (b); Alan White (d); George Harrison (dobro); Nicky Hopkins (p); Jim Gordon (d) King Curtis (s); Joey Molland, Tom Evans (g); Mike Pinder (tb)

Track listing:
Imagine (S); Crippled Inside; Jealous Guy; It's So Hard; I Don't Wanna Be A Soldier Mama; Gimme Some Truth; Oh My Love; How Do You Sleep?; How; Oh Yoko!

Running time:
39.31

Current CD:
5 24858 2

Further listening:
Mind Games (1973)

Further reading:
MOJO 42; We All Shine On: The Stories Behind Every John Lennon Song (Paul Du Noyer, 1997)

careful and caring about the fact that this important message would go around in a wider circle. Yes, of course he was talking about the whole album, but I think that Imagine was the message and the whole album was trying to push that song, too, in a way."

The song reached Number 3 in the US, but Lennon abruptly nixed a single release in Britain, preferring instead to concentrate on the hastily assembled Happy Xmas (War Is Over) campaign. This was indicative of how quickly his life had changed since the recording of *Imagine* in England's Green Belt. His politics had attained a militant edge, fuelled by his fascination for the frantic pace of life in New York. "I'm just sort of fascinated by it, like a fucking monster," he confessed. "I love it. I should have been born in the Village; that's where I belong." But he was more than aware of the dangers which lurked in the city. Spector had persuaded one of Lennon's musical heroes, the legendary King Curtis, to overdub a contribution after the main sessions were finished. A month later Curtis was stabbed to death by a vagrant outside his house in New York, in a disturbing portent of the fate of the creator of this beautiful, sardonic and, above all, human masterpiece.

Shirley Collins And The Albion Country Band
No Roses

Perhaps the single best English electric folk set.

Shirley Collins seemed the least likely of the established folkies to get involved with electric folk – a genteel Sussex artist who took her vocal style directly from the old singers and could scarcely have been more immersed in traditional song, having travelled around Britain and America collecting material with the researcher Alan Lomax. Yet she'd already broken a few barriers with her multi-cultural *Folk Roots, New Routes* album with Davey Graham in 1964 and the conceptual early music themes of *Anthems In Eden* with sister Dolly Collins in 1969 while the simple, understated depth of her 1970 album *Death And The Lady* had given direction to many bands of the day, notably Pentangle.

She was dubious when her husband Ashley Hutchings spoke of his plans to create a relevant, modern band exploring the spirit of English country dance bands of old but found she got a great kick out of fronting the Albion Country Band venture without remotely compromising her distinctively relaxed rural style.

"I remember talking to Ashley about what a dance band was," says one-time Albion Band member John Tams. "I said I thought it should sound like Joe Loss with Anne Shelton singing while people danced. Not long afterwards there was this big band with Shirley Collins doing Anne Shelton while people danced." It led to a lifetime of Albion Bands in different formats with hugely varying line-ups pursuing contrasting goals – and Collins was an early departure when her marriage to Hutchings broke up.

But *No Roses* remains appealing as an album that brilliantly matched a singer and musical style of apparently sharp contrast, driven by natural, inventive interpretations of some of the finest songs produced by the British tradition, notably the Coppers' Claudy Banks, Joseph Taylor's White Hare and, best of all, a spectacular theatrical treatment of The Murder Of Maria Marten.

Record label:
Mooncrest

Produced
by Sandy Robertson and Ashley Hutchings.

Recorded
at Sound Techniques, Morgan and Air Studios, London; summer, 1971.

Released:
October 1971

Chart peaks:
None (UK) None (US)

Personnel:
Shirley Collins (v, ag, banjo, a); Nic Jones (v, vn); John Kirkpatrick (acc); Maddy Prior (v); Richard Thompson (ag, g); Lol Coxhill (s); Ashley Hutchings (b); Simon Nicol (v, ag, g); Roger Powell (d); Tim Renwick (ag, g); Roy Wood (v); Francis Baines (g, hurdy gurdy); Dave Bland (dulcimer, concertina); Alan Cave (bassoon); Dolly Collins (v, p); Barry Dransfield (vn, v); Tony Hall (melodeon); Alan Lumsden (s); Dave Mattacks (d); Lal Waterson (v); Mike Waterson (v); Ian Whiteman (p); Royston Wood (v); Jerry Boys (e)

Track listing:
Claudy Banks; The Little Gypsy Girl; Banks Of The Bann; Murder Of Maria Marten; Van Dieman's Land; Just As The Tide Was A'Flowing; The White Hare; Hal-An-Tow; Poor Murdered Woman

Running time:
41.00

Current CD:
CRESTCD011

Further listening:
Battle Of The Field (1976)

Further reading:
www.folkicons.co.uk

The Master Musicians Of Jajouka

Brian Jones Presents The Pipes Of Pan At Jajouka

"The menace of darkness outside the circle of firelight,"
according to Rolling Stone.

Unwanted by Mick and Keef ("I have the feeling my presence is not required," was how Jones described the early *Let It Bleed* sessions), hounded by the fuzz in Britain, no longer able to play his guitar and mentally crumbling, Brian Jones fled to Morocco in the summer of 1968. Earlier in the year he had taken the producer Glyn Johns to record Gnaoua musicians, but had been unhappy with the results. In the Rif mountains near Tangiers, the artist Brion Gysin had taped Berber music for him, and he wanted more. When Jones arrived, the musicians happily re-enacted part of the 4,000-year-old Rites Of Pan for him. The musicians (all men) played pipes and drums, making unearthly sounds that whipped the participants into trances, seemingly possessed and unable to stop for hours. "I don't know if I possess the stamina to endure the incredible constant strain of the festival," Jones wrote in the sleevenotes, "such psychic weaklings has Western civilisation made of so many of us."

Jones returned to London certain he had uncovered a link between Africa and American music – a concept outside the scope of most pop musicians in the 1960s. Filled with enthusiasm, he turned tyro producer, swamping parts in electronic effects, adding keyboards and guitar wherever he felt they were required. Take Me With You sounds as if it's running backwards in parts, Your Eyes is scarily intense, and I Am Calling Out could be an Afro-Caribbean voodoo chant. "What exists here is a specially chosen representation of the type of music which is played and chanted during the festival," he wrote. "We apologise for the virtual inaudibility of the lead singer during the chanting of the women, but they are chanting an incantation to those of another plane. It was not for our ears."

The two sides were unbroken single tracks (the titles were not added until a 1995 re-release) and the total cost was more than £20,000. On the positive side, it was unquestionably unique – no other Moroccan music was commercially available in Britain. But then again, neither was Brian's LP – at least, not until two years after his death.

Record label:
Rolling Stones Records

Produced
by Brian Jones.

Recorded
in Morocco; 1968.

Released:
October 1971

Chart peaks:
None (UK) None (US)

Personnel:
Brian Jones (v, g, k); The Master Musicians Of Jajouka (v, d, pipes)

Track listing:
55; War Song; Standing And One Half; Take Me With You My Darling, Take Me With You; Your Eyes Are Like A Cup Of Tea; I Am Calling Out; Your Eyes Are Like A Cup Of Tea (Reprise)

Running time:
46.00

Currently unavailable on CD

Further listening:
Jajouka Between The Mountains (1996)

Further reading:
www.eyeneer.com/World/Nawa/Profiles/Jajouka

Van Der Graaf Generator
Pawn Hearts

The sound of the underground at its most unpredictable.

"The times were intense, and we were an intense, even scary band," remembers frontman/songwriter Peter Hammill. Back in 1971, things rarely got scarier than *Pawn Hearts*, VDGG's most traumatic album. Hammill's odyssey blurred searching, bad-trip visions with moments of blissful revelation; the complex arrangements owed much to 20th century classical music, contemporary jazz and psychedelia; the manic, end-of-tether results belied the progressive tag that's often been attached to the band. Unusually, there were few showy displays of virtuosity.

Emerging from the late '60s underground scene, VDGG's previous albums had won them keen college and continental followings. "Things were extremely open," says Hammill, "and that's the attitude we went in with. We were given more time than before, and we were aware that it was going to be an epic production. In the writing, I was trying to push things as far as they could go, and in the playing we were trying to pull many influences into one cohesive mess."

After rehearsals at a haunted house in Crowborough (where the inner sleeve photo was shot), the group spent around four weeks between July and September 1971 stretching Trident's studio technology. "A lot of effects had to be invented," says Hammill. Phasing involved running two stereo machines slightly out of sync by balancing a heavy ashtray on one of the reels. "At one stage during the mixing, we were using every tape-machine that Trident had in order to cope with the phasing, delays and repeats." While the basic structure of the album's three pieces was pre-planned, the VDGG ethos allowed room for improvisation. "We were a touring band at the time and we trusted each other to do the business when the red light went on." Some bridging sections were completely improvised, notably the start and finish of Lemmings and the Pictures segment of Plague Of Lighthouse Keepers, a complex, side-long segue of ten parts cross-faded together. "The mixing, which often involved six pairs of hands, was effectively a live performance," Hammill adds.

Pawn Hearts compelling, claustrophobic, carefully-hewn chaos is practically unique in pop.

Record label:
Charisma

Produced
by John Anthony.

Recorded
at Trident Studios, London;
July–September 1971.

Released:
October 1971

Chart peaks:
None (UK) None (US)

Personnel:
Peter Hammill (v, g, p); David Jackson (s, flute, v); Hugh Banton (k, o, p, Mellotron, syn, b, v, psychedelic razor); Guy Evans (d, pc, p); Robert Fripp (g); Robin Cable (e); David Hentschel (e); Ken Scott (e)

Track listing:
Lemmings (including Dog); Man-Erg; A Plague Of Lighthouse Keepers: i. Eyewitness; ii. Pictures/Lighthouse; iii. Eyewitness iv. SHM; v. Presence Of The Night; vi. Kosmos Tours; vii. (Custard's) Last Stand; viii. The Clot Thickens; ix. Land's End (Sineline); x. We Go Now

Running time:
45.06

Current CD:
1704616392

Further listening:
Hear the band limber up on H To He, Who Am The Only One (1970)

Further reading:
www.vub.ac.be/STER/KoenWWW/Ph/RefHome.html

Mickey Newbury
'Frisco Mabel Joy

Gritty songwriter crafts dark, stormy songs to the sound of the rain.

Mickey Newbury had a reputation as a composer of chirpy hits for the likes of Willie Nelson, Tom Jones and Kenny Rogers (the evocative psychedelia of I Just Dropped In To See What Condition My Condition Was In, later on the soundtrack of The Big Lebowski) when he landed a deal with Elektra to make his own records and, between 1969 and 1971, cut three albums of intensely personal music that bore little resemblence to his pop work. "I never really liked those early songs," he now admits.

Holed-up on a barge in Nashville, he'd often write while rain tumbled onto the roof and its melancholy rhythm soon began to permeate his work, so much so that all three albums – *Looks Like Rain*, *'Frisco Mabel Joy* and *Heaven Help The Child* – feature the sounds of those stormy nights.

"It seemed to be raining all the time back then. And I just seemed to turn it into sad songs," Newbury confirms. These were stories of loss, missed opportunity and road-weary misadventure, on *'Frisco Mabel Joy* they languish in a strange orchestral haze of minor chords, choirs, peeling bells, distant steel guitars and a gathering storm just in earshot. Although the album was recorded in Nashville, the only link to country music is Newbury's groggy twang of a voice, and the songs owe more to the blackest of gothic stories.

Opening with An American Trilogy, a medley of three Civil War songs fused to underline their gloominess, the mood is set for this study in despair. Elvis Presley's subsequent cover added drum rolls and whistles to play up the patriotic element. "I thought Elvis kinda missed the point," Newbury said later. "The idea was to emphasise that they were real folk songs, talking about real people." Newbury simply relied on the lyrics' inherent pain and poignancy to carry the weight. And his self-penned tunes mined a similarly dark vein; recurring orchestral themes enhancing their grandiose, weather-beaten feel. These tales of unfaithful lovers, a fondly-remembered past and a future that can't compete make *'Frisco Mabel Joy* a mood piece that aches to be wallowed in.

Record label:
Elektra

Produced
by Dennis Linde.

Recorded
at Cinderella Sound Studios, Nashville, Tennessee; 1970.

Released:
Autumn 1971

Chart peaks:
None (UK) None; (US)

Personnel:
Mickey Newbury (v,p); Dennis Linde (g); Wayne Moss (g); Charlie McCoy (hm); Weldon Myrick (s,g); Charles Navarro (c); Don Grant (vn); Norman Spicher (d); Farrell Morris (pc); Bobby Thompson (g, banjo); Beegie Cruser (k); James Isbell; James Capps and the Nashphilharmonic; with Dr John Harris; John Moss; Walter Sill and Bob Beckham

Track listing:
An American Trilogy; How Many Times (Must The Piper Be Paid For His Song); Interlude; The Future's Not What It Used To Be; Mobile Blue; Frisco Depot; You're Not My Same Sweet Baby; Interlude; Remember The Good; Swiss Cottage Place; How I Love Them Old Songs

Running time:
36.05

Currently unavailable on CD

Further listening:
Though not available as individual CDs, the ten albums Newbury released between 1969 and 1981 are compiled on eight CDs as The Mickey Newbury Collection. Lovers (1975) and The Sailor (1979) are also worth hearing.

Further reading:
No Depression (Grant Allen and Peter Blackstock,1999) www.mickeynewbury.com

Led Zeppelin
IV

Their fourth, untitled, album — also known as "Four Symbols"— turned them into untouchable superstars.

Led Zeppelin's blues-rock origins as The New Yardbirds were a little misleading. Both Page and Plant were as influenced by British folk music as they were by American blues and had begun to explore their fascination in earnest on their third album which — as a much more pastoral set than its predecessors — was coolly received by critics.

Jimmy Page took it badly, Robert Plant got on the defensive. "Plant Denies Soft Charge", trumpeted Record Mirror. "Now we've done *Zeppelin III* the sky's the limit," Plant declared. They'd been making full use of the emerging mobile studio technology, hiring The Rolling Stones' truck-mounted facility and parking it in the Hampshire countryside outside a former Victorian workhouse known as Headley Grange. Here, they'd cut some of *Led Zeppelin III* and after they'd got used to the damp and draughty accommodation, had grown to like the relaxed creative atmosphere it afforded.

"It gave us a chance to work at our own pace," recalls Jimmy Page. "It was a three-storey house with a huge hallway where we miked the drums. We'd have the amplifiers in other rooms and cupboards. It was an unconventional way to record but it certainly worked." The gargantuan sound of John Bonham's drums on When The Levee Breaks — captured by one microphone hanging down the house's central stairwell — has been imitated and sampled countless times. "We always wanted the drums to sound like real drums," Page proclaims, "but that hall made them sound like cannons."

The sound, indeed the whole album, became a benchmark for the future of heavy rock, as Page, Plant, Bonham and Jones definitively wove together their individual influences for the crunching riff of Rock And Roll, the sword and sorcery lyric of Battle Of Evermore and all points in between. But over the years, the record's wider pleasures have been overshadowed by rock radio's most-played album track of all time, Stairway To Heaven. It was begun in Island's Basing Street Studios in December 1970, Page having planned it as a 25-minute fusion of all their various styles, (although Plant has claimed, perhaps fancifully, that it started out as a reggae number). The mini-symphony was refined at the Grange, Page spending days on the solos and Plant coming up with the lyrics one evening in front of the fire.

Record label:
Atlantic

Produced
by Jimmy Page.

Recorded
at Headley Grange, Hampshire; Island and Olympic Studios, London; Sunset Sound, Los Angeles; December 1970 to June 1971.

Released:
November 1971

Chart peaks:
1 (UK) 2 (US)

Personnel:
Jimmy Page (g); Robert Plant (v, hm); John Paul Jones (b, k, syn); John Bonham (d); Sandy Denny (v)

Track listing:
Black Dog; Rock And Roll; The Battle Of Evermore; Stairway To Heaven; Misty Mountain Hop; Four Sticks; Going To California; When The Levee Breaks

Running time:
42.37

Current CD:
7567826382

Further listening:
Houses Of the Holy (1973); Physical Graffiti (1975)

Further reading:
MOJO 12A, 77; Led Zeppelin: The Definitive Biography (Ritchie Yorke, 1994); Hammer Of The Gods (Stephen Davis, 1985) www.led-zeppelin.com

"Stairway crystallised the essence of the band," says Page. "It was a milestone for us." The band's anti-marketing seemed geared to scupper their milestone's chances. No singles, no band name or even title on the muted, very un-rock sleeve. But all of that simply added to the record's mystique and majesty. The fans seized upon the brutal simplicity of Rock And Roll and the elaborate dynamic of Stairway with equal enthusiasm. Zeppelin ascended into the loftiest realms of the rock gods. This was the record that made them untouchable.

Sly & The Family Stone
There's A Riot Goin' On

Drug-addled weirdness and tuneful hits combine on one of pop's most perplexing records.

"Two years is a short time to wait for a work of genius," declared manager David Kapralik when the follow-up to his band's smash-hit 1969 album, *Stand!* was finished. Once scheduled as *The Incredible And Unpredictable Sly And The Family Stone*, the edgy and inscrutable record he delivered wasn't what anyone was expecting. "Unpredictable" was right enough. In 1970, the band had missed 26 out of 80 shows. Things were obviously awry chez Stone, a mock-Tudor mansion at 783 Bel Air, overrun by hangers-on, groupies, drug dealers and a psychotic pit-bull terrier named Gun, who'd attack anyone wearing a hat. In the small attic studio, Sly Stone (who used his real name, Sylvester Stewart, when producing) was trying to cut his masterpiece. But he'd also discovered PCP – a drug not so much mind-altering as brain-damaging – and added it to a frightening pharmaceutical shopping list. Riot sounds like it was recorded haphazardly. In fact, it was painstakingly compiled from hours of tape. There was constant overdubbing. Sly would sometimes work three days without sleep. Bobby Womack, Miles Davis, Billy Preston and others dropped by, but no one's too sure who made it to the final mixes (Preston almost certainly plays electric piano on Family Affair). Even long-serving drummer Gregg Errico is only certain he's on the spaced-out jam Africa Talks To You. (Family Affair marks one of the first recorded appearances of a drum machine.)

Jerry Martini recalls that Sly also used the sessions to get laid. "He'd ask women if they wanted to be on his album. They'd lay down some terrible vocal. Sly would get the goods and then erase [their voice]." That's why the $1m-budgeted Riot sounds murky. "The tape was worn out."

Though it topped the American charts, few who purchased this dense brew of stoned grooves and crazed voices could have known exactly what Sly was on about. Were the lyrics militant tirades or whacked-out paranoia? Was the irresistibly funky Family Affair wistful or pessimistic, the beautiful Running Away disturbed or playful? And what's with the yelling of "Timber!" or the yodelling on Spaced Cowboy? Why was an invisible title track listed at 0 minutes and 0 seconds? "It's so complex, words get in the way," offered the original liner notes, unhelpfully. Whatever, the all-positive, good-time Family Stone was over.

Record label:
Epic

Produced
by Sylvester Stewart.

Recorded
at Record Plant and 783 Bel Air, Los Angeles; Spring/Summer, 1971.

Released:
November 1971

Chart peaks:
31 (UK) 1 (US)

Personnel:
Sly Stone (v, k); Rose Stone (v); Freddie Stone (g); Bobby Womack (g, v); Larry Graham (b); Gregg Errico (d); Jerry Martini (ts); Cynthia Robinson (t); Billy Preston, Miles Davis, Johnny "Guitar" Watson, Herbie Hancock, James Conniff (e)

Track Listing:
Luv'N'Haight; Just Like A Baby; Poet; Family Affair (S); Africa Talks To You (The Asphalt Jungle); There's A Riot Goin' On; Brave & Strong; (You Caught Me) Smilin' (S/US); Time; Spaced Cowboy; Runnin' Away (S); Thank You For Talkin' To Me Africa

Running time:
47.40

Current CD:
4667770639 CD DIGIPACK

Further listening:
Fresh (1973); the Sly Stone solo album High On You (1975).

Further reading:
Sly And The Family Stone (An Oral History) – For The Record (1999); www.slyfamstone.com

Wings
Wildlife

McCartney's forgotten folly.

Just 18 months after the Beatles split, and Paul McCartney
was up the proverbial creek. *Ram* was ridiculed, and perhaps
Paul felt the need for the security of a band again. In August
1971 he announced that he had formed Wings with a drummer
he'd met during the New York *Ram* sessions and one of his old
heroes, Denny Laine (real name Brian Hines) once of The
Moody Blues, and intended to undertake an old-fashioned tour
by funky bus. The new band had cut their first album within
days of first meeting. McCartney proudly unveiled the result at
a lavish Come Dancing-style album launch. "Bip Bop,"
announced Paul tenderly on the opening track, "Bip bop-a-bip-
bip-bop a-bip-bop bip-bop-bay." Or some nonsense to that
effect. Critics could barely contain their contempt. *Wildlife*
quickly became the most reviled record in any Beatle's canon.
Plans to extract a single (the, ahem, reggae cover of Micky And
Sylvia's Love Is Strange) were hastily dropped. Paul has barely
mentioned the album since, and even Linda later conceded, "We
could have done it better."

Ah, but "could have" is not the same as "should have",
and time has shown that the McCartneys' misguided experiment
in off-the-cuff simplicity wasn't so mad, after all. For *Wildlife*'s
weaknesses back then are the very same factors that make it
fascinating today, a sparse, bare-bones defiance reaching back
into the infancy of rock'n'roll and forward to the lo-fi boom of
the '90s. Nonsense it may have been, but Bip Bop is a big
groove – Paul's meaty bass right up in the mix – and absurdly
catchy. Mumbo emerges as an archetypal McCartney rocker,
somewhere between Helter Skelter and Soily; and Tomorrow –
one of Paul's most surprsingly overlooked songs – could have
slipped into the *Abbey Road* medley. Dear Friend is a first-class,
Paul-at-piano heart-render, while the title track is an intricately
constructed six minute mantra awash with some utterly lovely
Linda harmonies. Indeed, comparisons between *Wildlife* and the
pre-Spector mix of the Beatles' *Let It Be* demonstrate that everything McCartney was now attempting with Wings, he had first
envisioned during those last, fraught months of The Beatles; and
would be bringing to fruition as the '70s developed. In other
words, Wings may have made some bigger albums, but they
never made a more distinctive one.

Record label:
Apple

Produced
by Paul McCartney.

Recorded
at Abbey Road, London; August, 1971.

Released:
December 7, 1971

Chart peaks:
8 (UK) 10 (US)

Personnel:
Paul McCartney (v, b); Denny Laine (g);
Linda McCartney (k, v); Denny Seiwell (d)

Track listing:
Mumbo; Bip Bop; Love Is Strange; Wild
Life; Some People Never Know; I Am Your
Singer; Bip Bop Line (uncredited on LP);
Tomorrow; Dear Friend; Mumbo Link
(uncredited on LP).

Running time:
39.41

Current CD:
CDP7892372 adds: Oh Woman Oh Why;
Mary Had A Little Lamb (S); Little
Woman Love

Further listening:
Band On The Run (1974); Wings At The
Speed Of Sound (1976)

Further reading:
The Paul McCartney Story (George
Tremlett, 1975)

David Bowie
Hunky Dory

The birth of a superstar

In mid-1971, 24-year-old David Bowie was being berated by his manager Tony Defries for dragging his heels. Mercurial of temperament and ambition – Bowie would announce variously at the time that he was a washed up old rocker or about to be bigger than Elvis – and distracted by the birth of his son, Bowie was taking his time over the follow-up to his under-noticed, futuristic proto-metal album *The Man Who Sold The World*. Spurred by the news from Defries that he had a mere £27 in the bank and freshly inspired by his recent acquaintanceship with New York's decadent art-rock crew (Messrs Pop, Reed and Warhol), within weeks Bowie had written and recorded enough material for two albums.

The first was the schizophrenic *Hunky Dory*. Side one was an attractive set with a misleadingly sunny, acoustic sound – all guitars and undulating piano – and remains among Bowie's most extravagantly melodic achievements. Both Changes and Oh! You Pretty Things were built on a reassuringly bouncy descending bass line, Life On Mars? (with what Wilfred Mellors called "near-lunatic shifts" of key, as the movie-going heroine dissolves into the film she watches) was Bowie's concerted effort to re-write My Way and Kooks was a Kinksy slice of optimism for his new-born son. The haunted self-examination of Changes and announcement of the obsolescence of the older generation (if not the human species) in Oh! You Pretty Things barely impacts upon a listener in thrall to the music's tunefulness, but side two adopts a grimmer tone and the darkness of Bowie's imagination (images of madness, drugs and cross-dressing abound) becomes more vivid. His nods to Warhol (on, erm, Andy Warhol), Dylan (Song For Bob Dylan) and The Velvet Underground (Queen Bitch) are snarling, ambiguously critical homages, while Bewlay Brothers is a remarkably evocative and impenetrably personal meditation on Bowie's schizophrenic half-brother Terry Burns.

Though a New York critic was sufficiently moved by the album to state that Bowie was "the most intelligent person to have chosen rock music as his medium of communication", Bowie's attention-grabbing "I'm gay" announcement and launch (only six months after *Hunky Dory*) of his career-changing alter-ego Ziggy Stardust meant it took a while for *Hunky Dory* to build its reputation as a classic. For many – despite a further 30 years of astonishingly disparate Bowie music – it remains his finest songwriting hour.

Record label:
RCA Victor

Produced
by David Bowie and Ken Scott

Recorded
at Trident Studios, London summer 1971

Release date:
December 1971

Chart peaks:
3 (UK) 93 (US)

Personnel:
David Bowie (g, p, v, s); Rick Wakeman (p); Mick Ronson (g, v); Trevor Bolder (b, t); Mick "Woody" Woodmansey (d)

Track listing:
Changes; Oh! You Pretty Things; Eight Line Poem; Life on Mars?; Kooks; Quicksand; Fill Your Heart; Andy Warhol; Song for Bob Dylan; Queen Bitch; Bewlay Brothers

Running time:
51.24

Current CD:
EMI 5218990

Further listening:
The Man Who Sold The World (1970); The Rise & Fall Of Ziggy Stardust And The Spiders From Mars (1973)

Further reading:
Loving The Alien by (Christopher Sandford, 1996), www.bowie.com; www.homeusers.prestel.co.uk/neukoln/

Faces
A Nod's As Good As A Wink

The quintessential lad rock knees-up.

By 1971, The Faces had an outlandish live reputation: boozy, boisterous and brash, they brought the house down in America but still hadn't got it together in the studio. Their debut *First Step* had reached Number 45 and then disappeared after a week, and the follow-up *Long Player* didn't fare much better. To make matters worse, Rod Stewart's solo career was skyrocketing: *Every Picture Tells A Story* and Maggie May had given him his first Number 1 album and single respectively. The fans were clamouring for more – and if they couldn't buy another Rod solo record, then the Faces were the next best thing.

"That's really when we came good," recalled Stewart. "The Faces as a band never surpassed *A Nod's As Good As A Wink*. Incredible album." Few would disagree. The Faces' third album broke their familiar recording pattern. Usually they'd meet in the pub before a session, stay until closing time and then wonder why the album took so long to complete. This time, with producer Glyn Johns bullying them into action, first takes were the order of the day.

"Glyn pulled us together and kept us focused," recalls organist Ian McLagan. "Rod and Kenny would start rattling their car keys about 10 o'clock because they couldn't wait to get out of the studio and go clubbing, while the two Ronnies and I were happier getting high and playing music all night. Glyn was the referee – he could vote a song in or out. We were quite happy to let him be the judge," explains McLagan. Of the nine tracks, four were Wood/Stewart compositions. Rod would sing an idea to Wood, who'd tinker with it and lay down a basic track. Rod would write the lyrics at home – a task he didn't relish: "I hate writing words, that's the hardest part. I'm not really a natural songwriter."

Stay With Me is the album's pinnacle. Their first hit single, an instantly catchy yell-along anthem with Stewart casting himself as a bog-brush haired misogynist demanding: "Just don't be here in the morning when I wake up." The strutting Miss Judy's Farm is a comic tale of sexual slavery, while the McLagan/Lane-penned You're So Rude is more tongue-in-cheek sleaze-rock. But the two Ronnie Lane compositions are more downbeat, Last Orders Please and the beautifully bleak, reflective folk ballad Debris – rumoured by Lester Bangs to be directed at Stewart: "Now we both know you got the money/And I wonder what you would've done/Without me hanging around."

Record label:
Warner Brothers

Produced
by Glyn Johns and the Faces.

Recorded
at Olympic Studios, London; summer 1971.

Released:
December 1971

Chart peaks:
2 (UK) 6 (US)

Personnel:
Rod Stewart (v); Ron Wood (g); Ronnie Lane (b); Ian McLagan (p, o); Kenny Jones (d)

Track listing:
Miss Judy's Farm; You're So Rude; Love Lived Here; Last Orders Please; Stay With Me (S); Debris; Memphis; Too Bad; That's All You Need

Running time:
36.11

Current CD:
7599259292

Further listening:
Good Boys When They're Asleep, a comprehensive 'best of' featuring the previously unissued Open To Ideas (1999).

Further reading:
All The Rage (Ian McLagan, 1998); MOJO 18; Smiler fanzine, online at http://members.aol.com/smilerfrg/rod/sminfo.htm

Bread
Baby I'm-A Want You

The fourth, most polished and best-selling of the soft-rock kings' five albums.

Although they delivered five albums, with enough world-class material to justify endless recompiling for decades to come, the original Bread recording era was remarkably succinct: 1969–72. Trailered by its feather-light title track, *Baby I'm-A Want You* was the apex of Bread's ascendency in the soft-rock pantheon and also the album debut of the group's finest line-up.

Originally conceived as a harmony-based pop-rock group, with an emphasis on quirky, three-minute songwriting in The Beatles vein – and specifically as an alternative to the lengthy indulgences of the West Coast acid rock acts – Bread began life as a trio. Spending most of the '60s in Los Angeles as successful session players and songwriters-for-hire, David Gates and James Griffin met during album sessions for Robb Royer's Pleasure Faire. Subsequently tiring of session work the pair, with Royer as Griffin's writing partner, embarked on their own project.

A superb first album, *Bread* failed to secure the sales it deserved, but shortly afterwards Gates' schmaltzy ballad Make It With You became a smash hit in both US and UK charts. Not necessarily representative of the group, it set the agenda – certainly for public expectations, and to an extent for group direction. In the subsequent battle for whose songs became singles, Griffin (essentially responsible for Bread's raunchier material) tended to lose out – a situation that would contribute, along with simple creative burn-out, to Bread's demise in 1973. But, as Gates has wisely observed: "Ultimately, soft rock was what we did best, and you can't really argue with success."

Baby I'm-A Want You opened with Mother Freedom, a disarmingly funky slab of heavy rock written by Gates in a style he christened "Bread Zeppelin". Inevitably, it fared weakly as a single. In an album brimming with exquisitely crafted material from all concerned – one, Down On My Knees, a rare and dynamic Griffin/Gates co-write – once again the biggest hits were by Gates alone: "Everything I Own was written for my dad, who had then just passed away. Diary was just a fictitious thing – it disappointed a lot of people who were hoping there really was a diary, but there never was!" Within a year, there was no more Bread either.

Record label:
Elektra

Produced
by David Gates.

Recorded
at Sound Recorders, Hollywood, California and Sound Labs, Hollywood, California; late 1971.

Released:
January 1972

Chart peaks:
9 (UK) 3 (US)

Personnel:
David Gates (v, g, b, Moog, vn); James Griffin (v, g, p); Larry Knechtel (k, b, hm, g); Mike Botts (d); Armin Steiner (e); James Griffin (associate producer)

Track listing:
Mother Freedom (S/US); Baby I'm-A Want You (S); Down On My Knees; Everything I Own (S); Nobody Like You; Diary (S/US); Dream Lady; Daughter; Games Of Magic; This Isn't What The Governmeant; Just Like Yesterday; I Don't Love You

Running time:
34.19

Current CD:
7559606782

Further listening:
Manna (1971); The Guitar Man (1972); David Gates And Bread: Essentials (1996)

Further reading:
Waiting For The Sun: Strange Days, Weird Scenes And The Sounds Of Los Angeles (Barney Hoskyns, 1996)

J.J. Cale
Naturally

Magical debut from the man who came to epitomise the term "laid back".

"WW hen I first saw John, he was playing guitar with an Elvis imitator in Tulsa," recalled Leon Russell, "so he's playing all the Scotty Moore stuff, he'd step out in front, take solos, and it was all very showbizzy. Then it seemed like when he started making his own records, he kind of gravitated towards the rear of the stage and played with his back to the audience. He had an amazing local reputation: when he played a black club in Tulsa called The Rose Room, he did all that stuff, it was just like Jackie Wilson or somebody, and then when he started making his own records it's kind of like he turned into Miles Davis or someone. Very odd!"

Jean Jacques Cale had been a stalwart of Tulsa, Oklahoma's music scene for several years before getting the chance to record his solo debut for his friend Leon Russell's new label Shelter Records. Already the wrong side of 32, Cale had led a chequered career which saw him try his hand at whatever musical mode was currently in fashion, starting with western swing in the '50s and taking in rock'n'roll (Johnnie Cale & The Valentines), country and even garage psychedelia as the '60s progressed, eventually releasing a tongue-in-cheek "hippie" album (A Trip Down Sunset Strip by The Leathercoated Minds) during a spell as studio engineer and session musician in Los Angeles.

It was an earlier recording that triggered his subsequent solo career, however, when Eric Clapton covered Cale's 1965 single After Midnight on his own 1970 debut solo album. "It was like discovering oil in your own backyard," Cale later commented, while Clapton explained, "I was tired of gymnastic guitar-playing, and when I listened to J.J. Cale records, I was impressed by the subtlety, by what wasn't being played." Clapton's interest prompted Cale's manager Audie Ashworth to invite him down to Nashville to make an album. Recorded at fabled country studio Bradley's Barn, *Naturally* showcased Cale's smoky murmur and liquid guitar style on his own country, blues and rockabilly grooves, with opener Call Me The Breeze, another version of After Midnight, and the album's first single Crazy Mama (US No.22, 1972) quickly becoming rock standards.

"'Mellow' and 'laid-back' are the two terms most

Record label:
A&M

Produced
by Audie Ashworth.

Recorded
at Bradley's Barn, Mt. Juliet, Tennessee;
September 29–October 4, 1970.

Released:
January 1972

Chart peaks:
None (UK) 51 (US)

Personnel:
J.J. Cale (v, g); Karl Himmel (d); Chuck Browning (d); Tim Drummond (b); Carl Radle (b); Norbert Puttnam (b); Bob Wilson (k); David Briggs (k); Jerry Whitehurst (k); Weldon Myrick (sg); Shorty Lavender, Buddy Spicher (fiddle); Walter Haynes (dobro); Mac Gayden (slide g); Ed Colis (hm); Diane Davidson (bv); Joe Mills (e); Jim Williamson (e)

Track listing:
Call Me The Breeze; Call The Doctor; Don't Go To Strangers; Woman I Love; Magnolia; Clyde; Crazy Mama (S); Nowhere To Run; After Midnight (S); River Runs Deep; Bringing It Back; Crying Eyes

Running time:
40.08

Current CD:
830042-2

Further listening:
His sophomore effort Really was a little funkier than his debut, while Okie achieved a near-perfect blend of low-key soul and country elements. Of the later albums, Travel-Log and Ten are the closest in quality to the earlier ones.

Further reading:
J.J. Cale interview in Q38; www.jjcale.com

applied to my style and I guess I go along with that," said Cale. "Most of it is medium-, slow-tempo, not really an aggressive in-your-face kind of thing. When I was a real young fellow and played in bands, just as a guitar player, I played a lot more rock 'n'roll, but when I got into songwriting and had to sing, since I only have about a two-note range it was easier to do mellow stuff and grooves."

Despite his backwoods image and the album's title, Cale – who has an engineering background – has always been a devoted techie, making countless modifications to his guitar to achieve his distinctive sound. *Naturally* even featured an early model of a drum machine. "I'm sure it wasn't the first," said Cale, "but it was in a very infant stage at that time. Four songs on that first album were with a drum-machine. The deal is, in those days people didn't know about it, so they didn't realise what it was." His fluid, weightless guitar style became a huge influence on Clapton, and especially on Mark Knopfler, who built on it the kind of high-profile career that would terrify the chronically shy Cale.

Nilsson
Nilsson Schmilsson

A less whimsical, more gruff Nilsson has his first big success.

At the start of 1971, Nilsson went back into the recording studio after almost a year's absence to make the album that would become his all-time best-seller, *Nilsson Schmilsson*. His first album of mostly original, non-soundtrack material in the two years since *Harry*, it was also his first recorded in London, and his first with producer Richard Perry. Perry, who was almost exactly a year younger than Nilsson and, like him, born in Brooklyn, NY, had a colourful resumé that included Tiny Tim's first two albums and Captain Beefheart's *Safe As Milk*. He was also a talented arranger – he'd worked on Nilsson's friend Ringo Starr's *Sentimental Journey*.

From its (to say the least) informal cover photo – Harry, unshaven and dishevelled in a dressing gown – to its tongue-in-cheek title, *Nilsson Schmilsson* was a surprising change from Nilsson's previous albums. Most surprising was that he had made such a great artistic leap. "What do you say to a man who writes The Puppy Song," he said later, "and then writes Jump Into The Fire? I really needed [to make that change], too, that was exactly what I was hoping would happen. That album was a great meeting [of minds]. I was so glad to meet Richard Perry, because he was thinking the same thing I was thinking at the same time: now let's go to work and do some rock'n'roll and get down!"

It was while in England that Nilsson heard and recorded the Badfinger's Without You. While the Badfinger version (on their 1970 album *No Dice*) still stands up, there is no question that Nilsson's version remains definitive. It topped the charts for four weeks in the US and five weeks in the UK, selling well over one million copies and earning Nilsson his second Grammy.

Nilsson Schmilsson spent nearly a year on the charts, spawning two more US hit singles, Jump Into The Fire and the Top 10 hit Coconut. The hard-rocking Jump Into The Fire was a completely left-field choice for a follow-up to Without You; "I wanted to do a fast song," Nilsson shrugged later. Fortunately, fans took it on its own merit and sent it up to Number 27. To this day, it is the only hit to feature a bass detuning, courtesy of legendary session man Herbie Flowers. Presented with the contrast between Jump Into The Fire and his earlier work, Nilsson countered "My earlier stuff had the same soul in it, only it was more subtle."

Record label:
RCA

Produced
by Richard Perry.

Recorded
at Trident Studios, London; between January and June, 1971.

Released:
January 1972

Chart peaks:
4 (UK) 3 (US)

Personnel:
Harry Nilsson (v, p, Mellotron); Richard Perry (Mellotron, pc); Roger Coolen (o); Gary Wright (p); Ian Duck (g); Caleb Quaye (g); Chris Spedding (g); John Uribe (g); Herbie Flowers (b); Klaus Voormann (b); Jim Gordon (d); Roger Pope (d); Jim Price (horns)

Track listing:
Gotta Get Up; Driving Along; Early In The Morning; The Moonbeam Son; Down; Without You; Coconut; Let The Good Times Roll; Jump Into the Fire; I'll Never Leave You

Running time:
35.48

Current CD:
ND83464

Further listening:
For the rocking Nilsson, the aptly-named follow-up, Son Of Schmilsson (1973); for the more delicate Nilsson, Harry (1969).

Further reading:
www.jadebox.com/nilsson

Isaac Hayes
Black Moses

Fourth album of seductive self-indulgent soul with a bitter-sweet undertow.

By 1971 Isaac Hayes was a cultural icon – a renowned writer and producer with David Porter for Stax, an esteemed solo artist and a Grammy and Academy Award winner for his third album, the soundtrack to Shaft. With the difficult prospect of writing the follow-up, he entered the recording studios in March of that year and emerged with this sprawling epic. Lavishly packaged with a fold out sleeve that formed a cross four feet high by three feet wide, it pictured Hayes as Moses, resplendent in a robe by the water.

It was Stax minder Dino Woodard who had dubbed Hayes with the Black Moses moniker. "I had nothing to do with it," admits Isaac, "I was kicking and screaming all the way. But when I saw the relevance and effect that it had on people, it wasn't a negative thing." With Hayes' increasing popularity and success however, came a downside. Production and presentation became more extravagant and more often than not completely over the top.

"There's a difference in his music from what he produced when he took a bus to the studio," explains Larry Shaw, Stax's creative editor and man behind the sleeve artwork, "as opposed to when he took a limousine". Yet *Black Moses* is arguably Hayes' most personal and emotionally intense work. He would often write about a love gone bad, but this time he was writing about it from experience. "I was going through the break-up of my marriage. I was heartbroken. That's the only way I could express myself," says Isaac. As a result, he doesn't remember the sessions with particular affection, they weren't much fun. At one point he had to call his secretary into the studio so that he could focus on her while singing, "I was at the mic, tears running down my face. I needed somebody to just hold on to at the time".

Of the 14 songs, three are extended Ike Raps – long, spoken narratives – and 12 are covers. Hayes had a knack of using a familiar song as the starting block for something new. The Jackson 5's Never Can Say Goodbye is stripped bare of its pop origins and reborn as a mammoth tear-jearker, A Brand New Me becomes sheer sensual celebration and Your Love Is Doggone Good completely overshadows The Whispers' original. And if all that wasn't enough, fans could also send off for their very own hand-woven Black Moses robe for a mere $24.95.

Record label:
Stax

Produced
by Isaac Hayes.

Recorded
at Stax Studios, Memphis; spring 1971.

Released:
February 1972

Chart peaks:
38 (UK) 10 (US)

Personnel:
Isaac Hayes (p, vibes, o, electric piano, v); Lester Snell (electric piano); Charlie Pitts (g, rg); Willie Hall (d, tambourine); Gary Jones (bongos, congas); Ronald Hudson (b); Hot Buttered Soul (bv); Sidney Kirk (p); The Bar-kays (bv); Pat Lewis (backing vocal arrangement)

Track listing:
Never Can Say Goodbye; (They Long To Be) Close To You; Nothing Takes The Place Of You; Man's Temptation; Never Gonna Give You Up; Medley: i. Ike's Rap II; ii. Help Me Love; Need To Belong To Someone; Good Love; Medley i. Ike's Rap III ii. Your Love Is So Doggone Good; For The Good Times; I'll Never Fall In Love Again; Part Time Love; Medley i. Ike's Rap IV ii. A Brand New Me; Going In Circles

Running time:
95.00

Current CD:
CDSXE2 033

Further listening:
essential soundtrack, Shaft (1971); Hot Buttered Soul – his debut album, including the epic By The Time I Get To Phoenix (1969); Isaac's Moods – a comprehensive introduction which unfortunately contains some abbreviated versions (1988).

Further reading:
Soulsville USA: The Story Of Stax Records (Rob Bowman, 1997)

Don McLean
American Pie

Anyone for money-spinning albatross.

J ust weeks before the single American Pie topped the US
charts in January 1972, Don McLean was a virtual unknown
outside the coffee houses and college campus bars of the US
folk circuit. Yet before winter was out, there were very few
record-buyers in the Western hemisphere who weren't
wondering whether the States had finally found a "new Bob
Dylan" for the '70s. The song had all the hallmarks of a truly
epochal recording, somehow managing in the era of Nixon and
Vietnam to both celebrate that nation's downhome values –
whisky-drinking good ol' boys, Chevvies taken to the levee,
rock'n'roll dances, high-school romances – while strongly
suggesting that the age of post-war innocence had long since
passed. The references to Buddy Holly's death in 1959 ("The day
the music died"), and veiled allusions to Elvis, Bob Dylan and
the Stones, add to the song's deeply symbolic undertow: but as
he refuses to shed any light on the lyrics himself, it's left to
being mostly a *feel* thing. Triumphant, elegiac, happy, sad –
American Pie is all these things and more.

Two years before American Pie's breakthrough, McLean
had been picked by Pete Seger to join a crew of folkies on The
Hudson River Sloop restoration benefit (sailing up the Hudson
river by day, singing and writing songs by night). The experience was invaluable, but McLean had to wait until his recording
contract with the Mediarts label was bought up by United
Artists for his big break. American Pie would probably have
made him famous just by itself, but the parent album of the
same name showed he was no one-trick pony. Most of the
tracks were set to a sparse backing of acoustic guitar and piano,
with songs like Winter Wood, Crossroads and Empty Chairs
offering quiet, reflective and profoundly felt meditations on a
screwed-up, morally bankrupt world, where birds still sing
despite the gloom; yet there were also occasional rock combo
arrangements – as on the title track and the chilling, anti-'Nam
statement The Grave – to give *American Pie* some rock muscle.

It was, though, McLean's ruminations on Van Gogh that
provided the album's second enduring triumph, his gentle,
precise picking and clean, arresting tenor ensuring that "Starry,
starry night, paint your palette blue and grey" is up there with
some of the most memorable opening lines of all time.

Record label:
United Artists

Produced
by Ed Freeman

Recorded
in New York, autumn 1971

Released:
February 1972

Chart peaks:
3 (UK) 1 (US)

Personnel:
Don McLean (v, ag), Lee Hays (a)

Track listing:
American Pie (Parts 1 & 2); Till
Tomorrow; Vincent; Crossroads; Winterwood;
Empty Chairs; Everybody Loves Me, Baby;
Sister Fatima; The Grave; Babylon

Running time:
36.10

Current CD:
EMI CDFA3023

Further listening:
Tapestry (1971) is his belatedly recognised debut and home to Castles In The
Air; American Pie – The Greatest Hits is
exactly what it says on the tin.

Further reading:
John Tobler's sleeve note on American
Pie – the Greatest Hits sketches out
the basics of his career; Billboard's book
of Number 1 singles offers an insightful
look into his craft. Also check out
www.don-mclean.com

Al Green
Let's Stay Together

Secular or sacred, he was soul's most seductive singer.

William Mitchell, mastermind of the unmistakable soft soul sound of Memphis's Hi Records, was pushing his protégé Al Green pretty hard during the recording of *Let's Stay Together*. As the hours wore on towards the 100 they would spend on just the title track, Green was growing increasingly frustrated.

"Al's like my son, but he objected a lot," recalls Mitchell in a soft drawl. "He said, 'Well, what you want?' I said, I want *YOU*. He's got a pretty voice and I wanted him to put that prettiness in it. Well, we got it. I think I captured everything I wanted to on that record."

Twenty-five years old at the time, Green was a rising star. He'd met Mitchell in 1969, and after flopping with Beatles covers and having a minor R&B hit with the Temptations' I Can't Get Next To You, the two men had refined their style, tapping both Green's gospel roots and Mitchell's background in jazz. In 1971 Tired Of Being Alone reached Number 11 on the pop charts, but Mitchell believed there was more room for Green to cross over to the white pop audience. The song he pinned his hopes on was Let's Stay Together, a gorgeous plea for love he'd co-written with Green and Al Jackson, drummer for the MGs.

"This was a transition record," recalls Mitchell. "Softer, more melodic, with more jazzy chords." Let's Stay Together would eventually top both the R&B and pop charts, making it the only Number 1 song of Green's long career. Over Mitchell's gently pulsing arrangement of strings, horns and vocals floats Green's ethereal voice, perhaps the most intimate in the music world. The lyrics sound like a lover's plea, but Green insists he was writing also about the social upheavals of the '60s.

"I was trying to figure out where we were all going. You know, 'Whether times are good or bad, happy or sad.'" Brotherhood was treasured at Hi. Situated in gritty south Memphis, the company was smaller than its crosstown rival, Stax, and, as run by Mitchell, very much a family affair. The core of the house band were the Hodges brothers, Teenie on guitar, Leroy on bass and Charles on keyboards. In a sweet if risky nod to brotherhood, Mitchell invited the neighbourhood winos in for this session.

Record label:
Hi Records

Produced
by Willie Mitchell.

Recorded
at Royal Recording Studios, south Memphis; summer and autumn of 1971.

Released:
March 1972

Chart peaks:
None (UK) 8 (US)

Personnel:
Al Green (v); Teenie Hodges (g); Charles Hodges (o, p); Leroy Hodges (b); Al Jackson (d); Howard Grimes (d); Wayne Jackson (t); Andrew Love (ts); Ed Logan (ts); James Mitchell (bs); Jack Hale (t); Willie Mitchell (k, a); Charles Chalmers (oa, bv); Sandra Rhodes (bv); Donna Rhodes (bv)

Track listing:
Let's Stay Together (S); La-La For You; So You're Leaving; What Is This Feeling; Old Time Lovin'; I've Never Found A Girl; How Can You Mend A Broken Heart; Judy; It Ain't No Fun To Me

Running time:
34.05

Current CD:
HILO152

Further listening:
Green Is Blues (1969); I'm Still In Love With You (1972); Call Me(1973)

Further reading:
Sweet Soul Music: Rhythm and Blues and the Southern Dream of Freedom (Peter Guralnick, 1986) has a good chapter; Take Me To The River, Al Green's Autobiography (2000)

Neil Young
Harvest

It transformed him into a singer-songwriter superstar, a role he has been systematically dismantling ever since.

1971 should have been the biggest year in Neil Young's recording life. The combined success of CSN&Y's *Deja Vu* and his own *After The Goldrush* had transformed him into the hottest property among the new breed of LA-based singer-songwriters. Unfortunately, he was in no position to take advantage of his new-found fame by combining his strengths as an electric and acoustic player. Back problems made it difficult for him to even hold an electric guitar, and doctors warned that he might well be confined to a wheelchair unless he underwent an operation to remove some damaged discs. During a slow convalescence, Young was allowed to remain on his feet for only a few hours a day. A laid-back musical style had been forced upon him quite literally: much of the album was written while under sedation, and recorded in a surgical back-brace. As the months passed demand for new product became all the more intense.

He already had a backlog of songs, some of which had been premiered in concert. The grandiose A Man Needs A Maid – featuring an arrangement by Young's longtime friend, Spector sidekick Jack Nitzsche, and recorded with the London Symphony Orchestra during a UK visit – contained some straightforward autobiography: laid up at his northern California ranch, he was watching a movie with a friend and fell in love with the actress, Carrie Snodgress, who would become the mother of his first child, Zeke. During a visit to Nashville, Young met producer Elliot Mazer who assembled a hand-picked team of local musicians. "They just learned the essence of the songs," Mazer recalls. "With somebody like Neil playing acoustic guitar and singing a song the complete vibe is out there. Those guys heard that and we got those tracks in one or two takes." Young's empathy with the musicians was underlined when they casually ran through Heart Of Gold in the first evening, completing a Number 1 hit in record time.

The album, too, quickly topped the charts on both sides of the Atlantic. Critics accused him of dumbing down at the time – "It can only be concluded that Neil Young is not one of those folks whom superstardom becomes artistically," said Rolling Stone, accusing him of "invoking most of the LA variety of superstardom's weariest clichés in an attempt to obscure his inability to do a good imitation of his earlier self" – and there

Record label:
Reprise

Produced
by Elliot Mazer, Neil Young, plus Jack Nitzsche and Henry Lewy; 1972.

Recorded
at Quadrafonic Studios, Nashville; Broken Arrow Studio no. 2, San Francisco; Barking Town Hall, London; Royce Hall, UCLA

Released:
March 1972 (UK); February 20, 1972 (US)

Chart peaks:
1 (UK) 1 (US)

Personnel:
Neil Young (g, v, banjo); Ben Keith (sg); Kenny Buttrey (d); Tim Drummond (b); Jack Nitzsche (p, slide g); John Harris (p); James Taylor (bv); Linda Ronstadt (bv); David Crosby (bv); Graham Nash (bv); Stephen Stills (bv); Danny Whitten (g, bv); Ralph Molina (d, bv); Billy Talbot (b, bv)

Track listing:
Out On The Weekend; Harvest; A Man Needs A Maid; Heart Of Gold (S); Are You Ready For The Country?; Old Man (S); There's A World; Alabama; The Needle And The Damage Done; Words (Between The Lines Of Age)

Running time:
37.38

Current CD:
7599272392

Further listening:
Comes A Time (1978); Harvest Moon (1992)

Further reading:
MOJO 10, 25, 44; Neil Young: Here We Are In The Years (Johnny Rogan, 1982)

was no denying that the album contained its share of saccharine. But *Harvest* can now be seen as simply another facet of Young's musical personality, representing the acoustic, pastoral idyll that usually preceded another barrage of electric howl. It changed Young's standing in the rock world to a degree that seemed unimaginable. Suddenly, he was at a level of fame that eclipsed even that of Crosby, Stills & Nash. Fears that he would take the easy road to MOR blandness, though, soon proved unfounded. Having a chart-topping single was "empty", Young found. "I thought the record was good, but I also knew that something else was dying." As he would later write, "the middle of the road became a bore"; he much preferred the ditches on either side.

Manassas

Manassas

Record label:
Atlantic

Produced
by Stephen Stills, Chris Hillman and Dallas Taylor.

Recorded
at Criteria Sound Studios, Miami, Florida; January–February 1972.

Released:
April 12, 1972

Chart peaks:
12 (UK) 12 (US)

Personnel:
Stephen Stills (g, v, p); Chris Hillman (b, v, mandolin); Al Perkins (sg, bv); Dallas Taylor (d); Joe Lala (congas, pc, bv); Paul Harris (p, k); Calvin Samuels (b); Byron Berline (fiddle); Bill Wyman (b); Sydney George (hm)

Track listing:
Song Of Love; (a) Rock'n'Roll Crazies (b) Cuban Bluegrass; Jet Set (Sigh); Anyway; Both Of Us (Bound To Lose); Fallen Eagle; Jesus Gave Love Away For Free; Colorado; So Begins The Task; Hide It So Deep; Don't Look At My Shadow; It Doesn't Matter; Johnny's Garden; Bound To Fall; How Far; Move Around; The Love Gangster; What To Do; Right Now; The Treasure (Take One); Blues Man

Running time:
72.00

Current CD:
7567828082

Further listening:
Déjà vu (1970); Down The Road (1973)

Further reading:
Crosby, Stills, Nash And Young: The Visual Documentary (1996).

CSN&Y renegade forms crack team whose legacy is this exemplary double.

Double albums were regarded as something of an indulgence by critics in the early '70s, but few complained about this one. Burning with creative zeal and egomaniacal ambition, Stephen Stills assembled the top players in his orbit and soon realized that their combined talents could not be contained within the context of a single album. Having already impressed with two solo albums, Stills seemed determined to display the full range of his abilities over four sides, pointedly titled The Raven, The Wilderness, Consider and Rock'n'Roll Is Here To Stay. The package proved the ultimate artistic CV, embracing bluegrass, country, pop, rock, R&B, blues and Latin. Remarkably, Stills sounds equally comfortable in each genre – a tribute to his canny choice of players, who include ex-Byrd Chris Hillman, country steel guitarist Al Perkins and Jamaican bassist Fuzzy Samuels.

Premiering the new band, Stills announced: "It's not totally a partnership but it's enough of a partnership that everyone's satisfied. It's better than *Crosby, Stills And Nash*, *Deja Vu* and my two solo albums. I'm really proud of it." Echoing the musical diversity, Stills displayed his abilities as a lyricist covering favourite themes like starcrossed love in the Judy Collins tribute So Begins The Task, ecology in Fallen Eagle and a quirky stab at philosophy in Move Around – "What do we do given life? We move around." Bill Wyman was on hand to co-write the bluesy Love Gangster and was supposedly so smitten with the septet that he briefly considered leaving the Rolling Stones to join their ranks. "I nearly jumped off a bridge when I found out about this," Stills roared.

Manassas embarked on a world tour, including appearances in the UK that are still spoken of with reverence by those lucky enough to have attended. Alas the group's unwieldiness ensured that they split after recording a less impressive second album. Unlike other superstar aggregations, they would never reform. Chris Hillman still regards their double album as a seamless piece of work. "A lot of people have said it should have been a single album, but I think it's a great double," he insists. "It's very rare for me to come from a project and say, 'That's wonderful'. Manassas had some really good players in it. It had the capacity to do anything from bluegrass to Latin. It was very rewarding and stimulating for the period it lasted."

Big Star
#1 Record

Debut by legendary underachievers whose influence can be heard in R.E.M., Teenage Fanclub and The Replacements.

Big Star's *#1 Record*? Ironic, of course. But few bands abandon hope before they begin. Although group member Alex Chilton had already experienced fame at its most fickle as the singer of '60s pop-soul hitmakers The Box Tops, the irony he applied to naming his new outfit and their debut album wasn't intended to be damning. Having grown up during the glory days of AM radio, that Beatles-fuelled age when great records often happened to be hits and vice versa, Big Star naturally believed that their own sparkling tunes might likewise rule the airwaves.

Chilton has become acutely uncomfortable with his reputation as a pop avatar. He tends to characterise himself as a fan of Memphis soul and blues who just happened to join a pop/rock group led by that city's biggest Anglophile. "I was joining Chris Bell's band and all I did was to fit in with his concept of the group," he claimed recently. In a 1987 interview, however, he admitted that his relationship with Bell, who co-wrote most of *#1 Record* with him, was one of shared sensibilities: "I loved British music myself. When I first got interested in rock'n'roll, it was when all the British stuff first started coming out. [From] '64 through '66, I thought music was great. But then in '67, when all this psychedelic Californian music started happening, people got more pretentious, but '64 to '66 was still three-minute songs and everything was fairly understandable."

Formed in 1971, Big Star were together only a few months before they went into Ardent Studios to record *#1 Record*. The intense chemistry between Bell and Chilton resulted in a clutch of original songs, none of which sounded like anything else out of Memphis – or anywhere, for that matter.

"After our first run-through of The Ballad Of El Goodo, I thought there was really something magic here," recalls drummer Jody Stephens. "I was so inspired by the songs, by what Alex and Chris were singing and how they sang it. It was a great feeling. For me, recording with Big Star was a Magical Mystery Tour, a trip to Disneyland." The transcendent longings of high-decibel rocker Feel and harmony-draped anthems like My Life Is Right, justified Stephens' enthusiasm, but the album was a flop and, by the end of 1972, Bell had quit to go solo.

Record label:
Ardent

No producer listed.

Recorded
at Ardent Studios, Memphis, Tennessee, late 1971–early 1972.

Released:
April 1972

Chart peaks:
None (UK) None (US)

Personnel:
Chris Bell (g, v); Alex Chilton (g, v); Andy Hummel (b, p, v); Jody Stephens (d, v); John Fry (executive producer)

Track listing:
Feel; The Ballad Of El Goodo; In The Street; Thirteen; Don't Lie To Me; The India Song; When My Baby's Beside Me; My Life Is Right; Give Me Another Chance; Try Again; Watch The Sunrise

Running time:
37.03

Current CD:
ACE AK028

Further listening:
Radio City (1974); Third (1978)

Further reading:
MOJO 75; http://frontlinearts.com/bigstar

Deep Purple
Machine Head

The album which brought us *Smoke On The Water*, the alma mater of every other '70s school rock band.

It's a story that's entered rock'n'roll myth: on December 6, 1971, Deep Purple arrived at the Montreux Casino, intending to take over the venue for two weeks and record their next album live. But the night before the sessions began, as the Casino hosted its last show of the season, a flare-gun-toting Zappa fan fired into the ceiling. The roof went up, the Casino burned down and Purple were suddenly homeless. A few alternatives presented themselves – a bank vault and a fall-out shelter among them – but the band eventually rented space at the Grand Hotel. They also had a day or so at the nearby Pavilion, and it was there that Purple made history. "We were kicked out because of the noise," bassist Glover recalls. "The only thing we recorded there was a riff of Ritchie's which we called Title #1, and the police were actually outside banging on the doors, the roadies were holding the doors shut while we recorded it – one can almost hear the banging as the song fades out. So we finished the track, but we really didn't think much of it. When we went back to it a week later it was, 'Oh, what are we going to write over this?' So we wrote something, put it on the album, and that was it." "It" just happened to be Smoke On The Water.

The sessions were tight. "What you get is what we did," says Glover. "There were no out-takes, no alternate versions. When I came to remaster *Machine Head* for the anniversary edition, that was the challenge. All there was were those eight songs and a little bit of banter – right at the end of Lazy you hear somebody, I think it's me, going 'wooh!' And that speaks volumes because there's so little else." Nevertheless, Purple wound up with what would be instantly proclaimed a hard rock classic, home to at least four future Purple live staples (Lazy, Smoke, Highway Star and Space Truckin' all reappear on the seminal *Made In Japan*) and, of course, repository of one of the most instantly recognisable riffs in rock.

"The funny thing is, when *Machine Head* came out the song we thought was going to be big was Never Before. We put a lot of work into that, a nice middle eight, polished performances, properly mixed. No-one ever expected Smoke to take off."

Record label:
Harvest

Produced
by Deep Purple.

Recorded
at Grand Hotel, Montreux; December 6–21, 1971.

Released:
April 1972

Chart peaks:
1 (UK) 7 (US)

Personnel:
Ian Gillan (v); Ritchie Blackmore (g); Roger Glover (b); Jon Lord (k); Ian Paice (d)

Track listing:
Highway Star; Maybe I'm A Leo; Pictures Of Home; Never Before; Smoke On The Water; Lazy; Space Truckin'

Running time:
37.44

Current CD:
31002

Further listening:
Deep Purple In Rock (1970); Made In Japan (1973)

Further reading:
Child In Time (Ian Gillan and David Cohen, 1994); www.deep-purple.com

Mellow Candle
Swaddling Songs

Overlooked folk classic. Yours for upwards of £500.

Had Clodagh Simonds and Alison O'Donnell been to a more permissive school, it's hard to say whether Mellow Candle's small legacy would have been so remarkable. But at the Holy Child Convent School in Killiney, Dublin, the '60s didn't get much of a look-in among all the Bible-reading and talking to God. As a result, the girls were forced to conduct their discourse with pop music beneath the bedsheets, covertly listening to Radio Luxembourg. These two very different lives – one for the days, the other at nights – finally started seeping into each other when Simonds, aged only 12, began to write a whole succession of baroque, hymnal pop songs on her parents' piano. One of them, *Lonely Man* featured lyrics that went, "Lonely man looking for the day/Damns the night whose stars have left him cold." This much we know because, amazingly, it was good enough to end up on *Swaddling Songs*.

By the time Simonds and O'Donnell formed their first band, briefly called The Gatecrashers, aged 15, their musical vision was complete. But it was four years before *Swaddling Songs* emerged. Events in the interim almost killed off Mellow Candle's appetite for music. They released just one single on Simon Napier-Bell's SNP label before it folded, forcing the girls to return to Dublin and complete their studies. This at least allowed Mellow Candle the time to expand into practitioners of peerlessly explosive psychedelic folk. John Peel caught them at the 1971 Wexford Festival and came away a fan: "The seeds of something good are there," he proclaimed.

A year later, now living in London, Mellow Candle had gathered the makings of an extraordinary album. Medieval pop gems like Heaven Heath and Reverend Sisters set the tone, punctuated by almost operatic excursions like The Poet And The Witch. Simonds and Williams' lyrics often depicted a merciless world, free of spiritual comforts. On paper, Mellow Candle's realm of "bold bright-eyed saints", "shadows of unicorns", "sailing angels", ravens crying "Beware!" and "Solstice [that] brings the chill winds to an end" should have amounted to the most enormous folly. Indeed, according to the CD reissue notes, Simonds is now "reluctant to consider the Mellow Candle album as anything other than an old if charming skeleton in the closet." A shame, because despite the indifferent reception that caused Mellow Candle to disband, *Swaddling Songs* repays repeated listening.

Record label:
Deram

Produced
by David Hitchcock.

Recorded
at Decca Studios, Tollington Park, London; December 1971.

Released:
April 1972

Chart peaks:
None (UK) None (US)

Personnel:
Clodagh Simonds (v, p); Alison Williams (v); David Williams (g, v); Frank Boylan (b, v); William A Murray (d)

Track listing:
Heaven Heath; Sheep Season; Silver Song; The Poet And The Witch; Messenger Birds; Dan The Wing (S); Reverend Sisters; Break your Token; Buy Or Beware; Vile Excesses; Lonely Man; Boulders On My Grave

Running time:
43.14

Current CD:
See For Miles (import) SEECD 404

Further listening:
The Virgin Prophet: Unreleased Sessions 1969–71 (1996) – unofficial collection of demos and unreleased recordings

Further reading:
http://website.lineone.net/~geoff.burton/mellowc/mellowc.html

The Rolling Stones
Exile On Main Street

The record that distilled the Stones mystique, often hailed as the greatest rock album ever made.

The album which holds pride of place in the Stones' mythology has a shambling, expansive feel on the surface, but is underpinned by a brooding, barbarous quality which reflects the trying conditions in which it was recorded. Having left Britain to avoid paying their taxes, the band set up shop for the summer in the basement of Keith Richards's villa in the south of France, recording on their 16-track mobile. The house had been the headquarters of the Gestapo during the Nazi occupation of France. The sessions turned into what's been described as "the biggest house party of Keith's hospitable career."

"It was a right sodding pain in the arse, actually," Mick Taylor recalls. "We bloody hated it almost from the moment we started work on it – thought it was crap. Keith wanted to trash it all and start again." In the makeshift studio there was barely room to accommodate the instruments. Engineer Andy Johns vividly remembers the swastika-shaped air-conditioning ducts, and overdubs being done in the kitchen while people were "sitting at the table talking; knives, forks, plates clanking."

"It was party time all the fucking time," agrees Taylor. "It's a wonder we got anything done, the place was so overrun with people. Plus it was damp and cold. Keith and I got boils. Very unpleasant." After some weeks, with no end in sight, Keith's wife Anita became volubly peeved about the occupying forces who'd invaded their home. Meanwhile, to the evident chagrin of Richards, Mick Jagger was away for much of the time with his heavily pregnant bride Bianca.

"Jagger came in and did a bit of poncing about as usual, but Keith guided that one to completion," confirms Taylor. "It was ideal for Keith because all he had to do was fall out of his bed, roll downstairs and voila, he was at work."

Material left in the can from *Sticky Fingers*, such as Sweet Black Angel (known to Keith as Bent Green Needles), was reworked and, though its looseness would suggest otherwise, work on every aspect of the album was fastidious. Tumbling Dice alone took almost two weeks to nail, with over 150 takes before one captured the groove Keith was seeking. In all, the sessions lasted for six months. A further six were spent mixing in Hollywood. Chaotic it may have been, but the group's chemistry was never again so strong.

Record label:
Rolling Stones Records

Produced
by Jimmy Miller.

Recorded
at Rolling Stones Mobile, Nellcôte, France;
May–September 1971.

Released:
May 12, 1972

Chart peaks: ·
1 (UK) 1 (US)

Personnel:
Mick Jagger (v, g, hm); Keith Richards (g, v, b, p); Bill Wyman (b); Charlie Watts (d); Mick Taylor (g, b); Nicky Hopkins (p); Ian Stewart (p); Bobby Keyes (s); Jim Price (t, tb); Bill Plummer (db); Jimmy Miller (pc); Al Perkins (psg); Mac Rebennack (o, bv); Tammi Lynn, Kathi McDonald, Clydie King, Jerry Kirkland, Shirley Goodman, Joe Green, Vanetta Fields (bv)

Track listing:
Rocks Off; Rip This Joint; Hip Shake; Casino Boogie; Tumbling Dice; Sweet Virginia; Torn & Frayed; Black Angel; Loving Cup; Happy; Turd On The Run; Ventilator Blues; Just Wanna See His Face; Let It Loose; All Down The Line; Stop Breaking Down; Shine A Light; Soul Survivor

Running time:
69.16

Current CD:
CDV 2731

Further listening:
Goat's Head Soup (1973)

Further reading:
The True Adventures Of The Rolling Stones (Stanley Booth, 1975)

Rory Gallagher
Live In Europe

Gallagher was the first real Irish rock star, this his only UK Top 10 album.

*L*ive In Europe was Rory's third solo album, recorded during a frenetic and extraordinarily creative 18-month period after splitting psychedelic power trio Taste at the height of their popularity. The two studio albums from 1971, *Rory Gallagher* and *Deuce*, chronicled Rory's maturing as an artist and introduced a more crafted and varied aspect to his work.

Gallagher had created his own sound on these albums, drawing from modern jazz, urban and Delta blues, hillbilly flat-picking, heads-down rock and Celtic folk. On slide and acoustic there was a passing affinity with Jimmy Page; his use of the guitar's volume controls, feedback and sublime tone was more akin to Free's Paul Kossoff; while quirky power-pop classics like Laundromat – along with In Your Town, one of only two previous recordings reprised on *Live In Europe* – doffed a cap to Pete Townshend. It was a potent, and very popular, concoction. "A lot of groups get annoyed with audiences that are too rowdy, but I think I know where the line is," said Rory in 1971. "You don't see the old greats on the blues scene preaching about sitting still."

With two posthumous Taste in-concert sets to compete with, *Live In Europe* had to be good, and it was: a definitive snapshot of what made Gallagher great on-stage. Two more concert albums appeared before his untimely death in 1995, but neither has the masterfully channelled energy nor breadth of palette as *Live In Europe* – purportedly the album that inspired future U2 members Adam Clayton and The Edge to form a band. This period marked the height of Rory's public and critical popularity. He did sessions for old heroes Muddy Waters and Jerry Lee Lewis, turned down serious invitations to join The Rolling Stones and Deep Purple, and ousted Eric Clapton as Best Guitarist in 1972's Melody Maker poll. The following year the title went to another non-Brit, Jan Akkerman from Dutch band Focus. They were both 'outsiders' who won.

"I never had the pleasure to meet him," says Akkerman, "but I knew his playing and I admired it. He was the king of the white blues players as far as I'm concerned." Many others have since agreed.

Record label:
Polydor

Produced
by Rory Gallagher.

Recorded
at various European shows;
February–March 1972.

Released:
May 1972

Chart peaks:
9 (UK) None (US)

Personnel:
Rory Gallagher (v, g, mandolin, hm);
Gerry McAvoy (b); Wilgar Campbell (d)

Track listing:
Messin' With The Kid; Laundromat; I Could've Had Religion; Pistol Slapper Blues; Going To My Home Town; In Your Town; Bullfrog Blues

Running time:
45.31

Current CD:
74465996852 adds: What In The World; Hoodoo Man

Further listening:
Rory Gallagher (1971); Deuce (1971)

Further reading:
MOJO 59; Irish Rock (Mark J Prendergast, 1987)

Spring

Spring

Brian Wilson borrows the immaculate sound and emotional focus of The Beach Boys' late '60s work for a girl group gem.

Brian Wilson's first non-Beach Boys production job was Shoot The Curl for The Honeys – Marilyn and Diane Rovell and their cousin Ginger Blake – released in May 1963. Brian produced three other Honeys singles, the last and best, Tonight Belongs To Me, recorded in late 1968. Like all Brian's extra-curricular production work, the tracks echoed The Beach Boys' style but were all commercial failures. Marilyn Rovell (Brian's future wife) and Diane would go on to sing backing vocals on Beach Boys albums well into the '70s. But in November 1971, the two of them – minus cousin Ginger – were reborn as Spring, and released a debut single, Carole King's Now That Everything's Been Said. They retained the Honeys' girl group sound but displayed a greater sophistication, and the evocation of wonder and loss in their vocals echoed *Pet Sounds*.

For Brian, Spring was an outlet for his talents unhampered by the commercial pressures of The Beach Boys, and recording at the Wilsons' home studios made for a relaxed and creative ambience. Marilyn, speaking at the time, explained: "The idea was to record all the songs that we ever loved. Brian helped out in all departments – he sang, arranged most of the backgrounds, wrote some of the songs and picked the material. He was very emotional throughout and would cry at the sessions because he liked a song so much he couldn't believe it." Most intriguing is Thinking About You, originally produced by Brian for Sharon Marie in 1964 but *Spring* also benefits from the presence of *Sunflower* tracks This Whole World and brother Dennis Wilson's lovely ballad Forever. This Whole World is a real high point, adding a bridge ("starlight, starbright") with a stunning harmony between Brian and the girls which tops the Boys' own version. Marilyn and Diane imbue these songs with extraordinary emotion and innocence.

Dynamic and expansive, *Spring* is an uncomplicated, unpretentious – and largely unheard – record, as fine as anything Brian Wilson ever produced.

Record label:
United Artists

Produced
by Brian Wilson, Stephen Desper and David Sandler.

Recorded
at Brian Wilson's studio; throughout 1970.

Released:
May 1972

Chart peaks:
None (UK) None (US)

Personnel:
Marilyn Rovell, Diane Rovell (v); Brian Wilson (v, all instruments, a)

Track listing:
Tennessee Waltz; Think 'Bout You Baby; Mama Said; Superstar; Awake; Sweet Mountain; Everybody; This Whole World; Forever; Good Time; Now That Everything's Been Said (S); Down Home

Running time:
40.33

Current CD:
REP4472WP

Further listening:
The Beach Boys, Sunflower (1970)

Further reading:
www.geocities.com/Heartland/8303/brian/honeys.htm

Wishbone Ash

Argus

"The British Allman Brothers" surprise themselves by recording a classic.

Formed in 1969 when Martin Turner and Steve Upton, remnants of a West Country beat group, advertised in Melody Maker for a new guitarist – and couldn't decide between Andy Powell and Ted Turner – Wishbone Ash became and remain, however fluctuating latterday line-ups have been, owners of a most distinctive 'sound'. Initially the British answer to the Allman Brothers – a twin lead guitar blues/boogie outfit – by their second album *Pilgrimage* (1971) influences of a decidedly more pastoral and English nature had been absorbed. Pentangle and Fairport Convention, for example, were of equal importance to guitarist Andy Powell as The Who, and by this stage the group were finding their feet as writers.

Incessant road work and the fearless door-openings achieved by their young American manager Miles Copeland had resulted in the group claiming Melody Maker's Brightest Hope award for 1971. *Argus*, their third album, would not only be their best-selling release but also, beyond question, their best work. It had been the happy combination of youthful energy, two weeks between touring to write the songs and a little convenient geography: "We were all living in the same street in the Ladbroke Grove area," says Andy Powell, "and I can remember the influences just tumbling out. Most of it was written on acoustic guitars, in each others bedsits – running from one bedsit to the next, exchanging ideas for guitar melodies, Martin feverishly writing out lyrics . . . There also was a lot of Bible-reading going on at the time. It was just a good spirit. But perhaps *Argus* promised a lot more than we delivered afterwards. I think we felt that we'd tapped into a spiritual vein and that we were opening our hearts out and maybe we got a bit self-conscious and didn't want to sound too pretentious."

In a way, Argus was Wishbone's *Led Zeppelin IV* – powerful, mystical, dynamic. Conversely, 1973's *Wishbone Four* was more akin to *Led Zeppelin III* (right down to its conception in a Welsh cottage). Not a bad record, it just wasn't strong enough to build on *Argus*' surprise success. Ted Turner retired with exhaustion and the band effectively moved to America – filling stadiums, but rarely recapturing what had made *Argus* so special. One curious footnote: the entire album was remixed by Martin Turner in 1989, though the tracks are only available dotted over two compilations, *Time Was* (1993) and *Distillation* (1997).

Record label:
MCA

Produced by
Derek Lawrence.

Recorded
at De Lane Lea Studios, London;
January–February 1972.

Released:
May 1972

Chart peaks:
3 (UK) None (US)

Personnel:
Martin Turner (v, b); Andy Powell (g, v); Ted Turner (g, v); Steve Upton (d); Martin Birch (e)

Track listing:
Time Was; Sometime World; Blowin' Free (S); The King Will Come; Leaf And Stream; Warrior; Throw Down The Sword

Running time:
45.08

Current CD:
MCLD 19085 adds: No Easy Road

Further listening:
4-CD box set of classic, live and rare Ash, Distillation (1997).

Further reading:
The Illustrated Collector's Guide To Wishbone Ash (Andy Powell, 1989); www.wishboneash.com

Stevie Wonder
Music Of My Mind

Stevie meets Tonto for electro.

At the age of 18, after six years of writing and singing big hits for Motown Records and Jobete Publishing, Stevie Wonder downed tools. He stopped recording and composing, fed up with his role on the Motown assembly line, and waited out his contracts for three years. In May 1971, he turned 21, came into the vast sum of royalties sitting in his trust fund, and was free from the shackles of the Motown machine. Determined to prove himself, he ignored Motown's urgings to work with their house producers and, instead, chose Bob Margouleff and Malcolm Cecil, who made records under the name Tonto's Expanding Headband. Stevie was taken by his bass player, Ronnie Blanco, to Tonto's studio in the Mediasound complex in mid-town NYC. Cecil recalls looking out the window and seeing Blanco standing there with some guy in shades and a pistachio green cape on. When Cecil realised it was Stevie, he dialled his partner Margouleff, imploring him to come over immediately. It was Memorial Day Weekend (the last weekend in May). Stevie sat down in the studio that Saturday afternoon, and by Monday night they'd recorded an amazing 17 tracks. Six of them became part of *Music of My Mind*.

Out of gratitude to Berry Gordy and Ewart Abner, owner and president of Motown, respectively, Stevie re-signed to Motown, delivering his first new album at the signing in December 1971. When Abner did not hear a traditional Stevie single on the album he was angry. But when the record was released in the first quarter of 1972 to critical raves, he changed his tune. *Music Of My Mind* started to sell to an across-the-board audience, a fact which was not wasted on Motown's marketing people. Three months into the release, they finally got behind the album with Superwoman, Happier Than The Morning Sun and Keep On Running garnering consistent airplay. It took two years before Motown sweetened the pot enough to re-sign Stevie to Jobete as a writer. It cost them $13 million and half the publishing which stayed with Stevie's Black Bull Music company.

Record label:
Motown

Produced
by Stevie Wonder.

Recorded
at Media Sound NYC, Electric Lady NYC, and Crystal Studios LA, California; May 1971–December 1971.

Released:
May 1972

Chart peaks:
None (UK); 21 (US)

Personnel:
Stevie Wonder (all instruments, v); Buzzy Feiten (g); Art Baron (tb); Lani Groves, Jim Gilstrap (bv); Malcolm Cecil; Bob Margouleff (e, syn programming)

Track listing:
Love Having You Around; Superwoman; I Love Every Little Thing About You; Sweet Little Girl; Happier Than The Morning Sun; Girl Blue; Seems So Long; Keep On Running; Evil

Running time:
48.06

Current CD:
Motown/Universal 5300282

Further listening:
The albums that followed belong together as a listening experience: Talking Book (1973), Innervisions (1973) and Songs In The Key Of Life (1976) complete a quartet that few, if any, artists might equal in a lifetime.

Further reading:
Stevie Wonder (John Swenson, 1994)
www.insoul.com/stevie

David Bowie

The Rise And Fall Of Ziggy Stardust And The Spiders From Mars

The alter-ego has landed.

" A star is born," proclaimed Melody Maker when Ziggy emerged. But it had been a helluva gestation, from Marquee R&B nights via Buddhism and the Beckenham Arts Lab to avant-garde mime. Now Bowie's moment had finally arrived and, under the wing of tough New York manager Tony DeFries and his MainMan set-up, he seized every opportunity to realise long-held dreams of fame.

The attention garnered by *Hunky Dory* – released just six months earlier – helped set the scene, as had the "confession" to the music press at the start of 1972 that he was "gay and always have been, even when I was David Jones".

Then came the first single, Starman, which revealed an androgynous glam creation to a generation of young dudes eager for flamboyant imagery and hard-edged pop. The new fans lapped up such gestures as the key Top Of The Pops appearance when Bowie, vermilion-haired in a skintight jumpsuit and painted nails, camply slung a provocative arm around Mick Ronson during the guitarist's solo.

Ziggy, an amalgam of Bowie's heroes Marc Bolan, Iggy Pop and Vince Taylor, is an apocalyptic rock star whose rise and fall comes just in time for the end of the world. Arguably pop's first post-modern construct, the album enabled Bowie to simultaneously explore and flaunt his own hunger for stardom. "No one has seen anything like this before," he boasted to pop potboiler George Tremlett in 1972. "That's what's missing in pop music now, entertainment. There's not much outrageousness left."

On *Ziggy*, the trusty Ronson marshalls the Spiders into providing a tough and concise musical backdrop which allows every song to shine. Highlights include remarkable scene-setter Five Years, the pre-punk hysteria exhibited on Star, magical bi-ballad Lady Stardust and the overwrought beauty of Rock'n'Roll Suicide. "Bowie has arrived – a worthy pin-up with such style," declared Melody Maker's Ray Coleman.

Some of the tracks had been around for a while: both Hang Onto Yourself and Moonage Daydream were given a test

Record label:
RCA

Produced
David Bowie and Ken Scott.

Recorded
at Trident Studios, London; September 1971–January 1972.

Released:
June 9, 1972

Chart peaks:
5 (UK) 75 (US)

Personnel:
David Bowie (g, s, v); Mick Ronson (g, p, v); Trevor Bolder (b); Mick Woodmansey (d)

Track listing:
Five Years; Soul Love; Moonage Daydream; Starman (S); It Ain't Easy; Lady Stardust; Star; Hang Onto Yourself; Ziggy Stardust; Suffragette City; Rock'N'Roll Suicide

Running time:
38.48

Current CD:
EMI CDP7944002 adds: John I'm Only Dancing; Velvet Goldmine; Sweet Head; Ziggy Stardust (2); Lady Stardust (2)

Further listening:
Aladdin Sane (1973)

Further reading:
MOJO 49; David Bowie's The Rise And Fall Of Ziggy Stardust And The Spiders From Mars (Mark Paytress, 1999)

run by Bowie under the name Arnold Corns, fronted by Ziggy clothes designer Freddie Burrell, but Bowie was also soaking up American rock influences. In the studio he warned engineer Ken Scott that he wasn't going to like the music "because it's much more like Iggy Pop . . . more rock'n'roll".

With the perma-outrageous Angie at his side and DeFries at the controls, Bowie willed his stardom into existence. Journalists were flown in from the US to witness a Ziggy showcase at Friars Club, Aylesbury and the British press were granted short interviews at the Dorchester. In reality, the Bowies were still ensconced in their £7 a week abode in Beckenham.

But not for long. *Ziggy* worked as well live as on record and Bowie's career obligingly went supernova. US music biz magazine Cashbox described *Ziggy* as "an album to take you into the 1980s". And many a decade beyond.

Aphrodite's Child
666

A double helping of Greek rock opera.

B orn Evangelos Odyssey Papathanassou in March 1943. As early as 1963 he was anxious to express his classical keyboard chops in a pop format and devised Aphrodite's Child, which – like much later UK equivalent The Nice – was a neo-classical rock trio: bass and drums providing the foundation while the Athenian wizard flew around a bank of keyboards.

They quickly became Greece's most extraordinary band and began to look further afield, moving to France in 1967. The bass player and singer was Egyptian born Demis Roussos, possessor of a remarkable, high sob of a voice, which was put to good use on their single, Rain And Tears, a hit all over Europe (making Number 27 in the UK) in 1968. An album *The End Of The World*, provided further European hits.

Feeling that wider acceptance was eluding them, the group disbanded and Vangelis returned to Greece to write with poet Costas Ferris. They came up with an extravagant vision of the apocalypse and the group reformed to record this ambitious rock opera complete with a Greek chorus, a posh English narrator, five minutes of female orgasm (Irene Pappas gasping "I am to come, I was" over and over, years before Clare Torry's throes of ecstasy on *Dark Side Of The Moon*), the massive 19 minute rock-out montage, All The Seats Were Occupied, and a charming, puzzling closing song Break (sung by drummer Lucas Sideras) which, when released as a single some time after the group had disbanded, almost made the British charts.

The album's lush arrangements were as startling as any of the progressive era and it have aged better than most, Vangelis having the vision not to lard the record with keyboard noodling but to use an appropriately broad and dark palette and to highlight the excellent playing of guitarist Silver Koulouris. Taxing and costly to make, when *666* failed to fanfare them world-wide, Aphrodite's Child split for the final time. Roussos soon found fame as a bizarre, rotund purveyor of lachrymose ballads that were avidly consumed by Europe's housewives. Vangelis later composed the popular and evocative soundtracks to Chariots Of Fire and Blade Runner.

Record label:
Vertigo

Produced
by Vangelis Papathanassou.

Recorded
at Europasonor Studios, France; 1971.

Released:
June 1972

Chart peaks:
None (UK) None (US)

Personnel:
Vangelis Papathanassou (o, syn, flute, pc, vibes, bv); Demis Roussos (b, v); Lucas Sideras (d, v); Silver Koulouris (g, pc); Harris Halkitis (b, ts, conga, bv); Michel Ripoche (tb, ts); John Forst (narration); Yannis Tsarouchis (Greek text); Irene Pappas (v); Roger Roche (e)

Track listing:
The System; Babylon; Loud Loud Loud; The Four Horsemen; The Lamb; The Seventh Seal; Aegean Sea; Seven Bowls; The Wakening Beast; Lament; The Marching Beast; The Battle Of the Locusts; Do It; Tribulation; The Beast; Ofis; Seven Trumpets; Altamont; The Wedding Of The Lamb; The Capture Of The Beast; *f*; Hic And Nunc; All The Seats Were Occupied; Break (S)

Running time:
78.10

Current CD:
838-430-2

Further listening:
It's Five O'Clock (1970); Vangelis's Earth (1974)

Everly Brothers
The Stories We Could Tell

Rock'n'roll duo retrace their upbringing on this countrified super-harmony excursion.

By 1970, the musical landscape the Everly Brothers had helped shape in the '50s had changed beyond all recognition. For the brothers themselves, successful records had become elusive and, apart from TV guest slots and some routine live work, their career was almost at a standstill. Don made the first break, cutting a truly unusual solo album for A&M that featured Ry Cooder, Spooner Oldham and various Flying Burrito Brothers among its guest players. Inspired by the experience, and enjoying playing with a new crowd brought together by their love of country music, Don saw a way forward for the Everly brand and reunited with Phil in 1972 to make this album, steeped in the emerging new-country sound.

Don and Phil created beautifully poignant arrangements that pointed at a whole new audience, using accomplices which included ex-Byrds, Burritos, Lovin' Spoonfuls and Delaney And Bonnie. Their 1968 album *Roots* had taken the brothers' back-porch past at face value, *Stories* married down-home earthiness to ultra-loose hippie idealism on a selection of songs by contemporary figures like Kris Kristofferson, Rod Stewart, Jessie Winchester, John Sebastian (in whose home the album was recorded) and multi-instrumentalist Dennis Linde. The Everlys themselves turned in breathtaking performances. Set against brooding, churchy keyboards and high, lonesome guitar, their close harmony work was spellbinding. There were tear-drenched ballads, melancholy tales of bar-room regret, Western rock opera in the David Crosby mould and the kind of Nashville gloom that comes with a spoonful of syrup. A timeless slice of Americana, a – mostly unheard – gem.

The following year's *Pass The Chicken And Listen* took the sound a stage further, but neither album revived the Everlys' career and their chronic sibling rivalry, which had spilled over into their love lives, finally exploded on stage in 1973, initiating a split which lasted for 10 years.

Record label:
RCA

Produced by
Paul A Rothchild.

Recorded
at the home of John Sebastian, California; 1972.

Released:
June 1972

Chart peaks:
None (UK) None (US)

Personnel:
Don Everly, Phil Everly, Dennis Linde (g,b,k,v); Geoff Muldaur (g); Wayne Perkins (g); John Sebastian (g, v, hrm); Waddy Watchel (g); Danny Weiss (g); Chris Ethridge (b); Clarence White (g); Ry Cooder (g); Buddy Emmons, Jerry McGee (slide g); Barry Beckett, Michael Fonfara (k); Spooner Oldham (k); Warren Zevon (k); Johny Barbata, Jim Gordon (d); Russ Kunkel (d); George Bohanon, Tommy Johnson (brass); Jeff Kent (v); Bonnie Bramlett (v); David Crosby (v); Delaney Bramlett (v); Graham Nash (v)

Track listing:
All I Really Want To Do; Breakdown; Green River; Mandolin Wind; Up In Mabel's Room; Del Rio Dan; Ridin' High (S); Christmas Eve Can Kill You; Three-Armed Poker-Playin' River Rat; I'm Tired Of Singing My Song In Las Vegas; The Brand New Tennessee Waltz; Stories We Could Tell.

Running time:
37.15

Current CD:
CAMDEN 74321 432552. Also contains eight of 12 tracks from Pass The Chicken And Listen

Further listening:
Roots (1968); Pass The Chicken And Listen (1973) and Don Everly's eponymous debut (1971) complete the picture.

Further reading:
The Everly Brothers: Walk Right Back (Roger White, 1998).
www.everly brothers.com

Alice Cooper
School's Out

Cooper's commercial breakthrough included an instant teen rebellion anthem.

Prior to the release of *School's Out*, Alice Cooper, the band, was regarded as a novelty act: grown men dressing up in women's clothes, churning out badly-played blasts of abrasive rage. But to their credit, they invented the horror hard rock genre, with their mutilation of rubber baby dolls, mock executions and, er, pillow fights. One of these resulted in the mutilation of a chicken at a Toronto pop festival in 1969, ensuring the band received universal censure from parents. The onstage theatrics outstripping their musical ability earned them the title of 'worst band in Los Angeles' from some pundits. After moving to a farm outside Detroit, Michigan and hooking up with 21-year-old Canadian producer Bob Ezrin, the band underwent a transformation, honing their musical skills by practising for up to 12 hours a day under his uncompromising tutelage. The iron-fisted work ethic paid off, with contemporary reviewers claiming that "Alice Cooper has finally found their voice".

"Bob Ezrin wasn't the sixth member of Alice Cooper, he was our George Martin," explained Alice Cooper. "We were actually a pretty good psychedelic band, and all of a sudden Bob came along and said, 'You know what? Everybody likes you guys. They love you guys. They love your show, they love everything about it, but there's no musical signature to this.' And so Bob made us stop touring, made us stop writing. He put us in a barn in Detroit for seven months and said, 'We work from 10 in the morning until 10 at night, and all we do is relearn how to be Alice.' He was taking us to another level, and what we didn't understand was we didn't have to give anything up to get there. What he did was make us scarier."

Heralded as a concept album, the entire record was inspired by old movies on late-night television. "We were really affected by West Side Story, but I don't know why. People connected us more with Clockwork Orange than West Side Story – the more modernistic kind of gang thing. But the track Gutter Cats Vs The Jets is a total tribute to West Side Story. If there's a theme in the album, it's gang mentality. The '50s and '60s gang were actually very much part of our life, and we identified with it."

Bob Ezrin concurs. "*School's Out* was recorded when the band was the happiest being Alice Cooper and working together

Record label:
Warner Brothers

Produced
by Bob Ezrin.

Recorded
at the Record Plant, New York and Alice Cooper Mansion, Greenwich, Connecticut; spring 1972.

Release date:
July 1972

Chart peaks:
1 (UK) 2 (US)

Personnel:
Alice Cooper (v); Michael Bruce (g, k); Glen Buxton (g); Dennis Dunaway (b); Neal Smith (d); Dick Wagner (g); Roy Cicala, Shelly Yakus (e)

Track listing:
School's Out (S); Luney Tune; Gutter Cat Vs The Jets; Street Fight; Blue Turk; My Stars; Public Animal #9; Alma Mater; Grande Finale

Running time:
35.59

Current CD:
7599272602

Further listening:
Love It To Death, (1971); Killer (1971), considered by aficionados to be Cooper's best studio album; Greatest Hits (1974)

Further Reading:
Me, Alice (Alice Cooper with Steven Gaines, 1976);
www.netfx.com/~mansion/cooper.html

and were the most respectful of what they were doing – and they were doing their best work. *Billion Dollar Babies* might have been better from an artistic point of view, but in terms of spirit *School's Out* was fabulous. This was the first time that they had ever used a big orchestra, which was fun for me – and kind of goofy and fun for the guys, because it was so incongruous."

"When we wrote [the song] *School's Out* we always said, 'What's the greatest three minutes in your life?'" Alice remembers. "There's two times during the year. One is Christmas morning, when you're just getting ready to open your presents. The greed factor is right there. The next one is the last three minutes of the last day of school when you're sitting there and it's like a slow fuse burning. I said, 'If we can catch that three minutes in a song, it's going to be so big'."

Randy Newman
Sail Away

The world's most sardonic liberal debunks God and America, and nearly charts.

"The feel's good. We don't care if we hit all the notes do we?" That was Randy Newman's cry whenever a melody started to elude him and the producers demanded take 23. "You see I have a real good ear, but I don't have absolute control over my voice," he would assert-confess.

Yet he made those wobbly tones a crucial part of his act. He came from a family of topnotch musicians; uncles Lionel and Alfred scored movies, while uncle Emil conducted the orchestra on *Sail Away*. Serving a songwriting apprenticeship at the legendary Brill Building – and much covered long before he began recording – Newman became an expert pianist and arranger, precise in every detail. But his voice carried the load of human frailty implied by his pithy lyrics. When, for instance, he failed pathetically to hit the high note at the end of Simon Smith And The Amazing Dancing Bear, it was only appropriate.

On his fifth album, *Sail Away*, he was as usual abetted by a friend since childhood in co-producer Lenny Waronker, and top-of-the-range session allies. His ambivalent playlets and in-character monologues lean more to big issues than before. But, like no other, he can handle it, touching every verbal subtlety with a moan of woodwind, a sigh of strings, or his own oblique little piano figures. Then the scratchy front-porch voice delivers the shocks. The 18th-century adman scamming Africans into slavery: "In America you'll get food to eat/Won't have to run through the jungle/And scuff up your feet" (Sail Away). The redneck advising on defence policy: "They don't respect us – so let's surprise them/We'll drop the big one and pulverize them/Boom goes London and boom Paree/More room for you and more room for me" (Political Science). God telling the human race where to get off: "[Man] chases round this desert/Cause he thinks that's where I'll be/How we laugh up here in heaven at the prayers you offer me" (God's Song (That's Why I Love Mankind)).

As often happened to Newman, some told him he was going too far with this last one, debunking people's faith. An atheist, Newman just thought it one of the best pieces he had ever written: "It all clicks together. Those are real good big jokes. I think believers will disagree with me, that's all. I don't wanna hurt anybody's feelings – except assholes and bigots maybe, but that's an extreme case."

Record label:
Reprise

Produced
by Lenny Waronker and Russ Titelman.

Recorded
at Amigo, Western and Poppi Studios, Los Angeles, Jan–Feb 1972.

Released:
July 1972

Chart peaks:
None (UK) 193 (US)

Personnel:
Randy Newman (v, p); Ry Cooder, Russ Titelman (g); Jim Keltner, Gene Parsons, Earl Palmer (d); Chris Ethridge, Wilton Felder, Jimmy Bond (b); Milt Holland (pc); Lee Herschberg (e)

Track listing:
Sail Away (S); It's Lonely At The Top; He Gives Us All His Love; Last Night I Had A Dream; Simon Smith And The Amazing Dancing Bear; Old Man; Political Science (Let's Drop The Big One); Burn On Big River; Memo To My Son (S/US); Dayton, Ohio, 1903; You Can Leave Your Hat On; God's Song (That's Why I Love Mankind)

Running time:
30.38

Current CD:
7599272032

Further listening:
12 Songs (1970); Good Old Boys (1974); Little Criminals (1977); Land Of Dreams (1988); Bad Love (1999) – best of a life's work; always witty, acerbic and joli laid.

Further reading:
MOJO 57

Jorge Ben
Ben

Peak for Brazilian superstar who energised the bossa nova.

Jorge Ben, the son of a Brazilian fishmonger and an Ethiopian immigrant mother, was a former choirboy and an aspirant footballer thwarted by injury when he began hanging out with a trendy crowd on Brazil's Copacabana beach. To entertain his new friends he started composing his own songs and, in 1963, was signed to Philips after just one appearance at The Bottle Club, a hot spot at the epicentre of the bossa nova boom. A&R man Armando Pittigliani was impressed by the young man's versatile voice – sometimes seductively gritty, sometimes sweetly falsetto (as in the brilliant early single Menina) – and his propulsive, compulsive guitar playing. Ben was an overnight sensation, selling over 100,000 copies of his debut Mas Que Neda (But It's Nothing) – which has since become a standard worldwide. He popularised a new strain of high-energy bossa nova, based around the Bantu tribe's maracatu rhythm. His distinctive acoustic guitar style – strumming rhythm parts while simultaneously picking out basslines – which he has described as "the beat of a samba school on its way out the door", was self-taught and hugely influential, particularly when he won the disapproval of bossa nova purists by plugging in his guitar and adding electric R&B feels to the Afro-Brazil-ian blend.

He has experimented with Afro, carnival, jazz and funk and made records with huge percussion-driven bands, small trios, lush, brassy orchestras and once even improvised an entire double album for guitar and voice with Gilberto Gil. He's sung about the Black Panthers (Take It Easy My Brother Charlie), Dostoyevski (As Rosas Eram Todas Amarelas) and his homeland's soccer stars (notably the masterful Umbabaraumba, included by David Byrne on the excellent *Beleza Tropical* compilation).But for this 1972 release he utilised a small band and extracted the maximum effect from his acoustic guitar playing and foot-stamping, creating sexy, irresistible dance music that's richly melodic too. The album's most famous song, the rousing Taj Mahal, had its chorus appropriated by Rod Stewart and Carmine Appice for D'Ya Think I'm Sexy (now co-credited to Ben). But practically every track is a corker.

The man who now "researches into alchemy" in his spare time was forced to adopt the recording name Jorge Ben Jor in 1989 for legal reasons, but still makes good music. However, it's his work of the '70s that's commonly held to be his career best, and has been cited as an influence by non Brazilian pop artists such as Beck and The Beastie Boys.

Record label:
Philips

Produced
by Paulinho Tapajös.

Recorded
at the Phonogram Studios, Brazil; 1972.

Released:
summer 1972

Chart peaks:
None (UK) None (US)

Personnel:
Jorge Ben (g, ag, 12-string guitar, v);
Osmar Milto (a); Luigi Taninho (e)

Track listing:
Morre O Burro Fica O Homem; O Circo Chegou; Paz E Arroz; Moiça; Domingo 23; Fio Maravilha; Quem Cochicha O Rabo Espicha; Caramba; Que Nega É Ess; As Rosas Eram Todas Amarelas; Taj Mahal

Running time:
37.16

Currently unavailable on CD

Further listening:
Jorge Ben – excellent 4-CD box set selected from all his Polygram recordings; O Bidu (Silencio No Brooklin) (1968) his one non-Polygram album of the '60s & '70s has the most peculiar, recorded in a wheelie-bin sound, but is good stuff too.

Further reading:
The Billboard Book Of Brazilian Music (1992)

Yes
Close To The Edge

Yes pull together their influences — pop, jazz, classical — to deliver one of progressive rock's most convincing extended pieces.

*C*lose To The Edge may sound like the most carefully conceived of concept albums, but its creation owed more to chance and deft tape editing. Yes's method of working up new material at the time involved everyone playing live in the rehearsal studio until the music either ground to a halt or someone made a mistake. The band would then go back a few bars and start again. With the tapes rolling, Eddie Offord or a tape operator would be feverishly taking notes. Thus the title piece was patched together from possibly 30 or 40 edits. According to Rick Wakeman, the take of the closing section had to be retrieved from a dustbin full of tape after Offord, working overnight on the master, had spliced on the wrong edit. "When we finally found the right section we were horrified because the sound did not match, there was lots more echo," Wakeman recalls. "But after a few listens it seemed to work, sort of opened the music out, so we reproduced the change when we played the piece live."

The arrival of the classically trained Wakeman had started to "professionalise" the band's methods of composition. On And You And I, Wakeman took Jon Anderson's tune and developed it into an 11-minute opus by varying the chord structure and tempo. Treatises have been written about Anderson's hippy-mystic lyrics, teasing out which lines exactly are inspired by Hesse, Hinduism or Bilbo Baggins. But Wakeman is dismissive: "It's a bit like McCartney's first words for Yesterday were 'scrambled eggs'. Jon used to just make up words in the studio, only he'd keep them if they sounded good." For all the "amateurism and shamateurism" that Bruford, the soon-to-depart drummer later complained of, Close To The Edge still holds together impressively as a work of sustained creativity and inspired playing. "Every element is utilised to enhance or modify mood," noted Rolling Stone, "and you never get the impression that a particular passage was included because Wakeman just found a hot new sound on his Moog and they had to get it in there." The tedium of Tales From Topographic Oceans may have followed, but Close To The Edge was a moment of greatness.

Record label:
Atlantic

Produced
by Eddie Offord and Yes.

Recorded
at Advision Studios, London; early summer, 1972.

Released:
September 13, 1972

Chart peaks:
4 (UK) 3 (US)

Personnel:
Jon Anderson (v); Chris Squire (b, v); Steve Howe (g, v); Rick Wakeman (k); Bill Bruford (d)

Track listing:
Close To The Edge: i. The Solid Time Of Change; ii. Total Mass Retain; iii. I Get Up I Get Down; iv. Seasons Of Man; And You And I: i. Cord Of Life; ii. Eclipse; iii. The Preacher And The Teacher; iv. Apocalypse; Siberian Khatru

Running time:
37.51

Current CD:
7567826662

Further listening:
Fragile (1972); Yessongs (1973)

Further reading:
Yes: The Authorized Biography (Dan Hedges, 1981); for an insight into the obsessive US fan's mind, read Music Of Yes (Professor Bill Martin, 1996); www.yesworld.com

Black Sabbath
Vol 4

Birmingham's heaviest sons record in a blizzard.

By the time Black Sabbath rented a mansion in Bel Air early in '72 to write their fourth album they'd been on the road for three years straight.

"We were completely fried," admits bass player Geezer Butler. "When we got to LA we had six million groupies, booze, coke and heroin – which we sniffed, we never shot up – everything. We were still pretending to enjoy it, but you could feel everyone changing." For drummer Bill Ward in particular, Los Angeles was not a good place to be. "I was getting a bad cocaine addiction. When we decided to try and kick back in LA things got worse because things were so available. Things started to sound different behind that wall of cocaine," states Ward. Such was their infatuation with cocaine that Sabbath decided to call the album Snowblind in tribute to their drug of choice. Their US label, Warner Brothers, baulked at the prospect. "They made us change the name of the album but we left a load of references to coke all over it!" laughs Ozzy Osbourne. "If you listen to the track Snowblind itself you can hear the word 'cocaine' being whispered in those quiet bits. I don't know why they didn't object to that. Maybe they didn't bother listening to it."

But there's a pervading sense of paranoia and self-loathing in songs such as Wheels Of Confusion, the brooding Cornucopia and the semi-acoustic ballad Changes. "Musically it's a good album," says Butler, "but, on a personal level, I think we all have mixed feelings about it." The strength of material like Tomorrow's Dream and the cantering Supernaut (resplendent with Ward's soulful drum break), hides the fact that *Vol 4* marked the beginning of the end for Sabbath. While it would take another seven years for the original line-up to finally split, their own excesses were causing the four friends from Aston to drift apart. "It was easy not to bother talking to each other because we were so fucked," states Ozzy.

"We went totally mad making that album," concludes Geezer. "The album cost around $65,000 dollars to make and we'd spent about $75,000 on coke. We also managed to wreck the house in Bel Air, with Ozzy having water fights with hose pipes inside the house all the time. I didn't realise how nuts we'd gone until I went home and the girl I was with at the time couldn't recognise me!"

"We wish to thank the great COKE-Cola Company of Los Angeles," states the sleeve.

Record label:
Vertigo

Produced
by Patrick Meehan and Black Sabbath.

Recorded
at The Record Plant, Los Angeles; spring 1972.

Released:
September 1972

Chart peaks:
(UK) 8; (US) 13

Personnel:
Ozzy Osbourne (v); Tony Iommi (g); Geezer Butler (b); Bill Ward (d); Colin Caldwell, Vic Smith (e)

Track listing:
Wheels Of Confusion; Tomorrow's Dream (S); Changes; FX; Supernaut; Snowblind; Cornucopia; Laguna Sunrise; St Vitus Dance; Under The Sun

Running time:
43.23

Current CD:
Essential ESM CD 304

Further listening:
The first six Black Sabbath albums – Black Sabbath (1970); Paranoid (1970); Master Of Reality (1971); Vol 4 (1972); Sabbath Bloody Sabbath (1973) and Sabotage (1975) – are described by Henry Rollins as "albums that you can't live without".

Further reading:
Mick Wall's None More Black feature, MOJO 49; live album Reunion (1998) also features a detailed biography written with the band's approval; www.black-sabbath.com

Sandy Denny
Sandy

Sandy's second solo album after quitting Fairport Convention.

Right from the start *Sandy*, with its lavishly glamorous David Bailey cover photo, was the one that Sandy Denny and Island Records believed would establish her as a solo act in her own right. Sandy will always be linked inextricably with Fairport Convention, even though she was with the band for barely 18 months before quitting in late 1969, immediately after the release of the landmark *Liege & Lief*. But, against all advice, Sandy decided to put her solo career on hold and instead formed Fotheringay – who broke-up after one album in 1970. Her engaging but ill-conceived solo debut, *The North Star Grassman & The Ravens*, sold to Fairport fans but did little to expand her audience beyond the university circuit. Sandy did win Melody Maker's prestigious Best Female Vocalist award two years running, and Robert Plant, who met her at the 1970 MM awards ceremony, later admitted: "Sandy (was) my favourite singer out of all the British girls that ever were." She was subsequently invited to sing on Battle Of Evermore for Led Zeppelin's fourth album in 1971, and also appeared in the ill-fated but star-studded stage version of *Tommy*.

So when it came to recording *Sandy* during the spring of 1972, it seemed – with the current vogue for female singer-songwriters such as Carole King, Carly Simon and Joni Mitchell – that the timing couldn't be better for Sandy Denny. The strength of *Sandy* lay in its diversity. Songs like It Suits Me Well, Sweet Rosemary and Bushes And Briars obviously drew on her enthusiasm for, and knowledge of, traditional folk music; while other original compositions – It'll Take A Long Time and Listen, Listen (Tony Blackburn's Radio 1 single of the week!) – displayed Sandy's more commercial side. Even her choice of covers was impeccable and distinctive – Dylan's Tomorrow Is A Long Time was given a rich country tinge; while Richard Farina's Quiet Joys Of Brotherhood (which she had earlier attempted with Fairport) was vividly a cappella, with only Dave Swarbrick's violin for added poignancy at its conclusion.

It remains a mystery why *Sandy* didn't sell. The original compositions were probably the best and most accessible of Sandy's whole career and, perhaps more significantly, her standing was at its highest. But within two years she was back with Fairport. *Sandy* was her crack at the title. And she should have been a contender.

Record label:
Island

Produced
by Trevor Lucas.

Recorded
at Sound Techniques and Island Studios, Basing Street, London; spring 1972.

Released:
September 1972

Chart peaks:
None (UK) None (US)

Personnel:
Sandy Denny (g, v, p); Richard Thompson (g, mn); Pat Donaldson (b); Timi Donald (d); Dave Swarbrick (vn); Pete Kleinow (ps); John Bundrick (p, o); Linda Peters (bv); John Wood (e)

Track listing:
It'll Take A Long Time; Sweet Rosemary; For Nobody To Hear; Tomorrow Is A Long Time; Quiet Joys Of Brotherhood; Listen, Listen (S); The Lady; Bushes And Briars; It Suits Me Well; The Music Weaver

Running time:
40.40

Current CD:
IMCD 132

Further Listening:
Who Knows Where The Time Goes (1985) 3-CD box set; Listen, Listen: An Introduction To Sandy Denny (1999)

Further Reading:
MOJO 55; Meet On The Ledge: Fairport Convention, The Classic Years (Patrick Humphries, 1997)

Genesis

Foxtrot

Prog-rock mavericks reach early creative peak.

The Charterhouse old boys Banks, Rutherford and Gabriel
had imported ex-Flaming Youth drummer Collins and
Fripp-freak guitarist Hackett for their third album, *Nursery
Cryme*, and – though stuffed with bright-eyed invention,
charming acoustic whimsy and black humour – it failed to grab
the imagination of an England more drawn to the blues rock of
Deep Purple and Led Zeppelin. Buoyed by interest in Europe,
Genesis jammed, rehearsed, argued and arranged their music
into a new set of pieces to be recorded as *Foxtrot*. Hackett
describes them as a "songwriting collective" though Banks
remembers "my tastes controlled the group more than the
others, perhaps because I got the most unpleasant if people
didn't agree with me."

Indeed, one producer lasted only a week, with the
band even by-passing usual man David Hitchcock in favour of
engineer John Burns. There was the archetypical Ancient Kings
mythology of Time Table and Can-Utility And The Coastliners,
the Mellotron-drenched sci-fi Watcher Of The Skies with its
maddening 12/8 rhythmic motif and a fantastic satirical mini-
opera Get 'Em Out By Friday. Gabriel's increasing sense of
theatre had made Musical Box and Harold The Barrel the highlights of the previous album, and his multi-voiced
characterisations in the evil-property-developer drama of
Friday were even more vivid. The centre-piece, however, was
the 23-minute Supper's Ready, a seven-part work of extraordinary power and imagination. Inspired in-part by a real-life
supernatural encounter experienced by Gabriel and his wife,
Supper's Ready was a remarkable patchwork achievement. It
ran the gamut of Genesis textures from bass pedal pomp to
enchanting acoustic passages to psychedelic music hall back to
anthemic, soulful rock in an exhaustingly rich exposition on
the forces of good and evil.

Gabriel remains close to and proud of it: "I felt like I
was singing from my soul – almost like singing for my life."
Foxtrot represented a turning point for the band's commercial
and artistic fortunes.

Openly disappointed by *Nursery Cryme*, manager Tony
Stratton-Smith was bowled over upon hearing their follow-up; "I
remember I had to wipe a tear from my eye. Everything that
one had believed about the band had come through."

Record label:
Charisma

Produced
by David Hitchcock.

Recorded
at Island Studios, London;
August–September 1972.

Released:
October 1972

Chart peaks:
12 (UK) None (US)

Personnel:
Tony Banks (o, mellotron, p, syn, 12
string, v); Steve Hackett (g, 12 string-g,
6 string solo); Phil Collins (d, v, pc);
Peter Gabriel (v, flute, bass d,
tambourine, oboe); Michael Rutherford (b,
bass pedal, 12 string-g, v, c)

Track listing:
Watcher Of The Skies; Get 'Em Out By
Friday; Time Table; Can-Utility And The
Coastliners; Horizons; Supper's Ready
(i. Lover's Leap, ii. The Guaranteed
Eternal Sanctuary Man, iii. Ikhnaton And
Itsacon And Their Band Of Merry Men,
iv. How Dare I Be So Beautiful, v. Willow
Farm, vi. Apocalypse In 9/8 (Co-starring
The Delicious Talents Of Gabble Ratchet),
vii. As Sure As Eggs Is Eggs (Aching
Mens' Feet)

Running time:
51.09

Current CD:
CASCDX1058

Further listening:
Nursery Cryme (1971); Selling England By
The Pound (1973)

Further reading:
www.genesis-path.com

Can
Ege Bamyasi

A more questing but approachable music from Germany.

In December 1971, Can left Schloss Norvenich, the castle in which they had recorded double-album *Tago Mago* and their astonishing debut *Monster Movie*, and moved their studio into an old cinema in Weilerswist, some 20 kilometres from Köln, nailing 1,500 army-surplus mattresses to the walls as sound-proofing, and renaming the location Inner Space in memory of the band's original name.

The first music recorded there was Spoon, which was used as the theme music for a popular television thriller, *Das Messer*. Released as a single, it became the group's only Number 1 hit (in Germany). It would be some while before the accompanying album could capitalise on its success, however, due to injunctions taken out by Abi Ofarim (yes, of Cinderella Rockefella fame), the group's former manager, which delayed its release until much later that year.

Recorded between December 1971 and the following June, the dark, rather bleak tone of *Ege Bamyasi* reflects the rainy weather and the onset of Michael Karoli's illness (he was hospitalised shortly after its completion with a perforated ulcer), Can being a band peculiarly sensitive to environmental conditions. For all that, it remains one of their most rewarding albums, an engaging blend of structure, improvisation and sensitivity ranging from the spirited abstraction of I'm So Green to the slow, sensuous waltz of Sing Swan Song, a Damo Suzuki piece to which Holger Czukay added an overture of babbling-brook water. Jaki Liebezeit's trademark cyclical drumming and Suzuki's impassioned vocal made a particular success of Vitamin C, which was also used as theme music, for the Sam Fuller thriller *A Dead Pigeon In The Beethovenstrasse*.

"I can't sing, so I use the voice as an instrument," explains the Japanese singer. "I'm not so much interested in anything in particular, that's why I sing about nothing. I improvise melody and texture too... Sometimes it sounds like English, French or German, but really it is the language of the Stone Age."

The album was completed bang on deadline by the inspired improvisation of Soup, which Irmin Schmidt describes as "one of the most spontaneous pieces we've ever done". The title derived from a can of okra (ladies' fingers) which they encountered in a Turkish restaurant; "it was the name of the manufacturer in Istanbul!"

Record label:
United Artists

Produced
by Can.

Recorded
at Inner Space Studio, Weilerswist, nr. Köln; 1971–72.

Released:
November 1972

Chart peaks:
None (UK) None (US)

Personnel:
Holger Czukay (b, e); Michael Karoli (g); Jaki Liebezeit (d); Irmin Schmidt (k); Damo Suzuki (v)

Track listing:
Pinch; Sing Swan Song; One More Night; Vitamin C; Soup; I'm So Green; Spoon (S)

Running time:
40.08

Current CD:
SPOON CD 008

Further listening:
All of Can's albums offer manifold delights, though those featuring vocalist Damo Suzuki (Tago Mago (1972), Ege Bamyasi and Future Days (1973)) have the most pleasing similarity of sound and purpose.

Further reading:
The Can Book (Pascal Bussy and Andy Hall, 1989); MOJO 41

Captain Beefheart And The Magic Band
Clear Spot

His most accessible offering. Includes ballads!

L egend had it that Captain Beefheart wrote the entire *Clear Spot* album in the course of an eight-hour car journey from Boston to Yale, and "transmitted" it to The Magic Band via harmonica (just as the parts for *Trout Mask Replica* had been painstakingly transcribed by John "Drumbo" French from Beefheart's piano demos), though in actual fact, several of the songs – including Low Yo Yo Stuff, Circumstances, Sun Zoom Spark and Clear Spot itself – were held over from the previous album *The Spotlight Kid*.

Clear Spot is a much slicker affair than its grumpy predecessor, in large part due to the more professional approach imposed on the band by producer Ted Templeman (once of Harper's Bizarre) – and the better studio afforded by their newly-enlarged budget. "Of course, there were still all the usual band blow-ups and fights, the same old shit," recalls Bill Harkleroad (Zoot Horn Rollo) in his book *Lunar Notes*. "This time, however, I got the feeling that Ted had taken Don to one side and said something along the lines of, 'I'm not going to put up with this.'" Whatever the reason, the end results offer the most rewarding rapprochement between the artistic and commercial imperatives of Beefheart's career – and thanks also to the general emphasis on love and sex, it became his biggest seller.

Driven along by the idiosyncratic engine-room of Artie Tripp and Oréjon – both refugees from Zappa's Mothers Of Invention – *Clear Spot* has a flexible muscularity lacking in some of the earlier albums, enabling Beefheart to carve his most elegant wrinkles yet on the R&B format. Also unlike previous recordings, overdubbing was employed extensively. "In some places there are actually tons of guitar parts," explains Harkleroad, "yet the actual parts themselves are so sparse, it doesn't feel like that."

As throughout The Magic Band's existence, Beefheart's solo composer credits remain a sore point with the other musicians. Zoot Horn Rollo, for instance, recalls creating "two mandolin parts, three electric guitar tracks, and two or three acoustic [guitar] tracks" on the beautiful Her Eyes Are A Blue Million Miles, which along with My Head Is My Only House Unless It Rains found Beefheart's lyricism at its most romantically inventive.

Record label:
Reprise

Produced
by Ted Templeman.

Recorded
in Los Angeles; 1972.

Released:
November 1972

Chart peaks:
None (UK) 191 (US)

Personnel:
Don Van Vliet (v, hm, wings on Singabus); Zoot Horn Rollo (solo g, steel appendage g, glass finger, mandolin); Rockette Morton (g, b); Ed Marimba aka Art Tripp (d, tattoos, pc); Oréjon aka Roy Estrada (b); Milt Holland (pc); The Blackberries (b, v); Russ Titelman (g); Donn Landee (e)

Track listing:
Low Yo Yo Stuff; Nowadays A Woman's Gotta Hit A Man; Too Much Time (S); Circumstances; My Head Is My Only House Unless It Rains; Sun Zoom Spark; Clear Spot; Crazy Little Thing; Long Neck Bottles; Her Eyes Are A Blue Million Miles; Big Eyed Beans From Venus; Golden Birdies

Running time:
37.16

Current CD:
7599-26249-2

Further listening:
Safe As Milk (1967)

Further reading:
Zoot Horn Rollo's Captain Beefheart Experience (Bill Harkleroad, 1998)
www.beefheart.com

Bobby Charles
Bobby Charles

Enigmatic teenage writer of rock'n'roll standards resurfaces after years in the wilderness to jam with The Band.

The word was that Bobby Charles was on the run when he showed up in Woodstock in 1971. The FBI was very interested in his whereabouts, apparently. Nevertheless, the 33-year-old "outlaw" was made to feel very welcome in the musical community that circulated around Bob Dylan and The Band. And no wonder, for Bobby Charles (born Robert Charles Guidry in February 1938), was well-respected among rock-'n'roll cognoscenti as the composer and originator of (See You) Later Alligator, one of rock's defining songs.

Charles, a Louisiana cajun boy, had written the tune, aged only 17, in 1955 with Fats Domino in mind. Fats turned it down so Bobby stayed in New Orleans and cut it himself for Chess. Decca's Milt Gabler seized on the song while scouting for material for Bill Haley. Their version sold millions worldwide; Bobby's died on the American R&B charts soon after record buyers discovered he was white. But he found acceptance as a writer, penning such classics as But I Do (Clarence Frogman Henry) and Walking To New Orleans (Fats Domino).

How he spent the '60s is a bit of a mystery, but when he decamped to Woodstock in the summer of 1971 he soon ran into old friend, guitar player Ben Keith. Ben introduced him to The Band and their manager, Albert Grossman, who promptly signed Bobby to his Bearsville label and put him in the studio with Rick Danko and producer John Simon, for some ramshackle, star-packed sessions that meandered well into the following year.

They cut a profoundly laid-back record, bound to appeal to fans of The Band — all of whom, apart from Robbie Robertson, appear on it. Charles's voice is relaxed, even a little careworn, and the playing is loose as a goose. One song sticks out, the beautiful Small Town Talk, a Charles/Danko collaboration that's as coolly mellow and gently groovy as anything by, say, J.J. Cale or Little Feat. It was released as a single in 1973, by which time Bobby had fallen out with Grossman. His album was allowed to languish in obscurity and its follow-up was never released. However, fans of easy-living Woodstock music hold this album up as a classic example. Charles later turned out to sing at The Band's Last Waltz show. But he was a reluctant live performer and his unwillingness to promote his music may be why he's currently only known to a lucky few.

Record label:
Bearsville

Produced
by Bobby Charles, Rick Danko and John Simon.

Recorded
at Bearsville Studios, Woodstock; December 1971–July 1972.

Released:
November 1972

Chart peaks:
None (UK) None (US)

Personnel:
Bobby Charles (v, g); Rick Danko (b, v); Levon Helm (bv, d), Garth Hudson (p, o, acc); Amos Garrett (g); Billy Mundi (d); Buggsy Maugh (b); Jim Colgrove (b); Ben Keith (g, sg); Mac Rebennac (p, pc); Geoff Muldaur (g); Richard Manuel (p, v); David Sanborn (s); Joe Newman (t); Bob Neuwirth (bv); Mark Harmon (e)

Track listing:
Street People; Long Face; I Must Be In A Good Place Now; Save Me Jesus; He's Got All The Whiskey; Small Town Talk; Let Yourself Go; Grow Too Old; I'm That Way; Tennesse Blues

Running time:
41.72

Current CD:
Essential ESM CD675

Further listening:
Bobby Charles (1983); Chess compilation of his '50s hits; Fats Domino Million Sellers (1970)

Further reading:
For the lowdown on The Band in Woodstock: Across The Great Divide (Barney Hoskyns, 1994)

Focus
Focus III

Look mum, virtuoso Euro classical-prog fusion!

The origins, discography and family tree of Focus are complex. Essentially formed when guitar whizz Jan Akkerman was kicked out of Dutch hard rockers Brainbox in late 1969 for jamming with the classically trained Van Leer's cabaret trio. A first single, House Of The King – thereafter assumed by everyone to be either Jethro Tull or some TV theme – was a European hit and subsequently appeared on the debut album *In And Out Of Focus* and later on this, their third. Akkerman claimed to have written it in five minutes to vent some angst the very night he left Brainbox.

Happening to have a generator on their first UK tour, in 1972, proved their making: the trip coincided with an electricity strike. The first of several legendary appearances on TV's Old Grey Whistle Test ensued and album two, *Moving Waves* – featuring the bizarre heavy-metal yodel-fest Hocus Pocus – was a cult hit.

By January 1973 Focus had two albums in the UK Top 30, two singles – Hocus Pocus and Sylvia – in the singles Top 20, and an even more frenzied version of Hocus Pocus heading for the US Top 10. Akkerman was voted that year's Best Guitarist in the Melody Maker poll, but a concert at the Rainbow Theatre, London – filmed and recorded for album number four – marked the end of an era. Musical differences had emerged and the eccentric Akkerman appeared to have become a part-time member. Living in England during 1972, he had become enamoured of renaissance lute music, glimpsed here on the beautiful Elspeth Of Nottingham – a love which was indulged further on his 1974 solo set *Tabernakel*. Like Eric Clapton, he seemed content to move away from guitar herodom, and later brushed aside an offer to work with Sting "because I didn't like his music".

Focus III, a luxuriant double set brimming with energy, improvisational brilliance, catchy tunes and exquisite taste, remains the moment of perfect balance between the ultimately uncontainable influences and aspirations at work.

Record label:
Polydor

Produced by
Mike Vernon.

Recorded
at Olympic Studios, Barnes; July 1972.

Released:
November 1972

Chart peaks:
6 (UK) 35 (US)

Personnel:
Thijs van Leer (v, k, alto flute, piccolo); Jan Akkerman (g, lute); Bert Ruiter (b); Pierre Van der Linden (d); George Chkiantz (e)

Track listing:
Round Goes The Gossip; Love Remembered; Sylvia (S); Carnival Fugue; Focus III; Answers? Questions! Questions? Answers!; Anonymous II; Elspeth Of Nottingham; House Of The King

Running time:
70.00

Currently unavailable on CD

Further listening:
Moving Waves (1971); the Akkerman solo albums Profile (1973) and 10,000 Clowns On A Rainy Day (1997), a live double featuring Focus material revisited for the first time in 20 years.

Further reading:
www.janakkerman.com (the official Akkerman site).

The Nitty Gritty Dirt Band
Will The Circle Be Unbroken

Great down-homers meet their country heroes.

The Dirt Band started out as a kind of zany jug band, good-timey, with more than a sprinkling of country influence. The line-up and the direction appeared to change almost weekly and members such as Jackson Browne and Chris Darrow soon moved on. Odd as it may seem, the band even turned up in a Hollywood musical during 1968, performing in Paint Your Wagon. That same year, The Byrds arrived in Nashville to record *Sweetheart Of The Rodeo*, while Dylan, who'd been working in the city since the mid-'60s, created *Nashville Skyline*. Bluegrass performers got in on the trend – Earl Scruggs made an album titled *Nashville's Rock* in 1970. It was in the wake of such activity that the long-hairs arrived in Music City to record with any country legends who would enter the studio with them. John McEuen, the band's banjo picker, was a bluegrass enthusiast. He talked Earl Scruggs into becoming involved, after which everything else fell into place, though some of the Nashville aristocracy remained suspicious. Jim Ibbotson later recalled auditioning for Wesley Rose, Roy Acuff's publisher. "We sat around his office and it was like 'Well, do you rape babies? Are you actually actively selling narcotics right now?'"

Ibbotson speculated on the use of heavy drums and wah wah pedals – real country rock. But, he later informed writer William Ruhlmann: "I realised my job on the record was to hold the door for Mother Maybelle and sing a little harmony here and there." In the event, each of the six main guest stars (Mother Maybelle, Acuff, Travis, Martin, Scruggs and Watson) performed four or five songs or instrumentals associated with them and what was regarded as a Nashville 'happening' veered increasingly towards the traditional side of things, while retaining just a mild hint of the Woodstock Nation. The title song, which opens and closes *Circle* encapsulated the event, with the whole cast – including wives, kids and anyone else who happened to be around – joining in for a final touch of spontaneity. The album quickly went gold, remarkable for a triple set. Robert Christgau hailed as "an instant classic – an intensely agreeable way into mountain music".

Record label:
United Artists

Produced
by William E McEuen.

Recorded
in Nashville; 1971.

Released:
November 1972

Chart peaks:
None (UK) None (US)

Personnel:
Jimmie Fadden (hm); Jeff Hanna (v, washboard, d); Jim Ibbotson (v, g, d); John McEuen (banjo, mandolin); Les Thompson (mandolin, v); Mother Maybelle Carter (v, g, a-harp); Earl Scruggs (g, banjo); Doc Watson (g, v); Jimmy Martin (g); Roy Acuff (v); Merle Travis (v, g); Vassar Clements (fiddle, g); Roy Huskey (b); Norman Blake (dobro); Pete 'Oswald' Kirby (dobro)

Track listing:
Grand Old Opry Song; Keep On The Sunny Side; Nashville Blues; You Are My Flower; The Precious Jewel; Dark As A Dungeon; Tennessee Stud; Black Mountain Rag; The Wreck On The Highway; The End Of The World; I Saw The Light; Sunny Side Of The Mountain; Nine Pound Hammer; Losin' You; Honky Tonkin'; You Don't Know My Mind; My Walkin' Shoes; Lonesome Fiddle Blues; Cannonball Rag; Avalanche; Flint Hill Special; Togary Mountain; Earl's Breakdown; Orange Blossom Special; Wabash Cannonball; Lost Highway; First Meeting; Way Downtown; Down Yonder; Pins And Needles; Honky Tonk Blues; Sailin' On To Hawaii; I'm Thinking Tonight Of My Blue Eyes; I Am A Pilgrim; Wildwood Flower; Soldier's Joy; Will The Circle Be Unbroken; Both Sides Now

Running time:
118.47

Current CD:
CDPB7465891/2

Further listening:
Uncle Charlie And His Dog Teddy (1970)

Further reading:
www.nittygritty.com

Lou Reed
Transformer

Reed's commercial breakthrough was powered by this irresistible broadside from the Wild Side.

On leaving the Velvet Underground in 1970, Lou Reed clerked for his accountant father and made a solo album which sold just 7,000 copies. Then David Bowie saved his career by offering to produce him.

In July 1972, Reed flew to London, rented a Wimbledon flat and set about making one of the quintessential New York albums. He had some brilliant material ready. Andy Warhol had offered the initial stimulus via the boggling suggestion that Reed write a musical with himself and Parisian couturier Yves St. Laurent. Oddly, Walk On The Wild Side emerged from a completely different, misconceived Broadway proposal. Candy [Darling], who "never lost her head even when she was giving head" was hardly the stuff of family entertainment but, as Reed leered: "I always thought it would be kinda fun to introduce people to characters they maybe hadn't met before, or hadn't wanted to meet."

But *Transformer* wasn't all scuzz. New York Telephone Conversation and Goodnight Ladies recall Noel Coward, recreating waspish Manhattan gossip, while the brief, brilliant Make Up depended on unexpected, but undeniable, *charm*: "The gay life at the moment isn't that great," Reed remarked. "I wanted to write a song which made it terrific." Perfect Day, bizarrely adopted by the BBC as an institutional anthem 25 years later, further baffled expectation with sweet sincerity but tempered it with a hint of self-loathing ("I thought I was someone else/Someone good"). Reflecting its lyrical scope, *Transformer* delivered equal parts Velvet Underground dirt rock and cute-to-comic oompah, with Herbie Flowers' virtuosity evident as much in the tubby tuba of New York Telephone Conversation as in the slinky bass of Walk On The Wild Side.

Despite extreme tantrums en route – Reed screaming, Bowie retiring to the studio toilet to curl himself around the pedestal in the foetal position – *Transformer* gave Reed his lifetime best chart placings in on both sides of the pond, and Bowie's choice, Walk On The Wild Side, proved his biggest hit single too (UK 10, US 16). Even so, Reed could often be heard lamenting the sham nature of his successful persona: "I mimic me probably better than anybody else. I created Lou Reed. I have nothing faintly in common with that guy, but I can play him well."

Record label:
RCA

Produced
by David Bowie and Mick Ronson.

Recorded
at Trident Studios, London; summer 1972.

Released:
November 1972

Chart peaks:
13 (UK) 29 (US)

Personnel:
Lou Reed (v, g); Mick Ronson (g, p, recorders); David Bowie (bv); Klaus Voorman (b); Herbie Flowers (b, string bass, tuba); Ronnie Ross (bs); John Halsey (d); Barry DeSouza (d); Ritchie Dharma (d)

Track listing:
Vicious (S/US); Andy's Chest; Perfect Day; Hangin' Round; Walk On The Wild Side (S); Make Up; Satellite Of Love (S); Wagon Wheel; New York Telephone Conversation; I'm So Free; Goodnight Ladies

Running time:
37.09

Current CD:
74321601812

Further listening:
Berlin (1973); Rock 'N' Roll Animal (1974)

Further reading:
Transformer: The Lou Reed Story (1995)

Bob Marley And The Wailers

African Herbsman

The conjunction of Lee Perry and The Wailers results in a definitive moment in reggae history.

A s the 1960s dribbled to a close, Bob Marley and his two cohorts in The Wailers were in a state of vexation. The stream of Jamaican hits they had enjoyed since the middle of the decade had all but dried up, they had fallen out with several producers, and attempts to establish themselves as an independent production force had foundered. In the small pool of the Jamaican music industry, their options were limited.

Help arrived from an unexpected source in the wiry, querulous shape of Lee 'Scratch' Perry, a 27-year-old producer who had amazed the island by scoring a major hit in Britain with a jaunty instrumental called Return of Django. Perry agreed to produce the troubled trio, immediately giving them a hit with Small Axe, a Marley song threatening to chop down Jamaica's 'big t'ree' record studios. Over the next year Perry coached the group in the back of his Beeston Street record store, frequently recording them at Randy's Studio a block across town. Under Scratch's inspired tutelage, the group's style mutated, leaving behind the doo-wop gymnastics of their early years in favour of a more visceral approach.

Marley, a ceaseless songwriter, found material to match; among his creations were the joyous Trench Town Rock and Lively Up Yourself, the fiercesome Duppy Conqueror (in which the singer casts himself as ghost-buster), the dreamy ganja song Kaya, and the cryptic, anguished reverie of Sun Is Shining. The partnership was at times stormy – the three Wailers beat Perry savagely when they suspected he was cheating them of royalties – but it produced reggae of a different order to almost anything else emerging from Jamaica, its soulful vocals and lyrical intricacy wound round the sparse but heavy rhythms conjured up by the young rhythm section of the Barratt brothers. The sides were, in effect, the template on which the group's subsequent success was built, many of the songs becoming cornerstones of Marley's live shows. Their release on 1971's *Soul Revolution* and this album in the following year, mark a turning point not just in Marley's career, but in the evolution of reggae music.

Record label:
Trojan

Produced
by Lee Perry.

Recorded
at Randy's Studio, Kingston, Jamaica; 1969–70.

Released:
December 1972

Chart peaks:
None (UK) None (US)

Personnel:
Bob Marley (v); Peter Tosh (v); Bunny Livingstone (v); Aston 'Family Man' Barrett (b); Carlton Barrett (d); Glen Adams (k); Alva Lewis (g); Lee Perry (e)

Track listing:
Lively Up Yourself (S/UK); Small Axe (S/UK); Duppy Conqueror (S/UK); Trenchtown Rock (S/UK); African Herbsman; Keep On Moving; Fussing and Fighting; Stand Alone; All In One; Don't Rock the Boat; Put It On; Sun Is Shining; Kaya (S/UK); Riding High; Brain Washing; 400 Years

Running time:
35.22

Current CD:
TRL62

Further listening:
The Complete Upsetter Collection, a six CD set gathers all known vocal, instrumental and DJ sessions resulting from these sessions (113 in all!). The Perry tracks are much anthologised elsewhere.

Further reading:
MOJO 16; Catch A Fire (Timothy White, 1983); Bob Marley: Conquering Lion Of Reggae (Stephen Davis, 1983); Bob Marley: Songs of Freedom (Chris Salewicz and Adrian Boot, 1995); Bob Marley (Scotty Bennett, 1997)

Steely Dan
Can't Buy A Thrill

Wryly cynical songs buffed to an impeccable shine.

When Gary Katz moved to Los Angeles to take up an A&R position with ABC Records, the first thing he did was persuade his employers that they should also hire a young songwriting duo he'd met in New York. Accordingly, Walter Becker and Donald Fagen soon found themselves on the West Coast, vainly trying to write songs to fit ABC artists like Three Dog Night, whilst secretly using the company's money to fund their own project, which became Steely Dan.

"We realised that to succeed, we would have to do these songs ourselves," recalled Walter Becker. "They were too odd, too out of context for the time. On the one hand, they expressed an odd sensibility lyrically, and they were musically unusual, because of the jazz and other harmonic elements."

With their old friend Denny Dias brought over from the East Coast, and Katz's acquaintances Jeff "Skunk" Baxter and Jim Hodder drafted in from Boston, they set about rehearsing their new material after hours in an accountant's office at ABC, before recording it at the Village Recorder studio in West LA.

"Before we did the first album," says Becker, "we presented pretty much finished arrangements to the musicians." Though Fagen had sung on the demos, he was unsure of his vocal capabilities, so Jim Hodder (on the rare debut single Dallas) and subsequently David Palmer (on Dirty Work and Brooklyn)were featured as singers, before Fagen was persuaded that the songs required his peculiar pipes.

"They have to be performed with a certain attitude," Fagen acknowledged, "I became singer by default, because I was the only one with the right attitude, even though I didn't consider myself a singer at the time." Proof of Fagen's capabilities came when the album's two hit singles established his sardonic nasal sneer as the band's characteristic trademark. The slinky mambo rhythm and electric sitar solo of Do It Again proved surprisingly irresistible over the airwaves, as did the rockier Reeling In The Years. The parent album has since become recognised as a genuine pop landmark, recorded with peerless clarity by their brilliant engineer Roger "The Immortal" Nichols, while the post-hippy cynicism of songs like Only A Fool Would Say That has come to be regarded as prefiguring the pervasive disillusion of the mid- to late-'70s.

Record label:
ABC

Produced
by Gary Katz.

Recorded
at Village Recorder, Los Angeles; 1972.

Released:
January 1973

Chart peaks:
None (UK) 17 (US)

Personnel:
Donald Fagen (v, k); Walter Becker (b, v); Denny Dias (g, electric sitar); Jeff 'Skunk' Baxter (g, sg); Jim Hodder (d, pc, v); David Palmer (v); Elliot Randall (g); Victor Feldman (pc); Jerome Richardson (s); Snooky Young (flugelhorn); Clydie King King, Shirley Matthews, Venetta Fields (bv); Roger Nichols (e)

Track listing:
Do It Again (S); Dirty Work; Kings; Midnite Cruiser; Only A Fool Would Say That; Reelin' In The Years (S); Fire In The Hole ; Brooklyn (Owes The Charmer Under Me); Change Of The Guard; Turn That Heartbeat Over Again

Running time:
41.02

Current CD:
MCAI 18862

Further listening:
The follow-up Countdown To Ecstasy (1973) bore evidence of hard touring, longer solos illuminating the songs; Pretzel Logic added jazzy touches to the classy pop songwriting, Katy Lied and The Royal Scam refined the formula further within a strictly studio/sessionman milieu; the hugely successful Aja delved even deeper into jazz.

Further reading:
MOJO 23; Steely Dan: Reelin' In The Years (Brian Sweet, 1994); www.steelydan.com

Stevie Wonder
Talking Book

Second instalment of Stevie's purple patch.

On May 13 1971, Stevie Wonder inherited a million dollar trust fund. Unlike most heirs to such fortunes, he'd earnt it all himself from the many hits he'd scored since the age of 12. By now, however, he was keen to break from the Motown production line. "I wasn't growing," he said in 1972. "I just kept repeating the Stevie Wonder sound, and it didn't express how I felt about what was happening out there." Instead, he set up his own autonomous company Taurus Productions and forced Motown to give him total artistic control. He then embarked on a mammoth solo recording session, sealing himself inside Greenwich Village's legendary Electric Lady Studios with his new toys, some Arp and Moog synthesisers. He'd often forget to eat or sleep attempting to get all the music bursting from his astonishingly fertile, newly unleashed mind down on tape.

Friend and publicist Ira Tucker recalls, "He'd call me at four in the morning and say 'Hey, we gotta go to the studio, right now.'" From the 40-ish songs he demoed, six appeared on *Music Of My Mind*. A succulent ballad suite, its meandering psychedelia was too introspective for the public. *Talking Book*, released just eight months later and drawing from the same song stock, revealed a more confidently extrovert figure. At the same time, after only a year, his marriage to Syreeta Wright was ending and *Talking Book* (aside from the brazenly political Big Brother) is essentially a meditation on love's closure and new beginning, complicated by the fact that Syreeta wrote the lyrics to wondrous break-up odes Blame It On The Sun and Lookin' For Another Love.

"I was too young, and I also dug another person," Stevie explained. That other person was Gloria Barley, the female vocalist on and subject of the soon-to-be-standard You Are The Sunshine Of My Life (and the reason it was tactfully held over from the previous year). Influenced by Billy Preston's keyboard work on 1972 hit Outa-Space, the album's distinctive fluttering keyboard sound was achieved by wiring a clavinet to the Arp synth. The two singles, You Are The Sunshine Of My Life and the devastating Superstition represented the polar opposites of his craft – generous spirited pop-soul and blaring street-funk – and both became among the biggest hits of the year. Constantly touching on jazz, Latin and rock music but settling on none, *Talking Book* revealed a teeming, unconstrained creative impulse that could do little wrong.

Record label:
Tamla

Produced
by Stevie Wonder, Malcolm Cecil and Robert Margouleff.

Recorded
at Air Studios, London; Electric Lady Studios, New York; Crystal Studios, Los Angeles; Record Plant, LA; summer 1971–autumn 1972.

Released:
January 1973

Chart peaks:
16 (UK) 3 (US)

Personnel:
Stevie Wonder (v, k, p, b, g, d, pc); Scott Edwards (b); David Ben Zebulon (pc); Jim Gilstrap, Lani Groves, Loris Harvin, Shirley Brewer, Gloria Barley and Debra Wilson (bv); Ray Parker Jnr, Jeff Beck, Buzzy Feton (g); Dave Sanborn, Trevor Lawrence (s); Steve Madaio (tp) Track listing: You Are The Sunshine Of My Life (S); Maybe Your Baby; You And I; Tuesday Heartbreak; You've Got It Bad Girl; Superstition (S); Big Brother; Blame It On The Sun; Lookin' For Another Love; I Believe (When I Fall In Love)

Running time:
43.30

Current CD:
1573542

Further listening:
Music Of My Mind (1972); Innervisions (1973)

Further reading:
Stevie Wonder – Written Musiquarium: 41 Hits Spanning His Career (Hal Leonard, 1999); www.insoul.com/stevie

Nick Drake
Pink Moon

Beyond folk, beyond singer/songwriterly convention, a stark, redemptive — and final — missive from an elusive talent.

Nick Drake's third and last album is, "far from bleak and ghoulish, it is a stark, sparingly beautiful meditation on redemption through spiritual trial," wrote Ian MacDonald in MOJO 74. Of the three albums that Drake recorded in his short lifetime, the debut, *Five Leaves Left*, represents the first flourish of promise, *Bryter Layter*, its full fruition. *Pink Moon* is the portent, the lingering remnant of a soul – and its muse – in retreat. This view is, of course, almost entirely retrospective, bolstered by the artist's tragically early death and the myths that have sprung up subsequently. Drake had in fact indicated immediately after the recording of *Bryter Layter* (partly as a reaction to that record's lavish production) that his next album was going to feature just him and his guitar, and at least one of *Pink Moon*'s songs, Things Behind The Sun (with its plaintive and prophetic refrain, "Who'll hear what I say?") had been written years earlier.

But Drake's crushing depression began exerting its grip after *Bryter Layter*. He started to take the anti-depressants that eventually killed him, and he became increasingly withdrawn from all those closest to him. Later in 1971, Island Records' head Chris Blackwell offered him the use of his villa in Portugal for a change of scene. On his return, Drake called engineer John Wood and announced he wished to record. He completed the record in two nights, took the tapes and left them – without telling anyone – in the reception of Island Records.

It was his masterpiece. The one that draws deserved comparisons with Van Gogh and Robert Johnson. More than merely the product of a troubled mind, as some have suggested, it is a confident record delivered with clarity and singularity of vision. Apart from the delightful eight bars of overdubbed piano which grace the title track, *Pink Moon* is just Nick Drake's voice and guitar. It leaves you no choice but to listen to what he has to say. Drake had never before written anything as apocalyptic and judgmental as the title track, while Parasite, with a four note melody which evokes church bells peeling, is an astoundingly specific cry of self-loathing and alienation. (Commentators rarely note Drake's black humour, evident in Parasite's "Changing a rope for a size too small/people all get hung".) Two tracks, Road and Know, have four lines of lyric and last for

Record label:
Island

Produced
by John Wood.

Recorded
at Sound Techniques, November 1971.

Released:
February 25, 1972

Chart peaks:
None (UK) None (US)

Personnel:
Nick Drake (g, v, p); John Wood (e)

Track listing:
Pink Moon; Place To Be; Road; Which Will; Horn; Things Behind The Sun; Know; Parasite; Ride; Harvest Breed; From The Morning

Running time:
28.00

Current CD:
IMCD 94 / 842 923-2

Further listening:
Five Leaves Left; Bryter Layter; the posthumous compilation Time Of No Reply. All are collected on the Fruit Tree boxed set (1991). Way To Blue: An Introduction To Nick Drake (1994) is an effective Best Of.

Further reading:
MOJO 74; Nick Drake: The Biography (Patrick Humphries, 1998)
www.algonet.se/~iguana/DRAKE/DRAKE.html

less than two minutes, yet both speak volumes. On Place To Be, Drake sang of a new-found maturity and reflective under-standing of the nature of things. He was 23. Within months of the album's completion Drake plunged into the depression from which he never re-emerged. He cut only a few more songs in his life. His mother found him dead in his bedroom on November 25, 1974. In *Pink Moon* he left behind the perfect testimony to his greatness.

In April 2000, the album suddenly appeared high on the Amazon.com best-seller's list after the title track was used in an American Volkswagen advert.

John Martyn
Solid Air

Weightless, melancholy folk-jazz never bettered by its maker.

John Martyn had two ways of making records in this period.
He'd either take his time, think each track through with
producer/engineer John Wood, who had a magical touch with
Martyn's music, and put together an album, or he'd go in with a
bunch of musical pals, lock the doors and create what was effectively a jam session, picking out the best of it at the end. The
stormy *Inside Out* is an example of the latter; *Solid Air*, his
masterpiece, was done by the first method.

It's such a harmonious record it's hard to see how it
could ever have been improved. Martyn, a tempestuous
Glaswegian who'd been on the London folk circuit since 1967,
had darkened his music without surrendering its acoustic base
or the innate virtuosity of his playing and singing. Previous
entries such as *Bless The Weather* or *Stormbringer* (the latter with
wife Beverly), were stepping slowly but steadily away from folk
and into singer-songwriter rock. A tougher feel was cautiously
imported into this record, although it came via Fairport
Convention's Dave Pegg and Dave Mattacks, who were hardly
heavy metal merchants. Jazz-directed players such as saxophonist
Tony Coe and acoustic bassist Danny Thompson, with whom
Martyn enjoyed a long relationship, added an improvisatory feel.
Martyn's own snapping guitar work was expanded by his new
fascination with fuzz and echo units, used to formidable effect
on the long, hallucinatory version of Skip James's blues I'd
Rather Be The Devil. Martyn's concerts with this set-up were
the place to hear him, though. Anyone who heard him live
during this period, particularly in the trio with Thompson and
drummer John Stevens, will never forget that music. The second
half of *Solid Air* is similarly memorable, with the sexy lilt of Go
Down Easy, John Bundrick's spellbinding chords on Dreams By
The Sea and Martyn's signature wish-you-well May You Never,
which was subsequently butchered by Eric Clapton. But one
always goes back to the title track, the vocals slipping in over
Thompson's long sliding notes, the vibraphone glinting in the
background, Coe's tenor sax drifting in like smoke, to catch the
essence of *Solid Air*. It was Martyn's tender tribute to his friend
Nick Drake, whose passing, 18 months after *Solid Air* was
released, he still refuses to discuss.

Record label:
Island

Produced
by John Martyn and John Wood.

Recorded
at Island and Sound Techniques Studios;
Nov–Dec 1972.

Released:
February 1973

Chart peaks:
None (UK) None (US)

Personnel:
John Martyn (g, v, syn); John Bundrick
(p, o, clavinet); Tony Coe (ts); Richard
Thompson (mandolin); Sue Draheim (vn);
Simon Nicol (autoharp); Neemoi Acquaye
(vibes); Danny Thompson (b); Dave
Pegg (b); Dave Mattacks (d); Tristan Fry
(vibraphone)

Track listing:
Solid Air; Over The Hill; Don't Want To
Know; I'd Rather Be The Devil; Go Down
Easy; Dreams By The Sea; May You
Never; The Man In The Station; The Easy
Blues

Running time:
34.53

Current CD:
IMCD585

Further listening:
Sunday's Child (1975); One World (1977)

Further reading:
come.to/johnmartyn

Pink Floyd
The Dark Side Of The Moon

A cult band goes stellar. At 30 million copies and rising, it's still the biggest selling album ever by a British band.

By late November 1971, Floyd watchers were complaining that the band had been coasting during live shows, and that, since Syd Barrett's demise, their albums – *Ummagumma* and *Atom Heart Mother* – had been high on ambition but only superficially entertaining. Most recent album *Meddle*, however, pointed a way out of this creative trough; the epic, side-long Echoes, though assembled from assorted fragments of music, approached the cohesion they'd been lacking.

After an American tour, the band convened at their London rehearsal studios to discuss the possibility of doing something new on their UK dates, only seven weeks away. Using the methods employed on Echoes, they began to work up some scraps – Roger's song Breathe, Rick's unused tune for the *Zabriski Point* soundtrack (Us & Them), and his chord sequence which was destined to become Great Gig In The Sky. But an adhesive concept was missing. It was Roger who provided it. "When [he] walked in with the idea of putting together one piece with this linking theme he'd devised, that was a moment," recalls Dave Gilmour. Roger's theme? Insanity and its catalysts – the demands of modern life: work, money, deadlines.

Gilmour admits that Waters did the majority of the subsequent writing, "while the rest of us went home to enjoy our suppers" on what was originally called *Eclipse: A Piece For Assorted Lunatics*. The new work was first road-tested in Brighton in January 1972. After a four-day stint at London's prestigious Rainbow theatre in February, a live bootleg of the piece – since retitled *The Dark Side Of The Moon* – appeared under record shop counters. Recording of the real thing began in earnest in June and was completed seven months later, though only 38 days were spent in Abbey Road while the Floyd undertook various obligations (tours, the La Valée film soundtrack, a ballet). They stretched the studio's resources to its limits, creating new reverb and delay effects, experimenting with the nascent Quadraphonic technology and mastering the VCS suitcase synthesiser.

With just six songs linked by instrumental interludes and sonic collage, the result was the Floyd's most succinct and approachable album, crammed with hooks and episodes of simple beauty. In places it's remarkably soulful too.

Record label:
Harvest

Produced
by Pink Floyd.

Recorded
at Abbey Road, London; June 1972–January 1973.

Released:
March 25, 1973

Chart peaks:
2 (UK) I (US)

Personnel:
Roger Waters (b, v, VCS3 synthesiser, tape effects); David Gilmour (g, v, VCS3); Richard Wright (k, v, VCS3); Nick Mason (p, tape effects); Dick Parry (s); Clare Torry (v on Great Gig In The Sky, bv); Les Duncan, Lisa Strike, Barry St. John (bv); Alan Parsons (e); Peter James (ae)

Track listing:
Speak To Me; Breathe; On The Run; Time; The Great Gig In The Sky; Money; Us & Them; Any Colour Your Like; Brain Damage; Eclipse

Running time:
42.57

Current CD:
CDEMD 1064 digitally remastered

Further listening:
Hear The Dark Side... sound evolve on the under-rated soundtrack Obscured By Clouds (1972).

Further reading:
MOJO 6, 20, 52, 73; Echoes (Cliff Jones, 1997); www.pinkfloyd.com

Though some elements may seem crass now, moments like Time's pivotal lines: "No-one told you when to run, you missed the starting gun" and "Hanging on in quiet desperation is the English way" retain their power and On The Run is surely acid-house 15 years before the fact. But it was the album's directness, in songs like Money and Us & Them, which won it unprecedented global approval. In America it remained in the Billboard 200 for an astounding 741 weeks — over 14 years.

Mahavishnu Orchestra
Birds Of Fire

John McLaughlin's virtuoso heavy-hitters deliver fusion's most explosive moment.

I f fusion later noodled off into high-brow muzak, for a few years in the early '70s this heady collision of jazz and rock was one of the most exciting styles on the block. Of the three great fusion bands – Weather Report, Return To Forever and the first Mahavishnu Orchestra – it was McLaughlin's outfit who came on loudest and fastest.

Their house style was a kind of heavy metal jazz, and their three soloists, propelled by Cobham's rolling thunder, could outgun any band on the planet. But *Birds Of Fire* is not all clatter, the Mahavishnus could also play with extreme delicacy, as on Thousand Island Park. According to McLaughlin, the band was at the top of its form after several long tours when it embarked on the second album. "We were on a wave, we were experiencing a success that was unforeseen, and we were making light-year jumps in terms of playing together, developing new ways of playing." The guitarist worked out most of the music with Billy Cobham in a New York rehearsal studio, with the others adding their parts later. McLaughlin says: "The album was recorded in two or three days, quite simply. It was a 24-track machine: we'd mike up the amps, mike up the drums, one, two, three, go. There would be two or three takes but invariably it would be the first take that had the magic. We always worked fast – we didn't have the budget to go and live in the studio like pop bands do."

Birds Of Fire possessed the same fierce, occasionally exhausting, intensity as its predecessor, *The Inner Mounting Flame*. But if the debut was for jazzers, the second record was more accessible to a rock audience, with its snatches of skewed blues, Hendrix-tinged guitar and strong tunes. Cobham's extraordinary drum attack stems in part from his belief that the band needed a second percussionist and he opted to do the work of two men. The album's visceral brew was given further mystique by McLaughlin's quaintly exotic song titles, inspired by his guru of the time, Sri Chinmoy.

McLaughlin believes the band's golden period lasted another year after the recording before personal clashes led to the break-up. Evidence of how much more this line-up had to offer came with the 1999 release of the band's shelved third studio album as *The Lost Trident Tapes*."

Record label:
CBS

Produced
by John McLaughlin.

Recorded
at Trident Studios, London; Electric Lady and CBS Studios, New York; August 1972.

Released:
March 1973

Chart peaks:
20 (UK) 20; (US) 15

Personnel:
John McLaughlin (g); Jan Hammer (k); Jerry Goodman (vn); Rick Laird (b); Billy Cobham (d); Ken Scott, Jim Green (e)

Track listing:
Birds Of Fire; Miles Beyond; Celestial Terrestrial Commuters; Sapphire Bullets Of Pure Love; Thousand Island Park; Hope; One Word; Sanctuary; Open Country Joy; Resolution

Running time:
40.29

Current CD:
CK66081

Further listening:
Live album Between Nothingness And Eternity (1974).

Further reading:
Go Ahead: The Music Of John McLaughlin (Paul Stump, 2000)

Roxy Music
For Your Pleasure

Roxy's crowning glory, created as Ferry's autocratic style clashed with Eno's urge to experiment.

*F*or Your Pleasure exudes confidence: from the stunning, punning opener, Do The Strand, to the pounding, repetitive epic, The Bogus Man, the rave-up of Editions Of You and the beautifully queasy In Every Dream Home A Heartache, this is a record that brims with bravado. After all, by the time Roxy Music (minus original member Graham Simpson, who was replaced by John Porter, the first in a series of revolving-door bass players) convened at Air Studios, they had good reason to feel upbeat. The success achieved in the few months since the release of their self-titled debut had overcome initial critical suspicion, and was consolidated by striking appearances on Top Of The Pops promoting non-album single Pyjamarama and sell-out tours all over the UK and Europe. But *For Your Pleasure*'s sheen – heightened by the use of 'is she/isn't he?' model Amanda Lear on the glossy cover – masked a deepening and ultimately unbridgeable gap between mainman Bryan Ferry and the band's increasingly mischievous electronic sprite Brian Eno.

Eno's limelight-grabbing stage antics had certainly not endeared him to Ferry, but at the heart of the matter was a major difference of musical opinion. Ferry favoured a structured approach to recording, one which had been achieved on the band's debut since songs had been written and rehearsed meticulously over a number of years. Eno, by contrast, was (and continues to be) a keen advocate of randomness, and the lack of preparation for album two allowed him to flourish.

"We did have some material, like For Your Pleasure, which was one of our first songs," says Eno. "But there weren't a lot of new tracks, and that suited me fine, because it meant we could invent the sound. The studio is my instrument. I didn't play the guitar or the oboe so I came into my own there. What resulted wasn't just the transmission of pre-existing ideas."

The spontaneity gave rise not only to the pulsating nine-minute epic The Bogus Man but also one of Roxy's most extraordinary conceits, In Every Dream Home A Heartache. Here Ferry's cool reflections on materialism are matched by an electronic backdrop which boils over as the track becomes a paean to an inflatable rubber doll. "In Every Dream Home came to life in the studio," confirms Eno. "What happened was that I was allowed to become a random element which stopped the

Record label:
Island

Produced
by Chris Thomas and Roxy Music.

Recorded
at Air Studios, London; spring 1973.

Released:
March 1973

Chart peaks:
3 (UK) 193 (US)

Personnel:
Bryan Ferry (v, p); John Porter (b); Andrew Mackay (oboe, s); Brian Eno (syn, tapes); Paul Thompson (d); Phil Manzanera (g)

Track listing:
Do The Strand; Beauty Queen; Strictly Confidential; Editions Of You; In Every Dream Home A Heartache; The Bogus Man; Grey Lagoons; For Your Pleasure

Running time:
42.21

Current CD:
Virgin ROXYCD2

Further listening:
Brian Eno, Here Come The Warm Jets (1974); Bryan Ferry, These Foolish Things (1973)

Further reading:
MOJO 21, 25; Unknown Pleasures: A Cultural Biography Of Roxy Music (Paul Stump, 1998); The Bryan Ferry Story (Rex Balfour, 1976)

rest of the band working in a traditional way." But therein lay Eno's fate. The conflict with Ferry spilled over into the dates to promote the album, with Eno deliberately extending synthesiser solos and increasing the volume to swamp out the singer. Within a couple of months Eno had quit the band.

"What Roxy Music lacks for me is one of the most important elements of my musical life, which is insanity," Eno told Geoff Brown of the Melody Maker. Ferry restricted his comments to the pithy: "Two non-musicians in a band is one too many." The pair immediately set about recording deeply contrasting solo albums. Nevertheless, together, and with the adventurous support of Manzanera, Mackay and Thompson, Eno and Ferry had delivered Roxy's finest three-quarters of an hour in *For Your Pleasure*, a fact now ruefully recognised by the frontman. "There's a completeness of mood about it," he says of the album. "Looking back I'm sad I didn't do more work with that line-up. But at the time I felt that was it. I didn't think we could make one better." Some might say they never did.

Terry Reid

River

Downbeat and dreamy curio from an unrequited next big thing.

T erry Reid was the man most likely to succeed as the '60s spiralled to a close. He was first noticed as a member of Peter Jay And The Jaywalkers. When Jimmy Page was recruiting for The New Yardbirds (later Led Zeppelin), it was Reid – clean-cut, cool and only 19 – who was first offered the role of vocalist. Recommending Robert Plant, Reid turned down the job. At first it seemed he'd made the right decision: his acclaimed solo debut with producer Mickie Most, *Bang Bang You're Terry Reid*, was followed by gigs opening for Cream, and a cover of his song Friends was a sizeable hit for British band Arrival. But after that, very little went as planned and a string of business and personal problems hobbled his career.

By 1973, Reid had moved to Atlantic Records. A quick scan of his bedraggled state on the gatefold of *River* is worth a thousand words: bearded, unkempt, far-away eyed and with a serious trouser problem, he's hardly the stuff of stardom. The music, however, is excellent. *River* progresses from pristine early '70s rock – with Reid's searing rock voice in full effect – to deep Southern fried soul (with accompanying slide from David Lindley), before it spins into outer space for side two's awesome trio of songs. The band dissolve from the title track on, until Reid is accompanied only by percussion. His voice swoops and floats, a strange amalgam of Tim Buckley and Dino Valente, his unplugged guitar drives the mesmeric backing. By Dream, the percussion is gone too and multi-tracked guitars drift by. Then, for the lengthy closer Milestones, Reid's vocal is reduced to a plaintive cry, a series of wordless, emotive sounds coaxed from deep within.

River functions as a kind of journey, the story of a man travelling inward and reaching the inarticulate core of his soul. Sadly, the album didn't work as a therapeutic self-exorcism, it reaped little attention at the time, has never been issued on CD and only occasionally turns up at record fairs, but it is a treasure; for just over half an hour you'd swear you were listening to a superstar.

Record label:
Atlantic

Produced
by Eddie Offord and Tom Dowd.

Recorded
in London, 1971 and Los Angeles, 1973.

Released:
April, 1973

Chart peaks:
None (UK) None (US)

Personnel:
Terry Reid (g, v); David Lindley (sg, slide g); Leo Miles (b); Conrad Isidore (d); Willie Bobo (pc)

Track listing:
Dean; Avenue; Things To Try; Live Life; River; Dream; Milestones

Running time:
36.26

Currently unavailable on CD

Further listening:
Nothing in Reid's sporadic output resembles River, but the promise is evident on Bang Bang You're Terry Reid (1968) and some fans swear by the mellow, Graham Nash-produced Seed Of Memory (1976)

Further reading:
Sleevenotes to BGO's 1992 reissue of Rogue Waves (1978).

The Wailers
Catch A Fire

The first crossover reggae album announces a new force in world pop.

T he music industry thought Chris Blackwell had taken leave of his senses. Not only had he signed an unknown Jamaican group, The Wailers, he had paid handsomely for them; £4,000 handed to the group to cut an album, £5,000 to prise Bob Marley from a previous deal with CBS and a cut of future profits. And for what? A reggae act? In 1972, reggae was regarded by most of the business with a disdain that verged on racism.

"Everyone told me I was mad, that I'd never see the money again," said Blackwell. The Island boss was confident he'd prove his critics wrong. A Jamaican himself, he had built his label by selling the island's hits to Britain's black community, had stayed in tune with what was happening back a yard, and saw the potential of the charismatic and prolific Marley. When writer Richard Williams, then working for Island, visited Kingston to check on progress at Harry J's Kingston studios, he was astonished: "I was prepared to find someone talented, but it quickly became obvious that Bob simply was Marvin Gaye, Bob Dylan or both."

The appearance of *Catch A Fire*, lavishly packaged as a giant Zippo lighter and promoted with the same fuss as, say, Roxy Music, confounded conceptions of reggae. Partaking of the same blighted urban romanticism as Gaye and Curtis Mayfield, its mix of militancy and mysticism helped lay bare the pomposity of a rock scene long since drained of the fervour of the '60s. Not that *Catch A Fire* didn't borrow some licks from rock. Once Blackwell had its master tapes, he secreted himself in Island's Notting Hill studios to sweeten and polish the sound of Trench Town for western ears. US guitarist George Perkins and keyboard player Rabbit Bundrick were among the uncredited names adding sheen. But the album remained the work of the group, or band, as they'd now become, with live appearances at London's chic Speakeasy club and on BBC TV to prove it. If all this succeeded in raising media eyebrows, and shifted The Wailers from Caribbean hitmakers to international cult, it didn't yet make them, or Marley, into superstars. That was to come.

Record label:
Island

Produced
by Bob Marley and Chris Blackwell.

Recorded
at Dynamic Sound Studios, Harry J Studios and Randy's Studios, Kingston, Jamaica; spring 1972.

Released:
April 1973

Chart peaks:
None (UK) None (US)

Personnel:
Bob Marley (v, g); Peter Tosh (v, g, k); Bunny Linvingstone (v, congas); Aston 'Family Man' Barrett (b); Carlton Barrett (d); Rabbit Bundrick (k); Carlton Lee, Stu Barrett, Tony Platt (e)

Track listing:
Concrete Jungle (S); Slave Driver; 400 Years; Stop That Train (S); Rock It Baby (UK/S); Stir It Up; Kinky Reggae; No More Trouble; Midnight Ravers

Running time:
33.51

Current CD:
Tuff Gong TGLCD1

Further listening:
Though 1973's Burnin' was a lesser work than its predecessor, it expanded the Marley canon and contained I Shot The Sheriff, whose cover by Eric Clapton did much to raise Marley's profile.

Further reading:
MOJO 16; Catch A Fire (Timothy White, 1983); Bob Marley: Conquering Lion Of Reggae (Stephen Davis, 1983); Bob Marley, Songs of Freedom (Chris Salewicz and Adrian Boot, 1995); Bob Marey (Scotty Bennett, 1997)

Mike Oldfield
Tubular Bells

Teenage social misfit's debut expands the horizons of the electric guitar like no-one since Hendrix.

"Record companies looked at me as if I was mad," says Mike Oldfield. "They all said, because there were no vocals, no words, no drums or anything, that it was not marketable." And who could blame them? Confronted by a hesitant, gawky, unself-confident teenager touting a 20 minute demo of multi-tracked guitar riffs cheaply recorded on a Bang & Olufsen tape machine borrowed from Kevin Ayers, any experienced A&R man would show him the door. And if the Arthur Lewis Band, for which Oldfield played guitar, hadn't been sent by chance to make test recordings at the soon-to-open Virgin Manor studio in Oxfordshire, Oldfield wouldn't have played his demo for studio boss Tom Newman.

"He was just a funny little hippie," recalls Newman, who nevertheless championed Oldfield's cause to reluctant Virgin boss Richard Branson, and won him some recording time.

In late 1972, Oldfield set to work in earnest, playing virtually all the instruments himself, cobbling *Tubular Bells* together from what Newman had first heard as "half a dozen little unconnected pieces", beginning with a motif inspired by US minimalist composer Terry Riley.

"It was very fashionable not to have everything in 4/4," points out Oldfield, "so I made one bar 7 beats and one bar 8 and then later realised that it had the complexity of Eastern music, the repetitiveness of Terry Riley and the technique of Bach. It just turned out by accident that it was a very nice listenable thing."

But, on hearing the completed masterwork, Branson was far from convinced. According to Newman, getting his hip capitalist boss to release the record "was like dragging stuff uphill through treacle." Ultimately though, it did become the first album released by Virgin. In the course of the '70s, it was outsold in the UK only by Simon And Garfunkel's *Bridge Over Troubled Water* and found American success after the theme was used in the soundtrack for The Exorcist. It was unquestionably the massive sales Oldfield generated which established not only the Virgin label (sold to EMI in March 1992 for £560 million) but, by extension, the entire Branson empire. By the dawn of the new millennium *Tubular Bells* had easily surpassed 25 million sales, not to mention spawning two sequels and an orchestral version. Not bad for a funny little hippy.

Record label:
Virgin

Produced
by Mike Oldfield, Simon Heyworth and Tom Newman.

Recorded
at The Manor, Shipton-on-Cherwell, Oxfordshire; November 1972.

Chart peaks:
2 (UK) 3 (US)

Released:
May 25, 1973

Running time:
48.47

Personnel:
Mike Oldfield (g, k, p, pc, v, b, taped motor drive amplifier organ chord, mandolin-like guitar, flageolet, Lowrey organ, glockenspiel, Farfisa organ); Jon Field (flutes); Lindsay Cooper (db); Mundy Ellis (bv); Sally Oldfield (bv); Steve Broughton (d); Viv Stanshall (Master of Ceremonies)

Track listing:
Tubular Bells Part One; Tubular Bells Part Two

Current CD:
CDV2001

Further listening:
The subsequent Hergest Ridge is pretty much an anagram of Tubular Bells. Tubular Bells II (1996) and Tubular Bells III (1999) didn't move the story on much, but Songs Of Distant Earth (1994) is arguably Oldfield's most intriguing full-length instrumental composition after Tubular Bells.

Further reading:
The Making Of Mike Oldfield's Tubular Bells (1993); http://tubular.net

Planxty

Planxty

The band who changed the face of Irish music.

C hristy Moore, long established as one of Ireland's most
beloved icons, still can't quite grasp his fortune in finding
the magic that dropped into his lap with Planxty. An old school-
friend of Donal Lunny, Moore – from Newbridge, County
Kildare – had quit his safe job in a bank to chance his luck on
the English folk circuit playing a mixture of standard fare,
rousing sing-alongs, comedy songs and the odd protest number.
His instinctive, intimate way with an audience was such that he
swiftly became one of the scene's biggest draws, even if a
lifestyle of heavy drinking and sleeping on people's floors did
him no favours. He was loved in a roustabout, Dubliners sort of
way and nobody – least of all Christy himself – could have
anticipated the consequences of his return to Ireland.

He gravitated to the infamous sessions in the village of
Prosperous which had become a magnet for the better young
Irish folk musicians of the day, and it was there he met up again
with Donal Lunny. Moore decided that his next album wouldn't
be the standard song collection, and that he would instead utilise
the vibrant new Irish sounds of pipes he was now hearing at
home. His next album – titled *Prosperous* – heavily featured the
brilliant young uilleann piper Liam Og O'Flynn, the dextrous
guitarist/mandolin player Andy Irvine and Lunny pulling all the
rhythmic strings. All four of them were so enthused and invigorated by the sounds they were creating that there was never much
doubt that they'd put the relationship on an official basis. The
band Planxty came out of it and – released on the back of lone
Irish hit single Cliffs Of Dooneen – made the album that still
stands as modern Irish folk's primary landmark.

"It was an amazing feeling to be part of it all," says
Moore. "I think we did know we were doing something special,
although it did seem very natural at the time." They were young
guys with energy and ideas to burn, and instantly pulled in a
new young audience to give the music a new impetus; but with
Liam Og O'Flynn in particular revered as one of the finest
pipers in the country, they retained the respect of the purists
with a total understanding and love of the roots of traditional
music. "I always felt that traditional music could be expanded in
the same way as contemporary music because people were used
to hearing a rhythm section," said Lunny. "But it was still hard
accompanying a piper as good as Liam in a way that didn't
dilute the music or affect its character."

Record label:
Polydor

Produced
by Phil Coulter.

Recorded
at Escape Studios, Kent; January 1973.

Released:
May 1973

Chart peaks:
None (UK) None (US)

Personnel:
Christy Moore (v, g, hm, bodhran); Andy
Irvine (v, g, mandolin, mandola, hm,
hurdy gurdy); Donal Lunny (v, g,
bouzouki, bodhran); Liam Og O'Flynn
(uilleann pipes, tin whistle); Barry
Ainsworth (e)

Track listing:
Raggle Taggle Gypsy/Tabhair Dom Do
Lamh; Arthur McBride; Planxty Irwin;
Sweet Thames Flow Softly; Junior Crehan's
Favourite/Corney Is Coming; West Coast
Of Clare; Jolly Beggar; Only Our Rivers;
Sí Bheag Sí Mhór; Follow Me Up To
Carlow; Merrily Kissed The Quaker; The
Blacksmith

Running time:
41.20

Current CD:
SHANCD79009

Further listening:
After The Break (1979) is especially
recommended. Check also the first self-
titled albums by the Bothy Band and
Moving Hearts. There's also a direct
lineage to the Riverdance soundtrack,
composed by Planxty member Bill
Whelan.

Further reading:
Bringing It All Back Home: The Influence
Of Irish Music (Nuala O'Connor, 1991);
Folk Roots 43 (www.froots.co.uk)

Can

Future Days

A chill-out classic long before the term was coined.

Compared to the somewhat bleak tone of its predecessor *Ege Bamyasi*, the ethereal ambience of *Future Days*, particularly the shimmering Bel Air suite which takes up the whole of side two, is like balm: the perfect accompaniment to a summer's day, as close to rustic bliss as technology gets. Appropriately enough, it was recorded (on twin two-track Revox machines) during the balmy summer of 1973, with the band on particularly empathic form. "Nothing is planned, both in the studio and on stage," explains Irmin Schmidt. "It sounds strange, but everybody in this group is a telepath. We never called it improvising, that was a very misleading term. What we improvised were forms, which we called 'instant composition'. It needs some time to come together: you've got to learn to listen to others, rather than just playing. We played every day, hours and hours, for years."

"We created a spiritual universe between us which allowed this kind of music," adds Michael Karoli. "If you take a mistake as a mistake, you don't get very far with improvisation. If you take a mistake as music as well, you get your ideas from the mistakes. I think our greatest strength was to let things happen."

Appropriately enough, the album's front cover contains both the I-Ching hexagram Ting (The Cauldron) and the Greek letter psi, representative of ESP. For Holger Czukay, Bel Air in particular represented the culmination of what he was trying to do with the bass: "I love it when Can gets the symphonic feeling that Bel Air has. It's when Michael and Irmin are just getting somewhere, and I put the counterpoint to it. That's something which Jack Bruce did so well with Cream."

Not all of the band were as convinced about the album's worth, however. Jaki Liebezeit, for instance, preferred the band's earlier work, when "...everybody just had a few notes he could play, so it stayed simple. But later our technical abilities increased...And then it really went off with *Future Days*, I think, it became too symphonic." Damo Suzuki, too, was disenchanted enough to leave the group: "It was really boring," he said later. "*Future Days* was musically very good, but it was really distant music for me, and more elemental than at the beginning, not so much of a freak out."

For all that, *Future Days* was widely acclaimed as Can's finest work yet, with NME's Ian MacDonald describing it as containing "more positive energy to the square centimetre than three barrels of brown rice".

Record label:
United Artists

Produced
by Can.

Recorded
at Inner Space Studio, Weilerswist, near Köln; 1973.

Released:
June 1973

Chart peaks:
None (UK) None (US)

Personnel:
Holger Czukay (b, e); Michael Karoli (g); Jaki Liebezeit (d); Irmin Schmidt (k); Damo Suzuki (v)

Track listing:
Future Days; Spray; Moonshake (S); Bel Air

Running time:
40.08

Current CD:
SPOON CD 009

Further listening:
All of Can's albums offer manifold delights, though those featuring vocalist Damo Suzuki (Tago Mago (1972), Ege Bamyasi (1972) and Future Days) have the most pleasing similarity of sound and purpose.

Further reading:
The Can Book (Pascal Bussy and Andy Hall, 1989); MOJO 41

Iggy Pop & The Stooges
Raw Power

The Stooges' last gasp, this time with new patron David Bowie.

"I felt doomed at the time, very doomed. No one was listening to me so I thought if we're going down then it's going to be very beautiful," says Iggy today.

Raw Power represented an astonishing comeback for The Stooges, who'd disappeared into junkie oblivion after being dropped by Elektra in 1971. Iggy had bounced back after a fateful meeting with David Bowie and Bowie's manager Tony DeFries while exiled to New York. Ignoring DeFries's plans for a transatlantic, *Transformer*-style collaboration with English sessioneers, Iggy brought over new Detroit hotshot guitarist James Williamson to London, and then the Asheton brothers, with Ron now grudgingly demoted from guitar to bass.

After rehearsing and demoing songs at various London studios, the revamped Stooges discovered a whole new work ethic: "There wasn't a lot of conflict at the time," says James Williamson. "We would just go into CBS studios every single night right after dinner, and just work pretty much until we were too tired to work any more. That was pretty much it. We weren't really doing drugs at that time."

Williamson's guitar style – firmly in the tradition of MC5-style Detroit metal – brought a new brutal muscle to the sound; counterpointed with Iggy's paeans to becoming a good-looking corpse: "I was singing about death trips way before any metal band got into that," he points out, "although that wasn't the whole story."

More conventional in structure than any other Stooges album, *Raw Power* was also bursting with memorable anthems. The album's mix, however, became a source of friction, when Tony DeFries rejected the original Williamson and Pop mix (which was subsequently bootlegged after being previewed on a Detroit radio station). Instead, The Stooges were forced to wait months until Bowie completed a live tour and had a day and a half free to mix the album. Making heavy use of a then-fashionable delay device called The Time Tube, Bowie's version lost much of the punch of the original. A 1997 remix by Iggy himself was far more brutal, VU meters firmly locked in the red, and it's this edition which is most widely available today.

Record label:
CBS

Produced
by James Williamson and Iggy Pop.

Recorded
at CBS Studios, London, September 10–October 6, 1972; mixed March 1973, Western Sound Recorders, Los Angeles.

Released:
June 1973

Chart peaks:
None (UK) 182 (US)

Personnel:
Iggy Pop (v, m); Ron Asheton (b); Scott Asheton (d); James Williamson (g); David Bowie (m)

Track listing:
Search And Destroy; Gimme Danger; Hard To Beat; Penetration; Raw Power; I Need Somebody; Shake Appeal; Death Trip

Running time:
33.57

Current CD:
4851762 Hard To Beat replaced by Your Pretty Face Is Going To Hell

Further listening:
Kill City (1978); live album Metallic KO (1977)

Further reading:
MOJO 29;
www.sonymusic.com/artists/IggyPop

Sly & The Family Stone
Fresh

Long-awaited follow-up to Riot revealed that even an incapacitated Sly could be more alive than most.

The two years since *There's A Riot Goin' On* had not proved any more peaceful. Drug busts, financial hassles, royally wasted TV appearances and rumours of dead bodies at his Bel Air home had accompanied the increasingly haunted figure of Sly Stone. When the new album was titled *Fresh*, few found its claim believable.

Lines like "I switched from coke to pep and now I'm a connoisseur" from opener In Time stretched credibility further. But it was supposed to mark a new beginning. Sly had finally split from manager David Kapralik and signed a new deal with CBS as Fresh Productions. "Sly was developing what he thought was the next step in music," says Robert Joyce who, at 19, had just been made the Family's new production manager at that time. "We were leaders in the field of what we were doing, but the pressure all fell back on him to keep it going. Keep it going. Keep everybody paid."

So Sly attempted to return to sunnier times. The album's a convincing stab at allying his previous album's sprawling, fragmentary voodoo (the mantric closer Babies Makin' Babies) with the upbeat pulse of his early work (witness the straight-ahead pop of If It Were Left Up To Me). Keep On Dancin' even explicitly reprises their first hit Dance To The Music.

Despite losing key members, legendary bassist Larry Graham and drummer Greg Errico, Sly still managed to coax brilliant performances from the Family. Tracks like Thankful 'N' Thoughtful took the funk to such new heights of complex syncopation, it almost appeared as though they'd mastered telepathy. The bass duties are mixed between Graham (who laid down some tracks before his exit), Rusty Allen and Sly himself. It was Sly who performed the stealthily creeping bassline on the outstanding single If You Want Me To Stay. In his usual self-referential mode, this song offered a message to his public claiming he would stick around on the scene as long as they realised that, "I've got to be me…".

Sadly, this 'me' proved to be a singularly unknowable entity. The single went to Number 12 in the US charts – it was to be his last hit. The epically swaying, end-of-night take on Que Sera, Sera got some radio play after rumours of an unlikely

Record label:
Epic

Produced
by Sly Stone, Hamp 'Bubba' Banks and Bro Fred.

Recorded
at Record Plant, and 783 Bel-Air, Los Angeles

Released:
June 1973

Chart peaks:
None (UK) 7 (US)

Personnel:
Sly Stone (g, k, v); Freddie Stone (g); Rose Stone (p, v); Jerry Martini (s); Rusty Allen (b); Andy Newmark (d); Little Sister (bv); Pat Rizzo (s); Cynthia Robinson (t); Larry Graham (b); Bob Gratts, Willie Greer, George Engfer, Tom Flye aka 'Superfly', Mike Fusaro, James Green, Chris Henshaw, Don Puluse, Roy Segal, Bill Schruggs, Richard Tilles (e)

Track listing:
In Time; If You Want Me To Stay (S); Let Me Have It All; Frisky (S/US); Thankful 'N'Thoughtful; Skin I'm In; I Don't Know (Satisfaction); Keep On Dancin'; Que Sera, Sera (Whatever Will Be Will Be)(S/UK); If It Were Left Up To Me; Babies Makin' Babies

Running time:
39.40

Current CD:
485170 2 A remastering mix-up means that this CD contains inferior test mixes that Sly had abandoned in 1972. Thus the only version currently available in Europe amounts to an anthology-style alternative version. The American edition appears to be taken from the correct masters, so look for an import.

Further listening:
There's A Riot Goin' On (1971); Sly Stone
solo album, High On You (1975)

Further reading:
MOJO 9; For The Record: Sly And The
Family Stone, An Oral History (Joel
Selvin, 1997); www.slyfamstone.com

romance between Sly and Doris Day. And Sly was still influential: Miles Davis was taken with In Time, using it as the blueprint for his own voodoo funk album, *On The Corner*.

But he was on his way to the point of no return. The cover shot, taken by Richard Avedon, portrayed Sly as full of high-kicking vitality. The effect was achieved by laying him out on a glass table and shooting from underneath.

Todd Rundgren
A Wizard, A True Star

Blue-eyed soul man takes a trip.

A n essential navigational aid for all astral travellers. Tucked
between the sweet-scented sattiva vibe of his 1972 double
album *Something/Anything* and the sprawling eponymous 1974
masterwork *Todd* came this, Rundgren's acid home-movie, his
Fantasia for one. Famously shy of the drug culture during his
time with The Nazz in the '60s, by the early '70s Todd had
finally taken the lysergic plunge. "Psychedelics brought me to an
awareness of myself that I'd no comprehension of previously,"
said Rundgren. "You don't know you're 'you' until you've had
your ego stripped away and you realise you're all that stuff."

The 'Wizard side', is a microcosmic encapsulation of an
acid trip, from take-off to landing and all stratospheric stop-offs
between. The trip begins and ends with interstellar anthem
International Feel ("Here we are again/The start of the
end/But there's more"), skims across the interplanetary terrain
of Disney's Never Never Land (Todd always was a shrewd and
iconoclastic judge of cover versions), gets horny and disintegrates into tiny molecules on Tic Tic Tic It Wears Off, You
Need Your Head, Rock and Roll Pussy and Dogfight Giggle,
glams up and gender-bends on You Don't Have To Camp
Around, glides majestically across the universe on Zen Archer,
gets the giggles again on Just Another Onion Head and Dada
Dali, before crashing and burning gloriously, emerging only
slightly singed by the multi-coloured flames on When The Shit
Hits The Fan.

Part two showcases Todd, the singer-songwriter, the
"True Star". Sometimes I Don't Know What To Feel and I Don't
Want To Tie You Down are emotionally raw ballads that Carole
King might have written. The sublime medley of I'm So Proud,
Ooh Baby Baby, and La La La Means I Love You pays homage to
his blue-eyed soul heritage, his heroes, and his home town of
Philadelphia. Cool Jerk and Is It My Name are Todd, the unre-
constructed cosmic buffoon, peeling off power chords and
goofing off at the same time. He was a self-promoting, self-
producing, self-sufficient polymath, ten years before Prince and
this was his finest hour.

Record label:
Bearsville

Produced
by Todd Rundgren.

Recorded
at Secret Sound, USA, 1972–1973.

Released:
June 1973

Chart peaks:
None (UK) 86 (US)

Personnel:
Mark 'Moogy' Klingman (k); John Seigler
(c, b); Randy Brecker (t); Dave Sanborn
(s); John Siomos (d); Ralph Shuckett (b);
Mike Brecker (s); Tom Cosgrove; Jean Yves
Lebout; Rick Deringer (g); Barry Rogers
(tb); Buffalo Bill Gelber (b)

Track listing:
International Feel; Never Never Land; Tic
Tic Tic It Wears Off; You Need Your
Head; Rock And Roll Pussy; Dogfight
Giggle; You Don't Have To Camp Around;
Flamingo; Zen Archer; Just Another
Onionhead; Dada Dali; When The Shit
Hits The Fan — Sunset Boulevard; Le
Feel Internationale; Sometimes I Don't
Know What To Feel (S/US); Does Anybody
Love You?; I'm So Proud/Ooh Baby
Baby/La La La Means I Love You/Cool
Jerk; Hungry For Love; I Don't Want To
Tie You Down; Is It My Name?; Just One
Victory

Running time:
53.04

Current CD:
ESM CD 673

Further listening:
Something/Anything (1972)

Further reading:
www.tr-i.com

Stevie Wonder

Innervisions

Mid-point of his great creative eruption.

The ultimate natural, an accomplished multi-instrumentalist by the time he was 10, by the early '70s Stevie Wonder was demanding new challenges which did not include compliance with his label's plan to make him "Stevie Wonder the entertainer, another Sammy Davis". Intrigued by new developments in electronic instruments, he asked for a tutorial from Tonto's Expanding Head Band synthesiser masters Malcolm Cecil and Robert Margouleff.

According to Cecil, he walked into the studio brandishing Tonto's *Zero Time* album, saying "'I don't believe all this was done on one instrument. Show me.' So we dragged his hands all over the Moog and he thought he'd never be able to play it."

Wonder remembered no such doubt: "It was definitely a lot of knobs to turn and push and levers to twist and pull up and down. But my concern was not as great as my eagerness to learn it."

Within weeks, he embarked on one of music's more magisterial tides of creativity. Often working 48 hours solid, in the course of a year he completed tracks that formed the basis of his next five albums.

The third of the sequence, *Innervisions*, confirmed his quality MOR side with love ballads Golden Lady and All In Love Is Fair, but really grasped lapels with the unrestrained anger and political punch of Living For The City. Hard-driving funk rams home the rage behind such lines as "To find a job is like a haystack needle/'Cause where he lives they don't use coloured people". Half-way through, it breaks off to run a highly compressed playlet in which the innocent boy "born in hard time Mississippi" is arrested and jailed for a drugs offence.

The joy was that Wonder took control of the machines and made them express his emotions, warm or raging, and follow his startling sense of where a limber melody or hip-jolting syncopation might lead. Playing almost everything on synthesisers, he powered through Higher Ground, Latin-swayed Don't You Worry 'Bout A Thing, set his anti-drug song Too High pulsing with tension (his 48-hour days ran on adrenaline, his first joint having put him off drugs forever).

The feeling is cornucopia.

Record Label:
Motown

Produced
by Stevie Wonder.

Recorded
at Record Plant, Los Angeles and Media Sound, New York; autumn 1971–spring 1973.

Released:
August 3, 1973

Chart peaks:
8 (UK) 4 (US)

Personnel:
Stevie Wonder (v, Arp & Moog synthesisers, p, electric piano, d); Malcolm Cecil, Scott Edwards, Willie Weeks (b); Dean Parks, David 'T' Walker, Ralph Hammer (g); Clarence Bell (o); Larry 'Nastyee' Latimer (congas); Yusuf Roahman (shaker); Sheila Wilkerson (pc); Lani Groves, Tasha Thomas, Jim Gilstrap (bv); Robert Margouleff, Malcolm Cecil (e, programming); Dan Barbiero, Austin Godsey (e)

Track Listing:
Too High; Visions; Living For The City (S); Golden Lady; Higher Ground (S); Jesus Children Of America; All In Love Is Fair; Don't You Worry 'Bout A Thing (S); He's Misstra Know-It-All (S, UK only)

Running time:
44.15

Current CD:
157 355-2

Further Listening:
Music Of My Mind, Talking Book (1972); Fulfillingness' First Finale (1974); Songs In The Key Of Life (1976)

Further reading:
Stevie Wonder (Constance Elsner, 1977); Stevie Wonder (John Swenson, 1986)

New York Dolls
New York Dolls

Rough-hewn punk primer.

"**G**et the glitter out of your asses and play," barked the producer to the New York Dolls from the safety of his side of the studio glass. That Todd Rundgren himself had hair in four garish colours not found in nature's rainbow is an indication of the bizarre spectacle that was the recording of the Dolls' debut album.

To the band, the sessions were just one more show. They dressed in their finest thrift-shop flash, and always had enough of an entourage present to constitute an audience for every take. Fortunately, there was plenty of music too.

"We'd been working on songs for a solid year," singer David Johansen says. "Once we started going out on the road and being rock stars, we got kind of lax in that department. That's not a terribly unique story, is it?"

Perhaps not, but few bands have delivered a debut this brash and assured. There was no basis for it: the Dolls had been turned down by every major label, finally winding up on Mercury, and even producer Rundgren admitted that their unschooled clatter wasn't his musical cup of tea. The Dolls noticed none of this, rocking on as if they were the center of the universe. They were a rough and raucous extension of the line that ran through The Rolling Stones to the MC5, adding the then-modern touch of sexual confusion to the mix. They more than compensated in energy and style what they lacked in musical grace. Johansen was no Jagger or Tyner vocally, but his attitude was dead-on. The self-taught Johnny Thunders let loose with jagged bursts of stun guitar, playing off the steady rhythm guitar of Sylvain Sylvain and (depending on his liquid/chemical consumption on the day) Arthur Kane's bass. Curiously, Rundgren chose to minimise the band's most powerful and accomplished musician – drummer Jerry Nolan – in the final mix.

Highlights include Personality Crisis, Looking For A Kiss, Trash and Jet Boy, but every other song (excepting a regrettable acoustic number) displays gloriously sloppy excellence. Johansen describes it as "a little jewel of urban folk art", but he's being modest. The album didn't make them the stars they imagined themselves to be but all the right people heard it as a call to arms. *New York Dolls* lit the fuse to punk, and contains enough attitude, enthusiasm and excess to incite more revolutions in the future.

Record label:
Mercury

Produced
by Todd Rundgren.

Recorded
at the Record Plant, New York; April 1973.

Released:
August 1973

Chart peaks:
None (UK) 116 (US)

Personnel:
Johnny Thunders (g); Sylvain Sylvain (g); David Johansen (v, hm); Arthur Kane (b); Jerry Nolan (d); Todd Rundgren (p, Moog); The Fantastic Buddy Bowser (s); Jack Douglas, Ed Sprigg

Track listing:
Personality Crisis; Looking For A Kiss; Vietnamese Baby; Lonely Planet Boy; Frankenstein; Trash (S/US); Bad Girl; Subway Train; Pills; Private World; Jet Boy (S/UK)

Running time:
42.42

Current CD:
Polygram 832-7522

Further listening:
In Too Much Too Soon (1974), second Polygram album; Lipstick Killers (1981) early demos; Red Patent Leather: Live In NYC 1975 (1984) end of the road.

Further reading:
From The Velvets To The Voidoids (Clinton Heylin, 1993); In Cold Blood: The Johnny Thunders Story (Nina Antonia, 1987)

Elton John

Goodbye Yellow Brick Road

The second of seven consecutive US number one albums underlined his status as a global superstar without peer.

From the pomp of the anticipation-building overture Funeral For A Friend, it was clear that this hulking masterwork betrayed a new set of concerns far removed from the country comforts and suburban dreams conjured up previously by lyricist Bernie Taupin: a growing obsession with the travails of fame (Candle In The Wind, Roy Rogers), excitement for primal rock 'n' roll energy (Saturday Night's Alright For Fighting, You're Sister Can't Twist); nostalgia (Goodbye Yellow Brick Road, Danny Bailey) and a decidedly confused attitude towards sexuality (All The Girls Love Alice). However the album's epic nature was achieved by accident. But for The Rolling Stones, everything would have been very different, according to producer Gus Dudgeon who points out that Mick Jagger recommended Byron Lee's Dynamic Studios in Kingston, Jamaica to Elton after a happy sojourn recording the Stones' *Goats Head Soup*.

But Dudgeon soon encountered problems. "It sounded amazing when I'd previously been there," says Dudgeon. "It had exactly what we were looking for, this massive bottom end [which adds bass to a recording]. Things were looking great until we set all the equipment up." The bottom end had inexplicably vanished. "It sounded fucking terrible," admits Dudgeon. After days of dickering, the team taped just one track, a rough run-through of Saturday Night's Alright For Fighting, before repairing to trusted standby the Château d'Herouville in France. Here the tight band of musicians raced through the 21 songs John had stockpiled while holed up in his Kingston hotel room waiting for the studio problem to be resolved.

"That's how it came out a double," says Dudgeon. "Elton just had more time to write than usual. None of us was particularly into doing a double, but the stuff he had was just too good." Although the impact of the fragile Candle In The Wind may now be forever dissipated by overfamiliarity in the wake of the mawkish Diana tribute, *Goodbye Yellow Brick Road* is stacked full of winners, from the touching I've Seen That Movie Too to the rambunctious Faces-pastiche Saturday Night's Alright For Fighting. There are few clunkers (the gruesome white boy reggae of Jamaica Jerk-Off should have been left in Kingston) but several hidden gems including the fragrant Sweet Painted

---

Record label:
DJM

Produced
by Gus Dudgeon.

Recorded
at Château d'Herouville, France; summer 1973.

Released:
October 1973

Chart peaks:
1 (UK) 1 (US)

Personnel:
Elton John (v, p, o, farfisa, mellotron); Dee Murray (b, v); Davey Johnstone (g, v); Nigel Olsson (d, v); David Henstchel (ARP synth); Del Newman (a); Prince Rhino (v); Kiki Dee (v); Ray Cooper (pc); Leroy Gomez (s)

Track listing:
Funeral For A Friend (Love Lies Bleeding); Candle In The Wind (S/UK); Bennie And The Jets (S); Goodbye Yellow Brick Road (S); This Song Has No Title; Grey Seal; Jamaica Jerk-Off; I've Seen That Movie Too; Sweet Painted Lady; The Ballad Of Danny Bailey (1909–34); Dirty Little Girl; All The Girls Love Alice; Your Sister Can't Twist (But She Can Rock'N'Roll); Saturday Night's Alright For Fighting (S); Roy Rogers; Social Disease; Harmony

Running time:
76.23

Current CD:
MCA 528159-2

Further listening:
Elton's other double album Blue Moves (1976)

Further reading:
Elton: The Definitive Biography (Philip Norman, 1992); www.eltonjohn.com

Lady and This Song Has No Title, which, combined with The Ballad Of Danny Bailey, apparently provided Billy Joel with an entire career template. Bennie And the Jets, replete with "live" atmosphere, remains as vibrant as ever, a fact recognised by contemporary urban artists such as Mary J Blige. And this was ever so. The track was released as a US single instead of Candle In The Wind as a response to airplay on R&B radio. "Being R&B lovers and big black music fans that got to our ego," confesses Elton.

As the release of the album was being finalised, Elton played the Hollywood Bowl, introduced in jokey style by Deep Throat star Linda Lovelace and a cast of royal and film star lookalikes. He trailed the album by playing many of its songs there and by selling out two nights at the historic venue. Within weeks *Goodbye Yellow Brick Road* had confirmed him as the biggest British star in the US since The Beatles.

Emerson, Lake And Palmer
Brain Salad Surgery

The master showmen of prog rock reach their creative and commercial zenith.

E merson, Lake And Palmer's torrid brew of keyboard savagery, wistful balladry and hot-wired classicism may seem an unaquirable taste to modern ears, but in 1973–74 they were the cat's knackers, the cutting edge, and stadium giants. Only Led Zeppelin, The Rolling Stones and The Who were bigger live draws, and none of them offered a set that took in Mussorgsky, Copland, Dave Brubeck and boogie-woogie. Here was a band cocky enough and clever enough to record William Blake and the astringent music of Argentine classical composer Alberto Ginastera for their fourth hit album.

Most of *Brain Salad Surgery* (working title was *Whip Some Skull on You*) was assembled at the band's Manticore Studios, an abandoned Odeon cinema in Fulham, London they had turned into a rehearsal and production centre. They worked in the upstairs foyer while the downstairs area was rented out to bands including Zeppelin and Jethro Tull.

Greg Lake remembers *Brain Salad Surgery* as a group effort, whereas previous albums were very much a question of each person thinking of ideas in solitude. Emerson had wanted to have a crack at Jerusalem since his Nice days, but only with Lake had he found an arrangement that worked. For Toccata, Emerson adapted a piece by Ginastera; but there was panic when, close to release, it was discovered that the venerable composer's approval was required. Emerson flew to his Swiss home with a tape, where, to his relief, Ginastera declared the adaptation diabolical. This was meant as a compliment: he gushed that Emerson had captured the malevolent essence of the music.

The album is dominated by the sci-fi suite Karn Evil 9, whose technical complexities built on their hit album *Tarkus*. The title was suggested by lyricist Pete Sinfield as a corruption of "carnival". A former IBM tape operator, Sinfield was also responsible for the 3rd Impression's theme of computers taking over humanity. A carnival of bombast and grungy early Moogs, there's a furious energy about this record and a real spirit of adventure: a couple of minutes of Toccata sound like prototype drum'n'bass.

Greg Lake says that the album came out of the band's "healthy days – as opposed to when everything became fragmented, ego-driven. Our creativity was at its very best."

Record label:
Manticore

Produced
by Greg Lake.

Recorded
at Olympic and Advision Studios, London; 1973.

Released:
November 19, 1973

Chart peaks:
2 (UK) 11 (US)

Personnel:
Keith Emerson (k); Greg Lake (v, b, g); Carl Palmer (d, drum synthesiser); Geoff Young (e)

Track listing:
Jerusalem; Toccata; Still You Turn Me On; Benny The Bouncer; Karn Evil 9 (1st Impression – Part 1); Karn Evil 9 (1st Impression – Part 2); Karn Evil 9 (2nd Impression); Karn Evil 9 (3rd Impression)

Running time:
45.04

Current CD:
ESM CD344

Further listening:
The eponymous first album (1970) and Tarkus (1971) stand up better than bloated later works.

Further reading:
www.dynrec.com/elp/ – the official site; www.brain-salad.com is a good fan site.

The Isley Brothers
3+3

Two generations of a great soul band come together.

During the '50s and '60s The Isley Brothers – Ronald, Rudolph and O'Kelly – had left an indelible mark on soul music with Shout, Twist And Shout and This Old Heart Of Mine, and influencing white pop from The Beatles on down. Then, self-producing and running their own label, T-Neck, they turned the tables by covering the likes of Stephen Stills, Jackie De Shannon, James Taylor and Bob Dylan.

Hearing the possibilities engineer/programmers Bob Margouleff and Malcolm Cecil opened up by introducing Stevie Wonder to synthesisers on *Music Of My Mind* (1972), the Isleys the duo to produce their next album. It was to be titled *3+3* because the three veteran brothers were joined officially by a triumvirate from the next generation, Ernie, Marvin, and 'cousin' Chris Jasper (they had appeared uncredited on the T-Neck albums while finishing college).

Led by the burly O'Kelly, patriarch of the clan, they came punctually to each session, as Margouleff notes: "They arrived prepared, knowing exactly what they wanted. They were a hard-working industrious group, no drugs or alcohol." If any Isley made a mistake, they had to endure O'Kelly's wrath.

With Ronald's timeless tenor in the lead, they tackled Seals and Crofts' Summer Breeze, the Doobie Brothers' Listen To The Music and James Taylor's ballad Don't Let Me Be Lonely Tonight. But their own That Lady (a new version of 1964 hit Who's That Lady) really served notice that The Isleys were back – and that there was a new guitar in town. His name was Ernie Isley, 17 and almost a reincarnation of Jimi Hendrix. At nine, he had stood transfixed when Hendrix was employed in the Isleys' backing band and begged guitar lessons from him. "Ernie's playing on That Lady was all done in one take and he was only rehearsing!" recalls Marvin proudly. "He'd play with the lights off facing the wall so he couldn't see anybody's expression. What he didn't see was us screaming, Ernie, don't stop! Keep it going! By the end we were jumping up and down and giving each other five. To us it was some of the baddest stuff we'd ever heard." Ernie himself remembers that, when he had finished, "Kelly looked at me for about 15 minutes straight without blinking. I felt like I had one foot on the ground and the other on Mount Olympus." That Lady and Summer Breeze were all over American radio in 1973–74 and ushered in the funky family's golden era, which endured well into the '80s.

Record label:
Epic

Produced
by The Isley Brothers.

Recorded
at Record Plant Studios Los Angeles, CA; 1973.

Released:
November 1973

Chart peaks:
None (UK) None (US)

Personnel:
Ron Isley (v); O'Kelly Isley (bv); Rudy Isley (bv); Ernie Isley (g); Marvin Isley (b); Chris Jasper (k); Truman Thomas (o); George Moreland (d); Bob Margouleff (e); Malcolm Cecil (e)

Track listing:
That Lady; Don't Let Me Be Lonely Tonight; If You Were There; You Walk Your Way; Listen To The Music; What It Comes Down To; Sunshine (Go Away Today); Summer Breeze; The Highways Of My Life

Running time:
38.56

Current CD:
4879372

Further listening:
It's Your Thing: The Story Of The Isley Brothers – a comprehensive, well-compiled 3-CD anthology.

Further reading:
www.isleybrothers.com

Tangerine Dream

Atem

One giant step for ambient music.

Tangerine Dream's 1971 album *Alpha Centauri* was dedicated "to those obliged to space"; its successor, the rhythmless double album *Zeit*, was almost all space. These predominantly keyboard-based, *kosmische* albums – "like Pink Floyd without the tunes" was how one commentator summed them up – sounded as if they had been conceived at the point where psychedelia had run its course. But the group were drug-free and Edgar Froese has a different explanation.

"We rather came from a background of painting, sculpting and graphic design, and viewed music as a sort of extension of our creativity – which was limited to concrete form and images in the other art forms," he says. "Music has a sense of abstraction, which has always fascinated us." If its predecessors had read like galactic charts set to music, *Atem* sounds as if Tangerine Dream had landed on one of those far-off worlds and were beaming back musical information. Although the results were more melodic, the group created a series of shifting, semi-fathomable atmospheres where individual instruments were often unrecognisable as they morphed together into new textures and timbres.

Live, the group had used backing tapes since the '60s to "increase the surreal atmosphere for the audience", as Froese puts it. Here the title track begins with a treated recording of breathing ("atem" means "breath" in German) and, taking the Pink Floyd comparison further, the Mellotron fanfares and tympani that usher in the track are reminiscent of that group's Sysyphus from their 1969 album *Ummagumma*. But former jazz drummer Chris Franke's tom-toms soon cut loose, whipping the processional into a cacophony that suddenly implodes, then drifts into a lengthy soundscape of sublime austerity, with keyboard notes hanging like sheets of mist. Fauni-Gena finds Froese's eerie, Debussyesque Mellotron in an alien glade surrounded by teeming, twitching animal life. "We made our own sound recordings at the coast of the North Sea and the bird houses of the Berlin Zoo," he explains. The echo repeats on Circulation Of Events, meanwhile, point towards the sequencer patterns that would become their trademark on their next album, the big-selling *Phaedra*. The band created potent music before and after, but *Atem* still stands as a unique world of sound, an evocative album of seductive strangeness.

Record label:
OHR

Produced
by Tangerine Dream.

Recorded
at Dierks Studios, Stommelen and Cologne; December 1972–January 1973.

Released:
November 1973

Chart peaks:
None (UK) None (US)

Personnel:
Chris Franke (o, VCS3, pc, v); Edgar Froese (Mellotron, g, o, v); Peter Baumann (o, VCS3, p); Dieter Dierks (e)

Track listing:
Atem; Fauni–Gena; Circulation Of Events; Wahn

Running time:
41.54

Current CD:
ESMCD 348

Further listening:
Green Desert, Edgar Froese and Chris Franke's extension of the Atem sound in this appetiser for Virgin Records, recorded in 1973 but not released until 1986.

Further reading:
MOJO 41; Digital Gothic: A Critical Discography Of Tangerine Dream (Paul Stump, 1997) www.tangerinedream.de

The Who

Quadrophenia

Another four-sided enigma from Pete & Co.

Hugely frustrated by the short-circuiting of his *Lifehouse* project (eventually released on six CDs in 2000) in 1973 Pete Townshend turned his ever conflicted creative emotions towards another grand concept, his to Mod, the movement which gave The Who identity.

The title did allude to the ultimately useless technology of quadraphonic sound, but more significantly to the four sides of the personality of central character Jimmy as he struggles to assert his identity in the face of peer pressure, drug confusion, family condemnation and sexual disappointment. To Townshend, it also reflected the split personality of The Who, "Roger the fighter, John the romantic, Keith the lunatic and Pete the self-dubbed 'beggar and hypocrite'".

Structurally, said Townshend, "It's a series of impressions, of memories. You see a kid on a rock in the middle of the sea, and this whole thing explains how he got there."

The band were less than enamoured with the whole idea. While Moon's alcoholism took its toll on his abilities, Daltrey remained staunchly unimpressed, complaining that his voice had been buried in the mix, and Entwistle growled that all the songs sounded the same to him.

But the quartet produced peak performances on songs such as 5.15, Dr Jimmy and Love Reign O'er Me. The adolescent frustration evoked by songs such as Sea And Sand and Cut My Hair proved that Townshend was still in touch with both his own generation and the teenage angst of any era. Moon was instructed to play every percussion instrument to hand, and as the album ends he hurls the tubular bells at his drumkit which noisily collapses in what one critic called "his last great moment on record".

"*Quadrophenia* is about The Who and what happens to us," Townshend explained at the time. "I left it open-ended on a note of spiritual desperation because we're in the middle of nowhere, not sure where we're going." He would tell concert audiences, "It's about growing up. At the end of the album the hero is in grave danger of maturing."

Not so The Who, though. On tour, technical problems resulted in more feuding. Townshend responded to Daltrey's complaints by hitting him over the head with a guitar. The singer's response was one mighty right hook which put his old friend in hospital with concussion. *Quadrophenia* was never played live again until 1996.

Record label:
Polydor

Produced
by The Who.

Recorded
at The Kitchen, Battersea, London and Ronnie Lane's Mobile; June 1972 and June 1973.

Released:
November 1973

Chart peaks:
2 (UK) 2 (US)

Personnel:
John Entwistle (b, horns, v); Roger Daltrey (v); Keith Moon (pc, v); Pete Townshend (g, v, syn); Chris Stainton (p); Chris Stamp, Pete Kameron and Kit Lambert (executive producers)

Track listing:
I Am The Sea; The Real Me (S/US); Quadrophenia; Cut My Hair; The Punk Meets The Godfather; I'm One; The Dirty Jobs; Helpless Dancer; Is It In My Head?; I've Had Enough; 5:15 (S); Sea And Sand; Drowned; Bell Boy; Doctor Jimmy; The Rock; Love Reign O'er Me (S/US)

Running time:
81.44

Current CD:
531 971-2

Further listening:
The Who Sing My Generation (1965)

Further reading:
MOJO 32, 82; Before I Get Old: The Story Of The Who (Dave Marsh, 1983); www.thewho.net

Paul McCartney And Wings
Band On The Run

The fraught fifth post-Beatles release that restored
McCartney's worldwide reputation.

H is solo and early Wings output was mourned and scorned
as wilfully shabby. The critical gush that greeted *Band On
The Run* was a sigh of relief that the man who'd helped set an
unmatchable standard for pop music in the '60s hadn't
completely lost it. Even John Lennon, who'd blown raspberries
at earlier efforts, called it "a great album – you can call them
Wings but it's Paul McCartney music. And it's great stuff."
Perhaps the key to its charms was the duress it was made under.
A week before the five-piece Wings were to fly to Lagos to
record *Band On The Run*, guitarist Henry McCullough stormed
out of the Mull Of Kintyre rehearsals, and six days later
drummer Denny Seiwell followed suit. Paul pushed on with just
Linda and ex-Moody Blues pal Denny Laine. Arriving in
Nigeria, the McCartneys were robbed at knife point and
relieved of, among other things, the sole demo tape of the songs
they were about to record. Paul was accused by irate locals of
intending to exploit Africa's music and musicians and, later still,
a doctor was called when it was thought McCartney was
suffering a heart-attack.

"It was a challenge to be in Lagos," he charmingly
understates, "and very uphill."

Work began at a ferocious lick once the fabulously
outmoded Studer 8-track desk had been dusted down and some
microphones were located in a cardboard box. It was, Laine
remembers, "like a home studio; nobody knew what we were
doing but us", though they took a day out to record Picasso's
Last Words at Ginger Baker's adjacent ARC Studios, on which
Baker appears using a fire-bucket full of gravel as a maraca. The
MO was basic in the extreme: "Normally me and Denny would
start it off with a couple of acoustics, like you would for a
demo," McCartney recalls, "then it would be me on drums, and
then we'd build it up like a sculpture." Back at AIR in London,
the tapes were transferred to 16-track for the overdubs and
Tony Visconti's sax, brass and orchestral scores.

The result was a jewel. *Band On The Run* has a tangible
vibe, McCartney's customary breezy confidence at last matched
by his inspiration. The title track – a three-theme tour de force
about some "rabbits on the run" – is an irresistible statement of
buoyant defiance, Jet is his best rocker since Back In The USSR,

Record label:
Parlophone

Produced
by Paul McCartney.

Recorded
at Arc and EMI Studios, Lagos, Nigeria;
September 1973.

Released:
December 1973

Chart peaks:
I (UK) I (US)

Personnel:
Paul McCartney (v, b, d, g, k); Denny
Laine (g, v); Linda McCartney (v, pc);
Howie Casey (s); Tony Visconti (a); Geoff
Emerick (e)

Track listing:
Band On The Run; Jet; Bluebird; Mrs
Vanderbilt; Let Me Roll It; Mamunia; No
Words; Picasso's Last Words; 1985

Running time:
41.09

Current CD
CDP7892402 adds second, documentary
CD

Further listening:
Mauled at the time but undergoing
reassessment, Ram (1971); Flaming Pie
(1997).

Further reading:
Beatles After The Break Up (Keith
Badman, 1999); Mark Lewisohn's sleeve
notes to the Band On The Run 25th
Anniversary Edition

boasting one of McCartney's all time great vocals, Bluebird is almost a parody of McCartney-esque beauty, Let Me Roll, it's repeated guitar riff becomes near-incantational. Even the question mark over his might-mean-something-probably-don't lyrics is answered by the delightfully sustained paean to rainfall, Mamunia, a pearl of naïve wisdom. The fun he has with Picasso's Last Words (Drink To Me) shows him not letting the absence of a proper song (he wrote it at a party to impress Dustin Hoffman) get in the way of a great track. Laine co-wrote the glorious slab of Wings harmony No Words with his husky tones a discernible part of the fabulous vocal arrangements throughout, but his suggestion that "the contribution of the three people was, you know, very equal" sounds a touch hopeful, with even McCartney regarding the resulting work as "nearly a solo album".

Macca was back to pseudo-democracy on the following few albums – consistently detrimental to the work – and by the next DIY venture (1980's hopeless *McCartney II*), something had definitely gone. Amazingly, doing it for himself again on 1997's *Flaming Pie*, something had definitely returned.

Dan Penn
Nobody's Fool

Debut solo album from stellar back-room boy, one of the decade's great songwriters.

"I made the record because I didn't have anything else to do," Penn explains with characteristic modesty. "There was no-one to cut, so I thought, cut you." Penn had composed his first hit by the age of 18 (for Conway Twitty) and spent the '60s helping invent country-soul as sessionman, producer and song-writer, first at Muscle Shoals and then at the American Sound studios in Memphis. By the end of the decade Penn had used some of his song-writing royalties (from hits such as the Box Tops' Cry Like A Baby, James Carr's Dark End Of The Street and Percy Sledge's Out Of Left Field) to establish his own studio, Beautiful Sounds; certainly an apposite name. This independence allowed Penn to step into the spotlight himself, but though – for example – I Hate You boasts one of the great soul vocals, Penn, typically, downplays the majesty of the performance ("I put too much echo on that one. I've never been real big on echo"). Elsewhere his voice is "dry" and typically laid-back: on the Mississippi symphony Raining In Memphis he resembles a mellow Elvis – though Penn insists he shares with The King a tendency to "waller" vocally – and on Ain't No Love he indulges in some splendid Otis Redding-style bravura. The album closes with three tracks which form a Southern white man's *What's Going On?* in miniature: "I guess I was a bit political at that point," Penn dead-pans. Prayer For Peace is a plea to end racial disharmony, complete with gospel choruses winging in from every point of the stereo picture. If Love Was Money is a rich girl/poor boy story zinging with sophisticated strings, while the extraordinary Skin returns to the problem of race. "I was working at Ardent (Memphis studio) and just found this two-track tape in my brief-case, I'd never seen it before in my life." The tape had a combination of distorted '40s film soundtrack and "backwards Christmas music" on it. Over this Penn dubbed his underplayed but emotive spoken vocal; an idiosyncratic coda to a beautifully played and often surprisingly experimental album.

"We didn't have synthesisers back then so we had to do things with tape speeds and editing," Penn recalls, "We were just having fun." That's what it sounds like, and at the time the album received good reviews but did next-to-nothing commer-cially. Only now is Penn being paid his true due as a performer, his recent tours with cohort Spooner Oldham (and a superb live album) attracting plaudits and many new converts.

Record label:
Beautiful Sounds

Produced
by Dan Penn.

Recorded
at Beautiful Sounds Studios, Memphis, Tennessee, "and some other nice places"; 1969–1971

Released:
1973

Chart peaks:
None (UK) None (US)

Personnel:
Dan Penn (v, g); Spooner Oldham (k); Mike Utley (k); Greg Redding (k); Jay Spell (k); Bill Phillips (k); Bergen White (vibes); Tommy Richards, Charlie Freeman, Tony Oterri, Marlin Greene (g); John Huey, Leo LeBlanc (steel gtr); Jim Johnson, David Hood (b); Dulin Lancaster, Roger Hawkins, Sammy Creason (d); Wayne Jackson (t); Andrew Love (s); Cargo, Jeanie Green, Mary Holiday, Ginger Holiday, Susan Dotson, Susan Coleman (bv); Nashville Strings & Horns; Memphis Horns; Memphis Strings; Bergen White (a)

Track listing:
Nobody's Fool (S/US); Raining In Memphis; Tearjoint; Time; Lodi; Ain't No Love; I Hate You; Prayer For Peace; If Love Was Money; Skin

Running time:
30.17

Current CD:
EE 4622

Further listening:
Do Right Man (1994). Moments From This Theatre (1999) is a fantastic stripped-down live album with long-time collaborator Spooner Oldham.

Further reading:
Say It One Time For The Brokenhearted (1998); It Came From Memphis (1995); Sweet Soul Music (1986)

Eno
Here Come The Warm Jets

Patenting glam punk on rush-recorded solo debut.

I t's said that the day Brian Eno left Roxy Music – June 21, 1973 – he wrote this album's standout track, the nagging and nasty pre-punk classic Baby's On Fire. At this distance, Eno can't confirm the story, but he does recall the sense of freedom after the acrimonious fall-out with Bryan Ferry during the recording of the band's second album *For Your Pleasure*.

"I was absolutely euphoric," he says. "I remember leaving my management offices on the King's Road the day I resigned and skipping and leaping down the road in delight. I felt so liberated." He quickly began recording at the very economical Majestic Studios in Clapham, south London, the total recording costs were £5,600.

"I was flat broke, having not been a songwriter with Roxy," he says. "It was very cheap but served its purpose – I needed a place where I could feel comfortable making mistakes. If a day was wasted it didn't cost me a fortune." Musicians included Chris Spedding, his Sharks bandmate Busta Cherry Jones – who Eno would later recall to help funkify Talking Heads – and all of Roxy Music except, of course, Ferry.

"I wanted to make a hard-sounding record, one that didn't try and hide its artifice and pretend it was a recording of a performance." To that end he ruled that there should be no reverb simulating a live sound, though producer Chris Thomas snuck it onto a couple of tracks. *Here Come The Warm Jets* (among the jumble on the cover's mantelpiece is a charming Victorian picture of a micturating maiden) retains a brittle, synthetic and thoroughly modern ring. Eno's playfulness is evident in his wordplay (The Paw Paw Negro Blowtorch) and while he sticks in the main to traditional song structure, they're interlaced with doo-wop harmonies, sub-Velvets white noise, stop-start rhythms, Beach Boys pastiche and faux-Roxyisms (during Dead Finks Don't Talk's jokey attack on Ferry he breaks into a spot-on parody of the Roxy mainman's braying vocal style).

However, once recording was over, Eno lost interest in the album, moving onto to the experimental collaboration with Fripp, *No Pussyfooting*. He even tried to persuade Island to abandon its release. "It seemed full of lost opportunities. This often happens though – I suffer from post-partum depression!" he says. "But fortunately they wouldn't listen to me and went ahead. I'm glad they did."

Record label:
Island

Produced
by Eno.

Recorded
at Majestic Studios, London; September 1973.

Released:
January 1974

Chart peaks:
26 (UK) 151 (US)

Personnel:
Brian Eno (v, k, snake guitar, syn, treatments); Andy Mackay (s, k); Robert Fripp (g); Phil Manzanera (g); Paul Rudolph (g, b); Chris Spedding (g); Busta Cherry Jones (b); John Wetton (b); Paul Thompson (pc)

Track listing:
Needles In The Camel's Eye; The Paw Paw Negro Blowtorch; Baby's On Fire; Cindy Tells Me; Driving Me Backwards; On Some Faraway Beach; Blank Frank; Dead Finks Don't Talk; Some Of Them Are Old; Here Come The Warm Jets

Running time:
41.40

Current CD:
ILPS 9268

Further listening:
Taking Tiger Mountain By Strategy (1974)

Further reading:
Paul Morley's sleevenotes to Enobox 2: Vocal (1993); enoweb at www.hyperreal.org

Gram Parsons
Grievous Angel

A touchstone of alternative country.

In his last year, the young man born into a wealthy family as Cecil Ingram Conner III had realised it was time to turn his life around. A paid up member of the Brian Jones Physical Abuse Programme, he tasted many of the Devil's most insidious pleasures in his quarter century. But, invigorated by the way his first solo tour and album (1973's *GP*) were received, Gram Parsons was now itching to mend his no-good ways and continue his winning streak. To do so would require a certain amount of sobering up.

When the *GP* tour ended in spring '73, he was already assembling songs for the follow-up. He was particularly enthused by his new singing partner, Emmylou Harris from Birmingham, Alabama (previously resident songstress in a Washington, DC bar until discovered by The Flying Burrito Bros). The ache in Parsons' cracked voice dovetailed perfectly with Emmylou's clear soprano. Although eyebrows were raised when Gram chose himself as the album's sole producer, by all accounts the sessions were magical. "There was a real sense of exhilaration, such an excitement," recalls Harris. "He would go back at the end of the day's recording just to listen to the songs we did and talk about the band we would put together, the tour we would do. There were so many plans. Because he loved that record. It just seemed like he was so strong, that's why his death was such a shock to me."

Parsons had come up with his most enduring songs: a heartfelt ballad to his deceased mother called Brass Buttons, the gorgeous left-at-the-altar tale of $1000 Wedding, the rockin' Ooh Las Vegas, and the poignant In My Hour Of Darkness which recounted the deaths of three close friends and subsequently seemed an omen for Parsons' own demise a few weeks after it was recorded. Add to this the terrifically cinematic Return Of The Grievous Angel and you have five country-rock standards. Supported by strong covers of Tom T. Hall and The Everly Brothers and with crisp, inventive playing from a band largely on hire from Elvis Presley's Vegas crew, this was the album Parsons had dreamed of.

Then, when he finished recording, he decided to go to the town of Joshua Tree in the Californian desert to celebrate. He celebrated himself to death, overdosing in his hotel room on a narcotic cocktail which stopped his heart. He was 26.

Record label:
Reprise

Produced
by Gram Parsons.

Recorded
at Wally Heider Studio 4 and Capitol Recording Studios, Hollywood; summer 1973.

Released:
January 1974

Chart peaks:
None (UK) None (US)

Personnel:
Gram Parsons (v, g); Emmylou Harris (v); Glen D Hardin (k); James Burton (g); Emory Gordy (b); Ronnie Tutt (d); Herb Pederson (g); Al Perkins (sg); Bernie Leadon (g, dobro); Byron Berline (fiddle, mandolin); ND Smart II (d); Steve Snyder (v); Linda Ronstadt (bv); Hugh Davies (e); Phil Kaufman, Kim Fowley, Ed Tickner, Jane & Joe Doe ("background blah blah on Northern Quebec Medley")

Track listing:
Return Of The Grievous Angel; Hearts On Fire; I Can't Dance; Brass Buttons; $1000 Wedding; Medley Live From Northern Quebec: Cash On The Barrelhead/Hickory Wind; Love Hurts; Ooh Las Vegas; In My Hour Of Darkness

Running time:
36.12

Current CD:
7599261082 adds: GP

Further listening:
Parsons first solo album, GP (1973); Gram Parsons & the Fallen Angels, Live, 1973 featuring Emmylou Harris and crew in concert.

Further reading:
Hickory Wind: The Life And Times Of Gram Parsons (Ben Fong-Torres, 1991); Gram Parsons: A Music Biography (Sid Griffin, 1985); www.gramparsons.com

Tangerine Dream
Phaedra

With one bound, the guitar becomes obsolete.

Nothing much prepared the record-buying public for *Phaedra*. Sure, rock stars had been dabbling with synthesisers since the late '60s, Terry Riley had composed works using layers of minimalist keyboards, and Tonto's Expanding Head Band had begun devising ways to give electronic music a rhythmic pulse. With *Phaedra*, though, it all came together into an accessible ambient brew, sending reviewers scrurrying to their thesauruses in search of alternative ways to say 'cosmic'.

It had started when German rock guitarist Edgard Froese formed The Ones in 1965. They played traditional rock instruments, quite contentedly, until May 15, 1967 — when they supported Hendrix and were stunned by him. Convinced they could never match Hendrix on guitars, switched to primitive synthesisers as soon as they became available, and started devising their own futuristic instrumental music.

In 1973 mindful that the unlikely success of Mike Oldfield's long-form instrumental *Tubular Bells* had established his Virgin label, Richard Branson offered them a five-year contract. Until they entered Manor Studios, Tangerine Dream's music had all been improvised. Now, however, the complexity of the latest synths and sequencers required them to impose some pre-arranged shape on their compositions. "Just tuning the instruments took several hours each day," recalls Froese. Working daily from 11am until 2am, they completed six and a half minutes of music in 11 days, before finally mastering the machines and finishing the rest in a frenzied week. Musical inspiration (and titles) were drawn largely from Greek, Egyptian and Indian mythology, but the swirling electronic dreamscapes with their constantly shifting patterns, gradual changes of pace and vast blocks of seemingly orchestral/choral sound, could be interpreted uniquely by every listener. Gordon Fletcher of Rolling Stone hailed the "three visionary German kids" and their "amazing record" as "an immensely enjoyable experience". Before long, *Phaedra* was the only album cover on which any self-respecting head would be seen rolling a joint. Despite its lack of similarity to anything preceding it, *Phaedra* earned gold discs in seven countries, and (along with their fellow-countrymen, Kraftwerk) paved the way for modern electronic music.'

Record label:
Virgin

Produced
by Edgar Froese.

Recorded
at The Manor, Shipton-on-Cherwell, Oxfordshire; November 20–December 11, 1973.

Chart peaks:
15 (UK) None (US)

Released:
February 20, 1974

Running time:
37.57

Personnel:
Edgar Froese (Mellotron, b, syn); Chris Franke (syn); Peter Baumann (k, syn, flute); Phil Becque (e)

Track listing:
Phaedra; Mysterious Semblance At The Strand Of Nightmares; Movements Of A Visionary; Sequent C'

Current CD:
TAND5

Further listening:
Stratosfear (1976), the point at which Tangerine Dream reached a perfect balance between innovation and proficiency.

Further reading:
http://www.tangerinedream.de/

Lamont Dozier

Black Bach

Euphoric, string-powered soul from revered Motown writer and producer.

Anyone who takes the mantle of a classical icon and has an illustration of himself as a weathered bust on the cover of their album might well be accused of being a little full of himself. But Lamont Dozier's unusual mid-'70s album does just that and he gets away with it.

Still only 32, Dozier had already had hits in his own right, written and produced dozens for Motown, formed his own labels and worked with everyone from The Four Tops and Supremes through to Chairmen Of The Board and Freda Payne. His lengthy relationship with Brian and Eddie Holland had made the Holland/Dozier/Holland writing and production team a household name. What else was there left to do but leave it all and start again?

He broke up the partnership, abandoned their HDH label and started to record for ABC Records. His 1973 solo album, *Out Here On My Own* had concentrated on simple narrative mixed with a little politics (the single Fish Ain't Bitin'). *Black Bach*, on the other hand, was a grand act of hubris, a lushly orchestrated soul symphony, silky, sweet and simmering with emotion.

He called in a huge band of seasoned players to fill out the sound. At times there was a cast of hundreds in attendance, choirs of angels accompanying Lamont's ruminations on life and love, as he stood centre stage hamming it up. Dark and brooding in places, euphoric elsewhere, it indicated his distance from the mini-soap operas he'd helped create at Motown. And set in among all this swirling grandeur is Dozier's solitary, rather plain voice commanding all of the attention. It many ways it could be viewed as a folly, exactly the kind of record one would expect from a proven writer of hits not known for his own vocal prowess, but with a lavish budget to play with — not dissimilar in many ways from Jimmy Webb's solo albums of the same period. Even so, that mix of conceit and wing-and-a-prayer experiment makes it fascinating too. Naturally it didn't sell and, like much on the ABC label, hasn't made it onto CD, so this classic soul folly has receded into myth.

Record label:
ABC

Produced
by McKinley Jackson.

Recorded
at ABC Recording Studio, Los Angeles, California; 1973.

Released:
February 1974

Chart peaks:
None (UK) None (US)

Personnel:
Lamont Dozier (v); Ray Parker Jr (g); Melvin 'Wah Wah' Ragin (g); Dean Parks (g); Greg Poree (g); Rick Straviski (g); Scott Edwards (b); Ronald Brown (b); Ed Greene (d); Sylvester Rivers, Sonny Burkes, McKinley Jackson, Ernest Vantrese (p); Clark E Sprangler (s); Eddie 'Bongo' Brown, Leslie Bass (pc); Jessica Smith, Patricia Hodges, Myrna Matthews, Edna Wright, Darlene Love, Julia Tillman, Maxine Willard, Oren Waters, Luther Waters, Marti McCall (v)

Track listing:
Shine; Put Out My Fire; Let Me Start Tonite (S/US); All Cried Out; Intermission; Prelude; Rose; Thank You For The Dream; I Wanna Be With You; Blue Sky And Silver Bird

Running time:
39.52

Currently unavailable on CD

Further listening:
While Out Here On My Own (1973) and the following Love And Beauty (1975) have some excellent songs, they lack the carefully-tempered power of Black Bach. They're certainly worth a listen as are any of his earlier Motown, Invictus and Hot Wax sides.

Further reading:
www.lamontdozier.com

Roy Harper
Valentine

Folk-rocker's most vivid and enduring collection.

A singular mix of hardcore hippy and unrepentant chauvinist, Harper is a folk singer who effected a superbly bloody-minded rapprochement with rock. Friends like Jimmy Page, Robert Plant, Keith Moon and Ian Anderson crop up on his various records from the early to middle '70s – his great period – and lend a little muscle to music which already had plenty of gristle in it. Harper could write effective protest-cum-political songs, such as the haunting South Africa, but his love songs – battered, intoxicated and helplessly personal – are his finest work. He made clever use of the studio, too: the earlier *Stormcock* was a soloistic tour de force, and his deployment of multi-tracking and reverb, in some ways similar to some of John Martyn's work of the same period, made the records intriguingly individual. But *Valentine* is his warmest and most affecting set.

"I don't know, man, I've listened to a lot of other singers," he said around this time, "but none of them have the burning intensity of my own work." Fair comment, except that Roy's intensity could as easily spill over into embarrassing wrong-headedness. "Equality yes, but when it comes to breast feeding, I just can't make it," he says about the preposterously nasty Magic Woman (Liberation Reshuffle), a completely daft demolition of women's lib; Forbidden Fruit is about sex with 13-year-old schoolgirls ("Sing it smiling with gentle integrity and a knowledge of the real world"). Small wonder that his personal kind of outrage fell out of sight when punk swept in, and although he has continued to make occasional records, he is a tough subject for rehabilitation. Better to remember him for his gorgeous elegies to a pastoral England which was already slipping quickly from view in 1974: Twelve Hours Of Sunset, Commune and above all his astonishingly lovely rendition of North Country, which effortlessly cuts Bob Dylan's version.

Record label:
Harvest

Produced
by Peter Jenner and Roy Harper.

Recorded
in 1974.

Released:
March 1974

Chart peaks:
27 (UK) None (US)

Personnel:
Roy Harper (g, v); Max Middleton (p); Tim Walker, Jimmy Page (g); Pete Sears (b); Keith Moon, Marty Simon (d) John Leckie (e)

Track listing:
Forbidden Fruit; Male Chauvinist Pig Blues; I'll See You Again; Twelve Hours Of Sunset; Acapulco Gold; Commune; Magic Woman (Liberation Reshuffle); Che; North Country; Forever.

Running time:
42.04

Current CD:
Science Friction HUCD015 adds: Home (studio); Too Many Movies; Home (live)

Further listening:
HQ (1998); Flashes From The Archives Of Oblivion (1974)

Further reading:
www.royharper.com

Richard And Linda Thompson

I Want To See The Bright Lights Tonight

His emergence as the major folk-rock artist of his generation and hers as the finest interpreter of his songs.

Linda Peters originally met Richard Thompson when she was recording a Kelloggs Cornflakes TV commercial at Sound Techniques studio at the same time Fairport Convention were recording Liege & Lief. She was already a close friend and big fan of Sandy Denny and, always insecure about her own singing, and desperately nervous in front of an audience, reluctant to assume duo status with Richard after they were married.

"I was always amazed by Richard's writing," said Linda. "He was very focused and constantly came up with these incredible songs. People sometimes said I should write more but how could I write when there's Richard in the house turning out all this amazing stuff?"

In fact, the fragile emotions she exuded provided the perfect foil for Richard's songwriting as it took on a new personality, rooted in a cinematic storytelling style and built around vivid, heartbreaking scenarios. If Richard's initial steps into a solo career with *Henry The Human Fly*'s modern take on the folk tradition were tentative and uneasy, he was audibly growing in confidence and flair with Linda as the conduit for his songs. Certainly the title track is a superior kind of pop song – covered as a single by Julie Covington – and the album is full of tracks that have long been accepted as classics by Thompson aficionados, brooding masterpieces like Down Where The Drunkards Roll, The Great Valerio and, most desperate of all, The End Of The Rainbow. Richard had invented a new, thoroughly English style of social commentary. You could see its roots in folk, but ever ready to launch into a blistering guitar solo, this was a modern rock album with a difference. The public didn't quite know what to make of it, setting Richard off on a familiar path of critical acclaim dampened by marketing confusion and commercial disappointment. It's been the story of his career ever since.

Record label:
Island

Produced
by John Wood and Richard Thompson.

Released:
April 1974

Chart peaks:
None (UK) None (US)

Personnel:
Richard Thompson (v, g); Linda Thompson (v); John Kirkpatrick (acc, concertina); Richard Harvey (horn, krummhorn); Trevor Lucas (v); Simon Nicol (g, k, v, dulcimer); Roy Wood (v); Timi Donald (d); Pat Donaldson (b); Brian Gulland (v, horn, krummhorn); Royston Wood (v); CWS Silver Band (horns); John Wood (e)

Track listing:
When I Get To The Border; The Calvary Cross; Withered And Died; I Want To See The Bright Lights Tonight; Down Where The Drunkards Roll; We Sing Hallelujah; Has He Got A Friend For Me; The Little Beggar Girl; The End Of The Rainbow; The Great Valerio

Running time:
36.45

Current CD:
IMCD160

Further listening:
Pour Down Like Silver (1975) an awesome study in bleakness. Richard's most rounded solo albums, Rumor And Sigh (1991) and Hand Of Kindness (1983).

Further reading:
Richard Thompson: Strange Affair (Patrick Humphries, 1997);

10cc
Sheet Music

Clever pop-single craftsmen make great album.

It looked like a novelty. In the glittery early '70s a decidedly unglamorous, denim-clad quartet of pasty-faced Manchester studioniks appeared with Donna, a doo-wop pastiche that sounded like The Beatles' Oh Darling; cartoon falsetto juxtaposed with dark brown bass vocals, limp hair, squinty drummer, moderate hit, goodbye surely? But no: Rubber Bullets, a cheery shuffle about the suppression of prisoners, complete with sadistic jokes ('I love to hear those convicts squeal/It's a shame these slugs ain't real') and super-dumb chorus, was a monster hit. But it was the follow-up – The Dean And I – that pointed the way; hook-stuffed but with an unpredictable structure and a pervading sense of the smarts, it signalled musicians of extraordinary gifts. Their second album, *Sheet Music*, proved they could also riff big, jump-cut into a rumba, harmonise like angels and make awful puns. "The Beach Boys of Good Vibrations; the Beatles of Penny Lane" gushed the Melody Maker, "[It] defies you to label it mere eclecticism, something akin to musical Dada," raved the NME.

The four writers, singers and multi-instrumentalists happily cross-fertilised in various co-composer permutations, attempting to impress each other. Later, it became clearer that this art-pop combo were really Godley/Creme (art) and Gouldman/Stewart (pop) but on *Sheet Music* the union was seamless.

"We had tremendous fun, we couldn't go wrong," remembers Gouldman. "We had to keep ourselves entertained and being the people we were, you couldn't get away with anything. No cliché was allowed unless it was so obvious, we wanted it like that."

The Worst Band In The World, a knowing satire on pop mediocrity, packed more invention into its two and a half minutes than could be found in the entire output of their glam contemporaries. Significantly, that particular Godley/Creme track failed as a single but Stewart/Gouldman's lighter though still relentlessly clever Wall Street Shuffle did the trick.

Gouldman: "We came close to sixth-form humour but it was too smart. Kevin and Loll were better at that than me and Eric but we got infected with it." Though 10cc went on to more elaborate recordings and bigger commercial success, *Sheet Music* represents their artistic peak.

Record label:
UK

Produced
by 10cc.

Recorded
at Strawberry Recording Studios, Stockport, Cheshire; winter 1973–1974.

Released:
May 1974

Chart peaks:
9 (UK) 81 (US)

Personnel:
Lol Creme (v, g, gizmo, p, k); Kevin Godley (v, d, pc); Graham Gouldman (v, b, g); Eric Stewart (v, g, p, k, e, m)

Track listing:
The Wall Street Shuffle; The Worst Band In The World; Hotel; Old Wild Men; Clockwork Creep; Silly Love; Somewhere In Hollywood; Baron Samedi; The Sacro-iliac; Oh Effendi.

Running time:
37.44

Current CD:
Repertoire REP4843WY, adds 18 Carat Man Of Means; Gismo My Way

Further listening:
Original Soundtrack (1975); How Dare You (1976)

Further reading:
The 10CC Story (George Tremlett, 1975); http://welcome.to/10cc www.page27.co.uk/tencc

Robert Wyatt
Rock Bottom

His second solo album, and debut for Richard Branson's burgeoning hippy-rock label.

Y ou'd think the title referred, ironically or otherwise, to Wyatt's state of mind following the tragic accident on June 1 1973 – he fell from a fourth-storey window – which left him paraplegic. However, the way Wyatt tells it, the mood was one of euphoria: "One of the things about lying around hospital for a year was that I was free to dream," he remarks today. "I was able to really think through the music. Most musicians are busy thinking about trying to pay their bills. If anything, the title alluded to the sea bed, to sleep and dreams."

Wyatt, to his eternal distress, had been expelled from The Soft Machine in 1970, shortly after cutting *The End Of An Ear*, a patchy avant-garde solo album. He subsequently made two excellent records under the name Matching Mole. But none of those records quite prepared the listener for the vivid inventiveness of this album.

It began life as the third Matching Mole record – and was mostly composed on the Venetian island of Guidecca while Wyatt's partner Alfreda Benge (who drew the cover image) worked as an assistant on director Nic Roeg's thriller Don't Look Now. Wyatt was "spending all day watching lizards on the walls of the house. To keep me occupied Alfreda bought me a basic little keyboard with a particular vibrato that shimmered like the water around us." Returning to London, Wyatt began rehearsing a new band and asked Pink Floyd's drummer, Nick Mason, to produce the record because he wanted to repay a favour. "I had a card from Robert asking me to produce the album about two days before he had his accident," says Mason. "It's one of the things I'm most proud of doing in 30 years of music, and I still find it very moving to listen to." After the accident Wyatt realised that he'd never drum or tour again, but neither would he be tied to one band of musicians. "In a way it gave me a new freedom," he reflects.

The next summer, the Virgin Mobile was tethered in a field outside a borrowed Wiltshire cottage and recording began. "I loved working with Robert," says Mason. "I remember one piece where he played the rhythm on an old tea tray. He was very focused, full of ideas. It's an important album, so personal, with some beautiful songs." Guided by Wyatt's plaintive Olde-England croon, the album's impressionistic drift had no precedent in the art-rock canon and has remained inimitable.

Record label:
Virgin

Produced
by Nick Mason.

Recorded
at The Manor, Oxfordshire and Mobile studio at Delphina's Farm, Little Bedwyn Wiltshire; February–March 1974.

Released:
July 26, 1974

Chart peaks:
None (UK) None (US)

Personnel:
Robert Wyatt (v, k, g, "James's drum"); Richard Sinclair (b); Laurie Allan (d); Hugh Hopper (b); Ivor Cutler (v); Mongezi Feza (t); Alfreda Benge (v); Gary Windo (bass clarinet tenor); Fred Frith (va); Mike Oldfield (g)

Track listing:
Sea Song; A Last Straw; Little Red Riding Hood Hit The Road; Alifib; Alife; Little Red Robin Hood Hit The Road

Running time:
39.34

Current CD:
HNCD 1426

Further listening:
Ruth Is Stranger Than Richard (1975); Nothing Can Stop Us – compilation (1982)

Further reading:
MOJO 64; www.strongcomet.com/wyatt

Average White Band
Average White Band

Average? Not hardly.

By early 1974 Average White Band seemed to have blown it. Their first album for MCA, *Show Your Hand*, had bombed. Their second was handed back to them unreleased. It looked grim. For about a week. Then they met Atlantic Records co-founder Jerry Wexler. He loved the songs on their MCA tape and by April they were at Criteria Studios, Miami, looking on bemused while soul immortals Wexler, Tom Dowd and Arif Mardin decided which of them should produce the revamped album. Eventually, they decamped to New York with Mardin. Seasoned pros permanently enraptured by James Brown, Donny Hathaway, Marvin Gaye and other soul greats, they responded eagerly.

"Arif was lovely, the bee's knees, he cared so much about what we were doing," says Hamish Stuart. "Even the engineer Gene Paul (Les Paul's son) got right behind us." Duly encouraged, they nailed it: the discipline, the ease, the funk. Although the songs on the second vinyl side were less strong, the band were all firing – viz Stuart's soaring falsetto on Person To Person, the booty-shaking architecture of Onnie McIntyre's guitar solo on The Isley Brothers' Work To Do, the judder of Alan Gorrie's bass on Got The Love, the saxmen's moan-and-thrust riffs and Robbie McIntosh's snap-crackle drumming throughout. However, to general surprise, the instrumental Pick Up The Pieces stood out. "The MCA version was like The JBs' Pass The Peas," says Stuart. "But we dug deeper, found an innovative groove. The moment we finished it we were all hysterically dancing round the room. Playing it back we just thought, 'God, that's us!'" But Stuart reckons it took him 20 years to digest subsequent events: "A surreal time. I've only recently started writing some songs about it." That September, at a showbiz party after a Los Angeles Troubadour gig, McIntosh died of "a strychnine-based heroin overdose" thinking he was snorting cocaine. Then, with the band in a hopeless spin, Pick Up The Pieces took off via black radio, crashing straight through the "blue-eyed soul" jibes. They all moved to the States and prospered until the early '80s. And if they needed further vindication the sampling era provided it as their records were repeatedly plundered by rap-R&B artists including TLC, Ice Cube and Utah Saints – an enduring tribute to McIntosh.

"Robbie strapped us to the groove," says Stuart. "He understood it better than any of us. He had an arranger's mind. He was the catalyst. It wouldn't have happened without him."

Record label:
Atlantic

Produced
by Arif Mardin.

Recorded
at Criteria Sound Studios, Miami, Florida; Atlantic Recording Studios, New York; April–May, 1974.

Released:
July 1974

Chart peaks:
6 (UK) 1 (US)

Personnel:
Alan Gorrie (v, b, g); Hamish Stuart (v, g, b); Roger Ball (k, s); Onnie McIntyre (g); Malcolm 'Molly' Duncan (s); Robbie McIntosh (d); Gene Paul (e)

Track listing:
You Got It; Got The Love; Pick Up The Pieces (S); Person To Person; Work To Do; Nothing You Can Do (S); Just Wanna Love You Tonight; Keepin' It To Myself; I Just Can't Give You Up; There's Always Someone Waiting

Running time:
40.24

Current CD:
CCSCD438

Further listening:
Soul Searching (1976) – decent follow-up

Further reading:
www.averagewhiteband.com

Neil Young
On The Beach

Young dreamily combines personal and political horror and creates his masterpiece. But nobody gets it.

In 1974, Crosby, Stills, Nash & Young reformed for one of the biggest arena tours of the decade. Halfway through, cunning plan or not, with no new CSNY album available Young put out his own LP. There was, as it happens, already one in the can – the corrosive *Tonight's The Night*, recorded with Crazy Horse after the heroin deaths of guitarist Danny Whitten and roadie Bruce Berry – but its release had been put on hold. Not, as his record company and some of his fans might have hoped, in favour of a more accessible, less harrowing album – many had still not forgiven him for the previous year's self-indulgent soundtrack, *Journey Through The Past* and live set *Time Fades Away* (which sounds riveting now but in those laid-back singer-song-writer times was deemed erratic and out of place). *On The Beach*, he told Rolling Stone, was "probably one of the most depressing records I've ever made", a statement with which most of the reviews at the time (NME – "It's a downer") concurred. Then, as he pointed out some years later, "It was only a reflection of what I was going through at the time." Things like divorce, death, dealing with celebrity, and the demise of the hippy dream.

Though closer examination would reveal more positive, cathartic aspects ("I'm deep inside myself," he sang, adding "but I'll get out somehow") and even sparks of dark humour, this was as raw and cathartic an album as Young had made. Since sepa-rating from actress Carrie Snodgress, with whom he'd had a son Zeke, Young had moved south from his Northern California ranch to his house in Malibu, on the beach, before making this record, on which neighbours Rick Danko and Levon Helm helped out. It wasn't just the estrangement that was occupying his thoughts, nor the fact that their son had been diagnosed as suffering from cerebral palsy, though these no doubt added to the prevalent feeling of paranoia and decay.

One theme – somewhat incongruous, perhaps, given his decision to rejoin the mammoth CSNY – was the hollowness of stardom. Others were the decline of American culture – although unnamed, Charles Manson (whom Young knew prior to the Family murder, having met the budding singer-songwriter at Beach Boy Dennis Wilson's house) and kidnapped heiress-turned-revolutionary Patty Hearst feature in the songs

Record label:
Reprise

Produced
by Neil Young with co-production from David Briggs, Mark Harman and Al Schmitt.

Recorded
at Sunset Sound, Hollywood and Broken Arrow Studios, San Francisco; 1974.

Released:
July 1974

Chart peaks:
42 (UK) 16 (US)

Personnel:
Neil Young (g, v, banjo, hm); Ben Keith (sg, p, bv); Billy Talbot (b); Ralph Molina (d); Tim Drummond (b, pc); Levon Helm (d); David Crosby (g); Rick Danko (b); George Whitsell (g); Graham Nash (p, hm, tambourine); Rusty Kershaw (sg)

Track listing:
Walk On (S); See The Sky About To Rain; Revolution Blues; For The Turnstiles; Vampire Blues; On The Beach; Motion Pictures; Ambulance Blues

Running time:
39.00

Currently unavailable on CD

Further listening:
Tonight's The Night (1975); Sleeps With Angels (1995)

Further reading:
MOJO 10, 25, 44; Neil Young: Here We Are In The Years (1982);
www.bosco.net/human-highway
www.neilyoung.com

Revolution Blues and Ambulance Blues — and the decline of American counterculture. "Sooner or later," he told the hippies in Walk On, "it all gets real."

When Young tried to add some of these songs to the CSN&Y set he met resistance — outright refusal when it came to the Manson-inspired number; what David Crosby would have called "a bummer". Vampire Blues had more of a note of resigned optimism: "Good times are coming," Young sang, "but they sure are coming slow," while the epic title track was a lament for Young as much as a lament for his adopted country.

It was a therapeutic album, signalling Young's emergence from a dark night of the soul, and analysing his past like a man three times his age, offering a fresh perspective on his future. Thankfully, the album was critically "rediscovered" quite soon. One month after the NME's negative review, assistant editor Ian MacDonald wrote: "*On The Beach* isn't, as previously interpreted, the fag-end of Neil Young's romance with rejection but actually a quite positive piece of work in the Merciless Realism bracket of Lennon's primal-scream period."

Blue Öyster Cult

Secret Treaties

'Heavy-metal' before it got speedy. The working title was Power In The Hands Of Fools.

Think Blue Öyster Cult and you inevitably think Don't Fear The Reaper. Great as that track was, there was much more to this inventive troupe. As this fine album attests.

"Personally, *Secret Treaties* is my favourite BÖC album," says Eric Bloom. "I was the only one who was single, so I did a lot of writing on it."

In 1974, the Blue Öyster Cult had a communal house/rehearsal den on Long Island, New York where Bloom composed the music for Subhuman and ME 262. By the time recording started at Columbia's 30th Street studio, though, BÖC's third album was shaping-up as the usual team-effort: outside influences included Lanier's girlfriend Patti Smith, whose *Poem Of Isadore Ducasse* inspired Career Of Evil, and Richard Meltzer, a former scribe for music magazine Crawdaddy, who supplied the Dada-esque lyric for Harvester Of Eyes. Co-producer Sandy Pearlman was BÖC's Svengali-figure. Like Meltzer, he'd written for Crawdaddy, but he'd also been instrumental in BÖC's inception, coined the term 'heavy-metal' to describe their music, and given 'Buck Dharma' his nick-name.

"Sandy would basically be the judge," says Donald Roeser. "There were a lot of ideas flying around for the album, so we needed somebody to be the Fuhrer."

The album's undoubted stand-out was Astronomy, its music written and arranged by the Bouchard brothers. The lyrics came from Imaginos, an epic poem Pearlman had written back in the '60s, and according to the fanzine Morning Final, the song's memorable chorus riff was inspired by Mick Ronson's work on Bowie's Panic In Detroit. When Metallica were looking for a BÖC song to cover on 1998's *Garage Inc.*, Astronomy was the obvious choice.

Upon its release, the album's sado-masochistic lyrics and a sleeve which pictured BÖC with a German ME 262 fighter-jet drew allegations of neo-Nazism. Bloom and Pearlman – both Jewish – thought this unlikely. Melody Maker's readers voted *Secret Treaties* Top Rock Album Of All Time in 1975. *Agents Of Fortune* would catapult the band to stadium-status.

Record label:
Columbia

Produced
by Murray Krugman and Sandy Pearlman.

Recorded
at Columbia Studios, New York

Released:
September 1974

Chart peaks:
None (UK) 53 (US)

Personnel:
Donald 'Buck Dharma' Roeser (g,v); Eric Bloom (g, v, k); Albert Bouchard (d,v); Joe Bouchard (b,v); Alan Lanier (k, g); Tim Geelan (e)

Track listing:
Career Of Evil (S/US); Subhuman; Dominance And Submission; ME262; Cagey Cretins; Harvester Of Eyes; Flaming Telepaths; Astronomy

Running time:
38.28

Current CD:
468 018 2

Further listening:
Tyranny And Mutation (1973)

Further reading:
www.blueoystercult.com;
http://members.aol.com/bocfaqman/

Supertramp
Crime Of The Century

Pop-prog rockers regroup, rethink and create a concept album that propels them towards stadium stardom.

By 1973 Supertramp had made two lacklustre albums and spent their time "bombing up and down the M1 in a Transit and playing Johnny B. Goode as an encore," according to Rick Davies. The band's financial backer, a Dutch millionaire called Stanley Miesegacs, announced he wanted to cut his losses. Their label, A&M, was also losing faith, but after Davies and Hodgson replaced the other band members, the company agreed to fund a stay at a Somerset farm where a new album would be created.

"This was the first time something had clicked," recalls Hodgson. "We knew we had a band, not just a hotch-potch of styles, and the music was working." Many of the players remember *Crime Of The Century* as the most enjoyable Supertramp record to make. An unknown and uncredited street musician played saw on Hide. For Rudy the band went to Paddington Station to tape the sound of trains, and to Leicester Square for crowd noises.

The album addresses the same themes of loneliness and lunacy that the Pink Floyd had tackled on *Dark Side Of The Moon* the year before. But it is only a concept album "in the loosest sense", says Hodgson. "There was a link from School to the opening line of Bloody Well Right, 'So you think you're schooling's phoney', and that's about as far as we took it. Listeners could take it further if they wanted." The music mixed the ambition and scale of prog rock with Hodgson's instinctive feel for a poppy melody, which drew in listeners who steered well clear of King Crimson or Gentle Giant's knottier constructions.

When Supertramp toured that year they played the first side in order, then newer songs that would later appear on *Crisis? What Crisis?* before ending with side two and no encore. "It was like a house catching fire, it just clicked with audiences," says Davies. "It was a magical time because before then we had only known absolute failure." With Dreamer becoming a British hit single, Supertramp's rise to the top had begun and their Dutch uncle, somewhat to his surprise, would soon get his £60,000 investment back.

Record label:
A&M

Produced
by Ken Scott and Supertramp.

Recorded
at Trident, Ramport Studios and Scorpio Sound, London; February–June 1974.

Released:
September 1974

Chart peaks:
4 (UK) 38 (US)

Personnel:
Roger Hodgson (v, g, p); Rick Davies (v, k, hm); John Helliwell (s, clarinet, v); Dougie Thomson (b); Bob Siebenberg (d); Ken Scott and John Jansen (e)

Track listing:
School; Bloody Well Right (S/US); Hide In Your Shell; Asylum; Dreamer (S/UK); Rudy; If Everyone Was Listening; Crime Of The Century

Running time:
44.10

Current CD:
393 647-2

Further listening:
Crises? What Crises? (1975); Even In The Quietest Moments (1977); Breakfast In America (1979) sees the band hit commercial peak.

Further reading:
MOJO 44; www.supertramp.com

Millie Jackson
Caught Up

Potent combo of lubricious talk and deep soul.

By 1973, Millie Jackson had tired of the men directing her recording career. She'd moved to Spring Records, had R&B hits with My Man Is A Sweet Man (a 1972 UK Number 50) and Hurt So Good (taken from the film Cleopatra Jones), but the positive reaction to her live performances – where she told down'n'dirty real-life stories between songs – suggested her audience could take something stronger, more in keeping with that saltier stage self.

"I had been doing If Loving You Is Wrong [with a long, spoken intro] for quite some time. So I just recorded what I had been doing live." Introducing material with a rap, in its pre-hip hop meaning of dialogue, had been a strong staple of soul music since the '60s, with Joe Tex and Isaac Hayes being particularly adept. In her rap on this song, Jackson sets up the story of a woman who realises that her relationship with a married man is at a critical stage: Will he or won't he leave his wife and kids for a life with her?

On the album's second side, Jackson reverses the viewpoint and takes the role of the 'wronged' wife in It's All Over But The Shouting, Bobby Womack's I'm Through Trying To Prove My Love To You and, an unexpected but effective choice, Bobby Goldsboro's Summer (The First Time), in which she sets up the sequel by reminiscing about the good times. Jackson had been impressed by the way Marvin Gaye segued tracks on *What's Going On*. She took the device further to build two complete stories for soul's first truly effective concept album.

Though *Still Caught Up*, the follow-up, is at least as good (and Jackson herself preferred it), the element of groundbreaking surprise gives *Caught Up* the slight advantage. Soon, raps by women soul singers from the point of view of wife or mistress or aimed at philandering male, proliferated. Millie's own style coarsened down the years, expletives went undeleted and the pursuit of outrage seemed to outweigh her pursuit of good material (*Back To The Sh*t* which pictured her on the lavatory, panties round her ankles, was a bit of a low point). But at her peak Jackson was one of the most distinctive and inventive of all soul performers, someone whose music really connected with its audience.

Record label:
Polydor

Produced
by Brad Shapiro and Millie Jackson.

Recorded
at Muscle Shoals Sound, Alabama and Criteria Studios, Miami.

Released:
October 1974

Chart peaks:
None (UK) 21 (US)

Personnel:
Jimmy Johnson, Pete Carr (g); Barry Beckett (k); David Hood (b); Roger Hawkins (d); Tom Roady, Brad Shapiro (pc); Mike Lewis, Brad Shapiro (oa)

Track listing:
If Loving You Is Wrong I Don't Want To Be Right; The Rap; If Loving You Is Wrong I Don't Want To Be Right (Reprise); All I Want Is A Fighting Chance; I'm Tired Of Hiding; It's All Over But The Shouting; It's Easy Going; I'm Through Trying To Prove My Love To You; Summer (The First Time)

Running time:
33.23

Current CD:
CDSEWM003

Further listening:
The rest of her "cheatin' trilogy": Still Caught Up (1975) and Free And In Love (1976). She starts to get saucier on Feelin' Bitchy (1978)

Further reading:
www.davidnathan.com/millie.htm

King Crimson
Red

Studio swansong from the most radical Crimson line-up.

O f the '70s Crimson albums, *Red* has endured best, even resonating with some of the pioneers of grunge – Kurt Cobain among them. But the record was made in what Bill Bruford remembers as "excruciating" circumstances. The original five-piece line-up had shrunk after the departures of, firstly, percussionist Jamie Muir, then violinist David Cross, worn down by the rigours of a punishing touring schedule and a live show that relied heavily on intense improvisation.

As the trio entered the studio morale was mixed; both Wetton and Bruford believed that the band was about to make a quantum leap into Top 10 success, as the Floyd had just done. Fripp, however, had been growing tired of trying to play intricate rock-jazz fusions to arena crowds who had come to boogie. He also felt that his freewheeling rhythm section was crowding him out. Then, the night before the sessions, the guitarist read a text by the mystical thinker J.G. Bennett that plunged him into spiritual turmoil.

"I had a glimpse of something – the top of my head blew off," he recalled later. In the studio the band leader found himself unable to function normally. Bruford says: "Robert had 'decided to withhold the passing of my opinion' which meant you'd do a take and you'd say, 'What did you think, Robert?' Nothing, nothing at all. He had decided the way to Nirvana was not to express an opinion – and it seemed to me that John Wetton and I more or less moved his hand about on the fretboard."

Fripp's head blown off or not, the results are remarkable. The angular guitar of the title track defined an avant-metal style that Fripp would come to revive years later. Providence gives a glimpse of the band's live power, while the epic Starless with its furious instrumental section and soaring reprise recalls the grandeur of the first line-up. But with the sessions over, Fripp unilaterally declared the band was finished. Announcing his disillusionment with the rock musician's lifestyle he went to a spiritual retreat – to the exasperation of fellow band members. But maybe Fripp's timing was right – *Red* is that rarest of records, the sound of a line-up quitting while ahead.

Record label:
Island

Produced
by King Crimson.

Recorded
at Olympic Sound Studios, London; July–August 1974. Providence recorded live at Palace Theatre, Providence, Rhode Island; June 30, 1974.

Released:
October 1974

Chart peaks:
45 (UK) None (US)

Personnel:
Robert Fripp (g, Mellotron); John Wetton (b, v); Bill Bruford (d); David Cross (vn), Mel Collins, Ian McDonald (s); Robin Miller (oboe); Marc Charig (cornet); George Chkiantz (e)

Track listing:
Red; Fallen Angel; One More Red Nightmare; Providence; Starless

Running time:
40.05

Current CD:
EGCD15

Further listening:
The posthumous Great Deceiver (1989) box set is the best document of the line-up's live ingenuity.

Further reading:
MOJO 73

The Raspberries
Starting Over

Last and greatest album by terminally misunderstood US power popsters.

File under: Self-Consciously Appropriate Album Title. When The Raspberries converged upon New York's Record Plant with longtime producer Jimmy Ienner to record *Starting Over*, they sported a new line-up and a new direction. Bassist Dave Smalley and drummer Jim Bonfanti were out, replaced, respectively, by Scott McCarl and Michael McBride. Musically, although their obsession with classic '60s pop raged unabated, they were out to shed their teenybopper image. Gone were the matching white suits, likewise the gimmicky album covers (which had contained raspberry puns, photos of raspberries, even a raspberry-scented scratch'n'sniff sticker).

The effort to assume a more mature face was driven at least in part by lead guitarist Wally Bryson. He had almost followed Smalley and Bonfanti out of the group, but Ienner convinced him to stay. "My condition was that Eric had to be real," Bryson later recalled. "See, I appreciated Eric, but he had to realize that he didn't have to be a copy of Steve Marriott, Paul McCartney, or Roger Daltrey. What had always been happening was that Eric would want our songs to sound like The Beach Boys, The Who or The Beatles. He'd say, 'Play a Who drum roll there, or play a Townshend guitar riff here.' I wanted us to be our own musical entity, not anyone else. I wanted us to be The Raspberries."

Perhaps Bryson was still smarting from the distant indignity of having to get two haircuts before Carmen would let him join the group. Carmen, for his part, felt persecuted, as he told a reporter in 1975: "When you're trying to write to please four people instead of yourself, it's very strange. It's very difficult to convince the public that you believe in yourself when half the band doesn't even believe in what you're doing."

Carmen's insecurities aside, it is unlikely that anyone listening to *Starting Over* would think that the band were anything but unified. Rather, the album is a shining example of what evangelists call 'the sandpaper ministry': the opposing forces sanded down one another's imperfections to a heavenly sheen, creating a result that was probably finer than any of them had in mind. Not that the group's intentions were purely artistic. They laid out their ambitions on the album's leadoff track, Overnight Sensation (Hit Record). Although the song

Record label:
Capitol

Produced
by Jimmy Ienner.

Recorded
at The Record Plant, New York City; April 1974.

Released:
October 1974

Chart peaks:
None (UK) 143 (US)

Personnel:
Eric Carmen (k, g, v); Wally Bryson (g, v); Scott McCarl (b, v); Michael McBride (d, v)

Track listing:
Overnight Sensation (Hit Record) (S); Play On; Party's Over (S); I Don't Know What I Want; Rose Coloured Glasses; All Through The Night; Cruisin' Music; I Can Hardly Believe You're Mine; Cry; Hands On You; Starting Over

Running time:
40.05

Current CD:
RPM 163 re-released as Power Pop, Volume 2; includes Starting Over and its predecessor, Side 3

Further listening:
The Raspberries' first two albums, The Raspberries (1972) and Fresh (1972), are available on a single disc, Power Pop, Volume One.

Further reading:
www.raspberries.net

barely made it into the US Top 20, it earned them the respect of rock critics such as Rolling Stone's Ken Barnes, who wrote, "Lyrically it's a refreshingly frank confession of the band's number one goal. Unlike those sensitive, questing souls, who profess to disdain their gold records, The Raspberries want that hit on the radio. And they know what it takes to get it — 'If the program director don't pull it / Then it's time to get back a bullet' is a far cry from the naive 'Please Mr. DJ, play my record' plaints of a decade ago."

Despite such praise, *Starting Over* sold poorly. The Raspberries disbanded less than six months after the album's release, leaving a gap on hit radio that would not be filled until the power pop movement that they helped inspire took flight. McCarl spoke for many fans when he later told a reporter, "I see The Raspberries as the American Badfinger, carrying on soon after The Beatles when it really wasn't in vogue to do it with that same three minute pop song thing."

Queen
Sheer Heart Attack

Imaginative third album triumph for over-the-top pop rockers.

The first couple of albums-worth of Queen's brand of densely layered, fantastical, post-Zeppelin heavy pop had met with vicious critical resistance ("the dregs of glam rock" went one review, "a bucket of stale urine" another), though the band were gradually finding a loyal audience. Their sonically flamboyant, elaborately arranged *Queen II* had yielded a Number 10 hit with Seven Seas Of Rye, but Brian May later admitted the album had perhaps "dished up too much for people to swallow". Having already cancelled a US tour due to May's arm infection, when he fell ill again during the initial sessions for *Sheer Heart Attack*, he worried that the band would replace him with another guitarist. However, with May's unique multi-layered contributions an intrinsic part of Queen's signature, the band carried on recording leaving space for his guitar parts which, when recuperated, he filled with powerful relish in an intense two week solo session – the guitar part on Killer Queen alone taking several days and 12 overdubs.

Much of the album continued to effectively combine and juxtapose extreme bombast (Brighton Rock – May's tour-de-force of stereo echo, Flick Of The Wrist – classic Mercury bile, Now I'm Here – May's parade of chunky riffs) with melodic delicacy (Lily Of The Valley – Mercury in mythological quest mode, Dear Friends – May's funeral hymn). However, the humour – whether heavy rock'n'roll (Stone Cold Crazy), ingenious banjo-driven '30s pastiche (Bring Back That Leroy Brown) – introduced a lighter touch that opened many ears, not least in Mercury's Killer Queen, a delightfully camp and amazingly inventive piece about a high-class whore.

"You almost expect Noel Coward to sing it," said Freddie. "It's one of those bowler hat, black suspender belt numbers – not that Noel would wear that." Suffering from restrictive management and deep suspicion from the press (they had a resistance to Freddie's showiness which an outrageous chest wig on the album's cover probably didn't assist in overcoming), reaching Number 2 in the UK with Killer Queen was a serious boost for the band.

May: "It was the turning point. It was the song that best summed up our kind of music and a big hit. And we desperately needed it as a mark of something successful happening to us."

Record label:
EMI

Produced
by Roy Thomas Baker and Queen.

Recorded
at Trident, Wessex, Rockfield and Air Studios; July–September 1974.

Released:
November 8, 1974

Chart peaks:
2 (UK) 12 (US)

Personnel:
Roger Taylor (d, v); Freddie Mercury (v, p); John Deacon (b, ag); Brian May (g, p, banjo)

Track listing:
Brighton Rock; Killer Queen; Tenement Funster; Flick Of The Wrist; Lily Of The Valley; Now I'm Here; In The Lap Of The Gods; Stone Cold Crazy; Dear Friends; Misfire; Bring Back That Leroy Brown; She Makes Me (Stormtrooper In Stilettos); In The Lap Of The Gods (Revisited)

Running time:
39.09

Current CD:
CDPCSD129

Further listening:
Queen II (1974); Night At The Opera (1975); Day At The Races (1976)

Further reading:
MOJO 69; Mercury (1996); Good Vibrations: A History Of Record Production (1996); www.queen-fip.com

Genesis

The Lamb Lies Down On Broadway

Eccentric English prog-rockers hit NYC.

Genesis's 1973 offering *Selling England By The Pound*, along with the minor hit I Know What I Like (In Your Wardrobe), had further established them as a vital and creative unit but they remained maverick outsiders of the progressive scene because of their continued focus on songwriting. For the next project, however, they wanted to pursue a concept and Peter Gabriel's idea of the semi-autobiographical, allegorical adventures of Puerto Rican New York street punk Rael was voted best idea. Gabriel has admitted that band democracy at this stage was "bullshit on my part, as there was only one story I was going to pursue", and further insisted on writing all the lyrics himself.

The band decamped to Led Zeppelin's rat-infested rehearsal cottage. Collins: "It was horrible, we spent three months in there driving each other crazy." Meanwhile, Gabriel, already feeling stifled by group life and suffering from his wife's infidelity with a close friend, temporarily left the band to pursue a vague film offer from William "The Exorcist" Friedkin but when it came to nothing "returned to a very murky reception," as he remembered. The band, by this time, had written a double album's worth of good music and Gabriel was way behind with the lyrics. Banks: "I felt we were separated at that point really." Hackett was not happy either: *The Lamb* happened despite me, not with me. I really felt it was indulgent and I couldn't get to grips with it or contribute something great in the guitar sense."

The ensuing double album remains Genesis's most controversial. Melody Maker's Chris Welch complained that they should "learn the importance of self-editing", but though extravagantly detailed, dense and difficult to follow, *The Lamb* is much more fun than it's often given credit for. The music is playful. Gabriel is a compelling central presence, the whole bubbles with good things, some (In The Cage, Carpet Crawlers) among the highest achievements in the Genesis oeuvre. After 102 live performances Gabriel left, sick of the rock life and the internal resentment (as he perceived it) of the attention he received as front man. Genesis went on to conquer the world with Phil Collins as lead vocalist.

Record label:
Charisma

Produced
by John Burns and Genesis.

Recorded
at Glosspant, Wales with the Island Mobile, mixed at Island, London; August–October 1974.

Release date:
November 1974

Chart peaks:
10 (UK) 41 (US)

Personnel:
Tony Banks (k); Steve Hackett (g); Phil Collins (d, v, pc); Peter Gabriel (v, flute); Michael Rutherford (b, 12 string); Brian Eno ('Enossification'); David Hutchins (e)

Track listing:
The Lamb Lies Down On Broadway; Fly On A Windshield; Broadway Melody Of 1974; Cuckoo Cocoon; In The Cage; The Grand Parade Of Lifeless Packaging; Back In N.Y.C; Hairless Heart; Counting Out Time; Carpet Crawlers; The Chamber Of 32 Doors; Lilywhite Lilith; The Waiting Room; Anyway; Here Comes The Supernatural Anaesthetist; The Lamia; Silent Sorrow In Empty Boats; The Colony Of Slipperman (Arrival, A Visit To The Doktor, Raven); Ravine; The Light Dies Down On Broadway; Riding The Scree; In The Rapids; It

Running time:
94.12

Current CD:
CGSCDX1

Further listening:
For a terrific 1975 live version, check Archive (1998)

Further reading:
www.genesis-path.com

Dr Feelgood
Down By The Jetty

*Scorching live act's debut gives pub rock a good name,
inspiring punk along the way.*

By the early '70s the blues seemed to have run out of puff.
After a decade of civil rights activity, young blacks were
turning their backs on an idiom associated with slavery days,
while white bands had sentenced the music to death by guitar
solo. In late 1974 four distinctly seedy looking saviours swaggered off their Canvey Island home on the Thames Estuary, to
produce a back to basics R&B album which helped revitalise the
form, and at the same time laid the foundations of a further
revolution. After a year of garnering rave gig reviews at the
vanguard of the pub rock movement, Dr Feelgood went into the
studio with The Who's *Live At Leeds* engineer Vic Maile.

"A beautiful guy," recalls guitarist and songwriter Wilko
Johnson. "He was the only person who called to ask how I was
after the band bust-up in 1977. But we had terrible arguments
during the recording. I was inexperienced and a bit cocky and I
said, 'Can't we all play and you stick up a microphone?'"

Drummer, John 'The Big Figure' Martin remembers: "I
was a bit disappointed. I was a struggling musician and wanted
the whole studio bit, but Wilko wouldn't do any overdubs, so
the tracks seemed a bit thin on stereo playbacks."

"It was never our intention to be deliberately Luddite
releasing it as a mono mix," claims Wilko. "In fact I thought we
were a very forward looking band, it just sounded better that
way." Lee Brilleaux's gritty vocalisms and Sparks' and Martin's
solid but agile rhythm section played their part. But it was
Johnson's extraordinary, cubist, simultaneous rhythm and lead
playing which provided the main thrust. ("I tried to copy The
Pirates' Mick Green, but got it wrong!") The inexorable drive of
She Does It Right, the industrial, quasi-bluebeat of Roxette, the
choppy, soul-funk of Keep It Out Of Sight each possessed a
visceral impetus which seemed to point a way ahead. Gary
Valentine of Blondie confirms this: he recalls attending a 1975
New York party with Johnny Thunders, Richard Hell, Talking
Heads and the Ramones among others. *"Down By The Jetty* was
played over and over. Dr Feelgood inspired everyone there that
night to go on."

Record label:
United Artists

Produced
by Vic Maile.

Recorded
at Rockfield Studios, Monmouth; August
26–September 1 and November 25–27,
1974; Jackson's Studios, Rickmansworth;
September 23, 1974; Dingwall's, London;
July 8, 1974 (live recording).

Released:
December 1974

Chart peaks:
None (UK) None (US)

Personnel:
Lee Brilleaux (v, hm); Wilko Johnson (g,
v, k); John B 'Sparko' Sparks (b); John
'The Big Figure' Martin (d, pc); Barry
Andrews (k, s); Brinsley Schwarz (s)

Track listing:
She Does It Right (S/UK); Boom Boom;
The More I Give; Roxette (S/UK); One
Weekend; That Ain't The Way To Behave; I
Don't Mind; Twenty Yards Behind; Keep It
Out Of Sight; All Through The City;
Cheque Book; Oyeh; Bonie Moronie; Tequila

Running time:
40.51

Current CD:
GRANDCD05

Further listening:
Malpractice (1975); Stupidity (1976) (a
superb live album, Number 1 in Britain);
Solid Senders by Wilko Johnson's Solid
Senders (1978); Going Back Home (Wilko
Johnson, 1998); Wilko was also with Ian
Dury And The Blockheads for the album
Laughter.

Further listening:
Down By The Jetty (1997); No Sleep Till
Canvey Island: The Great Pub Rock
Revolution (2000); www.drfeelgood.de

Gene Clark
No Other

Taking singer-songwriter rock to its logical extreme, one of the most extravagant productions of the era.

Despite his wonderful work with The Byrds, Gene Clark was always one of rock's most frustrating underachievers. He quit The Byrds just as they were reaching new peaks with his composition Eight Miles High, completed one of the first LA singer-songwriter albums and pioneered country rock, but never received the recognition he deserved.

Maybe it was his reluctance to tour, but his solo albums failed to sell, leaving him in a precarious position in the early '70s. The Byrds' 1973 reunion album provided a much-needed spotlight for his songwriting talents, and although the work was panned on release most critics acknowledged the quality of Clark's contributions. Asylum founder and starmaker David Geffen was sufficiently impressed to offer Clark the chance of a lifetime with a big budget album. Producer Thomas Jefferson Kaye approached the project like a man possessed and boasted of recording an album that resembled a cross between The Beatles' *Sgt. Pepper* and Brian Wilson's *Pet Sounds/Smile*. Clark was living in pastoral bliss in Mendocino and, while looking over the ocean, composed a series of strange but arresting songs, quite unlike anything he had previously written.

"I was strongly influenced at that time by two other artistes," he explained. "Stevie Wonder's *Innervisions* and The Rolling Stones' *Goat's Head Soup*. When I was writing *No Other* I concentrated on those albums a lot, and was very inspired by the direction of them – which is ironic because *Innervisions* is a very climbing, spiritual thing, while *Goat's Head Soup* has connotations of the lower forces as well. But somehow the joining of the two gave me a place to go with *No Other*, and I wanted it to go in a powerful direction."

Clark crafted an intriguing fusion that includes gospel, country and choral, music and has a rich, cinematic feel. It should have elevated Clark to a new standing in the rock marketplace, but sales were disastrous. Thereafter, Clark was consigned to the cult fringe and increasingly dependent on questionable money-spinning reunions with former Byrds colleagues. He was bitterly disappointed by the commercial failure of *No Other*. Some reckon he never fully recovered from the blow. The great album remains scandalously unavailable on CD in either the US or UK and cries out for reappraisal.

Record label:
Asylum

Produced
by Thomas Jefferson Kaye.

Recorded
at The Village Recorder, West Los Angeles; early 1974.

Released:
January 1975

Chart peaks:
None (UK) None (US)

Personnel:
Gene Clark (v, g); Lee Sklar (b); Butch Trucks (d); Russ Kunkel (d); Michael Utley (p); Craig Doerge (k); Joe Lala (p); Richard Greene (vn); Chris Hillman (mandolin); Ted Machell (c); Bill Cuomo (o); Jerry McGee (g); Danny Kootch (g); Jesse Ed Davis (g); Steve Bruton (g); Buzzy Feiten (g); Tony Reale (e); Joe Tuzen (ae)

Track listing:
Life's Greatest Fool (S); Silver Raven; No Other; Strength Of Strings; From A Silver Phial; Some Misunderstanding; The True One; Lady Of The North

Running time:
39.00

Current CD:
AMC Y6066

Further listening:
Gene Clark With The Gosdin Brothers (1967); White Light (1971); Two Sides To Every Story (1976)

Further reading:
The Byrds: Timeless Flight Revisited (1997)

Led Zeppelin
Physical Graffiti

Led Zeppelin's first for their nascent label, Swan Song, was preceded by over one million advance orders.

Almost eighteen months in the making, *Physical Graffiti* began life in November 1973, when the band moved en masse into Headley Grange in Hampshire. They started work just as Jimmy Page was finishing up his music for Lucifer Rising, a film by Kenneth Anger, who shared Page's interest in the occult. Then, after a bout of illness, John Paul Jones announced to manager Peter Grant that he was seriously thinking about giving it all up to be the choirmaster at Winchester Cathedral. Grant told him to take a few weeks off to think it over. Recording was postponed until the following February, a month after the band announced the formation of Swan Song Records.

Unapologetic for the long lapse between releases, Robert Plant told reporters, "On the surface, this band might not appear to be a hive of industry, but when we do get something together it's always something that we're all completely satisfied with."

Finally, after long delays, and skirmishes over the album's sleeve art – which originally sported images of Aliester Crowley, Lee Harvey Oswald and two photos of the band in drag – Led Zeppelin returned to rock's frontlines with their most ambitious work ever, spanning genres, tempos, and once again contrasting bombastic, rock-solid tunes alongside folksy spiritual quests, most notably the Eastern-tinged Kashmir. (At the time the band penned the song – originally titled Driving Into Kashmir – none of them had set foot in India.) Page had been contemplating putting out a double-disc for some time and went on a scavenger hunt in the band's vaults, unearthing outtakes from their previous albums and grafting them to the band's more recent compositions, giving a sprawling view of what they were capable of — from the innocence of Ten Years Gone, which was inspired by Plant's first girlfriend who demanded he choose between her and the music, to the anthemic Houses of the Holy, which was recorded for the band's album of the same name, yet strangely never used.

At the height of their powers, and already wearing the thorny crown of rock legends, Graffiti exposes Led Zeppelin's more human side. For instance during the recording of In My Time of Dying you can hear drummer John Bonham coughing and then saying, "That's going to be the one, isn't it?" Also left

Record label:
Swan Song/Atlantic

Produced
by Jimmy Page.

Recorded
at Ronnie Lane's Mobile at Headley Grange, the Rolling Stones' Mobile and Olympic Studios, London; November1973–July 1974.

Released:
February 25, 1975

Chart peaks:
1 (UK) 1 (US)

Personnel:
Jimmy Page (g); Robert Plant (v, hm); John Paul Jones (b, k, mellotron); John Bonham (d); Ian Stewart (p); Eddie Kramer, George Chkiantz, Andy Johns, Ron Nevison (e); Peter Grant (executive producer)

Track listing:
Custard Pie; The Rover; In My Time Of Dying; Houses Of The Holy; Trampled Underfoot (S/US); Kashmir; In The Light; Bron-Yr-Aur; Down By The Seaside; Ten Years Gone; Night Flight; Wanton Song, The; Boogie With Stu; Black Country Woman; Sick Again

Running time:
82.15

Current CD:
7567924422

Further listening:
Led Zeppelin Remasters (1990) — the 54-track compilation pulls material from the nine studio albums, with some previously unreleased stuff.

Further reading:
Led Zeppelin: The Definitive Biography (Ritchie Yorke, 1994); Hammer Of The Gods: The Led Zeppelin Saga (Stephen

Davis, 1985); Led Zeppelin: Heaven and Hell (Charles R Cross, Erik Flannigan, Neal Preston, 1991); www.led-zeppelin.com

in the mix are the sounds of a supersonic jet in Black Country Woman, and then the phrase "We gotta leave the airplane in."

Jimmy Page simply explains it by saying, "We were in that frame of mind in those days. That album's really good because we were having a long run working as a band, and it really shows. We had this beautiful freedom that we could try anything, do anything, which was what the beauty of how the band was, and how the music was made as opposed to how things are today. A band today has to constantly try to keep its head above water."

Within two weeks of its release *Graffiti* was perched at the top of the US charts, (reportedly selling over 500 copies an hour at one point), pulling all of the band's previous five albums in its wake, back onto the Billboard album charts, making them the first band ever to have six albums on the Top 200. In the UK it was a more modest success, enjoying just one week at the top.

Bob Dylan
Blood On The Tracks

Dylan's astonishing 1975 return to form, a suite of songs prompted by the emotional fallout of his failing marriage.

Commonly regarded as the only one of his later albums able to stand comparison with his innovative '60s work, *Blood On The Tracks* finds the songwriter both more sensitive and more bitter than he'd been since 1966, in a series of emotionally-charged narratives and reflections that defies simple assessment. One of rock's most mature albums. As so often in Dylan's career, uncertainty and procrastination presaged the eventual appearance of *Blood On The Tracks*, with the album being scrapped a few weeks before its delivery date, as he hurriedly re-recorded some tracks with a scratch band in Minneapolis. The sudden change came so late in the production schedule that early copies of the album came with not only the wrong musician credits, but also liner notes by journalist Pete Hamill (not the Van Der Graaf Generator singer) which quoted lyrics that had since been changed. It is typical of Dylan's unreliable judgement concerning his own output that when the out-takes appeared shortly after on the *Joaquin Antique* bootleg, most hardcore Dylan aficionados (including close friends like Robbie Robertson and Joni Mitchell) preferred the abandoned original versions of some songs – particularly Idiot Wind, which is transformed from an eerie, reflective piece into something altogether more scathing and strident at the Minneapolis sessions. (With customary contrariness, the out-take eventually released on *The Bootleg Series Vols 1–3* is not the one originally scheduled for release, either!)

Seeking a more acoustic sound after the rock-band settings of *Planet Waves*, Dylan employed Eric Weissberg's folk group Deliverance for the New York sessions, though ultimately only bassist Tony Brown appeared on the record. The band's three guitarists were apparently expected to follow Dylan's fingering largely by instinct, a situation not helped by his open D tuning. "If it was anybody else," said Weissberg later, "I would have walked out." For all that, the songs recorded by Dylan and Brown (with overdubs added later by organist Paul Griffin and pedal-steel guitarist Buddy Cage) are amongst the album's more affecting, particularly Shelter From The Storm, Simple Twist Of Fate and the concluding Buckets Of Rain. But when Dylan played a test-pressing of the album to his brother David, he was persuaded that some of the songs sounded too thin and bare,

Record Label:
CBS

Produced
by Bob Dylan.

Recorded
at Columbia A&R Studios, New York, September 1974 and Sound 80 Studios, Minneapolis, December 1974.

Released:
February 1975

Chart peaks:
4 (UK) 1 (US)

Personnel:
Bob Dylan (v, g, hm); Chris Weber (g); Ken Odegard (g); Tony Brown (b); Bill Peterson (b); Paul Griffin (k); Greg Imhofer (o); Bill Berg (d); Buddy Cage (sg); Phil Ramone (e)

Further Listening:
Tangled Up In Blue (S); Simple Twist Of Fate; You're A Big Girl Now; Idiot Wind; You're Gonna Make Me Lonesome When You Go; Meet Me In The Morning; Lily, Rosemary And The Jack Of Hearts; If You See Her, Say Hello; Shelter From The Storm; Buckets Of Rain.

Running time:
51.53

Current CD:
4678422

Further listening:
Only a few albums compare with Blood On The Tracks, most notably Another Side Of Bob Dylan (1964), his first "personal" work, occasioned by his break-up with girlfriend Suze Rotolo. Of his other albums dealing in matters of the heart, Blonde On Blonde (1966) and Time Out Of Mind (1997) are to be preferred to the comparatively dismal Empire Burlesque (1985).

Further reading:
Dylan Behind The Shades (Clinton Heylin, 1991)

and ought to be re-done with a group of local Minneapolis musicians. Accordingly, a few days after Christmas Dylan went into a local studio to re-cut half the tracks, of which only Tangled Up In Blue really matched the emotional acuity of the earlier version. The results were rush-released a few weeks later, and despite the circuitous nature of its development, the two sessions' material meshed together well enough to form one of Dylan's most attractive and purely enjoyable albums – an extraordinary achievement, given the often harsh, painful nature of the subject matter.

Neil Young
Tonight's The Night

Young's painful, personal requiem to Crazy Horse guitarist Danny Whitten and roadie Bruce Berry.

Desperate, bleak and emotionally cathartic, the wasted vocals and ragged production of *Tonight's The Night* were the antithesis of the consumer-friendly *Harvest*. It took two years to release it, and nobody, his record company thought, would buy it. That they did bears testament to Young's post-CSNY marketability as much as to the album's undoubted brilliance – the best part of the 'doom trilogy' that encompassed *Time Fades Away* and *On The Beach*.

In November '72 Danny Whitten, friend and Crazy Horse guitarist, died of a dose of heroin bought with the $50 Young gave him when he fired him. It was, said Young, "traumatic". It didn't help when the following summer, while working in a Hawaii with Crosby, Stills And Nash on an aborted album, he learned that his roadie Bruce Berry had also OD-ed.

Back in LA, Young got together with the remains of Crazy Horse, Nils Lofgren, Ben Keith and several crates of tequila in a Hollywood rehearsal room. In two live, loud, late-night sessions-come-wakes they recorded nine of the album's 12 songs. Trying to capture their late friends' states of mind they got wasted "right out on the edge, where we knew we were so screwed up that we could easily just fall on our faces" and waited "until the middle of the night until the vibe hit us and just did it," Young told Rolling Stone.

The label might have stopped its release but they couldn't stop him doing the songs live. A month later a dishevelled Young wearing a white jacket and sunglasses stumbled onstage at LA's Roxy, launching the *Tonight's The Night* tour. The band shared the stage with a palm tree, wooden Indian, old piano and silver glitter platform boots. A similar set-up came to Britain. Audiences who had no idea of the provenance of this furious, fucked up, moving music – among its highlights a raw cover of Crazy Horse's Downtown, the poignantly lovely New Mama (inspired by the birth of his son) and the agonizing Borrowed Tune (whose melody the lyrics confess were stolen from the Stones, Young being "too wasted to write my own") were often hostile or confused. Said manager Elliot Roberts, "Neil was sort of dribbling out of the side of his mouth on that tour, the mood was so down." Finally appearing in 1975, the album still stands up as one of the most honest and harrowing in rock.

Record label:
Reprise

Produced
by David Briggs and Neil Young, with Tim Mulligan, Gabby Garcia and Elliot Mazer.

Recorded
at Studio Instrument Rentals Rehearsal Hall, Hollywood; Broken Arrow; and live at Fillmore East, San Francisco, August and September 1973.

Released:
June 1975

Chart peaks:
48 (UK) 25 (US)

Personnel:
Neil Young (v, g, p, hm); Nils Lofgren (g); Billy Talbot (b, v); Ralph Molina (d); Ben Keith (sg, v)

Track listing:
Tonight's The Night; Speakin' Out; World On A String; Borrowed Tune; Come On Baby Let's Go Downtown; Mellow My Mind; Roll Another Number (For The Road); Albuquerque; New Mama; Lookout Joe; Tired Eyes; Tonight's The Night Part II

Running time:
44.58

Current CD:
7599272212

Further listening:
Time Fades Away (1973); On The Beach (1974)

Further reading:
Neil Young: The Rolling Stone Files (1994); Neil And Me (Scott Young, 1997); www.hyperrust.org/

Guy Clark
Old No. 1

A Lone Star answer to Nashville's Outlaw movement,
possibly the best country-folk album of the 1970s.

I f there was a theme to Guy Clark's music it was Texas.
Not the Texas of cattle drives and shoot-outs, but the
Texas whose citizens work hard and drink cases of Lone Star
beer while arguing about whose chilli is the hottest and whose
woman is the sweetest.

Clark's first album was named *Old No. 1* with real foresight and no little accuracy. Texas music. Clark, whose photos
graced albums by the psychedelic pioneers The 13th Floor
Elevators, came from the same Texan circuit as Townes Van
Zandt and fresh-faced San Antonio youngster Steve Earle. *Old
No. 1* wove together several threads of Texan sound and hasn't a
duff cut on it.

"The album wasn't meant to have a theme, and it didn't
really occur to me it had one till I went back and looked at it
later as a solid body of work," recalled Clark recently. "Now I
can appreciate how all the pieces fell together. It's a collection
of songs about life as I knew it in Monahans, in Rockport and
later on in Houston and Austin."

Rightly considered a classic today, the album represents
the sympathetic Lone Star state response to the country establishment, drawing Dixie's folk and country audiences closer
together, and gave the contemporary alt-country crowd another
icon. These days, Clark lives off his substantial songwriting
royalties.

Record label:
RCA

Produced
by Neil Wilburn.

Recorded
at RCA Studios, Nashville; spring 1975.

Released:
August 1975

Chart peaks:
None (UK) None (US)

Personnel:
Guy Clark (g, v); Mike Leech (b); Jerry
Kroon (d); Jerry Carrigan (d); Larrie
London (d); Chip Young (g); Pat Carter (g,
bv); Steve Gibson (g); Dick Feller (g); Jim
Colvard (g); Reggie Young (g); Hal Rugg
(ps, dobro); Jack Higgs (dobro); David
Briggs (p); Chuck Cochran (p); Shane
Keister (p); Lea Jane Berinati (p, bv);
Johnny Gimble (fiddle); Mickey Raphael
(hm); Rodney Crowell (bv); Emmylou Harris
(bv); Gary B White (bv); Florence Warner
(bv); Steve Earle (bv); Sammi Smith (bv)

Track listing:
Rita Ballou; L.A. Freeway; She Ain't Goin'
Nowhere; A Nickel For The Fiddler; That
Old Time Feeling; Texas 1947; Desperados
Waiting For The Train; Like A Coat From
The Cold; Instant Coffee Blues; Let Him
Roll

Running time:
36.20

Current CD:
74321588 132 adds Texas Cooking

Further listening:
Almost as hot is Old No. 1's follow-up
Texas Cooking (1976); a late period
comeback of sorts, Boats To Build (1992);
Keepers: Live Recording (1997) which
doubles as a greatest hits package.

Further reading:
Who's Who In Country Music (Hugh
Gregory, 1993)

Curtis Mayfield
There's No Place Like America Today

The former Impression brings biting social commentary, messages of hope and love songs.

In his Impressions days, Curtis Mayfield had written with a sharp eye for social injustice, a keen ear for striking melody and an optimistic heart for the future of mankind. Quitting the group in 1970, he ploughed much the same furrow as a solo act and crossed over to the mass market with the Superfly soundtrack. Thereafter he strode on boldly with the somewhat darker *Back To The World*, but by the time he settled to record *There's No Place Like America Today*, disco had become a prime mover in the market place. He would not follow that trend just yet.

The scene is set by the striking album-sleeve painting – in front of a huge billboard whose poster depicts an All-American WASP family grinning hugely and heading off for the sunshine in their shiny automobile, a line of black Americans queue dejectedly. For what? Welfare? A soup kitchen? The American Dream? The specifics do not matter. The sharp disparity in potential happiness and actual comfort of the characters is plainly stated. The looming high-rise offices of Mammon.

Starting with the tough, cautionary tale of Billy Jack, victim of a casual shooting, and When Seasons Change (there is no difference for the hard-up, victimised and oppressed), thereafter Mayfield seamlessly shifts between the reality of Blue Monday People and Hard Times to the more tender passages of the exquisite So In Love and the positive note on which he ends, Love To The People.

Long since dubbed the 'gentle giant of soul', Mayfield's well-attuned sensitivity as a singer of his own material is matched by the simple and subtle promptings of the band. But the album's tone and content were at odds with the commercial successes of the day.

"One of my favourite albums was one that didn't sell at all – *America Today*," Mayfield told Black Music magazine in 1979. "I felt a need to say those things. When you become creative, you're not worried so much about making money as speaking on certain things. It's no more than an artist painting a picture – this is the way it's just got to be."

Never exactly a superstar, but always hugely respected and admired, Mayfield was still working hard, enjoying his

Record label:
Buddah

Produced
by Curtis Mayfield

Recorded
at Curtom Studios, Chicago. February 1985

Release Date:
August, 1975

Chart Peaks:
None (UK) None (US)

Personnel:
Curtis Mayfield (v,k,g); Rich Tufo (k); Lucky Scott (b); Quinton Joseph (d); Gary Thompson, Phil Upchurch (g); Henry Gibson (congas, bongos)

Track listing:
Billy Jack; When Seasons Change; So In Love; Jesus; Blue Monday People; Hard Times; Love To The People

Running Time:
35.30

Current CD:
NEMCD401 adds Give Get Take Have

Further Listening:
Curtis (1970); Roots (1971); Superfly (1972); Back To The World (1973); People Get Ready: The Curtis Mayfield Story (1996)

Further Reading:
www.curtismayfield.cjb.net.

music and delivering his message of hope when, on stage in August 1990 he was crushed by a falling lighting rig and paralysed from the neck down. While he was in hospital his house burnt to the ground. Despite it all, Curtis kept as active in music as possible but missed being able to play his guitar, though he found he could sing for short periods and started occasional work on a new album, *New World Order* which was finally released in 1997. In 1998 he lost a limb due to diabetes, which had been triggered by his accident. Finally, this brave, noble king of soul music died on the morning of December 26, 1999 at North Fulton Regional Hospital in Roswell, Georgia, a suburb of Atlanta.

Eno
Another Green World

Instrumental-dominated release which provided Bowie with his Berlin trilogy template.

U ntil *Another Green World*, Brian Eno's post-Roxy Music card had been marked as that of an arch dilettante.

But Eno's serious side had already begun to emerge with the establishment of the world's first ambient imprint Discreet Music. Eno had also immersed himself in the work of soundtrack maestros such as Nino Rota and Ennio Morricone resulting in the cinematic lushness of this excellent collection.

The dandified glam piss-taker of solo debut *Here Come The Warm Jets* had been replaced by a short-haired fellow of studious demeanour. "I'd worked out that I was interested in building picture landscapes, soundscapes," he says now. "The impressionistic soundtrack music I was listening to was made to complement visuals, and I wanted to make similar music which was less personality-based, more evocative of times or places."

Eno created the soundbeds for the tracks at his home studio before presenting them to musicians he had assembled from the ranks of regular collaborators (Fripp, Cale) and selected fellow travellers (Collins, Rudolph, Melvin). Each was encouraged to play as awkwardly as possible as Eno and producer Rhett Davies whittled away at a total of 36 tracks.

"I had these sonic experiments and then tried to see what we could do with them to make music in the studio," says Eno, who rejects the opinion that this album is where he started to flex his minimalist muscles. "I like unfinished things – a musical idea seems to be more powerful if you are operating on the cusp because you start a picture and create a proposition which lets the listener fill in the rest. So these songs are actually minimalist by accident. I'd also been listening to a lot of music by the Mahavishnu Orchestra, I really liked their singularity – they didn't sound like anything else. Each piece of music could be like a jewel."

Which is exactly what is achieved here – an album full of jewels, from the opening squall of Sky Saw to the baroque of St Elmo's Fire, the motorik of In Dark Trees and the exotica of Zawinul/Lava, the beautiful Becalmed and the somnolent Spirits Drifting. Decades after its release *Another Green World* continues to live up to its title, offering the listener entry to an opulent aural plain.

Record label:
Island

Produced
by Brian Eno and Rhett Davies.

Recorded
at Island Studios, London; July–August 1975.

Released:
September 1975

Chart peaks:
None (UK) None (US)

Personnel:
Brian Eno (v, snake guitar, syn, treatments); Phil Collins (d); Percy Jones (b); Rod Melvin (p); Paul Rudolph (g, anchor bass); John Cale (va); Robert Fripp (g)

Track listing:
Sky Saw; Over Fire Island; St Elmo's Fire; In Dark Trees; The Big Ship; I'll Come Running; Another Green World; Sombre Reptiles; Little Fishes; Golden Hours; Becalmed; Zawinul/Lava; Everything Merges With The Night; Spirits Drifting

Running time:
41.10

Current CD:
EGCD21

Further listening:
Before And After Science (1977)

Further reading:
Paul Morley's sleevenotes to Enobox 2: Vocal (1993); http://noc.pue.udlap.mx/eno/

Glen Campbell
Rhinestone Cowboy

Precise, multi-million-selling MOR.

By the mid-'70s, Glen Campbell's career as a bankable recording artist seemed over. It was several years since his interpretation of Jimmy Webb's tryptich of haunting, ballads – By The Time I Get To Phoenix, Galveston, Wichita Lineman, all located in the South – had made him a worldwide superstar, and his time was now spent on the golf course, making movies or cutting lacklustre religious and country albums. Even a much-anticipated collaboration with Webb, 1974's *Reunion*, had nose-dived spectacularly. Then, while driving home one evening in late 1974, Campbell heard a song on the radio that he thought might revive his chart fortunes. Capitol A&R chief Al Coury agreed to hear it on the condition that Campbell first listen to a song *he* believed would do the same trick: as it turned out, they'd both picked the same tune, Rhinestone Cowboy.

A flop for its author Larry Weiss the previous year, the song seemed tailor-made for Campbell, its story of a jaded country star pounding "the dirty sidewalks of Broadway" as unnervingly autobiographical as Jimmy Webb's late '60s songs. "With that record, I was determined that the lyrics call attention to themselves," recalls Campbell. "This was the first time I had ever made a record in which the words needed to shine above my singing. I recorded the vocal melody, then overdubbed my voice harmonising with myself. I thought this duet would compel listeners to focus on the words."

Teaming up with pop producers/writers Dennis Lambert and Brian Potter, an album was constructed around the concept of a compromised, 40-something country star at odds with the fruits of his fame. From the conviction and fluidity of his honey-sweet tenor, you could tell that Campbell – then having drink, drug and marital problems – felt a rare affinity with the material: on Comeback, Count On Me, Miss You Tonight and the delightful Country Boy ("Looking back, I can remember a time when I sang my songs for free!"), it seemed as if Glen was confiding the infernal woes of his own life, then a well-kept showbiz secret. Side two had a looser collection of covers, Johnny Cunningham's subtly melancholic Pencils For Sale, Randy Newman's gorgeous Marie and, as a fitting finale, Mann and Weil's We're Over.

Rhinestone Cowboy resurrected Campbell's global profile in one fell swoop.

Record label:
Capitol

Produced
by Dennis Lambert and Brian Potter.

Recorded
at Sound Labs, Hollywood; summer 1975.

Released:
October 1975

Chart peaks:
38 (UK) I (US)

Personnel:
Glen Campbell (v, ag); Dean Parks, Ben Benay (g); Scott Edwards (b); Michael Omartian, Dennis Lambert (k); Ed Greene, Dave Kemper (d)

Track listing:
Country Boy (s); Comeback; Count On Me; I Miss You Tonight; My Girl; Rhinestone Cowboy (S); I'd Build A Bridge; Pencils For Sale; Marie; We're Over

Running time:
33.25

Currently unavailable on CD

Further listening:
The 2-CD selection The Capitol Years (1999) anthologises his career to 1977, and includes the near-legendary, Brian Wilson-penned and produced Guess I'm Dumb from 1966.

Further reading:
It's all in the great man's own, brutally honest account of his life, Rhinestone Cowboy (Glen Campbell with Tom Carter, 1994)

Dion
Born To Be With You

Both born in the Bronx, Dion DiMucci and Phil Spector team for a mouth-watering album.

A t the end of the '60s, John Lennon had coaxed Phil Spector out of retirement to produce Instant Karma and doctor The Beatles' Let It Be. Spector went on to greater things, producing George Harrison's *All Things Must Pass* and Lennon's *Imagine*. Two near fatal car crashes later, Spector decided to set up another label, Phil Spector International in the UK in 1975.

Dion had had his problems too. Drug addiction had almost caused his career to falter completely in 1964, but by the end of the '60s he had re-emerged as a singer-songwriter. At Christmas 1968, he even hit the US Top 10 with Abraham, Martin And John. Though they were raised in the same part of New York, Spector didn't really know Dion until they worked together on this LP. On the liner notes he writes: "As kids, we probably threw rocks at the same gangs, at each other. We fought the same wretched battles rooted in boredom and bigotry. And it was the same music that saved us from (destroying) ourselves."

With its dedication to Lenny Bruce, Spector's close friend who died in 1968, *Born To Be With You* has also taken on a reputation as music to take drugs to. But it's not a bleak work, it's an uplifting record, five of the six Spector productions being quite magnificent. The Wall Of Sound orchestra – featuring many of Spector's regular musicians: drummers Hal Blaine and Frank Kapp, guitarists Barney Kessel and Dennis Budimir, horn players Steve Douglas, Jay Migliori and Nino Tempo among them – is as sharp as ever. The songs have pedigree too, best of all being Barry Mann and Cynthia Weil's pleading Make The World Love Me, where Dion's voice somehow manages to soar above the towering mix. Two songwriting collaborations with Spector stalwart Gerry Goffin continue the mood of introspection, Only You Know and In And Out Of Showers. Finally, there's the Phil and Dion collaboration He's Got The Whole World In His Hands: a strange hybrid of gospel and pop which sounds modern enough to have been recorded 20 years later.

Born To Be With You was Phil Spector's last great record. Meanwhile, Dion continued to make well received albums like 1978's *Return Of The Wanderer* and 1989's *Yo Frankie*. As Spector claimed in his liner notes: "He is also a GREAT artist. I hope

Record label:
Phil Spector International

Produced
by Phil Spector.

Recorded
at A&M Studios, Los Angeles; September 1975.

Release date:
October 1975

Chart peaks:
None (UK) None (US)

Personnel:
Dion DiMucci (v, g); The Wall Of Sound Orchestra; Nino Tempo (a)

Track listing:
Born To Be With You (S); Make The World Love Me; Your Own Backyard; He's Got The Whole World In His Hands; Only You Know; New York City Song; In And Out Of Showers; Good Lovin' Man

Running time:
35.20

Currently unavailable on CD

Further listening:
Runaround Sue (1998)

Further reading:
http://yodion.com

Al Green
Al Green Is Love

Green's comeback album after serious injury.

C hoosing between any of Al Green's '70s albums is a tough task, and it might seem perverse to pick the most misanthropic and idiosyncratic of all of them. But *Al Green Is Love* crystallises the dilemma at the heart of Green's music, and at the core of soul itself: the conflict between the sacred and the profane. On The Love Sermon, six and a half minutes of near-madness, preacher Green seems to be berating some of the more wayward members of his flock, but he still manages to sneak through the line "I want to do everything for you that all the married men won't do." It comes as no surprise his father sacked him from the family gospel quartet after catching young Al listening to Jackie Wilson.

Green was coming off the back of a period of both astonishing success and personal turmoil. He had already scored 12 gold records in the US, but less than a year earlier had suffered terrible burns after an attack by an ex-girlfriend (who then shot herself). What was going through his mind when he started these sessions is open to conjecture, but the results range from child-like lyrics (Rhymes) to classic pop-soul (L-O-V-E, later covered in a memorable mismatch by Edwyn Collins' Orange Juice) to stream-of-consciousness confession (The Love Sermon) and pure rhythmic grooving (Love Ritual). As always, producer Willie Mitchell covers the music in the dusty patina of the Hi Records sound, and sometimes Green seems to be disappearing into a box. But there is always that peerless voice. Nobody else really comes close to Green's gentle, musing tenderness on a ballad. I Didn't Know is close to eight minutes as he goes through his repertoire of voices, from mewling, bird-like falsetto to half-spoken growl, and presents himself for our mercy. As with all Green's records, there is a lot of barefaced machismo here, but it dissolves in the cracks of his shape-changing artistry. As MOJO's Barney Hoskyns put it, he is "the jester of soul, a meta-singer, a cat narcissistically chasing its own tail". This is one of Green's last performances before he committed more fully to the gospel over soul, and it's an amazing transition.

Record label:
Hi Records

Produced
by Willie Mitchell and Al Green.

Recorded
at Royal Recording Studios, Memphis;
1975.

Released:
October 1975

Chart peaks:
None (UK) 28 (US)

Personnel:
Al Green (v); Teenie Hodges, Larry Lee
(g); Charles Hodges (o, p); Archie Turner,
Michael Allen (p); Leroy Hodges (b);
Howard Grimes (pc); Congo Lou (congas);
Wayne Jackson (t); Jack Hale (tb);
Andrew Love, Lewis Collins (ts); James
Mitchell (bs); The Memphis Strings;
Rhodes, Chalmers & Rhodes, Duncan
Sisters (bv)

Track listing:
L-O-V-E (Love); Rhymes; The Love Sermon;
There Is Love; Could I Be The One; Love
Ritual; I Didn't Know; Oh Me, Oh My
(Dreams In My Arms); I Gotta Be More
(Take Me Higher); I Wish You Were Here

Running time:
41.12

Current CD:
HILO157

Further listening:
Call Me (1973)

Further reading:
From A Whisper To A Scream (1991)
and autobiography Take Me To The River
(2000)

Jade Warrior
Waves

Obscure British instrumental duo cut sonic hymn to oceans, whales, truth and beauty.

"Whale sounds from recording all notes of organ, splicing them together then running tape through by hand + sine wave generator." On the inner sleeve of *Waves*, Jade Warrior decided to explain how their music was made. It revealed their painstaking methods – such as recreating whale calls as their own music rather than borrowing a library recording – but it hardly conveyed their emotional and aesthetic intensity. Friends for 15 years since they met as forklift truck drivers and discovered a shared love of jazz, Tony Duhig and Jon Field had wandered in the penumbra of rock's glory years until, in the early '70s, they formed Jade Warrior as a prog rock band. They sounded a bit like Jethro Tull and recorded for Vertigo. When that folded, they dropped the vocals, kept the name – triggered by their own passion for Japanese culture and Kurosawa movies in particular – and betook themselves to Island (Steve Winwood recommended them to label owner Chris Blackwell). At which they became an "exclusive club of two and did our floaty stuff", as Field puts it. Through four widely ignored albums, they strove to capture the pristine notions of ideal beauty inspired in them by years of chewing over matters Oriental and philosophical.

Waves found them tense with one another, abraded by the impossibility of commercial success with the music they longed to make. But still, says Field, they could resolve their differences into "complete musical harmony. We were push-and-pull, that's how it worked, that's how we reached the golden road". Boundlessly imaginative-cum-happy-accidental, they reached for the heavenly sound they imagined. At night in the Oxfordshire countryside, they would park speakers in the fields, the microphones 400 yards away, so that Duhig's "distant" guitar solos really were just that. The birdsong at the start of side two (as was) arose from Duhig flinging open the studio window at 4am to take a leak, as musicians will, and being overwhelmed by the dawn chorus.

Wordless *Waves* is a drama, a meditation, a composition of entrancing grace. Even so, Field still views it with some rue: "Really, we always made the same album under different names and the number of albums we made is the extent of our failure to get it right." He recalls a '70s interview in which his late friend Duhig was asked whether he would describe Jade Warrior as a pop group. "No, it's not popular music," he said. "It's more *un*popular music." But great.

Record label:
Island

Produced
by Jon Field and Tony Duhig.

Recorded
at The Manor, Shipton-on-Cherwell, Oxfordshire; The Argonaut, Little Venice, London; May–August 1975.

Release date:
October 1975

Chart peaks:
None (UK) None (US)

Personnel:
Jon Field (flute, oboe, clarinet, c, p, pc, bv); Tony Duhig (g, bv); Steve Winwood (Moog, p); Dave Duhig (g); Graham Morgan (d); Nick Glossop, Tom Newman (e)

Track listing:
The Whale; The Sea; Section See; Caves; Wave Birth; River To The Sea; Groover; Breeze; Sea Part Two.

Running time:
42.46

Current CD:
314524140-2

Further listening:
Floating World (1974), Kites (1976), The Way Of The Sun (1978), or complete Island CD anthology Jade Warrior: Elements (1995) – the isolated striving for elegance and grace continues.

Further reading:
www.feghoot.ml.org;
www.radagast.org/jade-warrior

Paul Simon
Still Crazy After All These Years

The summit of Simon's post-Garfunkel creative surge.

Effectively, this album covered the continuing aftermath of two divorces. In 1970, Simon and Garfunkel had separated to go solo musically. In 1975, Simon and Peggy, his wife of six years, were formalising their break-up while he wrote and recorded *Still Crazy After All These Years*.

Naturally, this shaped the songs. "That's what was happening," he said, ruefully. "I guess I have an easier time expressing myself in song than in real life." But the marital divorce stirred him to seek reconciliation in his fractured friend-ship with Garfunkel by offering him a song – even if he proposed My Little Town as something 'nasty' to offset the sugary nature of his former partner's solo repertoire.

The domestic emphasis in Simon's life may have contributed to the ethnic explorations of his first two solo albums being put on hold. But he stayed with producer Phil Ramone who shepherded him through nine months of sporadic progress until he emerged with his most consistent, coherent and profoundly communicative album – the Brill Building musical craftsmanship acquired in his youth, sharpened by inquisitive imagination and matched by lyrics which were subtle yet clear, never blurred by his tendency to run for cover behind poetic obfuscation.

Unusually, this was a successful album built on a prevailing sense of doubt. Gone At Last, the glorious gospel track driven by the late Richard Tee's piano, is the only unbri-dled expression of happiness. The other songs all carry questions and hints of sour irony in either the lyrics or acidic musical comments; in the hit single 50 Ways To Leave Your Lover the turmoil of breaking up is set against a rigid military beat (the "You just slip out the back, Jack" chorus inspired by a rhyming game Simon played with his son).

Significantly, the only track which didn't work well was Silent Eyes. A Jew wanting to write about the Holocaust, he drifted into the fatal trap for artists dealing with history and politics of expressing how *he felt* about the Holocaust, calling for attention to himself rather than the event. But that was just one (well-meant) false step. Simon advertised the temporary rapprochement with Garfunkel by singing with him on American TV's Saturday Night Live. The album a huge hit, he stopped recording for five years.

Record label:
CBS

Produced
by Paul Simon and Phil Ramone (except My Little Town produced by Simon, Art Garfunkel, Ramone)

Recorded
January–September 1975.

Release date:
October 1975

Chart peaks:
6 (UK) 1 (US)

Personnel:
Paul Simon (v, g); Pete Carr, Joe Beck Jerry Friedman, Hugh McCracken (g); Barry Beckett, Leon Pendarvis (p); David Hood, Tony Levin, Gordon Edwards (b); Roger Hawkins, Steve Gadd, Grady Tate (d); Mike Brecker, Phil Woods (s); Ralph McDonald (pc); Bob James (electric p); Toots Thielemans (hm on Night Game); Richard Tee (p on Gone At Last); Art Garfunkel (duet v on My Little Town); Phoebe Snow, Valerie Simpson, Patti Austin, The Jessy Dixon Singers, The Chicago Community Choir (bv); Burt Szerlip, Glen Berger (e)

Track listing:
Still Crazy After All These Years (S, US only); My Little Town (S); I Do It For Your Love; 50 Ways To Leave Your Lover (S); Night Game; Gone At Last (S, US only); Some Folks' Lives Roll Easy; Have A Good Time; You're Kind; Silent Eyes

Running time:
34:33

Current CD:
Warner Brothers 7599-25591-2

Further listening:
Graceland (1986) – Simon busts the anti-apartheid cultural boycott but finds soulmates in South Africa.

Further reading:
MOJO 50. Simon And Garfunkel: The Definitive Biography (Victoria Kingston, 1996); http://paul.simon.org

Queen
Night At The Opera

The pinnacle of Queen's achievements, a monstrous, marvellous magnum opus.

Freddie Mercury was playing a powerful ballad from the point of view of someone who had 'just killed a man' for producer Roy Thomas Baker when he suddenly stopped, saying "this is where the opera section comes in." Baker fell about laughing but knew what he meant.

Baker: "I had worked with the D'Oyly Carte Opera at Decca so I knew a lot about vocals and the way vocals are stressed, so I was probably one of the few people in the pop world who knew what he was talking about."

There ensued a series of marathon sesssions overdubbing, bouncing-down (the resulting distortion accidentally contributes to Queen's 'saturated' sound) and splicing to realise Mercury's grandiose vision. Baker: "Every time Freddie would come up with another Galileo I would add another piece of tape to the reel which was beginning to look like a zebra crossing whizzing by." The band didn't mind spending so much time on Freddie's baby, they knew it was a monster and were united in insisting that the unedited six-minute track should be the single (though Baker remembers Roger Taylor locking himself in a cupboard until his I'm In Love With My Car was allowed on the B-side). Meeting managerial and record company resistance, the band got a white label to Kenny Everett who 'accidentally' played it 14 times in one weekend creating huge interest and it went on to be, along with the groundbreaking promo film, a milestone in pop music, revered and reviled in equal extremes. Wisely, it was placed at the end of an album which, though rigorous and resourceful, couldn't hope to top Mercury's ludicrous masterpiece.

Beautifully paced and programmed, the album opens with the remarkably sustained viciousness of Mercury's revenge-in-song Death On Two Legs that brickwalls into the hilariously carefree Lazing On A Sunday Afternoon. Further highlights include Deacon's delightfully breezy You're My Best Friend (showing he was the only one in Queen who could write a straightforward pop song), May's sprawling, atmospheric Prophet's Song, the cheeky pastiches Seaside Rendezvous and Good Company (May combining George Formby with an astounding guitar-created swing band) and Mercury's gorgeous ballad Love Of My Life. Freddie said Queen would be "the Cecil B De Mille of rock, always wanting to do things bigger and better." With *Night At The Opera* they achieved it.

Record label:
EMI

Produced
by Roy Thomas Baker and Queen.

Recorded
at Sarm, Roundhouse, Olympic, Rockfield, Scorpio and Lansdowne; August–November 1975.

Released:
November 21, 1975

Chart peaks:
1 (UK) 4 (US)

Personnel:
Roger Taylor (d, v); Freddie Mercury (v, p); John Deacon (b, ag); Brian May (g, p, ukelele, harp)

Track listing:
Death On Two Legs; Lazing On A Sunday Afternoon; I'm In Love With My Car; You're My Best Friend; '39; Sweet Lady; Seaside Rendezvous; The Prophet's Song; Love Of My Life; Good Company; Bohemian Rhapsody; God Save The Queen

Running time:
43.11

Current CD:
CDPCSD130

Further listening:
Queen II (1974); Sheer Heart Attack (1974); Day At The Races (1976)

Further reading:
Mercury (Laura Jackson, 1996); Good Vibrations: A History Of Record Production (Mark Cunningham, 1996); www.queen-fip.com

Peggy Lee
Mirrors

Autumn-years rumination makes high art of high camp.

Having sold-out their interests in Red Bird records, songwriters Jerry Lieber and Mike Stoller moved on to a pet project of philosophy-drop-out Jerry Lieber's, a song adaptation of Thomas Mann's story Disillusionment.

"It's an example in existentialist thinking, like Heidegger and Camus," said Leiber, "and I was fascinated by it." Lieber presented Stoller with spoken vignettes voicing nonchalant disappointment with a fire, a circus, a love affair and encroaching death but in the absence of a sung linking passage to bind the vignettes together, Stoller composed some music and Leiber some lyrics, separately. When they compared them "we didn't have to change one syllable or anything," remembers Stoller. "It's the only time that's ever happened."

Peggy Lee loved the song – Is That All There Is? – and recorded it; a further cry from Leiber/Stoller's rock'n'roll songs of the '50s like Hound Dog and Yakety Yak could hardly be imagined. With something of Irving Berlin and Kurt Weill in the song's tenor, it was arranged by Randy Newman – having a similar elliptical orchestral ebb and flow to his early work – and Lee's performance was adult and heady. Her record company, Capitol, hated it, refusing to issue it. So she traded an appearance on a TV show she didn't want to do for the record's release. It became a nationwide hit, winning Lee a Grammy and revitalising her career.

Six years later, the same team – minus Newman but plus brilliant arranger Johnny Mandel – fashioned a series of similarly toned songs for *Mirrors*, which combined new tunes with numbers from failed Lieber/Stoller musicals into a kind of concept. Lee explained: "It's like a voyage of the mind, a vehicle for moving from thought to thought, place to place, person to person. You can make up your own endings. There's a sort of question mark – on purpose, not by accident."

Mauled by rock critics at the time, to some ears it remains camp and pretentious – a smokey-voiced blonde wordily straining for profundity amongst banjo-punctuated oom-pah grooves, and a trancelike life's-a-circus atmosphere. To others it's a rich, alluring piece of mature cabaret whose complex musical palette is matched by resonant, psychologically dense lyrics and wise, world-weary performances.

Record label:
A&M

Produced
by Jerry Leiber and Mike Stoller.

Recorded
at A&M Studios, Hollywood; Record Plant, New York; 1975.

Released:
November 1975

Chart peaks:
None (UK) None (US)

Personnel:
Peggy Lee (v); Johnny Mandel (oa, conductor); Hank Cicalo, Bob Ludwig (e)

Track listing:
Ready To Begin Again (Manya's Song); Some Cats Know; I've Got Them Feelin' Too Good Today Blues; A Little White Ship; Tango; Professor Hauptmann's Performing Dogs; The Case Of M.J.; I Remember; Say It; Longings For A Simpler Time

Running time:
39.07

Currently unavailable on CD

Further listening:
Is That All There Is? (1969)

Further reading:
Miss Peggy Lee (Peggy Lee, 1989); www.geocities.com/Broadway/Stage/2481/home.html

Bob Marley & the Wailers

Live

Transcendent, career-defining show caught on record.

The 1975 tour that launched *Natty Dread* turned the year into an *annus mirabilis* for Marley. The last tour, with Peter and Bunny still in the group, had been a disaster – playing shabby venues amid a biting winter. Marley had realised that to succeed in a world defined by slick rock and soul acts, his live shows had to be honed into a sharper force. Bass player Family Man Barrett became his musical lieutenant, tightening up a band in which American guitarist Al Anderson now had a role, while Marley himself developed a shamanic stage presence. Floundering for a description of the phenomenon, the Village Voice called him "the Mick Jagger of reggae" when he played New York in June. By the time the tour arrived in Britain, Marley fever had begun to break out. Demand for tickets to his concerts exceeded availability several times over, with the two London Lyceum shows mobbed by people trying to get in. Inside, the atmosphere resembled a muggy night in Kingston.

"The first night, the intensity and the vibe were just nuts," said Steve Smith, who helped Chris Blackwell record the second night's show on The Rolling Stones' Mobile for what is widely regarded as one of the handful of truly great live albums. "They opened up the roof because it was so hot."

The sweaty passion of the occasion is palpable on *Live*, where the audience's waves of emotion surge from the speakers along with the band's music. "The recording would never have been as good as it was if it hadn't been for Dave Harper, who mixed the live sound out front," said Smith. "So much of the mix is to do with those live hall mikes, and you can hear that in No Woman, No Cry."

No Woman No Cry was one of the night's surprises – transformed from a slight piece on *Natty Dread* (where it was mysteriously speeded up) to become what Smith described as "the ultimate singalong." When the live version was released as a single, it became Marley's first UK hit ("the damn thing just jumped off the radio," said Smith) and one of his enduring anthems. "At the Lyceum it was, like, 50-50 black and white", said Dennis Morris. "And those 2,000 people spread the word to 20,000 people, who then spread it to another 50,000. No-one had ever seen a performer like that before." No small thanks to that concert, Bob Marley – 30 years old when he stepped onto the Lyceum stage – would become a legend.

Record label:
Island

Produced
by Steve Smith and Chris Blackwell.

Recorded
at the Lyceum, London; July 1975.

Released:
November 1975

Chart peaks:
38 (UK) None (US)

Personnel:
Bob Marley (v, g); Aston 'Family Man' Barrett (b); Carlton Barrett (d); Al Anderson (g); Tyrone Downie (k); Rita Marley (v); Judy Mowatt (v); Marcia Griffith (v); Dave Harper, Phill Brown (e)

Track listing:
Trenchtown Rock; Burnin' And Lootin'; Them Belly Full; Lively Up Yourself; No Woman No Cry (S); I Shot The Sheriff; Get Up, Stand Up

Running time:
35.44

Current CD:

Further listening:
Natty Dread (1975); Rastaman Vibration (1976). A lesser, but still entertaining live album was Babylon By Bus (1978).

Further reading:
Catch A Fire (Timothy White, 1983); Bob Marley (Stephen Davis, 1983); Bob Marley: Songs of Freedom (Chris Salewicz and Adrian Boot, 1995); Bob Marley (Scotty Bennett, 1997); MOJO 16; www.bobmarley.com

Joni Mitchell
The Hissing Of Summer Lawns

Joni stays two steps ahead.

izarrely, Rolling Stone critics declared *Hissing Of Summer Lawns* Worst Album Of The Year. In mitigation, Mitchell was too musically fleet of foot for many a '70s pundit. After David Crosby 'discovered' her in 1968, she recorded a sequence of pristine, confessional, acoustic albums. But with the naked exposure of *Blue* (1971), she said, "I felt at the end of that phase. I was still lonely at moments, but I was damned if I was going to write about it any more."

Her next three albums saw her working rather rowdily with Tom Scott's brass-based LA Express, and following well publicised romances with Graham Nash, Leonard Cohen and James Taylor – at the end of her 1974 tour she set up home in a Bel Air hacienda with the band's drummer, John Guerin. Apparently, they spent their time playing cribbage and backgammon – while casting a beady eye over the svelte suburbs around them. Dropping the horn section, she gathered up her big box of Camels, crate of red wine, some classy session friends, and set off for the neighbourhood mega-studio to transport her sound to a supple, subtle jazziness beyond genre definition. Her observations focused on women, as in the film Diary Of A Mad Housewife, women trapped in rooms full of furniture: "There must be something more! What's missing?" These characters populate the title track (co-written by Guerin), Don't Interrupt The Sorrow, Shades Of Scarlett Conquering and, by implication, Harry's House/Centrepiece. The obvious eyebrow-raiser is Jungle Line's concatenation of Burundi drums, Moog, gymnastic voice and bloody clever lyrics: "In a low-cut blouse she brings the beer/Rousseau paints a jungle flower behind her ear" (Henri Rousseau the Impressionist, that is). It laid out her theme of man's innate primitivism, the well-watered lawn as a delusion of civility, Los Angeleno sophistication as an almighty bluff. But the final track, Shadows And Light, went even further, proffering elegant reflections on "blindness and sight, wrong and right" drenched in whole choirs of harmonised minor-key Mitchells.

Twenty-five years on, *Hissing of Summer Lawns* is said to be Prince's all-time favourite album. Mitchell thought rather well of it herself, remarking in her sleevenote that "This is a total work conceived graphically, musically, lyrically and accidentally – as a whole."

Record label:
Asylum

Produced
by Joni Mitchell.

Recorded
Burbank Studios, Los Angeles, summer 1975.

Released:
November 1975

Chart peaks:
14 (UK) 4 (US)

Personnel:
Joni Mitchell (v, g, k, p); Robben Ford, Jeff Baxter, Larry Carlton (g); Victor Feldman (p); Joe Sample (electric piano); John Guerin (d); Max Bennet, Wilton Felder (b); Chuck Findley (horn); Bud Shank (s, flute); Graham Nash, David Crosby (bv); James Taylor (bv, g); Henry Lewy (e); Ellis Sorkin (ae)

Track listing:
In France They Kiss On Main Street; The Jungle Line; Edith And The Kingpin; Don't Interrupt The Sorrow; Shades Of Scarlett Conquering; The Hissing Of Summer Lawns; The Boho Dance; Harry's House/Centerpiece; Sweet Bird; Shadows And Light

Running time:
42.26

Current CD:
7559-60332-2

Further listening:
Her acoustic apogee, Blue (1972); Chalk Mark In A Rainstorm (1988) – eccentric highlight: Mitchell duets with Billy Idol; Both Sides Now (2000), smoky club jazz covers gloriously sung.

Further reading:
MOJO 12A, 57; The Complete Poems And Lyrics (Joni Mitchell, 1997); Both Sides Now (Brian Hinton, 1998)
www.JoniMitchell.com/

Patti Smith
Horses

Rimbaud goes garage, a new way forward with a poet's debut album.

"Five crazed neo-punks" – according to guitarist Lenny Kaye – played CBGB's club on the Bowery in New York, four to five nights a week for nine straight weeks, then rehearsed in Times Square behind a huge billboard before decamping to Electric Lady to make a debut album almost christened *Land*. Smith, a rock lover who'd had several volumes of poetry published in the early '70s, had been experimenting with music as a vehicle for some time, and had cut a stirring single, Hey Joe/Piss Factory, with Kaye and Richard Sohl in 1972. Joined by Ivan Kral and Dee Daugherty they began to develop into a popular act and were spotted by Clive Davis and signed, rather incongruously, to his rather mainstream Arista label. The album they made was a splurge of garage abandon, pop hooks and high-wire improvisation around Smith's wildcard role as Baudelaire's kid sister – a record embracing "the sea of possibilities", as she sings on Land.

Kaye's abiding memory is combating John Cale's will to make a more traditionally arranged record. "It was strange to us because we'd chosen him for his artistic ability, but he was into The Beach Boys at the time. He made us stand for what we believed, to challenge our artistic notions of who we wanted to be, which pushed us out onto the edge."

Unleashed upon a moribund music scene, the effect of *Horses* was startling. This and The Ramones' first album are the records most often cited as the catalysts for punk: raw examples of how music might have been. But it's maybe not too surprising that few who were inspired by it subsequently took up Patti's model of tumbling free-form beat poetry declaimed over semi-improvised garage rock. It was a daring, complex trick to pull off. Even Smith herself couldn't really repeat the recipe.

"All we were trying to do," she reflected in 1995, "was to rekindle people's spirit and motivate new people to keep going. We really looked at it as our prime mission, so when people say good things about it, it really does make me feel good. It makes me feel like we achieved what we set out to do."

Record label:
Arista

Produced
by John Cale and Alan Lanier.

Recorded
at Electric Lady Studios, New York City;
September–October 1975.

Released:
November 1975

Chart peaks:
None (UK) 47 (US)

Personnel:
Patti Smith (v, g); Lenny Kaye (g); Ivan Kral (g, b); John Cale (b); Richard Sohl (p); Jay Dee Daugherty (d); Bernie Kirsh (e)

Track listing:
Gloria (In Excelis Deo) (S); Redondo Beach; Birdland; Free Money; Kimberly; Break It Up; Land: Horses/Land Of A Thousand Dances/La Mer; Elegie

Running time:
43.07

Current CD:
07822188272

Further listening:
Radio Ethiopia (1976) was less focused, less appealing. After an extended hiatus due to a broken back, Patti returned with Easter (1978), a more conventional, radio-friendly sound.

Further reading:
MOJO 33; The Complete Poems And Lyrics (Patti Smith, 1999)

Keith Jarrett
The Køln Concert

At three million copies, this improvised live recording is the biggest selling piano record ever.

Few great albums have been made by artists apparently on the verge of falling asleep: *The Køln Concert* is one of them. Jarrett, in the midst of a European solo tour, reckons he hadn't slept for 24 hours when he arrived at the Cologne concert hall to tackle an audibly substandard piano. Avoiding the instrument's tinny high notes, he concentrates on pulsing rhythmic patterns in the middle register whose hypnotic repetition may have had something to do with his exhaustion. The resulting album – a musical triumph over adversity – contains fewer harmonic adventures than normal but a simplicity and passion that resonated far beyond Jarrett's jazz following.

The pianist, a Miles Davis veteran, had been performing improvised solo shows for about two years before the Cologne date, conjuring up music that see-sawed between his classical training and the jazz, gospel and blues he loved. Before the Cologne show, however, Jarrett was feeling less than inspired. With Manfred Eicher, manager of the fledgling ECM label, driving, he had spent a long day travelling by car from a Lausanne date, trying fruitlessly to catnap. The pair arrived exhausted and at the hall discovered that of the two Bosendorfer pianos in the city, the wrong one had been delivered. There was a row but the removal team's lorry had already left. Jarrett went back to his hotel and tried again to sleep without success. A late meal at an overheated Italian restaurant was bolted down while Jarrett and Eicher discussed whether to scrap plans to tape the sold-out show. Eventually they decided that since the engineers had already been paid, they might as well have a document of the gig.

Jarrett says he was fighting off waves of fatigue as he headed for the stage. "When I finally had to play it was a relief because there was nothing more of this story to tell. It was 'I am now going out here with this piano . . . and the hell with everything else.'" Listening to the tape later on the tour, the pair decided that, dodgy piano or no, the performance had something special – and the resulting record duly received rave reviews. The album's sales helped turn the tiny ECM label into a major European force and won Jarrett the kind of across-the-board recognition that only a handful of living jazzmen have achieved.

Record label:
ECM

Produced
by Manfred Eicher.

Recorded
in Oper der Stadt, Cologne; January 24, 1975.

Released:
1975

Chart peaks:
None (UK) None (US)

Personnel:
Keith Jarrett (p); Martin Wieland (e)

Track listing:
Part I; Part IIa; Part IIb; Part IIc

Running time:
67.33

Current CD:
8100672

Further listening:
The world is not short of solo Jarrett, veering from the transcendental to the predictable. Solo Concerts (1973) and Concerts (1981) are among the very best.

Further reading:
Keith Jarrett: The Man And His Music (Ian Carr, 1992);
www.bruchez.org/olivier/music/keith
Keith Jarrett discussion group

June Tabor
Airs And Graces

Tabor's first serious album release established her as England's premier female interpreter of traditional song.

Tabor, a former Oxford University student, worked in a library and was (by choice) only a part-time singer when she made this album on a shoestring budget. Many years later she was still hanging on to her day job, fearful that turning professional and singing on a daily basis would blunt her desire and commitment to her music. To this day she becomes so emotionally immersed in her performance she will end a particularly emotional song in tears: "I sang The Band Played Waltzing Matilda at Inverness Folk Festival and I couldn't finish it because I was crying and the whole audience was crying," she remembers. In the end she stopped performing the song – written by Scotsman Eric Bogle after watching in despair the Anzac Day parades in Australia – altogether, because she felt that singing it on a regular basis would diminish its importance, but it still has an enormous impact and must rank as one of the greatest anti-war songs ever written.

The album also includes a powerful version of John Tams' melancholy song about funfairs, Pull Down Lads – which put him on the map as a major songwriter. But dominant is Tabor's icily moving a cappella voice performing serious child ballads like Waly Waly, Young Waters and Bonny May. It gave her the platform to move on to greater things, but despite recording the high profile *Silly Sisters* duet album and touring with Maddy Prior she stayed true to her roots in the folk clubs and stuck to her strict beliefs about the sanctity of traditional song. Her music subsequently evolved to include a partnership with Martin Simpson, an album and tour with the Oyster band, an album of jazz standards, work with the Creative Jazz Orchestra and a natural move towards French *chansons*.

As a landmark for English folk music and pure traditional singing, however, *Airs And Graces* remains a must.

Record label:
Topic

Produced
by Paul Brown.

Recorded
at Sound Techniques Studios, London;
November 1975.

Released:
March 1976

Chart peaks:
None (UK) None (US)

Personnel:
June Tabor (v); Nic Jones (g, fiddle); Jon Gillaspie (p, o, bassoon); Victor Gamm (e)

Track listing:
While Gamekeepers Lie Sleeping; Plains Of Waterloo; Bonny May; Reynardine; The Band Played Waltzing Matilda; Young Waters; Waly Waly; The Merchant's Son; Queen Among The Heather; Pull Down Lads

Running time:
38.53

Current CD:
TSCD298

Further listening:
The upbeat, fun partnership with Maddy Prior, Silly Sisters (1986); hitting another vocal peak with demanding, rewarding mostly contemporary material on Aqaba (1988); her celebrated collaboration with the Oyster band, Freedom And Rain (1990)

Further reading:
Folk Roots magazine, www.froots.co.uk

Thin Lizzy
Jailbreak

*The record that established Lizzy as the rockers who even
the punks could love.*

"We knew we had to get it right with *Jailbreak*," Phil
Lynott reflected almost a decade after the album's
release. "Because if we didn't, we'd be stuck playing Whiskey In
The Jar for the rest of our lives."

Almost three years had elapsed since Thin Lizzy burst
into the British chart with their epic rearrangement of a traditional Irish drinking song and, since that time, their reputation
as one of the hardest rocking bands on the circuit had soared
towards the heavens. Their vinyl appeal, however, remained
locked in the past, and Lynott continued, "we knew we were
moving in the right direction with *Fighting* (#60 the previous
summer); and to be honest, I think Springsteen helped –
suddenly there was this Yank writing the same kind of songs as
we were, the romantic street-fighting thing, and maybe people
started looking around for something similar, a little closer to
home."

The Boys Are Back In Town, the first single from this
new album, set the stage effortlessly – swaggering, lawless,
mercilessly punched along by Gorman and Robertson's twin
guitars. But as the hottest summer in living memory unfolded
over the UK, the song's own mood of impending menace
captured more than the meteorological heat – punk was taking
its first, tentative steps in the *barrio* bars of the capital and, is it
simply hindsight talking or did Lynott really zap a social mood
which even its practitioners had yet to fully comprehend?

"I don't know," he admitted. "Of course we were going
out to the clubs, we were aware of the bands coming up behind
us, but what you have to remember is, before *Jailbreak* took off,
we were still playing the same places they were, the Greyhounds
and Nashvilles and Dingwalls. Who were the boys? We all were."
Jailbreak is Lizzy's masterpiece, but it wasn't to be the final
word on the subject. Two years later, the double *Live And
Dangerous* readdressed five of the album's finest moments; both
singles, the rebellious thunder of Emerald, the seething Warriors
and the rollicking Cowboy Song ("lonesome trail" rhymed with
"certain female" – how can anybody resist?), and imbibed them
all with even greater meaning. Not only were the boys back in
town, they'd stuck around as well. And what they had wrought
would never be undone.

Record label:
Mercury

Produced
by John Alcock.

Recorded
at Ramport Studios, London; winter 1975.

Released:
March 1976

Chart peaks:
10 (UK) 18 (US)

Personnel:
Phil Lynott (v, b, acoustic g), Scott
Gorman (g), Brian Robertson (g), Brian
Downey (d)

Track listing:
Jailbreak (S); Angel From The Coast;
Running Back; Romeo And The Lonely
Girl; Warriors; The Boys Are Back In
Town (S); Fight Or Fall; Cowboy Song;
Emerald

Running time:
36.16

Current CD:
532294-2

Further listening:
Dedication: The Very Best Of (1991)

Further reading:
MOJO 2; Phil Lynott – The Rocker (Mark
Putterford, 1998); www.thinlizzyfan.com

Kiss

Destroyer

Fourth studio album by stack-heeled New York cartoon rockers is their first to top the million mark in the US.

Between January 1974 and mid-'75 Kiss allegedly relied on then-manager Bill Aucoin to overload his credit cards in order to obtain the necessary tour support to keep the band on the road. By the end of '75, however, their legwork had paid off forcing the double album *Alive!* set to crash into the US Top 10. In a bid to raise the stakes for that all-important fourth album, Kiss recruited Bob Ezrin whose work included several Alice Cooper albums including the chart-topping *Billion Dollar Babies* set. Sharing the songwriting on seven of the nine *Destroyer* tracks, Ezrin added a suitably grandiose edge to the proceedings – the overblown pomp of Great Expectations and the keyboard interlude on Flaming Youth, an otherwise typical chest-beating Kiss number.

Opener Detroit Rock City, a tribute to Kiss's Motor City stronghold, boasts a lengthy intro which catalogues the death of a drink-driver in Pontiac, Michigan – the newscast and subsequent sound of the wreckage being cleared from the road. Ominous, brooding but anthemic, the track sets the tone for the entire album. Paul Stanley's King Of The Night Time World is pure machismo, while the thumping God Of Thunder allows Gene Simmons to unleash his demonic persona to full effect. Anthems such as Shout It Out Loud and Do You Love Me are dumb-ass glam nuggets furnished with a layer of production gloss courtesy of Ezrin. Top 10 single Beth, a weepy ballad about life on the road penned and sung by drummer Peter Criss in his best *faux* Rod Stewart rasp, is the album's biggest track, providing Kiss with a wave-your-lighters-in-the-air live show-stopper. *Destroyer* was one of Kiss's most accomplished and ambitious albums, and their first million-seller, kick-starting the second phase of the band's career.

In the next two years, just as punk broke in the UK, Kiss became America's hottest live attraction, developing a larger-than-life stageshow (see the inside sleeve of *Alive II*) alongside a range of merchandise that extended from lunch-boxes to lawnmowers and, later, even cars. In short, Kiss – literally – sold their audience a rock'n'roll dream, and reaped considerable financial benefits. Their influence upon the next generation of American rock bands should not be underestimated.

Record label:
Casablanca

Produced
by Bob Ezrin.

Recorded
at The Record Plant, New York; summer 1975.

Released:
May 1976

Chart peaks:
22 (UK) 11 (US)

Personnel:
Paul Stanley (v, g); Gene Simmons (v, b); Ace Frehley (g, v); Peter Criss (d, v)

Track listing:
Detroit Rock City; King Of The Night Time World; God Of Thunder; Great Expectations; Flaming Youth (S); Sweet Pain; Shout It Out Loud (S); Beth (S); Do You Love Me

Running time:
34.06

Current CD:
824 149

Further listening:
Alive II (1977)

Further reading:
Kiss And Sell: The Making Of A Supergroup (CK Lendt, 1997) – the band's former business manager spills the beans on Kiss's marketing strategies.

Steve Miller Band
Fly Like An Eagle

Charisma-free, but classy, the cosmic hippy / downhome R&B crossover.

Brought up in Texas and San Francisco, Steve Miller benefited from his doctor father's fondness for having star musicians round for tea. With house guests ranging from Les Paul through T-Bone Walker to Charlie Mingus, he grew up usefully apprised that "musicians had funny manners and funny habits", but also believing it would do no harm to learn how to play a bit.

In '60s San Francisco, his skill distinguished him from the run of hippy bands while his fondness for peace-and-love lyrics linked him handily to the new cosmic mainstream. Astutely, in 1967 he secured from Capitol the best contract any artist had achieved up to that time. Then, less cleverly, he slave-drove himself through eight albums in six years. But after *The Joker* (1973) sold a million, already 30 and having finally "snapped" on the road, he took a break. It turned out that he could sneak away from the public eye very easily because, according to Rolling Stone, he was rock's "most faceless top-ranked performer". Miller knew it and liked it that way. "I don't want to be a personality," he said. "I like to slip in and out of other characters." So, playfully, in his songwriting he had concealed himself behind personas like The Gangster Of Love on *Sailor* (1968) and the sleazeball Maurice (that's Maureece) on *Recall The Beginning . . . A Journey From Eden* (1972).

For two years he worked mostly at home, creating *Fly Like And Eagle* (1976) and *Book Of Dreams* (1977), both seductively coherent mergers of late-blooming psychedelia with grunty R&B. The rough and the smooth – juxtaposed by Miller's pithy guitar and whipped-cream vocals – work like rye bread with honey. There's an irresistible slippiness to cool rockers Mercury Blues, Take The Money And Run and Rock 'N Me and a sense of airiness, flight even, to his insouciant digressions into hoedown with Dance, Dance, Dance, soul with Sam Cooke's You Send Me and spooky blues with Sweet Maree (abetted by Muddy Waters' harmonica player James Cotton). Developing into a careful planner, Miller promoted the album with a break-even theatre tour when he could have played arenas for big money: "The show will start at eight sharp – hopefully it'll be the ultimate rational concert." And he got a result: more than 4 million American sales each for *Fly Like An Eagle* and its successor. With which he bought a farm in Oregon and withdrew to conduct sporadic musical activities as the mood took him.

Record label:
Mercury

Produced
by Steve Miller.

Recorded
at Steve Miller's home in Marin County and CBS Studios, San Francisco, California; June 1974–December 1975.

Released:
May 1976

Chart peaks:
11 (UK) 3 (US)

Personnel:
Steve Miller (v, g, Roland, sitar, g); Gary Mallaber (d, pc); Lonnie Turner (b); James Cotton (hm); Mike Fusaro (e)

Track listing:
Fly Like An Eagle (S, US only); Space Odyssey; Wild Mountain Honey; Serenade; Dance, Dance, Dance; Mercury Blues; Take The Money And Run (S); Rock 'N Me (S); You Send Me; Blue Odyssey; Sweet Maree; The Window

Running time:
37.44

Current CD:
EAM CD 041

Further listening:
Sailor (1968), The Joker (1973), Abracadabra (1982) – the other times when Miller's sleek self-confidence opened out to become really seductive.

Further reading:
Clippings-zines on Steve Miller (available direct from David Housden, tel 00 44 (0)1945 870065); www.stevemillerband.com or www.gangster-of-love.com

Ramones

Ramones

Four skinny jerks from New York tear down rock music and start again.

Clocking in at under 30 minutes and sounding the death knell for flares, Ramones is one of the most exciting and influential records in rock'n'roll. Though it seemed to have come of the blue, the band had been honing their sound for two years.

"It was born out of a chemical imbalance between me, Dee Dee and Johnny," says Joey Ramone. "Rock'n'roll had got so bloated and lost its spirit. We stripped it down and reassembled it under the influence of The MC5, The Beatles and the Stones, Alice Cooper and T Rex. We had all the songs worked up before we went in, we were always good like that. The Ramones was always about having fun. Fun disappeared in 1974, there were too many serious people out there at that time."

Joey remembers that they tried putting the bass and drums through one channel, with guitars and vocals through the other, but neither method worked.

"That approach was far too retro," states producer Craig Leon (also the scout who'd brought the group to Sire). "[Ramones] was recorded on the graveyard shift, very quickly, then we mixed and remixed the whole thing in one night. Each song was recorded slower than its live counterpart because the studio metronome would only go up to 208 beats per minute!"

Of course, the band's "dumb" image was just an act: the subtlety and intelligence at work evidenced in the application of a joyous Brill Building pop instinct to a compressed metal wall of sound.

The Ramones went on to even greater glory with Leave Home and Rocket To Russia, but their debut was the crucial broadside, a defining statement, a wake-up call.

Record label:
Sire

Produced
by Craig Leon and Tom Erdelyi (aka Tommy Ramone).

Recorded
at Plaza Sound, Radio City Music Hall, New York City;

Released:
May 1976

Chart peaks:
None (UK) 111 (US)

Personnel:
Johnny Ramone (g); Joey Ramone (v); Dee Dee Ramone (b); Tommy Ramone (d)

Track listing:
Blitzkrieg Bop; Beat On The Brat; Judy Is A Punk; I Wanna Be Your Boyfriend; Chain Saw; Now I Wanna Sniff Some Glue; I Don't Wanna Go Down In The Basement; Loudmouth; Havana Affair; Listen To My Heart; 53rd & 3rd; Let's Dance; I Don't Wanna Walk Around With You; Today Your Love, Tomorrow The World

Running time:
29.14

Current CD:
7599-27421-2

Further listening:
Try the exhilarating double It's Alive (1979), effectively a live greatest hits.

Further reading:
The Ramones, An American Band (Jim Bessman, 1993); www.officialramones.com

Aerosmith
Rocks

Their sex-and-drugs-fuelled fourth album is the nearest thing yet to a rock festival on record.

Inspired and honed by an increasingly successful three years on the road, with all the lurid sex-and-drugs excesses that encompassed, this sinewy, horny, heavy rock album found Aerosmith at the peak of their powers – and of their drug intake. If the previous year's *Toys In The Attic* had marked the Boston band's shift from wannabe British blues-rockers (the Stones, Yardbirds and Zeppelin were critics' usual comparisons) to all-American, superstar stadium-rockers, *Rocks* marked the shift, according to Joe Perry, "from a bunch of musicians dabbling in drugs to a bunch of addicts dabbling in music."

In early 1976, when they backed a mobile recording truck into The Wherehouse to start preproduction, Aerosmith were one of the biggest bands in America. *Toys* was gold, all three of their albums were in the charts, and sales had topped three million. This accounts for *Rocks'* confident swagger, from the metal-funk of Get The Lead Out, the Black Sabbathy power of Nobody's Fault and the lighter-wielding ballad Home Tonight to the punch-along, powerhouse opening anthem Back In The Saddle, which aimed for "this larger-than-life vibe, to bring the band right into the middle of the kid's head when he put on his phones in his bedroom at night."

The album, Jack Douglas said, "had to make a big statement about how loud and hard they were, how unapologetic they felt about being who they were – this brash, rude, sexual, hardcore rock band." The band's two core obsessions – sex and drugs – were both well represented; Rats In The Cellar inspired by the death of their dealer during the recording, and Back In The Saddle by a discussion in the studio about Gene Autry whom Tyler was convinced was referring to "fucking". *Rocks* shipped platinum, an immediate hit, and would become probably the biggest influence on the next generation of US stadium-rockers such as Van Halen and Guns N'Roses, whose Slash cites it as the album that made him pick up a guitar. A review in American rock magazine Creem summed it up: "Coming after a brief era when rock'n'roll fans were bombarded with the exaggerated sexual ambiguity of Alice, Bowie and Reed, it must be reassuring to have a band that knows everything we've wanted to know about sex all along: it's dirty."

Record label:
CBS

Produced
by Jack Douglas and Aerosmith.

Recorded
at the Wherehouse, Waltham, Massachusetts; Record Plant, New York; February–March 1976.

Release date:
June 1976

Chart peaks:
None (UK) 3 (US)

Personnel:
Steven Tyler (v); Joe Perry (g); Brad Whitford (g); Tom Hamilton (b); Joey Kramer (d); Jay Messina (e)

Track listing:
Back In The Saddle; Last Child; Rats In The Cellar; Combination; Sick As A Dog; Nobody's Fault; Get The Lead Out; Lick And A Promise; Home Tonight

Running time:
34.25

Currently available CD:
4749652

Further listening:
Toys In The Attic (1975); Pump (1989); Get A Grip (1993); Nine Lives (1997)

Further reading:
Walk This Way: The Autobiography Of Aerosmith (Stephen Davis, 1998)
www.aerosmith.com

Parliament
Mothership Connection

*The Parliafunkadelicment thang goes universal as Clinton
marries serious funk to a comic-book tale.*

In 1974 the wildly prolific and continually inventive George
Clinton, tired of trying to make Funkadelic a commercial
success and unsure about their immediate direction, reactivated
the name of his former vocal group, The Parliaments, and
signed them as Parliament to Neil Bogart's new label,
Casablanca.

Classically trained keyboard player Bernie Worrell had
brought a greater sense of order to the arrangements, the
Horny Horns from James Brown's band meant a sharp new
colour in the mix, and the younger recruits, Bootsy and Phelps
Collins and Frank Waddy, infused the band with a fresh energy,
just as they had James Brown's orchestra. The new sound was
called P-Funk. The final ingredient was lyrics, written by Bootsy
and Clinton, that set up an unlikely tale of intergalactic struggle
for the funk which unravelled like some particularly perverse
soap opera over two subsequent albums.

Typically, Clinton played it to the hilt, laying inspiration
for the songs at the door of extraterrestrial intervention. He
and Bootsy, he said at the time, were driving along a highway in
Canada when a solid beam of light hit their car. "I told Bootsy
to step on it . . .ever since then things have really begun to
happen. It was like somebody out there saying they were hip to
the Mothership and approve."

More likely is the confluence of great dance music
honed after years of touring and studio work, Clinton's innate
sense of cool, copious amounts of drugs and a visual flair far
removed from the mohair suits and slick dance steps associated
with virtually every top male black act. P-Funk (Wants To Get
Funked Up) and Give Up The Funk (Tear The Roof Off The
Sucker), were Parliament anthems to set alongside Funkadelic's
Get Off Your Ass And Jam, while Handcuffs introduced new
singer Glen Goins and the title track unveiled Star Child,
leading character in the space battle for funk and dance that
would evolve between Dr Funkenstein and Sir Nose
D'Voidoffunk. Dense, freewheeling, goodtiming music with its
crazy head in the stars. It might have been baffling to outsiders
but the hip bought it by the truckload, P-Funk stormed the
charts.

Record label:
Casablanca

Produced
by George Clinton.

Recorded
at United Sound, Detroit, Hollywood
Sound, Hollywood; Autumn 1975.

Released:
June 1976

Chart peaks:
None (UK) 13 (US)

Personnel:
George Clinton (v); Calvin Simon, Fuzzy
Haskins, Raymond Davis, Grady Thomas
(bv); Bootsy Collins (v, b, g, d, pc); Fred
Wesley, Maceo Parker, Michael Brecker,
Boom, Joe Farrell (horns); Cordell Mosson
(b); Gary Shider (g, bv); Michael Hampton
(g); Glen Goins (bv, g); Tiki Fulwood,
Jerome Brailey, Gary Cooper (d, pc);
Bernie Worrell (k, syn)

Track listing:
P-Funk (Wants To Get Funked Up) (S);
Mothership Connection (Star Child);
Unfunky UFO; Supergroovalistic-
Prosifunkstication; Handcuffs; Give Up The
Funk (Tear The Roof Off The Sucker) (S);
Night Of The Thumpasorus Peoples

Running time:
38.19

Current CD:
AA8245022

Further listening:
The Clones Of Dr Funkenstein (1977);
Funkentelechy Vs The Placebo Syndrome
(1977); Parliament Live: P-Funk Earth
Tour (1977); Funkadelic's One Nation
Under A Groove (1978)

Further reading:
MOJO 34; http://ourworld.compuserve.com/
homepages/PJebsen/links.htm

Rush
2112

Half hard rock, half concept album that spawned numerous sci-fi metal imitations. Side one features Alex Lifeson tuning-up in a cave.

Some collective consciousness has decreed that Rush be eternally unhip, but the Toronto band's fourth album was an instantly intriguing gambit. Side one – the concept side – was heavily-influenced by the novelist and philosopher·Ayn Rand, and imagined a futuristic society ruled by priests who had banned musical instruments as the setting for an examination of human freewill. That's gotta work for you!

A quarter-century on, the album's *mise-en-scène* raises a smile, but at the time, teenage metal fans thought they'd found the Holy Grail.

Lyricist Neil Peart's penchant for extended ruminations had been established on 1975's *Caress Of Steel*, but if this was a poor-seller which left the band with everything to prove, *2112* was a brilliantly-executed riposte.

"I grew up in the suburbs and it was all very prosaic and dull," said Peart of the sci-fi fascination he shared with a large portion of his audience, "so I started getting interested in all those kinds of things just in the belief that there must be a more interesting world out there. Consequently you get tied up in all that, and whether you believe it or not really doesn't matter. It becomes an escape. I can understand it from the kids' point of view, having been that way myself. And as a writer, fantasy is really an excellent vehicle for expressing ideas in their purest sense, without any preconceptions. There's nothing better than having your own made-to-order extraterrestrial world."

Much of side two offered more traditional fare. The lyrics of A Passage To Bangkok – later a live favourite – read like a hash menu at an Amsterdam cafe, and Something For Nothing – the kind of song which would later prompt Pavement's Steven Malkmus to wonder how Geddy Lee's voice got so high – works its magic with little more than a few power-chords. Lifeson's lead-guitar work is at its best on The Twilight Zone, where he makes spine-tingling use of the false-harmonic technique which was becoming his trademark. Only the slush-laden ballad Tears let the side down.

Showcasing the kind of chops that would regularly see them top "best musician" polls, Lee, Lifeson and Peart – "I don't know about numerology or anything mystical but there's

Record label:
Mercury

Produced
by Rush and Terry Brown.

Recorded
at Toronto Sound Studios, Ontario, Canada; 1975–1976.

Released:
June 1976

Chart peaks:
None (UK) 61 (US)

Personnel:
Geddy Lee (b, v); Alex Lifeson (g); Neil Peart (d); Hugh Syme (k); Terry Brown (e)

Track listing:
2112: I Overture; II The Temples of Syrinx; III Discovery; IV Presentation; V Oracle: The Dream; VI Soliloquy; VII Grand Finale; A Passage To Bangkok; The Twilight Zone; Lessons (S); Tears; Something For Nothing

Running time:
38.52

Current CD:
534 626-2

Further listening:
A Farewell To Kings (1977)

Further reading:
Rush Visions: The Official Biography (Bill Banasiewicz, 1988); www.oceanrush.com www.blarghnet.com/supper/rush/index.html #top

something good about three people," he said – created a spirited galaxy of riffs which eclipsed their Zeppelin-esque roots.

The album also saw them lay the foundations of a sound which would establish them as one of the premier hard rock acts of the '80s and '90s. Fans of *2122* include Beck, who used to play live with a sticker of the Rush star logo on his guitar. By November 1977, the album was certified gold, and by November 1995 triple platinum.

Boz Scaggs
Silk Degrees

Slick and soulful music for satin-sheet-sliding. Allegedly caused hump(!) in the US population graph.

When William Royce (Boz) Scaggs began work on his *Slow Dancer* album in 1974, he forsook recording with his road band in favour of studio musicians for the first time since his debut album in the late '60s. A lot of Detroit/Motown expatriates turned up at those Los Angeles sessions including famed bassist James Jamerson. Scaggs knew he was on the right track, but was prevented from artistic closure by the total-control tactics of producer/writer/artist Johnny Bristol.

So, for his next effort, Scaggs dumped Bristol and turned to Columbia staff producer Joe Wissert, who had been doing wonderful things with Earth, Wind & Fire. Together, they assembled a rhythm section of studio up-and-comers including drummer Jeff Porcaro, bassist David Hungate and keyboardist/arranger David Paitch (the three soon to become the nucleus of the band Toto). The chemistry between the musicians and Scaggs' material was inspiring. Wissert wisely stepped back and let magic take place, offering only the occasional suggestion or tie-breaking vote in a musical "discussion". Along with guitarists Fred Tackett and Louie Shelton, and the cream of LA's horns-for-hire, they produced a slick, uptown, soulful goo that slid right down inside your best dancin' shoes.

The resultant collection, named after a discarded Scaggs lyric, was immediately embraced by American radio. Lowdown, We're All Alone, What Can I Say and Lido Shuffle billowed creamily out of car speakers and pumped out of the dance clubs. Scaggs vocals moved up a notch as he essayed the material in the manner of an authoritative, yet laid-back white-boy Al Green. Later artists, such as Bobby Caldwell or middle-period Robert Palmer, built careers on the musical foundation of *Silk Degrees*. Photographer Moshe Brakha's evocative cover shot showed an apparently-despondent Scaggs sitting on a seaside park-bench facing left, while a glimpse of a woman's nicely manicured hand indicates her exit stage right. On the back, Scaggs is nowhere to be seen, but the woman's hand remains on the right, apparently frozen in time by the proceedings. Lowdown was awarded a Grammy for best R&B song in 1976, and album sales soared to four million. The following year, when work began on the follow-up, *Down Two, Then Left*, squabbles from the past year over who wrote what, availability, and scheduling prevented the same line-up from being reprised. So it was for one time only that Scaggs delivered the goods with a great batch of songs and sympathetic studio stringers who perfectly matched his muse.

Record label:
CBS

Produced
by Joe Wissert.

Recorded
at Dav-Len Studios and Hollywood Sound, Los Angeles; 1975.

Released:
September 1976

Chart peaks:
37 (UK) 2 (US)

Personnel:
Boz Scaggs (g, v); David Paitch (k, arr); David Hungate (b); Jeff Porcaro (d); Fred Tackett (g); Louie Shelton (g); Tom Perry (e)

Track listing:
What Can I Say (S); Georgia; Jump Street; What Do You Want The Girl To Do; Harbor Lights; Lowdown (S); It's Over (S); Love Me Tomorrow; Lido Shuffle (S); We're All Alone

Running time:
41.33

Current CD:
Columbia 4719682

Further listening:
The album before, Slow Dancer (1974); the album after, Down Two Then Left (1977); a sprinkling from all 13 solo albums on two CDs: My Time: A Boz Scaggs Anthology (1999).

Stevie Wonder
Songs In The Key Of Life

Only the third album ever to enter the US charts at Number 1 (after two by Elton John), where it stayed for 14 weeks.

Back in the mid-'70s, a two-year gap between albums seemed interminable. Two years after *Fulfillingness' First Finale*, Stevie was seen around LA in a T-shirt that proclaimed "We've nearly finished". It had been made for him by engineer Gary Olazabal, who was, according to Stevie, "very patient."

After signing his first contract with Motown as an adult, Wonder had produced an astonishingly sustained run of four excellent albums in a creative partnership with programmers and arrangers Malcolm Cecil and Bob Margouleff. Having signed a new seven-year deal for $13 million in 1975, he began, then aborted, two albums, *Fulfillingness' Second Finale* and *Let's See Life The Way It Is* and severed his ties with Cecil and Margouleff before delivering this double-plus masterpiece.

This was the first album where Stevie called all the shots. The sweep of styles, from the big-band jazz of the Ellington tribute Sir Duke, via the string-driven street opera of Village Ghetto Land through the driving polemic of Black Man, is the broadest of any Wonder album. Bursting with inspiration, Stevie would spend literally days on end recording, up to 72 hours at a stretch without food or sleep.

Many things held up recording: new songs that simply had to be included; a chase around Los Angeles maternity wards to obtain the first cries of a new-born baby for Isn't She Lovely; experimenting with new gadgets like the Yamaha Electrone Polyphonic Synthesizer GX10 (which produced the most convincing synthesized strings anyone had heard to that date); even – it was reported at the time – Stevie's dissatisfaction with the cover art! If Wonder's tardiness would become a matter of legend, few could dispute that the delays paid off here. "I wanted it to be the very best I can do," declared Stevie with a note of triumph in his voice. Released on a tidal wave of hype, it was kept from the UK peak by Abba's *Greatest Hits*.

Record label:
Motown

Produced
by Stevie Wonder.

Recorded
at Crystal Industries Inc., Los Angeles; Hit Factory, New York City; Record Plant, Los Angeles; Record Plant, Sausalito, California; 1975–76.

Released:
October 16, 1976

Chart peaks:
2 (UK) 1 (US)

Personnel:
All instruments played by Stevie Wonder. Additional parts by: Mike Sembello, Ben Bridges, Dean Parks, George Benson, WG 'Snuffy' Walden (g); 'Sneaky Pete' Kleinow (sg); Nathan Watts (b); Ray Pound, Greg Brown (d); Greg Philinganes, Herbie Hancock (k); Ronnie Foster (o); Gary Olazabal, John Fischbach (e)

Track listing:
Love's In Need Of Love Today; Have A Talk With God; Village Ghetto Land; Contusion; Sir Duke (S); I Wish (S); Knocks Me Off My Feet; Pastime Paradise; Summer Soft; Ordinary Pain; Isn't She Lovely; Joy Inside My Tears; Black Man; Ngiculela/Es Una Historia/I Am Singing; If It's Magic; As; Another Star (S)

Running time:
86.53

Current CD:
1573572 adds: Saturn; Ebony Eyes; All Day Sucker; Easy Goin' Evening (My Mama's Call)

Further listening:
Stevie's incredibly fecund patch in the '70s has not been matched by much he's done since, though Hotter Than July (1980) includes such great pop moments as Masterblaster and Lately.

Abba

Arrival

Abba's fourth album irrevocably transformed them from Swedish pop curiosity to worldwide phenomenon.

In the summer of 1976 Abba were invited to perform at the most exclusive Swedish social event of the year – a Stockholm ball celebrating the wedding of King Carl Gustaf and Silvia Sommerlath. Dressed in bizarre medieval costumes they decided to perform a new song Björn and Benny had written six months earlier, Dancing Queen. The reaction was extraordinary. Sweden, which had been coolly sceptical of their success thus far, elevated them to musical royalty, erroneously assuming they'd written the song in honour of the new ruler and Dancing Queen embarked on a startling journey of its own, becoming Abba's first and only American chart-topper, and eventually becoming a front-line gay anthem.

"I hope," said Björn when *Arrival* was finally released six months behind schedule, "people will stop assuming we're one hit wonders." The NME didn't, dismissing it as "patent rubbish", but for most other commentators it was the album that finally earned them respect, albeit grudging. Björn and Benny had all but eradicated the trashier influence of manager Stig Anderson from the songwriting and provided a vindication for pure pop song as a valid art form. "Our difficulty was always to get rid of the Eurovision stamp and it was especially hard in England where they were used to groups coming over from the continent and not lasting very long, but with *Arrival* we were finally accepted," said Bjorn.

It also, briefly, cracked America. Partly due to Agnetha's terror of live audiences, an even greater terror of flying and a hatred of being parted from daughter Linda, Abba were reluctant to spend time in the States, and once announced they'd never tour the US until they had a chart-topper. When Dancing Queen hit Number 1 there in April '77 they ran out of excuses, but there remained something half-hearted about their American adventure and they never enjoyed the success there that they knew in the rest of the world.

Arrival also included the classic Knowing Me Knowing You (a-ha!) and Money Money Money which apart from showing Björn and Benny's willingness to poke fun at themselves, also hinted at musical ambitions beyond a three-minute pop format into the world of musicals. Years later they achieved it, working with Tim Rice on Chess, but for most people in the late '70s Abba's vindication of the three-minute format and their search for the perfect pop record was enough. Here's where they found it.

Record label:
Epic

Produced
by Benny Andersson and Björn Ulvaeus.

Recorded
at Metronome Studios, Stockholm;
January–February 1976.

Released:
November 5, 1976

Chart peaks:
1 (UK) 20 (US)

Personnel:
Agnetha Fältskog (v); Anni-Frid Lyngstad (v); Benny Andersson (syn, p, accordion, k, marimbas, chimes, v); Björn Ulvaaeus (ag, g, v, a); Janne Schaffer (ag, g); Ola Brunkert (strings, d); Lars Carlsson (horn); Anders Dahl (strings); Malando Gassama (pc); Anders Glenmark (ag, g); Roger Palm (strings, d); Lasse Wellander (ag, g); Michael B Tretow (e); Sven-Olof Walldoff (a)

Track listing:
When I Kissed The Teacher; Dancing Queen (S); My Love My Life; Dum Dum Diddle; Knowing Me Knowing You (S); Money Money Money (S); That's Me (S); Why Did It Have To Be Me?; Tiger; Arrival

Running time:
33.16

Current CD:
Polydor 5339812

Further listening:
The massively successful compilations Abba Gold (1992) and More Abba Gold (1993) tell the complete story, but for deeper intrigue try the thematic, moody The Visitors, (1981).

Further reading:
MOJO 66. ABBA: The Name Of The Game (Andrew Oldham, Tony Calder and Colin Irwin, 1995); ABBA: The Music Still Goes On (Paul Snaith, 1994); www.abbasite.com

The Eagles
Hotel California

Erstwhile proponents of that Peaceful Easy Feeling get real and metaphorical too.

"We wanted it all. Peer respect, Number 1 singles and albums, great music and a lot of money," said Glenn Frey, summing up The Eagles shortly after they recorded *Hotel California*. His co-frontman and rival Don Henley added: "I was driven, a man possessed." But weren't they the epitome of '70s soft rock's slumberous laid-back genre? Frey elucidated: "The only difference between boring and laid-back is a million dollars."

Before *Hotel California* they had shuffled their citified country rock – exemplified by vapid hits Take It Easy, Peaceful Easy Feeling and so on – across to the rockier sound of *One Of These Nights* (1975). This and US chart-topping compilation, *Their Greatest Hits 1971-1975*, left their blatant greed satiated, their longing for esteem less so because critics still scorned them. So, with original member Bernie Leadon replaced by Joe Walsh, just when The Eagles might have succumbed to complacency they were fired up as never before.

Aiming a touch high, they decided "the Eagles' Bicentennial album" should express everything they felt about America post-'60s, post-Vietnam, post-Watergate. With the title track and Life In The Fast Lane they had songs which slicked their way into the singles charts while bearing durable, era-defining metaphors. "The Hotel California is something that was elegant, but now is decadent – we think this album represents the whole world, not just California," Henley proclaimed.

Although Victim Of Love came on like *faux* Bad Company, the key songs were well supported by tough-tender tales of innocence and experience in New Kid In Town and Wasted Time, while the seven-minute final track, The Last Resort, was at least a valiant sacrifice on the altar of saying it all in one song about the state of the world and the world of the state.

Personally the antithesis of their cool image, The Eagles effectively burned themselves out making *Hotel California*. Recording between tour dates, for weeks on end their daily timetable read "gig, airport, fly to Miami, record all night, airport, fly to next gig, gig, airport." At the end of it, Henley boasted of chalking up his first stomach ulcer at 29 and Frey simply insisted, "We've tried harder than we ever tried before."

Henley argued that their concept extended to satirising "the kind of limbo we are experiencing in the music business while we are waiting for the next big surge of inspiration". Then came punk and, as it happened, The Eagles never made another good record.

Record label:
Asylum

Produced
by Bill Szymczyk.

Recorded
at Criteria Studios, Miami, and The Record Plant, Los Angeles, March–October 1976.

Release date:
December 1976

Chart peaks:
2 (UK) 1 (US)

Personnel:
Don Henley (v, d, pc, syn); Glenn Frey (v, clavinet, p, g); Don Felder (v, g, ps); Joe Walsh (g, v, p, organ, syn); Randy Meisner (v, guitarone); Bill Szymczyk, Allan Blazek, Ed Mashal, Bruce Hensal (e)

Track listing:
Hotel California (S); New Kid In Town (S); Life In The Fast Lane (S); Wasted Time; Wasted Time (reprise); Victim Of Love; Pretty Maids All In A Row; Try And Love Again; The Last Resort

Running time:
43.28

Current CD:
7559-60509-2

Further listening:
One Of These Nights (1975) – big step on the way from LA dudes posing as desperadoes to self-discovery as ironic rockers.

Further reading:
To The Limit: The Untold Story Of The Eagles (Marc Eliot, 1999).
www.eaglesfans.com

Johnny 'Guitar' Watson
Ain't That A Bitch

Smash-hit disco comeback by veteran bluesman.

When disco started cutting a swathe through black American music in the early '70s, it put a whole generation of musicians out of work. But while scores of his blues and soul contemporaries were consigned to obsolescence, one-time Texas bluesman Johnny 'Guitar' Watson hit paydirt with one of the biggest dance albums of the '70s, winning a Grammy nomination as best new vocalist – at the age of 41: "I'm saying to myself, is this a joke? But better late than never is what I always say."

Watson had scored several small hits in a staggeringly eclectic career, but the big time eluded him until British blues producer Mike Vernon suggested an unlikely partnership.

"He tells me this guy Dick James is looking to start a new label. I found out later they didn't really expect a big success, it was possibly a tax write-off."

If Dick James, publisher of The Beatles and mentor of Elton John, was really hoping for a tax write-off, he met with failure of Producers-size proportions. Given *carte blanche* in the studio, Watson crafted an outrageously over-the-top epic, combining synth bass, Vocoders, spiky funk guitar, and outrageously witty lyrics.

"Man, when I recorded that album I had a serious ego problem, I felt like I could do anything – and somehow it all worked, it was the strangest thing. I did all the horns on studio time, said to the musicians, bring your manuscript and your horn and play what you want when you get there! Then when I told the promotion people what the title of the album was they were going 'Jeez, this man is crazy.' But Dick [James] was great, he was saying 'if that's what Mr Watson wants, that's what we'll do!'"

The wit and timeliness of the writing helped *Ain't That A Bitch* crossover into R&B and Pop markets, going gold in the process; the recording quality would help make it a favourite for shop assistants demonstrating hi-fi systems, while his pristine but organic grooves would later see him sampled by Snoop Doggy Dogg, Dr Dre and others.

Record label:
DJM

Produced
by Johnny 'Guitar' Watson.

Recorded
in Los Angeles, 1976.

Released:
1976

Chart peaks:
None (UK) None (US)

Personnel:
Johnny 'Guitar' Watson (v, g, b, k); Emry Thomas (d); Tommy Roberson (tb); Paul Dunmall (s); Peter Martin (tp)

Track listing:
I Need It; I Want To Ta-Ta You Baby; Superman Lover; Ain't That A Bitch; Since I Met You Baby; We're No Exception; Won't You Forgive Me Baby

Running time:
34.28

Current CD:
NEMCD774

Further listening:
A Real Mother (1977) and Funk Beyond The Call Of Duty (1978) repeat the irresistible funk formula; Ace compilation Hot Like TNT (1996), of early single sides like Gangster Of Love shows how far ahead of his time Watson was.

Further reading:
MOJO 80; Portrait Of The Blues (Paul Trynka, 1997)

Boston

Boston

Super-melodic AOR, custom-built for US radio, sold zillions.

U ntil it was overtaken by Whitney Houston's efforts in
1986, *Boston* was the fastest-selling debut album in history.
Band lynchpin Tom Scholz – inventor of the Rockman micro-
amp – was a studio boffin who'd graduated from the
Massachusetts Institute Of Technology. When he married guitars
reminiscent of an airbrushed Thin Lizzy with Brad Delp's
gymnastic yet emotive vocals, America melted.

Scholz was a perfectionist: every note here is just how
he wanted it. The band re-recorded several tracks on the West
Coast with producer John Boylan, but much of the album
consists of the original 12-track demos recorded at Scholz's
home studio in Watertown.

The undoubted stand-out was More Than A Feeling, the
ultimate AOR anthem. Slick as the song is, it has surprising
links with grunge: Kurt Cobain later acknowledged that its
chorus riff had partly inspired Smells Like Teen Spirit. Hitch A
Ride and Peace Of Mind aired contrasting views on the
American Dream, but most of the album's lyrics chewed the
familiar fat of sex (Let Me Take You Home Tonight), drugs
(Smokin'), and rock'n'roll (Rock'N'Roll Band).

Three US Top 40 singles set Boston's ball rolling, and
Boston eventually sold over 15 million copies.

When Scholz laboured for two years over the follow-up,
CBS grew impatient. The company rush-released the new record
as soon as Scholz released the tapes, and it went on to shift six
million units. The title was a misnomer: *Don't Look Back* was a
virtual re-write of its predecessor.

Record label:
Epic

Produced
by John Boylan and Tom Scholz.

Recorded
at Foxglove Studios, Watertown,
Massachusetts; winter 1975; Mastered at
Capitol Studios, Hollywood, and The
Record Plant, Los Angeles; spring 1976.

Released:
January 1977

Chart peaks:
11 (UK) 3 (US)

Personnel:
Brad Delp (v, g); Tom Scholz (g, k);
Barry Goudreau (g); Fran Sheehan (b);
Sib Hashian (d)

Track listing:
More Than A Feeling (S); Peace Of Mind
(S); Foreplay; Long Time (S); Rock'N'Roll
Band; Smokin'; Hitch A Ride; Something
About You; Let Me Take You Home
Tonight

Running time:
37.47

Current CD:
4894122

Further listening:
Don't Look Back (1978)

Further reading:
www.boston.org

David Bowie
Low

The first of Bowie's "Berlin" trilogy of collaborations with Brian Eno.

After the Neu!-influenced motorik of *Station To Station*, Bowie delved deeper into his Krautrock influences for *Low*, collaborating with Eno on this breakthrough work which brought the notion of "industrial music" experimentation to a mainstream audience. Using a basic group of Carlos Alomar, George Murray and Dennis Davis, Bowie decamped to Berlin, where he and Eno worked in complementary ways to open up exciting new paths for mainstream pop. "There was a very clear separation of jobs," recalls Eno. "Mine was to make musical settings in which something could happen, which suited me fine – I love being the scene-painter – and David, of course, is just great at stepping into things like that and becoming the actor. It suited both of our temperaments." Bowie was so charged-up by the experience that he employed the widest instrumental palette of any of his albums, while Eno added his distinctive patina of synths, tapes and treatments to the songs. At the time, however, Bowie was away from the studio for long stretches dealing with a protracted court case, so Eno worked on some tracks alone, intending to use them himself if they weren't deemed appropriate for *Low*. "A couple of those things on the second side, like Warszawa, started out of that process," he says. "As soon as David heard it he said, 'Get me a mic,' and just did this whole thing. He's very fast when he gets going, really a brilliant singer – I don't think people realise how finely he can tune his singing, in terms of picking a particular emotional pitch: it's really scientific, the way he does it. He'll say, 'I think that's slightly too theatrical there, it should be more withdrawn and introspective,' and he'll go in and sing it again, and you'll hear this point four of a degree shift which makes all the difference. That's what he's good at: he picks up the mood of a musical landscape, such as the type I might make, and he can really bring it to a sharp focus, both with the words he uses and the style of singing he chooses."

Balancing one side of angular electronic pop with one of more experimental tone poems, the album was a striking reaffirmation of the power of musical imagination at a time of Luddite retrenchment in rock, enabling Bowie to be one of the few glam-rock stars to successfully withstand the onslaught of punk with his reputation intact. It remains one of the pinnacles of his career.

Record label:
RCA

Produced
by David Bowie and Tony Visconti.

Recorded
at Château d'Herouville, France, and Hansa By The Wall; West Berlin; October 1976.

Released:
January 1977

Chart peaks:
2 (UK) 11 (US)

Personnel:
David Bowie (v, g, k, s, syn, tapes, c, pump bass, hm, vibes, xylophone, pc, Chamberlain); Eno (syn, k, Chamberlain, treatments, v); Carlos Alomar (g); George Murray (b); Dennis Davis (pc); Roy Young (p, Farfisa organ); Ricky Gardener (g); Iggy Pop (v); Mary Visconti (v); Eduard Meyer (c); Peter & Paul (k)

Track listing:
Speed Of Life; Breaking Glass; What In The World; Sound And Vision (S); Always Crashing In The Same Car; Be My Wife (S); A New Career In A New Town; Warszawa; Art Decade; Weeping Wall; Subterraneans

Running time:
38.54

Current CD:
5219070

Further listening:
The subsequent Heroes (1977) further developed the Bowie/Eno association, though by Scary Monsters (and Super Creeps) (1980) their joint inspiration was getting somewhat thinner on the ground.

Further reading:
MOJO 19; www.davidbowie.com

The Damned

Damned Damned Damned

The first British punk album.

S peed – in both senses of the word – was of the essence. The first UK punk band to release a single (New Rose, October 1976), the first to hit daytime television (performing Neat Neat Neat on Supersonic), the first to visit America, it was inevitable The Damned would also be first to release an album, and what a little monster it was. With (as Brian James succinctly puts it) "a honkful of toot" to sustain them and six months of gigging behind them, even producer Nick Lowe later confessed that he did little more than watch while The Damned slammed through their live set.

"We treated it like a gig," explains James. "We went in and just bashed it down – I know that was Nick's nickname, Basher Lowe, 'Bash it down and tart it up in the mix' – but that's what we did. There were one or two numbers we had to do a second take on like Feel The Pain, because we weren't playing it live so much, and a couple of minuscule guitar bits on top – like on New Rose, there was a little guitar overdub on the middle eight. But that was it. It was just like a gig."

Written in haste, the songs represented punk's first public steps, with a couple – Stab Yor Back, So Messed Up – trailing the obligatory hail of gob. Yet for every slobbering three-chord blur in the Ramones mould, there was a genuine gem: Fish, which dated back to James' days with legendary rehearsal-room heroes, London SS; New Rose, of course; Feel The Pain – described by James as "our Jonathan Richman number" – and Fan Club, one of rock's most honest examinations of its audience, with a classic riff thrown in. Who said these punks couldn't write or play? Not that The Damned themselves went along with the punk-rock tag. Rat Scabies insists, "They were pop songs that were there to be played today and thrown away. That was the whole point." The Damned's brand of anarchy was resolutely playful, as the pie-fight sleeve-art attests. Neither was there any thought of longevity. "We never expected anything to last fucking 20 years," muses Rat. "The point was simply to do it."

Record label:
Demon

Produced
by Nick Lowe.

Recorded
at Pathway Studios, London; late 1976.

Released:
February 1977

Chart peaks:
36 (UK) None (US)

Personnel:
Dave Vanian (v); Brian James (g); Captain Sensible (b); Rat Scabies (d)

Track listing:
Neat Neat Neat (S); Fan Club; I Fall; Born To Kill; Stab Yor Back; Feel The Pain; New Rose (S); Fish; See Her Tonite; I Of The 2; So Messed Up; I Feel Alright

Running time:
31.34

Current CD:
FIENDCD91

Further listening:
Neat Neat Neat (Demon 3-CD box, 1997); The Dripping Lips (fronted by Brian James) Ready To Crack? (1998)

Further reading:
The Light At The End Of The Tunnel by Carol Clerk (1987)

Fleetwood Mac
Rumours

Internal romantic fall-out creates an AOR milestone, and Fleetwood Mac's first trans-Atlantic chart-topper.

Unity was never Fleetwood Mac's strongest point. Twelve musicians in eight years – 15 if you include the ersatz Mac sent on tour by a former manager in 1974 – ensured a family tree which was more of a small forest. But the discord they were accustomed to was as nothing to what was unleashed here: it was the stuff of soap opera. Stevie was breaking up with Lindsey, Christine was breaking with John, Mick and his first wife were separating and he was becoming close to Stevie, with liberal quantities of coke on hand to further fuel the paranoia. *Rumours* was less a collection of songs, more a bag of emotional crutches for the members to batter one another with.

"It was crucifyingly difficult at certain points," Mick Fleetwood admits, describing the frosty atmosphere in the studio. Compared to the three months it took to record their previous album, *Rumours* took a year, as private heartache became public property and every lyric, it seemed, became a source for further conflict. Buckingham took his rage out on his guitar, turning in a couple of solos (Go Your Own Way and Don't Stop) of soul-searing intensity; Christine McVie buried hers in the sonorous delicacy of Songbird; Nicks draped hers in the tragedy of Dreams and the vicious Gold Dust Woman. Fleetwood smashed hell out of the drums. "Stevie did her first take of Gold Dust Woman in a fully lit studio and, as take followed take, she began withdrawing into herself," recalls Mick. "So we dimmed the lights, brought her a chair, a supply of tissues, a Vicks inhaler, a box of lozenges for her sore throat and a bottle of mineral water. And on the eighth take, at four in the morning, she sang the lyric straight through to perfection."

The key to *Rumours*, however, lay in The Chain, the one song which turned all the betrayal and bitterness around and pinpointed what Fleetwood remembers as the sole unifying factor in all the turmoil. "We were so engrossed in what we were doing, realizing that we'd been given an opportunity, as individuals and as a band, that may only come once in a life-time. And to throw it away would have been a sin. That's how we looked at it. That's how we got round all the other stuff, the bedroom stuff." Self-explanatory and, ultimately, self-fulfilling, the brooding, mantric Chain was the album's only band composition and became the creed which has since been woven into the musical and personal fabric of Fleetwood Mac: no matter what happens, you must never break the chain.

Record label:
Warners

Produced
by Fleetwood Mac, Richard Dashut and Ken Caillat.

Recorded
at Record Plant, Sausalito and LA; Wally Heider Recording Studios, LA; Criteria Studios, Miami FL; Davlen Recording Studio; North Hollywood; Zellerback Auditorium, UC Berkeley (Songbird).

Released:
February 1977

Chart peaks:
1 (UK) 1 (US)

Personnel:
Christine McVie (v, k, syn); Stevie Nicks (v); Lindsey Buckingham (g, v); John McVie (b); Mick Fleetwood (d)

Track listing:
Second Hand News; Dreams (S); Never Going Back Again; Don't Stop (S); Go Your Own Way (S); Songbird; The Chain; You Make Loving Fun (S); I Don't Want To Know; Oh Daddy; Gold Dust Woman

Running time:
39.58

Current CD:
7599 27313 2

Further listening:
The previous year's Fleetwood Mac, the calm before the storm.

Further reading:
Mick Fleetwood: My Life And Adventures With Fleetwood Mac (1990); www.repriserec.com/fleetwoodmac

Television
Marquee Moon

Not quite art rock but not quite prog or punk, the cult US outfit produce one of rock's most accomplished debuts.

By the mid-'70s, Television had became a focal point of the New York scene and were instrumental in persuading CBGB's manager Hilly Kristal to give a platform to some of the city's more *outré* musical units – themselves included. Malcolm McLaren was so impressed by the group – not least by bass player Richard Hell's ripped T-shirt – that he offered to manage them. The group recorded demos with Brian Eno (which Island were keen to release as an album) and with Blue Öyster Cult's Allen Lanier, but the group turned down a number of major label offers while waiting for the right deal. Hell left in 1975 and was replaced by ex-Blondie bassist Fred Smith, who added both a solidity and rhythmic flexibility. The group developed rapidly as a unit, in a collective style which reflected their musical influences: Smith and Richard Lloyd came from a more rock'n'roll background, Billy Ficca was a jazz enthusiast, while Tom Verlaine was interested in all points between The 13th Floor Elevators and Albert Ayler.

"Television rehearsed for six to seven days a week for four to six hours a day," Lloyd explains. "So we were both really roughshod musicians on one hand and desperadoes on the other, with the will to become good." Once Television signed to Elektra, Verlaine was keen not to have a name producer tell them what to do in the studio. So the job went to engineer Andy Johns who had worked in conjunction with producer brother Glyn, most famously with The Rolling Stones. "He had got some of the great guitar sounds in rock," says Lloyd.

Marquee Moon captured the group's new-found chemistry in action, sounding like nothing else around at the time. The tension generated between Lloyd and Verlaine's guitars was crucial, the players swapping between rhythm and melodic lines, sometimes several times per song. The soloing is superb, from Verlaine's dive-bombing runs on Friction to Lloyd's sublime cameo on Elevation.

Press reaction was ecstatic in the UK (though less so in the US), with NME immediately putting Television on its front cover. Lloyd: "There was a certain magic happening, an inexplicable certainty of something, like the momentum of a freight train. That's not egoism but, if you cast a spell, you don't get flummoxed by the results of your spell."

Record label:
Elektra

Produced
by Andy Johns and Tom Verlaine.

Recorded
at A&R Studios, New York City; September 1976.

Released:
February 1977

Chart peaks:
28 (UK) None (UK)

Personnel:
Tom Verlaine (v, g, k); Richard Lloyd (g, v); Fred Smith (b, v); Billy Ficca (d)

Track listing:
See No Evil; Venus; Friction; Marquee Moon (S/UK); Elevation; Guiding Light; Prove It (S/UK); Torn Curtain

Running time:
45.54

Current CD:
7559-60616-2

Further listening:
Adventure (1978), the group's untimely swansong; hear them cut loose live in the same year on double CD set, The Blow-Up.

Further reading:
http://www.slip.net/~rivethed/tvsite.htm

The Clash
The Clash

Soundtrack to 1977's 'Summer of Hate' and the totemic album of the English punk insurrection.

Mick Jones' claim that "I was so into speed I don't even recall making the first album" was undoubtedly an exaggeration, but by February 10, 1977, when the The Clash arrived at CBS Studios (where five years earlier Iggy and The Stooges had recorded *Raw Power*) things were certainly moving fast. The group had played their first show a mere eight months earlier, had inked their £100,000 contract with CBS just weeks before, and still hadn't written enough songs to fill their first long-player. As they swaggered into the Soho studios in their artfully paint-spattered clothes – causing the receptionist to mistake them for workmen – The Clash brought more attitude than expertise.

Engineer Simon Humphrey recalled that "They wouldn't shake my hand because I was a hippy." And their raw live sound was self-evidently discordant in the unyielding environment of the studio. Strummer's taped-together Fender, in particular, made such a din that CBS sent across a brand-new Telecaster from Soho Square, which he resolutely refused to play. Such was his pub-rock background that Strummer was unable to sing without simultaneously scrubbing out rhythm guitar, but for most of the session he was left unplugged, meaning *The Clash* bears little of his playing.

The sessions, which took place over three, four-day weekends, proved imponderable to producer Mickey Foote and his engineer. None of the group liked to be first to arrive; if they were, they would vanish for an hour or two, each thereby missing the others. An entire session could vanish through this competition in cool. "There was a rivalry between Mick and Joe," said Humphrey. "One of them would turn up and say, 'Who else is here?' and I'd say, 'Actually Mick you're the first one.' He'd say 'Fuck that!' and bugger off. Then Joe would turn up and say 'Where's Mick?' and I'd say, 'He was here earlier but left.' So Joe would say 'Bloody hell!' and storm off. Then they'd all reconvene later on." There were other problems; drummer Terry Chimes (derisively named 'Tory Crimes' on the cover) had already been flung out of the group, but since they could find no replacement, he played on the album anyway.

From this muddle of inexperience, ideological posturing and amphetamine overload, a magnificent record somehow

Record label:
CBS

Produced
by Micky Foote.

Recorded
at CBS Studios, London; February 1977.

Released:
April 1977

Chart peaks:
12 (UK) 100 (US)

Personnel:
Joe Strummer (g, v); Mick Jones (g, v); Paul Simonon (b); 'Tory Crimes' Terry Chimes (d); Simon Humphrey (e)

Track listing:
Janie Jones; Remote Control (S); I'm So Bored With The USA; White Riot (S); Hate And War; What's My Name; Deny; London's Burning; Career Opportunities; Cheat; Protex Blue; Police And Thieves; 48 Hours; Garageland

Running time:
34.00

Current CD:
4687832. The American edition of the album had a different track listing, adding Clash City Rockers, Complete Control, I Fought The Law, Jail Guitar Doors and (White Man) In Hammersmith Palais and removing Deny, Protex Blue and 48 Hours. Cat. no: EK63883

Further listening:
The mini-album Black Market Clash (1980) and The Story of The Clash (1991) include out-takes from '77.

Further reading:
MOJO 71; The Last Gang In Town by Marcus Gray (1996); The Illustrated History (Chris Salewicz and Adrian Boot, 1996); http://members.tripod.com/~casbahclub

emerged, one which distilled punk rock's intoxicating brew of anger, boredom and excitement better than any other. To go with its barking vocals, leering choruses and ram-a-lam guitar (all much copied) was snappy sloganeering; the dole queue moan of Career Opportunities, the confrontation of White Riot, the anti-Americanism of I'm So Bored With The USA (ironic given the band's later infatuation with the country). Its two-minute songs zipped past, requiring six minutes of clumsy white reggae on Police And Thieves for padding. In America Rolling Stone hailed it as "the definitive punk album" but CBS were nonetheless loath to release it there, relenting only after 100,000 import copies were sold. They had realised what Jones had claimed all along: "It ain't punk, it ain't new wave. Call it what you want, all the terms stink. Call it rock'n'roll."

Kraftwerk
Trans-Europe Express

Landmark Euro-electronica. The future starts here.

Trans-Europe Express marked the culmination of the "romantic impressionist" style which Kraftwerk had initially developed a few years earlier with their hit transport tribute Autobahn. The idea for the new album came from a friend, Paul Alessandrini, who took Ralf Hütter and Florian Schneider to lunch in a restaurant in the Gare De Lyon station in Paris. As they watched the trains arriving and departing beneath them, Alessandrini told them: "With the kind of music you do, which is kind of like an electronic blues, railway stations and trains are very important in your universe – you should do a song about the Trans-Europe Express."

Back at their Kling Klang Studio a short distance from Düsseldorf Station, Kraftwerk set about devising the electronic analogues of train sounds that would power their new work. Both Arthur Honegger's 1923 symphonic poem Pacific 231 and Pierre Schaeffer's 1948 proto-sampling piece Étude Aux Chemins De Fer had previously featured train noises sculpted into musical shape – but this was the first time that synthesisers had been employed to mimic the metronomic click-clack of railways. "We were fascinated with train sounds and machine sounds," explained Ralf Hütter. "They create certain rhythm patterns that are very dynamic and stimulating, and at the same time monotonic, repetitive. We called it Electronic Ballet."

The melodies were better than any Kraftwerk had come up with before, particularly on the wryly self-deprecatory Showroom Dummies and the opening track Europe Endless, which developed the theme of trans-European cultural unity, serenading the "parks, hotels and promenades" of the continent's great cities. This theme was emphasised in the superb packaging, which presented Ralf, Florian and their two electronic drummers as ultra-bourgeois sophisticates at a time when punk was the height of fashion. The album has stood the test of time significantly better than their punk contemporaries' work, becoming the single most important influence on future developments in techno from Detroit to Tokyo, and revolutionising the course of black American music courtesy of Afrika Bambaataa's sampling of the Metal On Metal section of the title track on his seminal hip hop cut Planet Rock. It remains one of the most affectionately regarded works of electronic music.

Record label:
Capitol

Produced
by Ralf Hütter & Florian Schneider.

Recorded
at Kling Klang Studio, Düsseldorf and the Record Plant, Los Angeles; 1976–77.

Released:
April 1977

Chart peaks:
49 (UK) None (US)

Personnel:
Ralf Hütter (v, electronics); Florian Schneider (v, electronics); Karl Bartos (electronic pc); Wolfgang Flur (electronic pc); Peter Bollig (e); Bill Halverson (e)

Track listing:
Europe Endless; The Hall Of Mirrors; Showroom Dummies (S); Trans-Europe Express (S); Metal On Metal; Franz Schubert; Endless Endless (S)

Running time:
42.44

Current CD:
CDP 7 46473 2

Further listening:
The ensuing albums The Man-Machine and Computer World further refine the formula. The earlier Autobahn and Radio-Activity are like preparatory sketches, while their very earliest albums are more experimental and improvisatory.

Further reading:
Kraftwerk: Man, Machine And Music (Pascal Bussy, 1999); MOJO 41; comprehensive links site at: web.bham.ac.uk/busbykg/kraftwerk/links.html

The Beatles
Live At The Hollywood Bowl

Sounds like a beat group inside one of Concorde's engines. Fantastically exciting.

Recorded for possible release at the height of Beatlemania by Voyle Gilmore – one of the house producers for The Beatles' American label Capitol – but turned down by the band and label as poor quality, the Hollywood Bowl concert tapes weren't seriously considered until Phil Spector (so the legend goes) – fresh from his contentious salvage job on *Let It Be* – took the 3-track recordings to the acetate stage in readiness for release on Apple in 1971.

With The Beatles in litigation, the project was shelved until 1977 when George Martin was asked to prepare the tapes for release. He wasn't keen: he remembered the '64 show as an unsatisfactory performance ("the boys didn't sing too well during the shows: they had no foldback speakers so they couldn't hear themselves") and was further dismayed to find the mixing on the 3-track tapes hadn't isolated the vocals: "I found guitar and voices mixed on the same track and the recording seemed to concentrate more on the wild screaming of 18,700 kids than on The Beatles on-stage." Having trouble finding a 3-track machine that worked ("Eventually we found an old one which we prevented from overheating by having a vacuum cleaner in reverse blowing cool air into it"), Martin and Geoff Emerick transferred the recordings to 24-track and edited the best of two shows a year apart into a continuous concert record.

Appearing 11 years after the Beatles had given their last concert, it wasn't the most refined live recording but it certainly countered the myth that The Beatles were actually not very good on-stage ("Good in the studio, rubbish live," Charlie Watts was heard to mutter as recently as 1997). As well as conveying a palpable excitement, there's a musical fervour and commitment that entirely fails to convey the tiredness and growing cynicism the band later admitted to feeling about the shows of the period. And with the absence of vocal foldback, that anything of musical value occurred in the face of the wall of hysteria that overwhelmed them (and, on the record, us) is miraculous.

It was deleted from the catalogue in the mid-'90s to make way for the live cuts on the *Anthology* releases.

Record label:
Parlophone

Produced
by Voyle Gilmore and George Martin.

Recorded
at the Hollywood Bowl; August 1964 and August 1965.

Released:
May 6, 1977

Chart peaks:
1 (UK) 2 (US)

Personnel:
John Lennon (g, v, o); Paul McCartney (b, v); George Harrison (g, v); Ringo Starr (d, v); Hugh Davies (concert engineer 1964); Pete Abbott (concert engineer 1965); Geoff Emerick (remixing)

Track listing:
Twist And Shout; She's a Woman; Dizzy Miss Lizzy; Ticket To Ride; Can't Buy Me Love; Things We Said Today; Roll Over Beethoven; Boys; A Hard Day's Night; Help!; All My Loving; She Loves Me; Long Tall Sally

Running time:
28.30

Not currently available on CD

Further listening:
Anthology 1 (1996), Anthology 2 (1996)

Further reading:
Beatles: An Illustrated Record (Roy Carr and Tony Tyler, 1978)

Tom Waits
Small Change

Recorded live in the studio, the jazziest of Waits' records.

Tom Waits was discovered at the Troubadour Club's amateur night by manager Herb Cohen (Frank Zappa/Tim Buckley) and quickly established himself as one of LA's most peculiar singer-songwriters. On his first album *Closing Time* he was twangy-voiced and mellow, with a country-ish tinge to his songs. (One early composition Ol' 55 was covered by The Eagles on *On The Border*). But then, from *The Heart Of Saturday Night* onwards, he began to write about, and live, a bohemian, flophouse lifestyle, taking on the persona of a sentimental, grizzly-voiced barfly and motel poet howling at the moon.
     Small Change sums up Waits' chequered relationship with jazz and beat poetry. Meticulously written and spontaneous in feel, it is the closest any artist has come to making a jazz record that the jazz audience never heard or cared about. Waits wanted to use Zoot Sims for the saxophone role, but the ever-busy Sims was double-booked, and instead he got the marvellous Lew Tabackin, a pro's pro among session men and the perfect choice for the date. The greatest single track Waits has ever created is Step Right Up, a seemingly improvised flow of street barking – actually carefully planned – which Tabackin and the superlative team of Jim Hughart and veteran West Coast drummer Shelly Manne underscore and elevate with the most exciting playing imaginable. Even Waits is taken out of himself: listen to the way he suddenly spills out the line "Change into a nine-year-old Hindu boy/Get rid of your wife!" – an explosive piece of surrealism which his subsequent albums, no matter how accomplished, have rarely matched.
     In some ways *Small Change* is a farewell to a tradition of West Coast musicianship. Shelly Manne, who had already been a fixture of Californian jazz and session work for three decades, probably played the stripper-music beat on Pasties And A G-String with a nostalgic grin on his face. The work which these musicians had enjoyed in Californian studios for the past 20 years was drying up, and Waits's decision to use these masters of their craft was already quaint. The studied poetry of his previous records – and his carefully nurtured gravelly timbre – was by now sufficiently lived-in to give this album an entirely plausible feel, even though in 1976 this kind of music was as idiosyncratic as his more out-there later work. But for now, Waits sticks with the woozy romanticism which makes this

Record label:
Asylum

Produced and engineered
by Bones Howe.

Recorded
at Wally Heider Recording, Hollywood 15–20 July 1976.

Released:
May 1977

Chart peaks:
None (UK) 89 (US)

Personnel:
Tom Waits (v, p); Lew Tabackin (ts); Jim Hughart (b); Shelly Manne (d)

Track listing:
Tom Traubert's Blues; Step Right Up; Jitterbug Boy; I Wish I Was In New Orleans; The Piano Has Been Drinking (Not Me); Invitation To The Blues; Pasties And A G-String; Bad Liver And A Broken Heart; The One That Got Away; Small Change; I Can't Wait To Get Off Work

Running time:
50.02

Current CD:
7559-60612-2

Further listening:
Foreign Affairs (1977)

Further reading:
www.officialtomwaits.com

period of his music so affecting. Bad Liver And A Broken Heart is a sodden unrequited valentine; Small Change is pure reportage, something he would later come at much more obliquely; I Can't Wait To Get Off Work is a blue-collar farewell that would melt the heart of the sternest boss. The Piano Has Been Drinking is a delicious comic gem. While Waits' subsequent records deal with similar territory (albeit in different ways), he never made more humane and moving music than this. Some years later Tom Traubert's Blues was pilfered by Rod Stewart, to the dismay of many.

Muddy Waters
Hard Again

A career-defining masterpiece of Chicago blues in one great — and final — burst of creativity.

When recording his earlier, legendary sides for Chess Records the man born McKinley Morganfield was usually alotted only enough studio time for cutting four songs. Singles were the order of the day at Chess, as elsewhere then, and when enough singles had been issued a few were collected for an album release. The label's initial forays into the LP market for Muddy resulted in psychedelic blues misfires like *Electric Mud* (1968). When Muddy Waters signed to Blue Sky at the behest of Johnny Winter he was assured that things would be different. They were.

With Winter producing and playing guitar, Muddy recorded four fine albums in a row before his death in 1983. *Hard Again* is the best, a culmination of everything he stood for and a personal triumph for both him and Winter, who'd been battling a heroin addiction. Recorded in a small studio — Muddy and his band were set up downstairs with the mics bleeding into one another for a rich ambient sound — there were few over-dubs. Winter was upstairs with no window or video monitor to see the band and had to keep running up and down the stairs to help adjust the mics or play guitar.

"The sessions for *Hard Again* were my favourite we did," recalled Pine Top Perkins, "they proved we still had it as a band and that Muddy still had it as a singer. The blues hadn't left us." Winter wisely chose a selection of old and new Muddy mate-rial. They returned to old chestnuts like Mannish Boy (a thumping great version that opens the album and sets the agenda), I Want To Be Loved (the Stones' first ever B-side) and I Can't Be Satisfied. Muddy also wrote new tunes — his hilarious The Blues Had A Baby And They Named The Baby Rock'n'Roll (co-written with Brownie McGhee) and the powerful punch of Bus Driver. *Hard Again* was named by a proud Waters who claimed that that's what this music made him.

Record label:
Blue Sky

Produced
by Johnny Winter.

Recorded
at The Schoolhouse, New York; winter 1977.

Released:
May 1977

Chart peaks:
None (UK) None (US)

Personnel:
Muddy Waters (v, g); Johnny Winter (g, miscellaneous screaming); James Cotton (harp); Pine Top Perkins (p); Bob Margolin (g); Charles Calmese (b); Willie "Big Eyes" Smith (d)

Track listing:
Mannish Boy (S); Bus Driver; I Want To Be Loved; Jealous Hearted Man; I Can't Be Satisfied; The Blues Had A Baby And They Named The Baby Rock'N'Roll (#2) (S); Deep Down In Florida; Crosseyed Cat; Little Girl

Running time:
45.66

Current CD:
SNY344492

Further listening:
The best of Muddy's Blue Sky years Hoochie Coochie Man (1993); Muddy Waters: The Chess Box (1989)

Further reading:
www.muddywater.com; Bluesland: Portraits Of Twelve Major American Blues Masters (Pete Welding and Toby Byron, 1992)

Cheap Trick
In Color

Boisterous, hook-laden missing link between '60s British pop and American arena.

W hen the first Cheap Trick album came along it confused the hell out of people. Here was a band with no apparent history, just a reputation for having played every bar-room across the Midwest of America. Cheap Trick's black and white sleeve added to the puzzlement. Were they New Wave and, if so, why did they look more like Queen? Add to that the sound of the record itself; stylish high-power pop but noisily mixed – it was too harsh and too fast to be pop, too pop and too lyrically weird to be metal and, too heavy *and* too pop to be New Wave.

In Color came along just six months later. Producer Steve Douglas, whose Aerosmith connections had helped clinch their deal with Epic, was gone, along with his blitzkrieg live/studio sound. He was replaced by Tom Werman, another heavy rock producer but with a cleaner sound that emphasised their melodies and hooks – of which there were plenty – and their up-close-and-personal vocals. The band have subsequently suggested they'd have preferred their natural sound – "The way we sound in person when you come to see the band," as bassist Petersson put it – but this was Cheap Trick *In Colour* and bright, bold colours at that. Despite the slicker production, the guitars still fizz and the energy level is still off the scale. The 10 songs, all written by guitar player Rick Nielsen – "I'm not sure what the reason is; they like to go out more than I do" – are shoe-horned into 30 boisterous minutes littered with Anglophilia: The Move, The Beatles and The Who, and even more notably Gary Glitter and The Sweet. Picking up early on the glam connection, Kim Fowley had once advised Nielsen to put his colleague Bun E. Carlos on a diet and dress him like David Bowie.

Thanks to incessant touring – no great sacrifice; Cheap Trick were always a touring band, spending three years on the road before recording their first album – the album nudged into the lower reaches of the American charts, though failed to ignite UK audiences. Japan, however, was a different matter. The Rockford, Illinois band were fast becoming superstars. Two years later their live-in-Japan album *Cheap Trick at Budokan* – recorded amidst scenes like The Beatles at Shea Stadium – would be their breakthrough, making a UK hit single of a beautifully tinny live version of I Want You To Want Me.

Record label:
Epic

Produced
by Tom Werman.

Recorded
at Kendun Recorders, Los Angeles; early summer 1977.

Released:
August 1977

Chart peaks:
None (UK) 73 (US)

Personnel:
Robin Zander (v, rg); Tom Petersson (b, v); Bun E Carlos (d); Rick Nielsen (g, v)

Track listing:
Hello There; Big Eyes; Downed; I Want You To Want Me (S); You're All Talk; Oh Caroline; Clock Strikes Ten; Southern Girls; Come On, Come On; So Good To See You

Running time:
31.05

Current CD:
491230 2 adds: Oh Boy; Southern Girls (2); Come On, Come On (2); You're All Talk (2); Goodnight

Further listening:
Heaven Tonight (1978)

Further reading:
Reputation Is A Fragile Thing: The Story Of Cheap Trick (Mike Hayes with Ken Sharp, 1998); www.cheaptrick.com

Dennis Wilson
Pacific Ocean Blue

The Beach Boy least-likely-to delivers the band's first solo masterpiece.

Dennis Wilson was never allowed the level of involvement in the early Beach Boys' successes he might have liked. Indeed, he'd only been grudgingly allowed into the band at the insistence of his mother. His role of drummer and band heart-throb established, such was Dennis' unreliable nature, the others became increasingly happy to keep him at arm's length. But when big brother Brian became unreliable too, The Beach Boys needed any decent songs they could get. With poet and lyricist Steve Kalinich, Dennis submitted two for the *Friends* album, the delightful Little Bird and Be Still. Be With Me, Slip On Through, Forever, Celebrate The News, Make It Good, Cuddle Up and Only With You and his Sound Of Free solo single all served to build his confidence. His increasingly emotional and epic contributions suggested that Brian wasn't the only great mind in the group after all.

While his singing wasn't as sweet as his brothers', there was a distinctive, tender quality to his voice, suggesting that under the rakish exterior lurked a sensitive soul.

"Dennis and I used to sit up in his tree-hut and talk about how we would like to change and help influence the world towards peace, and helping all the sick kids," Kalinich recalls. "Despite all the things you read about Dennis, there was that side of him that wanted to give."

Finally, in 1977, he recorded something exactly the way he wanted it. *Pacific Ocean Blue* allowed Dennis to bear his soul. The songs were given expansive, dreamy settings in delicately complex arrangements. The musical landscape was oceanic too: powerful, motive and uplifting.

The majestic opener, a plea for a simpler, more natural life, River Song, was co-written with brother Carl Wilson. After that, the bulk of the songs dealt with the theme of love, though from a more wistful, almost metaphysical viewpoint than The Beach Boys' optimistically adolescent take. The Dennis version of romance was fatalistic, mordant even. Two of the album's most chillingly lovely songs – Time and You And I – were written with his wife, Karen Lamm Wilson, most of the others were composed with co-producer and long-standing friend Gregg Jacobson.

"There was never talk about money or success or death,"

Record label:
Caribou

Produced
by Dennis Wilson and Gregg Jacobson.

Recorded
at Brother Studios, Santa Monica, California; 1976–1977.

Released:
September 16, 1977

Chart peaks:
None (UK) None (US)

Personnel:
Dennis Wilson (v, k, d); Ed Carter (g, b); Earl Mankey (g); Jamie Jamerson (b); Hal Blaine (d); Ricky Fataar (d); Curt Boettcher, Bruce Johnston, Karen Lamm Wilson, Billy Hinsche, Ed Tuleja, Gregg Jacobson, Alexander Hamilton and The Double Rock Baptist Choir (bv); Stephen Moffitt (e, m)

Track listing:
River Song; What's Wrong; Moonshine; Friday Night; Dreamer; Thoughts Of You; Time; You And I; Pacific Ocean Blues; Farewell My Friend; Rainbows

Running time:
37.25

Currently unavailable on CD

Further listening:
Beach Boys, Sunflower (1972)

Further reading:
The Nearest Faraway Place (Timothy White, 1994);
www.cabinessence.com/dennis/

remembers Kalinich, who collaborated on Rainbows with Dennis and Carl. "There was only talk about the work, about the creativity."

It's quite easy to imagine that the warm critical reception which welcomed *Pacific Ocean Blue* would have given rise to mixed emotions within The Beach Boys' camp. Its release came only five months after the official band album, *The Beach Boys Love You* and in terms of coherence, sound and a mature sense of purpose, it beat that album hands down. Dennis was suitably buoyed to begin preparing tracks for a second album with the working title of *Bamboo* which never made it to the finishing line. Two of the best songs, Baby Blue and Love Surrounds Me, were used for The Beach Boys' *LA (Light Album)* in 1979. Several others showed strong new directions, but, as Dennis let his life drift into more excesses than even he could handle, plans for the second release petered out.

Dennis Wilson drowned in 1983.

Ian Dury
New Boots And Panties

Thirty-five-year-old wordsmith and art teacher becomes roguish uncle to the nation.

As with many of the flag-bearers of the New Wave, Ian Dury was not inexperienced. He had previously combined his massively charismatic leadership of pub-rock banditti Kilburn And The High Roads, with a lecturing post at Canterbury College Of Art; and had released several records well before Punk Year Zero. After the dissolution of the Kilburns, Dury formed a songwriting team with ex-Byzantium guitarist and pianist Chaz Jankel.

"Drummer Charlie Charles and me played together in Loving Awareness, and went out as a pair for sessions," says bass-playing Blockhead, Norman Watt-Roy. "We got a call from Alvic Studios in Wimbledon to work on some demos. They were for Ian and Chaz. We clicked straight away. I just remember us laughing our heads off all the time. I'd never heard anything as funny as Clever Trevor before. We went into Workhouse Studios a few weeks later; straight in and just banged 'em out. We were given quite a free hand, everyone was throwing ideas in. Ian and Chaz were into dancey grooves, they wanted a foot-tapping feel."

Chaz and Ian's loosely-drawn manifesto was gloriously realized from the off. The lubricious, Cockney funk of Wake Up And Make Love With Me gives way, with a typical stroke of genius, to the rocking Sweet Gene Vincent – the best tribute song ever. Breezing and wheezing through a touching paean to his father, My Old Man, and the effortlessly witty, reconstructed music hall of Billericay Dickie, Dury and his posse of supremely versatile players close the album with a trio of the most complex, powerful punk tracks of the era. On Blockheads, Dury berates Essex ladism, at the same time displaying an awareness that there's a bit of Blockhead in all men. The opening 30 seconds of Plaistow Patricia (a volley of swearing removed from subsequent CD reissues) are genuinely disquieting, while Blackmail Man is two minutes of the fastest jazz-wank in the East End.

Watt-Roy: "I've played on a lot of records and this is the only one I still listen to. I remember when we all went to Blackhill's (Ian's management) to listen to it. Elvis Costello was there. Afterwards he said it was the most complete album he'd ever heard." Charles Shaar Murray of the NME described *New Boots* as "the working man's *Tubular Bells*". The public concurred, and the maverick indie label Stiff had their first Top 10 album. Ian Dury, Doctor Johnson of the Doctor Marten, had arrived.

Record label:
Stiff

Producer:
not listed.

Recorded
at Workhouse Studios, Old Kent Road, London; 1977.

Released:
September 1977

Chart peaks:
5 (UK) None (US)

Personnel:
Ian Dury (v); Chaz Jankel (g, k, bv); Davey Payne (s); Norman Watt-Roy (b); Charlie Charles (d); Laurie Latham (e); Geoff Castle (syn); Ted Speight (g)

Track listing:
Wake Up And Make Love With Me; Sweet Gene Vincent (S/UK); I'm Partial To Your Abracadabra; My Old Man; Billericay Dickie; Clever Trevor; If I Was With A Woman; Blockheads; Plaistow Patricia; Blackmail Man

Running time:
37.10

Current CD:
AHLCD57 adds: Sex And Drugs And Rock And Roll

Further listening:
Do It Yourself (1979); Laughter (1980); Mr Lovepants (1998)

Further reading:
No Sleep 'Til Canvey Island: The Great Pub Rock Revolution (Will Birch, 2000); Sex And Drugs And Rock'n'Roll (Richard Balls, 2000); www.iandury.co.uk www.blockheads.co.uk

Richard Hell And The Voidoids

Blank Generation

New York punk innovator belatedly makes LP. Too clever by half for most punks.

Richard Hell is placed, rightfully, at the epicentre of punk's origins. This is chiefly on account of the fact that in 1975 Malcolm McLaren noted Hell's penchant for ripped T-shirts and plundered it wholesale for his Chelsea boutique, for the Sex Pistols, and consequently for the entire punk look.

But Hell was far more important and influential than merely for his innovative fabric abuse. Changing his surname from Myers to Hell was no Tin Pan Alley star makeover, *à la* Ziggy Stardust. This was Hell's chosen life. The title track of this album revealed an agenda which was rapidly misinterpreted: rather than being a literal exhaltation of nihilism, Hell meant blank as in autonomy. But his literate lyrics were always too smart for most New Wavers. All of these songs are about identity, relationships, the transience of sex, mortality – a world where life, as the title track puts it, was "God's consolation prize".

Hell also had a great sense of rock'n'roll history, captured perfectly in a storming version of the Fogerty brothers' Walking On The Water (actually the most minimalist track on the album) recorded at a time when nobody was talking about Creedence Clearwater Revival. The other great thing about this record is guitarist Robert Quine – the balding antithesis of all the punk clones from central casting. Quine's spluttering guitar work owes more to free jazz than to the Chuck Berry-on-amphetamine histrionics of most punk. Probably the most 'punk' thing the Voidoids could have done, in fact.

Record label:
Sire

Produced
by Richard Gottehrer and Richard Hell.

Recorded
at Electric Ladyland and The Plaza, New York; 1977.

Released:
September 1977

Chart peaks:
None (UK) None (US)

Personnel:
Richard Hell, (b, v), Robert Quine (g, bv), Ivan Julian (g, bv); Marc Bell (d)

Track listing:
Love Comes In Spurts; Liars Beware; New Pleasure; Betrayal Takes Two; Down At The Rock And Roll Club; Who Says?; Blank Generation (S); Walking On The Water; The Plan; Another World;

Running time:
32.10

Current CD:
7599261372

Further listening:
The Kid With The Replaceable Head/I'm Your Man (1979)

Further reading:
MOJO 77; England's Dreaming (Jon Savage, 1992); www.richardhell.com

Iggy Pop
Lust For Life

Iggy's acknowledgement as punk's founding father is marked with his first Top 30 UK hit.

From the exhilarating opening groove, now familiar via the movie Trainspotting and a host of commercials, *Lust For Life* proclaims itself Iggy Pop's most effervescent, vital album – one that saw his collaborator David Bowie at a towering peak in his songwriting – accompanied by a stunningly inventive band. The album found Iggy, who'd enjoyed a modest career revival with his previous Bowie collaboration, *The Idiot*, in a newly-optimistic mood: "I was living on coke, hash, red wine and German sausages, I had my own little place with cold water showers, and I was the happiest person in the world." Where *The Idiot* had been a Bowie-influenced experimental affair, *Lust For Life* was determinedly an Iggy album, recorded in two weeks of nocturnal sessions at Hansa Studio 1 overlooking the Berlin Wall.

Practically every song was written and conceived in the studio, with Iggy revelling in his new industrious work ethic. He'd show up at the studio with vocal or instrumental snippets on his tape recorder, and argue into the night with Bowie: "There was a lot of friction going on. But on the other hand we were both really into the project, The thing was written in one day, he came down and sat at the piano and we taped about eight things like that." Bizarrely, the album's title track came from the signature oompah band theme to German public television, spotted by Bowie; Iggy's words incorporated William Burroughs references, while the whole affair was powered forward by the superb sibling rhythm section of Hunt and Tony Sales ("I put everything into those songs," says drummer Hunt. "I fooled myself into thinking it was a proper band.").

The optimism and electricity generated in the studio is exemplified by the closing fade-out of Success, where Iggy ad-libs lines about buying expensive rugs, while Bowie and the Sales brothers, singing the backing vocals live, try not to break into hysterics. Sadly, much of the confidence seemed misplaced in the subsequent months, for, following the death of Elvis Presley on August 16, 1977, RCA dedicated its pressing plants to churning out Presley material, all in-store RCA promotions were withdrawn and Presley memorial material put in its place. Iggy's greatest solo album was forgotten in his homeland, the unfortunate victim of the King's terminal event atop the commode.

Record label:
RCA Victor

Produced
by Bewlay Bros (Iggy Pop and David Bowie).

Recorded
at Hansa Tonstudios, Berlin, Germany; June 1977.

Released:
September 1977

Chart peaks:
28 (UK) 120 (US)

Personnel:
Iggy Pop (v); Carlos Alomar, Ricky Gardiner (g); Tony Sales (b); Hunt Sales (d); David Bowie (p)

Track listing:
Lust For Life; Sixteen; Some Weird Sin; The Passenger; Tonight; Success (S); Turn Blue; Neighborhood Threat; Fall In Love with Me

Running time:
40.41

Current CD:
CDOVD278

Further listening:
The Idiot (1976)

Further reading:
MOJO 29; I Need More (Iggy Pop, 1996); www.theroc.org/mus-link/bands/i/iggypop.htm

Steely Dan
Aja

Steely Dan's most sophisticated and commercially successful work, a masterpiece of session layering.

Recorded at immense cost over many months at various Los Angeles studios, with one song (Peg) added later in new York, *Aja* stands as a monument to the apparently limitless perfectionism of Steely Dan songwriters Walter Becker and Donald Fagen.

"I think because of the kind of music we were doing, it seemed to us that it should be real seamlessly put together and have a high level of polish to make it work," explains Becker. Accordingly, the album credits read like a Who's Who of '70s session players, with only their old friend Denny Dias retained from the original Steely Dan line-up – and then only as one of three guitarists on the title track, a multi-sectioned suite based on an oriental motif and boasting a sterling sax solo from Weather Report's Wayne Shorter. This was typical of the new Steely Dan, which after "dumbing down" their ambitions in order to kick-start its career, had now re-inflated them to way beyond their original expectations.

And with unprecedented expectations came unprecedented measures, with each of the album's seven songs being recorded several times over by different combinations of expensive session musicians, to allow Becker and Fagen to decide which particular accents of rhythm and style best suited a particular song. At its most absurd, this strategy resulted in a parade of no fewer than seven top guitarists being called in to try and find the right guitar solo for Peg, a search called off only when Jay Graydon came up with the elegantly pirouetting break that graces the released track. "A lot of times we didn't know what we wanted," admits Becker. "Other times, we just wanted it to be better, so we'd keep trying for another take. Many days we'd make guys do 30 or 40 takes and we'd never listen to any of them again, because we knew none of them were any good; but we just kept hoping that somehow it was just going to miraculously get good."

Along with hints about the album's jazzier style, Becker and Fagen had previously warned that, after the fuss that had been made over the previous album *The Royal Scam*'s title track (a political parable about Puerto Rican immigrants in New York), the new songs would have no social significance. They were, however, some of the most emotionally satisfying the duo

Record label:
ABC

Produced
by Gary Katz.

Recorded
in Los Angeles and New York; 1976–77.

Released:
September 1977

Chart peaks:
5 (UK) 3 (US)

Personnel:
Donald Fagen (v, k, police whistle); Walter Becker (b, g); Denny Dias (g); Larry Carlton (g); Lee Ritenour (g); Steve Khan (g); Jay Graydon (g); Dean Parks (g); Chuck Rainey (b); Victor Feldman (k, vibes, pc); Joe Sample (k); Michael Omartian (k); Paul Griffin (k, bv); Don Grolnick (k); Paul Humphrey (d); Steve Gadd (d); Bernard Purdie (d); Rick Marotta (d); Ed Greene (d); Jim Keltner (drm, pc); Gary Coleman (pc); Tom Scott (s, lyricon); Wayne Shorter (s); Pete Christlieb (s); Clydie King King, Shirley Matthews, Venetta Fields, Rebecca Louis, Tim Schmit, Michael McDonald (bv); Roger Nichols (e)

Track listing:
Black Cow (S); Aja; Deacon Blues (S); Peg (S); Home At Last (S); I Got The News (S); Josie (S/US only)

Running time:
39.56

Current CD:
MCLD19145

Further listening:
Earlier Steely Dan albums didn't have quite as noticeable a jazz influence, but the later Gaucho (1980) and comeback album Two Against Nature (2000) are comparable in terms of texture, accent and attitude.

Further reading:

MOJO 23; Steely Dan: Reelin' In The Years
(Brian Sweet, 1994); www.steelydan.com

ever came up with, featuring celebratory portraits of high-spirited girls (Peg and Josie), Zen-like reflections on satiety (Aja and Home At Last), and a touchingly *simpatico* tribute to bohemian losers (Deacon Blues). Fusing pop and jazz in a subtle, seamless alloy entirely at variance with the leaden jazz-rock riffing of their "fusion" contemporaries, *Aja* proved to be the band's most popular album, eventually selling in excess of five million copies.

Johnny Thunders And The Heartbreakers
L.A.M.F.

The only punk band who could sing about the street-gang lifestyle with authority.

When heroin becomes more of an interest than music it is tough to keep your career going. Ex-New York Dolls Johnny Thunders (*né* Genzale) and Jerry Nolan managed both for a while, and their band had quite a reputation, but simply because of their music. Managed by ex-Warhol protégé Leee Black Childers, they were invited in late 1976 by Malcolm McLaren, who had briefly managed the Dolls, to fly to London and join the Sex Pistols/Damned/Clash Anarchy Tour. The tour was a mess of cancelled gigs and rescinded payments, but Childers got the band exposure through packed-out London concerts and they were soon signed to Track Records. Several singles appeared – Chinese Rocks sold 20,000 copies in its first week of release. Track asked Pete Townshend acolyte Speedy Keen (his telltale nickname marking him as the perfect Heartbreakers producer) to hurry up the album.

It took several weeks to record at two studios, six months to mix at *five* different studios and still it wasn't right. The initial sound of *L.A.M.F.* (Like A Mother Fucker) was murky; though it's likely that Track's mastering – rather than the mix – was responsible for the sonic problems. By the time *L.A.M.F.* came out, the Heartbreakers had a UK following but most of the musicians, club owners and record company people they'd dealt with hated them: it's not easy working with junkies. But the album was a rocks-off affair from start to finish; not so much punk rock as NYC toughs playing elemental rock'n'roll for dancing or pogo-ing It was like updated Eddie Cochran, noted Jake Riviera perceptively, or at least Eddie Cochran with a $125 a day habit. Some of the songs (Pirate Love, Going Steady) were leftovers from the Dolls days – yet this was classic stuff; you could bet any song's title would be repeated at least half a dozen times, welded to a riff Gene Vincent would've killed for.

Record label:
Track

Produced
by Speedy Keen and Daniel Secunda.

Recorded
at Essex Studios and Ramport Studios, London; February–March 1977.

Released:
October 3, 1977

Chart peaks:
55 (UK) 55; (US) None

Personnel:
Johnny Thunders (v, g); Walter Lure (v, g); Billy Rath (b, v); Jerry Nolan (d)

Track listing:
Born To Lose; Baby Talk; All By Myself; I Wanna Be Loved; It's Not Enough (S/UK); Chinese Rocks (S/UK); Get Off The Phone; Pirate Love; One Track Mind; I Love You; Going Steady; Let Go

Running time:
40.04

Current CD:
FREUD CD445 remixed and issued as L.A.M.F: The Lost '77 Mixes adds: Can't Keep My Eyes Off You; Do You Love Me?

Further listening:
Thunders' first solo effort So Alone (1978)

Further reading:
In Cold Blood: The Authorised Biography Of Johnny Thunders (Nina Antonia, 1987); http://home.eol.ca/~ifftay/thunders.htm

Electric Light Orchestra
Out Of The Blue

The least fashionable band of its day reach preposterous peak.

ELO's brand of space-age, orchestral Beatley rock had struggled in the early days to click with a mass audience, but the more band *auteur* Jeff Lynne allowed his writing to come from his pop heart, the more successful they became. Initial ELO albums had been lugubrious affairs, straining to combine a Walrus density with progressive rock weight.

Lynne: "I thought it was cool to write long songs. It took me ages to get that violin out of my arse!"

The first three albums featured brutal-toned cellos but with 1974's *Eldorado* using a full orchestra, the sound attained a lighter touch as Lynne surrendered to his Beatles instincts; John Lennon even said if The Beatles had made records in the '70s, they'd be like ELO music. Lynne loved that. *A New World Record* (1976) was an international breakthrough spawning three hit singles and the pressure was on for the follow-up. Deciding upon a double, Lynne set himself three weeks in a Swiss chalet to write two albums worth of songs. "For the first four days I couldn't get a thing. I just looked at all that equipment and thought, What a funny job I have!" The juices started flowing and though Mr Blue Sky took a week to finish ("I pounded the chord sequence for nine hours in a row one day"), he wrote 13 new songs in a fortnight. Three months in Munich with their favourite engineer Mack produced this magnificent, ridiculous smorgasbord of Beatles/Beach Boys/Bee Gees/Roy Orbison nicks, echo effects, extravagant call-and-response backing vocal hooks, monolithic slabs of Louis Clark strings and choir, and a sackful of great pop tunes.

The words meant little (Lynne was often finishing them at the vocal sessions), the mother spaceship sleeve was a thematic red herring (though the motif was adopted as a stage for the tour) and critics were scornful (Sounds: "Why does the female preying mantis eat its mate after orgasm? Why do ELO sell so many records?"). But the feel-good bounce of Mr Blue Sky (surely one of *the* great uplifting pop records) the mock-epic Standing In The Rain and the power ballads Steppin' Out and Big Wheels are the inspired work of a singular pop craftsman and have worn amazingly well. There were advance orders of four million for the album, and though their next, *Discovery* (1979), was even more successful, *Out Of The Blue* is Lynne's pinnacle.

Record label:
Jet

Produced
by Jeff Lynne.

Recorded
at Musicland Studios, Munich; May–July 1977.

Release date:
October 1977

Chart peaks:
4 (UK) 4 (US)

Personnel:
Jeff Lynne (v, g, k, a); Bev Bevan (d); Richard Tandy (k, a); Kelly Groucutt (b, v); Mik Kaminsky (v); Hugh McDowell (c); Melvyn Gale (c); Louis Clark (a, oa)

Track listing:
Turn To Stone; It's Over; Sweet Talkin' Woman; Across The Border; Night In The City; Starlight; Jungle; Believe Me Now; Steppin' Out; Concerto For A Rainy Day; Standin' In The Rain; Big Wheels-Summer And Lightning-Mr Blue Sky; Sweet Is The Night; The Whale; Birmingham Blues; Wild West Hero

Running time:
70.16

Current CD:
Epic 450885 9

Further listening:
Eldorado (1974); A New World Record (1976); Discovery (1979)

Further reading:
The Electric Light Orchestra Story (Bev Bevan, 1980)

Sex Pistols
Never Mind The Bollocks — Here's The Sex Pistols

Punk rock crash-lands in the mainstream, just as the Sex Pistols fall apart.

By April 1977, the Sex Pistols had been thrown off both EMI and A&M, and shunted around a succession of London recording studios. Manager Malcolm McLaren was holding back from signing to Virgin, but the Pistols were still motivated enough to finally commence the recording of their debut album. Though countless demos were recorded with their soundman, Dave "Boss" Goodman, their two A-sides thus far — Anarchy In The UK and the aborted A&M single God Save The Queen — had been produced by Chris Thomas, hired on account of Paul Cook's fondness for his work with Roxy Music. The template for Pistols recordings had thus been set, and the vast majority of tape was gleefully filled by Steve Jones' piled-up guitars.

"Phil Spector's my inspiration as a rock producer," Jones told NME. "So what I wanted to get was a new Wall of Sound."

"I was a bit bored making that album," John Lydon recalls now. "There were something like 21 guitar tracks laid down and only two tracks for vocal. I did most of the songs all the way through, one or two takes, and that's it. And I got very annoyed."

The first phase of work was halted by the Pistols' signing to Virgin on May 12, 1977. Two weeks later they released God Save The Queen, and reached the height of their infamy in the summer of Elizabeth's Silver Jubilee. This impacted on the second spurt of recording: on June 18, having worked on Holidays In The Sun, John Lydon, Chris Thomas and engineer Bill Price were attacked by a gang of irate royalists. Inevitably, it was Lydon they were after: the damage inflicted on one of his hands was permanent. Against such a background, it's amazing the record was ever finished. Also weighing against the Pistols was the ineptitude of their new bass player: Sid Vicious made no audible contribution to the album at all (though he's alleged to be buried somewhere in the mix of Bodies), leaving the playing of brutally simple, root-note bass parts to Jones.

It was late September, a month after the legendary SPOTS tour (Sex Pistols On Tour Secretly), before the LP was

Record label:
Virgin

Produced
by Chris Thomas.

Recorded
at Wessex Studios, London; May–September 1977.

Release date:
October 1977

Chart peaks:
1 (UK) 106 (US)

Personnel:
John Lydon aka Johnny Rotten (v); Steve Jones (g, b); Paul Cook (d); John Ritchie aka Sid Vicious (b); Bill Price (e)

Track listing:
Holidays In The Sun (S); Bodies; No Feelings; Liar; God Save The Queen (S); Problems; Seventeen; Anarchy In The UK (S); Submission; Pretty Vacant (S); New York; EMI

Running time:
38.30

Current CD:
CDVX2086

Further listening:
8LP demos on There Is No Future (1999) and Early Daze (1992); the entire Pistols canon on Kiss This (1992)

Further reading:
Classic Rock Albums: Never Mind The Bollocks (Clinton Heylin, 1998); England's Dreaming (Jon Savage, 1992); Sex Pistols: The Inside Story (Fred and Judy Vermorel, 1987)

finalised. Its working title – God Save The Sex Pistols – was jettisoned, though confusion still surrounded the final track-listing. So it was that 10,000 initial copies omitted Submission, slipped into the package as a one-sided single. Such hiccups mattered little: *Bollocks* was deservedly lauded as a epochal triumph. "It's all speed, not nuance," said Rolling Stone, "and the songs all hit like amphetamines or the plague, depending on your point of view."

Jacques Brel
Brel

Belgium's great chansonnier *bids adieu.*

Jacques Brel was in a bad way when he arrived in France for the sessions that would comprise his final recordings. He had been in semi-retirement for a decade, during which time his Anglophone profile had never been higher, thanks to Scott Walker (Jackie et al), Alex Harvey (Next) and Terry Jacks (who had heard The Beach Boys toying with Seasons In The Sun). But it was when he was diagnosed as having terminal cancer (he was a 100 filterless-a-day man) that the effects of mortality, a common subject of his songs, came into focus. He was 48.

From his home in the South Pacific, he wrote to old collaborator Jouannest and label boss Eddie Barclay, wondering if they would be interested in some of his "nonsense". Jouannest was the first to hear Brel's demos; the timbre of his voice had deepened, his ability with lyrics was still there, but the melodies were boring. This was no discouragement because, by tradition, *chansonniers* concentrated on the words, tunes would only distract the listener.

In the studio, Brel's enthusiasm evaporated. His fast-failing health meant he wanted as few hassles as possible and could only manage a maximum of three takes for each song. If it sounded off — and it often did — then tough. Barclay, unaware of the singer's impending death, started formulating plans for an album of duets with Streisand as a way of breaking America once again. How this would have worked is anyone's guess, as Brel still aligned himself with the French refuseniks who wanted to repel American influences — allowing, of course, for the wah-wah pedal on Les F?

As soon as recording was completed, Brel took off, determined to avoid giving any interviews and insisting on a low-key release. Nevertheless, the record company embarked on an unparalleled marketing campaign, creating an air of mystery that was only alleviated the day before release, when radio stations were finally allowed to play the album. Within 24 hours, 650,000 copies had been bought in France alone. The subject of constant intrusion by the French press, Brel himself hung on another 11 months, commenting only that he hated the sleeve.

Record label:
Barclay

Produced
by Gerhard Lehner.

Recorded
in Paris, September 1977.

Released:
November 1977

Chart peaks:
None (UK) None (US)

Personnel:
Jacques Brel (v); Gerard Jouannest (p); Marcel Azzola (accordion); Francois Rauber (o)

Track listing:
Jaures; La Ville S'Endormait; Vieillir; Le Bon Dieu; Les F?; Orly; Les Remparts De Varsovie; Voir Un Ami Pleurer; Knokke-Le-Zoute Tango; Jojo; Le Lion; Les Marquises

Running time:
48.30

Currently available CD:
810 537 2

Further listening:
Ce Gens-La (1966) — the LP that introduced Jackie, Mathilde and Tango Funèbre to the world; Quand On N'a Que L'Amour, a two-CD best of. For Brel in English, Scott Walker Sings Jacques Brel (culled from Scott 1–3) is ample proof of why Brel considered Scott the foremost interpreter of his work.

Further reading:
Jacques Brel: The Biography (1998)

Suicide

Suicide

Proto-punk electronic rock'n'roll; Elvis and The Seeds with the technology of tomorrow.

Alan Vega and Martin Rev were the first to use the term "punk" in a musical context, when they put on something called "A Punk Music Mass" at a New York art gallery in 1971.

"Everybody else in the world has claimed it – Richard Hell, Legs McNeil – but I don't give a shit, we were the first," says Vega. "I liked the juxtaposition of the words 'punk' and 'mass' – they just don't go with one another. It was like a poetry thing. And five or six years later, it's a movement! Whoever would have thunk it?"

When that happened, however, the punk movement's music bore little or no relation to the strange, edgy hybrid that Vega and Rev had developed, though compared to the dreary three-chord thrash-merchants, Suicide were undeniably the real punk iconoclasts. Martin Rev was a free-jazz pianist whose sonic experiments had led him to delve into primitive electronic devices by the time he hooked up with Alan Vega at the Project For Living Artists, a gallery space for which the latter served as caretaker. Influenced by garage bands like The Seeds and electronic peers such as the Silver Apples, they devised a scary new kind of pop music which used Rev's machines to generate a backdrop of electronic pulses and poignant melody lines, over which Vega would intone melodramatic tales of urban low-lifes, lovers and losers, in his feverish Presley vocal pastiche. Suicide's live shows were always tense, confrontational events, the duo being regarded as contravening punk style laws, but by the time they came to record their debut album for Marty Thau's Red Star label, they had developed a set which mixed social-realist tales of urban dystopia like the 10-minute tragic opus Frankie Teardrop with erotic dreams like Cheree.

"They're basically true stories," claims Vega. "Cheree's about a girlfriend of mine, for instance. I wrote about people I knew, and Marty did the same with the music. There was a little time for love here and there, but mostly it was a horror story!" Though their music had at least as powerful an adrenalin surge as anything thrown up by punk, they were hopelessly out of step with the era's musical fashions; accordingly, their debut album remained very much a cult item, a fate shared by their subsequent releases.

Record label:
Red Star

Produced
by Craig Leon and Marty Thau.

Recorded
at Ultima Studios, Blauvelt; New York, 1977.

Release date:
November 1977

Chart peaks:
None (UK) None (US)

Personnel:
Alan Vega (v); Martin Rev (electronics)

Track listing:
Ghost Rider; Rocket USA; Cheree; Johnny; Girl; Frankie Teardrop; Che; Cheree (remix); I Remember; Keep Your Dreams

Running time:
43.56

Current CD:
BFFP133CDL adds live tracks: Mr Ray; Las Vegas Man; 96 Tears; Keep Your Dreams; I Remember; Harlem; 23 Minutes Over Brussels

Further listening:
The Ric Ocasek-produced follow-up, Alan Vega/Martin Rev – Suicide (1980), is a smoother and sleeker variant on the same formula. Vega's solo albums (such as Collision Drive (1981) and Saturn Strip (1983)) explore techno-rockabilly territory, while Martin Rev's solo efforts are electronic instrumentals (although Cheyenne is largely backing tracks from the second Suicide album).

Further reading:
www.multimania.com/jes/music/suicide2.htm

Throbbing Gristle
Second Annual Report

A lo-fi blueprint from the heart of the Death Factory.

In the basement of an old East End knitting factory situated on the fringes of Hackney's London Fields parkland – once a giant burial pit for plague victims – Throbbing Gristle assembled *Second Annual Report* in the latter half of 1977. Their use of disturbing subject matter and improvised, synthesised sound, created from hand-built and customised instruments, was so uncompromising, that it took "rebelliousness" to a level undreamt-of in the punk climate and identified a new musical genre: industrial music.

"We were absolutely antithetical to rock'n'roll at that point," declares vocalist Genesis P-Orridge, "We really didn't care if anybody liked it, or if we sold any records. Mark Perry of Sniffin' Glue had famously said, 'Learn three chords now form a band.' I said, 'Learn none at all.' To play chords was to plug back into the tradition on some level."

Set against a deep ambient roar, speech samples, synth screeches and uncontrolled feedback, the barely coherent words of Slug Bait, the opening section of live excerpts that fill side one, drew from two recent murder cases, with P-Orridge assuming the role of psychopathic killer. Altogether now: "I pull out your baby/I chew its head off with my teeth/As you bleed to death I kill it."

The subject of murder wasn't new to a rock audience, but the viewpoint was. The piece wasn't *about* the event, it sounded like it *was* the event. The assortment of punks, artists, critics and politicians that saw this performance at the ICA in October 1976, stood dumbfounded afterwards. It was meant, as P-Orridge later reflected, "To confront ALL assumptions in ALL aspects of the culture. Considered mischief with a motive of evaluation and rejuvenation of the medium itself."

The headline-grabbing ICA event, called Prostitution, was to mark the transformation of Coum Transmissions, a seven-year-old performance-art collective, into Throbbing Gristle. As Coum, P-Orridge and fellow founder Cosey Fanni Tutti had performed internationally, using mutilation, bodily fluids and pain to confront personal fears and public taboos, and, as with Gristle gigs, "to deliberately build situations of emotional and creative crisis, that have to be resolved instantly," says P-Orridge. If Coum were barely tolerated in the art world, then Throbbing Gristle would be an abomination to rock.

Record label:
Industrial Records

Produced
by Throbbing Gristle

Recorded
at The Death Factory, Hackney, London;
May–September 1977

Released:
November 1977

Chart peaks:
None (UK) None (US)

Personnel:
Genesis P-Orridge (b, violin, v); Peter Christopherson (t, tapes, processing); Cosey Fanni Tutti (Raver and Satelite guitar); Chris Carter (k, rhythms, m)

Track listing:
Industrial Introduction; Slug Bait – ICA; Slug Bait – Live at Southampton; Slug Bait – Live at Brighton; Maggot Death – Studio; Maggot Death – Southampton; Maggot Death – Brighton; After Cease To Exist – The Original Soundtrack of the Coum Transmissions Film.

Running Time:
39.56

Current CD:
Mute TGCD2 includes: Zyclon B Zombie; United

Further Listening:
D.O.A (1978); 20 Jazz Funk Greats (1979); Journey Through A Body (1981)

Further Reading:
Wreckers Of Civilisation: The Story of Coum Transmissions and Throbbing Gristle (Simon Ford, 1999)

To their surprise, the initial 785 copies of the album sold out quickly, mostly through Rough Trade. The title reflected the band's journalistic intentions, and darkly mimicked corporate speak. Released on their own Industrial Records label, it was the model independent release: totally self-financed and recorded on a portable Sony cassette recorder with a condenser mic that was simply placed opposite the band to record their gigs or studio sessions – a financial limitation but fortuitous send-up of studio professionalism. The technique also gave the recording its volatile, nightmarish quality. "It has," says P-Orridge, "a perfect ambiguity that one cannot create consciously."

Roberta Flack
Blue Lights In The Basement

The fifth gold album by the most impassive of the great soul divas.

She has been out of the limelight for so long that it's difficult to remember that Flack was once a major figure. Her first real success came in 1972 when The First Time Ever I Saw Your Face (from her excellent 1969 debut *First Take*) belatedly became a hit after its use in the movie Play Misty For Me. Of all her records, this is the most resourceful, the most thoughtful, the best of her essays on grown-up soul.

Flack was no spring chicken – she was pushing 40 when she made this set – and if Michael Jackson was a kid setting the pace in black pop, Flack was a vanguard representative of what was happening at the other extreme, the adult soul which had been formulated in her albums and those by The Detroit Spinners, Al Green and others. She has a rather sombre voice, somewhat akin to Nina Simone and Carmen McRae; jazz-directed singers who, like Flack, often accompanied themselves on piano. Although there's some joyful music here – Fine, Fine Day and the delicious revision of The Box Tops' hit, Soul Deep – Flack suggests a comfortable kind of happiness. Why Don't You Move In With Me goes on to suggest that "we could be a family", a search for domestic bliss which fades away on the meltingly beautiful 25th Of Last December. Some of the best songwriters of the era are represented here – Gwen Guthrie, Eugene McDaniels, Rachel Perry – and there is what, unhappily, turned out to be one of the final examples of her many duets with Donny Hathaway, who died a little over a year after the album was made (he fell from a hotel room window).

Blue Lights – her last great work – is beautifully played, too. Flack began working in piano bars in the '60s, and she knew many of the best cats to hire. In its latest remastering, the record has a somewhat eccentric sound, but Flack herself had an idiosyncratic way in the studio; a perfectionist, but not technically very adept at the board, she needed assistance to get records finished, even though she is still credited – Rubina Flake is a pseudonym for Roberta Flack.

Record label:
Atlantic

Produced
by Rubina Flake, Joe Ferla and Eugene McDaniels.

Recorded:
Spring 1977.

Released:
December 1977

Chart peaks:
None (UK) 8 (US)

Personnel:
Roberta Flack (v, k); Reggie Lucas, Hugh McCracken, Jeff Mironov, John Tropea, David Spinozza (g); Michael Kamen (oboe); Harry Whittaker, Ronnie Foster, Don Grolnick, Paul Griffin, Rob Mounsey, Leon Pendarvis (k); Anthony Jackson, Will Lee, Basil Fearrington (b); Howard King, Steve Gadd, Jimmy Wong, Idris Muhammed, Allen Schwarzberger (d); Mtume, Crusher, Jimmy Maeulin, Dave Carey, Gary King (pc); Donny Hathaway (v)

Track listing:
Why Don't You Move In With Me; The Closer I Get To You; Fine, Fine Day; This Time I'll Be Sweeter; 25th Of Last December; After You; I'd Like To Be Baby To You; Soul Deep; Love Is The Healing; Where I'll Find You

Running time:
41.22

Current CD:
Warner Brothers 3282791

Further listening:
First Take (1969); Feel Like Makin' Love (1975).

Billy Joel
The Stranger

Italian guy with chip on shoulder finally hits the big time.

Phil Ramone made the difference. With four almost great albums behind him, Billy Joel needed the guidance of a master producer to hit the bull's-eye he'd been missing. "The band had been under the gun with other producers, having to prove themselves, and also, there were always studio players, who were good but who weren't me," Joel said in 1978. "Phil liked my guys right off the bat. He heard them play the songs and said, 'Don't play any different than you play on the road – be the rock'n'roll animals that you are.' We did songs in five takes instead of 15 or 20. He was one of the guys. We'd throw around ideas, kick the songs around, try them different ways and get them right. Sometimes we'd throw pizza at each other."

Appropriately, there was a song called Scenes From An Italian Restaurant, a McCartney-ish suite of three wildly different sections sewn tastefully together. And anywhere else you dropped the needle you found a winner: the 16-note ivory attack-ack-ack of Moving Out, the cabaret swank of Vienna, the gorgeous balladry of She's Always A Woman and the fiery acoustic rocker Only The Good Die Young (Joel on the song's banned status: "As soon as kids found out that there was some authority that didn't want them to hear it, they went out and bought it in droves and it became this big hit"). The album's most enduring song, Just The Way You Are, almost didn't make the cut.

"I didn't like it very much," Joel says. "We were in the studio listening back to it and I was not even gonna put it on the album, then Linda Ronstadt and Phoebe Snow showed up and they said, 'You've got to put that on the album!' I said, 'Yeah, you think so?' And they just pleaded with me to put it on the album. So I'm going to listen to what women say. I put it on the album."

Record label:
CBS

Produced
by Phil Ramone.

Recorded
at A&R Recording, New York, 1977

Released:
December 1977

Chart peaks:
25 (UK) 2 (US)

Personnel:
Billy Joel (p, v, k); Doug Stegmeyer (b); Liberty DeVitto (d); Richie Cannata (s, clarinet, flute, k); Phil Woods (s); Steve Khan, Hiram Bullock, Steve Burgh, Hugh McCracken (g); Dominic Cortese (acc); Richard Tee (k); Ralph McDonald (pc); Phoebe Snow, Lani Groves, Gwen Guthrie, Patti Austin (bv); Patrick Williams (oa); Jim Boyer (e)

Track listing:
Moving Out (Anthony's Song) (S); The Stranger; Just The Way You Are (S); Scenes From An Italian Restaurant; Vienna; Only The Good Die Young (S); She's Always A Woman; Get It Right The First Time; Everybody Has A Dream

Running time:
40.17

Current CD:
4911842

Further listening:
The Nylon Curtain (1982)

Further reading:
www.turnstiles.org

Gerry Rafferty
City To City

Bolshy, reclusive songwriter's landmark of Scottish soft-rock.
Immortalised by a sax motif.

G erry Rafferty was a gifted man not cut out for fame. After
cutting his teeth with comedian Billy Connolly in The
Humblebums, he first tussled with the big time after forming
Stealer's Wheel – self-styled "Scots version of Crosby Stills Nash
And Young" – with fellow songwriter Joe Egan. Rafferty quit as
their debut album, produced by Lieber and Stoller, no less, was
released, only to return when Stuck In The Middle With You
(1973) charted in Britain and America, but only on condition
that Egan sacked the rest of the band. Two albums later they
broke up, with Rafferty no longer speaking to Egan and about
to embark on a three-year legal battle with their management.

But then came *City To City*, Baker Street and a further
short-lived struggle with the horrors of wealth and public
approbation. Never before can an album's commercial success
have been built so squarely on one sax solo. As Baker Street
rose to Number 3 in the UK and, after a live airing on David
Frost's American TV show, Number 2 in the States, the album
took off towards five million sales and even ended *Saturday
Night Fever*'s six-month run at the top of the US album chart.
Session star Raphael Ravenscroft's mournful plaint became an
unforgettable calling card for the melancholy beauty of much of
City To City. Yet Ravenscroft was called into the session only as
an afterthought when Rafferty and co-producer Hugh Murphy –
his one career-long colleague – decided mutually that the guitar
line they had earmarked for the song wasn't happening.

In America, the label had big plans for Rafferty, fondly
imagining that, with his gift for sensitive lyrics and radio-friendly
melodies, they had found a tunesmith of Paul McCartney stature.
But they swiftly discovered his reluctance to be a superstar. He
resisted all overtures for a major tour there, opting instead for
the studio and a quiet family life on his farm in Kent. His
subsequent solo albums described the same downward parabola as
Stealer's Wheel's, both commercially and, it must be said,
artistically. However, the durable power of Rafferty's best soft-
rock standards was acknowledged in the '90s when Quentin
Tarantino revived Stuck In The Middle With You for the Reservoir
Dogs soundtrack and Baker Street was covered by house crew
Undercover (1992, Number 2 in the UK singles charts) and ex-
Nirvana drummer Dave Grohl's Foo Fighters (1997).

Record label:
United Artists

Produced
by Hugh Murphy and Gerry Rafferty.

Recorded
at Chipping Norton Studios;
September–October 1977.

Released:
January 1978

Chart peaks:
6 (UK) 1 (US)

Personnel:
Gerry Rafferty (v, k, p); Gary Taylor (v,
b); Barbara Dickson (v); Jerry Donahue
(g); Andy Fairweather-Low (g, d); Rab
Noakes (v); Roger Brown (v); Hugh Burns
(g); BJ Cole (sg); Brian Cole (Dobro, sg);
Tommy Eyre (k, brass, a); Barry Hammond
(e); Nigel Jenkins (g); Paul Jones (hm);
Glen LeFleur (pc, d); Vivienne McAuliffe (v);
John McBurnie (v); Mick Moody (g); Hugh
Murphy (v, tabla); Declan O'Doherty (e);
Graham Preskett (fiddle, mandolin, v);
Raphael Ravenscroft (s); Henry Spinetti (d);
Joanna Carlin (v); Willie Ray (acc)

Track listing:
Ark; Baker Street (S); Right Down The
Line (S); City To City (S); Stealin' Town;
Mattie's Rag; Whatever's Written In Your
Heart (S); Home And Dry (S/US); Island;
Waiting For The Day

Running time:
51.12

Current CD:
EMI CDFA3119

Further listening:
Humblebums (1969) and Stealer's Wheel
(1972) demonstrate Rafferty's innate
sense of melody. For less sophisticated
but endearing pre-City To City Rafferty,
try Can I Have My Money Back? (1971).

Further reading:
www.redstone-tech.com/gerry

The Adverts

Crossing The Red Sea With The Adverts

Punk pioneers leave it too late to make their mark on album, but do it anyway.

During the first months of 1977, Gaye Advert – smudged make-up, faded denims, ripped leathers – was a punk icon to rival Johnny Rotten. Stiff Records stuck her on the sleeve of One Chord Wonders, The Adverts' first 45, and lookalikes sprouted everywhere. These were different times, but not that different: the presence of a near-inanimate woman bassist quickly aroused suspicions about the band's musical abilities, doubts that were seemingly confirmed when a ragged version of Bored Teenagers turned up on an EMI various artists live album taped at the Roxy. When Gary Gilmore's Eyes (inspired by a Death Row killer's wish to leave his eyes to science) gatecrashed the UK Top 10 in August, The Adverts were poised to become New Wave heavyweights. Instead, the one-chord wonders soon began to resemble wonders of a less celebrated kind: the one-hit variety.

Had *Crossing The Red Sea* . . . made it into the shops that summer, things would have been different. Instead, it was November before the band committed their well-practised set to tape, having signed to Anchor, a subsidiary of US major ABC. Once within the unpunkish walls of Abbey Road, they recorded and mixed the album in two weeks with a minimum of overdubs. The songs, all staccato rhythms and Glam-like choruses, sparkled with unabashed energy and an endearing air of amateurism. Sophistication was provided by Smith's gallant attempt to wrestle with the dilemmas of the new punk age. It was all here: the untrained resolve (One Chord Wonders, Bored Teenagers), liberation (Bombsite Boy, New Church), confusion (No Time To Be 21) and a healthy dollop of cynicism (Safety In Numbers, The Great British Mistake). In sum it was an exemplary summation of a remarkable few months in rock, but by February 1978, when it eventually appeared, The Adverts were *passé*.

"I was writing conventional songs in an unconventional way," Smith explains, "but there was this dumbing down – Oi! bands and punk copyists who thought that punk rock was only about putting on a leather jacket and playing at 100mph." Caught in the crossfire between a new conservatism and the post-punk experimental scene, and hampered by ABC's decision to shut down Anchor prior to its release, *Red Sea* instead became the Great Lost Punk Album. After a poorly received follow-up, 1979's *Cast Of Thousands*, the group folded.

Record label:
Bright

Produced
by John Leckie.

Recorded
at Abbey Road, London; November 1977.

Released:
February 1978

Chart peaks:
38 (UK) None (US)

Personnel:
TV Smith (v); Gaye Advert (b); Howard Pickup (g); Laurie Driver (d)

Track listing:
One Chord Wonders (S); Bored Teenagers; New Church; On The Roof; Newboys; Bombsite Boy; No Time To Be 21 (S); Safety In Numbers (S); Drowning Men; On Wheels; Great British Mistake. Current CD adds earlier recordings found on two singles: Gary Gilmore's Eyes; Bored Teenagers; Safety In Numbers; We Who Wait – plus two cuts, Gary Gilmore's Eyes; New Day Dawning, taped at the album sessions but dropped from the final running order.

Running time:
32.00

Current CD:
ESMCD 451

Further listening:
The Punk Singles Collection (1997)

Further reading:
MOJO 78

Nick Lowe
Jesus Of Cool

Pub rocker and honorary punk crests the New Wave.

"I was never a punk. I was definitely pub rock. Bit like Paul Weller really." Thus, Nick Lowe, the Renaissance man of the snug bar defines his late '70s creative self. The former bassist with Brinsley Schwarz found himself co-opted by the punk movement when he became the first artsist to release a single on Stiff Records (So It Goes/Heart Of The City)

"Punk was really an attitude thing, and I liked that, but I was raised in playing good." Because he knew his way around a studio but wasn't averse to recording quickly and cheaply, Nick found himself in demand as a producer for arriving artists such as The Damned and Elvis Costello. His bash-it-down philosophy earned him the soubriquet "Basher" Lowe. And he applied all he'd learned from pub to punk when cutting his first solo album. "I deliberately messed things up a bit in the production," he says. "I'd put a tambourine up too loud or mix the vocals too low: generally leave things a bit undercooked, or at least cooked in a ragamuffin style. At the time I was just a frustrated music bloke, there was a lot of horrible prog rock and old singer-songwriter stuff around so anything that changed the status quo was all to the good."

I Love The Sound Of Breaking Glass encapsulates this disillusionment perfectly: "I need the noises of destruction/ When there's nothing new." The brittle piano weirdness that accompanies the loping, funky bass and the laid-back vocal captures the spirit of New Wave better than a hundred rowdier tracks. The rest of the album is a delicious jamboree bag of different "throwaway ideas", in Lowe's typically self-effacing esti-mation. The Beach Boys collide with Billy J Kramer on Little Hitler. No Reason adopts reggae. Shake And Pop, one of several songs to take a lyrical knife to the throat of the music biz, lurches like a drunken Chuck Berry. In complete contrast, Marie Provost is a ghoulish country-rock tale of a dead woman eaten by her dog, while Nutted By Reality begins as disco-funk and then transmogrifies into a Fab Four-styled novelty number.

"We were the first generation for whom music had gone round a full cycle. We could strike poses and play games. I suppose you could call it ironic rock." In the US, where the British title was thought to be a bit racy, they lifted the copy from a British advertisement for the album, calling it *Pure Pop For Now People*.

Record label:
Radar

Produced
by Nick Lowe.

Recorded
at Pathway and Eden Studios.

Released:
February 1978

Chart peaks:
22 (UK) None (US)

Personnel:
Nick Lowe (v, b, g); Dave Edmunds (v,g); Billy Bremner (g); John Turnbull (g); Bob Andrews (k); Andrew Bodnar (b); Norman Watt-Roy (b); Steve Goulding (d); Terry Williams (d); Charlie Charles (d)

Track listing:
Music For Money; I Love The Sounding Of Breaking Glass (S); Little Hitler (S); Shake And Pop; Tonight; So It Goes; No Reason; 36" High; Marie Provost; Nutted By Reality; Heart Of The City

Running time:
33.12

Currently unavailable on CD.

Further listening:
Labour Of Lust (1979); The Impossible Bird (1994)

Further reading:
No Sleep Till Canvey Island: The Great Pub Rock Revolution (Will Birch, 2000) Stiff: The Story Of A Record Label (Bert Muirhead, 1983) available from www.theturkeyzone.co.uk www.dbd.co.uk/nicklowe

Buzzcocks
Another Music In A Different Kitchen

Definitive New Wave pop album: rousing hooks, racetrack riffs, experimental leanings.

Catapulted into action after witnessing an early Sex Pistols performance, this Manchester-based band had virtually crumbled at the start of 1977 after frontman Howard Devoto quit. He'd regarded the release of the self-financed Spiral Scratch EP as the final realisation of an ambition. "Me and Pete decided to carry on," recalls Steve Diggle. "Pete took over the vocals, I switched from bass to guitar and we developed the twin-guitar style that became the classic Buzzcocks sound."

Two singles, Orgasm Addict and What Do I Get?, and a constant round of touring kept the band's profile high throughout 1977 but it was the punk-pop elegance of their spring 1978 debut album that sealed their reputation. "We'd toured that set for months," says Diggle, "so we knew the songs inside out. It was just ready to explode onto the tape." No punk-era album rivals *Another Music* in terms of its boundless effervescence, though Diggle acknowledges that the band's youthful enthusiasm was matched by Martin Rushent's assured approach to the production. "What you hear is what we did," he states, "but he was great to work with. We'd record three backing tracks for each song, choose the best, then add overdubs. Nothing was laboured, and there was none of this, 'We'll get it right in the mix' attitude. It wasn't overproduced yet it still sounded unique."

Being installed in a major-league studio like Olympic also had its advantages. "It was a massive room which enabled us to get a good drum sound. But we'd also bought these tiny H/H combo amps which allowed us to get a good sustain sound without having to crank up the volume levels. They were vital in obtaining that buzzsaw guitar feel."

Essentially a studio translation of the band's live set, *Another Music* was nevertheless easier on the ear than most punk-era albums. Despite being laden with hooks (I Don't Mind was just one of several potential singles), the record also hinted at greater experimentation. Moving Away From The Pulsebeat, which hung on a hypnotic John Maher rhythm and was even circulated to DJs as a club 12-inch, wasn't the only track to betray a Krautrock influence.

Record label:
UA

Produced
by Martin Rushent.

Recorded
at Olympic Studios, Barnes, London;
December 28, 1977–January 31, 1978.

Released:
March 1978

Chart peaks:
15 (UK) None (US)

Personnel:
Pete Shelley (g, v); Steve Diggle (g, v);
John Maher (d); Steve Garvey (b); Doug
Bennett (e)

Track listing:
Fast Cars; No Reply; You Tear Me Up; Get
On Our Own; Love Battery; Sixteen; I
Don't Mind (S); Fiction Romance;
Autonomy; I Need; Moving Away From
The Pulsebeat

Running time:
35.39

Current CD:
724382830924 adds Love Bites (1998)
Real World; Ever Fallen In Love (With
Some One You Shouldn't've?) (S);
Operator's Manual; Nostalgia; Just Lust;
Sixteen Again; Walking Distance; Love Is
Lies; Nothing Left; ESP; Late For The
Train

Further listening:
Singles Going Steady

Further reading:
Buzzcocks: The Complete History
(Independent Music Press, 1995)
www.buzzcocks.com

"Autonomy was inspired by Can. It was my attempt at impersonating a German taking off an Englishman," says Diggle. "The album had lots of influences and directions. People forget that. We weren't just about singles." The first few thousand copies were issued in carrier bags with the record's catalogue number on one side and the word "Product" on the other: a typically witty gesture from one of the most powerful and intelligent bands of the epoch.

Pere Ubu
The Modern Dance

Singular, uncompromising art-punk debut.

Pere Ubu were college drop-outs – five young men who saw no point in "half-assed art" – who came together in Cleveland, Ohio, where a healthy music scene had been thriving since the early 1970s. But it was, to many, the epitome of Nowheresville. They convinced themselves that the weight of history had fallen on their shoulders: they were destined to move rock music forward, but resigned themselves to anonymity. "This is a very, very powerful atmosphere to work in," says David Thomas. "The utter hopelessness of it, in that no one would know, and the knowledge that this was unique."

Tightened up by playing every week at the Pirate's Cove club in the industrial zone known as The Flats, and with two stunning singles (30 Seconds Over Tokyo and Final Solution) under their belt, Pere Ubu went for broke on their debut album. They recorded it in a couple of weeks at the out-of-town Suma Sound, with Ken Hamann, who had been working since the '40s and whose CV included engineering for The Lemon Pipers and Grand Funk Railroad. He captured the band's idiosyncratic creativity at flashpoint and the finished work was as radical as they intended.

Non-Alignment Pact opens with Allen Ravenstine's unpredictable EML synthesizer emitting an uncomfortable, abrasive signal to which guitarist Tom Hermann responds with a Chuck Berry-style riff, a launch pad for a song which marries avant-garde experimentalism with rock'n'roll clout. The urban sprawl of Street Waves is typical, with the group's rolling groove and Thomas' whooping wail of a voice buffeted by toxic waves from the synth, but there are also poignant moments such as the melancholic Chinese Radiation. Critics, especially in the UK, raved. Pere Ubu were tagged "industrial", which was only partly useful; although the music was dark and intense, there was melody and absurdist humour in there too; the group never saw their environment as an industrial wasteland. "Its greatest influence on us was the notion of sound as a powerful, poetic tool," says Thomas. And far from remaining unknown, the group have produced consistently intriguing music for over two decades.

Record label:
Mercury

Produced
by Pere Ubu with Ken Hamann.

Recorded
at Suma, Cleveland, Ohio; November 1977.

Released:
April 1978

Chart peaks:
None (UK) None, (US)

Personnel:
David Thomas (v, musette); Tom Herman (g); Allen Ravenstine (EML syn, s); Tony Maimone (b); Scott Krauss (d); Ken Hamann (e); Paul Hamann, Mike Bishop (ae)

Track listing:
Non-Alignment Pact; The Modern Dance (S/US); Laughing; Street Waves (S/US); Chinese Radiation; Life Stinks; Real World; Over My Head; Sentimental Journey; Humor Me

Running time:
39.15

Current CD:
Cooking Vinyl COOKCD141

Further listening:
The quickly written, but equally impressive follow-up, Dub Housing (1978)

Further reading:
www.dnai.com/~obo/ubu/

Van Halen
Van Halen

Hard-rock colossus blows the competition out of the water.

By 1978, heavy metal already needed re-inventing. Fortunately, Van Halen had the blueprint. Guitarist Eddie was an alchemist, his licks influential, his virtuosity always tempered by *joie de vivre*. Frontman David Lee Roth was his perfect foil; a charismatic peacock in Spandex. After a demo financed by Kiss's Gene Simmons led to a contract with Warner's, staff producer Ted Templeman (Captain Beefheart, Montrose) took charge of the band's debut.

The lean, testosterone and Jack Daniels-fuelled performances featured few overdubs. Ostensibly, Templeman's job was to capture live performances already perfected on the Pasadena/Santa Barbara bar circuit. Most tracks hover around the three-and-a-half-minute mark, evidencing a strong pop sense, bolstered by Eddie and bassist Michael Anthony's falsetto harmonies. Roth – ever the preener – moots his sexual prowess throughout; on his cover of John Brim's Ice Cream Man, you sense the "push-ups" he's offering have little to do with dairy produce.

In a 1996 interview with Smashing Pumpkins' Billy Corgan, Eddie confided that the instrumental showpiece Eruption was an afterthought recorded in one pass at Templeman's suggestion. "And there's a mistake at the top end of it," he added. "To this day, whenever I hear it, I always think, Man, I could've played it better."

It was a flaw nobody else noticed, and Eddie – then aged 22 – dominated this record. Like Jimmy Page, he had a keen appreciation of the hook riff, evident herein a startling reworking of The Kinks' You Really Got Me, and his own Ain't Talking 'Bout Love. Two decades later, Apollo 440 would pay homage, pairing the latter song's intro with a drum'n'bass loop on Ain't Talkin' 'Bout Dub. When Van Halen toured with Black Sabbath after this album's release, the Brummie's leaden riffs suddenly seemed *passé*, and a coup by the support act was widely reported. Soon, Los Angeles would spawn a host of copycat bands, but none of them had Eddie's talent or Roth's easy wit. *Van Halen* eventually sold over six million copies.

Record label:
Warner Brothers

Produced
by Ted Templeman.

Recorded
at Sunset Sound Recorders, Hollywood; 1977.

Released:
April 1978

Chart peaks:
34 (UK) 19 (US)

Personnel:
David Lee Roth (v); Edward Van Halen (g); Michael Anthony (b); Alex Van Halen (d); Don Landee (e)

Track listing:
Runnin' With The Devil (S); Eruption; You Really Got Me (S); Ain't Talkin' 'Bout Love (S/US); I'm The One; Jamie's Cryin'; Atomic Punk; Feel Your Love Tonight; Little Dreamer; Ice Cream Man; On Fire

Running time:
35.34

Current CD:
7599273202

Further listening:
Van Halen II (1979)

Further reading:
Crazy From The Heat (David Lee Roth, 1998) www.van-halen.com

Kraftwerk
The Man-Machine

The Düsseldorf Dynamos add a sardonic political overview to their romantic-realist style.

*T*he *Man-Machine* was the album which ushered in the age of electronic pop, clearing the ground for everyone from The Human League and Depeche Mode to Daft Punk and Pole. Like its predecessor *Trans-Europe Express*, it was another concept album, offering a sly, ambiguous commentary on the relationship of man and machine, and the dehumanisation of man in industrial society. The group were intrigued, for instance, to learn that the Russian word for "worker" is "robotnick", although in interviews Ralf Hütter expressed an altogether more sanguine attitude to the man-machine interface.

"The dynamism of the machines, the 'soul' of the machines, has always been a part of our music," he claimed. "We are playing the machines, the machines play us, it is really the exchange and friendship we have with the musical machines which make us build a new music."

The marshalling, in revolutionary red and black, of the dynamic diagonals of the Russian constructivist El Lissitzky for the album's cover art cleverly conveyed the paradoxical Utopian promise and totalitarian threat of the early 20th-century modernist notion of "machine art" which Kraftwerk were effectively resurrecting. The album's pristine, machine-tooled presentation of tracks with titles like Neon Lights, Spacelab, The Robots and (most pertinently) Metropolis further drove home its theme of antique modernity: these are all dated, nostalgic visions of the future, polished and shiny with the awed glow of conviction, before the notion of modernism began to rust. Even the album's hit single The Model, ostensibly a hymn to unattainable beauty, deals with a woman determined to present herself to the world as object rather than subject, a malleable robot to dress up in our desires.

The music itself was sleeker and more gracefully minimal than before, while the rhythm tracks were so infectious that Whitfield Records' Leanard Jackson, flown in from LA to mix some of the tracks, was surprised to find himself dealing with four white Germans, rather than the black musicians he imagined had laid down the grooves. Derived from hours of improvisation, the tunes were slowly chipped into shape by the group – literally, "machined" until they gleamed – while a new order of fastidious complexity was applied to the hypnotic

Record label:
Capitol

Produced
by Ralf Hütter and Florian Schneider.

Recorded
at Kling Klang Studio, Düsseldorf;
1977–78.

Released:
May 1978

Chart peaks:
9 (UK) None (US)

Personnel:
Ralf Hütter (v, electronics); Florian Schneider (v, electronics); Karl Bartos (electronic pc); Wolfgang Flur (electronic pc); Joschko Rudas, Leanard Jackson (e)

Track listing:
The Robots (S); Spacelab (S); Metropolis; The Model (S); Neon Lights (S); The Man-Machine.

Running time:
36.10

Current CD:
CAO460392

Further listening:
The preceding Trans-Europe Express (1977) and ensuing Computer World (1981) feature the mature Kraftwerk operating on a plateau rarely approached by other electronica acts. The earlier Autobahn (1974) and Radioactivity (1975) are like preparatory sketches, while their earliest albums are more experimental and improvisatory. The later remix album The Mix (1991) re-tools their hits with new rhythmic undercarriage.

Further reading:
MOJO 41; Kraftwerk: Man, Machine And Music (Pascal Bussy 1997); Kraftwerk:

From Düsseldorf To The Future (With
Love) (Tim Barr, 1998)
www.kraftwerk.com

electronic percussion: a track like the nine-minute Neon Lights
might seem relentlessly repetitive on first listen, but deeper
attention reveals that each of the little drum fills which punctu-
ates its progress is different from the rest.

Provisionally entitled *Dynamo*, the album went on to sell
over 100,000 copies in the UK and 200,000 in France, in the
process becoming a much-beloved cornerstone of electronic
pop.

Steve Reich
Music For 18 Musicians

American composer creates his most important crossover work.

Ask any minimalist composer about their work and the first thing they'll do is deny any allegiance to the M word. Steve Reich is no exception. He asserts that it was simply a convenient way of describing composers who, in the '60s, broke away from the rigorous complexity of modern classical composition – Reich himself, Philip Glass and Terry Riley, for example. Early on, Reich's main interests were phase and rhythm. On Come Out, two identical tapes of speech were run slightly out of phase, producing a hallucinatory effect.

A former jazz drummer, Reich later studied percussion in Ghana, and Balinese gamelan music in the US. Both styles inform works like *Drumming*. He also enjoyed the repetition and clarity of line in everything from Bach to Junior Walker's Shotgun. In 1973, Reich composed the mind-boggling sonic mesh of Six Pianos and the gamelan-like Music For Mallet Instruments, Voices And Organ. The following year, work began on what was to become his best-known instrumental work, *Music For 18 Musicians*. A composition of 12 parts all played along a basic rhythmic pulse, each discrete part, or cell, gradually mutating via augmentation. What looks dry and academic on paper is in fact sublime, with moments of stunning beauty – particularly in the multiple piano sections, and the huge arcs of bass clarinets and voices that crop up as a recurring motif.

It has become immensely influential; its rippling waveforms have found their way into DJ sets, and Reich's signature is heard on music produced by Tortoise, Pan Sonic, Alec Empire, The Orb, Aphex Twin and particularly German techno of the early '90s – a situation the composer is delighted with. "Bach and other baroque composers were writing dance forms; sarabands and gavottes that derived from the street," he notes. "This is the state of affairs until we get to Schoenberg who builds a wall between serious music and the trash out there in the street. That is totally artificial and out of kilter with the history of Western music. Now, if we can talk about what the techno groups are doing, or what they've learned from my music, I can feel inside my heart: Gee, that's great. That's the way it should be."

Record label:
ECM

Produced
by Rudolph Werner.

Exact recording
location and date unknown.

Released:
spring 1978

Chart peaks:
None (UK) None (US)

Personnel:
Shem Guibbory (vn); Ken Ishii (c); Elizabeth Arnold (v); Rebecca Armstrong (v); Pamela Fraley (v); Nurit Tilles (p); Larry Karush (p, maraccas); Gary Schall (marimba, maraccas); Bob Becker (marimba, xylpohone); Russ Hartenberger (marimba, xylophone); James Preiss (metallophone, p); Steve Chambers (p); Steve Reich (p, marimba); David Van Tieghem (marimba, xylophone, p); Glen Velez (marimba, xylophone); Virgil Blackwell (clarinet, bass clarinet); Richard Cohen (clarinet, bass clarinet); Jay Clayton (v, p); Klaus Hiemann (e)

Track listing:
Pulse; Sections I-X; Pulse

Running time:
56.31

Current CD:
8214172

Further listening:
Octet/Music For A Large Ensemble/Violin Phase (1980) took the Music For 18 Musicians style to another level of sophistication.

Further reading:
www.slis.keio.ac.jp/~ohba/Reich/srindex.html

Willie Nelson
Stardust

At 55, the touchstone country songwriter goes Broadway and Hollywood with smash-hit results.

William Nelson was the real thing. As a kid he worked in the cottonfields near his hometown, Abbott, Texas, for $3 a day. But that didn't make him a purist. Having toiled away for years as a songwriter without himself becoming a star performer, in the early '70s he grew his hair, took to hippy hats, switched from booze to hash – and began to pick the rhinestones off the Nashville sound. In 1975, with his CBS debut *Red Headed Stranger* he defied accepted practice by insisting on creative control, secured by self-production. Commercial fears were allayed when it headed for a million sales at a time when "country hit" meant around 200,000. But label misgivings revived when he announced *Stardust* as a collection of standards drawn from writers like Hoagy Carmichael (the title track and Georgia On My Mind), Irving Berlin (Blue Skies) and the Gershwins (Someone To Watch Over Me). Columbia said he was crazy; the album wasn't country. Nelson said: "Who cares?"

He explained that, as a poor boy, radio had provided his musical education. Frank Sinatra was his favourite singer. The *Stardust* idea crystallised when Bing Crosby died in October 1977. "It was a big gamble," he acknowledged. "Until I met Booker [T Jones, of the MGs, producer, on a beach in Los Angeles] I wasn't sure how well I could do it because of my limited musical ability. These are complicated songs. They have a lot of chords in them." But with the Stax maestro arranging sparse, though warm, settings – a touch of piano, a sliver of strings – Nelson delivered the lovely essence of these honoured songs. Like Carmichael himself or Jimmy Durante, he never seemed much of a singer. But consider the aching gentleness of Moonlight In Vermont or the restrained fervour of Someone To Watch Over Me; it turns out that he hits the notes and jockeys the beat so fluently that performance becomes intimate conversation. Atlantic Records founder Jerry Wexler, who worked regularly with Aretha Franklin, wrote that Nelson, whom he produced a couple of times, shared Sinatra's "gift for incredible vocal *rubato* – prolonging one note, cutting short another, swinging with an elastic sense of time that only the finest jazz singers understand".

Stardust stayed in the American Top 200 for over two years, sold four million and, commercially, set country on the road to Garth Brooks.

Record label:
CBS

Produced
by Booker T Jones.

Recorded
at Emmylou Harris's house, southern California, on The Enactron Truck, early 1978.

Released:
June 1978

Chart peaks:
None (UK) 30 (US)

Personnel:
Willie Nelson (v, g); Bobbie Nelson (p); Paul English (d); Rex Ludwig (d); Jody Payne (g); Bee Spears (b); Chris Ethridge (b); Mickey Raphael (hm); Booker T Jones (o, p); Bradley Hartman, Donivan Cowart (e)

Track listing:
Stardust; Georgia On My Mind; Blue Skies; All Of Me; Unchained Melody; September Song; On The Sunny Side Of The Street; Moonlight In Vermont; Don't Get Around Much Anymore; Someone To Watch Over Me

Running time:
37.09

Current CD:
4952452, adds: Scarlet Ribbons; I Can See Clearly Now

Further listening:
Red Headed Stranger (1975), Nelson's country groundbreaker

Further reading:
MOJO 14; Heart Worn Memories: A Daughter's Personal Biography Of Willie Nelson (Susie Nelson, 1987); Willie Nelson Sings America (Stephen Opdyke et al, 1998); www.willienelson.com

Bruce Springsteen
Darkness On The Edge Of Town

After suing his manager, Springsteen rages. The cars are metaphors, the darkness is real.

S talled for more than a year by a legal wrangle with manager Mike Appel, Springsteen achieved severance on May 28, 1977. Two days later, with the E Street Band, he walked into Atlantic Studios, New York, to start recording his fourth album. Much changed, he was determined to take total control of his career. At the same time, with *Born To Run*'s co-producer, Ivy League rock critic Jon Landau, becoming both a close friend and his new manager, Springsteen embraced a previously alien world of cultural experience, beginning with old movies. John Ford's The Grapes Of Wrath and various *films noirs*, American and French, gave him a political and emotional backdrop for his stories about "people who are going from nowhere to nowhere". At 28, in Promised Land, he sang, "Mister, I ain't a boy, no, I'm a man." Frustration off the leash, he worked fast, recording 16 songs, choosing 10.

While love and sex still seethed in his lyrics, now he acknowledged older generations too, with profound feeling for their hard lives – especially in Factory's portrait of an archetypal worker representing his own father's wasted-life bitterness. "Darkness" loomed everywhere. Springsteen noted that because Clarence Clemons' sax style was too "in-your-face" for this setting, he was given less to do this time. Guitar stood in because "it has a little more distance". But the sound of *Darkness On The Edge Of Town* is at once sombre *and* wild.

Angry rather than celebratory, it sold much less well than its predecessor. Yet it deepened Springsteen's appeal. There are conspicuously great songs: just soak in the orgasmic rush of Candy's Room followed by the slow, fathomless grief of Racing In The Streets. But *Darkness On The Edge Of Town* also touches inexplicable emotions through visceral detail, like the measured melancholy tread of Roy Bittan's piano and Springsteen's own frantic high harmonies which run almost subliminally through most tracks as if he had an anxiety-wracked second self in the studio with him. Writing and performing, he reflected on his family and their hard, poor lives as never before.

"I see my sister and her husband," he said. "These are people, you can see something in their eyes. I asked my sister, What do you do for fun? I don't have any fun, she says. She wasn't kidding." Which is part of the reason why, in a more upbeat contemporary reflection on the meaning of rock'n'roll, he concluded, "The whole idea is to deliver what money can't buy."

Record label:
CBS

Produced
by Jon Landau and Bruce Springsteen.

Recorded
at The Record Plant, New York;
July–December 1977.

Released:
June 1978

Chart peaks:
16 (UK) 5 (US)

Personnel:
Bruce Springsteen (v, g, hm); Clarence Clemons (s, pc); Danny Federici (o); Roy Bittan (p); Garry Tallent (bs); Steve Van Zandt (g); Max Weinberg (d); Jimmy Iovine (e)

Track listing:
Badlands (S); Adam Raised A Cain; Something In The Night; Candy's Room; Racing In The Street; The Promised Land (S); Factory; Streets Of Fire; Prove It All Night; Darkness On The Edge Of Town

Running time:
42.31

Current CD:
CD86061

Further listening:
The familial darkness between the rock'n'roll hollering on The River, then utter societal gloom descends with the solo Nebraska. Born In The USA (1984) and Tunnel Of Love (1987)

Further reading:
MOJO 17, 62; Born To Run: The Bruce Springsteen Story (Dave Marsh, 1979); www.backstreets.com (US)

Talking Heads
More Songs About Buildings And Food

Itchy agit-pop angst meets Egghead.

The comparative commercial failure of Talking Heads' first album led the group's mentors to the conclusion that a less traditional production was needed to maximise the creative tension between pop-minded bassist Tina Weymouth and art-house eccentric David Byrne. They'd signed to Sire for big bucks and, as yet, they were far away from justifying the tireless press acclaim. Byrne's agit-pop storytelling had attracted an intelligent cult following and his tales of everyday tedium, crazed psychopaths and the vagaries of the business world had indicated that Talking Heads were on the verge of something quite spectacular. But if Byrne was to realise his vision of a shallow Generation X-styled America, juiced with the small-town weirdness of a David Lynch film, it wouldn't be easy.

Neither backdrop at that point even existed. Meanwhile, in a parallel universe, former Roxy Music man Brian Eno had already struggled over the same musical juxtaposition on his solo albums *Here Come The Warm Jets* and *Taking Tiger Mountain*. By '78 he'd given up on clever pop and gone ambient but he had an armoury of production techniques and a penchant for clipped rhythmic guitar and dubbed percussion that fully complemented Byrne's off-kilter worldview.

To satisfy the collision of well-grooved soul and their sense of technocratic removal, Talking Heads were wrapped in a cocoon of phased effects, looped sounds and echoey snare snaps. It was the perfect backdrop for Byrne's jerky dance and it left enough space for the rest of the group to play like a hothoused pick-up band. Even the album's cover of Al Green's Take Me To The River, which was a minor hit, managed to process a classic slice of Gospel hyperventilation into a sterilised laboratory-controlled groove. *More Songs About Buildings And Food* checks out the world from a safe distance, a sensation fully realised on the closing cut, The Big Country in which the Byrne acts like the pilot of a space capsule orbiting his former world. It's like an album of intimate and very personal songs but heard through Clingfilm.

It was a success but the delicate Weymouth/Byrne axis was rattled by the arrival of Eno. "They're like two 14-year-old boys making an impression on each other," Weymouth moaned. "By the time they finished working together for three months, they were dressing like one another... I can see them when they're 80 and all alone. There'll be David Bowie, David Byrne and Brian Eno, and they'll just talk to each other." The triad lasted one more album.

Record label:
Sire

Produced
by Brian Eno and Talking Heads.

Recorded
at Compass Point, New Providence, The Bahamas; March–April 1978.

Released:
July 1978

Chart peaks:
21 (UK) 29 (US)

Personnel:
David Byrne (v, g, pc); Chris Frantz (d, pc); Jerry Harrison (o, p, syn, g, bv); Tina Weymouth (b); Brian Eno (syn, g, pc, bv); Tina And The Typing Pool (bv on The Good Thing)

Track listing:
Thank You For Sending Me An Angel; With Our Love; The Good Thing; Warning Sign; The Girls Want To Be With The Girls; Found A Job; Artists Only; I'm Not In Love; Stay Hungry; Take Me To The River (S); The Big Country

Running time:
41.48

Current CD:
7599274252

Further listening:
The previous September's Talking Head '77 sets out Byrne's song style and the following Fear Of Music (1979) and Remain In Light (1980) refine it and develop the Eno-patented production techniques.

Further reading:
www.talking-heads.net What The Songs Look Like: The Illustrated Talking Heads (David Byrne and Frank Olinsky, 1987)

Blondie
Parallel Lines

Skinny-tied new Yorkers combine punk, New Wave and disco to world-beating effect.

Despite being the last act out of the original New York punk scene to be offered a record deal, the blonde ambition of ex-Playboy Bunny girl Debbie Harry and her mop-topped male colleagues paid off, when *Parallel Lines* became such a critical and commercial success that, by early 1979, Blondie had apparently become the biggest band on the planet.

Despite an early reputation as a bit of a novelty act (fellow CBGB act Patti Smith told them to "get the fuck out of rock'n'roll"), UK hits Denis and (I'm Always Touched By Your) Presence Dear (from *Plastic Letters*) showed that a bunch of punks written off in their own city could cross over into the uncertain arena of pop.

Mike "if you can't make hit singles, go chop meat somewhere" Chapman of the infamous Chinnichap production line (Sweet, Smokie, Suzi Quatro, Mud, Racey) was a risky choice for the producer's chair. But the band had a taste for more commercial success.

When Chapman listened to their demos for the album, he was rather taken with something called The Disco Song, a tune that had been skulking in their set since 1975 but hadn't made the cut on either their debut or *Plastic Letters*. It was played apologetically in a *faux*-reggae rhythm, but Chapman saw its potential and persuaded them to do it with a full-on funk swagger. The band really went for it, laying down a storming groove with a Roland Rhythm Machine and, according to Stein, "a bass-line copped from Goldfinger". They retitled the result Heart Of Glass.

"We didn't expect the song to be that big," Stein recalls. (This is borne out by the fact that it's buried at track four, side two on the original LP.) "[It was] a novelty item to put more diversity into the record. But it [turned out to be] a mark in history. It brought black and white music together. We weren't thinking about selling out, we were thinking about Kraftwerk and Eurodisco."

Chapman taught Blondie the importance of tightening arrangements and honing the backing tracks to a glossy perfection. Critic Lester Bangs enthused. "The thing that makes *Parallel Lines* so assuredly avant-garde is precisely that it's so airtight and multiple-choice. This is it. The masterpiece."

Record label:
Chrysalis

Produced
by Mike Chapman.

Recorded
at the Record Plant, New York; June–July 1978.

Released:
September 1978

Chart peaks:
1 (UK) 6 (US)

Personnel:
Jimmy Destri (k); Frank Infante (g); Chris Stein (g); Nigel Harrison (b); Clem Burke (d); Deborah Harry (v); Pete Coleman (e)

Track listing:
Hanging On The Telephone (S); One Way Or Another (S/US); Picture This (S); Fade Away And Radiate; Pretty Baby; I Know But I Don't Know; 11:59; Will Anything Happen?; Sunday Girl (S); Heart Of Glass (S); I'm Gonna Love You Too (S/US); Just Go Away

Running time:
41.26

Current CD:
CCD1192

Further listening:
Eat To The Beat (1979); The Platinum Collection (1994) collects both sides of every Blondie single up to 1982, plus a handful of interesting early demos. Deborah Harry's Def, Dumb And Blonde (1989), which saw her reunited with Mike Chapman, is the sharpest of her solo albums.

Further Reading:
MOJO 63; Making Tracks: The Rise Of Blondie (Debbie Harry, Chris Stein and Victor Bockris, 1998); www.blondie.ausbone.net

From the gutsy Hanging On The Telephone to the luscious Sunday Girl – a paean to Debbie's pet moggy – the success of *Parallel Lines* is down to a mixture of sweet '60s girl-group harmonies and edgy New Wave arrangements. It also spawned some enduring candy-coated punk-pop anthems in Pretty Baby, Fade Away And Radiate (featuring guitar wizard Robert Fripp) and 11:59, which many of their contemporaries would have given their skinny ties to use as singles.

Wire

Chairs Missing

Raising the stakes in the UK post-punk scene.

If punk came as a shock, Wire were more shocking still.
Although they cut their teeth playing at the the (in)famous
Roxy in London's Covent Garden, they shared as many differences as affinities with the rest of that scene. Initially the band
refused to release singles, and while their 21-song, 1977 debut
Pink Flag may have been the most brutally pared-down album of
the era, it was released on Harvest courtesy of Nick Mobbs,
who had also signed Pink Floyd to the label. And, horror,
guitarist Bruce Gilbert was already over 30.

Gilbert admits the group learnt to play on *Pink Flag*, but
they were fast learners – halfway through that album they were
already experimenting in the studio and writing new songs. "A
lot of material didn't survive the process of touring and the
process of starting to record *Chairs Missing*," he says. "We were
moving so quickly that things came and went in the blink of an
eye."

By the time they were set to record the album, virtually
all generic New Wave moves had been left behind. Gilbert: "We
could go through lots of variations on themes and experiment
with a confidence that, with a bit of practice, any structures that
were unorthodox or slightly unusual we would eventually be
able to handle." From the staccato chords of opener Practice
Makes Perfect onwards, there was a new-found sense of
dynamics and syncopation taking over from their former
straight-ahead rigidity, with producer Mike Thorne's keyboards
adding new textures. The ferocious Mercy clocked in at nearly
six minutes, while songs like Marooned showed a more reflective approach. As an example of the band's often impenetrable
humour, on Outdoor Miner they set a lyric about entomology
to a gorgeous pop tune.

The album was well-received, apart from the odd sneer
that it carried a Syd Barrett influence – a view Gilbert refutes
totally. *Chairs Missing* is direct, powerful and bursting with ideas,
and catches a group on the cusp of a journey that was to see
them constantly move on throughout their on/off, 20-year
course. Meanwhile, their music has exerted a widespread
influence – not least on '90s Britpop.

Record label:
Harvest

Produced
by Mike Thorne.

Recorded
at Advision Studios; summer 1978.

Released:
September 1978

Chart peaks:
48 (UK) None (US)

Personnel:
Colin Newman (v, g); BC Gilbert (g);
Graham Lewis (b, v); Robert Gotobed (d);
Mike Thorne (k, syn); Kate Lukas (flutes);
Paul Hardiman (e)

Track listing:
Practice Makes Perfect; French Film
Blurred; Another The Letter; Men 2nd;
Marooned; Sand In My Joints; Being
Sucked In Again; Heartbeat; Mercy;
Outdoor Miner; I Am The Fly (S/UK); I
Feel Mysterious Today; From The Nursery;
Used To; Too Late

Running time:
42.20

Current CD:
CDGO2065

Further listening:
Pink Flag (1977); 154 (1979); Behind
The Curtain (1994), a collection of live
tracks and early demos circa 1977–1978

Further reading:
Wire: Everybody Loves A History (Kevin S
Eden, 1991)

The Police
Outlandos D'Amour

Unlikely stadium rock band's debut.

It was proof of Miles Copeland's managerial skill that he managed to sell The Police to A&M as a punk group. They were signed on March 22, 1978 after a gig at London's Nashville Rooms, and began a run of underachievement and ill-advised side projects: Roxanne flopped in April, and the group went their separate ways during the summer – Sting spent six weeks filming Quadrophenia, while Stewart Copeland (former drummer with Curved Air) recorded two bizarre singles under the pseudonym Klark Kent.

Their debut album was largely in the can, having been worked on since January at Surrey Sound, a rather shabby establishment in the unlikely environs of Leatherhead (since hugely upgraded): "It was a cruddy, funky place with egg cartons on the wall," remembered Sting. Copeland Sr had persuaded the Gray brothers to assist the band with its recording for little more than £1,500, and they also found themselves having to mediate with a group who were clearly not getting on (Mike Noble, then an A&R man for A&M, claims he was attracted to the band by "the incredible tension between Sting and Stewart – they loathed each other"). One incident flared up around Andy Summers' difficulty getting to grips with the guitar part for Hole In My Life. Aware that Sting fancied himself as a guitar player, he tetchily suggested that he play it himself. Sting refused, only to find Copeland offering his services.

The studio, though dingy, had its advantages – chiefly, a large sloping roof that allowed Copeland to creatively vary his drum sound. This was just one of the benefits arising from the trio's musical experience, reflected in an album which – for all the energised charge of Next To You, Peanuts and Truth Hits Everybody – had a far more varied palette than most of the New Wave dreck appearing at the time. In that sense, *Outlandos D'Amour* was instrumental in proving that virtuosic rock had a post-punk future. Most crucial of all was The Police's grasp of reggae.

"Bob Marley was the link," said Sting. "Roxanne has a real Bob Marley feel. He's half-white, so he's sort of a cultural go-between, a cornerstone. Once you get past Marley, you can get past the rest of reggae and understand it more clearly." After moderate success in America, a re-released Roxanne reached Number 12 in the UK in April 1979, and *Outlandos* was belatedly given its commercial just desserts.

Record label:
A&M

Produced
by The Police.

Recorded
at Surrey Sound Studios, Leatherhead; January–August 1978.

Released:
October 1978

Chart peaks:
6 (UK) 23 (US)

Personnel:
Sting (b, v), Andy Summers (g, v); Stewart Copeland (d, v); Nigel Gray, Chris Gray (e)

Track listing:
Next To You; So Lonely (S); Roxanne (S); Hole In My Life; Peanuts; Can't Stand Losing You (S); Truth Hits Everybody; Born In The '50s; Be My Girl – Sally; Masoko Tanga

Running time:
38.50

Current CD:
CDMID126

Further listening:
A&M box set, Message In A Box (1993)

Further reading:
Sting: Demolition Man (Christopher Sandford, 1998); www.stingchronicity.co.uk

Siouxsie And The Banshees
The Scream

Fiercely individualistic punks arrived late with debut album; it still sounded way ahead of its time.

Starting life as suburban Sex Pistols' acolytes dressed in fetish clothing, Sioux and Steve Severin – with guitarist Marco Pirroni and Sid Vicious on drums – improvised a debut at the 100 Club in September 1976.

Over the next 18 months, a new-look Banshees stabilised around a set of songs inspired by the Velvet Underground's atonality and Nico's bellow, a Bowie-like misanthropy and a "pure punk" antipathy towards 12-bar rock'n'roll. The mystique piled up, hastened by two extraordinary sessions for John Peel, some uncompromising interviews and a rash of "Sign The Banshees" graffiti daubed on record company walls.

"We hyped it up a lot," admits Steve Severin, "but most A&R men were too scared to come and see us because most of our shows erupted into violence. Then, out of the blue, we wrote Hong Kong Garden."

Polydor won the battle for the band's signature and, in August 1978, released Hong Kong Garden on 45. That same month, the Banshees entered RAK to record an album with rookie producer Steve Lillywhite. Severin: "We went into the sessions with a sense of relief, an arrogance that thrived on the burden of expectation, and a lot of frustration. We had this incredible sense of striving for the unattainable and we trusted no one. And we were nervous that Lillywhite would dilute the sound. He didn't understand the 'attitude' but in the end it didn't really matter – everything was in the performances."

"The album was written before going into the studio," Sioux recalls. "We had a clear idea of the sound we wanted and our set-up was very simple. All the tracks were played live with overdubs added later."

Severin adds: "Years of festering ideas and minutes of technique! Everything was bold, strong strokes. We threw away the clichés and patched together what was left."

Angular, artful and seething with contempt, *The Scream* took punk's anti-rock'n'roll rhetoric seriously: psychological breakdown (Jigsaw Feeling, Suburban Relapse), disease (Nicotine Stain) and Charles Manson (Helter Skelter) enhanced the dystopian mood. "I still think the segue from Pure into Jigsaw Feeling is one of rock's scariest moments," maintains Severin. "Here's our calling card. Get out of that!"

Record label:
Polydor

Produced
by Steve Lillywhite & Siouxsie And The Banshees

Recorded
at RAK, London, mixed at De Lane Lea, London, August 1978

Release date:
October 1978

Chart peaks:
12 (UK) None (US)

Personnel:
Siouxsie Sioux (v), John McKay (g), Steven Severin (b), Kenny Morris (d).

Track listing:
Pure; Jigsaw Feeling; Overground; Carcass; Helter Skelter; Mirage; Metal Postcard (Mittagessen); Nicotine Stain; Suburban Relapse; Switch

Running time:
38:26

Current CD:
839 008-2

Further listening:
The funereal follow-up, Join Hands (1979), inspired a host of gothic impersonators, none of whom matched the Banshees' dazzling run of singles, compiled on two collections, Once Upon A Time and Twice Upon A Time.

Further reading:
Entranced: The Siouxsie and The Banshees Story (Brian Johns, 1988).
www.vamp.org/Siouxsie/

Blame it on suburbia, "that wonderful land of manicured lies and stifling conformity", says Sioux who, like Severin, was living in Bromley at the time. "Where else do you find such fertile breeding grounds for disparate malcontents?"

The Jam
All Mod Cons

The Jam establish themselves as the class of '76's most popular graduates.

The first months of 1978 were hardly happy for The Jam. Their second album, *This Is The Modern World*, had been released in November 1977 to a barrage of flak, and the criticism impacted on Paul Weller's nerve. He sought comfort in his new relationship with Gill Price – but love seemed to dim his muse yet further. In February 1978, The Jam released the single News Of The World, an alarmingly weak Bruce Foxton song that betrayed the fact that the group were stalling. To cap it all, the following month saw them packed off on a US tour with Blue Öyster Cult. They returned to the UK to begin work on a third album in an understandably miserable state, and pre-production work in a country house found them atrophying further.

Their mentor, Polydor A&R man Chris Parry, heard the new material and passed judgement. "This is shit," he told his charges. Paul Weller took swift action, moving back in with his parents in Woking and re-immersing himself in some of his favourite music – The Kinks in particular. "There was a feeling we were being written off," he says now. "That pressured me into writing *All Mod Cons*. It was me proving myself."

By June, The Jam had started to rally. The scabrous Billy Hunt was recorded as their next single – but on the advice of producer/impresario Mickie Most, they instead released their reading of Ray Davies' David Watts (intended as a double A-side with A Bomb In Wardour Street, but favoured by radio). It reacquainted the trio with the charts, if hardly serving notice of a creative renaissance. Back in the studio, though, a triumph was taking shape: sharp, pop-minded but admirably innovative. "I'd like to be able to write minute-and-a-half, two-minute classics," Weller had told the NME. "If I could write a mini-opera in 1.5 minutes, that'd be great. I had an idea to write a three-minute song, where you'd got about 15 different tunes in one song. I'd just like to experiment. I've got loads of ideas." His aspirations were smeared all over the album: in the layered, effects-laden coda of In The Crowd, the shimmering ballad Fly, The Place I Love – one of Weller's best-ever compositions – and the single that proved that The Jam were now on era-defining form. Down In The Tube Station At Midnight was released on October 6, 1978 to a fiercely appreciative response. *All Mod Cons* appeared a month later, and still stands as The Jam's finest half-hour.

Record label:
Polydor

Produced
by Vic Coppersmith-Heaven.

Recorded
at RAK Studios, London; May–September 1978.

Released:
November 3, 1978

Chart peaks:
6 (UK) None (US)

Personnel:
Paul Weller (v, g, p, hm); Bruce Foxton (b, v); Rick Buckler (d, pc); Greg Jackman, Roger Bechirian (e); Chris Parry (associate producer)

Track listing:
All Mod Cons; To Be Someone (Didn't We Have A Nice Time); Mr. Clean; David Watts (S); English Rose; In The Crowd; Billy Hunt; It's Too Bad; Fly; The Place I Love; 'A' Bomb In Wardour Street (S); Down In The Tube Station At Midnight (S)

Running time:
38.20

Current CD:
537 419-2

Further listening:
In The City (1977); Sound Affects (1980)

Further reading:
A Beat Concerto (Paolo Hewitt, 1996)

X-Ray Spex
Germ Free Adolescents

Pointed social critique wrapped up in punky, three-minute pop.

There was a moment in the early summer of 1978 when X-Ray Spex seemed to be the punk "band most likely to". Three singles, each more accomplished and successful than the last, had taken the band from Roxy Club makeweights to Top Of The Pops regulars. And in brace-wearing Poly Styrene, dressed in brightly coloured thrift-shop chic, they featured one of the era's more engaging anti-stars. By the following spring, it had all gone wrong. All the wit with which Poly had attacked consumerism and other contemporary ills had vanished and, unable to divorce art from commerce, she quit rock'n'roll for Krishna.

It was a far cry from the couldn't-care-less demeanour of her early performances when, with schoolgirl sax-player Lora Logic in tow, Poly and X-Ray Spex provided welcome relief from the pageant of Pistols imitators at the Roxy early in 1977. By the summer, the group had enough material for an album and, after a bidding war, signed to Virgin who released the debut 45, Oh Bondage Up Yours. One of the year's more startling singles, it was punk minimalism topped with a vocal to match the singer's idiosyncratic visual appeal. But the group were dropped, re-emerging on EMI who, rather appropriately, given Poly's lyrical concerns, offered an advertising budget that exceeded the band's advance. April 1978's The Day The World Turned Day-Glo, featuring a brass section, hinted at a growing sophistication and it worked. Identity gave the band a second Top 30 hit that summer, but by then Poly was suffering her own personality crisis.

"Get rid of the synthetic life," she advised the nation's youth through the pages of the Daily Mirror. "Go back and be natural." By the time the band's only album appeared, in November, Poly had grown bored of punk, pop and fame. Asked about the direction of her new music in the television documentary Who Is Poly Styrene?, she shrugged: "Maybe it'll turn into the sound of a Hoover."

Weeks later, she'd packed it in, leaving X-Ray Spex with a brief if memorable legacy. Lyrics like "I know I'm artificial/But don't put the blame on me/I was reared with appliances in a consumer society," epitomised Poly's dichotomy: part-fury, part-resignation, X-Ray Spex blew hot and cold between kitsch and deeper knowledge.

Record label:
Virgin

Produced
by Falcon Stuart.

Recorded
at Essex Studios. 1978

Released:
November 1978

Chart peaks:
30 (UK) None (US)

Personnel:
Poly Styrene (v); Jak Airport (g); Paul Dean (b); Rudi Thompson (s); B.P. Hurding (d); John Mackenzie Burns (e); Andy Pearce (ae)

Track listing:
The Day The World Turned Day-Glo (S); Obsessed With You; Genetic Engineering; Identity (S); I Live Off You; Germfree Adolescents (S); Art-I-Ficial; Let's Submerge; Warrior In Woolworths; I Am A Poseur; I Can't Do Anything; Highly Imflammable (S); Age; Plastic Bag; I Am A Cliché

Running time:
35.46

Current CD:
1704618132 adds: Oh Bondage Up Yours! (S)

Further listening:
None of Poly's subsequent solo albums compare to this.

Further reading:
www.comnet.ca/~rina/xrayspex.html

Marvin Gaye
Here, My Dear

Marvin's raw soul-opera memoir. Might be his very best work.

For too many years the reputation of *Here, My Dear* rested on its stature as one of the most poisonous alimony settlements of the 20th century and it had been dismissed as an impenetrable, self-indulgent mess. But, in recent years, it has dawned on fans that in its heartbreaking honesty usually heard only in m'learned friends' chambers, this double album describes love, its decline and a couple's painful separation with an intensity unique in pop and in a complex musical setting that reveals new corners with every listen.

Marvin was 20 when he married 37-year-old Anna Gordy, one of Motown-boss Berry Gordy's three sisters. She became a source of inspiration and support to him from Pride And Joy through Stubborn Kind Of Fellow and continued to be so post-bliss. He called her his "motivational force" but their marriage was stormy and childless. Marvin met new love Janis Hunter in 1973 and had two children with her. Anna finally sought a divorce in March 1977.

Notoriously bad with money, Marvin didn't have an awful lot to offer by way of a settlement, so the judge took his lawyer Curtis Shaw's suggestion that all the proceeds of Gaye's next record should go to his former wife.

"At first I thought I'd put out a lot of garbage for the album, there was no stipulation that it had to be a good one," Marvin said later. "Why should I break my neck when Anna was going to wind up with the money?" But once he was persuaded to start work, he lived and breathed the record. "I did that record out of a deep passion. It became a compulsion. All those hearings and depositions, accusations and lies . . . I knew I'd explode if I didn't get all that junk out of me."

Here, My Dear took three months in his own studio in Hollywood, a set-up which came complete with waterbedded living quarters. Marvin tended to sing in the control room, sitting at the mixing desk, overdubbing new vocal parts alongside his previous tracks until the melodies emerged. "I sang and sang until I drained myself of everything I'd lived through." When it was done, Marvin invited Anna to a playback but stayed up in the studio's apartment while she listened to it – saying almost nothing to engineer Art Stewart – and left.

With sleeve art depicting a Monopoly-type game called

Record label:
Motown

Produced
by Marvin Gaye; Anger co-produced by Gaye, Delta Ashby and Ed Townsend

Recorded:
Marvin Gaye's Studio, Hollywood, California. August–November 1977.

Released:
December 1978

Chart Peak:
None (UK) 26 (US)

Personnel:
Marvin Gaye (v, bv, k, syn), Nolan Smith (t), Charles Owen, Fernando Harkness (ts), Ernie Fields (as), Frank Blair (b), Bugsy Wilcox (d), Gary Jones, Elmira Collins (pc), Gordon Banks, Wali Ali (g)

Track listing:
Here, My Dear; I Met A Little Girl; When Did You Stop Loving Me, When Did I Stop Loving You; Anger; Is That Enough; Everybody Needs Love; Time To Get It Together; Sparrow; Anna's Song; When Did You Stop Loving Me, When Did I Stop Loving You (Instrumental); A Funky Space Reincarnation (S); You Can Leave, But It's Going To Cost You; Falling In Love Again; When Did You Stop Loving Me, When Did I Stop Loving You (Reprise)

Running time:
73.18

Current CD:
Motown 530 253-2

Further listening:
For an excellent overview of his career hear The Master a near-faultless 4-CD box set (1995). Marvin's other undervalued albums are the ones that sandwich Here, My Dear – I Want You (1976) and his last Motown album, In Our Lifetime (1981).

Further reading:
Divided Soul (David Ritz, 1985); I Heard
It Through The Grapevine (Sharon Davis,
1991); Trouble Man (Steve Turner, 1999)

"Judgement" and liner notes by his lawyer, the album was
released to almost universal critical disdain: it sounded too
much like an act of spite and revenge, they said, it was too
long, it was baffling, it was a downer. Its admittedly barmy
single, Funky Space Incarnation, was one of Marvin's biggest-
ever flops and *Here, My Dear* was deleted only a few years later,
the Gordy family's dismay at its bitterness towards Anna cited as
a prime reason.

From this distance it can be seen as a gripping,
passionate work that's full of good music; and if Marvin doesn't
come out of it exactly smelling of roses, at least his candour
was brave and revealing. Since Marvin's murder, Anna's opinion
of the record has mellowed and, in the '90s, she sanctioned its
reissue on CD. "It's taken me a while," she said, "but I've come
to appreciate every form of Marvin's music, even songs written
in anger."

Stiff Little Fingers
Inflammable Material

The first great UK punk record to emerge from the provinces.

With the exception of Siouxsie And The Banshees, the original cabal of '76 punk bands – Pistols, Clash, Damned, Buzzcocks, etc – had all cut records by 1977, inspiring a wave of imitators. Formed in Belfast, Stiff Little Fingers interpreted punk's received aesthetic – anti-Establishment growling, brisk tempos, barked delivery – more literally than most and, at the suggestion of journalist and mentor Gordon Ogilvie, turned to "The Troubles" in Northern Ireland for their inspiration.

Recorded in London – where the band had relocated in late 1978 – with an advance from independent record shop/label Rough Trade, *Inflammable Material* captured the bleak, violent and unpredictable mood of their strife-ridden hometown. A profoundly felt frustration and anger came across in songs like Suspect Device, State Of Emergency and Alternative Ulster, all lent a ferocious edge by singer Jake Burns throat-shredding vocals and the cauterising attack of his and Cluney's sand-blasted rhythm-lead guitar parts.

"The album was recorded in a basement in Cambridge, and took about two weeks in total," recalls Burns. "There are only a couple of guitar overdubs on the whole record – it was basically just the live set put down. Lots of it is hopelessly out of tune, but even now you can tell we meant it."

Despite its ferocious mien, the album has a musicality and subterranean humour than lifts it high above other "second-generation" punk albums. Heard in stereo, the twin guitar work is innovative, unforced and occasionally volcanic – especially on their punk-rock reworking of Bob and Rita Marley's Johnny Was (a blatant homage to The Clash's covering Junior Murvin's Police And Thieves) – while the doowop pastiche on the middle-eight of Barbed Wire Love and nimble chord changes and inauguaral open-string riff of Alternative Ulster show an instinctive understanding of pop dynamics.

Lyrically, Burns' collaborations with Ogilvie create some of the most frank and startling images to come out of the new wave: White Noise tackled racism, Suspect Device described the then seemingly insoluble political situation of Ulster and Closed Close offered a list of ironic clichés agianst a robotic art-rock groove. Two years late, perhaps, but worthy of its place among the pantheon of UK punk classics.

Record label:
Rough Trade

Produced
by Geoff Travis and Mayo Thompson.

Recorded
at Spaceward Studios, Cambridge; winter 1978–79.

Released:
February 1979

Chart peaks:
14 (UK) None (US)

Personnel:
Jake Burns (g); Henry Cluney (g); Ali McMordie (b); Brian Faloon (d)

Track listing:
Suspect Device (S); State Of Emergency; Here We Are Nowhere; Wasted Life; No More Of That; Barbed Wire Love; White Noise; Breakout; Law And Order; Rough Trade; Johnny Was; Alternative Ulster (S); Closed Groove

Running time:
41.16

Current CD:
CDP 7921052

Further listening:
All The Best (1991), 2-CD retrospective of the classic Chrysalis years

Further reading:
Record Collector 152; www.slf.com; www.murkworks.to/slf/

Brian Eno
Music For Airports

Sound specifically devised to suit a particular space, ushered in the era of ambient music.

As the most obviously intellectual exponent of '70s British art-rock, Brian Eno found himself seriously wrong-footed by the Luddite intervention of punk, which placed a great premium on intense, non-cerebral reactions to whatever stimuli floated past its protagonist's gaze.

By comparison, Eno's musical interests had become all the more reflective as the decade had proceeded, culminating in this landmark work, the first release on his new Ambient label. As with so many of his pieces, it was partly inspired by a particular quality of another composer's work.

"My friend Peter Schmidt made me a tape of all the slow movements from the late Haydn quartets – there are six of them – arranged so there were nice shifts between them," he explains. "It was a fabulous tape to listen to, because it just pretty much stayed in the same place. I had already done *Discreet Music*, which was intended to do just that, stay in one place for a while, and *Music For Airports* was an extension of that, the idea that the new job of music could be to create a location. It didn't have to tell you anything, or guide you in any way when you got there, it just made the space for you to be there."

The space in this case was the airport, whose emotional stresses and strains Eno intended to soothe away by a kind of aural massage – much the same intention as muzak, but less patronising and less damaging to treasured musical memories. Effectively, it was the world's first chill-out album. Comprising an unhurried series of recurring piano figures (played by Robert Wyatt) suspended in an ambient haze, the gentle, non-specific, ruminative quality of *Music For Airports* owed more to the innovations of "quiet" avant-garde classical composers like John Cage and Morton Feldman than any pop or rock antecedents, and was all the more shocking for appearing in the midst of the punk *Putsch*. It has actually been employed in several airport spaces, with great success.

"A lot of things like *Music For Airports* came out of that Borgesian idea that you could invent a world in reverse, by inventing the artefacts that ought to be in it first," says Eno. "You think of what kind of music would be in that world, then you make the music and the world forms itself around the music. This American ensemble called Bang On A Can have

Record label:
Ambient

Produced
by Brian Eno.

Recorded
in London and Conny Plank's Studio, Cologne; 1978.

Released:
March 1979

Chart peaks:
None (UK) None (US)

Personnel:
Brian Eno (syn, tapes, treatments); Christa Fast, Christine Gomez, Inge Zeininger (bv); Robert Wyatt (k); David Hutchins, Conny Plank, Rhett Davies (e)

Track listing:
1/1; 1/2; 2/1; 2/2

Running time:
42.20

Current CD:
EGEDC17

Further listening:
Eno has subsequently released a varied selection of ambient-music albums, including Ambient 4: On Land (1982), Thursday Afternoon (1985), The Shutov Assembly (1992) and Neroli (1993).

Further reading:
MOJO 19; MOJO 55;
www.hyperreal.org/music/artists/brian_eno/discog.html

done a live musical facsimile of *Music For Airports*, and what they've come up with is so moving: because you know it's humans playing it, it's suddenly invested with all this concentration and feeling, a tear-jerking quality that isn't really there in the original, which was originally conceived as deliberately austere and unemotional."

The Roches
The Roches

Heady mix: the three sisters' punk-folk debut produced by King Crimson's Robert Fripp.

Late '70s New York was a good place to peddle music with a difference and The Roches certainly fitted that bill. Warner Brothers noticed them tearing up Greenwich Village clubs with a delightfully squiffy combination of folk, jazz, barbershop and girl-group harmonies – delivered with an intensity that bordered on dissonance. The company had also recently signed Fripp as a producer and in late 1978 this slightly odd pairing got hitched.

Terre Roche recollects him as "the only producer we worked with who believed in recording what came out of the artist rather than creating it in the studio. Much of that album was in fact recorded live sitting around in a semi-circle playing acoustic guitars and singing." Fripp puts it a little more technically: "To get a radio hit you mix everything to the middle. The Roches didn't need that kind of crass strength. I mixed the album so any point along a line from left to right speaker is equally valid as a listening perspective." Hence the sleeve line, "Produced In Audio Vérité".

A comparison of the first two tracks illustrates the variety and power of the collection. The opener, We, is a goofball signature tune in The Monkees Theme mould, replete with vaudevillian vocal curlicues: "We are Maggie and Terre and Suzzy/We don't give out our ages/And we don't give out our phone numbers." The quite magical Hammond Song follows. The long, close-harmony washes that drive the track recall the very best of another set of siblings, the West Coast Wilsons, but with further piquant twists. The lyrics hint at a split within the trio caused by a lover as a single voice defies the unity of the chorale. "Remember we were a family, with all the underlying heaviness," says Suzzy. "At the same time there was a lot of love on that first record." Terre concludes, "Even though our sound was softer I always felt that issuing our album in the iconoclastic climate of punk/new wave was a definite boon".

Influential New York Times critic John Rockwell made it his favourite record of the year, but, more importantly, the genre-busting inheritance of The Roches' debut lives on in the work of successful female artists from k.d. lang to Liz Phair.

Record label:
Warner Brothers

Produced
by Robert Fripp.

Recorded
at the Hit Factory, New York;
September–November 1978.

Released:
March 1979

Chart peaks:
None (UK) 64 (US)

Personnel:
Suzzy Roche (v, g); Maggie Roche (v, g, syn); Terre Roche (v, g); Robert Fripp (g); Tony Levin (b); Jim Maelen (pc); Larry Fast (syn); Ed Sprigg (e); Jon Smith (ae)

Track listing:
We; Hammond Song; Mr Sellack; Damned Old Dog; The Troubles; The Train; The Married Men; Runs In The Family; Quitting Time; Pretty And High.

Running time:
39.59

Current CD:
Warner Bros. 3298-2

Further listening:
Nurds (1980); We Three Kings (1990) and Can We Go Home Now? (1995)

Further reading:
Folk Roots January–February 1996 (www.froots.demon.co.uk); Dirty Linen September–October 1995 (www.futuris.net) www.roches.com

Lowell George
Thanks, I'll Eat It Here

Solo jaunt for Little Feat star with a tragic outcome.

By the close of 1975, Little Feat's implied leader, Lowell George, was rapidly losing interest. "The guy was moving past the notion of a group," remembers Martin Kibbee, Lowell's former bandmate and songwriting partner in pre-Feat combo The Factory. "When we started out, Frank Zappa was our mentor. It was his show and he knew what he wanted and if you didn't like it, *adios!* That's what Lowell was shooting for, ultimately. The idea of having a band that's a democracy with all members as business partners with artistic input; there's a downside to that if you're an artist with a unique vision, which he was."

Although he'd produced all of Feat's albums since *Sailing Shoes*, Warner Brothers were apprehensive about Lowell producing what would become *Time Loves A Hero*, possibly mindful of his rapacious cocaine use at this point. But Lowell used their reluctance to his advantage, agreeing to the appointment of producer Ted Templeman for the Feat album in return for an advance for a solo record. Thus, in early 1976, Lowell began work. Recordings would continue piecemeal over a two-and-a-half-year period, sessions slotted around increasingly fraught Little Feat tours and recordings. Lowell worked wherever he happened to be, with whomever was around to help out – the glitterati of the LA session scene or a mariachi band plucked from a local Mexican restaurant. Such a variety of players, and the numerous locations, contributed to the album's charming inconsistency, kept in check by imaginative production and George Massenberg's masterful engineering.

Aiming for a commercial record, Lowell wanted to focus on his singing, thus there's little of his signature slide playing, although he does roll out a pretty flawless solo on his version of I Can't Stand The Rain. Only four cuts are originals, but all the elements of his musical personality are there: his unique humour and skewed vision (Cheek To Cheek – with the aforementioned mariachi band), his playfulness (Himmler's Ring), sensitivity (Find A River), tight-but-loose grooves and sincere, flowing singing. 20 Million Things boasts a vocal that aches with tenderness and demonstrates his knack for just letting a song fall effortlessly out of his mouth.

As liberating as it was, work on the album also paralleled the disintegration of his relationship with Little Feat, his

Record label:
Warner Brothers

Produced
by Lowell George.

Recorded
at Sunset Sound, Sound Factory West, Hollywood Sound Recorders, at home with Wally Heider's mobile. 1976–79

Released:
April 1979

Chart peaks:
None (UK) None (US)

Personnel:
Fred Tackett (g), Ritchie Hayward, Jim Keltne, Jim Gordon, Jeff Porcaro, Mike Baird (d), Chuck Rainey (b), Bill Payne, David Foster, Nicky Hopkins, Gordon DeWitte, David Paich, Jimmy Greenspoon (k), Herb Pederson, JD Souther, Bonnie Raitt, Van Dyke Parks (v) and many others.

Track listing:
What Do You Want The Girl To Do; Honest Man; Two Trains; I Can't Stand The Rain; Cheek To Cheek; Easy Money; 20 Million Things; Find A River; Himmler's Ring

Running time:
31.34

Current CD:
2-3194 adds Heartache

Further listening:
As Time Goes By: The Very Best Of Little Feat (1995)

Further reading:
MOJO 8.

failing health – which included severe backaches and hospitalisation with hepatitis – and the worsening of his bad habits which, just weeks after the album's release, ultimately led to the 34-year-old singer's fatal heart attack while on tour to promote it. Rather than exploit his demise, Warners withdrew promotion and allowed the album to fade into the background of rock history.

"The fun that we had I really haven't had since," says Kibbee. "He was a very inspiring guy. You felt you were working on something important, because he loved it so much it just rubbed off on you. It was not about money and careers, we just loved the music. The fact that we were being allowed to do this blew our minds."

Sister Sledge
We Are Family

On a working sabbatical from Chic, Edwards-Rodgers wrote and produced a disco classic.

S igned by Atlantic in 1973, and by 1975 working with Bert de Coteaux and Tony Silvester, the four Sledge Sisters from Philadelphia were primed for success by the small hit Mama Never Told Me off their *Circle Of Love* album. At the time, two sisters were working their way through university, one was at art college and the fourth, lead singer Kathie, was still in high school. The Chic mainmen ensured the sisters' graduation by skilfully fashioning for them an instantly appealing pop-soul album that lit up the peaking disco market with classy ballads, infectious dance tracks and the trademarked sound of Nile Rodgers' rhythm guitar and Bernard Edwards' impossibly nimble and fluid bass playing, solidly grounded by Tony Thompson's imposing drumming.

"They came to us with a complete package they had written," said Joni Sledge, "songs they felt were what we were about from our other records and seeing us at different shows. But the song We Are Family was written after they met us." That said, the methods of Rodgers and Edwards working on Sister Sledge did not differ wildly from their preparation and recording of a Chic album. "Chic are into a strict way of doing things. For example, they'll teach you the song in the studio 'cos they feel like you shouldn't know anything about it before you record it. It's kinda strange working that way. They'll teach you line by line and say, 'OK we'll record it up to that much.' Then there are certain songs where they'll say, 'OK take it away, do what you want for the rest of the song.' They have definite ways of doing it and you have to do it that way. At first I found it kinda hard to adjust to but I learned to respect what they were doing."

Just as well, because Chic gave the Sledges their best, and best-selling album. The title track, an anthem of family, sexual and (disco) cultural solidarity; the floating, dreamy Lost In Music; the poppy Thinking Of You; the disco paean He's The Greatest Dancer; all highlight a set that, along with Chic's Greatest Hits, continue to define the best of sophisticated dancefloor pop.

Record label:
Atlantic

Produced
Bernard Edwards and Nile Rodgers.

Recorded
at the Power Station, New York; 1978

Released:
April 1979

Chart peaks:
18 (UK) 3 (US)

Personnel:
Kathie, Debbie, Kim and Joni Sledge (v);
Nile Rodgers (g); Bernard Edwards (b);
Tony Thompson (d); Robert Sabino, (p,
clavinet); Andy Schwartz (p); Raymond
Jones (Fender Rhodes); Sammy Figueroa
(pc); Alex Foster, Jean Fineberg (s); Jon
Faddis, Ellen Seeling (t); Barry Rogers
(tb); Alex Foster (flute); Alfa Anderson,
Norma Jean Wright, David Lasley, Diva
Gray, Luther Vandross (bv); Karen Milne,
Cheryl Hong, Marianne Carroll (strings);
Gene Orloff (concert master)

Track listing:
He's The Greatest Dancer; Lost In Music;
Somebody Loves Me; Thinking Of You; We
Are Family; Easier To Love; You're A
Friend To Me; One More Time

Running time:
40.45

Current CD:
122715872

Further listening:
Dance Dance Dance: The Best Of Chic
(1991); The Very Best Of Sister Sledge
1973–93 (1993)

Joy Division
Unknown Pleasures

Punk's darkest forces reach Manchester and signal a new grey dawn.

S id Vicious may have died a victim of his punk's-court-jester mythology, but there was nothing remotely comic-book about Joy Division's Ian Curtis, a mild misanthrope whose thin skin left him prey to life's rotten realities. This enigmatic frontman, whose "dying insect" stage act mirrored his own epilepsy, found some solace in punk's distressed aesthetic until the early hours of May 18, 1980, when he hanged himself. In this light, his work inevitably sounds like an extended suicide note. From its austere, Peter Saville-designed monochrome sleeve in *Unknown Pleasures* was an exemplary exercise in sorrow.

On the face of it, the band were four pool-playing lads from the less-fashionable parts of Manchester who'd been fired up by the Sex Pistols and taken under the wing of manager Rob Gretton and Factory boss Tony Wilson. After a ragged start as Warsaw, Joy Division were soon artfully distilling the contemporary malaise in a way that belied their untrained origins. Much of that artfulness was down to producer Martin "Zero" Hannett. Not that the band quite understood why. "When we played the album live, the music was loud and heavy. But we felt that Martin had toned it down, especially with the guitars," complained Bernard Sumner later. "The production inflicted this dark, doomy mood over the album."

Hannett, whose lifestyle later killed him, countered: "They were a gift to a producer because they didn't have a clue." Certainly, what chronicler Jon Savage described as Hannett's "shiny, waking-dream production gloss" lent a magisterial quality to the material, but *Unknown Pleasures* wasn't solely the product of a headstrong producer bullying musicians who didn't know better.

A year earlier, Joy Division had recorded an album for RCA which was scrapped after creative differences with the producers.

By April 1979, having worked with Hannett on two songs for a Factory compilation, the band had virtually perfected the album in rehearsal. What Hannett – a kind of punk Phil Spector – did was to separate the instruments and cloak the material in his customary metallic reverb. The drums, augmented by a drum machine, ran like clockwork (Disorder), the bass worked the melodies (Insight), the guitar rifts, strangely

Record label:
Factory

Produced
by Martin Hannett.

Recorded
at Strawberry Studios, Stockport, April 1979.

Released:
June 1979

Chart peaks:
71 (UK) None (US)

Personnel:
Ian Curtis (v); Peter Hook (b); Bernard Dicken (alias Sumner) (g); Stephen Morris (d)

Track listing:
Disorder; Day Of The Lords; Candidate; Insight; New Dawn Fades; She's Lost Control; Shadowplay; Wilderness; Interzone; I Remember Nothing

Running time:
38.50

Current CD:
Factory/London 228223

Further listening:
The stakes were raised further for the follow-up, Closer, recorded weeks before Curtis's suicide. The 4-CD collection, Heart And Soul, provides the complete picture.

Further reading:
MOJO 8; Touching From A Distance: Ian Curtis And Joy Division (Deborah Curtis; 1995); www.warren.org.uk/music/joyd.html

reminiscent of old Black Sabbath chord sequences (New Dawn Fades), were used for texture, and Curtis's weary, occasionally explosive vocals (She's Lost Control) added an unremittingly bleak lyricism. The singer insisted that the sessions took only four-and-a-half days; at least as much time would have been spent at the mixing-desk creating what was arguably the first post-punk album.

The B-52's
The B-52's

Courageously-coiffeured Southerners playing toy instruments invade the New York punk scene. With hilarious results!

When producer/Island Records MD Chris Blackwell first saw The B-52's on the New York club circuit, they'd already composed virtually two albums' worth of material on the long road journeys from Athens, Georgia. Captivated by their brittle sound, rudimentary instruments and sci-fi nightmare stage clothes, he began recording them at his Compass Point Studios before he'd even signed them to the label. The contrast with their penniless life on the road was unforgettable.

"We went to Chris's house and out in his boat," Kate Pierson recalls, "and we were amazed by all the studio equipment. We had this really spare sound which was built around the style of Ricky's Mosrite guitar, a really classic surf guitar sound. He used lots of open tunings inspired by Joni Mitchell; if he broke a string he'd often work the guitar parts out just on the other five as we were so broke we couldn't afford to buy any new ones. And with all this studio gear we imagined we'd have a much fuller sound – you know, really pumped up! We were shocked when we heard the record. We thought it would sound so much better! But Chris's genius was to record us exactly as we sounded on stage, everyone playing the same parts they played live and all on the same instruments. So I played my Farfisa organ and the guitar part on Hero Worship. His genius was to decide it should stay sparse and punky and edgy and really capture the quirkiness of the band."

The album took just over three weeks to record – "the basic tracks, me and Cindy in one vocal booth, Fred in another, and then some overdubs. And once Chris had made this one decision about our sound, he basically put his feet up on the console and smoked pot. I mean he *directed* the whole thing but he was very 'mellow'. Another producer could have over-produced, got session musicians in, who knows what could have happened." Breathlessly conflating '50s kitsch and proto-New Wave garage spunk – and hingeing on the contrast between the girls' Day-Glo harmonies and Fred Schneider's declamatory camp – The B-52's sold over 500,000 copies worldwide, practically without radio play. Three albums later, they would find themselves in pole position in the MTV-fuelled US New Wave derby. Pierson fondly remembers one shell-shocked review of that epic first record: "They are *not* going to import their American trash aesthetic over here!"

Record label:
Island

Produced
by Chris Blackwell.

Recorded
at Compass Point Studios, Nassau, Bahamas; March–April 1979.

Released:
July 1979

Chart peaks:
22 (UK) 59 (US)

Personnel:
Kate Pierson (k, v, g); Fred Schneider (v, walkie-talkie, toy piano, k); Ricky Wilson (g, smoke alarm); Keith Strickland (d, pc); Cindy Wilson (v, bongos, g, pc); Robert Ash (e)

Track listing:
Planet Claire; 52 Girls; Dance This Mess Around; Rock Lobster; Lava; There's A Moon In The Sky (Called The Moon); Hero Worship; 6060-842; Downtown

Running time:
39.25

Current CD:
IMCD1

Further listening:
Wild Planet (1980); Cosmic Thing (1989) contains their huge comeback hit Love Shack.

Further reading:
www.b52s.net

AC/DC
Highway To Hell

Aussie rockers finally break the States six months before the death of vocalist Bon Scott.

Their UK success established with 1977's *Let There Be Rock* and cemented with follow-ups *Powerage* and the live *If You Want Blood, You've Got It*, AC/DC now turned their attention to the States. Two years of near non-stop touring on the "highway to hell", as Angus called the road in America, was starting to do the trick. What would finally tip the balance, their record label figured, was a more polished album, so they upped the budget and prised the band away from Australia. Next, producers Harry Vanda and (Angus and Malcolm's brother) George Young packed them off to the States with former Hendrix engineer Eddie Kramer who'd recently had hits producing Aerosmith and Kiss.

It did not go well. "We thought, We can't work with him," said Malcolm Young, "but the label were going to drop us if we didn't. It was a tricky situation. Finally our manager did a bit of wheeling and dealing and managed to get a tape to Mutt Lange, a friend of his, then known for producing New Wave acts like Graham Parker and The Boomtown Rats. We told Kramer, We're having tomorrow off, we need a break, and we went in and wrote nine songs in one day and whacked them off to Mutt. He got straight back and said he wanted to do it and the rest is history."

Lange spent three weeks with AC/DC in London's Roundhouse Studios, walking a tightrope between the simplicity that the band wanted and the polished production the label was paying for. AC/DC's first million-seller, it was stuffed with air-punching rock anthems and the band's trademark solid riffs and quickly became a staple at teenage headbangers' booze-fuelled parties on both sides of the Atlantic.

As sales grew, so did their notoriety. The album attracted the unwelcome attention of America's Moral Majority, who castigated them from pulpits and picketed their shows. It didn't help when LA serial killer Richard Ramirez, aka "the Night Prowler", was arrested in an AC/DC T-shirt, claiming that his rapes and Satanic rituals were inspired by the song Night Prowler and the band's name, which he reckoned stood for Anti-Christ/Devil's Child. Meanwhile, the song Touch Too Much proved prophetic. Early the next year, at the end of another mammoth tour, Bon Scott was found dead in a car in London. The singer, the coroner said had "drunk himself to death".

Record label:
Atlantic

Produced
by Robert John "Mutt" Lange.

Recorded
at Roundhouse Studios, London; June 1979.

Released:
August 1979

Chart peaks:
8 (UK) 17 (US)

Personnel:
Bon Scott (v); Angus Young (g); Malcolm Young (g); Cliff Williams (b); Phil Rudd (d); Tony Platt (e)

Track listing:
Highway To Hell; Girls Got Rhythm; Walk All Over You; Touch Too Much; Beating Around The Bush; Shot Down In Flames; Get It Hot; If You Want Blood (You've Got It); Love Hungry Man; Night Prowler

Running time:
39.40

Current CD:
7567924192

Further listening:
Let There Be Rock (1977); Bon Scott And The Fraternity: Complete Sessions 1971–2 (1972)

Further reading:
MOJO 51; AC/DC – The Kerrang! Files! (Malcolm Dome, 1995)

Chic

Risque

After a clutch of hit singles, the Chic groove moves up a gear. Get down to the perfect beat.

There comes a time when all pop formulas reach a plateau of perfection. Motown did that in the '60s. James Brown nailed down the definitive "one" in the early '70s and in an 18-month period at the end of that decade Nile Rodgers and Bernard Edwards produced a clutch of albums for Chic, Sister Sledge and Diana Ross that crystallised the essence of hi-gloss funk. The state of the art sounded like this.

Magic moments abound; the climatic one note string parts on My Feet Keep Dancing courtesy of The Chic Strings, Bernard Edwards' trademark percolator bass, bubbling away under My Forbidden Lover, vocalists Alfa Anderson and Luci Martin chanting out their wish lists on Good Times like little disco haikus. That song's bass line established a legacy that ran through Queen's Another One Bites The Dust, The Sugarhill Gang's Rappers Delight, and out into soul music's pool of definitive riffs.

Risque celebrated black people moving on up, and Good Times ("Halston, Gucci, Fiorucci") was as much of a barometer of black aspirations in the late '70s as any civil rights song was in its time. The band's visual sophistication was matched by some of the leanest, yet most opulent dance music ever made. Everything as immaculate as Chic's wardrobe. Even the lyrics are styled to suit the rhythms.

Only when you glance at the lyric sheet do you notice that the sultry A Warm Summer Night has but five lines, twenty words. Such economy can be devastating – both lyric and treatment of Will You Cry (When You Hear This Song) are as achingly understated as Bacharach and David at their finest. Put Tony Thompson's crisp drumming, Bernard Edward's infectious bass and Nile Rodgers icy guitar chops together and what do you get? Grooves that defined an era.

Record label:
Atlantic

Produced
by Bernard Edwards and Nile Rodgers.

Recorded
at The Power Station, New York; 1979.

Released:
August 1979

Chart peaks:
29 (UK) 5 (US)

Personnel:
Nile Rodgers (g); Bernard Edwards (b); Tony Thompson (d); Raymond Jones (k); Robert Sabino (k); Andy Schwartz (k); Karen Milne, Cheryl Hong, Karen Karlsrud, Valerie Haywood (strings); Bob Clearmountain (e)

Track listing:
Good Times (S); A Warm Summer Night; My Feet Keep Dancing (S); My Forbidden Lover (S); Can't Stand To Love You; Will You Cry (When You Hear This Song); What About Me

Running time:
34.50

Curremt CD:
AMCYII8

Further listening:
C'est Chic (1978); and other Bernard Edwards and Nile Rodgers productions: Sister Sledge, We Are Family (1979); Diana Ross, Diana (1980)

Further reading:
The Death Of Rhythm And Blues (Nelson George, 1988)

Ry Cooder
Bop Till You Drop

Cooder's flair and care has an odd covers collection singing with one sweet voice. World's first digital rock album, allegedly.

Widely regarded as a maestro following session stints with Captain Beefheart, The Rolling Stones and Little Feat, Ry Cooder tended to believe he never got anything right. In 1978, commenting on earlier endeavours to Rolling Stone, he reckoned he had strayed "right off the map" with the Hawaiian accents of his Chicken Skin Revue tour in 1976–77 and that with 1978's *Jazz* he had then fallen into sterile "archivism" by "trying to revive traditions in a cute academic way – too much of that and you get relegated as a quirk artist, somebody people can't listen to without wearing their fucking think caps all the time". Still, he felt more confident about this R&B collection: "The style of song is well suited to my weird voice. The idea is to blend warm vocal arrangements and the guitar sound so that one leans on the other."

He knew what he was about. *Bop Till You Drop* sparkled and flowed like a stream over rocks. Opening with Mort Shuman and Doc Pomus' Little Sister offered a familiar point of reference, but the priapic hustle of Elvis Presley's version was replaced by an intricate weave of guitars and the high, keening harmonies of Bobby King and friends. While this was Cooder at his most charming, he was quite willing to get down and dirty too. He performed to Oscar standards in character as the would-be stoic trying to break off an affair with his best friend's woman in Arthur Alexander's Go Home, Girl. Then he switched to bug-eyed street-corner lecher for his own hometown song Down In Hollywood ("She's showing everything she's got, mm-mm") and slapstick yarn-spinner for Shuman and Jerry Ragovoy's Look At Granny Run Run (a pre-Viagra tale of how Grandpaw got overstimulated by a new pill).

An album steeped in what one critic called "the unruffled intensity of the groove", it did quite well commercially. But Cooder remained concerned about the desultory chart action he achieved: "I've always been aware that my records didn't sell real well. At one time it didn't matter. But it's hard not to worry now. You have to try to get your numbers up." He never could and, during the 1980s, he moved on to write movie soundtracks for a living while promoting ethnic music as a passionate hobby – which eventually led to his catalysing The Buena Vista Social Club phenomenon, an improbable worldwide hit album by a group of internationally unknown Cuban pensioners.

Record label:
Warner Brothers

Produced
by Ry Cooder.

Recorded
at Warner Brothers Recording Studio, north Hollywood, California; 1979.

Released:
August 1979

Chart peaks:
36 (UK) 62 (US)

Personnel:
Ry Cooder (v, g); David Lindley (g); Ronnie Barron (g,o); Patrick Henderson (o); Jim Keltner (d); Tim Drummond (b); Milt Holland (pc); Bobby King, Herman Johnson, Chaka Khan, George "Biggie" McFadden, Randy Lorenzo, Pico Payne, Greg Prestopino (v, bv); Lee Herschberg (e)

Track listing:
Little Sister (S/UK); Go Home, Girl; The Very Thing That Makes You Rich (Makes Me Poor) (S/UK); I Think It's Going To Work Out Fine; Down In Hollywood; Look At Granny Run Run; Trouble, You Can't Fool Me; Don't You Mess Up A Good Thing; I Can't Win

Running time:
39.50

Current CD:
7599273982

Further listening:
Chicken Skin Music (1976) – Tex-Mex Hawaiian R&B and it works! Buena Vista Social Club (1998) – not a Cooder album, but his final immersion in another culture.

Further reading:
www.geocities.com/BourbonStreet/Delta/7969/

Bob Dylan
Slow Train Coming

Dylan in born-again Christian album shock!

How could the coolest man in the world undergo a conversion to fundamentalist Christianity? Chronologically, after the Rolling Thunder Revue chaos, in 1977 his wife Sara divorced him and won custody of their five children, the following year his obsessional autobiopic *Renaldo And Clara* bombed. Elvis Presley's death caused him unwonted upset. Dylanology suggests that Bob's Damascene moment occurred on November 17, 1978, in a hotel room after a show in Tucson, Arizona. His own account goes: "There was a presence in the room that couldn't have been anybody but Jesus . . . Jesus put his hand on me. . . . I felt my whole body tremble. . . I truly had a born-again experience, if you want to call it that."

At once, he began writing religious songs. Slow Train and Do Right To Me Baby (Do Unto Others) appeared in soundchecks. Then, back home in California, he joined a sect called the Vineyard Fellowship and attended daily Bible study classes for three months. In May 1979, he flew to Muscle Shoals for 11 days of recording. Inspired in every sense, his dark admonitions retrieved the cold ferocity of early protest songs like Masters Of War. Recruited after Dylan saw Dire Straits play in Los Angeles a few weeks earlier, Mark Knopfler sounded like an enraged B.B. King, while Muscle Shoals stalwart Barry Beckett on piano played brimstone from the minatory intro to Gotta Serve Somebody through to the grim Gospel precisions of When He Returns.

Some resented his going Christian as a betrayal of shared values – perhaps even worse than his going electric in 1965 – Dylan's temporary tendency to on-stage denunciation of sinners confirmed that he'd embraced all the nastier aspects of fundamentalism. "Art can lead you to God," he proclaimed. "I think that's the purpose of everything. If it's not doing that, what's it doing? It's leading you the other way."

Controversy helped *Slow Train Coming* become his second-best-selling album after *Desire*. He thumped Bible for three more albums then moved on. As Eric Clapton remarked: "Bob goes through changes. Sometimes he's a heavy drinker, sometimes dry. Sometimes he's into dope, then not. He can disappear with a carload of Mexicans. No phase is the final one."

Record label:
CBS

Produced
by Jerry Wexler and Barry Beckett.

Recorded
at Muscle Shoals, Alabama; May 1979.

Released:
August 1979

Chart peaks:
2 (UK) 3 (US)

Personnel:
Bob Dylan (v, g); Mark Knopfler (g); Tim Drummond (b); Barry Beckett (k); Pick Withers (d); Muscle Shoals Horns (horns); Carolyn Dennis, Helena Springs, Regina Havis (bv); Gregg Hamm (e)

Track listing:
Gotta Serve Somebody (S); Precious Angel; I Believe In You; Slow Train; Gonna Change My Way Of Thinking; Do Right To Me Baby (Do Unto Others); When You Gonna Wake Up; Man Gave Names To All The Animals; When He Returns

Running time:
46.39

Current CD:
Columbia 32524

Further listening:
Those who consider his "religious phase" an aberration might consider and enjoy the moral fervour of The Freewheelin' Bob Dylan (1963) and the sombre contemplation of mortality in Time Out Of Mind (1997)

Further reading:
Song And Dance Man III: The Art Of Bob Dylan (Michael Gray, 1999); www.bobdylan.com

Gang Of Four
Entertainment!

Clangorous, post-punk, post-Marxist masterpiece put dance-ability on the New Wave agenda.

Gang Of Four formed in 1977 at Leeds University, describing themselves as a "fast rivvum and blues band", but by the time they recorded *Entertainment!* they were light years ahead of that. However, there were still loud echoes of Dr Feelgood's guitarist Wilko Johnson in the choppy, abrasive stylings of Andy Gill – "Yes, I thought Wilko was brilliant. Ska and reggae were also big influences – that's where I got the ideas about dropping instruments in and out, creating spaces." On the strength of the well-received Damaged Goods EP, Gang Of Four signed to mega-corporation EMI.

"We could have hidden away on Rough Trade, say, but we wanted people to hear our music," explains Gill. "EMI gave us money and let us get on with it. The sessions were pretty fraught as we were a very argumentative band. I would try to impose certain syncopated drum patterns on Hugo, and he'd throw his sticks at me and storm off. We didn't know much about studio techniques, but I knew I wanted a dry sound. We used transistor amps as an anti-rockist gesture – trying to get away from that warm Marshall feel."

The slashing punk-funk and the half-shouted, discursive vocals succeed brilliantly in conveying the sense of anomie the group felt. "We looked at our lives and the lives of our friends and came up with a simple rather than a simplistic view of modern capitalism. I mean we didn't tell anyone to go and smash WH Smith's windows."

On the lop-sided strut of Natural's Not In It, vocalist Jon King agonises over "The problem of leisure/What to do for pleasure" before concluding "This heaven gives me migraine." The sublimely sour feedback of Anthrax opens into an equally bitter lyric: "Love'll get you like a case of anthrax." I Found That Essence Rare is almost pop, albeit in a gnarly, Buzzcocks way. The press lapped up the challenging conflation of intellect, innovation and intuition and R.E.M.'s Michael Stipe commented that "*Entertainment!* shredded everything that came before it. I stole a lot from them."

Record label:
EMI

Produced
by Andy Gill, Jon King and Rob Warr.

Recorded
at the Workhouse, Old Kent Road, London; May–June 1979.

Released:
September 1979.

Chart peaks:
45 (UK) None (US)

Personnel:
Jon King (v, melodica); Andy Gill (v, g); Hugo Burnham (d, bv); Dave Allen (b, bv); Rick Walton (e)

Track listing:
Ether; Natural's Not In It; Not Great Men; Damaged Goods; Return The Gift; Guns Before Butter; I Found That Essence Rare; Glass; Contract; At Home He's A Tourist; 5.45; Anthrax

Running time:
39.43

Current CD:
CZ 541

Further listening:
Solid Gold (1981); Songs Of The Free (1982) and 100 Flowers Bloom (1998), a 2-CD compilation. Bassist Dave Allen helped found Shriekback.

Further reading:
Booklet by Jon Savage accompanying 100 Flowers Bloom; a booklet by Greil Marcus accompanying A Brief History Of The 20th Century compilation.
www.emdac.demon.co.uk/phil/gof/gof_indx.html

Al Green
The Belle Album

The Reverend Al ascends the pulpit to deliver a soulful sermon on life, love and God.

For soul singers, the opposing pulls of the spiritual and the sexual, of God and get-down!, are well-chronicled fact. That this should be the case is not surprising, because gospel had been a major source of '60s soul voices and a prominent component of the singing style and song structure. From Little Richard and James Brown, whose leadership of the jail choir earned him the recommendation for parole which set in train events that ended with the development of funk, to genuine sons and daughters of the church, Sam Cooke and Aretha Franklin, it was rare to find a soul singer who did not owe at least part of his or her style to gospel.

Green was no different – his father sacked him from The Green Brothers gospel quartet when Al was caught listening to rock'n'roll – and, like Little Richard, he felt a strong and constant tug back to the church. With producer Willie Mitchell in Memphis, Green became one of the very best soul acts of the early '70s, his delicacy of phrasing and inimitable tone bringing to earthy songs such as Tired Of Being Alone, Let's Stay Together, Love And Happiness and Here I Am (Come And Take Me). But the inspiration of church was never far from the surface: "I was a plain old Baptist Pentecostal born-again in the middle of a rock'n'roll career," he admitted. Indeed, Take Me To The River, Full Of Fire and the like are clearly spirituals in all but name.

In 1976 Green bought the First Church of Full Gospel Tabernacle in Memphis, installing himself as pastor. The following year he split with Mitchell and announced his new direction with *Belle*, a perfect commingling of the sacred and the secular, the line "It's you I want, but it's Him that I need" in the title track capturing the opposing pulls on Green's emotions and reflected throughout the album by the churning I Feel Good and the gentler ripple of Feels Like Summer.

Green took an accidental fall from the stage in 1979 as a warning from his God. "I was moving towards God, but I wasn't moving fast enough. That was God's way of saying I had to hurry up." He wouldn't make another soul album until 1993.

Record label:
Hi

Produced
by Al Green.

Recorded
at American Music, Memphis; Spring/Summer 1979

Released:
September 1979

Chart peaks:
None (UK) 103 (US)

Personnel:
Al Green (v, g); Reuben Fairfax Jr (b, bell lyre); James Bass (g); Leon Thomas (clavinet, Fender Rhodes); Johnny Brown (p, Fender Rhodes); Fred Jordan (Fender Rhodes, Roland String Ensemble, Polyphonic Orchestron); John Toney (d, Syndrum); Rob Payne (Syndrum); Ardis Hardin (d); Buddy Jarrett (alto); Darryl Neely, Fred Jordan (t, flugelhorn); Ron Echols (ts, bs); Margaret Foxworth, Linda Jones, Harvey Jones (bv)

Track listing:
Belle (S); Loving You; Feels Like Summer (S/US); Georgia Boy; I Feel Good; All 'N' All; Chariots Of Fire; Dream

Running time:
41.15

Current CD:
HILO160

Further listening:
Al Green Gets Next To You (1971); Let's Stay Together (1972); I'm Still In Love With You (1972); Call Me (1973), and the surprisingly good Don't Look Back (1993)

Further reading:
Take Me To The River (Al Green, 2000)

Gary Numan
The Pleasure Principle

Gary Numan's first "official" solo album, establishing him as the first international synth-pop star.

Inspired by the freakish, individualistic personae of his adolescent icons David Bowie, Lou Reed, Iggy Pop and Marc Bolan, at the end of the '70s Gary Numan fleshed out his punk band The Tubeway Army into a garagey electronic band. The alienated sci-fi drone of the single Are Friends Electric? was swiftly followed to the top of the charts by *Replicas*. However, it was the 21-year-old Londoner's completely guitar-free follow-up, *The Pleasure Principle*, which took the world by storm.

Recorded in a tiny London studio, Numan built his Moog-dominated, techno-rock sound around soaring keyboard lines, piano, strings, heavy percussion and clipped, monotone vocals.

"I concentrated on a very rich, layered, poly-Moog sound," he says. "In the late '70s, synthesizers provided an opportunity for people without any great musical training or ability to make pop music. You could rent them fairly cheaply, record them in little studios and they would sound incredibly powerful."

By sticking to one-word song titles, avoiding choruses and selling himself with an image of doleful introspection framed in the neon tubes of his promo videos and massive stage shows, Numan scored his second UK Number 1 album and single of 1979. The single was Cars, a cold, symmetrical, electro-disco track featuring tambourine and handclaps, which also made the Top 5 in the States. It was to open the floodgates to a new wave of aloof, image-conscious, British suburban synth artists like The Human League, Depeche Mode and Soft Cell, effectively signalling the end of UK punk.

This cultural shift towards synthesizers and showbiz led to a massive critical assault on Numan by a rock press who still clung to punk's "authentic" guitar-driven thrills. In spite of continued bad press, Cars kept rebounding back in to the Top 20 (its latest incarnation, Armand Van Helden's hip hop cut-up Koochy), while *The Pleasure Principle*'s lesser-known track, Films, has been credited by the likes of Afrika Bambaataa and The Beastie Boys as one of hip hop's original breakbeats.

The album's angular, rhythmic style has also been cited by techno pioneers like Moby, The Orb and Juan Atkins as playing a significant role in the birth of modern dance music,

Record label:
Beggars Banquet

Produced
by Gary Numan.

Recorded
at Marcus Music, London, spring 1979

Released:
September 1979

Chart peaks:
1 (UK) 16 (US)

Personnel:
Gary Numan (v, k); Paul Gardiner (b); Christopher Payne (k, va); Cedric Sharpley (d, pc); Billy Currie (v); Garry Robson (bv); Rikki Sylvian, Harvey Webb (e)

Track listing:
Airlane; Metal; Complex (S); Films; M.E.; Tracks; Observer; Conversation; Cars (S); Engineers

Running time:
41.12

Current CD
BBLO 10CD adds: Random; Oceans; Asylum; Me! I Disconnect From You (Live); Bombers (Live); Remember I Was Vapour (Live); On Broadway (Live)

Further listening:
Replicas (1979); Telekon (1980); Exile (1997)

Further reading:
Praying To The Aliens (Gary Numan and Steve Malins, 1997), plus all of Numan's catalogue features extensive sleevenotes www.numan.org

while Nine Inch Nails, Marilyn Manson, Blur, Tricky and Smashing Pumpkins have all referenced the cold, paranoid fantasies portrayed on Metal and Complex. According to Trent Reznor of Nine Inch Nails, "It painted an emotional place that wasn't pleasant to be in. It seemed creepy science fiction in an unpleasant way."

Reissued in 1998, *The Pleasure Principle* was hailed as a "spooky" classic, completing a gradual, 20-year critical reversal which recently inspired Spin magazine to conclude: "Against all odds, history has vindicated Numan."

The Residents
Eskimo

Anonymous San Franciscan art pranksters break the commercial ice with their vision of life up North.

The Residents are perhaps best known for the giant eyeballs they wear on their heads, first used on the cover of *Eskimo*, their sixth album and the record most often credited with establishing them as emperors of experimentalism. "It's without doubt one of the most important albums ever made, if not the most important," raved MOJO's Andy Gill, then writing for the NME. An overstatement, maybe, but *Eskimo* still has the power to unsettle, amuse and enchant.

On previous records the band had given pop music a deliciously weird going-over (try their version of Let's Twist Again in German on *Third Reich And Roll*) and written a synth-driven pseudo-opera (*Not Available*). *Eskimo* purported to be an accurate representation of Inuit music and culture, supposedly made using the five-note Eskimo scale and traditional instruments.

Drummer Chris Cutler (Henry Cow, Pere Ubu) played percussion on the album. "It was all recorded in their own studio at 444 Grove St, San Francisco. There were a few roto-toms and some other bits and bobs. I was more or less given a free rein. I didn't have any music to play along to. They made me sit in a fridge and breathe Arctic air which had been brought back in Thermos flasks by their guru N. Senada." Cutler smiles. "All, none or some of the above might be true."

There is no doubt The Residents did research Eskimo life, but the piece seems as much a comment on the nature of American society. The bitter, almost constant synth swooshes (Don Preston, ex-Mothers Of Invention) which denote the Arctic wind also conjure up a sense of urban alienation, and the guttural chants which make up the vocals are quite obviously distorted English. The repeated phrase "Coke adds life" stands out in particular, while the Angakok (priest) bears a striking resemblance to a Southern US preacher. The album closes with the beautifully melodic, quasi-prog of Festival Of Death; a release from the often atonal but enthralling depiction of births, hunts and snow madness that has gone before. The first 10,000 copies were pressed in Arctic White vinyl and it went on to sell 100,000 – amazing for an own label issue at the time. The following year they put out an eight-minute edit of the album called *Diskomo*, set, unsurprisingly, to a disco beat. Cool.

Record label:
Ralph Records

Produced
by The Residents.

Recorded
at 444 Grove Street, San Francisco; April 1976–May 1979.

Released:
September 1979

Chart peaks:
None (UK) None (US)

Personnel:
The Residents and Snakefinger [Phil Lithman] (v, all instruments); Don Preston (s); Chris Cutler (d, pc)

Track listing:
The Walrus Hunt; Birth; Arctic Hysteria; The Angry Angakok; A Spirit Steals A Child; The Festival Of Death

Running time:
39.06

Current CD:
CD 016

Further listening:
Meet The Residents (1974); Third Reich And Roll (1976); Commercial Album (1980); 25th Anniversary Box Set, Very good 4-CD package with informative booklet (1997).

Further reading:
Meet The Residents: America's Most Eccentric Band (Ian Shirley, 1998)
www.residents.com

The Slits

Cut

The band nobody wanted to sign defy detractors with the most sophisticated album of 1979.

W hen The Slits lost drummer Palmolive in autumn 1978, it looked as if the game was up. The band had little to show for an 18-month career except a mass of (usually) bad press highlighting their shortcomings, some traumatic support slots on tours with The Clash and The Buzzcocks, and, more recently, another scotched record deal. But within a year, The Slits turned it round with an album that banished the "punk incompetents" tag forever.

The band's close ties with The Sex Pistols and The Clash initially worked in their favour, winning them press interest and prestigious gigs. Yet rock's inherent sexism soon characterised The Slits as New Wave novelties or unwelcome intruders – though the band, particularly the precocious Ari Up, were more than capable of handling themselves.

An extraordinary radio session recorded in spring 1978 for John Peel was evidence of new musical muscle too. "Punk pulled everything apart," says Viv Albertine. "We dissected what we said, what we wore and how we sounded. We certainly didn't want to play 12-bar like every other band."

Through a mixture of accident and design, The Slits had become the great white hope of the post-punk avant-garde. But the band's rejection of convention drew them closer to black music – reggae in particular – which they'd discovered through Don Letts, Roxy Club DJ and, briefly, the band's manager: "They had a real affinity with the rebel aspect of the music and the culture," he says. According to Albertine, "Dub seemed to have a femininity about it; it was more fluid." After a shambolic late '78 tour with The Clash with new drummer Budgie on board, the group landed a deal with Island, and recruited Dennis "Blackbeard" Bovell as producer. The punky-reggae party was about to begin. From being the band nobody wanted to sign, The Slits became the sound of the future.

"They were way ahead of their time," insists Letts. "They took reggae's emphasis on the bassline over melody and guitars. And *Cut* used the mixing-desk as an instrument." The results were shocking – not least to the group's core following, who expected robustly recorded versions of the band's avant-punk live set. Instead, hitherto impenetrable songs like Newtown, Instant Hit and So Tough were transformed into hi-tech

Record label:
Island

Produced
by Dennis Bovell.

Recorded
at Ridge Farm Studios, London; spring 1979.

Released:
September 1979

Chart peaks:
30 (UK) None (US)

Personnel:
Ari Up (v); Viv Albertine (g, v); Tessa Pollitt (b, v); Budgie (d); Mike Dunne (e)

Track listing:
Instant Hit; So Tough; Spend, Spend, Spend; Shoplifting; FM; Newtown; Ping Pong Affair; Love And Romance; Typical Girls; Adventures Close To Home

Running time:
31:59

Current CD:
8425502

Further listening:
The Peel Sessions (1992)

Further reading:
www.comnet.ca/~rina/slits.html; Lipstick Traces: A Secret History Of The Twentieth Century (Greil Marcus, 1990)

exercises in spatial tension with Budgie's inventive percussion centre stage. However, the group's decision to pose nude – albeit covered in mud and irony – for the album's sleeve prompted further controversy, and despite portraying themselves as prophet-like modern primitives on subsequent releases, cultural confusion eventually got the better of the band and their effectiveness dwindled. *Cut*, however, remains a vital document. One suspects that if it had been made in a less male-dominated climate it would be far more celebrated today.

Marianne Faithfull
Broken English

A '60s icon shreds her past.

After cramming enough living into the '60s to last any normal lifetime, Marianne Faithfull effectively retired for the first half of the '70s – though it's probably more accurate to say that her drug habit retired *her*. She resurfaced with a couple of pleasant but insipid country-pop sets, but these were no preparation for the emotional fireball of *Broken English*.

"Punk made the album possible," she has commented. "Vast stadium tours, crazed male ego-driven bands, pop grandiosity in general – these were not my thing at all. The hard, defiant, honest world of punk showed me where and how I fitted in, where I could be relevant."

The title track is an indictment of the Cold War superpowers' posturings – though the undercurrents of her own psychic turmoil are also pretty apparent. The closer is a torrent of foul-mouthed abuse aimed fairly obviously at inconstant lover Ben Brierley, which makes that turmoil all-too plain – though, surprisingly, she didn't write it: poet Heathcote Williams did. "I told Heathcote, 'I would *die* to sing these lyrics.'" But "sing" barely describes the haunting, ravaged keen that characterises her delivery throughout, and which contrasts so startlingly with the folkie warble of her '60s recordings. The settings, too were a departure: an understated, hypnotic mesh of synths and guitars that made her livid vocals all the more stark.

Several songs seem like attempts to dump the baggage handed to her by early media fame. Her splendid cover of Lennon's Working Class Hero trashes the (inaccurate) picture of her as privileged daughter of the aristocracy, while The Ballad Of Lucy Jordan – pre-empting the grittier narratives of her Kurt Weill period – portrays the suicide of a suburban housewife denied any taste of the glamorous life which Marianne herself experienced. "The public's preconceived image of me has always been a thorny problem," she says. "But singing those songs was not a clever, conscious, detached move on my part, it was an intensely emotional decision that I deeply felt."

The only respite from the lamentations comes with the hope/black humour of Witches' Song – "inspired by an exhibition of drawings by Goya on a visit to the Prado in 1967 with Mick Jagger". The final line runs, "Remember death is far away and life is sweet." Marianne had been to Hell and back, and knew the value of life. *Broken English* has the songs to prove it.

Record label:
Island

Produced
by Mark Miller Mundy.

Recorded
at Matrix Studios, London; May–July 1979.

Released:
October 1979

Chart peaks:
57 (UK) 82 (US)

Personnel:
Marianne Faithfull (v); Barry Reynolds (g); Steve York (b); Terry Stannard (d); Joe Maverty (k); Steve Winwood (k); Dyan Birch, Frankie Collins, Isabella Dulaney (bv); Jim Cuomo (s); Guy Humphries (g); Morris Pert (pc); Darryl Way (vn); Ed Thacker, Bob Potter (e)

Track listing:
Broken English (S); Witches' Song; Brain Drain; Guilt; The Ballad Of Lucy Jordan (S); What's The Hurry; Working Class Hero; Why D'Ya Do It

Running time:
37.46

Current CD:
IMCD11

Further listening:
Strange Weather (1987) – in which older, wiser, croakier Marianne reprises songs from earlier in her career as cabaret standards; A Secret Life (1995) – a lush collaboration with Angelo Badalamenti; Vagabond Ways (1999) includes the extraordinary Incarceration Of A Flower Child, written by Roger Waters almost three decades previously.

Further reading:
Faithfull (Marianne Faithfull with David Dalton, 1995); www.planete.net/~smironne

Madness
One Step Beyond

Debut album from the Southern branch of the ska revival.

Many great bands emerged from the vibrant, hybrid jungle of pub rock, punk and New Wave in late '70s Britain, but few more enduring than the self-styled Nutty Boys from North London, Madness. They first leapt to prominence when their version of Prince Buster's song, The Prince, was a hit on The Specials' 2-Tone label.

"We used to go and watch Ian Dury a lot," recalls guitarist Chris Foreman. "Though we were basically ska we had a lot of other strings to our bow, just like Ian. There was a bit of a [label] feeding frenzy after The Prince was a hit, but we didn't want to be pigeonholed as 2-Tone. We met Dave Robinson from Stiff and Clive Langer (ex-Deaf School) on the circuit, and when Clive said he wanted to produce us we were like, wow! because we really liked his band. Basically, the album was our live set. We got it all recorded in about two weeks. The production was great because Alan (Winstanley – engineer) was a bit of a perfectionist, but Clive liked things when they sounded a bit wrong – Lee's sax for example. Once it was so out of tune that it had almost come back in! I remember when Clive wanted to put strings on Night Boat To Cairo, we thought it was a bit poncey, but Clive said he'd pay for the sessions if we didn't like the result. We liked it."

The exuberance of the songs and performances on *One Step Beyond*, from the irresistibly danceable bluebeat of the title track to the cod cool jazz of Razor Blade Alley, marked Madness as more than promising newcomers. But it was the classic, faintly melancholic pop of My Girl and Bed And Breakfast Man (recalling the domestic dramas purveyed by the Fabs and Kinks) which suggested that they were a good bet for the long term. The British took the album and the group to their hearts. After the furrowed brows of punk, fun was clearly what the pop nation needed. Madness broke the ice at parties while hinting at a sophistication that would give them more chart hits than practically any other British '80s outfit.

Record label:
Stiff

Produced
by Clive Langer.

Recorded
at TW Studios, Hammersmith, London;
May–June 1979.

Released:
October 1979

Chart peaks:
(UK) 2; (US) None

Personnel:
Graham "Suggs" McPherson (v); Mike Barson (k); Chris Foreman (g); Mark Bedford (b); Lee Thompson (s, v); Dan Woodgate (d, p); Chas Smash (v); Alan Winstanley (e)

Track listing:
One Step Beyond (S/UK); My Girl (S); Night Boat To Cairo (S/UK); Believe Me; Land Of Hope And Glory; The Prince (S/UK); Tarzan's Nuts; In The Middle Of The Night; Bed And Breakfast Man; Razor Blade Alley; Swan Lake; Rockin' In A Flat; Mummy's Boy; Chipmunks Are Go!

Running time:
39.00

Current CD:
Virgin CDOVS 133

Further listening:
Absolutely (1980); 7 (1981); Presents The Rise And Fall (1982)

Further reading:
www.madness.co.uk;
www.outrageouscreations.com/madness

The Specials
Specials

Cracking debut from Coventry's punk-ska innovators and social commentators.

By 1979 punk was stagnating and this multi-racial Coventry septet – who began in 1977 as The Coventry Automatics – were about to sweep the nation with their new beat – an intensified, aggressive fusion of punk and ska they called 2-Tone. Hair worn into a suedehead crop, dressed in Fred Perry shirts, mohair and tonic three-button suits, Crombies and tasselled loafers and bearing an attitude that had zero tolerance for bullshit, their sharp political awareness, biting sarcasm and cynical humour became the voice for many of Britain's disillusioned youth.

They'd first come to public attention as The Special AKA when they supported The Clash on their On Parole tour. A liaison with Clash manager Bernie Rhodes and a move to London proved abortive and the group decided to return home and cut their own record. By this time their live performances were becoming the stuff of legend – powerful, effulgent and terrifying, it was difficult to distinguish the band from their rude-boy following and stage invasions were *de rigueur*. Their first release on their own 2-Tone label was Gangsters, a rough-hewn tip of the hat to Prince Buster's Al Capone. Incredibly, it made the Top 10. Aligning their label with Chrysalis Records they entered TW Studios in their home town to record their first album.

"Everyone was pissed," admits Jerry Dammers, "We spent most of our time in the pub over the road from the studio." Nevertheless *Specials*, produced by Elvis Costello, captures the group's raw, breathless energy immaculately. Of the 14 tracks, four are skanking standards – Prince Buster's Too Hot, The Maytals' Monkey Man, Clement Seymour Dodd's You're Wondering Now, and A Message To You Rudy which features the inimitable trombone of Rico Rodriquez, who also featured on Dandy Livingstone's original.

Eight of the remaining tracks were penned by founder member Dammers (real name Gerald Dankin) including the bitter Too Much Too Young which borrowed heavily from Lloyd Charmers' risqué Birth Control, Doesn't Make It Alright with it's call for racial harmony, "Just because you're a black boy/Just because you're a white/It doesn't mean you've got to hate him/Doesn't mean you've got to fight/It doesn't make it

Record label:
2-Tone

Produced
by Elvis Costello.

Recorded
at TW Studios, Coventry; summer 1979.

Released:
October 1979

Chart peaks:
4 (UK) 84 (US)

Personnel:
Terry Hall (v); Neville Staples (v); Jerry Dammers (o); Roddy Radiation (g); Lynval Golding (g); Horace Panter (b); John Bradbury (d); Rico Rodriquez (horns); Dick Cuthell (horns); Chrissie Hynde (bv)

Track listing:
A Message To You Rudy (S/UK); Do The Dog; It's Up To You; Nite Klub (S/UK); Doesn't Make It Alright; Concrete Jungle; Too Hot; Monkey Man; (Dawning Of A) New Era; Blank Expression; Stupid Marriage; Too Much Too Young; Little Bitch; You're Wondering Now

Running time:
40.41

Current CD:
Chrysalis CCD 5001 adds: Gangsters

Further listening:
comprehensive best of The Specials Singles (1989); More Specials (1980). In The Studio (1984).

Further reading:
You're Wondering Now: A History Of The Specials (Paul Williams, 1995); The Two Tone Story (George Marshall, 1991); www.two-tone.co.uk

alright", the pro-active positivity of It's Up To You and Nite Klub, with it's instantly identifiable lyric, "I don't want to dance in a club like this/All the girls are slags and the beer tastes just like piss."

"I can only write about things that make me angry or I feel strongly about," Dammers later commented. A month after the album's release The Specials and their ska stable mates The Selecter and Madness all performed separately on the same edition of Top Of The Pops — 2-Tone's moment had clearly arrived with some force.

The Clash
London Calling

A seismic shift from punk recasts them as a kind of rocka-billy, pop, reggae jukebox.

L ondon Calling is without question the most enduring record to come out of the UK punk scene. Something in its musical scope, gush of ideas and feel-good rock'n'roll Zen brings to mind two other legendary doubles: Dylan's *Blonde On Blonde* and the Stones' *Exile On Main Street*. In fact, it's confusing to think of this as a "punk" record at all: *London Calling* was a celebration of the music The Clash enjoyed long before they became New Wave iconoclasts – blues, reggae, ska, soul, jazz, funk, rocka-billy. It was, as Strummer would put it, "probably our greatest moment".

The Clash's love affair with black American music had never been far from the surface but their interest was really re-awakened when they first toured the States in early '79, with Bo Diddley as support and a revved-up cover of Sonny Curtis' I Fought The Law in their set.

On returning to England, they donned brothel creepers and grew quiffs and work began on *London Calling* at a Pimlico rehearsal space. Between tea breaks and football games, a torrent of material was unleashed. Strummer was particularly loquacious: his increasingly complex lyrics taking the band's socio-political interests into new areas – the Spanish Civil War, cocaine-addled US company executives, Hollywood movie stars, impending apocalypse – while sticking with staple Clash fare like tower-block alienation, other pop stars and what it's like to be in The Clash. Meanwhile, Paul Simonon challenged the Strummer/Jones writing monopoly with Guns Of Brixton, a nervy punk-reggae hybrid brilliantly arranged by Jones.

After a demo version of the album was left on the tube by roadie Johnny Green, CBS insisted that they bring in a "proper" producer – so they dug out legendary '60s DJ, Svengali and lovable nutcase Guy Stevens (who'd produced Free and Mott The Hoople among others) from semi-retirement, and booked into Wessex Studios in Highbury. Stories from those sessions are legendary: Guy pouring beer in the piano and sleeping under the mixing desk, Guy swinging a ladder at Mick Jones' head, Guy throwing chairs across the room to get the vibe going.

Johnny Green: "It was the opposite of their previous album, *Give 'Em Enough Rope*, because it was all about energy

Record label:
CBS

Producer:
Guy Stevens

Recorded:
Wessex, London, summer 1979

Released:
December 1979.

Chart peaks:
9 (UK) 27 (US)

Personnel:
Joe Strummer (v, g), Mick Jones (g), Paul Simonon (b), Topper Headon (d), Micky Gallagher (k), Bill Price (e)

Track listing:
London Calling (S); Brand New Cadillac; Jimmy Jazz; Hateful; Rudie Can't Fail; Spanish Bombs; The Right Profile; Lost In The Supermarket; Clampdown; The Guns Of Brixton; Wrong 'Em Boyo; Death Or Glory; Koka Kola; The Card Cheat; Lover's Rock; Four Horsemen; I'm Not Down; Revolution Rock; Train In Vain (S/US)

Running time:
65:09

Current CD:
Columbia: Clash 3

Further listening:
The On Broadway (Sony) box set provides a meaty career overview, with the bonus of some rare archive tracks; the 2-CD The Story Of The Clash (Sony) is good for beginners; otherwise you really need to digest the albums individually.

Further reading:
The Last Gang In Town by Marcus Gray (Fourth Estate); A Riot Of My Own by Johnny Green (Indigo); feature MOJO 71.

levels. There was a high level of communication, people talking about their lives and circumstances."

The sessions kicked off with a cover of Vince Taylor's British rock classic Brand New Cadillac, which set out the band's stall as *nouveau* Teddy punks. This set the tone for two other covers celebrating their rude-boy fixation: The Rulers' Wrong 'Em Boyo and Revolution Rock. Some songs, like Rudie Can't Fail and The Card Cheat, felt as if they were long lost Jamaican/American greats but were actually Clash originals. The *coup de grâce*, though, came in the form of Mick Jones' lightly funky Train In Vain, a touching love song inspired by The Slits' Viv Albertine, added at the last minute (and hence not listed on the original sleeve).

When it was released in December 1979, with a brilliant Ray Lowry cover pastiching Elvis's first LP from Pennie Smith's shots of the group's second US tour, *London Calling* secured The Clash's reputation. Twenty years on, it remains a brilliant, unusual record, whose musicality – Topper's jazzy drumming, Mick Jones inventive guitar, Simonon's rock-solid dub-level bass, the thoughtful brass and piano overdubs – is matched only by Strummer's gift for impassioned vocals and inspired ad-libs. Worthy of Rolling Stone's 'Best album of the '80s' award.

Pink Floyd
The Wall

Claustrophobic double concept album whose bleak themes appeared to permeate its makers.

Someone once conducted a poll among the millions who purchased *The Dark Side Of The Moon* to discover why they liked it: they found it was Pink Floyd fans' favourite album to have sex to. No-one has undertaken a survey of the equally large numbers who purchased *The Wall*, so the use they make of an album about alienation, fascism, sadomasochism and despair, inspired by a rock star's hatred of his audience, remains a matter for conjecture.

A multi-level musical, lyrical, psychological and architectural concept that became a film starring Bob Geldof and one of the most elaborate theatrical stage shows ever, featuring Gerald Scarfe's animations, *The Wall* was sparked by an incident that closed the *Animals* tour. Waters, so disillusioned by stadium shows that he spat at a fan and fantasised about dropping bombs on the audience, said he would only perform again behind a wall. It also instigated the break-up of the band – starting with Rick Wright's dismissal during recording and ending with Waters' departure after *The Final Cut*. Bob Ezrin, one of three credited producers, called the atmosphere in the studio "war" – admittedly a "very gentlemanly" war "as they're English".

But the sessions – which took place outside of Britain for the very same tax reasons that prompted the album's genesis (finding themselves bankrupt with a huge tax bill thanks to poor financial mismanagement, the band agreed to make one of the two putative solo projects Waters had been writing) – also had successful moments of what Gilmour called "the last embers of Roger's and my ability to work collaboratively together". Though most songs were Waters compositions, Comfortably Numb started out as a part-written Gilmour song which, with Waters' lyrics, became one of the album's – and the band's – most affecting and memorable numbers.

Another collaboration – this time between Waters and Ezrin, who suggested the disco beat – produced hit single Another Brick In The Wall [Part II]. Its dark themes appeared to mirror the turmoil in the lives of its creators, both in and out of the studio. "Everybody," said Ezrin, "was going through amazing stuff in their individual lives, and we all brought our pain and our weakness and our foibles and our peculiarities to the table. But in the final analysis it produced what is arguably

Record label:
EMI

Produced
by Bob Ezrin, Roger Waters and David Gilmour; co-produced by James Guthrie.

Recorded
at Superbear, France; Miravel, France; Producers Workshop, Los Angeles; CBS, New York; April–November 1979.

Released:
December 1979

Chart peaks:
3 (UK) 1 (US)

Personnel:
Roger Waters (v, b); David Gilmour (v, g); Rick Wright (k); Nick Mason (d); Bruce Johnston, Toni Tennille, Joe Chemay, John Joyce, Stan Farber, Jim Haas, the children of Islington Green School (bv); James Guthrie (e); Nick Griffiths, Patrice Quef, Brian Christian, Rick Hart, John McClure (e)

Track listing:
In The Flesh?; The Thin Ice; Another Brick In The Wall [Part I]; The Happiest Days Of Our Lives; Another Brick In The Wall [Part II] (S); Mother; Goodbye Blue Sky; Empty Spaces; Young Lust; One Of My Turns (S); Don't Leave Me Now; Another Brick In The Wall [Part III]; Goodbye Cruel World; Hey You; Is There Anybody Out There; Nobody Home; Vera; Bring The Boys Back Home; Comfortably Numb (S); The Show Must Go On; In The Flesh; Run Like Hell (S); Waiting For The Worms; Stop; The Trial; Outside The Wall

Running time:
75.83

Current CD:
8SNY68519

Further listening:
Dark Side Of The Moon (1973);

Roger Waters' solo debut, The Pros And Cons Of Hitch-Hiking (1984); Various, The Wall: Live In Berlin (1990); the Floyd's own rendering of The Wall live, Is There Anybody Out There? (2000).

Further reading:
Saucerful Of Secrets: The Pink Floyd Odyssey (Nicholas Schaffner, 1991); www.pinkfloyd.com

the best work of that decade and maybe one of the most important rock albums ever made."

THE
1980s

Elvis Costello And The Attractions
Get Happy!!

Twewnty golden nuggets of Stax-influenced pop.

During preparations for *Get Happy!!* Elvis Costello was spied leaving legendary Camden record shop Rock On with armfuls of '60s soul and R&B albums. "I was listening to a lot of the music I'd loved when I was 15, such as Motown and Stax," admits Elvis, and, clad in its deliberately distressed, retro sleeve, with a packed tracklisting including a cover of obscure Sam & Dave tune I Can't Stand Up For Falling Down, *Get Happy!!* is indeed informed by the taut songwriting and muscular musicianship of the heyday of soul. Thus Booker T's Time Is Tight riff emerges on Temptation, one of the core trilogy of songs completed by Opportunity and Possession. This last was written about a waitress in a cafe near the studios in Amsterdam, and is described by Costello as "a total lust song, it has nothing to do with any art concept".

Nevertheless, artfulness abounds, from the jittery ska tones of Black And White World and Human Touch to the lovelorn country of Motel Matches and the impressionistic shadowplay of B-Movie. A frantic reading of The Merseybeats' classic I Stand Accused is complemented by such frenetic originals as Riot Act and Man Called Uncle, all of which belie the "wasted" condition of the band after two and a half years of solid touring and recording.

Rather than wearing them down, the tough schedule had produced a lean and powerfully efficient unit which left no space for the frontman to over-indulge in wordplay. It's not all retro either; Elvis drew on a range of contemporary influences too. He had just produced The Specials' debut album and had been enjoying Berlin-era Bowie on tour. At one stage, apparently, the upbeat High Fidelity was tailored like *Station To Station* "in a ponderous heavy metal style".

Although there's no direct musical evidence of his Bowie/Eno fascination, the album has a thoroughly modern ring, due in some part to the decision to scrap the original set of "wretched arrangements" in favour of "a more rhythmic accompaniment than the tricksy, nervy backing we'd been using", thereby marking a departure from the skinny-tied, New Wave sound associated with his first three albums. The Attractions maintain a manic pace on *Get Happy!!*'s 20 tracks,

Record label:
F Beat

Produced
by Nick Lowe.

Recorded
at Wisseloord Studios, Hilversum, Holland; October 1979. New Amsterdam recorded at Archipelago Studios, London; summer 1979.

Released:
February 1980

Chart peaks:
2 (UK) 11 (US)

Personnel:
Elvis Costello (v, g); Steve Nieve (k); Bruce Thomas (b), Pete Thomas (d)

Track listing:
I Can't Stand Up For Falling Down (S); Black & White World; 5ive Gears In Reverse; B Movie; Motel Matches; Human Touch; Beaten To The Punch; Temptation; I Stand Accused; Riot Act; Love For Tender; Opportunity; The Imposter; Secondary Modern; King Horse; Possession; Man Called Uncle; Clowntime Is Over; New Amsterdam (S); High Fidelity (S)

Running time:
48.23

Current CD:
DPAM5 adds: Girl's Talk, Clowntime Is Over (Version 2); Getting Mighty Crowded; So Young; Just A Memory; Hoover Factory; Ghost Train; Dr Luther's Assistant; Black And White World (demo); Riot Act (demo); Love For Tender (demo); Hoover Factory (demo); Ghost Train (demo).

Further listening:
Trust (1981); Booker T. And The MGs, Soul Limbo (1968); The Specials, Specials (1979)

Further reading:
The Big Wheel (Bruce Thomas, 1990); Let Them All Talk: Elvis Costello (Brian Hinton, 1999)

five of which are under two minutes long. In the UK the good-will created by Costello's biggest hit to date, Oliver's Army from predecessor *Armed Forces*, helped the first single – I Can't Stand Up For Falling Down – reach number four in the charts. And in the States, the album's Top 20 status was in part due to mainstream patronage by the likes of Linda Ronstadt, who had recently included three Costello songs on her latest album. *Get Happy!!* lives up to its title as Costello's most enthusiastic and life-affirming collection.

The Cramps

Songs The Lord Taught Us

Ladies and gentlemen, please welcome psychobilly — and one of the most exciting live outfits ever.

To this day, The Cramps are one of the greatest live outfits ever to walk the planet. "At the time rock'n'roll had turned into 'rock music' and we just wanted to get it back to what it was in the beginning," says singer Lux Interior. "We wanted the same simplicity you find with a Shadows Of Knight song, an early rockabilly number or the Velvet Underground."

The band were introduced to producer Alex "Big Star" Chilton by New York photographer friend Stephanie Chernikowski and as Lux remembers — "Immediately he was fun; not snobbish or arty. He's a wild person in the true sense of the word, and a little too honest, which doesn't earn him a lot of friends." Through Chilton's Memphis connections the band booked time in Sam "He-who-discovered-Elvis" Phillips' studio. Guitarist Poison Ivy recalls, "We just kept pinching ourselves. We couldn't believe we were there." The sessions were disjointed; often due to lack of financial support from the record company or the fact that various engineers couldn't/wouldn't work with Wildman Chilton.

"Alex would get drunk. . . we'd pick him up off the console. . .!" deadpans Lux. "We just played and played – ripped through, no overdubs, all in the same room. It was a bit Dada. If you're out of control you're bound to make new things." They captured some of the most visceral performances ever committed to vinyl. From the break-neck hillbilly boogie of The Johnny Burnette Rock'n'Roll Trio's Tear It Up, to grinding '60s garage stomps – witness their terminally sleazy manifesto Garbageman – the combo obviously knew their history and lived it as well, amalgamating their primal influences with a timeless punk swagger. The twin guitars of Rorschach and Gregory conjure up shards and shrouds of feedback and then rip them with knife-sharp single-note runs from the Link Wray How-To manual. "I loved the New York Dolls' guitar sound," says Ivy. "anyone could be doing anything, swooping in and out."

Over the top Lux howls paeans to outsiders everywhere: "I was a teenage werewolf/Braces on my fangs/A Mid-West monster with the highest grades."

"There's a lot more metaphor and autobiography in our songs than people realise," notes Ivy. "In Ohio (Lux's birthplace) we felt very isolated..."

Record label:
IRS

Produced
by Alex Chilton.

Recorded
at the Sam C Phillips Recording Studio, Memphis; July–September 1979.

Released:
April 1980

Chart peaks:
None (UK) None (US)

Personnel:
Lux Interior (v); Poison Ivy Rorschach (g); Bryan Gregory (g); Nick Knox (d)

Track listing:
TV Set; Rock On The Moon; Garbageman; I Was A Teenage Werewolf; Sunglasses After Dark; The Mad Daddy; Mystery Plane; Zombie Dance; What's Behind The Mask?; I'm Cramped; Tear It Up; Fever (S/UK)

Running time:
36.55

Current CD:
EMI/Zonophone 4 93836 2 adds: I Was A Teenage Werewolf (with false start); Mystery Plane (original mix); Twist And Shout (original mix); I'm Cramped (original mix); The Mad Daddy (original mix)

Further listening:
Gravest Hits (EP, 1979); Psychedelic Jungle (1981); A Date With Elvis (1986); Flamejob (1994)

Further reading:
The Wild, Wild World Of The Cramps (Ian Johnston, 1990)
www.geocities.com/thecrampspage

Getting a satisfactory final mix proved difficult, Chilton apparently rejecting one mix "because it sounded too good". Finally Chilton, Ivy and Lux came up with what Lux calls "an engineer's nightmare!" Ivy reckons it's a little "swimmy sounding", lacking the razor edge of the band's live shows. Nevertheless, it certainly sounded like no one else at the time, the album was ecstatically reviewed, and The Cramps spawned many imitators, none of whom could match either the seriousness or the humour of the originators.

It says on the spine of the original record "File Under Sacred Music". They are not joking.

Smokey Robinson
Warm Thoughts

A soul legend grows old gracefully.

Smokey Robinson had had a difficult time of it in the '70s. His albums were still stickered with the old Motown legend, "The Sound Of Young America", but in 1980 he was turning 40, and in the eight years since quitting The Miracles he hadn't achieved a terrific amount of solo success. But the previous year had seen him hit a new vein of excellence with *Where There's Smoke*, the most vibrant album he'd yet made, climaxing with the gorgeous hit, Cruisin'. *Warm Thoughts* — though it didn't quite have the same impact — now sounds like the perfect follow-up.

What he was seeking was a synthesis of his hit-machine vitality with the romanticism that had always drenched his writing, blending it all into something which a mature black audience could identify with. He might have blueprinted Motown's pop style with the likes of Going To A Go-Go, but Tears Of A Clown was more like the real Smokey. So his songwriting began to grow darker and more pensive, even if he never gave up on the cheeky wordplay which was another of his hallmarks. Nobody else would try and get away with a title like Into Each Rain Some Life Must Fall, even if that is the darkest and most wrenching of all the tracks on offer here. There are lighter pieces too, such as the irresistible Let Me Be The Clock ("For the time of your life, I'm a cuckoo I know"), but the centrepiece is What's In Your Life For Me, a deeply considered piece of songwriting with the subtlest melodic and harmonic shifts.

After all those years of having the highest, creamiest tenor in black music, Smokey's voice was beginning to thicken, yet it still touched peaks and skipped over bar lines in ways which must have been the despair of some of his rivals. His great records of the '80s — *Being With You, Essar, Yes It's You Lady* — continued to build on what he had set out to do on this record. But despite the big hit he scored with the title track of *Being With You*, his audience continued to drift away, which must have hurt such a great artist. Today, he is more interested in golf than music.

Record label:
Motown

Produced
by Smokey Robinson.

Recorded
at Motown Studios, Hollywood; 1980.

Released:
April 1980

Chart peaks:
None (UK) 14 (US)

Personnel:
William "Smokey" Robinson (v); Sonny Burke, Roderick Rancifer (k); Marv Tarplin, Phil Upchurch, David T Walker, Melvin "Wah Wah" Ragin, L Marlo Henderson (g); Wayne Tweed, Kenneth Burke, Scott Edwards (b); James Gadson, Scotty Harris (d); James Sledge (congas); Michael Jacobsen (c); Fred Smith (f, s); Cheryl Cooper, Ivory Davis, Claudette Robinson, James Sledge, Patricia Henley Talbert (bv)

Track listing:
Let Me Be The Clock; Heavy On Pride (Light On Love); Into Each Rain Some Life Must Fall; Wine, Women And Song; Melody Man; What's In Your Life For Me; I Want To Be Your Love; Travelin' Through

Running time:
36.31

Not available on CD

Further listening:
Where There's Smoke (1979); Being With You (1981)

Further reading:
Smokey: Inside My Life (1990)

X

Los Angeles

LA's accessible and influential answer to New York and London punk.

It was believed that punk would never take off in Los Angeles. Life was too sunny, too easy. X believed otherwise.

The embryonic X was Florida native Christine Cervenka and Baltimore's John Doe (born John Dukac) who met at a poetry workshop where Doe, entranced by Cervenka's poetry, mooted the idea of putting her lyrics to music in a band.

"I'm no dummy," says Exene (who changed her first name in lapsed Catholic support for Christ having His name dumped out of Christmas, as in Xmas). "The first thing I asked was, 'What about my publishing?'"

Doe recruited rockabilly guitar whiz Billy Zoom who had played in Gene Vincent's final bands, and found drummer DJ Bonebrake at an open audition. Bonebrake won the drummer's seat when he showed up with a piccolo snare, a drum which cracks through any music like a rifle shot. The quartet's image was strong: Doe's greaser's hair fell in his face as he pummelled his bass and howled, exotic Exene sang Beat poetry lyrics against bizarre atonal melodies, Zoom stood with legs apart and a stupid grin on his boyish face wailing riff after riff, leaving Bonebrake as the straight man, the grad student who wandered into the wrong group. This first album was largely their live set. It was produced by Doors keyboardist Ray Manzarek, largely because he was the only hip name to come backstage at the Whiskey and tell Doe that his band could actually go places. They did, and they didn't.

After *Los Angeles* it all began to fragment into thrash metal, cowpunk, surf punk, hardcore, straight edge, roots rock and even spoken word. But for a brief moment the Beat-meets-punk songs of John Doe and Exene Cervenka caught lightning in a jar.

Record label:
Slash

Produced
by Ray Manzarek.

Recorded
at Golden Sound Studios, Hollywood; January 1980.

Released:
April 1980.

Chart peaks:
None (UK) None (US)

Personnel:
John Doe (b, v); Exene Cervenka (v); Billy Zoom (g); DJ Bonebrake (d); Ray Manzarek (k)

Track listing:
Your Phone's Off The Hook But You're Not; Johnny Hit And Run Paulene; Soul Kitchen; Nausea; Sugarlight; Los Angeles; Sex And Dying In High Society; The Unheard Music; The World's A Mess It's In My Kiss

Running time:
28.05

Currently unavailable on CD

Further listening:
Wild Gift (1981); More Fun In The New World (1983)

Further reading:
Make The Music Go Bang!: The Early LA Punk Scene (edited by Don Snowden, 1997); Beyond And Back: The Story Of X (Chris Morris, 1983)

Linton Kwesi Johnson
Bass Culture

Anglo-Caribbean dub poetry. Sounds good, kicks like a mule.

Naturally, most great albums come from people who have dedicated their lives to music – whole-heartedly, if not monastically. But Linton Kwesi Johnson always had too much on the go to make that commitment. Moving from Jamaica to Brixton, London, when he was 11, he did well academically, graduating with a sociology degree. He worked in the civil service and factories for a while, but his passion flowed through black political activism and poetry (published regularly from 1973 on). In 1977 he recorded his first album *Dread Beat An' Blood*. Initially credited as Poet And The Roots, he was so well connected culturally and politically that his backing band, assembled by Dennis Bovell, comprised the cream of British-based reggae. Between his sleek, deep speaking voice and the musicians' syncopating sensitivity a new genre, dub poetry, was created. Johnson's third album, *Bass Culture*, proved its apogee.

Mostly, it took a sparse, hard line; Street 66 pugnaciously defying a police raid on a house party and Inglan Is A Bitch angrily lamenting abuses suffered by England's first generation of West Indian immigrants. But, with the title track and Reggae Sounds – both published as poems five years earlier – Johnson took a daring leap into cultural and intellectual territory hardly ever touched on in reggae (or any other kind of pop music). He explained that these songs were "basically talking about art and experience – I don't want too much eyebrows raised now! I mean they're about how you feel and how you translate that into meaningful entertainment that inspires and motivates at the same time." Rarely can street life and academic training have blended so naturally. He wrote and spoke and played the sinuous unity of word, music, rhythm and fighting oppression. It was Gerard Manley Hopkins as militant reggae: "Shock-black bubble-doun-beat bouncing/rock-wise tumble-down sound music;/foot-drop find drum, blood story,/bass history is a moving/is a hurting black story" (Reggae Sounds); "Muzik of blood/black reared/pain rooted/heart geared; all tensed up/in the bubble an the bounce/an the leap an the weight-drop/ SCATTA-MATTA-SHATTA-SHACK!/what a beat!" (Bass Culture). But perhaps it was one of those moments when an artist shoots so high, makes it, and has nothing left to say. After *Bass Culture* Johnson devoted himself to community politics, journalism and teaching, recording only one more album of new material.

Record label:
Mango

Produced
by Linton Kwesi Johnson and Blackbeard.

Recorded
at Gooseberry Sound Studios, London, 1980.

Released:
May 9, 1980

Chart peaks:
46 (UK) None (US)

Personnel:
Linton Kwesi Johnson (v); Vivian Weathers, Floyd Lawson (b); Jah Bunny, Winston Curniffe (d); John Kpiaye (g); Dennis Bovell, Webster Johnson (k); James Danton (s); Henry Tenyue (s, t); Dick Cuthell (t); Rico (tb); Julio Finn (hm); Clinton Bailey, Everald Forrest (pc); John Caffrey, Mark Lusardy, Dennis Bovell (e)

Track listing:
Bass Culture; Street 66; Reggae Fi Peach; Di Black Petty Booshwah; Inglan Is A Bitch; Loraine; Reggae Sounds; Two Sides Of Silence

Running time:
31.08

Current CD:
RRCD 26

Further listening:
Tings An' Times (1990) – brief return to recording, ten years on but still sharp.

Further reading:
Dread Beat & Blood (Bogle-L'Ouverture, 1975), Inglan Is A Bitch (Linton Kwesi Johnson, 1980)

Magazine
The Correct Use Of Soap

Gloomy art-rockers' happiest hour.

Signed by Virgin on the strength of a three-track demo, Manchester's Magazine cut sombre and intellectual figure. Their 1978 debut, *Real Life* caused a considerable critical and commercial splash; the follow-up, *Secondhand Daylight* only a ripple in comparison. For the difficult third album, Devoto resolved to work quicker and to highlight the talents of McGeoch, whose impressively versatile guitar sound had been squeezed out by keyboards on the previous album. Hannett (who'd worked with Devoto on the Buzzcocks' Spiral Scratch EP) was not Devoto's first producer of choice – Tony Visconti, John Barry and Sly Stone had all been requested – but his work with Joy Division and the fact that he had shared a flat with keyboardist Dave Formula secured him the job.

Twenty years on, Devoto – who has long since quit the music business and now works at a photographic agency – regards *The Correct Use Of Soap* as his band's best studio work. The outright anger of its predecessors was smoothed out and replaced with a percolating existential irritability although, Devoto claims, "it was more hurt. I was in a spiritually difficult place at that time. My father had died when we were on tour in America for the first time the previous summer – that chucked me into a spin – and I had also fallen in love in various places in the world. I was a very confused person. Even a year later, at the end of *Magic, Murder And The Weather* [Magazine's final studio album from 1981], I was still on the same psychic curve – down, down, down."

Curiously, this presents a brighter, more uptempo Magazine, demonstrating McGeoch's creative way with the subverted Johnny B Goode riff and subtle jazz nuance, alongside their more familiar, brooding Roxy Music and Bowie inflections. The inclusion of the Sly Stone classic – which they had been playing live as a final encore for some time – helped demolish Magazine's reputation as arty and difficult depressives, despite Devoto's downbeat delivery, which he borrowed directly from the funkmeister's Thank You For Talkin' To Me Africa version.

The Correct Use Of Soap was also significantly the result of Devoto's desire "to get a bit more straightforward"; he stopped wearing make-up on stage and began to withdraw from the band's press commitments, harbouring a deep-seated feeling that the end for him was not far off. This was clinched when

Record label:
Virgin

Produced
by Martin Hannett.

Recorded
on the Manor Mobile at Summa rehearsal studios, Chelsea and The Townhouse, London; December 1979 and February 1980.

Released:
May 1980

Chart peaks:
28 (UK) None (US)

Personnel:
Howard Devoto (v); John McGeoch (g, bv); Barry Adamson (b); John Doyle (d, pc); Dave Formula (k); Laura Teresa (bv)

Track listing:
Because You're Frightened; Model Worker; I'm A Party; You Never Knew Me; Philadelphia; I Want To Burn Again; Thank You (Falettinme Be Mice Elf Agin) (S); Sweetheart Contract; Stuck; A Song From Under The Floorboards (S)

Running time:
39.36

Currently unavailable on CD

Further listening:
Real Life (1978); Secondhand Daylight (1979); Devoto solo album Jerky Versions Of The Dream (1983); The Unanswerable Lust (1988), as Luxuria; box set Magazine ... Maybe It's Right To Be Nervous (2000)

Further reading:
www.buzzcocks.com/SecretPublic/SP_main/Devoto/body_devoto.html

McGeoch quit after a European tour to join Siouxsie And The Banshees. He proved almost impossible to replace and, despite the release of another album a year later, for Magazine the writing was by now most definitely on the wall.

Peter Gabriel
Peter Gabriel (III)

Gabriel astounds with his third and best solo album.

After leaving Genesis in 1975, Peter Gabriel had taken time off when he "grew cabbages and made babies" but continued to write songs. Following a frustrating period of trying to compose for other artists ("I was unhappy not to be in control of the arrangements"), he emerged with his debut solo album early in 1977. Over the following three years Gabriel re-established himself as a vital songwriter and uniquely charismatic performer and amazingly – given the sweeping-away-the-old-guard spirit of the times – he retained a credibility that his contemporaries must have wondered at.

That credibility was never higher than when Nick Kent in the NME gave Gabriel's third album a full-page review saying "I don't expect to hear a better record all year." From the rumbling threat of Intruder to the stone-faced outrage of Biko, *Peter Gabriel* (or *Melt*, as it's sometimes called, a reference to the striking cover and to distinguish it from the other three albums with the same title) is a model of intelligent, potent rock music. The mini presidential assassination movie Family Snapshot, the forceful And Through The Wire (featuring Paul Weller on searing rhythm guitar) and the ingenious and melodic hit Games Without Frontiers, were all decorated with disturbing, visceral textures and driven by an extraordinary cymbal-free drum track. Although producer Steve Lillywhite had been involved in notable "drum sound" albums (Siouxsie And The Banshees' *The Scream* among them), it was when Genesis pal Phil Collins was hammering out a tom-and-snare pattern and engineer Hugh Padgham was experimenting with gated reverb effects that Gabriel was inspired, writing Intruder there and then.

Gabriel: "I was certain it was a landmark drum sound. Now I get annoyed when people say I have copied Phil's sound." Collins, meanwhile, was annoyed not to be given more than "drum pattern" credit for the song itself.

The anthemic Biko was a heartfelt song of sorrow for the South African situation, some time before such things were fashionable. "I was disappointed it wasn't a hit," says Gabriel. "I had really hoped it would be an anthem against apartheid." It had its impact in time however, with Little Steven citing it as the inspiration behind his Sun City project. Gabriel went global soon after *Peter Gabriel III*, playing the rock-star-with-a-conscience with considerable artistry and dignity.

Record label:
Charisma

Produced
by Steve Lillywhite.

Recorded
at Bath with the Manor Mobile and the Townhouse, London

Released:
June 1980

Chart peaks:
1 (UK) 22 (US)

Personnel:
Kate Bush (bv); Phil Collins (d); Peter Gabriel (v, k); Larry Fast (k); Robert Fripp (g); John Giblin (g); Dave Gregory (g); Tony Levin (stick); Jerry Marotta (d); Dick Morrisey (s); Paul Weller (g); Morris Pert (pc); David Rhodes (g); Hugh Padgham (e)

Track listing:
Intruder; No Self Control; Start; I Don't Remember; Family Snapshot; And Through The Wire; Games Without Frontiers; Not One Of Us; Lead A Normal Life; Biko

Running time:
45.34

Current CD:
PGCD3

Further listening:
Peter Gabriel (1977); Peter Gabriel (1978); So (1986)

Further reading:
Peter Gabriel (Spencer Bright, 1999); www.petergabriel.com

AC/DC
Back In Black

*With Bon Scott dead, AC/DC unleash their new frontman
— and catapult to megastardom.*

Twenty years on, *Back In Black* still makes the hair stand up
on the back of the neck. It was recorded only weeks after
vocalist Bon Scott was found dead in a parked car in London
after a too-good night out on the town and — unsurprisingly
given the circumstances — is a lethal combination of wild and
barely suppressed emotion, anger at Bon for leaving them and a
wilful determination to carry on.

"There was a nothingness around everyone," says
Malcolm Young. "At the funeral Bon's dad said 'You can't stop,
you've got to find someone else', and our manager came up
with a list of singers — but we weren't interested. We thought,
we can't replace Bon. He was unique." Material for a follow-up
to the previous year's breakthrough album *Highway To Hell* had
been started with Bon, who actually played drums on the
demos. Finally, fed up with "sitting around moping", Malcolm
and Angus got together to play and decided to keep going. The
man chosen to sing was someone Bon himself had once recommended — Brian Johnson, ex-Geordie, possessor of a powerful,
abrasive, drain-cleaner-gargling voice and an ebullient, down-to-
earth personality. He joined them in a Bahamas studio with
Highway To Hell producer Mutt Lange.

"We'd got the title before we'd even written a word",
remembers Malcolm. "Angus said, 'Why not call it *Back In Black*
and make a black album cover as a tribute to Bon?' It was a hard
album to make but it had its magic moments." Matching their
turbulent mood swings, the Bahamas was being hit by hurricanes
and stalked by a machete-wielding killer. Inside the studio the
band closed ranks and focussed on the record — they jettisoned
the earlier lyrics to start from scratch with their new frontman.
The result was an album stuffed with rock anthems: You Shook
Me All Night Long; Rock And Roll Ain't Noise Pollution; the
sombre tolling bell of opener Hell's Bells — soon to become a
stage prop. Lange gave a polished, powerhouse metal production
to their trademark riffs and grinding beat. "He wanted to take
the sound a bit further," said Malcolm, "and he got it bang-on.
That album still impresses everyone for its production." Leaving
the Bahamas for the New York mixing room after a week off, the
band gathered for the playback. "We thought, 'Fucking hell, this
is a monster.'" It was. Over ten million people bought it in the
US alone. The band were megastars.

Record label:
Atco

Produced
by Robert John "Mutt" Lange.

Recorded
at Compass Point Studios, Bahamas; April
and May 1980.

Release date:
July 1980

Chart peaks:
1 (UK) 4 (US)

Personnel:
Brian Johnson (v); Angus Young (g);
Malcolm Young (g); Cliff Williams (b); Phil
Rudd (d); Tony Platt (e)

Track listing:
Hell's Bells; Shoot To Thrill; What Do You
Do For The Money Honey; Given The
Dog A Bone; Let Me Put My Love Into
You; Back In Black; You Shook Me All
Night Long; Have A Drink On Me; Shake
A Leg; Rock And Roll Ain't Noise
Pollution

Running time:
40.42

Current CD:
4951532

Further listening:
Highway To Hell (1979) and Let There
Be Rock (1977), featuring original
vocalist Bon Scott; Flick Of The Switch
(1983) and The Razor's Edge (1999)
featuring Johnson.

Further reading:
MOJO 79; AC/DC — The Kerrang! Files!
(Malcolm Dome, 1995) www.acdc.rock.com

Echo And The Bunnymen
Crocodiles

*Universally lauded debut from the group nearly called
Mona Lisa And The Grease Guns who made overcoats hip.*

In the fertile late '70s scene which centred around Liverpool
club Eric's, musicians were hanging out, talking up their act
and making their first tentative steps. Echo And The Bunnymen's
first recordings – like The Teardrop Explodes – were stiff-
limbed affairs. A session for John Peel in 1979 which showcased
rudimentary songs like I Bagsy Yours (later retitled Monkeys),
and their debut single, Pictures On My Wall, the same year,
sounded hesitant, flat and linear, bound by the restrictions of
their primitive drum machine. The press initially greeted them
as a substandard version of Neil Young – bad news indeed for
musicians inspired by Bowie, The Velvets, The Doors and The
Thirteenth Floor Elevators.

With manager Bill Drummond urging them to get a
drummer, the teenage Pete De Freitas was recruited. His tough,
imaginative playing had a galvanising effect. Added to Ian
McCulloch's pin-up potential – "The first rock'n'roll beauty
contest of the '80s" was Paul Morley's assessment of a show
with The Psychedelic Furs and The Teardrop Explodes at the
Lyceum in March 1980 – the effect on their popularity was
spectacular. Said Rob Dickins, who signed them to Warner's
new Korova imprint after seeing that show himself, "The singer
looked so charismatic. He was beautiful. His voice had that Jim
Morrison ring to it. The songs weren't well-formulated, but you
saw 'Star' in neon above his head."

By the time the band came to record *Crocodiles*, the old
untogetherness had vanished completely, replaced by an expansive, melodramatic sound. "We found we were capable of doing
something good," said McCulloch, "That album just opened up
possibilities." On Going Up, the supple rhythm section acted as
a launch pad for guitar lift-off, before the song drifted into a
delicious, spacey coda – McCulloch drolly intoned that there
were not enough people with flowers in their hair, a sentiment
also mischievously scratched in the run-out groove, which got
them labelled in some quarters as "psychedelic", at a time when
the jury was out on whether or not that was cool.

"Whoever the turd was who first said that, they should
chop his head off," said McCulloch after being constantly asked
about the band's drugs intake. "It doesn't mean anything,
'psychedelic'. If only rock critics could learn to be as original as

Record label:
Korova

Produced
by David Balfe, Bill Drummond and Ian
Broudie.

Recorded
at Rockfield and Eden Studios; summer
1979.

Released:
July 1980

Chart peaks:
17 (UK) None (US)

Personnel:
Ian McCulloch (v, g); Will Sergeant (g);
Les Pattinson (b); Pete De Freitas (d);
David Balfe (k); Hugh Jones (e); Rod
Houison (e)

Track listing:
Going Up; Stars Are Stars; Pride; Monkeys;
Crocodiles; Rescue (S/UK); Villiers Terrace;
Pictures On My Wall; All That Jazz;
Happy Death Men

Running time:
32.53

Current CD:
2292 42316-2

Further listening:
Heaven Up Here (1981); Porcupine
(1983); Ocean Rain (1984)

Further reading:
www.bunnymen.com

we are. If the music's got a dreamlike quality, maybe it comes from dreams. It doesn't have to be drug-induced. We get drunk like once in a blue moon but that's about it."

On the title track – with its ferocious cross-cutting guitars – and the relentless on-beats of the apocalyptic All That Jazz, the band also proved they could rock, while the sublime Rescue, released as a single, became the student soundtrack to the summer. *Crocodiles*, as NME predicted, would become "one of the contemporary rock albums of the year."

The Soft Boys
Underwater Moonlight

Second from cult Cambridge crew led by Robyn Hitchcock, inheritor of Syd Barrett's mantle of strange.

"I went into the music business with negative expectations and they were all fulfilled," says Robin Hitchcock. The Soft Boys may have supported several of the big-hitters in the late '70s days of punk and glory, but it wasn't really their scene. "We were really a psychedelic pub-rock band, scared of getting hit by a flying audience member."

The combo put out one ill-conceived single for Andrew Lauder's trendy Radar Records before re-grouping to release the over-complicated, intermittently brilliant album *A Can Of Bees.* "You can't listen for too long without getting a migraine," sighs Hitchcock. Yet from this general gloom the absolutely scintillating *Underwater Moonlight* emerged.

"It became a simpler and happier band. Matthew (Seligman) joined and he was a far more straight-ahead player than Andy (Metcalfe) – and he liked his pop, and Kim liked his pop, and I began to feel I could write songs rather than ideas with music attached." The opening trio of tracks bears this out. The wonderfully malevolent I Wanna Destroy You sounds likes hell's Bee Gees backed by The Who. Kingdom Of Love is a melodic jewel; British Art'n'B circa '66 – lyrical oddness, held aloft by a golden guitar riff. Positive Vibrations rushes to the sea on torrents of jangling guitar, sitar and harmonies borrowed from the American West Coast.

"[Producer] Pat Collier was a graduate of the '60s school of guitar. He knew how to make a little money go a long way. Kim and I only had volume pedals but he made us sound brilliant. I remember writing the cheque for the I Wanna Destroy You session, it was £30." Rew's versatile, vigorous playing is certainly a key element in the album's success, but at the very centre stands Hitchcock: a looming, oneiric poet with a singular sense of humour – "I would ramble all through time and space/ Just to have a butcher's at your face/ You're the one I love or so it seems/ Because you've confiscated all my dreams." Whether on the Beefheart-style slash'n'burn of Old Pervert or the perfect pealing beauty of Queen Of Eyes, Hitchcock commands the ring. The album barely made a dent at the time, but since then many bands (including R.E.M.), have acknowledged its influence. Rew went on to have hits with Katrina And The Waves, while Hitchcock's solo career continues to swim against the tide and continues to delight, much like *Underwater Moonlight.*

Record label:
Armageddon

Produced
by Pat Collier (except Spaceward sessions – produced by studio staff).

Recorded
at Spaceward, Cambridge; Summer 1979; Alaska and James Morgan Studios, London; early 1980.

Released:
July 1980

Chart peaks:
None (UK) None (US)

Personnel:
Robyn Hitchcock (g, k, v); Kimberley Rew (g, b, syn, v); Morris Windsor (d, v); Matthew Seligman (b); Andy King (sitar); Gerry Hale (vn)

Track listing:
I Wanna Destroy You (S/UK); Kingdom of Love; Positive Vibrations; I Got The Hots; Insanely Jealous; Tonight; You'll Have To Go Sideways; Old Pervert; The Queen Of Eyes; Underwater Moonlight

Running time:
35.36

Currently unavailable on CD

Further listening:
A Can Of Bees (1979); Invisible Hits (1983); The Soft Boys: 1976–1981 (1993); Solo – Hitchcock: I Often Dream Of Trains (1984); Eye (1990) Rew: Tunnel Into Summer (2000)

Further reading:
MOJO 53; Ptolemaic Terrascope; March 1995 and April 1998 (www.terrascope.com)
www.robynhitchcock.com
www.kimber leyrew.com. Good fan sites – www.fegmania.org and www.glasshotel.net/gh

Dead Kennedys
Fresh Fruit For Rotting Vegetables

Baroque-punk venom from San Francisco.

Ten years after San Francisco was hippy capital of the world, a new countercultural force took root in the city, led by a band whose very name spat in the face of the previous decade's idealism. Dead Kennedys' guitarist East Bay Ray: "We were trying to restore what the hippies believed in: tolerance for experimentation, the do-it-yourself thing and the questioning of authority." Song titles such as Kill The Poor and Forward To Death, however, hardly shouted Love and Peace. "Well, Biafra was into shredding people lyrically. But basically we just wanted people to think for themselves. We wanted to wake people up with a two by four."

After building a ferocious live reputation and establishing their own groundbreaking label – Alternative Tentacles – they went in to record their debut. The band produced it themselves (producer "Norm" was actually engineer Oliver Dicicco's cat) and R. Pepperell (East Bay Ray) received a "Production Assistance" credit on the original sleeve. He attributes the record's artistic success to group discipline. "Everyone in the band had a work ethic and a craftsmanship ethic: a commitment to not letting things slide. We had a budget of about $6000 and we stuck to it. It helped that we had all been in rock bands before, and had the ability to express the musical ideas in our heads – we could stop on a dime and go off in another direction."

This facility is apparent throughout what must qualify as the most musically complex punk record ever made. When Ray starts invoking Wagner, Arabian scales and Ravel's Bolero in an explanation of the classic California Über Alles he's not bullshitting. The sudden appearance of an oompah-band waltz section in Chemical Warfare is another case in point. All these elements are welded together by vocalist Jello Biafra's human theremin impersonation, Ray's loud but startlingly variable guitar playing, a kick-corporate-ass rhythm section and a heavy dose of warped humour. "We didn't see ourselves as a Top 40 proposition," says Ray. "We thought this might be our only chance, so we just put everything in." The album was a critical and commercial success, and gave the DKs several more chances to berate the bad guys and energise the good guys, making a damn fine noise in the process.

Record label:
Cherry Red

Produced
by "Norm".

Recorded
at Mobius Music, San Francisco; Spring 1980.

Released:
September 1980

Chart peaks:
33 (UK) None (US)

Personnel:
Jello Biafra (v); East Bay Ray (g); Klaus Flouride (b, v); Ted (d); Paul Roessler, Ninotchka (k); 6025 (g)

Track listing:
Kill The Poor (S/UK); Forward To Death; When Ya Get Drafted; Let's Lynch The Landlord; Drug Me; Your Emotions; Chemical Warfare; California Über Alles (S); I Kill Children; Stealing People's Mail; Funland At The Beach; Ill In The Head; Holiday In Cambodia (S); Viva Las Vegas

Running time:
32.49

Current CD:
CDBRED10

Further listening:
Lard: The Last Temptation Of Lard (1990), Biafra's side-project with Ministry members Al Jourgenson and Paul Barker.

Further reading:
www.geocities.com/Athens/Forum/3111/dk.htm

Talking Heads
Remain In Light

*David Byrne looks to Africa, lightens up, influences a gener-
ation of musicians and sells very few records indeed.*

Things did not look good when Talking Heads assembled in
the Bahamas to start recording their fourth album, *Remain
In Light*. According to bassist Tina Weymouth, long-time Heads'
producer Brian Eno was reluctant to become involved again,
having fallen out with David Byrne during recording of their
collaborative album, *My Life In The Bush Of Ghosts*. Within a
week, engineer Rhett Davies quit in frustration, and Byrne has
confirmed that there was tension between himself and
Weymouth over the direction of the music.

He has said, for example, "We were really intrigued and
excited by the formal aspects of African music." She, however,
insisted, "No-one discussed with us the fact that we were going
to be playing in an African style."

Nevertheless, what they created was a whole new direction, not just for Talking Heads but for '80s rock in general.
With the quartet expanded by the addition of horns, extra
percussion and voices, they moved away from traditional songwriting by improvising songs in the studio, diving headlong into
the complexities of African polyrhythms and replacing Byrne's
urban paranoia with more affirmative lyrics.

"I think the music was important in that," says Byrne.
"The anxiety of my lyrics and my singing didn't seem appropriate to this kind of music. This music is more positive, though
a little mysterious at the same time."

The other vital ingredient was Eno, taking a much more
active part in the music here than on previous Talking Heads
albums. Eno's fingerprints are everywhere, from vocal
harmonies and counterpoints to layered ambient sounds, lyrics
and rhythmic devices.

Guitarist Chris Frantz confirms that "The barriers
between musician and producer were being broken down
because we were writing the songs in the studio."

"An album of brave inventions and haunting textures,"
drooled NME on release, but Rolling Stone nailed it even better
with "Scary, funny music to which you can dance and think,
think and dance, dance and think, *ad infinitum*."

Predictably, though, the world wasn't ready for doing
two things at once. "It was the worst-selling Talking Heads
album ever," points out Frantz. Tightly formatted American

Record label:
Sire

Produced
by Brian Eno.

Recorded
at Compass Point, Nassau, Bahamas;
Sigma Sound, New York; Eldorado, Los
Angeles; 1980

Released:
October 8, 1980

Chart peaks:
21 (UK) 19 (US)

Personnel:
David Byrne (g, b, k); Adrian Belew (g);
Jerry Harrison (g, b, k); Tina Weymouth
(b, k); Chris Frantz (d, k); Brian Eno
(k, b, v); Nona Hendryx (v); Jon Hassell
(t, horns)

Track listing:
Born Under Punches (The Heat Goes
On); Crosseyed And Painless; The Great
Curve; Once In A Lifetime (S); Houses In
Motion (S); Seen And Not Seen; Listening
Wind; The Overload

Running time:
40.04

Current CD:
7599260952

Further listening:
The seeds of this new Talking Heads can
be found in My Life In The Bush Of
Ghosts by David Byrne and Brian Eno
(1981). Although released after Remain In
Light, it was recorded earlier.

Further reading:
Talking Heads (Jerome Davis, 1986).
www.talking-heads.net

radio found it impossible to programme because, as Byrne recalls, "The reaction we heard was that it sounded too black for white radio and too white for black radio."

By the end of the '80s, however, *Remain In Light* featured at Number 4 in Rolling Stone's selection of the decade's greatest albums, and it continues to attract new converts to its irresistibly quirky stew of traditional and avant-garde elements.

Nic Jones
Penguin Eggs

Melody Maker's Folk Album Of The Year takes the English folk revival to a new level of contemporary relevance.

There were strong clues on this magnificent album that Jones was heading into bold new territory, busy writing his own material and gleefully passing it off as traditional music to a folk scene still hung up on the niceties of history. He always was a colourful, wilful character who'd think nothing of turning his back on the audience or singing gibberish if he didn't think they were listening. "I once sang the same song twice in a row and no-one noticed!" he says with some triumph. "People didn't want me to write my own songs, they only wanted to hear traditional material, so I'd just do it and everyone would assume it was traditional. Other times I'd re-write traditional songs or stick in new verses. Nobody ever knew."

Penguin Eggs had such vitality, and Jones' modern guitar arrangements had such a contemporary feel, his appeal was surely on the verge of stretching way beyond the folk scene, which had long held him in reverence since his days running a club in Essex and his early tentative steps with the group The Halliard. But less than two years after recording the album, he was on the last leg of a long drive home from a gig in the early hours when he was involved in an appalling crash with a lorry and critically injured. It's assumed he fell asleep at the wheel, but Nic himself has no recollection of the accident. He was subsequently partly paralysed and although able to re-learn the guitar and play at home, he has not appeared on stage since.

"That's not important," he says with typical modesty. "I enjoy playing but I'm not bothered about appearing in public, I'm happy to play for my own satisfaction. There's plenty of others around to do it, they don't need me." Happily there has been a widening awareness of his influence in recent years, partly due to the rise of Kate Rusby, who cites Jones as one of her main inspirations. "I listen to him all the time and *Penguin Eggs* is a brilliant album," she says. "Sadly I never saw him play but the biggest thrill of my career was when he came to one of my gigs in York. I was so nervous but he sat in the front row and beamed all the way through and congratulated me after. Lovely man."

Record label:
Topic

Produced by
Tony Engle.

Recorded
at Livingstone Studios, London; late 197

Released:
October 1980

Chart peaks:
71 (UK) None (US)

Personnel:
Nic Jones (v, g, fiddle, a); Dave Burland (v); Tony Hall (melodeon); Nic Kinsey (e) Billy Kinsley (e)

Track listing:
Canadee-I-O; Drowned Lovers; Humpback Whale; Little Pot Stove; Courting Is A Pleasure; Barrack Street; Planxty Davis; Flandyke Shore; Farewell To The Gold

Running time:
45.14

Current CD:
TSCD411

Further listening:
The earlier The Noah's Ark Trap (1977) gave lots of clues to the direction Jones was heading for Penguin Eggs. For an excellent collection of obscurities and live recordings In Search Of Nic Jones (1998).

Further reading:

Motorhead
Ace Of Spades

Metal's excess and punk's attack; Lemmy's filthy, speed-propelled, biker-rock zenith.

"*A*ce Of Spades" said Black Sabbath's Ozzy Osbourne, "is a fucking killer."

The trio, formed by vicar's son Lemmy after Hawkwind threw him out (his drug intake, amazingly, too much even for them), were in Ozzy's opinion "the ultimate heavy-metal band". And their debut appeared just as the UK rock press had announced heavy metal's death at the hands of punk.

"I don't think our music has anything to do with heavy metal," Lemmy argued. "I think we sound more like punk, when you get into it, with the speed we play. And I'm a fucking cobbled-together bass player– I'm supposed to be playing rhythm guitar."

In the beginning their audience, made up mostly of Hell's Angels, was small. But, by 1979, their following had expanded into a substantial cult, which included many punks. That year had seen the release of three Motorhead albums. *On Parole* was a weak reissue, but the other two were classics. *Overkill* and *Bomber* had established their reputation as the loudest, fastest, nastiest band in rock. Thus it was a confident band who took a short break from their hectic live schedule –"I like to keep it concise," said Lemmy, "smack them in the face and split. Short, sharp shock" – to record Ace Of Spades.

"That whole time we knew that we were on a roll. I wish I could remember everything that happened – I'm sure that there's someone out there that does. I'm just fucked if I can!"

But if life in the Motorhead camp had become a blur, *Ace Of Spades* provided the perfect soundtrack to the band's endless hangover. A combination of vodka, Jack Daniel's, Special Brew, speed and general road-dog debauchery resulted in tracks like Jailbait (complete with a pre-take belch), Love Me Like A Reptile, Fast And Loose, (We Are) The Road Crew and The Chase Is Better Than The Catch (often introduced by Lemmy onstage as The Face Is Better Than The Snatch).

It was their biggest hit – UK Top 5. And though still not scraping the US charts, the album's influence Stateside was formidable, helping to catalyse the '80s thrash and speed-metal genres that spawned Slayer, Anthrax and Metallica. "If there wasn't a Lemmy and a Motorhead, there wouldn't be a

---

Record label:
Bronze

Produced
by Vic Maile.

Recorded
at Jackson's Studios, Rickmansworth;
August 4–September 15, 1980.

Released:
October 1980

Chart peaks:
4 (UK) None (US)

Personnel:
Lemmy (v, b); "Fast" Eddie Clarke (g);
Phil "Philthy Animal" Taylor (d)

Track listing:
Ace Of Spades (S); Love Me Like A
Reptile; Shoot You In The Back; Live To
Win; Fast And Loose; (We Are) The Road
Crew; Fire, Fire; Jailbait; Dance; Bite The
Bullet; The Chase Is Better Than The
Catch; The Hammer

Running time:
36.37

Current CD:
ESMCD912 adds: Dirty Love; Please Don't
Touch; Emergency

Further listening:
Hawkwind's Space Ritual (1973), featuring
Lemmy, is classic UK acid rock, while
Overkill (1979); Bomber (1979) and No
Sleep 'Til Hammersmith (1981) capture
Motorhead at their most thrilling during
the post-punk years of the late '70s
and early '80s.

Further reading:
The Illustrated Collector's Guide To
Motorhead, (Alan Burridge and Mick
Stevenson, 1999); www.imotorhead.com

Metallica," claimed Metallica drummer Lars Ulrich in December 1995, celebrating Lemmy's 50th birthday at LA's Whiskey A-Go-Go club.

The thunderous Spaghetti Western-inspired title track (itself a Top 20 single) was resurrected for use in an advert for Pot Noodles in '90s – around the same time that the critics who had dismissed Motorhead as "the worst band in the world" started mentioning their name in the same sentence as bands like The Stooges and The MC5.

The Jam
Sound Affects

Pop psychedelia meets the Gang Of Four: Weller's great post-punk statement is his most sophisticated album.

Between 1977 and 1980 The Jam barely had time to draw breath. How were they coping? "I came to the sessions for *Sound Affects* with only three, maybe four songs pre-written," Paul Weller admits. "Vic [Coppersmith-Heaven: long-time group producer] copped a lot of flak for the time it took to make, and it was frustrating, but if the songs weren't there. Anyway the pressure of constantly touring and recording ain't such a bad thing for a young band."

To judge by the results, released barely twelve months after the excellent *Setting Sons*, Weller was thriving on it. "*Sound Affects* is my favourite Jam record. We kept to our fundamental sound but stretched it a bit." The stretching went two ways. Firstly it involved exploring textures which moved them closer to post-punk contemporaries such as the Gang Of Four and Wire. Witness the gangly dissonance, startling dub vocal effect and French coda of final track Scrape Away. But there's also Start's obvious homage to The Beatles' Taxman ("Yeah, I know! I've always thought there was more James Brown to it though") through to gentle psych-rock experiments such as the backwards guitar interlude before Dream Time, and the bluebottle which buzzes its way between speakers before the acidic ska of Music For The Last Couple.

"Special stereophonic Japanese fly that was," recalls Weller wryly. "I think it was in the drum booth with Rick so I thought, Why not." Lyrically, Weller was on a bookish kick. "A poem by a bloke called Paul Drew inspired That's Entertainment. I was reading Geoffrey Ashe's Camelot And The Vision Of Albion and a lot of Shelley at the time too." His admiration for Percy Bysshe extended from the poet's aesthetic (That's Entertainment's reference to the "tranquility of solitude") to his politics: the repeated chant of "They know that God created all men equal" on Man In The Corner Shop. Weller, still only 22, had crafted a record of precocious maturity. The critics saw it as his *Revolver* and the British public bought it in barrowloads. The Jam's next and final offering, *The Gift*, was their only Number 1 album, but *Sound Affects* is their masterpiece.

Record label:
Polydor

Produced
by Vic Coppersmith-Heaven and The Jam.

Recorded
at Town House Studios, London;
June–October 1980.

Released:
November 28, 1980

Chart peaks:
2 (UK) 72 (US)

Personnel:
Paul Weller (v, g, p); Bruce Foxton (v, b); Rick Buckler (d, pc),.

Track listing:
Pretty Green; Monday; But I'm Different Now; Set The House Ablaze; Start (S); That's Entertainment (S/Import); Dream Time; Man In The Corner Shop; Music For The Last Couple; Boy About Town; Scrape Away

Running time:
35.29

Current CD:
537 421–2

Further listening:
All Mod Cons (1978) and Setting Sons (1979) are the two other classic Jam albums.

Further reading:
The Jam: The Modern World By Numbers (Paul Honeyford, 1995);
www.geocities.com/SunsetStrip/Towers/6411/links1.html

Phil Collins
Face Value

Genesis drummer launches solo career fuelled by marriage breakdown.

Already respected – for his early '70s Genesis work – as one of rock's most musical drummers, Phil Collins' profile had risen since 1975 when he replaced Peter Gabriel as lead vocalist; his sunny, blokeish style and commercial writing ability helped the band attain stadium status. By 1980, it was time to make a solo album. His workaholism had taken its toll on his marriage (in his absence, wife Andrea had dallied with a decorator) and Collins found himself alone, noodling angry songs in his home studio. Please Don't Ask – a remarkably vulnerable and moving separation song – had already appeared on Genesis's *Duke* but there was plenty more where that came from. If Leaving Me Is Easy and You Know What I Mean adopted a heartfelt, winningly plaintive style and I Missed Again had a jaunty frustration as expressed by the brittle Earth Wind And Fire horns. It wasn't all gloom though: The Roof Is Leaking maintained a hopeful tone in the face of poverty-stricken rural struggle and the Stephen Bishop-like This Must Be Love celebrated his new relationship with Jill Tavelman.

But the most memorable track was the opener In The Air Tonight, a brooding piece of unambiguous fury ("Well if you told me you were drowning/I would not lend a hand"), finally exploding with an apocalyptic drum fill treated to Hugh Padgham's customised concrete-room-gated-reverb effect, forever to be known as the Phil Collins Drum Sound. Collins performed it on Top Of The Pops with a paint pot on his piano, a symbol his wife took very personally; Andrea: "Implying decorator, implying affair, implying that was what happened to our marriage when that wasn't what happened at all."

Face Value went on to sell over 4 million copies, Genesis records started to sound like Phil Collins records and his solo follow-up; 1984's *Hello, I Must Be Going*, continued the revenge/catharsis-through-song theme, much to Andrea's dismay; "I didn't understand why he wasn't writing incredible love songs for Jill. To go on and on as he did was very mean." Though he and Genesis went on to do amazing business through the '80s and '90s, as Collins became housewife's choice so the music got less interesting. With his ubiquity an irritant to the impartial observer, Collins rarely recaptured that balance between creativity and the un-self-conscious expression that makes his solo debut so valuable.

Record label:
Virgin

Produced
by Phil Collins with Hugh Padgham.

Recorded
at Old Croft, the Townhouse and Village Recorder, LA; 1980.

Released:
February 1981

Chart peaks:
1 (UK) 7 (US)

Personnel:
Phil Collins (v, k, d); Darryl Steurmer, Eric Clapton (g); John Giblin (b); Alphonso Johnson (b); Ronnie Scott, Don Myrick (s); Louis Satterfield (tb); Rhamlee Michael Davis, Michael Hawis (t); Joe Partridge (sg); Shankar (vn, tamboura)

Track listing:
In The Air Tonight (S); This Must Be Love; Behind The Lines; The Roof Is Leaking; Droned; Hand In Hand; I Missed Again (S); You Know What I Mean; Thunder And Lightning; I'm Not Moving; If Leaving Me Is Easy (S); Tomorrow Never Knows

Running time:
40.36

Current CD:
CDV 2185

Further listening:
Duke (Genesis, 1980); But Seriously (1989)

Further reading:
Phil Collins (Ray Coleman, 1997)

Dick Gaughan
Handful Of Earth

Folk Roots magazine's 'Album of the '80s', re-established the passionate Scot as one of Britain's most committed folk singers.

"*H*andful Of Earth blew me away when I heard it, Gaughan's commitment to the songs is remarkable," said Billy Bragg. "In many ways it goes beyond folk music but everything you ever believed folk music could and should be is there. I toured East Germany with him before the Wall came down and I watched him in awe." Wherever you go on the British — and indeed more informed American — folk circuit, the reaction is the same.

"Dick gets inside a song like no-one else and proved himself a truly great singer," said June Tabor of the former member of traditional Celtic group Boys Of The Lough and folk-rock band Five Hand Reel. Even Gaughan himself, a modest man passionately opposed to any form of celebrity, knew he'd taken the traditional song form to fresh heights of intensity and stirring power on *Handful Of Earth*.

"After I made it I felt, Well that's it, I'm not going to do anything better. It was the best I could do, the best blend of songs I could find. I was fresh again after coming out of the whole Five Hand Reel band period, I'd done a record with Andy Irvine, I had a whole load of ideas to juggle about and the years and years of frustration all went into *Handful Of Earth*. After that I had to do something different, there was absolutely no point in trying to remake *Handful Of Earth*."

So just as Paul Brady decided his *Welcome Here Kind Stranger* represented a peak for Irish traditional song and boldly spun off into a brave new career as a singer-songwriter, Gaughan's music also took on a new turn with a hard political edge and adventurous experiments with rock arrangements, even including an improvised modern-jazz album with percussionist Ken Hyder (*Fanfare For Tomorrow*). But *Handful Of Earth* remains his masterwork, turning well-known ballads like Erin-Go-Bragh and Both Sides Of The Tweed into passionate Scottish anthems and restoring politics to the front line of British folk music with Workers Song and Leon Rosselson's emotive story of the Diggers' revolt The World Turned Upside Down, which became a modern classic covered, among others, by Billy Bragg. Other songs on the album were also widely covered, including the poignant Song For Ireland, now constantly heard performed by Irish bar bands and buskers, but oddly enough written by an Englishman, Phil Colclough.

Record label:
Green Linnet

Produced
by Dick Gaughan and Robin Morton.

Recorded
at Temple Studios, Scotland; late 1980.

Released:
March 1981

Chart peaks:
None (UK) None (US)

Personnel:
Dick Gaughan (v, ag, g); John Cunningham (k, whistle); Phil Cunningham (k, whistle); Stewart Isbister (b); Brian McNeill (fiddle, b); Robin Morton (e)

Track listing:
Erin-Go-Bragh; Now Westlin Winds; Craigie Hill; The World Turned Upside Down; The Snows They Melt The Soonest; Lough Erne; First Kiss At Parting; Scojun Waltz; Randers Hopsa; Song For Ireland; Workers Song; Both Sides Of The Tweed

Running time:
43.21

Current CD:
TSCD419

Further listening:
Redwood Cathedral (1999), while Gaughan's interest in taking folk music to more intense levels is demonstrated on A Different Kind Of Love Song (1983). His most political work is True And Bold: Songs Of The Scottish Miners (1986), his most left field is the improvised jazz collaboration with Ken Hyder, Fanfare For Tomorrow (1985).

Further reading:
Folk Roots, September 1996. Dick Gaughan also runs his own informative website, www.dickalba.demon.co.uk

The Birthday Party
Prayers On Fire

A terrifying cartoonish trip to rock's psychotic edge.

To the often uninspiring post-punk landscape of the early
'80s, The Birthday Party brought a bug-eyed, lurching
intensity, crooked humour and a magpie's eye for musical styles.
The keynote was excess: "I write a hell of a lot of lyrics when
I'm really drunk," notes Nick Cave. "When we were recording
Prayers On Fire, I was fairly drunk the whole time."

The group had returned to their native Australia to
record, after spending a miserable 10 months trying to make
their mark in Britain. By all accounts the studio was an open
house, but from this inebriated mayhem a perversely disciplined
album emerged. Hometown band Equal Local ("They were an
avant-garde outfit," remembers guitarist Rowland Howard.
"They'd stand in line and tap their feet frantically all at the same
time") dropped in to contribute the menacing, big-band brass
riff to Nick The Stripper.

Cave's splenetic delivery displays the mixture of self-
loathing and self-aggrandisement which often marks great
performers; a flailing, barking, spidery Elvis brutalised by punk.
The muscular cross-rhythms worked up by the band point at a
stew of influences: The Velvets (Ho-Ho), Kurt Weill (Just You
And Me) and Pere Ubu (Cry), with strongly flavoured scraps of
country (Capers), rockabilly (A Dead Song) and jazz-blues
(Yard) thrown in for good measure. Though the band deny any
knowledge of Captain Beefheart before the sessions, he seems
like the presiding deity. King Ink encapsulates the album's lyrical
sideswipe: "King Ink feels like a bug swimming in a soup
bowl/Oh! Yer! Yer! What a wonderful life – Fats Domino on the
radio." This dislocation mirrors engineer Tony Cohen's memory
of the time: "At the time we thought we'd made a Little River
Band-style record, horrible and slick. Now, looking back, of
course it's not."

Contemporary critics raved; the band went on to record
the utterly feral *Junkyard*, but drug problems and personality
clashes would derail them. Howard formed Crime And The City
Solution while Cave went solo, and Harvey played for both.
Prayers On Fire has moments that they've never bettered.

Record label:
4AD

Produced
by The Birthday Party.

Recorded
at Armstrong's Audio Visual Studios,
Melbourne and Richmond Recorders;
December 1980–January 1981.

Released:
April 1981

Chart peaks:
None (UK) None (US)

Personnel:
Nick Cave (v, k, s, d); Rowland S Howard
(g, v, s); Mick Harvey (k, g, pc); Tracy
Pew (b); Phil Calvert (d); Phillip Jackson
(t); Mick Hunter, Stephen Ewart (brass);
Tony Cohen (e)

Track listing:
Zoo-Music Girl; Cry; Capers; Nick The
Stripper (S/Aus); Ho-Ho; Figure Of Fun;
King Ink; A Dead Song; Yard; Dull Day;
Just You And Me

Running time:
35.09

Current CD:
GAD 104 CD adds: Blundertown; Kathy's
Kisses

Further listening:
Junkyard (1982); best of, Hits (1992);
Live 1981–1982 (1999); Nick Cave From
Here To Eternity (1984)

Further reading:
Bad Seed (Ian Johnston, 1996);
www.thebirthdayparty.com

Journey
Escape

Former jazz-rockers deliver AOR colossus. It spent over a year in the US Top 20.

*E*scape was Journey's Whopper with cheese; soft-rock in a bun; histrionics with fries. It paved the way for Foreigner, Styx and REO Speedwagon, and '80s America gobbled it up. "In the heat with a blue jean girl/Burnin' love comes once in a lifetime," sang Steve Perry on Stone In Love. It was hardly Keats, but tagged to Neal Schon's stoked power-chords, even the most clichéd memory of rock-chick action seemed delicious.

The album saw Jonathan Cain replace Gregg Rolie on keyboards, and as co-writer of all ten tracks, Cain helped Journey to perfect a sound which one less-than-enamoured critic described as "advanced jukebox Muzak". On Open Arms – soppy enough to warrant a 1995 cover by Mariah Carey – they were guilty as charged, but Don't Stop Believin's update on Springsteen's Born To Run ethic proved irresistible.

Reviewing Journey's seventh album, Rolling Stone joined the dissenters, positing that they "could be any bunch of fluff-brained sessioneers with a singer who sounds like a eunuch." Perhaps they meant *unique*. Perry could be melodramatic, certainly, but on Mother Father, his easy slides from soprano to alto demonstrate an extraordinary ability. Elsewhere, former Santana member Neal Schon's performance on Still They Ride was equally impressive, the notes of his guitar solo cascading with an attack and fluidity which Eddie Van Halen was amongst the first to acknowledge.

Who's Crying Now, Don't Stop Believin' and Open Arms all went Top 10 Stateside, and *Escape* eventually sold in excess of nine million copies. Its success prompted the band to collaborate with Data Age Incorporated on the *Escape* video game, an Atari 2600 product whose plot involved escorting Journey from the stage to the Scarab Escape Vehicle pictured on the album's cover. Naturally, obstacles en route included love-crazed groupies.

Journey's 1983 follow-up *Frontiers* sold a respectable enough six million. By now, though, Perry was constantly at loggerheads with Valory and Smith, whom he eventually sacked. So, not all sweetness and light, then.

Record label:
CBS

Produced
by Mike Stone and Kevin Elson.

Recorded
at Fantasy Studios, Berkeley, California; spring 1981.

Released:
August 1981

Chart peaks:
32 (UK) 1 (US)

Personnel:
Steve Perry (v); Neal Schon (g,v); Jonathan Cain (k,g,v); Ross Valory (b,v); Steve Smith (d); Wally Buck (ae)

Track listing:
Don't Stop Believin'; Stone In Love; Who's Cryin' Now; Keep On Runnin'; Still They Ride; Escape; Lay It Down; Dead Or Alive; Mother, Father; Open Arms

Running time:
42.43

Current CD:
486662 2

Further listening:
Frontiers (1983)

Further reading:
journey.simplenet.com;
www.journeythe band.com

The Human League
Dare

Self-conscious synth minimalism evolves into chart-topping New Romantic ear candy.

S uzanne Sulley burst into tears the day Don't You Want Me went to Number 1 in America. Not only had it knocked the mawkish Ebony And Ivory off the top, it's success also vindicated Phil Oakey's decision to replace the band's synth-whiz founders Martin Ware and Ian Craig-Marsh with a pair of unknown disco dollies. Nobody expected the League to bounce back from the split. Across two albums preoccupied with a modish synthetic brutalism, the Sheffield quartet had poised itself between post-punk experiment and chart pop. But it was Ware and Marsh's baby all the way – Oakey was just the figurehead who sounded faintly uncomfortable reciting Being Boiled, and Adrian Wright was just simply uncomfortable, before and after the split. Especially after. "He hated us," Catherall recalled. "Wouldn't even say hello in the mornings."

Under the intuitive guidance of co-producer Rushent and engineer Dave Allen, however, the animosity turned to instinctive chemistry. "When we first heard Sound Of The Crowd," Sulley told Smash Hits, "it was just thump-crash-thump-crash, and straight away we said 'definite hit'. You could dance to it." Musically, Catherall and Sulley's contributions were restricted to the deep mix harmonies which haunted half the album. But the sight of them onstage as the material took shape, Sulley "flailing like an octopus", as Oakey put it, and Catherall "completely out of time", instilled new discipline into the band's writing, and direction to their style. You could dance to all of it. Sound Of The Crowd, Love Action and Open Your Heart were hits even before Dare's Halloween release; and if Don't You Want Me distorted everything afterwards, still its enormity could not detract from the remainder of the album. Even in deadly earnestness (Seconds lamenting the death of John Lennon, the chilled paranoia of Darkness), Dare was riddled with infectious confections.

Record label:
Virgin

Produced
by Martin Rushent and the Human League.

Recorded
at Genetic Sound Studios, 1981.

Released:
October 31, 1981

Chart peaks:
1 (UK) 3 (US)

Personnel:
Philip Oakey (v, syn); Joanne Catherall (v); Susanne Sulley (v); Ian Burden (syn); Jo Callis (syn); Philip Adrian Wright (syn)

Track listing:
The Things That Dreams Are Made Of (S, US only); Open Your Heart (S); The Sound Of The Crowd; Darkness; Do Or Die; Get Carter; I Am The Law; Seconds; Love Action (S); Don't You Want Me (S)

Running time:
40.48

Current CD:
CDV2192

Further listening:
Love And Dancing (1982)

Further reading:
www.andwedanced.com

The Police
Ghost In The Machine

Truly global rock from a disintegrating group who used their frustration to create a deeply ambitious album.

"**V**ery horrible," says Sting of the making of *Ghost In The Machine*. "Very dark. Miserable. Our marriages were breaking up, our marriage was breaking up, and yet we had to make another record." This most problematic phase of The Police's progress was enacted against an idyllic backdrop: the Caribbean island of Montserrat.

The band and newly-hired producer Hugh Padgham arrived on June 15, 1981. For all his stresses, Sting in particular seemed to relish the environment – and for a reggae-inflected band, this was a perfect temporary home. Back in the UK, 2-Tone was at its peak, and ska – as evidenced by Spirits In The Material World, Hungry For You and Rehumanize Yourself – was a clear influence on the album. But Padgham's deep-pile production took the music somewhere completely new, as did Sting's increasingly ambitious lyrics. His clear socio-political stance meant that the album, named after an Arthur Koestler book, would forge his reputation as an exemplar of pretension.

On the musical side, *Ghost* saw The Police kicking back – given their problems, probably a smart move. "It was a please-yourself album," said Sting. "Our previous records were experiments in commercialism. I'd been obsessed with the idea of coming up with a commercial record. *Ghost* doesn't have that concern. It's just us." So it was that he ended up playing a quadruple-tracked saxophone part on Hungry For You, and gleefully contributing to the hilariously over-egged coda of Every Little Thing She Does Is Magic – taped not in Montserrat, but during a stopover in Quebec. Sandwiched between such tomfoolery was The Police's most serious song to date: Invisible Sun, the rumbling attempt to empathise with the IRA's hunger strikers, into which they poured all their creeping misery to stunning effect.

Lofty lyrical themes, an almost jazzy combination of relaxation and musical sophistication, and a retrospective admission that The Police were coming apart – it's not unreasonable to see *Ghost In The Machine* as the first Sting solo album. On his return to the UK, Sting played a brief solo set at a London gala for Amnesty International, during which Eric Clapton was heard to mutter: "Sting has arrived". He wasn't far wrong.

Record label:
A&M

Produced
by The Police and Hugh Padgham.

Recorded
at AIR Studios, Montserrat; Le Studio, Quebec; June–August 1981.

Release date:
October 1981

Chart peaks:
1 (UK) 2 (US)

Personnel:
Sting (v, b, k, s); Andy Summers (g, k, v); Stewart Copeland (d); Jean Roussel (k)

Track listing:
Spirits In The Material World; Every Little Thing She Does Is Magic; Invisible Sun; Hungry For You (J'Aurais Toujours Faim De Toi); Demolition Man; Too Much Information; Rehumanize Yourself; One World (Not Three); Omegaman; Secret Journey; Darkness

Running time:
41.10

Current CD:
CDMID162

Further listening:
A&M box set Message In A Box (1993)

Further reading:
Sting: Demolition Man (Christopher Sandford, 1998); www.stingchronicity.co.uk

Black Flag
Damaged

A US hardcore milestone, marking the vocal debut of Henry Rollins.

"**A**s a parent... I found this an anti-parent record." The words stuck on to the first 25,000 copies of *Damaged* were lifted from a statement made by MCA's Al Bergamo, defending his company's decision not to distribute Black Flag's incendiary debut album. However, thanks to the group's own DIY sales work, MCA were already too late: the record was shipping to stores across the country. *Damaged* was out.

In his diary, Henry Rollins described Black Flag's live show as "the ultimate soundtrack to a full-scale riot". Listening to *Damaged* it's easy to see what he meant. More anti-everything than anti-parent, Black Flag's first full-length LP explodes with frustration, alienation and unrestrained rage. From the opening air-raid warning riff of Rise Above to the agonised slo-mo grind of Damaged II, they hold nothing back. Black Flag took on all-comers: Spray Paint and Police Story are anti-authority, TV Party and Six Pack satirical sideswipes at apathetic beer culture. Depression and Damaged I spill over with self-loathing, while No More and What I See spew pure malevolence.

The music itself is a riot of adrenalised, distorted metal cranked out by a group possessed, as though they'd only get the one chance to leave their mark. Greg Ginn's molten guitar combined rhythm and lead in a mangled collision, scrawling riffs across the group's runaway rhythmic blur. Rollins, then the new guy, says of Ginn: "He was relentless... he would tape the head-phones to his head so they wouldn't fly off."

Henry himself had much to prove: in the audience barely two months previously, the DC punker found himself thrown into the deep end in LA by a group itching to record. He had little choice but to meet them head-on: "I would sing as hard as I could every time. I didn't know anything about pacing myself." It shows – words are spat out with a rasping, untrained aggression like punk primal-scream therapy.

Black Flag would go on to record several excellent albums and, alongside groups like Minor Threat and the Dead Kennedys, help to establish an independent touring and distribution network which would lay the groundwork for the global domination of groups like Nirvana and Green Day. But they would struggle to recapture the power and intensity of *Damaged*.

Record label:
SST

Produced
by Spot and Black Flag.

Recorded
at Unicorn Studios, Hollywood; September 1980.

Released:
November 1981

Chart peaks:
None (UK) None (US)

Personnel:
Henry Rollins (v); Greg Ginn (g); Dez Cadena (g, v); Charles Dukowski (b); Robo (d); Spot, Francis Buckley (e)

Track listing:
Rise Above; Spray Paint; Six Pack; What I See; TV Party; Thirsty And Miserable; Police Story; Gimmie Gimmie Gimmie; Depression; Room 13; Damaged II; No More; Padded Cell; Life Of Pain; Damaged I

Running time:
34.47

Current CD:
SST 007

Further listening:
The First Four Years (1984); My War (1984); Slip It In (1984); Rollins Band, Life Time (1988)

Further reading:
Get In The Van (Henry Rollins, 1994); Turned On: A Biography of Henry Rollins (James Parker, 1998)

Iron Maiden
Number Of The Beast

From Brit-metal hopefuls to globe-straddling concern.

Number Of The Beast is the album which succeeded in turning Iron Maiden into a household name in Britain, affording them a global reputation which they enjoy to this day. It showcases the new-found songwriting confidence exhibited by band leader and bass player Steve Harris – hook-filled metal nuggets like Run To The Hills, and the title track (resplendent alongside moments of atmospheric melodrama such as Hallowed Be Thy Name) still form the cornerstone of any Maiden set some 20 years later: testament to Harris' ability. Equally significant is the arrival of vocalist Bruce Dickinson. Recruited by ebullient manager Rod Smallwood in the beer tent at the Reading Festival, Bruce replaced the wayward Paul Di'Anno in the late summer of '81 and fittingly had his photo snapped with the band cradling a pint of Ruddles in a local boozer. Dickinson had confidence by the lungful.

"When I first joined I thought I could be the best damned singer this band had ever had," he explains. "I knew that they were ready to do things properly, that the set-up was there. It really was a case of when things were going to happen. When I heard the material for the album that they'd been working on, I knew they were ready."

The release of Run To The Hills in February 1982 confirmed Bruce's initial suspicions, smashing its way into the UK charts at Number 7. Primed by a 20-date UK tour, the album charged to the top of the charts on release. Despite the odd moment which hasn't weathered well (such as opener Invaders), *Number Of The Beast* is best viewed as an ambitious step forward which paid incredible dividends. While Maiden's peers like Angel Witch, Saxon and Diamond Head enjoyed faltering homegrown reputations, Maiden began carving out an international career which would lead to worldwide album sales in excess of 40 million.

Record label:
EMI

Produced
by Martin "Farmer" Birch.

Recorded
at Battery Studios, London;
November–December 1981.

Released:
March 1982

Chart peaks:
1 (UK) 33 (US)

Personnel:
Bruce Dickinson (v); Steve Harris (b);
Dave Murray (g); Adrian Smith (g);
Clive Burr (d); Nigel Hewitt-Green (e)

Track listing:
Invaders; Children Of The Damned; The Prisoner; 22 Acacia Avenue; TheNumber Of The Beast (S); Run To The Hills (S); Gangland; Total Eclipse; Hallowed Be Thy Name

Running time:
44.55

Current CD:
4969180

Further listening:
Killers (1981); Powerslave (1984); the landmark double live set, Live After Death (1985)

Further reading:
Run To The Hills (Mick Wall, 1999);
www.ironmaiden.com

Toto
IV

Muso sextet named after the dog in The Wizard Of Oz clean up at the 1982 Grammys.

Despite huge success with their 1978 single Hold The Line, *IV* found Toto with everything to prove. *Turn Back* (1981) had been dismissed as an album which favoured a self-conscious virtuosity over songs. On *IV*, they remedied this, writing strong pop melodies and making sure that most tracks were at "power-ballad" pace. For a band composed of session-musicians whose previous credits included Miles Davis and Steely Dan, this showed considerable restraint.

The recording process was anything but insular. Toto employed five engineers, six sound-recordists and a host of fellow session players. This last group included yet more Porcaro brothers. Band members Steve and Jeff were now joined by Mike Porcaro, who played cello on Good For You, and Joe Porcaro, who was responsible for the marimba hook on Africa. The final extravagance was a spell at Abbey Road to record James Newton Howard's string arrangements. By now Toto were well over budget, but they sensed they would recoup. For many, *IV* conjures little more than pony-tailed bass-players sipping Pepsi, but it's enjoyable, just as Baywatch is enjoyable. Highlights include Rosanna, written for the actress Rosanna Arquette, and I Won't Hold You Back, its production reminiscent of Richard Carpenter until Lukather's lovelorn vocal segues to a fiery guitar solo. More curious is Paich and J Porcaro's Africa, all congas and airy analogue synth. Reportedly the rest of the band were as bemused as the public by the song's lyrics : "I know that I must do what's right/ Sure as Kilimanjaro rises above the Serengeti", sings Paich, before repeatedly blessing the rain. How odd.

When *IV* won a gob-smacking six Grammys including best album, some cited nepotism, claiming that the band knew almost everybody on the voting panel. Either way, Joe Public was as taken as the Academy, and on the back of five hit singles, *IV* eventually sold over three million copies. When Hungate left before the accompanying tour, and Kimball followed suit, Toto's remaining members decided to return to their day jobs before starting on a follow-up. Lukather's next session was Michael Jackson's *Thriller*. Which was nice.

Record label:
CBS

Produced
by Toto.

Recorded
at Sunset Sound and Record One, Los Angeles; Abbey Road, London; 1981.

Released:
April 1982

Chart peaks:
4 (UK) 4 (US)

Personnel:
Bobby Kimball (v); Steve Lukather (g, v); David Paich (k,v); Steve Porcaro (k,v); Jeff Porcaro (d, pc); David Hungate (b); Lenny Castro (pc); Mike Porcaro (c); Joe Porcaro (marimba); James Newton-Howard (oa); The Martyn Ford Orchestra (strings); Al Schmitt, Tom Knox (e); Greg Ladanyi (e, m)

Track listing:
Rosanna (S); Make Believe (S); I Won't Hold You Back (S); Good For You; It's A Feeling; Afraid Of Love; Lovers In The Night; We Made It; Waiting For your Love (S); Africa (S)

Running time:
42.18

Current CD:
450088 2

Further listening:
Isolation (1984)

Further reading:
www.toto99.com

Marshall Crenshaw
Marshall Crenshaw

A walking encyclopedia of '50s and '60s rock and R&B, Crenshaw mounts a one-man revolution against '80s slickness.

At a time when radio meant Survivor's Eye Of The Tiger and Steve Miller's Abracadabra, Marshall Crenshaw arrived like rock'n'roll's long-lost son. "I felt at odds with what was going on," Crenshaw says of that summer of 1982. "Part of my approach on the first album was choosing certain things as influences and rejecting others. I was doing this kind of private rebellion in my mind."

He rejected what he called "throw-away pop". Instead, the singer chose sturdy golden-era influences: Buddy Holly, the pleasing dink of a Spector session glockenspiel, the "oohs" of The Beach Boys and the streamlined song design of Motown and The Beatles. Impressed by his home demos, Warner Brothers signed him and let him self-produce. But the transition from apartment to New York's Record Plant was rough.

"I was a little overwhelmed by 24-track equipment because I was used to working on 4-track," Crenshaw says. "I wasn't really getting the sounds and I was in over my head. The other thing that got to me was we were really under pressure to make a good record. There were high expectations."

The MO of cutting bass and drums together, then overdubbing guitars and vocals, captured a rough-and-ready spirit in tracks such as There She Goes Again, Rockin' Around In NYC. and She Can't Dance, while Cynical Girl benefitted from more deliberate layering.

"When I recorded that at home I had one Vox 12-string," Crenshaw recalls. "When we did it at the Record Plant, there are 14. It really gets the buzzing thing going on – like a big bees' nest."

Shortly before recording his debut, Crenshaw had been playing John Lennon in the stage show Beatlemania. "We were in the studio on December 8, 1981, which was exactly a year after John had been shot. And the day he got shot, he'd been in the Record Plant. So we all stopped working that day and sat around and talked about John Lennon. Everybody there had known him. It made me think that if he'd been alive, I probably would've met him. That was exciting for me."

Record label:
Warner Brothers

Produced
by Richard Gottehrer and Marshall Crenshaw.

Recorded
at The Record Plant, NYC; January 1982.

Released:
May 15, 1982

Chart peaks:
None (UK) None (US)

Personnel:
Marshall Crenshaw (g, v); Robert Crenshaw (d, v); Chris Donato (b, v); Tony Garnier (b); Michael Osborn (pc); Thom Panunzio (e)

Track listing:
There She Goes Again; Someday, Someway (S); Girls...; I'll Do Anything; Rockin' Around In NYC; The Usual Thing; She Can't Dance; Cynical Girl; Mary Anne; Soldier Of Love; Not For Me; Brand New Lover

Running time:
38.35

Current CD:
BSK-3673 2

Further listening:
Field Day (1983), Number 447 (1999)

Further reading:
www.marshallcrenshaw.com

The Cure
Pornography

Most bands are happy when they make their greatest album. The Cure broke up.

The NME review called it "Phil Spector in hell"; Robert Smith simply describes it as hell.

"I look back on it as just a crazed month, I was incredibly driven to make that album. It would be impossible for me to make an album like *Pornography* again. I was deranged, standing there screaming at people."

It *was* an intense album, even on the post-punk, proto-Goth yardstick by which the Cure were then measured. The culmination of a three-year cycle launched by 1980's *17 Seconds*, and following hard on the heels of the funereal *Faith*, *Pornography* was brutal, despairing and very, very ugly. But it was not, Smith insisted, "a violent album. If anything, it was about the inability to be violent."

The opening lyric sets the scene, Smith's vocal rising above 100 Years' crumbling castle wall of sound to insist, "It doesn't matter if we all die."

It was only later that he admitted that quite the contrary was on his mind; "I hate the idea that you'd die for your audience, [but] I was rapidly becoming enmeshed in that around the time of *Pornography*, the idea that Ian Curtis had gone first and I was soon to follow. I wasn't prepared for that to happen."

He just wasn't certain how to prevent it, and *Pornography* howls his frustration through the fractured wedding march of Siamese Twins ("I chose an eternity of this"); the numbing horror of Hanging Garden; and onto the cathartic rancour of the title track, composed the previous Christmas on a chemical vacation at Steve Severin's house.

Relentless in its density, a totalitarian battering where even the silences between tracks scream, *Pornography* is unlike any other Cure album. Childhood fancies like Bowie, Steve Harley and Alex Harvey, so vividly peeping through past (and future) Smith compositions, are nowhere to be seen; and though Smith has returned to the sounds of *Pornography* on several occasions since then (*Disintegration*, *Blood Flowers*), he has never reprised its intensity. And with good reason.

"It's like rereading old diaries. That period, I tend not to dwell on too much, because it wasn't much fun."

A few months later, Simon Gallup is thrown out after a violent quarrel on tour in Europe and Robert Smith joins

Record label:
Fiction

Produced
by The Cure and Phil Thornally

Recorded
at RAK Studio One, London, Jan–Feb 1982

Release date:
May 1982

Chart peaks:
8 (UK) None (US)

Personnel:
Robert Smith (v, g, k), Simon Gallup (b,k), Laurence Tolhurst (d, k)

Track listing:
One Hundred Years; A Short Term Effect; The Hanging Garden (S); Siamese Twins; The Figurehead; A Strange Day; Cold; Pornography

Running time:
43.22

Current CD:
CD FIX 7

Further listening:
The raw, cuter beginnings on Three Imaginary Boys (1979) — released in the US as Boys Don't Cry, the darkness thickens on Faith (1981), Disintegration (1989) is cited by Smith as the second part of a Pornography trilogy with Blood Flowers (2000) as its culmination.

Further reading:
Faith (Dave Bowler and Bryan Dray, 1995)

Siouxsie And The Banshees. The next incarnation of The Cure, fanfared by the electropop of Let's Go To Bed in December '82 and The Walk the following year will be very different from *Pornography* – comparatively jolly, some might say. Smith, though eternally glum, will never again seem quite so serious.

John Cale
Music For A New Society

Ex-Velvet Underground man's tenth album and deliberately, the hardest sell of them all.

"**I** wanted to do a *Marble Index*," Cale admits, invoking Nico's most glacially bleak album, a record he also produced. "What I was most interested in was the terror of the moment." Coming down from the sonic attack of *Honi Soit* – coming down, indeed, to the point where even he had to confess, "there were some examples where songs ended up so emaciated they weren't songs any more," Cale cast an eye back over a catalogue which had already been described as psychotic, and decided to show people precisely what psychosis really was.

"The songs were very difficult. They were entrenched in a certain *ennui* or angst that a lot of people associate with John Cale." Centring everything on his voice, adapting instrumentation not because it fit the songs but because it added to the atmospheres, *New Society* was sparse, cracked and scary. In his autobiography, Cale acknowledges that the spirit of the Velvet Underground hung heavily over the proceedings, the sense of "breaking things down into their lowest common denominator and seeing how much tension can be created between the individual parts".

Disembodied whispers and laughter cut through Thoughtless Kind; ghostly orchestral snatches give wife Rise, Sam And Rimsky-Korsakov its sole hope of melody; the ironic juxtaposition of Beethoven's Ninth (Song To Joy) and Cale's Damn Life. Even Close Watch, reprised from 1975's *Helen Of Troy* and the closest thing to a beautiful love song Cale has ever admitted to, is torn apart and turned in on itself, while Changes Made, the solitary rocker – included at his label's insistence to keep the whole affair from being too wrist-slashing – has the opposite effect entirely, bursting out to remind listeners of everything the rest of the album has rejected. But even though it was bleak, Cale had no fears about its effect. "It wouldn't make people jump out of windows," he shrugs. "They just wouldn't buy the damned album."

Record label:
Island

Produced
by John Cale.

Recorded
at Skyline Studios, New York; 1982.

Released:
August 1982

Chart peaks:
None (UK) None (US)

Personnel:
John Cale (v, g, k); DJ Young (g); Alan Lanier (k); David Lichtenstein (d); Risé Cale (v); John Wonderling, Mike McLintock, Robert Elk, Pipe Major Tom FitzGibbon ("accompanying musicians")

Track listing:
Taking Your Life In Your Hands; Thoughtless Kind; Sanities; If You Were Still Around; Close Watch; Broken Bird; Chinese Envoy; Changes Made; Damn Life; Rise, Sam And Rimsky-Korsakov

Running time:
44.38

Current CD:
YMCD 003 adds In The Library Of Force

Further listening:
for its twin, Marble Index by Nico (1969); for its corollary, Sabotage (1980)

Further reading:
What's Welsh For Zen (John Cale and Victor Bockris, 2000)

Kate Bush
The Dreaming

From pop star to cult artist in one peculiar, brilliant album.

When Kate Bush — a white-faced, red-lipped, flyaway-haired siren squalling mystical, sexy hippy-chick lyrics in the voice of a banshee — appeared in January 1978 singing Wuthering Heights, jaws dropped. People didn't know whether to laugh or listen harder. Those who chose the latter — and by 1981 there had been enough of them to support three hit albums and ten hit singles — heard an endearingly eccentric prodigy of rare creativity and singular style. Her music had evolved from piano-driven orch-rock into adventurous and unique soundworlds which utilised her unusual vocal mannerisms and light surrealism to increasingly powerful effect, as in Breathing, a claustrophobic creation concerning post-nuclear birth.

In 1981, writing a song a night to a drum machine (inspired by Peter Gabriel) she eventually felt compelled to "sever all the links I had had with the older stuff", in order to maximise the potential of her new, rhythmically assertive material. She had felt too easily influenced by other people; that meant saying goodbye to engineer Jon Kelly and producing *The Dreaming* herself. Always driven by the artistic rather than the business impulse (finding live work an unbearable personal upheaval, she quit it in '79), it took over a year and cost a small fortune with Kate finding it the most technically, artistically and emotionally demanding project of her life. But she was proud of the finished product, a dark, imposingly sophisticated and aggressive record of thundering rhythms and ethnic textures, acrobatic vocal effects and murky lyrics, full of inventive twists — the 5/4 groove of Sat In Your Lap, the chilling screams on Pull Out The Pin, All The Love's moving parade of voices saying "goodbye" on an answerphone.

Some soon-to-be-familiar aspects of the Fairlight — the then-vogueish sampling instrument used throughout — make some of the music rather "of its time", but its commitment, its unreasonable intensity and daffy combination of Vietnam/Aboriginal/*film noir*/escapologist imagery still impresses. Press and public alike were confused. Its density was attacked as overproduction, its ambiguousness as wilful obscurity. Kate: "Maybe the album is more difficult for people than I meant it to be. It isn't intended to be complicated." Just as the mainstream were getting used to her, she made *The Dreaming* — her "she's gone mad" album; if there had been any doubt of the dichotomous pop star/artist balance, there wasn't now.

Record label:
EMI

Produced
by Kate Bush.

Recorded
at Townhouse, Abbey Road, Odyssey, Advision; 1981–82

Released:
September 1982

Chart peaks:
3 (UK) None (US)

Personnel:
Kate Bush (Fairlight, v, k, p); Jimmy Bain (b); Ian Bairnson (g); Brian Bath (g); Rolf Harris (didgeridoo); Paddy Bush (hm, mandolin, stick); Geoffrey Downs (t); Percy Edwards (sound effects, v); Stuart Elliott (d); Dave Gilmour, Gordon Farrell, Paul Hardiman, Gary Hurst (v); Preston Heyman (d, stick); Sean Keane (vn) Dave Lawson (syn), Donal Lunny (bouzouki), Alan Murphy (g), Liam O'Flynn (whistle, uillean pipes), Del Palmer (b, v), Esmail Sheikh (d), Danny Thompson (b), Richard Thornton (choir), Eberhard Weber (b)

Track listing:
Sat In Your Lap; There Goes A Tenner; Pull Out The Pin; Suspended In Gaffa; Leave It Open; The Dreaming; Night Of The Swallow; All The Love; Houdini; Get Out Of My House

Running time:
42.25

Current CD
CDP7463612

Further listening:
Never Forever (1980); Hounds Of Love (1985)

Further reading:
www.gaffa.org

The Psychedelic Furs

Forever Now

After critical panning of their second album, British post-punk outfit make a do-or-die plunge Stateside.

I t was the dreaded "difficult third album" for The Psychedelic Furs. Having enjoyed across-the-board critical acclaim and Top 20 success in Britain with their decidedly edgy, agreeably gloomy debut in 1980, the band found the follow-up just one year later fell on hostile reviewers' ears and was greeted by a resoundingly indifferent public. Recognising that US college radio wielded serious muscle in terms of introducing leftfield music to a youthful, pre-MTV, record-hungry market, Butler and band decided to try and make a go of it in the States. Trimmed to a four-piece after the sackings of original members Roger Morris (guitarist) and saxophonist/keyboardist Duncan Kilburn (the latter because he and Butler were constantly at loggerheads), the Furs set about steering away from the intensely moody material of their first two releases towards a tougher, more textured sound, with greater emphasis on song structure.

"*Forever Now* was really charting new territory for us," says guitarist John Ashton. "We knew a lot of what we were doing was taking a chance, but we didn't have too much to lose. We thought, if we fail with this one, so what?" The choice of Todd Rundgren as producer – over Steve Lillywhite, who had produced the first two LPs – was a deliberate attempt to give the band an aesthetic reboot. His well-known fondness for British music was a good counter to the Furs' early love of American bands – most notably Iggy and The Stooges, MC5 and the Velvet Underground – and he had already expressed an interest in the Furs' work. It was Rundgren who brought in Flo and Eddie as backing vocalists and supported the band's wish to use cello.

"He was very affable, a really sweet guy," says Ashton of Rundgren, "and he had some great ideas." The album was recorded not in the famous Utopia Studios proper, but in a small room on Rundgren's property in Mink Hollow Road in Lake Hill – the adjacent village to Bearsville – in around six weeks. Remembers Ashton: "There was snow on the ground at Easter – about three feet of it, which we weren't used to – and we were walking around wearing bin liners up to our waists, at least, Richard was. On this album, we wanted to strip the sound back, to get away from trying to make every single thing

Record label:
CBS

Produced
by Todd Rundgren

Recorded
at Utopia Sound Studios, Bearsville, NY, April/May 1982

Release Date:
September 1982

Chart peaks:
20 (UK) 61 (US)

Personnel:
Richard Butler (v), John Ashton (g), Tim Butler (b), Vince Ely (d, pc), Gary Windo, Donn Adams (horns), Ann Sheldon (cello), Mark Volman, Howard Kaylan (bv), Todd Rundgren (k, s, e), Chris Andersen (e)

Track listing:
President Gas (S/US); Love My Way (S); Run And Run; Merry-Go-Round; Sleep Comes Down; Forever Now; Danger (S); You & I; Goodbye; No Easy Street

Running time:
40: 57

Current CD:
CB38261

Further listening:
The Psychedelic Furs (1980); Love Spit Love, (1994) Love Spit Love formed by Butler after the demise of the Furs

Further reading:
www.sonymusic.com/artists/ThePsychedelic Furs

sound louder than everything else. *Forever Now* is the sound of a band finding another direction and I'd be telling a huge untruth if I said we weren't interested in hit singles – we were. That's what bands are supposed to do."

The Furs bagged an American hit, Love My Way in February 1983 but it was a revised version of Pretty In Pink (ironically, from the lambasted second album), the song which inspired a movie, which was to really make their name, three years later. *Forever Now* delivered a clutch of darkly addictive, hook-laden yet existentially uneasy pop songs (President Gas, Love My Way, Forever Now), along with the brooding, psychedelic nod to The Beatles that is the cello-decked Sleep Comes Down. Although by no means the most successful, it remains the most cohesive, assured and definitively Furs-like of their albums.

The Dream Syndicate
The Days Of Wine And Roses

A fanfare from California's Paisley Underground, a guitar-rock anomaly in synth-dominated times.

T he Dream Syndicate invented the Californian Paisley Underground scene, which brought chiming guitars and a '60s aesthetic back into fashion in the early 1980s. Following the success of a self-released EP, the band were signed by punk label Ruby/Slash for the recording of their watershed guitar-soaked, neo-psychedelic LP. Syndicate leader Steve Wynn remembers that recording was off to a shaky start.

"We got to the studio at around 7pm for a graveyard session, and no one was there to meet us. We just sat around by the front door with our instruments in the car and took turns going to Kentucky Fried Chicken for greasy bits of bird." The entire album was knocked out from midnight till 5am. "We weren't nervous or intimidated – we were pretty carefree about what we did."

Wynn set about melding Karl Precoda's free-associative guitar assaults with his own dreamy drone-poems. "We always figured we would just push everything to an extreme, have fun, make noise and not worry about the end result," he says. But producer Chris D. had other ideas for the studio novices. "I encouraged Chris to push Karl's guitar and my harmonica on the outro of Until Lately into the extreme red, driving it to the point of white noise," says Wynn. "He finally threw up his hands and said, 'If you want your record to sound terrible you can do what you want, but it's a bad idea.' I'm glad that we held our ground and that saner minds didn't prevail."

Mercifully, level heads were also absent when it came to the construction of the unrelenting title cut, which distils the band's unwieldy essence into one tight seven-minute jam – an unthinkable act in itself in 1982. It's sloppy, but its primitive nature is what has elevated the album to legendary status in some quarters, particularly among fellow musicians: Kurt Cobain and The Black Crowes' Chris Robinson both claiming inspiration from it.

Record label:
Rough Trade

Produced
by Chris D.

Recorded
at Quad Teck Studio, Los Angeles;
September 1982.

Release date:
October 1982

Chart peaks:
None (UK) None (US)

Personnel:
Steve Wynn (g,v); Karl Precoda (g);
Kendra Smith (b, v); Dennis Duck (d);
Pat Burnette (e)

Track listing:
Tell Me When It's Over (S); Definitely Clean; That's What You Always Say; Then She Remembers; Halloween; When You Smile; Until Lately; Too Little, Too Late; The Days Of Wine And Roses

Running time:
41.32

Current CD:
23844-2

Further listening:
The Day Before Wine And Roses, Live At KPFK (1995); Steve Wynn solo album, Kerosene Man (1990)

Further reading:
www.stevewynn.net

Donald Fagen
The Nightfly

Steely Dan frontman fashions affectionate tribute to his "faux-luxe" jazz-fan adolescence.

Though its sleek jazz-pop lines were not too far-removed from later Steely Dan albums like *Aja* and *Gaucho*, the subject matter of Donald Fagen's debut album marked a striking departure from his earlier work. Originally intended to be titled *Talk Radio*, it eschewed Steely Dan's usual sardonic distance in favour of autobiographical closeness, offering a sentimental view of his own childhood development. In unprecedentedly autobiographical songs like IGY (International Geophysical Year) and New Frontier he depicted the hopes and dreams of a late-'50s adolescence lived in the shadow of the Cold War, while the title track evoked the sense of cultural liberation provided by distant R&B and jazz DJs (like his "Lester the Nightfly") for teenagers stranded in soulless suburban developments hundreds of miles away.

The Nightfly was recorded with the usual painstaking attention to detail that had marked the later Steely Dan albums, using the same top session players. But where Dan had always striven to record the basic grooves in real time, this time Fagen, enamoured of the new 32-track digital recorder that engineer Roger Nichols had chosen to record on, opted to overdub each part separately. This introduced a whole new range of difficulties into the recording process. Apart from the usual teething problems associated with new technology, the musicians found they were being asked to accomplish the virtually impossible: pianist Michael Omartian objected strongly when asked to set the groove of the title track on his own, with nothing to play against but a soulless click-track; even worse was to come when Fagen demanded subtle timing differences between the left- and right-hand piano parts on a cover of Lieber and Stoller's Ruby Baby – eventually, the parts were recorded simultaneously by Omartian and Greg Phillinganes sitting together at the same keyboard.

The album was an immediate critical success upon its release, nominated for seven Grammy Awards including Album Of The Year. But Fagen himself regretted making it almost immediately, slipping into a bad case of writer's block which ensured there would be no follow-up album for more than a decade.

"I wanted to do an autobiographical album, and I really

Record label:
Warners

Produced
by Gary Katz.

Recorded
at Soundworks Digital Audio/Video Recording Studios, New York; Village Recorders, Los Angeles; Automated Sound, New York; 1981–82.

Release date:
October 1982

Chart peaks:
44 (UK) 11 (US)

Personnel:
Donald Fagen (v, k, synth blues harp, a); Greg Phillinganes (k); Michael Omartian (k); Rob Mounsey (syn); Hugh McCracken (g); Larry Carlton (g); Dean Parks (g); Rick Derringer (g); Steve Khan (g); James Gadson (d); Jeff Porcaro (d); Ed Green (d); Steve Jordan (d); Anthony Jackson (b); Chuck Rainey (b); Marcus Miller (b); Abraham Laboriel (b); Will Lee (b); Randy Brecker (t, flugelhorn); Dave Tofani (s); Michael Brecker (s); Ronnie Cuber (s); Dave Bargeron (tb, euphonium); Valerie Simpson (bv); Zack Sanders (bv); Frank Floyd (bv); Gordon Grody (bv); Daniel Lazarus (bv); Leslie Miller (bv); Starz Vanderlocket (pc); Roger Nichols (e, pc).

Track listing:
I.G.Y. (S); Green Flower Street; Ruby Baby (S); Maxine; New Frontier (S); The Nightfly; The Goodbye Look; Walk Between Raindrops

Running time:
38.53

Current CD:
7599236962

Further listening:
All Steely Dan's albums, particularly the later, jazzier ones (Aja and Gaucho), offer hints at Fagen's direction here; his own follow-up Kamakiriad — released 11 years later! — refines the form in the service of a fanciful sci-fi theme.

Further reading:
Donald Fagen: The Nightfly (Donald Fagen, 1983) www.steelydan.com
www.seanet.com/~stalfnzo/

put everything I knew into the *Nightfly* album," he recalled later. "And after that I really wasn't inspired to do anything. I fell into a bit of a depression for a while. I think, that like a lot of artists, especially in the music business, I was young and successful, and I was basically still an adolescent. I started to address some of these things with *The Nightfly*, and I got really scared after it was done; I felt I'd exposed myself in a way that I wasn't used to doing, and I kind of retreated psychologically from that."

Michael Jackson
Thriller

A motherlode of hit singles — seven out of nine tracks. One of the biggest albums in pop history.

Off The Wall had sold 12 million copies worldwide and was on the UK charts for 173 weeks spawning five hit singles (four in the US). In the three subsequent years Jackson became a background voice for hire as he studied other acts' production and studio performance techniques. Eventually, with the same team in place and the majority of the writing from the same sources (four from Jackson; three from Rod Temperton, including the title track), recording began.

Reflecting the feeding frenzy about his private life in the press, a couple of the tracks (notably Billie Jean and opening track Wanna Be Startin' Somethin') simmered with the hurt, anger and paranoia that would set the agenda for the rest of his century's life and work.

Whereas *Off The Wall* was recorded at, for the late '70s, considerable speed with no loss of due care and attention to detail, *Thriller* was meticulous in planning and execution, to the point of obsessiveness.

Soul and R&B were downgraded and the emphasis shifted to dance pop and rock. Guitarist Eddie Van Halen was brought in to add edge to Beat It and Temperton's title track became a marvellous, comic rock-soul horror vignette with veteran thesp Vincent Price Hammering it up; the innovative, expensive videos from these tracks shattered MTV's unspoken racial barrier.

A duet with Paul McCartney (The Girl Is Mine) maintained a relationship started with *Off The Wall*'s Girlfriend. Recalling the sessions, the musicians spoke of painstaking preparations — drummer Ndugu Chancler set up in a room by himself as he did eight or nine takes of Billie Jean in three hours; Louis Johnson bringing four of his collection of basses to the party before settling on the Yamaha. To end on more stats, because that is what the exhaustively marketed album represented in the end: in the seven months to June 1983, a time when the record industry was in recession, *Thriller* sold a million copies a month. In addition to 1983's Album Of The Year, *Thriller* won eight other Grammys. It was just what the '80s needed to hear, a record that equated extravagance with success.

Record label:
Epic

Produced
by Quincy Jones.

Recorded
at Westlake Audio and Ocean Way Studios, Los Angeles; 1981–82

Released:
December 1982

Chart peaks:
1 (UK) 1 (US)

Personnel:
Michael Jackson (v, bathroom stomp board, drum case beater); Greg Phillinganes (Rhodes, k, syn); Bill Wolfer (syn, k, programming); Steve Porcaro (syn, programming); Michael Boddicker (syn, emulator, vocoder); David Paich, David Foster, Rod Temperton, Brian Banks (syn); David Paich (syn, p); Tom Bahler (Synclavier); Brian Banks, Anthony Marinelli (programming); Greg Smith (Synergy, syn); David Williams, Dean Parks, Steve Lukather, Eddie Van Halen, Paul Jackson (g); Louis Johnson, Steve Lukather (b); Jeff Porcaro, Ndugu Chancler (d); Paulinho da Costa (pc); Jerry Hey, Gary Grant (t, flugelhorn); Larry Williams (s, flute)

Track listing:
Wanna Be Startin' Somethin' (S); Baby Be Mine; The Girl Is Mine (S); Thriller (S); Beat It (S); Billie Jean (S); Human Nature (S); P.Y.T. (Pretty Young Thing) (S); The Lady In My Life

Running time:
42.15

Current CD:
MILLEN4

Further listening:
Off The Wall (1979); Bad (1987)

Further reading:
Michael Jackson: The Magic and the Madness (J Randy Taraborelli, 1992)

U2

War

U2's coming-of-age album, epic and compelling.

When U2 began writing their third album *War*, a pervading sense of desperation hung over them.

"The first two albums had gone well," says guitarist The Edge, "but they'd hardly taken the world by storm. We knew our future was hanging in the balance."

Alone in a seaside cottage in Howth, North Dublin, the guitarist began to stockpile ideas on a primitive Tascam 4-track while his bandmates took a holiday. He knew time was precious. Weighed down by the size of the quartet's financial debt to Island Records and suffering post-tour fatigue, The Edge briefly considered quitting the band. But gradually the bones of Sunday Bloody Sunday and Seconds appeared – and, thanks to an Adam Clayton bassline written on the road, New Year's Day was soon shaping up nicely too.

Lyrically, *War* found U2 politically charged and pre-irony, Bono's passionate beliefs colouring many of the songs. Drowning Man was full of Old Testament imagery, 40 was Psalm 40, and Sunday Bloody Sunday – famously misconstrued as a rebel song by some Irish Americans – urged both Republicans and Nationalists "to claim the victory Jesus won". No surprise, then, that booze and chemical stimulants weren't part of the recording equation – as Kid Creole's Coconuts discovered when they dropped by to sing on Surrender.

Another guest was future Waterboy Steve Wickham, invited to play on Drowning Man after a chance meeting with The Edge at a bus stop. Steve Lillywhite's production on the track is impressionistic, the chiming acoustic guitars and Wickham's fiddle awash with reverb. Elsewhere, on Like A Song and Two Hearts Beat As One the producer's raw, almost skifflish approach feeds on U2's post-punk energy.

Reportedly, '40' – a track which would close many U2 live shows on subsequent tours – was almost omitted from the final tracklisting. "Steve said, 'This is a great tune, but it's not going to work without some drastic edits,'" says The Edge. Two whole sections were ditched at the 11th hour and, impressed by the results, Bono improvised his vocal on the spot.

The album topped the UK charts and peaked at Number 12 in the US. Stadium gigs beckoned, and a more generous budget from Island for 1984's *The Unforgettable Fire* yielded a far more sculpted sound.

Record label:
Island

Produced
by Steve Lillywhite and Bill Whelan.

Recorded
at Windmill Lane, Dublin;
October–December 1982.

Released:
February 1983

Chart peaks:
1 (UK) 12 (US)

Personnel:
Bono (v, g); The Edge (g, p, ls, v); Adam Clayton (b); Larry Mullen Jr (d); Steve Wickham (vn); Kenny Fradley (tp); Cheryl Poirier, Adriana Kaegi, Taryn Hagey, Jessica Felton (bv); Paul Thomas (e)

Track listing:
Sunday Bloody Sunday; Seconds; New Year's Day (S); Like A Song?; Drowning Man; The Refugee; Two Hearts Beat As One (S); Red Light; Surrender; '40'

Running time:
42.10

Current CD:
IMCD 141

Further listening:
October (1981)

Further reading:
Unforgettable Fire: The Story Of U2 (Eamon Dunphy, 1988); www.atu2.com

Aztec Camera
High Land, Hard Rain

Aztec Camera's debut album, a romantic counterpoint to the post-punk scene.

A t the age of 16, Roddy Frame announced to his English teacher he was quitting school to pursue a career as a pop star. Having learnt his chops via jazz gigs with his father in the working men's clubs of East Kilbride, near Glasgow, he'd already secured a record deal with pioneering Scottish indie label Postcard.

Label boss Alan Horne had immediately recognised the quality of Roddy's poetic ruminations on love and life, set to complex folk-jazz-pop arrangements: Bert Jansch, Neil Young and Wes Montgomery were all influences. Moving down to London after the success of singles Just Like Gold and Mattress Of Wire, Frame signed to Rough Trade and decamped to Eastbourne to record an album.

"Scritti Politti [fellow Rough Trade artists] were a big influence on me at the time," recalls Frame. "I'd hooked up with John Brand and Bernie Clarke, and they seemed dead right to me. John knew a lot about Neil Young and liked to smoke a joint. We went down and recorded the album at International Christian Communications in Eastbourne at night. We went out to the beach in the morning: it was very exciting, very intense and we stayed there for about a month. Bernie Clarke did a lot of the arrangements – there were so many complicated details."

After kicking off the flamenco-inflected Oblivious, with the enchanting lick "They call us lonely when we're really just alone", *High Land, Hard Rain* journeys through Roddy's fragile teenage psyche, from the elegiac We Could Send Letters to the rousing Walk Out To Winter, thick with melodious semi-acoustic chording and poetic observations about the bleak '80s scene. Even at its most melancholic, a spirit of optimism and romance prevails, as testified by the yearning strains of The Bugle Sounds Again ("Grab that Gretsch before the truth hits town!") and the closing off-the-cuff rag Going Down The Dip, a reference to Roddy's East Kilbride local, The Diplomat.

Listening today, the only flaws relate to the production: the flanged drums and the occasionally over-reverbed confluence of instruments – Hammond, acoustic, first-take vocals. But overall this remains a wonderful insight into a flourishing talent.

Record label:
Warner Brothers

Produced
by John Brand and Bernie Clarke.

Recorded
at International Christian Communications, Eastbourne; spring 1983.

Released:
May 1983

Chart peaks:
22 (UK) 129 (US)

Personnel:
Roddy Frame (v, g, hm); Campbell Owens (b); Bernie Clarke (o, p); Dave Ruffy (d, pc); John Brand (e)

Track listing:
Oblivious (S); The Boy Wonders; Walk Out To Winter (S); The Bugle Sounds Again; We Could Send Letters; Pillar To Post (S); Release; Lost Outside The Tunnel; Back On Board; Down The Dip

Running time:
38.40

Current CD:
4509-92849-2 adds: Haywire; Orchid Girl; Queen's Tattoos

Further listening:
Mark Knopfler-produced follow-up Knife (1984) was a disappointment, but the straight-ahead white soul pop of Love (1987) – which gave Frame his biggest hit singles – and the rockier Stray (1990) proved him an enduring tunesmith. Later albums returned to a more stripped-down approach.

Further reading:
Record Collector 244; Blue Suede Brogans: Scenes From The Secret Life Of Scottish Rock Music (Jim Wilke, 1992)

Billy Bragg
Life's A Riot With Spy Vs Spy

Cheaply made, budget-priced, half-a-debut launches a punk-folk hero.

"If you look at what else was in the charts in 1982–83 you can see why *Life's A Riot* proved a success," says Billy Bragg, "all that hyped-up New Romantic stuff – then this comes out and it is a true solo effort. It appealed to both the singer-song-writer crowd and the punks who couldn't relate to New Romanticism but loved the guitar sound and the minimalism."

Bragg, broke in south London, had almost despaired of ever making an album after various false starts with record companies. A homemade demo received a good notice in Melody Maker and led to a publisher offering further recordings providing they were just Billy and his guitar. He recorded solidly for three days ("There are about 15 different versions of A New England alone," says Bragg), directly onto quarter-inch tape with just in-house producer/engineer Oliver Hitch pressing the buttons and telling Billy when to start.

Masquerading as a TV repairman, Bragg then blagged his way into Charisma Records and met A&R man Peter Jenner (Pink Floyd's first manager) who liked the tapes and promised to issue them as a mini-album as there was a bit of money left over in his budget. He pressed 5,000 and got the brilliant Barney Bubbles to design the cover. "The record industry has to come to terms with the colossal scale of unemployment, especially for young people," Jenner said at the time. "Our philosophy is that it's the idea, the song, the personality, the talent that matters, not the technology, the hype or the styling. Billy's album in both price and quality is a foretaste of lots more to come."

Songs as potently bare as To Have And Have Not and The Man In The Iron Mask gave plenty of notice that here was a singer-songwriter with the charge of The Clash and the social focus of Woody Guthrie. Plugger Jeff Chegwin heard Radio 1 DJ John Peel say on air he'd do anything for a mushroom biryani. He and Bragg went straight round to the nearest curry house and drove to Radio One with Peel's dinner, asking only that he listen to *Life's A Riot* in return. It worked. The same night Peel thanked Bragg for the vegetable curry and played The Milkman Of Human Kindness. He was on his way. A Peel session followed, swiftly pursued by a string of ecstatic reviews and Bragg's own persuasively full-on live performances up and down the country did the rest. Reissued by Go-Discs, it quickly sold 110,000 copies and entered the charts.

Record label:
Utility

Produced
by Oliver Hitch.

Recorded
at Park Street Studio, London; February 1–3, 1983.

Released:
May 1983

Chart peaks:
30 (UK) None (US)

Personnel:
Billy Bragg (v, g); Oliver Hitch (e)

Track listing:
The Milkman Of Human Kindness; To Have And Have Not; Richard; A New England; The Man In The Iron Mask; The Busy Girl Buys Beauty; Lovers Town Revisited

Running time:
15.10

Current CD:
Cooking Vinyl COOKCD 060 (Back To Basics) compiles all of Riot with Brewing Up With Billy Bragg (1984) and the Between The Wars EP (1985).

Further listening:
Between The Wars EP (1985), The Internationale (1990). There's a useful best-of accompanying his album William Bloke (1996). Also outstanding is collaboration with Wilco, setting newly-discovered Woody Guthrie lyrics to music on Mermaid Avenue (1998).

Further reading:
Still Suitable For Miners: Billy Bragg, The Official Biography (Andrew Collins, 1998)

King Sunny Ade
Synchro System

The first African pop album to be recorded in London.

W hen Ade was signed to Chris Blackwell's Island label in 1982, there was a definite impetus to bring some overview of African pop to a western audience suddenly hungry for new flavours in an increasingly international dance and club scene. But was Ade a pop musician, his band a team of faithful stalwarts – or was he an overlord of dance music in the manner of Hamilton Bohannon, submerging his own personality within the groove? It was hard to tell, and that confusion was one reason why Ade and his music remained mostly within a marginalised following.

His first set for Island, *Juju Music*, was an anthemic introduction to his Nigerian sound, less about the helium-toned guitars which dominated much other African pop, and more about the choral harmonies of his many singers and the jittery polyrhythms of the talking drummers and percussionists. But the subsequent set, *Synchro System*, recorded in London under the stewardship of Martin Meissonier, was the most determined bid to shape Sunny's groove and make it amenable to foreign ears. Meissonier carefully distinguished each element in the band in his mixes, so the voices sailed over the simmering percussion below and the guitars twanged out the little trademark rifts which set each composition apart. Ade and Meissonier himself then thickened the broth with just enough keyboard colour to fill out the ensembles.

It remains an abstract, a frozen picture of what The African Beats were like rather than a celebration of their art. There could be no substitute for seeing this glorious group, but even on record the music still sounds intensely vivid. Ade's own curiously small voice, a little whispery instrument in the mix, is as singular a part of *Synchro System* as the percussive chatter of the drums, or the cheery call-and-response of the other vocalists. Island pursued their ambitions with Ade for one further record, the even groovier *Aura*, but then they let him go.

Record label:
Island/Mango

Produced
by Martin Meissonier.

Recorded
at Music Works, London.

Released:
July1983

Chart peaks:
93 (UK) None (US)

Personnel:
King Sunny Ade (g, v); Segun Mori, John Akpan, Bob Ohiri, Elder Osei (g); Demola Adepoju (steel g); Jonah Bonsu (k); Felili Lawal (b); Fatioke Abiodun (agogo); Gani Alashe (shekere); Michael Babatola (maracas); Alhaji Timmy Olaitan, Rasaki Aladokun (talking drums); Mioses Akanbi (d); Shina Abiodun (congas); Femi Owomoyela, Jacob Ajakaye, Matthew Olojede, Niyi Falaye, Tunde Demiola (v)

Track listing:
Synchro Feelings- Ilako; Mo Ti Mo; Penkele; Maajo; Synchro System; E Saiye Re; Tolongo; E Wele; Synchro Reprise

Running time:
38.56

Current CD:
1625397372

Further listening:
Juju Music (1982); Aura (1984)

Further reading:
The Rough Guide To World Music (1994)

R.E.M.
Murmur

Pivotal work of the '80s American rock renaissance, finding perfection in understatement.

Following gruelling but ultimately unsuccessful demo sessions with English pop producer Stephen Hague (Pet Shop Boys, Human League, New Order), which had seen R.E.M. do over 40 takes of Catapult, only to have Hague later overdub synthesizers without their knowledge, the group reassembled with Mitch Easter (who had produced their *Chronic Town* EP) and Don Dixon to make their debut album. The more easy-going mood of the sessions at Reflection Studios enabled the group to record most of the songs in one or two takes, while Easter and Dixon suggested unusual ways of personalising the tracks. A recording of Bill Berry playing pool was layered into the song We Walk; the track 9-9 was played back over speakers and re-miked to give it a different sound; and the album's opening track Radio Free Europe was presaged by a mysterious buzzing echo effect achieved by filtering Mike Mills' bass through a noise gate.

In contrast to the band's raucous live performances, meanwhile, many of the recorded versions were built around acoustic guitars, as REM discovered the breakthrough folk-rock style that would revolutionise American rock in the '80s. The track Laughing, for instance, featured Buck, Mills, Easter and Dixon strumming together, double-tracked to produce a wall of eight acoustic guitars. Much of the album's indefinable magic comes from the air of mystery that surrounds it, from the cover photograph of kudzu, a vine common to the American south, to the unusually murky, "pillowy" mix and Michael Stipe's unnaturally quiet vocals, which bear out the album's title. In some cases, this was because the lyrics were developed from sounds rather than meanings.

"I purposely did not want any of the lyrics understood," said Stipe of Radio Free Europe. "The main reason for that was that I hadn't written any of the words yet, so I just kind of blabbered over the whole single."

On 9-9, by contrast, it was a semantic strategy. "We deliberately recorded it so you would never be able to decipher any of the words except the very last phrase, which is 'conversation fear', which is what the song is about," explained Stipe. Despite the occasional inaudibility, it was still clear which kind of matters were exercising Stipe's muse: apathy and commitment (Talk About The Passion), humiliation and contempt

Record label:
IRS

Produced
by Mitch Easter and Don Dixon.

Recorded
at Reflection Studio, Charlotte, North Carolina; January 1983.

Release date:
August 1983

Chart peaks:
None (UK) 36 (US)

Personnel:
Michael Stipe (v); Peter Buck (g, k); Mike Mills (b, k, bv); Bill Berry (d, bv); Don Dixon, Mitch Easter (e)

Track listing:
Radio Free Europe (S); Pilgrimage; Laughing; Talk About The Passion (S); Moral Kiosk; Perfect Circle; Catapult; Sitting Still; 9-9; Shaking Through; We Walk; West Of The Fields

Running time:
44.11

Current CD:
CDMID129

Further listening:
Virtually all of R.E.M.'s albums are required listening for any aware listener. The follow-up Reckoning (1984) was a further refinement of the Murmur sound; the Joe Boyd-produced Fables Of The Reconstruction (1985) initiated the '80s folk-rock revival; Life's Rich Pageant (1986) and Green (1988) adopted a harder, more political tone; Out Of Time (1991) thrust gently popwards; but only Automatic For The People (1992) carried the same kind of atmospheric weight as their debut. Later albums were rockier and generally less intriguing.

Further reading: Remarks:
The Story Of REM (Tony Fletcher, 1993);
REM Inside Out: The Stories Behind
Every Song (Craig Rosen, 1997)

(Laughing), cultural imperialism (Radio Free Europe) and moral proscription (Moral Kiosk).

Lighter and janglier than later R.E.M. albums, its blend of Byrdsome guitar arpeggios, contrapuntal vocal harmonies and flexible rhythms proved hugely influential over the subsequent decade. It was an immediate critical success on its release in 1983, going on to be voted Album Of The Year in Rolling Stone and placing second in the Village Voice's prestigious end-of-year critics' poll. It says much for its character that despite the band's subsequent globe-girdling fame, *Murmur* has retained all of its mystery and magic.

Tom Waits
Swordfishtrombones

Barfly troubadour Waits takes the weird way out of a cul-de-sac.

In the '70s, Tom Waits' vivid song world of plump-hearted street loners and five-and-dime losers had earned him critical acclaim and a healthy cult status, but there was a sense that he'd taken the Bones Howe-produced, gruffly sentimental, seedy lounge approach as far as it would go.

"I was getting lazy," Waits admitted. "I used to hear everything with a tenor saxophone, I had a very particular musical wardrobe." Halfway through scoring Francis Ford Coppola's movie One From The Heart in 1980 as a "lounge operetta about two years too late" he got in "a humbug" and left to write *Heartattack And Vine* before returning to complete the movie score.

It was a time of upheaval for Waits: he had split with girlfriend Rickie Lee Jones and moved to New York, met and married Kathleen Brennan and was keen to break the album-tour cycle of his existence. He credits his new wife with not only saving his life – there were reports that the line between himself and the drunken, broken characters in his songs was getting worryingly thin – but also with giving him the confidence to break with his old management and production team. "She knew that I was interested in a lot of diverse musical styles that I'd never explored before on my own records," Waits said. "She started playing a lot of records for me, the seminal idea for that record really came from Kathleen." That record was *Swordfishtrombones*, vocally and lyrically recognisably Waits, but musically amounting to a re-invention. Weill-esque stomps, semi-abstract instrumental vignettes, malformed minor blues all set in an extraordinary soundworld of harmonium and sledge-hammers, organ and metal aunglongs, twisted electric guitar and bell plates, trombone and glass harmonica; "a kind of a demented little parade band" or "mutant dwarf orchestra" as Waits variously had it.

The music was influenced by Harry Partch – a musician inspired by the American hobo existence and maverick instrument inventor of the '30s and '40s – and assisted by Partch's gramolodium player Francis Thumm, but Waits insists on back-crediting his wife as chief inspiration. "She really co-produced that record with me, though she didn't get the credit." The disturbing, surprisingly spacious music ("I liked the holes in it as

Record label:
Island

Produced
by Tom Waits.

Recorded
at Sunset Sound, Los Angeles; July–August 1982.

Released:
September 1983

Chart peaks:
62 (UK) None (US)

Personnel:
Tom Waits (syn, fiddle, g, harmonium, o, v); Crystal Gayle (v); Victor Feldman (pc); Shelly Manne (d); Bill Reichenbach, Dick Hyde (tb); Pete Jolly (p, accordion); John Lowe, Lanny Morgan (wind); Les Thompson (hm); Ronnie Barron (k); Eric Bikales (o); Larry Taylor (b); Bob Alcivar (p); Randall Aldcroft (tb, horn, s); Dennis Budimir (g); Larry Bunker (d); Anthony Clark (bagpipes); Greg Cohen (b, acoustic b); Teddy Edwards (s); Chuck Findley (t); Richard Gibbs (hm); Carlos Guitarlos (g); Stephen Hodges (hm, d); Richard Hyde (tb); Jack Sheldon (t); Gayle LaVant (horn); Jeff Porcaro (pc); Emil Richards (vibraphone); Joe Romano (tb, t); Anthony Stewart (bagpipes); Fred Tackett (banjo, g); Big John Thomassie (d); Francis Thumm (hm, a); Donald Waldrop (tuba); Clark Spangler (syn programming)

Track listing:
Underground; Shore Leave; Dave The Butcher; Johnsburg, Illinios; 16 Shells From A Thirty-Ought-Six, Town With No Cheer; In The Neighbourhood (S); Just Another Sucker On The Vine; Frank's Wild Years; Swordfishtrombone; Down, Down, Down; Soldier's Things; Gin Soaked Boy; Trouble's Braids; Rainbirds

Running time:
40.31

Current CD:
IMCD 48

Further listening:
Rain Dogs (1985); Frank's Wild Years
(1987)

Further reading:
Tom Waits (Terry Staunton and John
Aizelwood, 1999); www.officialtomwaits.com

much as I liked what was in them") was tantamount, as MOJO's Barney Hoskyns pointed out, to "throwing a gigantic spanner in the works". It was too much for his record company, Asylum, who passed on it, leaving Waits free to sign with Island and exploit his new-found inspiration and sometimes official creative partnership for another seven, increasingly ambitious albums.

Ruben Blades
Buscando America

The first crossover salsa album, and a calling card for a major Hispanic star.

By 1982 Ruben Blades had grown weary of prowling New Yorica's salsa ghetto. Other *salseros* might dance more slickly or dress more flamboyantly, but none was smarter than the Panamanian singer, a trained lawyer whose ambition was to become President of Panama.

Over the last five years, Blades' fruitful partnership with trombonist and producer Willie Colon had given him massive success; the pair's 1978 album *Siembra* (Seed) was a *cause célèbre*, Blades' song Pedro Navaja an anthem for Hispanic emigrants. Part of Blades' message was that North and South Americas were a continuum – "We are all Americans," he declared – yet his music remained little known outside of the *barrios*.

After falling out with Fania Records, and with Colon, Blades decided what he needed was a cross-over album. The result was *Buscando America* (Discovering America), an ambitious attempt to cross-pollinate salsa for a wider audience.

The blast of doo wop that opens the album served notice that this was no ordinary salsa record. Instead of the rich brass arrangements provided by Colon there were, gasp, synthesizers, while elsewhere Blades switched between singing and rap. The sleeve, meanwhile, carried the lyrics in both Spanish and English. Alongside typically Blades social cameos like Decisiones was El Padre Antonio, a song about the murdered El Salvadorean priest Oscar Romero, and Desapariciones, which mourns the "disappeared" of Latin America's dictatorships.

Buscando America worked for Blades in several ways. For the mainstream media an opinionated Latin singer able to articulate the Hispanic viewpoint made a good story. *Buscando America* also introduced Blades to a white music audience and even extended his appeal among Latin listeners for whom much salsa was vulgar and disreputable.

"Instead of just looking at the street corner for my subjects, I looked down the neighbouring street, then the city, then the world," he explained. Liike Blades' previous work, the record enlarged Latin music's own conception of what it was and could become, setting a precedent that artists like Gloria Estefan would later follow. The synths sound creaky today, otherwise *Buscando* still delivers.

Record label:
Elektra

Produced
by David Rodriguez and Ruben Blades.

Recorded
at Eurosound Studios, New York;
May–August, 1983.

Released:
October 1983

Chart peaks:
None (UK) None (US)

Personnel:
Ruben Blades (v, g, maraccas); Mike Vinas (g); Oscar Hernandez (p); Eddie Montalvo (tumbadoros, pc, bv); Louie Rivera (pc); Ralph Irizarry (timbales, pc); Ray Adams (d)

Track listing:
Decisiones; GDBD; Desapariciones; Todos Vuelven; Caminos Verdes; Padre Antonio Y El Moniguillo; Buscando America

Running time:
39.01

Current CD:
EA60352

Further listening:
1988's English language album Nothing But The Truth featured collaborations with Lou Reed and Elvis Costello, while 1996's La Rosa de Los Vientos [The Rose of the Winds] bagged a Grammy.

Further reading:
Salsa (Sue Steward, 1999)

Bruce Springsteen
Born In The USA

Springsteen mingles big heart and big ideas and goes global.

Quite consciously still growing up in his early thirties, after *The River* (1980) Springsteen took time out to digest diverse issues such as the onrush of wealth and fame, his lack of a long-term girlfriend, and his encounters with political campaigners including the Vietnam Veterans Of America. Then, on January 3, 1982, at his house in Holmdel, New Jersey, on an old reel-to-reel he suddenly recorded more than a dozen songs. He thought it was a demo. But when he and The E Street Band reconvened in May at The Power Station these ferocious vignettes resisted every arrangement they came up with. Springsteen was bemused – until he decided the demo *was* an album. The solo, grim, hit-free *Nebraska* came out that September and sold sparsely, but enhanced Springsteen's reputation as an artist of integrity.

However, back in May, something seismic did happen. One day, he stood alone in the studio and began to doodle a riff around a song which had sounded feeble on the Holmdel "demo". Just then the band arrived and, forthwith, slammed out one of the iconic tracks of the decade, Born In The USA. "I said, Roy, get this riff," Springsteen recalled. "He just pulled out that sound on the synthesizer (the opening fanfare). We played it two times and our second take is the record." Over the next three weeks they recorded five more songs.

Then, with Springsteen involved in *Nebraska* and his closest friend Van Zandt leaving to go solo, the band album got sticky again. Even though Springsteen wrote 70 songs start to finish, finding the right ones was the problem. They squeezed out My Hometown in February 1983, Bobby Jean and No Surrender the following autumn – along with Cover Me, originally written for disco queen Donna Summer in spring 1982 – and Springsteen finally came up with Dancing In The Dark in March 1984 ("It was just like my heart spoke straight through my mouth without even having to pass through my brain"). The peculiarly Springsteenian dark pop smash hit completed *Born In The USA*'s enormous emotional span, from the title track's agonised roar of anger about the Vietnam aftermath to the priapic bedroom intensity of I'm On Fire, the hard-rocking blues of I'm Going Down and the quiet father-and-son intimacy of My Hometown.

Record label:
CBS

Produced
by Bruce Springsteen, Jon Landau, Chuck Plotkin and Steve Van Zandt

Recorded
at The Power Station and The Hit Factory, New York; May 1982; February, August and October–November 1973; March 1974.

Released:
June 1984

Chart peaks:
I (UK) I (US)

Personnel:
Bruce Springsteen (v, g); Roy Bittan (p, syn); Clarence Clemons (s); Danny Federici (k); Garry Tallent (b; Steve Van Zandt (g); Max Weinberg (d); Toby Scott (e)

Track listing:
Born In The USA (S/US); Cover Me (S); Darlington County; Working On The Highway; Downbound Train; I'm On Fire (S); No Surrender; Bobby Jean; I'm Goin' Down; Glory Days (S); Dancing In The Dark (S); My Hometown (S)

Running time:
46:19

Current CD:
Columbia CD86304

Further listening:
Nebraska (1982), Born In The USA's mirror image, and the Tracks (1998), box set of outtakes because it's very good and sets his most commercial album in a career context. Darkness On The Edge Of Town (1978) and Tunnel Of Love (1987)

Further reading:
MOJO 17, 62; Glory Days: Bruce
Springsteen In The 1980s (Dave Marsh,
1987); www.backstreets.com (US)

But, as an event, everything about it was grand-scale. It took Springsteen to the world. He was in his pomp, the greatest blue-collar rock star ever. Also, inevitably, heading for a fall.

The Specials

In The Studio

"Difficult" third album helped to liberate a political freedom fighter and spelled the end of 2-Tone.

"I had to write the third Specials album without The Specials. Not an easy thing to do," recalls Jerry Dammers, founder member and chief songwriter. One week The Specials were top of the singles chart with Ghost Town, soundtracking 1981's week of inner-city riots; the next they were in tatters, as vocalists Terry Hall and Neville Staples and guitarist Lynval Golding left without warning to form the Fun Boy Three. Announcing a return to the group's original name of Special AKA and recruiting singer Stan Campbell, Dammers locked himself in the studio. He emerged occasionally to release a single, but it was three years before he delivered this brave, inspired, non-ska mix of lounge-jazz muzak and dub-reggae, a record which proved that there was such a thing as a blend of politics and pop which was effective on both counts.

It was not an easy album to make, even by "difficult third album" standards. Tracks were rewritten, reworked and re-recorded over and over again. It took so long, in fact, that the Fun Boy Three's entire career was over by the time this album came out. The intense Housebound, an agoraphobic nightmare rumoured to be directed at Terry Hall, could just as easily have described Dammers himself, holed up in the control room day and night for 36 months. Day after day would be spent singing the same line repeatedly until the perfectionist Dammers was satisfied. The one exception was its best-known track, Nelson Mandela – Dammers' spontaneous freedom chant took a mere four days to complete. Produced by Elvis Costello (who'd also produced The Specials' debut), the song featured The Beat's Rankin' Roger and Dave Wakeling and the return of Lynval Golding. The brutal War Crimes ("From the graves of Belsen, to the ruins of Beirut/I can still see people dying") made for a gloomy single, but there's also a taste of Dammers' cynical humour on What I Like Most About You Is Your Girlfriend, the only Specials track to feature his deadpan lead vocals.

By the time the album was ready it was attracting attention as an expensive folly and was, unfairly, judged accordingly. It sold poorly and became the group's swansong. A combination of contractual obligations and financial ruin made it the last album Dammers has released.

Record label:
2-Tone

Produced
by Jerry Dammers, Dick Cuthell, Dick Cuthell and Jerry Dammers, Elvis Costello.

Recorded
at Woodbine Studios, Air Studios, Vineyard and Phoenix Studios, Wessex Studios, London; between September 1981–83.

Release date:
June 1984

Chart peaks:
34 (UK) None (US)

Personnel:
Jerry Dammers (p, o); Gary McManus (b); Stan Campbell (v); Rhoda Dakar (v); John Shipley (g); John Bradbury (d); Rico Rodriquez (tb); Dick Cuthell (cornet, flugel horn); Andy Aderinto (s); Egidio Newton (bv); Caron Wheeler (bv); Naomi Thompson (bv); Claudia Fontaine (bv); Horace Panter (b); Tony "Groko" Utah (congas); Roddy Radiation (g); Nick Parker (vn)

Track listing:
Bright Lights (S/UK); The Lonely Crowd; What I Like Most About You Is Your Girlfriend (S/UK); Housebound; Night On The Tiles; Nelson Mandela (S); War Crimes (The Crime Is Still The Same) (S/UK); Racist Friend (S/UK); Alcohol; Break Down The Door

Running time:
42.42

Current CD:
CCD 5008

Further listening:
The Specials Singles (1991); their debut album The Specials (1979), a vicious mix of punk and ska; More Specials (1980), their second album, with its experimental excursions into soul, rockabilly, ska and easy listening.

Further reading:
You're Wondering Now: A History Of The Specials (Paul Williams, 1995); The 2-Tone Story (George Marshall, 1991)

SOS Band
Just The Way You Like It

The birth of one of the '80s' most distinctive sounds.

Jimmy Jam and Terry Lewis, respectively the keyboard player and bassist with Minneapolis funk band The Time, had just finished recording Just Be Good To Me for the SOS Band's fourth album, *On The Rise*. It was one of a number of projects in a burgeoning production career, but now they were at Atlanta airport waiting for the flight to San Antonio where they were due to link up with The Time for a gig. They got snowed in, never made the show and were sacked by Prince, The Time's keeper. It was a firing that launched Jam and Lewis' full-time production career.

Other acts – notably Janet Jackson and Alexander O'Neal – had bigger worldwide hits with Jam and Lewis, but no one better defined the producers' sound than the SOS Band. They'd created the blueprint – lush synth pads, plushly thudding drums, liquid bass – in Tell Me If You Still Care and the thundering Just Be Good To Me on *On The Rise*, which signalled a switch in focus onto Mary Davis' voice with its rich tone and slightly husky edge. Weaned on the productions of Gamble and Huff and Rodgers and Edwards, Jam and Lewis had worked with the SOS Band since their third album, 1982's imaginatively titled *III*, and by now knew the band's strong points. With thick washes of keyboard and a gentle, measured pace, opening track No One's Gonna Love You creates a ripe atmosphere and romantic mood that Davis' reading exploits to the full. Weekend Girl expands the palette and the tougher title track closes the first side of the vinyl release as the best-conceived and executed Jam-Lewis recording. The final three tracks – the uptempo dancer Body Break, the perky Feelings and the ballad I Don't Want Nobody Else – were written by the band and are much what one would expect from an experienced team (they had been Santa Monica, house band at Atlanta's Regal Room). This split of material between band and producers creates a tension, a fine balance between ballad and beat, emotion and dance, but the Jam and Lewis tracks, strongly featuring Davis, are, by some distance, the pick.

Record label:
Tabu

Produced
by Jimmy Jam and Terry Lewis with SOS Band.

Recorded
at Master Sound, Atlanta and Creation Audio, Minneapolis; 1983–84

Released:
August 1984

Chart peaks:
29 (UK) 12 (US)

Personnel:
Mary Davis (v); Jason "TC" Bryant (k, v); Abdul Raoof (t, v); Bruno Speight (g), Jerome "JT" Thomas (pc, d); John Simpson (b); Billy Ellis, Sonny Killebrew (s); Terry Lewis, Monte Moir, Leticia Peterson, Gwendolyn Traylor, Joyce Irby, Jimmy Jam (bv). Additional musicians: Jimmy Jam, Terry Lewis, Stewart Hanley, Lloyd Oby

Track listing:
No One's Gonna Love You; Weekend Girl; Just The Way You Like It; Break Up; Feeling; I Don't Want Nobody Else; Body Break

Running time:
45.58

Currently unavailable on CD

Further listening:
Check the brilliant On The Rise (1983) with its excellent side one suite; and two more commercially successful Jam and Lewis productions, Janet Jackson's Control (1986) and Alexander O'Neal, Alexander O'Neal (1985)

Further reading:
www.flytetyme.com

Hüsker Dü
Zen Arcade

Minneapolis trio emerge from the highly-charged early '80s US hardcore scene with winningly melodic double set.

The way Bob Mould picks his guitar *à la* A Hard Day's Night at the end of opening track Something I Learned Today provided a big clue to what Hüsker Dü intended with this record. By the time *Zen Arcade* arrived in 1984, Hüsker Dü had already forged a fearsome reputation, with their 1982 debut, *Land Speed Record* the epitome of snarling, super-fast hardcore. But come *Metal Circus* a year later, the group's love of The Beatles and The Byrds was beginning to seep through – they even released their version of the latter's Eight Miles High as a single in spring 1984. When pressed in interviews at the time, Bob Mould professed – tongue no doubt firmly in cheek – that Hüsker Dü had passed the punk test on a number of occasions. He also asserted that they knew they wrote good songs; Grant Hart maintained that their music had always had a "serious pop edge". By the time of *Zen Arcade*, the group were covering ground as if taking an idiosyncratic, high-speed overview of contemporary America.

Hart's Pink Turns To Blue and Mould's Chartered Trips showed that Hüsker Dü had two accomplished and complementary songwriters and singers – they even sang harmonies together. Harnessed to the group's formidable firepower, the combination was irresistible. Indeed, few, if any, groups have touched the concentrated ferocity of a song such as I'll Never Forget You; a howl of wounded rage set to dragster-speed riffing.

On a double album like *Zen Arcade*, you could argue a certain percentage of filler is necessary to give the listener some breathing space, but all the tracks here have a role, even Hart and Mould's piano cameos. The 14-minute, live-in-the-studio instrumental, Reoccurring Dreams – which got the group dubbed as the hard-core Grateful Dead – shows off the Hart/Norton rhythm section as a particularly propulsive unit, while Mould's guitar forays sound like entire cities being laid to waste; "No overdubs or fancy stuff", the sleevenotes proclaim. Every track is a first take – except two that they started too fast – which again saw them "passing the punk test". Hüsker Dü soon gained a reputation as one of the '80s' most influential rock groups, and although they streamlined their music later on, *Zen Arcade* captures them at their most adventurous. As to those Beatle influences, a couple of years later they were playing Ticket To Ride in concert.

Record label:
SST

Produced
by Spot and Hüsker Dü.

Recorded
at Total Access, Redondo Beach, California; October 1983.

Released:
September 1984

Chart peaks:
None (UK) None (US)

Personnel:
Bob Mould (g, v, b, pc, p); Greg Norton (b, bv); Grant Hart (d, v, pc, p, g); Spot (e)

Track listing:
Something I Learned Today; Broken Home, Broken Heart; Never Talking To You Again; Chartered Trips; Dreams Reoccurring; Indecision Time; Hare Krsna; Beyond The Threshold; Pride; I'll Never Forget You; The Biggest Lie; What's Going On; Masochism World; Standing By The Sea; Somewhere; One Step At A Time; Pink Turns To Blue; Newest Industry; Monday Will Never Be The Same; Whatever; The Tooth Fairy And The Princess; Turn On The News

Running time:
70.25

Current CD:
SST CD 027

Further listening:
New Day Rising (1985), and Flip Your Wig from later the same year.

Further reading:
world.std.com/~thirdave/hd.html

Lloyd Cole And The Commotions
Rattlesnakes

Glasgow University graduates plunder four decades of music and Eng. Lit. to produce clever and successful debut.

In the early and mid-'80s a gaggle of young groups emerged from the post-punk wreckage to strike a blow for song-writing craftsmanship. Scritti Politti, The Smiths and Prefab Sprout all knew their onions, but arguably Lloyd Cole And The Commotions produced the best first shot of the lot. Drummer Stephen Irvine remembers its genesis.

"Neil, Lloyd and Blair were in a soul band before I joined. With Lawrence (son of Lonnie Donegan) and myself involved it took an altogether less blue-eyed soul feel."

That feel still plays a very important part on *Rattlesnakes* however: witness the Tony Joe White-like funkiness and luxu-riant strings of Speedboat, or the Philly-derived beats and falsetto vocal of Patience.

"We rehearsed a lot, refining as we went. By the time we got our deal, Paul Hardiman (producer) was exactly what we needed. We wanted to work with him after hearing *Soul Mining* by The The. He knew exactly how to get each of us to perform to the best of our abilities."

Irvine has another theory as to why *Rattlesnakes* still feels fresh today. "Thankfully we all had our eyes on vintage equip-ment when we signed, and didn't go for the new sounds and effects that were in vogue in 1984 but seem so dated now. Phew."

The Commotions clearly played a good team game but Cole was the star. His wavering, protean voice – a vessel of the vulnerable and the knowing, proved to be the ideal vehicle for his sour-sweet musings, "She's got cheekbones like geometry and eyes like sin/And she's sexually enlightened by Cosmopolitan."

Cole was also a compulsive and fearless namedropper: Truman Capote, Leonard Cohen, Grace Kelly and Simone de Beauvoir all rub shoulders in his songs. Forest Fire was a time-less pop-soul gem blessed with a sublime build that climaxed in howling art-rock guitar. Charlotte Street possessed the kind of riff that stiffened the backbone of the British Invasion and the undulating Byrdsian guitar figures kept several songs flying high.

It was all very knowing, and Cole's inability to resist a

Record label:
Polydor

Produced
by Paul Hardiman.

Recorded
at The Garden, Shoreditch, London; March and June 1984.

Released:
October 12, 1984

Chart peaks:
13 (UK) None (US)

Personnel:
Lloyd Cole (g, v); Neil Clark (g); Blair Cowan (k); Lawrence Donegan (b); Stephen Irvine (d, p); Anne Dudley (a)

Track listing:
Perfect Skin (S); Speedboat; Rattlesnakes (S); Down On Mission Street; Forest Fire (S); Charlotte Street; 2CV; Four Flights Up; Patience; Are You Ready To Be Heartbroken?

Running time:
36.06

Currently unavailable on CD

Further listening:
Easy Pieces (1985); solo album Bad Vibes (1993)

Further reading:
www.lloydcole.com

literary reference got up some noses, but he judged his balancing act between artifice and instinct perfectly, making *Rattlesnakes* utterly right for its time. Though he continues to produce decent albums to this day — and has subsequently made some impact in the US — Cole has never seized the moment in quite the same alluring way.

Julian Cope
Fried

Former Teardrop's experiment in acoustic psychedelia went unappreciated in the age of The Thompson Twins.

It's the turtle shell that everyone notices first. Confirmation that, yes, drug-addled Julian Cope really is nuts! For Cope though, posing with a turtle shell on his back was a pre-emptive strike.

After The Teardrop Explodes split, Cope was aware that critics were tiring of his acid consumption, some even suggesting that he might go the same way as Syd Barrett. To a Barrett fan like Cope, though, this hardly constituted a warning. Undeterred by the critical pasting administered upon 1984's *World Shut Your Mouth*, he immediately resumed work and decamped to Cambridge in defiant mood.

"If these records have to be my *TB Sheets* or *Starsailor* [obscure gems by Van Morrison and Tim Buckley]," wrote Cope in his autobiography, "then so be it."

On arrival, his first move was to write a protest song of sorts. Bored with a climate in which every Tom, Dick and Tears For Fears was heralding their new record as "unlike anything you've ever heard before", Cope went the other way: "I decided that if it hadn't been done before, then I wasn't interested."

Drawing on a 400-year-old tradition, he wrote the primitive, pulsing Reynard The Fox (a song which he later cited as the inspiration for his archaeological tome, The Modern Antiquarian). Happy with the direction things were taking, he stuck a picture of Brian Wilson on the wall – to be consulted in times of crisis– and abandoned clothing for the remaining sessions, feeling that people would hear the nakedness. Oddly, you knew exactly what he meant. A clutch of desolate ballads, all strummed minor chords and catatonic Hammond organs, lent substance to the Syd Barrett comparisons. But such comparisons sold short the stark lucidity of Me Singing, Torpedo and Laughing Boy – performances which could induce a Glastonbury of goosepimples on the thickest of skins.

Unsurprisingly, Cope's record company hated it, not least for the turtle shell. They attempted to make a hit of its one indisputable moment of pop majesty, Sunspots. But to the public, even that conveyed something of the strangeness in which it was recorded: Cope perched atop a huge arched window attempting to hoover it clean, whilst his also-tripping producer discussed drums with the photo of Brian Wilson.

Record label:
Mercury

Produced
by Stephen Lovell.

Recorded
at Spaceward Studios, Cambridge; July 1984.

Released:
November 1984

Chart peaks:
87 (UK) None (US)

Personnel:
Julian Cope (v, g, b, o); Donald Ross Skinner (g); Steve Lovell (g); Brother Johnno (g); Chris Whitten (d)

Track listing:
Reynard The Fox; Bill Drummond Said; Laughing Boy; Me Singing; Sunspots (S); The Bloody Assizes; Search Party; O King Of Chaos; Holy Love; Torpedo

Running time:
42.50

Current CD:
523 370-2 adds: I Went On A Chourney; Mic Mak Mok; Land Of Fear

Further listening:
Peggy Suicide (1991); Jehovahkill (1992); Interpeter (1996); Julian Cope And The Teardrop Explodes: Floored Genius: The Best Of Julian Cope And The Teardrop Explodes (1992)

Further Reading:
MOJO 73; Head On/Repossessed – brilliant, funny autobiography chronicling the Teardrops and solo years until 1990; www.headheritage.co.uk

Needless to say, it tanked, and Cope was dropped. Some kind of revenge was afforded in 1987 by the successful bombast of *Saint Julian*, but it was only when Cope tapped back into his progadelic roots with 1991's *Peggy Suicide* that he truly rediscovered his form.

Frankie Goes To Hollywood
Welcome To The Pleasure Dome

The extravagant soundtrack to the biggest UK sensation of 1984.

"They have the wit of The Beatles, the decadence of The Rolling Stones and the wildness of the Sex Pistols." That was how one tabloid paper reacted to the Frankies back in 1984 and for once the reporting was absolutely spot-on. The Liverpudlians dominated the singles charts as no act had done since the golden age of Merseybeat. They equalled Gerry & The Pacemakers' hoary chart statistic with three consecutive chart-toppers from inception (a record since smashed by The Spice Girls, Westlife *et al*), and positively thrived on controversy. They were first glimpsed in 1982 on TV show, The Tube, cavorting to an early version of Relax in skimpy, black-leather bondage gear.

At a time when gay pop stars remained in the closet, Holly Johnson and Paul Rutherford brazenly flaunted their preferences. As Johnson accurately observed, "Frankie Goes To Hollywood might not have been part of an identifiable movement as the Sex Pistols had been, but the ideas of stylish pleasure and guilt-free sexuality perfectly matched the mood of the period." They even inspired a high-street fashion boom with their sloganeering T-shirts emblazoned with cryptic Frankie Says . . . commands. Musically, they were always operating at the sharp end of technology with studio boffin Trevor Horn and his team spending months at the Fairlight (a high-end sampling and sequencing rig) formulating their sound.

By the time this album was completed the group were the biggest-selling UK singles act in years. In order to take full advantage of their massive media profile, the record was as elaborately packaged as possible. And, prematurely for such novices, it was a double. The Frankies' talents were spread rather thinly over four sides, filler included lacklustre reworkings of Springsteen's Born To Run, Edwin Starr's War and Gerry Marsden's Ferry Cross The Mersey. Most agreed that this would have made a far better single album, but such reservations were forgotten amid the clamour to purchase the record.

On reflection, it's still the classic singles here that prove most arresting – the pulsating and erotic Relax, the awesome, dramatic Two Tribes and the sumptuous string-laden The Power Of Love. The following year they tried for a fourth Number 1 with the admittedly strong title track but by then Frankie fever had waned. What they left behind was a glowing reminder of a band burning themselves out in incandescent glory.

Record label:
ZTT

Produced
by Trevor Horn.

Released:
November 1984

Chart peaks:
1 (UK) 33 (US)

Track listing:
Well...; The World Is My Oyster; Snatch Of Fury; Welcome To The Pleasure Dome (S); Relax (S); War; Two Tribes (S); Ferry Cross The Mersey; Born To Run; San Jose; Wish; Krisco Kisses; Black Night White Light; The Only Star In Heaven; The Power Of Love (S); Bang

Personnel:
Holly Johnson (v); Mark O'Toole (b, v); Paul Rutherford (v); Brian Nash (g); Peter Gill (d); Anne Dudley (oa, k); Steve Lipson (e)

Running time:
70.11

Current CD:
CID 101

Further listening:
Liverpool (1986)

Further reading:
A Bone In My Flute (Holly Johnson, 1994)

The Minutemen
Double Nickels On The Dime

Ferociously articulate speed funk and political shouting from California.

Californian hardcore, like any other punk-based movement, fed on the intensity of the present, but its high-on-life buzz, distinguished it from the nihilism of UK punk-affiliated music. Some of the major players were even constructivist in their thinking. None more so than The Minutemen, whose five years of performing evolved into a kind of critique of both rock music and the real world, which D Boon's songs and playing broke down into tiny, angry fragments.

Like their SST label-mates Hüsker Dü, with whom they engaged in some friendly competition (the first edition of this set, originally a double LP, has "Take that, Huskers!" etched into the vinyl), The Minutemen were thinkers from an age when agitprop still had a foothold just outside the rock mainstream. Because they were, in most respects, a hard-playing rock three-piece, their early records were speedball deliveries of songs that often barely breached the one-minute barrier, but by the time they made *Buzz Or Howl Under The Influence Of Heat*, a 1983 EP, Boon had expanded his lyric-writing to accommodate the song form as most listeners knew it. You could hear this three-man team making themselves into tougher, less wayward players, and the subject matter and the vision was getting increasingly deadeye in its precision.

Double Nickels On the Dime is their marathon masterpiece. Cut over a pair of two-day sessions, the group nailed 45 songs. Boon's diehard leftism informs most of the lyric commentary, from bits and pieces like Shit From An Old Notebook to There Ain't Shit On TV Tonight, a miniature personal manifesto that ends on "No more lies! We are responsible." Mike Watt contributes some lighter notes, and they also do covers of Van Halen's Ain't Talkin' About Love and Steely Dan's Doctor Wu — these men were music fans as much as politicians. But Boon was a man in a hurry. "My skin keeps the storm inside," he sings on Storm In My House, and in this thin-sounding but tight and momentous record, with nothing throwaway despite the huge number of songs, he sang his epitaph. He was killed in a highway accident while the band was on tour in Arizona in December 1985, and The Minutemen were no more.

Record label:
SST

Produced
by Ethan James.

Recorded
at Radio Tokyo, Venice, California;
November 1983 and April 1984.

Released:
1984

Chart peaks:
None (UK) None (US)

Personnel:
D Boon (g, v); Mike Watt (b, v); George Hurley (d); Ethan James (e)

Track listing:
D's Car Jam/Anxious Mo-Fo; Theatre Is The Life Of You; Viet Nam; Cohesion; It's Expected I'm Gone; #1 Hit Song; Two Beads At The End; Do You Want New Wave Or Do You Want The Truth?; Don't Look Now; Shit From An Old Notebook; Nature Without Man; One Reporter's Opinion; Political Song For Michael Jackson To Sing; Maybe Partying Will Help; Toadies; Retreat; The Big Foist; God Bows To Math; Corona; The Glory Of Man; Take 5, D; My Heart And The Real World; History Lesson-Part II; You Need The Glory; The Roar Of The Masses Could Be Farts; ***** Mr Robot's Holy Orders; West Germany; The Politics Of Time; Themselves; Please Don't Be Gentle With Me; Nothing Indeed; No Exchange; There Ain't Shit On TV Tonight; This Ain't No Picnic; Spillage; Untitled Song For Latin America; Jesus And Tequila; June 16th; Storm In My House; Martin's Story; Doctor Wu; Ain't Talkin' About Love; Little Man With A Gun In His Hand; The World According To Nouns; Love Dance.

Running time:
79.14

Current CD
import SSTCD 028

Further listening:
Post-Mersh Vol 3 (1989)

Dire Straits
Brothers In Arms

The first CD to sell a million, statistics and reputation have served to obscure its artistic worth.

The sound of a voice, the sound of a guitar – what was it about *Brothers In Arms*? A receding hairline, a headband, a sweaty vest – Dire Straits *fashionable*? Never. More than any other chart phenomenon of the '80s, the album passed unexplained, inexplicable. But Knopfler had led the band's music through constant change and development from the sharp pub rock which first attracted London local radio interest in 1977. He began writing much longer pieces (notably, the 14-minute Telegraph Road from their previous studio album, 1982's *Love Over Gold*). He added keyboard players Alan Clark and, for *Brothers In Arms*, Guy Fletcher. If his growly voice and crying guitar remained the band constants, everything else was on the move.

In the winter of 1983–84, after hectic months producing albums for Bob Dylan and Aztec Camera, and getting married, he set time aside to write Dire Straits' next. With no premonitions of grandeur and rarely satisfied with his own work anyway, he would fiercely criticise the songs – Your Latest Trick he could never understand, One World was "horrible". The phrase "brothers in arms" had lodged in his brain after a conversation with his father who noted that the communist USSR supported the (then) fascist military dictatorship of Argentina in the Falklands War. But the song generalised the soldier's plight and Knopfler felt he failed to sustain the potential theme of war (what is it good for? or similar) through the album.

Yet the evidence is that, unless studio performance really did alchemise dross, he underrated his basic work. The characteristic dense melancholy of the title track – soon a favourite at funerals – and Your Latest Trick, the old-time rocking strut of Money For Nothing and Walk Of Life, the neat tonal fit of the less distinctive songs proved irresistible. The album topped charts in 24 countries, driven by Money For Nothing, Dire Straits' first American Number 1 single. It was a sour, sneery monologue transcribed, Knopfler says, almost verbatim from a New York electrical shop owner denouncing the "yo-yos" and "faggots" who played their guitars on the MTV. Even that he credited to the influence of Randy Newman: "Maybe I wouldn't have written that kind of character song but for him – you have to put yourself in other people's shoes."

Record label:
Vertigo

Produced
by Mark Knopfler and Neil Dorfsman.

Recorded
at Air Studios, Montserrat; The Power Station, New York; Air Studios, London; November 1984–April 1985

Released:
May 17, 1985

Chart peaks:
1 (UK) 1 (US)

Personnel:
Mark Knopfler (v, g); John Illsley (b, bv); Alan Clark (k); Guy Fletcher (k, bv); Omar Hakim, Terry Williams (d); Neil Dorfsman (e); Sting (bv)

Track listening:
So Far Away (S); Money For Nothing (S); Walk Of Life (S); Your Latest Trick; Why Worry; Ride Across The River; The Man's Too Strong; One World; Brothers In Arms (S)

Running time:
54.35

Current CD:
9252642

Further listening:
Their first, Dire Straits (1978), and their last On Every Street (1991) – striking entrance, graceful exit.

Further reading:
Mark Knopfler: An Unauthorized Biography (Myles Palmer, 1991); www.mark-knopfler-news.co.uk (includes link to brothersinarms.com fan site)

Prefab Sprout

Steve McQueen

Majestic second album from County Durham's finest.

Prefab Sprout's *Swoon* (1983) — with its jump-cut melodies, quasi-jazz/fusion changes and oblique lyrical twists — remains a breathtakingly impressive debut. Its author, Paddy McAloon, isn't so sure: "The things that people mistook for cleverness were terrible ignorance. We were very insular and just evolved a weirdly overdeveloped, strange style, our own little world." Thomas Dolby, a pop artist at the technological cutting edge, was guesting as singles reviewer on BBC Radio One and in despair at the quality of the music until he heard Don't Sing from *Swoon* and thought, "this soulful Geordie voice over frantic acoustic guitars and harmonica was the best thing I'd heard for ages." The band, listening in, got in touch with Dolby and asked him to produce their next album.

Paddy: "I gave him a huge collection of songs and almost all the ones he picked were from 1979, long before Swoon." The resulting album was called *Steve McQueen* because "he was really good in an un-arty sort of way" (Paddy) — rather unlike the record itself — but released as *Two Wheels Good* (with extra tracks) in the USA after objections by the actor's estate. Better focused and more approachable than their debut, it was among the freshest, brightest records of the '80s, full of twisting, memorable songs, luminous textures and solid grooves. Songs like Appetite and Goodbye Lucille #1 established McAloon's reputation as one of pop's great mavericks: a lyricist of range, depth and ambition; a chordsmith and melodist of daring originality; a craftsman of fiercely individual discernment. As it happened, Paddy agreed: "I know I'm probably the best writer on the planet," he said in 1985, "who are my rivals?"

Another time, however, he was keen to acknowledge his producer's contribution to *Steve McQueen*; "I was so much in awe of what Dolby had done to shape it, I kind of thought, This is his record, he's made this really good." A modest hit was eventually achieved with the umpteenth re-release of When Love Breaks Down and the Sprouts went on to greater commercial success with *From Langley Park To Memphis* (1988) and perhaps even grander artistry with *Jordan The Comeback* (1990), but as Thomas Dolby observes, "there's something magical about the *Steve McQueen* album, an openness and expectation that none of us have touched since." Refined and sophisticated as the album appears to the listener, it's surprising that Dolby adds, "I'm sure it's partly because we didn't really know what we were doing."

Record label:
CBS

Produced
by Thomas Dolby.

Recorded
1985

Released:
June 15, 1985

Chart peaks:
21 (UK) None (US)

Personnel:
Paddy McAloon (g, v); Wendy Smith (bv); Martin McAloon (b); Neil Conti (d); Thomas Dolby (k)

Track listing:
Faron Young; Bonny; Appetite; When Love Breaks Down; Goodbye Lucille #1; Hallelujah; Moving The River; Horsin' Around; Desire As; Blueberry Pies; When The Angels

Running time:
45.22

Current CD:
Sony 466336 2

Further listening:
Swoon (1983); From Langley Park To Memphis (1988); Jordan The Comeback (1990)

Further reading:
http://users.deltanet.com/~plockton/sprout.html

Kate Bush
Hounds Of Love

Crowning glorious album from the UK's most influential female artist ever.

"It was my 'She's gone mad' album," said Kate Bush in the late '80s, looking back at *The Dreaming* (1982). That seemed to be the verdict from record company and public alike as the album completed her commercial decline over four albums from a million sales for *The Kick Inside* (1978) to 60,000. But her reaction to relative failure was to make complete her escape from her girlhood role as "the company's daughter" into womanly independence. From July 1983, she invested a slab of her royalties in upgrading the studio she had set up in a barn at her parents' farmhouse on the outskirts of South-East London. A 48-track desk and a Fairlight synthesizer-sampler meant she could record much of the album there.

"In music you have to break your back before you even start to speak the emotion," she said. "The way I work is very experimental and when you're in a studio that's costing a phenomenal amount every hour it puts too much pressure on you. It zaps creativity."

Freed from increasing debt to the label, she pressed ahead with the transition from writing at the piano to building from a rhythm track – something she had learned via guesting on a Peter Gabriel album. At last, she was able to blend writing, recording and production into one untrammelled creative process. From these ideal circumstances emerged an album embodying her belief that "art is a tremendous sensual-sexual expression" and "the communication of music is very much like making love".

Reflecting the last days of vinyl dominance, *Hounds Of Love* divides down the middle. The A-side's five songs are unconnected but brilliant tracks, springing vibrantly from Bush's focus on rhythm – be it the percussive gallop of Running Up That Hill (A Deal With God) or the frantic pulsing of the Medici Sextet's strings on Cloudbusting. The second side is a suite – Bush didn't mind using the unfashionable term "concept". Her imagination careens around various ideas that haunted her: the fear of being trapped beneath ice (derived from Houdini's autobiography); the image of Ophelia drowning (from Hamlet, a romantic painting by Edward Millais and an obscure canvas she had bought a few years earlier in which the corpse is afloat in sewage). Bush switchbacks through time, referring to witches

Record label:
EMI

Produced
by Kate Bush and Jon Kelly.

Recorded
at Bush family's farmhouse studios, Kent; mixed at Windmill Lane and Abbey Road. January 1984–June 1985.

Released:
September 1985

Chart peaks:
1 (UK) 30 (US)

Personnel:
Kate Bush (k, v); Kevin McAlea (syn); Alan Murphy, Brian Bath (g); Del Palmer, Eberhard Weber, Danny Thompson (b); Stuart Elliott, Charlie Morgan (d); Johnathan Williams (c); Liam O'Flynn (uillean pipes); John Sheahan (whistles, vn); Paddy Bush (balalaika, dijeridoo); Donal Lunny (bouzouki); Morris Pert (pc); The Medici Sextet (strings); Richard Hickox Singers (v).

Track listing:
Running Up That Hill (S); Hounds Of Love (S); The Big Sky (S); Mother Stands For Comfort; Cloudbusting (S); And Dream Of Sheep; Under Ice; Waking The Witch; Watching You Without Me; Jig Of Life; Hello Earth; The Morning Fog

Running time:
47.34

Current CD:
E21S25239

Further listening:

The Sensual World (1989). Although not currently available, the EMI100 reissue of Hounds Of Love includes additional tracks: The Big Sky (Meteorogical mix); Running Up That Hill (12-inch mix); Be Kind To My Mistakes; Under The Ivy; Burning Bridge; My Lagan Love. Box set This Woman's Work (1990) contains all her albums up to, but not including, The Red Shoes (1993), her only inconsistent work, and has two CDs of excellent non-album material.

Further reading:

www.paradiseplace.org.uk provides links to the best Kate Bush sites; http://gaffa.org

and astronauts, drawing in traditional fiddles and all manner of Fairlight noises and effects, while the emotional tone sweeps from enervated torpor (And Dream Of Sheep), through terror (Waking The Witch) to redemptive warmth (The Morning Fog).

Throughout, perhaps more potent than any other aspect of an electrifying album, her voice is remarkable, a church organ of range and colour that still never loses the urgent intimacy of the impassioned artist.

Dexy's Midnight Runners
Don't Stand Me Down

Chart-topping young soul rebels make their most ambitious album; sales plummet and acclaim eludes them.

D exy's Midnight Runners had already released two best-selling albums and a couple of Number 1 singles (Geno and Come On Eileen) before embarking on their most ambitious and misunderstood project. Mainman Kevin Rowland spent an age fashioning this work but, as months passed into years, many of the group's younger fans had moved on. When the album finally appeared, the critics savaged it and Rowland effectively sabotaged its chances by initially refusing to extract a single from it. It quickly fell off the charts. All of which was a terrible injustice as the record was the most challenging and passionate of Rowland's tempestuous career.

"I stand by the work," Rowland insists. "I think it's really good. But I was a very misplaced person around *Don't Stand Me Down*. I found the success I'd achieved with Dexy's to be quite meaningless. I felt like a workhorse, working for the record company, going around the world promoting product. It just felt like it had nothing to do with me anymore. It was all very uncreative so I started searching for something with a bit more meaning. I'd been reading about Ireland around 1983 so I thought that's what I'll do — Irish Republicanism, and socialism too. I'd go on marches and walks. *Don't Stand Me Down* was originally going to be a much more political album but I think fear made me tailor it more personally in the end."

The album's centrepiece is the extraordinary This Is What She's Like, which combines a treatise on the essence of a woman with sarcastic diatribes on the ignorance of the English upper-middle classes. Musically, it merges opaque dialogue with Beach Boys' harmonies and a coda of Stax-style horns. Other tracks are equally inventive, although One Of These Things proved a bit too close to Warren Zevon's Werewolves Of London for comfort, prompting a successful copyright claim from Zevon.

Time has seen the album re-evaluated as a classic, which has prompted debate about why it failed on release. Many point to the cover which featured the remaining Dexys dressed immaculately in expensive Ivy League suits like upmarket chartered accountants. Rowland disagrees: "The real reason people didn't buy it is because they never heard it. The only song played on the radio was the butchered version of This Is What She's Like seven or eight weeks after the album came out. It was too late — and that was my mistake."

Record label:
Mercury

Produced
by Kevin Rowland, Helen O'Hara, Alan Winstanley and Billy Adams.

Recorded:
Spring 1984–July 1985, Montreux; Matrix Studios, London; Outside Studios, Reading; Selectsound, Hertfordshire; Electric Ladyland, New York.

Released:
September 1985

Chart peaks:
22 (UK) None (US)

Personnel:
Kevin Rowland (v); Billy Adams (g, rg, v); Helen O'Hara (vn, v); Nicky Gatfield (s, v); Vincent Crane (p); Tim Dancy (d); Julian Littman (mandolin); Jimmy Patterson (tb); Tommy Evans (steel g); Robert Noble (o, syn); John Edwards (b)

Track listing:
The Occasional Flicker; This Is What She's Like (S); My National Pride [previously titled Knowledge Of Beauty]; One Of Those Things; Reminisce Part Two; Listen To This; The Waltz.

Running time:
54.37

Current CD:
CRECD 154

Further listening:
For contrast, their classic debut Searching For The Young Soul Rebels (1980).

Further reading:
Essay in Love Is The Drug (John Aizlewood, 1994)

The Fall
This Nation's Saving Grace

Raucous, long-serving Mancunian shower add a hint of California sun, get a decent producer and hit a career peak.

At the turn of this century, The Fall had clocked up a 23-year career. Mark E Smith can claim to be not only the most credible survivor of the original punk era, but also the keeper of one of the most enduring visions in the history of rock. The Fall has always been Smith's vision; founder and sole original member, legendarily as caustic and difficult as he is dedicated, Smith's allegiance to punk was largely thanks to the galvanising power of its DIY ethic. The Fall's uniquely primitive sound (which has been expanded – but rarely departed signifi-cantly – from its original blueprint) owes more to the garage punk of '60s America, the raw attack of vintage rockabilly, and the hypnotic repetition of Can and the Velvet Underground. Smith's vocal style – the mad bark of a bellicose street hawker – is a one-off; the greatest non-singer who isn't Lou Reed.

In their eighth awesome year, many of The Fall's more conservative fans were resenting the creeping commercial influ-ence of Mark's new American wife, guitarist and co-writer Brix. Although the new Fall were hardly about to upset Duran Duran, Brix was indeed staunchly in love with the pop history of her native California, which was reflected in the bright strum of her Rickenbacker and the accessibility of her melodies. "Even with the old songs," she said in a 1984 interview, "I think I add some shadow and light to them. I give it a lot of drive, as well as adding some 'glamour' to it all."

Still widely thought to be their finest album, *This Nation's Saving Grace* catches The Fall at a moment of thrilling congruity, playing to their strengths with great clarity. Thanks to John Leckie, their first truly skilled producer, Bombast rages harder than any previous Fall song to that point, while LA uses the group's trademarks in service of what can fairly be described as a pop song. The meeting of the marginal and the mainstream proved winning here, taking The Fall into the UK Top 30, and making them look as though they belonged there.

Record label:
Beggars Banquet

Produced
by John Leckie.

Recorded
at Music Works, London and Chapel Lane, Hereford; June–July 1985.

Released:
September 1985

Chart peaks:
54 (UK) None (US)

Personnel:
Mark E Smith (v, g); Brix Smith (lead g, v); Stephen Hanley (b); Karl Burns (d); Simon Rogers (k, g, b); Craig Scanlon (rhythm g)

Track listing:
Mansion; Bombast; Barmy; What You Need; Spoilt Victorian Child; LA; Gut Of The Quantifier; My New House; Paintwork; I Am Damo Suzuki; To Nkroachment: Yarbles

Running time:
65.56

Current CD:
BBL 67 CD adds: Vixen; Couldn't Get Ahead; Petty (Thief) Lout; Rollin' Dany; Cruisers Creek

Further listening:
458489 A Sides (1990), The Wonderful And Frightening World Of The Fall (1984); Palace Of Swords Reversed (1987)

Further reading:
www.visi.com/fall (The Official Fall Website)

The Waterboys
This Is The Sea

They called it "The Big Music". They were right.

The first two Waterboys albums – particularly 1984's *A Pagan Place* – had introduced what became known as "The Big Music", a sound that requires the overused adjective "widescreen". "The song The Big Music [from *A Pagan Place*] was about seeing God's hand in the world," says Scott today. "But it became this catch-all term; I've seen it used to refer to lots of groups – U2, Simple Minds – and I always took it to mean the cinematic sound of *A Pagan Place* and *This Is The Sea*." Writing for *This Is The Sea*, he was inspired – as ever – by Patti Smith's *Horses*, but also Van Morrison's *Astral Weeks* and Television's *Marquee Moon*; and also, if only by default, U2 – with whom he'd toured. "I wasn't influenced by U2's music in the slightest – good band that they are – but I was influenced by the size of their audience. I did exactly the music that was in my heart but, at the same time, I'd been playing to a big audience [and] it had given me an aim."

Much of the pre-production was done at Seaview, Karl Wallinger's home studio. "I'd be trying out ideas; Karl would record it all and chip in with a bass part or a synthesizer part and stack up reverbs until the sound in his speakers seemed like a place to inhabit." Recording was delayed as Scott tried different personnel combinations: "When I look at it now it seems quite fast, but it didn't at the time. There was a period in Hastings with one co-producer that didn't work out, then we got someone else in, then I did some stuff on my own, then one of the other guys came back: there was a lot of coming and going."

Opening with the heady, goosebump-inducing trumpet intro to Don't Bang The Drum – cooked up by Scott and trumpeter Roddy Lorimer under the influence of Miles' *Sketches of Spain* – *This Is The Sea* proved all the "coming and going" worthwhile. It's an epic, furiously alive record, infused with a sweeping spirituality (The Pan Within, Spirit) and an energising anger – Old England (with crowd noise from a Prince bootleg) is a scathing critique of Thatcher's Britain, Be My Enemy a rapid-fire "ode to paranoia" warning foes to expect vengeance.

The album's most famous track began its life in New York. Scott's then-girlfriend had asked him if it was easy to write songs. Answering "yes", he took an envelope and immediately wrote the first verse of The Whole Of The Moon. The rest

Record label:
Ensign

Produced
by Mike Scott, Mick Glossop, John Brand and Karl Wallinger.

Recorded
at Amazon, Park Gates, Townhouse and other studios; March–July 1985 .

Released:
September 1985

Chart peaks:
37 (UK) None (US)

Personnel:
Mike Scott (v, g, p, k); Karl Wallinger (k, b, bv); Anthony Thistlewaite (s); Roddy Lorimer (tp); Chris Whitten, Kevin Wilkinson, Pete Thomas (d)

Track listing:
Don't Bang The Drum; The Whole Of The Moon (S); Spirit; The Pan Within; Medicine Bow; Old England; Be My Enemy; Trumpets; This Is The Sea

Running time:
42.37

Current CD:
CDP3215432

Further listening:
A Pagan Place (1984); The Secret Life Of The Waterboys (1994) – excellent compilation of outtakes and rarities; The Whole of The Moon – The Music Of Mike Scott And The Waterboys (1998) – useful compilation also rounds up some of Scott's stripped-down solo work; A Rock In The Weary Land (2000) – his best record since This Is The Sea.

Further reading:
www.waterboys.co.uk

of the lyric took months, but the finished song remains one of Scott's finest to date and his biggest hit.

The year after *This Is The Sea*, Scott moved to Ireland, where fiddler Steve Wickham and accordion virtuoso Sharon Shannon helped colour the folky "raggle-taggle" palette of *Fisherman's Blues* and *Room To Roam*. It was The Whole Of The Moon, though, which raised Scott's profile again in 1991 when ravers adopted it as a come-down anthem, prompting a re-release which won him an Ivor Novello award for songwriting in 1992.

"I think it has a lot of power," says Scott of *This Is The Sea* today. "From when I began in bands at 15 or 16, there's a progression that reaches its climax with the finishing of [that record]. The only thing I could do afterwards was do something different; all my youthful rock dreams were achieved on *This Is The Sea.*"

Jesus And Mary Chain
Psychocandy

Studied rebellion from leather 'n' Ray-Ban's-clad feedback Führers.

L auded as "the new Sex Pistols" by the music press, the Jesus And Mary Chain's blink-and-you-miss-'em live shows quickly became antagonistic affairs. One infamous North London Polytechnic gig in 1985 ended in a riot. "We really believed we could seriously change the way people made music," frontman Jim Reid explained laconically.

It was a far cry from their first appearance supporting mild-mannered jangle-merchants The Loft at Alan McGee's London club The Living Room. With heads down and backs to an audience of 15 people, there was no trace of the self-conscious abrasiveness that would soon become their trademark. By the time of Creation Records' debut single, Upside Down, the JAMC were courting controversy and the A&R men were in a frenzy.

Psychocandy was like no other debut LP. Describing themselves as "Eighties beatniks with an image that is shoddy but stylish", the Mary Chain made an exhilarating, intoxicating Wall Of Sound. Beneath that chaotic Velvet Underground-style white noise hid dark but beautifully crafted melodies worthy of Phil Spector. Recorded at Southern Studios and produced by the group – they didn't trust outsiders – all egos were left at home. It didn't matter who played what: the Reid brothers were after the perfect sound. Much swapping of instruments took place to get the parts down. As Jim explained: "Guitars look good. That's all we really care about."

Drugs were in plentiful supply. "We only take acid and speed!" the band declared, which explained in part the deranged, manic edge to their sound. The 14 tracks (all written by Jim and William on acoustic guitar – "The noise came later," admitted William) include album opener Just Like Honey, three minutes of bleak romanticism that strikes up with the opening drumbeats from The Ronettes' Be My Baby, and the angry, acidic pop of Never Understand. The Living End and In A Hole are driller-killer drones and the yearning, reflective Something's Wrong clocks in as the longest track at four minutes.

Before the album's release, Bobby Gillespie had already returned to Primal Scream. "He only played drums to help us out of our mess when Murray Dalglish left," said Jim. Although *Psychocandy* was hardly designed to set the mainstream alight, by the following August the JAMC would reach Number 13 in the singles chart with their Some Candy Talking EP.

Record label:
Blanco Y Negro

Produced
by The Jesus And Mary Chain.

Recorded
at Southern Studios, London; summer 1985.

Released:
November 1985

Chart peaks:
31 (UK) None (US)

Personnel:
Jim Reid (v, g); William Reid (g, v); Douglas Hart (b); Bobby Gillespie (d)

Track listing:
Just Like Honey (S); The Living End; Taste The Floor; The Hardest Walk; Cut Dead; In A Hole; Taste Of Cindy; Never Understand (S); Inside Me; Sowing Seeds; My Little Underground; You Trip Me Up (S); Something's Wrong; It's So Hard

Running time:
38.50

Current CD:
2292420002 adds: Some Candy Talking (S)

Further listening:
Follow-up Darklands (1987) – more mood-swing existentialism minus the feedback; Barbed Wire Kisses (1988) – assorted A- and B-sides and outtakes; Stoned And Dethroned (1993), a foray into reflective country rock with cameos from Shane McGowan and Mazzy Star's Hope Sandoval.

Further reading:
www.amniisia.com/aprilskies/net/

Shaun Davey And Rita Connolly

Granuaile

The most accessible of his singular folk-rock/orchestral epics.

Born in Belfast, Shaun Davey drifted into music while studying fine art at the Courtauld Institute in the early '70s through a brief folk-rock collaboration with James Morris, who subsequently founded Windmill Lane Studios. Returning to Ireland, Davey made a living with advertising jingles while pursuing the unprecedented concept of fusing uillean pipes with orchestra.

The fruits of that vision, *The Brendan Voyage*, thrust him into prominence in the early '80s but *The Pilgrim*, an almost ruinously colossal follow-up, was less well received. *Granuaile* was a direct reaction against composing on such a scale, yet still honed further what was by then Davey's trademark fusion of traditional Irish instrumentation (principally O'Flynn's pipes) within a European classical framework (here, a particular echo of Vivaldi) and coloured with a rock sensibility.

Known in legend as Granuaile, Grace O'Malley forged a long life as a "pirate queen" – storming castles, rustling cattle and commanding the warships that dominated the west of Ireland during the socially and politically turbulent Elizabethan era. Having enjoyed Anne Chambers' biography, Davey recreated O'Malley's story as a gripping, dynamic and richly drawn song-cycle written specifically as a vehicle for Rita Connolly, who had already cameod sensationally in *The Pilgrim*. The result was both moving and dramatic, integrating orchestral instruments fully into a small group context and conjuring O'Malley's spirit of defiance and the atmosphere of time and place.

Granuaile was aired twice before its recording and several times subsequently, including an RTE televised performance at the Greenwich Festival in 1987 for which Davey had added modest revisions – notably replacing the light relief of The Dismissal with Hen's March. This track plus two further Greenwich takes, deemed superior, featured on the subsequent CD version (a policy favoured also on the eventual CD revision of *The Pilgrim*). Davey subsequently returned to large-scale orchestral works before settling into a routine of highly regarded film, television and theatrical scoring. He also wrote songs for, and produced, two Connolly solo albums; yet both

Record label:
Tara

Recorded:

Produced
by Shaun Davey.

Released:
December 1985

Chart peaks:
None (UK) None (US)

Personnel:
Rita Connolly (v); Liam O'Flynn (uillean pipes); Des Moore (g); Donal Lunny (bouzouki, bodhran); Helen Davies (harp); Carl Gerraghty (sax); Marian Doherty (harpsichord); Noel Eccles (dr, pc); Gareth Hudson (c); 22-piece chamber orchestra; Brian Masterson (e)

Track listing:
Dubhdarra; Ripples In The Rockpool; The Defence Of Hen's Castle; Free And Easy; The Rescue Of Hugh De Lacy; The Dismissal; Death Of Richard-An-Iarainn (intro); Death Of Richard-An-Iarainn; Sir Richard Bingham; The Spanish Armada; The New Age

Running time:
45.10

Current CD:
Tara CD 3017

Further listening:
The Pilgrim (1983), and the Connolly solo albums Rita Connolly (1992) and Valparaiso (1995).

Further reading:
Granuaile (Anne Chambers, 1984)

the singer, who rarely performs live, and *Granuaile* – last staged in Mayo in 1992 – remain monstrously under-known.

Nevertheless, like *The Pilgrim*, revised and resurrected for the first time in 10 years for a Dublin performance in March 2000, *Granuaile* may yet enjoy a renaissance: "Rita's been muttering about it recently," says Davey. "I'm proud of it and I don't believe it's been performed enough. So, yes, if the opportunity arose I would revise it again!"

Robert Cray
Strong Persuader

A million-seller and Grammy-winner, the biggest blues record of the '80s.

Although Stevie Ray Vaughan was arguably a more in-demand performer, it was Robert Cray who rekindled the blues as a popular music in the '80s. He'd gone the usual route of blues artists since forming his first band in 1974 (with bassist Richard Cousins, a long-term confederate), playing the small-time live circuit and cutting records for independent labels with only a modest reach. But his 1985 triple-header with Albert Collins and Johnny Copeland, *Showdown!*, was a Grammy-winner and an album that was more widely reviewed in the rock press than most blues albums could normally hope for. On the strength of this, Cray signed to Mercury. Assisted by a shrewd press and media campaign, he was suddenly fêted as a brilliant young practitioner of the blues. *Strong Persuader* won him a second Grammy and went on to sell over a million.

Cray was fortunate in his producers, Bromberg and Walker, who also had a hand in some of the most effective songs. They made the most of Cray's lean, clear voice, untypical of the coarse-grained blues shouters which many people associated with the form; his taut and wiry guitar solos; his funky, modest but skilful band. Cray's *métier* was meanness, a cruel persona which he filtered into these songs like a brutal alter ego. But he was clever about distancing himself from his artistic self: he refers to the character as "Young Bob", the dark side of the real Robert. That makes the cold-eyed stud of Right Next Door (Because Of Me) or the homicidal cuckold of Smoking Gun into plausible fantasy figures that Cray steps inside for just long enough; I Guess I Showed Her is the other side of the coin. Though he sings the occasional 12-bar, Cray essentially put his faith in R&B as a more expansive music, and his later records found him moving towards a sort of rocking soul music, with less of the blues in it. None, though, have been as successful as this one, either critically or commercially, although the best of the follow-ups, *Don't Be Afraid Of The Dark*, does include some of his toughest material. For a period, he was successful enough to be courted by some of the biggest names in music: he even turned down an offer from Michael Jackson to appear on *Bad*.

Record label:
Mercury

Produced
by Bruce Bromberg and Dennis Walker.

Recorded
at Stage and Sound and Haywood's, Los Angeles; 1986.

Released:
January 1986

Chart peaks:
34 (UK) 13 (US)

Personnel:
Robert Cray (g, v); Peter Boe (k); Richard Cousins (b); David Olson (d); Lee Spath (pc); The Memphis Horns; Bill Dashiell (e)

Track listing:
Smoking Gun; I Guess I Showed Her; Right Next Door (Because Of Me); Nothin' But A Woman; Still Around; More Than I Can Stand; Foul Play; I Wonder; Fantasized; New Blood

Running time:
39.26

Current CD:
Mercury 830568-2

Further listening:
Don't Be Afraid Of The Dark (1988)

Further reading:
www.rosebuds.com/cray/

Anita Baker

Rapture

From waitress to '80s soul phenomenon and home again in eight years.

In 1980, Arista had bought the Ariola label and with it the contract of modestly successful Detroit soul band Chapter 8, which they allowed to lapse. Legend has it that the executives at Arista thought the lead singer — one Anita Baker — wasn't good enough. Returning to Detroit, Baker worked as a short-order cook, a waitress and eventually as a legal secretary.

In 1982 she got an offer from Otis Smith (who had signed Chapter 8 to Ariola) to record on his new Beverly Glenn label. The album that appeared was *The Songstress* (1983) which got her some attention, though the label's slowness in agreeing to a follow-up album resulted in Baker signing with Elektra, while still earning her living in a law firm.

Partly funding the recording herself (hence the "executive producer" credit she gets on the sleeve), she hired ex-Chapter 8 member Michael J Powell as producer and surrounded by ace sessioneers recorded *Rapture* which, from the sheen of Baker's skin on the album cover to the sensuous and precise music within, was a flawless product. When provocative new trends in black music were exploding from the street by the month, Baker kept her head and made a traditional (i.e., with its roots in the '70s) soul record with brooding, slow-burn minor tunes of romantic celebration and earthy longing. Baker's voice was an extraordinarily rich, restrained instrument that was further distinguished from many soul divas by a Sarah Vaughan-like jazz sensibility in her phrasing, the best example of which is the delightful series of improvised choruses on the fade of Been So Long.

Bolstered by the hit singles Sweet Love and Caught Up In The Rapture, the album won two Grammys and went on to sell over six million worldwide, establishing Baker as a genuine soul star of the late '80s and one of the all-time pop vocal greats. The follow-on albums did well enough but betrayed the common weakness of much glossy soul, succumbing to an under-inspired if efficient formula.

While fans of her artistry await a proper jazz album (she appeared on two tracks of pianist Cyrus Chestnut's eponymous CD in 1998), her leisurely approach to recording in the '90s bears out her famously quoted maxim; "You leave home to seek your fortune and, when you get it, you go home and share it with your family."

Record label:
Elektra

Produced
by Michael J Powell, except No One In The World; produced by Marti Sharron and Gary Skardina.

Recorded
in LA, autumn 1985.

Released:
March 1986

Chart peaks:
13 (UK) 11 (US)

Personnel:
Anita Baker (v, executive producer); Vesta Williams, Darryl Phinnessee, Natalie Jackson, Lynn Davis, Phillip Ingram, Jim Gilstrap, Alex Brown, Bunny Hull, Barry Diament (bv); Jimmy Haslip, Fred Washington, David B Washington (b); Robert Feist, Sir Gant, Randy Kerber (k); Lorenzo Brown, Paulinho Da Costa, Lawrence Fratangelo (pc); Paul Chiten, Greg Phillinganes (syn); Donald Griffin, Greg Moore, Dean Parks, Michael J Powell (g); Ricky Lawson, Arthur Marbury (d); Don Myrick (s); Warren Woods (finger snaps)

Track listing:
Sweet Love (s); You Bring Me Joy; Caught Up In The Rapture (s); Been So Long; Mystery; No One In The World; Same Old Love; Watch Your Step

Running time:
37.09

Current CD:
7559604442

Further listening:
The Songstress (1983); Giving You The Best That I Got (1988); Compositions (1990)

Further reading:
www.aub.dk/~tj/anitamain1.htm

The Bulgarian National Radio And Television Chorus

Le Mystère Des Voix Bulgares

World music that inspired Californian hippies then, over a decade later, topped the UK indie charts.

The Bulgarian State Radio and Television Female Vocal Choir had been assembled in 1951 by Philip Koutev, a composer whose task it was to use traditional music to advocate communism. The members of the choir brought to it their own region's folk songs, which were transformed into vehicles for six-part lead vocals and complex harmonies for 24 voices. Among the outsiders to be gripped by the new sound was Marcel Cellier, a Swiss engineer and part-time ethnomusicologist who spent 15 years in Bulgaria, much of it in the archives of the Bucharest Institute For Folklore. In 1966, Elektra's Nonesuch label released the album *Music Of Bulgaria*, and Koutev's choir struck a chord with the West Coast hippies. "They're like Angels, exceptionally pure," said Jerry Garcia, before sitting down to write Uncle John's Band, the opening track on *Workingman's Dead*, based on Bulgarian village music.

In the '80s, Cellier licensed his archives to Philips in France, entitling the resulting albums *Le Mystère Des Voix Bulgares*, the mystery, he claimed, lay somewhere between the "beauty of perfection and the perfection of beauty". A tape of the first volume found its way into the hands of Bauhaus's Peter Murphy in 1985, who played it to Ivo Watts-Russell. Ever-willing to use his label to indulge his passions (witness This Mortal Coil), the boss of 4AD then started searching for the source and discovered Cellier's LPs. 4AD released *Le Mystère Des Voix Bulgares* the following spring, while on a roll with The Cocteau Twins and Colourbox. Word-of-mouth recommendations meant the album quickly achieved cult status and Elektra took up the baton in the States. In an odd side-effect of their global success, the choir started using the album title as its recording and touring name. Though not the first Bulgarian compilation, Le Mystère took eastern European music to a level of acclaim hitherto unimaginable.

Record label:
4AD

Produced
by Marcel Cellier.

Recorded
throughout various Bulgarian villages.

Released:
April 1986

Chart peaks:
None (UK) None (US)

Personnel:
Yanka Roupkina (solo v); Kalinka Vatcheva (solo v); Stefka Sabotinova (solo v)

Track listing:
Pilentze Pee; Svatba; Kalimankou Denkou; Strati Na Angelaki Doumasche; Polegnala E Pschenitza; Messetschinko Lio Greïlivko; Breï Yvane; Erghen Diado; Sableyalo Mi Agontze; Pritouritze Planinata; Mir Stanke Le; Schopska Pesen; Polegnala Todora

Running time:
36.53

Current CD:
CAD603CD

Further listening:
Le Mystère Des Voix Bulgares, vols 2–4; Village Music Of Bulgaria (various artists)

Peter Gabriel

So

Eleven years after Genesis, his Grammy-winning world/pop/dance hit harvest.

It had been four years since Gabriel's fourth album. His head brimming with ideas, he had been working on film treatments (including an aborted project with cult director Alejandro Jodoroswky, a movie based on *The Lamb Lies Down On Broadway*) which led to writing soundtrack music (*Birdy – Music From The Film* appeared on an album the year before *So*). He was also organising WOMAD, his annual festival of world music and art, which in turn led to his decision to take time off to upgrade his studio in the Wiltshire countryside and "explore this hybrid of non-European music and electronics". As the British press hailed him variously as a "pioneer" or a "cultural imperialist", Gabriel recorded a German-language version of his fourth album. Its producer, he later discovered, was having an affair with Gabriel's wife. Gabriel, meanwhile, had domestic complications of his own: an affair with actress Rosanna Arquette. Going along with a friend's advice, the Gabriels entered therapy. It was in this emotionally turbulent state – living apart from his family, seeing Arquette whenever possible – that Gabriel made his US breakthrough *So*.

One could speculate as to the cause – the combination of lust and loss, the tension between freedom and free-falling, a feeling of having to prove himself – but the quality and variety of songs on Gabriel's first album with a title was outstanding. Sledgehammer, its best-known track, was a sexy, funky tribute to the R&B bands Gabriel had loved as a teenager. Wayne Jackson of The Memphis Horns was brought in to lead the horn section; and Gabriel had even considered hiring funkmeister Nile Rodgers to produce before opting to stick with Daniel Lanois, with whom he had worked on *Birdy*.

The world music influences were also evident: Youssou N'Dour was a guest performer (Jim Kerr was another); and Mercy Street's *forro* rhythm-track was recorded in Rio with Brazilian percussionist Djalma Correla, before, back in his home studio, Gabriel added Fairlight synthesizers and an English folk melody. Owning his own studio and its inherent lack of clock-watching might have been responsible for the time it took to make the album (various tracks, including In Your Eyes and Mercy Street, were completely rewritten between the album's start and end), but it can also claim

Record label:
Virgin

Produced
by Daniel Lanois and Peter Gabriel.

Recorded
at Real World, England and Polygram Studios, Rio De Janeiro; February–December 1985.

Released:
May 1986

Chart peaks:
1 (UK) 2 (US)

Personnel:
Peter Gabriel (v, k, p); David Rhodes (g); Daniel Lanois (g); Tony Levin (b); Manu Katche (d); Kate Bush (v); Youssou N'dour (v); Laurie Anderson (v); Nile Rodgers (g); Kevin Killen (e)

Track listing:
Red Rain (S); Sledgehammer (S); Don't Give Up (S); That Voice Again; In Your Eyes (S); Mercy Street; Big Time (S); We Do What We're Told (Milgram's 37); This Is The Picture (Excellent Birds)

Running time:
46.25

Current CD:
PGCD 5

Further listening:
Peter Gabriel IV (1982)

Further reading:
Peter Gabriel, An Authorised Biography (Spencer Bright 2000); www.petergabriel.com

credit for some fascinating experiments in electro-ethnic cross-pollination.

A highlight was the evocative, gospel-tinged duet with friend Kate Bush, Don't Give Up, the album's second hit single. The first, and even bigger, hit was Sledgehammer (UK Top 5; American Number 1). Its ubiquitous promo clip – dancing oven-ready chickens; animated fruit whirling about Gabriel's stop-motion face – was showered with awards.

One track that in the end did not make it onto *So* was Sagrada, inspired by Gaudí's church in Barcelona. Gabriel, who believed that great buildings were haunted by their creator's spirit, had found a new passion: he wanted to create his own great building. Or *buildings* – his next project, he hoped, would be a kind of Gabriel-land, an educational alternative theme park. This, as well as WOMAD, soundtracks, charity concerts, art projects, his Real World record label and multi-media company, would occupy him for the next six years before he followed up *So* with *Us* – the album that documented his eventual separation from both Arquette and his wife.

The Smiths
The Queen Is Dead

The Smiths' most rounded album saw them established as the most celebrated independent band of the decade.

Financial wrangling, management changes and a long-winded dispute with their record company, Rough Trade, were the backdrop to the recording of the Smiths' third studio album. Bassist Andy Rourke had recently been fired from the group and replaced by Craig Gannon, but was back on board by the time they entered the studio.

"My main memory is of darkness," recalls Johnny Marr. "Both literally and metaphorically. It was winter and we were in self-imposed isolation."

Marr was feeling the pressure of public scrutiny and hitting the bottle.

"I felt like I was diving into a mire and [had to hold] onto the belief that I was coming out the other end. It certainly was my darkest hour, which made it bad for everybody else. We'd got over the curve which most bands don't, and I had this feeling that, if we're going to take our place among the greats then we had to get ourselves in the frame of mind that created great stuff. I knew exactly what was expected of us, which was to do something that was genuine art."

The intense, satiric title track mirrored Morrissey's mindset with a brutal and occasionally comic depiction of contemporary England plagued by moral and spiritual bankruptcy.

"I think that's my favourite Smiths lyric," says Marr, "brilliant in the true sense." It set the scene for a rich panorama of sound and colour, embracing the romantic melodrama There Is A Light That Never Goes Out, the maudlin self-absorbed I Know It's Over, the frivolous musichall romp Frankly Mr Shankly and uproariously camp, Carry On-styled Some Girls Are Bigger Than Others.

Delayed by several months due to legal injunctions, the album finally emerged in the summer of 1986 and effectively elevated the Smiths to a new creative and commercial level.

"At the end we knew that we'd done it and whether or not people were going to accept it was beside the point," notes Marr. "It was time to get back on the bus and start touring again. Job done."

The tour was a riotous affair. "There was perfect musical unity between myself, Mike and Andy," says Johnny. "It was a

Record label:
Rough Trade

Produced
by Morrissey and Marr.

Released:
June 1986

Chart peaks:
2 (UK) 70 (US)

Personnel:
Morrissey (v); Johnny Marr (g, p); Andy Rourke (b) Mike Joyce (d). Stephen Street (e)

Track listing:
The Queen Is Dead; Frankly, Mr Shankly; I Know It's Over; Never Had No One Ever; Cemetry Gates; Bigmouth Strikes Again (S); The Boy With The Thorn In His Side (S); Vicar In A Tutu; There Is A Light That Never Goes Out; Some Girls Are Bigger Than Others

Running time:
37.06

Current CD:
WEA 4509918962

Further listening:
Meat Is Murder (1985), Strangeways, Here We Come (1987).

Further reading:
Morrissey & Marr: The Severed Alliance (Johnny Rogan, 1992).

dream for me to play. Mike was just behind me and Andy fitted in the middle. That's the way we worked. I had something with Mike and Andy that I won't have playing with any other people."

As for Morrissey, he confirmed that beneath all the doom and drama lay a clever writer with a rich vein of comic irony. Whatever else they accused him of, critics finally acknowledged his role as one of rock's most sardonic humorists.

Run DMC
Raising Hell

Rap momentarily mates with metal and is propelled over-ground.

In 1986, rap was little more than five years old, and still in thrall to a set of references that had been defined at the dawn of the '80s. Run DMC came out of the old world and promptly defined an altogether new one. In 1985, they were on tour with Kurtis Blow, Whodini and the Fat Boys as part of a package called "Fresh Fest"; one year later they released the album and single that revolutionised the rap form. Rubin had added metallic touches to LL Cool J's 1985 album *Radio*, but *Raising Hell* showcased the decisive melding of the two forms, when Run DMC duetted with Aerosmith on Walk This Way.

"I remember that the idea was met with some question at first," recalls Rubin, "but they listened to the song and wrote all the words down and started thinking 'We can do this.' The Aerosmith guys came down and played the guitars. Then Steven [Tyler] sang his chorus vocals first, and then Run did the rhymes and Steven joined in. We did it all in a day."

The group's account is of a rather more sceptical view of the idea than Rubin suggests ("Yo! This is hillbilly gibberish bullshit!" said McDaniels when presented with a lyric sheet), but the track's brutal brilliance was self-evident. It was one of three rock-based cuts on *Raising Hell* – there was also It's Tricky, based on a sample of The Knack's My Sharona, and the title track, on which Rubin once again scrawled his fuzz-toned musical signature. Even the more straight-laced rap songs utilised a hard-hitting aesthetic that was new to the rap milieu. The best example was My Adidas, a fantastically minimal track on which Run DMC paid tribute to their favourite brand of sneaker. It also introduced the rap world to corporate sponsorship: after the album's release, producer and manager Russell Simmons took an Adidas executive to a Run DMC show, and within seconds of the song's opening had clinched a deal.

All that apart, the importance of *Raising Hell* – which sold over five million copies in the US – lay in its destruction of the last few fences that stood in the way of rap's dominance of American pop culture. "It was important in that it brought it to the mainstream and it showed people rap was 'music'," says Rubin. "It allowed hip hop into homes it had never been in before."

Record label:
Profile

Produced
by Russell Simmons and Rick Rubin.

Recorded
at Chung King House Of Metal, NYC.

Released:
July 1986

Chart peaks:
41 (UK) 3 (US)

Personnel:
Joseph Simmons aka Run (v); Darryl McDaniels aka DMC (v); Jason Mizell aka Jam Master Jay (DJ, k, pc); Sam Sever (programming); Daniel Shulman (b); Rick Rubin (g); Steven Tyler (v); Joe Perry (g) Steve Ett, Andy Wallace, Jay Burnett (e)

Track listing:
Peter Piper (S); It's Tricky (S); My Adidas Walk This Way (S); Is It Live; Perfection; Hit It Run; Raising Hell; You Be Illin' (S) Dumb Girl; Son Of Byford; Proud To Be Black

Running time:
39.53

Current CD:
PCD1217

Further listening:
King Of Rock (1985); also, hear Rubin's rap/rock hybrid take shape on LL Cool J's Radio (1985)

Further reading:
The Hip Hop Years (Alex Ogg with David Upshal, 1999); www.thadweb.com/rundmc

Elvis Costello
Blood And Chocolate

Underrated career peak featuring the garage sound of "a band falling apart".

By 1986, life was becoming complicated for Elvis Costello. A failed marriage and two disappointing and over-produced flops – *Punch The Clock* and *Goodbye Cruel World*, both made with the production team of Clive Langer and Alan Winstanley – had directed him into a creative impasse characterised by manic name changes (he is billed here as Napoleon Dynamite). Hanging out with The Pogues as producer of their defining album *Rum Sodomy & The Lash* may not have been recommended his doctor, but it stabilised Costello emotionally by hooking him up with Caitlin O'Riordan. She promptly gave up her duties as The Pogues' bassist and married him.

Earlier in the year, Costello had ventured outside the Attractions for an entire album, the stunning *King Of America*, which was produced by his hero T-Bone Burnett and featured a shifting cast of sessioneers, including the legendary James Burton. "*King Of America* showed me one of the problems on the records we'd done with Clive and Alan – the band was simply falling apart," says Costello. And fall apart they did, gloriously, on *Blood And Chocolate*. With old hand Nick Lowe at the helm, Costello and the rest of the Attractions convened for one last blow-out. Lowe set up the band in one room at Olympic Studios, deliberately allowing their sounds to bleed into each other.

"We set up and played as loud as we did on-stage," recalls Costello. "It was a really primitive record – just one mic in the middle of the studio. That's the only way we could achieve that low dynamic." Opening track, Uncomplicated, sets the tone in title and sound: chiming guitars, bellowed vocals, distorted bass, hulking drums, cheesy keyboards. Throughout, Costello's concerns remain constant: romantic possession, betrayal and disgust overlaid with a biting wit and surreal paranoia, as evidenced on the album's first single, the Dylanesque epic Tokyo Storm Warning, which conjures up a wealth of queasy imagery from KKK conventions to "Disney abattoirs". Described as "a protest song", Tokyo Storm Warning reached Number 73 in the charts – not surprising given its lyrical savagery and six-minute duration. Costello's shaky hand with singles was displayed when he followed up with I Want You. 'Maybe releasing two six-minute singles back to back wasn't the

Record label:
F-Beat

Produced
Nick Lowe with Colin Fairley.

Recorded
at Olympic Studios, London;
February–April 1986.

Released:
September 15, 1986

Chart peaks:
16 (UK) 84 (US)

Personnel:
Napoleon Dynamite [aka Elvis Costello]
(v, g); Steve Nieve (k); Bruce Thomas
(b); Pete Thomas (d)

Track listing:
Uncomplicated; I Hope You're Happy Now;
Tokyo Storm Warning (S); Home Is
Anywhere You Hang Your Head; I Want
You (S); Honey Are You Straight Or Are
You Blind?; Blue Chair; Battered Old Bird;
Crimes of Paris; Poor Napoleon; Next
Time Round

Running time:
47.52

Current CD:
Demon DPAM 12

Further listening:
Spike (1989); Best Of (1999); the best
of the Warners Years on Extreme Honey
(1997)

Further reading:
The Big Wheel (Bruce Thomas, 1990); Let
Them All Talk: Elvis Costello (Brian
Hinton, 1999); www.elvis-costello.com

way to do it," he says. The central flaw in pitching I Want You at a mass audience was that the track, though certainly the high-point of the album, is arguably the most twisted love song ever recorded, a tale of deception and all-consuming jealousy spat out over a menacing musical backdrop.

"There were quite a few scores being settled on that record," admits Costello, who adds that the crude recording technique added resonance to the songs. "On I Want You, everything you hear on the last minute is all from my vocal mic — you can hear the band only when they're bleeding through onto my voice."

With *Blood And Chocolate*, Costello finally bid farewell to the musical set-up which had supported him for nearly a decade. From there, diversity became a watchword as he sought out fresh genres and new collaborative partners. But never did he better this underrated collection of bitter Valentines.

Paul Simon

Graceland

After a decade in the wilderness, Simon's songwriting gifts are re-invigorated with the energy of African music.

To suggest that *Graceland* contributed to the downfall of apartheid may be an overstatement but, in retrospect, it's certainly hard to rationalise the barrage of flak Paul Simon endured for working with the South African musicians who inspired this genre-busting album.

"*Graceland*'s instincts were right," he insists, "and it called into question a lot of thinking, which is good."

Even in Simon & Garfunkel, he had championed world music (cf El Condor Pasa) long before it became a *cause célèbre*, but the fusion of Western pop with township jive, *kwela* and *mbaqanga* styles on *Graceland* coincided serendipitously with the revitalising of Simon as a songwriter. "It started in 1984," Simon explained when the album was released. "A friend gave me a cassette of an album called *Gumboots: Accordion Jive Hits, Volume 2*." Surprised and impressed by how much this technically simple, happy music reminded him of the '50s rock'n'roll he'd grown up with, Simon went to Johannesburg in February 1985 to seek out the African musicians on *Gumboots*, hoping to collaborate with them on a new album. For more than a year, recording in Africa, the UK and various American locations, Simon brought together a unique combination of extraordinary musicians whose remarkable skills added texture, harmony, sound and playing technique previously unimaginable in the confines of Western pop.

For Simon, who had previously started with melodies and lyrics and then arranged them for a record, this process offered an exciting new way to create. "I thought, I have enough songwriting technique that I can reverse this process and write this song after the tracks are made. If I have a really good track and I write a good song, well then my chances of making a good record are vastly improved over the other way of working. And in the process of working in that way, I discovered different ways of turning the form around, from constantly listening to the way African guitarists and the bass players were altering what they were playing from verse to verse."

Heart-stopping moments abound – the first hit of Ladysmith Black Mambazo's vocal harmonies in Homeless,

Record label:
Warner Brothers

Produced
by Paul Simon.

Recorded
in Johannesburg, New York, Lafayette, Los Angeles and London; February 1985–May 1986.

Chart peaks:
1 (UK) 3 (US)

Released:
October 4, 1986

Personnel:
Paul Simon (v, g, b, synclavier); Chikapa "Ray" Phiri, Adrian Belew (g); Demola Adepoju (g); Morris Goldberg (penny-whistle); Alex Foster (as); Leonard Pickett (ts); Ronald E Cuber (bs, bass saxo-phone); Earl Gardner, John Faddis, Randy Brecker, Lewis Michale Soloff, Alan Rubin (t); David W Bargeron, Kim Allan Cissel (tb); Rob Mounsey (k); Forere Motloheloa, Bagithi Khumalo (b); Vusi Khumalo, Isaac Mtshali (d); Youssou N'Dour, Makhaya Mahlangu, Babacar Faye, Assane, Thiam, Ralph McDonald (pc); Ladysmith Black Mambazo, The Everly Brothers, Linda Ronstandt (v, bv); Los Lobos, Good Rockin' Dopsie And The Twisters

Track listing:
The Boy In the Bubble (S); Graceland (S); I Know What I Know; Gumboots; Diamonds On the Soles Of Her Shoes; You Can Call Me Al (S); Under African Skies (S); Homeless; Crazy Love Vol II; That Was Your Mother; All Around The World Or The Myth Of Fingerprints

Running time:
43.10

Current CD:
7599254472

Further listening:
Still Crazy After All These Years (1975) offers fairly conclusive proof that Paul Simon comes closer than any of his contemporaries to being the late-20th-century Cole Porter; Rhythm Of The Saints (1990).

Further reading:
freespace.virgin.net/r.kent/ has links leading to several excellent sites.

Baghiti Khumalo's mercurially slithering basslines in You Can Call Me Al – but it's the coherence and vision of *Graceland* as a whole that elevates it into the pantheon of classic rock albums. "Every groove is a small miracle," said Charles Shaar-Murray in New Hi-Fi Sound. "He has indeed made an excellent album."

XTC
Skylarking

The artistic and commercial renaissance of Swindon's finest.

O nce the brightest sparks of the British New Wave, XTC had been struggling to find their niche since main man Andy Partridge's debilitating – and, as it turned out, permanent – stage fright of 1981 had precluded touring. After the triumph of *English Settlement* of the same year, their last two albums *Mummer* (1982) and *Big Express* (1984) had seen the band's profile dip from cutting-edge craftsmen to negligible, arcane eccentrics – their psychedelic spoof project *The Dukes Of Stratosphere* (1985) had, embarrassingly, outsold both. A restless Geffen (XTC's US label) suggested Todd Rundgren produce the next album and guitarist Dave Gregory was genuinely excited by the potential of the Rundgren-Partridge meld: "What a fantastic pool of minds. Of course I'd reckoned without the ego problem."

Todd selected the demos and programmed the running order into a concept. Partridge: "He picked everything of Colin's and half of mine. And I thought, Am I that crap suddenly? Is Colin that brilliant?"

In the studio, Rundgren was musically dazzling but poisonously sarcastic. Gregory: "It was just nasty and unnecessarily unpleasant. Todd got the measure of Andy's conceit and Andy rose to the bait every time."

The band rowed furiously, Colin left temporarily and, after his third attempt at mixing, Todd signed off and XTC had *Skylarking*, an album of gloriously warm, pastoral psychedelia which entirely belied the tumult of its making.

The most coherent and, perhaps, most likeable work of XTC's career, Partridge's brilliance here takes on an appealing pastel hue, while Moulding's five excellent songs are a personal triumph which balance the personality of the record beautifully; Rundgren's luscious production manages to make XTC sound both less and more like themselves.

Partridge: "At the time I felt like disowning it. I thought, Jesus, this man's killed our career.' But I think he actually brought something out in us that we didn't know how to bring out, he did us a great favour."

Relegated from the album to the B-side of Grass – *Skylarking*'s first single – was an odd, angry little atheist's song of Andy's called Dear God, which Partridge regarded as a "petulant failure" but American college radio had picked up on,

Record label:
Virgin

Produced
by Todd Rundgren.

Recorded
at Utopia Sound Studios, Woodstock, NY and Soundhole Studios, San Francisco; spring 1986.

Released:
October 1986

Chart peaks:
90 (UK) 70 (US)

Personnel:
Andy Partridge (v, g); Colin Moulding (v, b); Dave Gregory (v, g, p, k, chamberlain); Prairie Prince (d)

Track listing:
Summer's Cauldron; Grass (S); The Meeting Place; That's Really Super, Supergirl; Ballet For A Rainy Day; 1000 Umbrellas; Season Cycle; Earn Enough For Us; Big Day; Another Satellite; Mermaid Smiled; Dear God (S/US); The Man Who Sailed Around His Soul; Dying; Sacrificial Bonfire

Running time:
45.42

Current CD:
CDV2399

Further listening:
English Settlement (1981); Oranges And Lemons (1989); Apple Venus Volume 1 (1999)

Further reading:
MOJO 64; XTC Song Stories (XTC and Neville Farmer, 1998) www.chalkhills.org

causing a furore in the process. "Mail was 50 per cent 'This is fantastic you've voiced what I've been thinking for years' and 50 per cent 'You're going to roast in hell.'" A Florida radio station received a bomb threat about it and a disaffected student held a New York State school secretary at knifepoint, demanding the track be played over the school PA. Dear God was hastily reinstated on *Skylarking* and XTC found a whole new audience.

Beastie Boys

Licensed To Ill

The Never Mind The Bollocks for the '80s hip hop generation.

In 1985, Def Jam chief Russell Simmons received a call from Madonna's management. They were under the impression that he represented the Fat Boys: would they be interested in being the support act on the Like A Virgin tour? Without missing a beat, Simmons passed over the fact that he nothing to do with the corpulent rappers and instead recommended the Beastie Boys. The result was the honing of the obnoxious Beastie persona, as MCA, Mike D and Ad Rock performed to arenas of teenage girls who hated them.

In the wake of that tour, the trio completed the recording of their debut album with Simmons' Def Jam partner, Rick Rubin. To save money most of the work was done in the early hours, after the Beasties and their mentor had been partying in the New York clubs. This hedonistic mood permeates the album: The New Style, She's Crafty, No Sleep Till Brooklyn, all brim with beery hyperactivity. But for all the party-hearty atmosphere, *Licensed To Ill* was rightly acclaimed as a bold step forward for rap. Rubin had developed the rock-hip hop collision on both LL Cool J's *Radio* (1985) and Run DMC's *Raising Hell* (1986), and the Beastie Boys' debut was the pinnacle of this approach. The opening seconds of Rhymin' And Stealin', using sampled drums from Led Zeppelin's When The Levee Breaks, said it all: this was rap music that pilfered a great deal of heavy metal's brute power.

Much of the album was also knowingly funny, as the Beastie Boys revelled in gonzoid lairiness based not only on old-school rap *braggadocio*, but a clear love of rock cliché: No Sleep Till Brooklyn takes its lyrical lead from Motorhead's We Are The Road Crew. Then there was Fight For Your Right – gloriously moronic metal topped with giggle-strewn exhortations to teenage rebellion. The LP was to swiftly endear itself to every misunderstood adolescent in the Western world – and still does.

"What boggles my mind," says Mike D, "is that *Licensed To Ill* remains one of the biggest-selling catalogue records. We never envisaged the longevity and neither did Russell Simmons. He was used to rap records being big for maybe a couple of months. It still sells something like 500,000 a year. I wonder if it's people wearing out their old copies, or 14-year-old kids just getting into it now. Either way, it's too weird."

Record label:
Def Jam

Produced
by Rick Rubin and the Beastie Boys.

Recorded
in New York, 1986

Released:
November 1986

Chart peaks:
7 (UK) I (US)

Personnel:
Michael Diamond (v); Adam Horovitz (v); Adam Yauch (v); Kerry King (g); Rick Rubin (g, programming); Steve Ett (e)

Track listing:
Rhymin And Stealin; The New Style (S); She's Crafty (S/UK); Posse In Effect; Slow Ride; Girls (S/UK); Fight For Your Right (S); No Sleep Till Brooklyn (S); Paul Revere; Hold It Now Hit It (S); Brass Monkey; Slow And Low; Time to Get Ill

Running time:
44.33

Current CD:
527 351–2

Further listening:
Pre-rap Beasties on Some Old Bullshit (1994); The Sounds Of Science(1999)

Further reading:
Rhyming And Stealing: A History Of The Beastie Boys (Angus Batey, 1998)

The The
Infected

One young Londoner vents his brooding spleen at Thatcher's Britain.

L ike its immediate predecessor, *Soul Mining*, *Infected* was a record fuelled by speed, vodka and Ecstasy, but its prevailing claustrophobic mood was far from euphoric. "*Infected*, to an eerie, ultimately disturbing extent is like 1986 trapped on vinyl," claimed the NME on its release.

Lyrically, the album dealt with such diverse subjects as US militarism, the male sex drive, and what mainman Matt Johnson described as the "greed culture" of Thatcherism. When he began writing the album, Johnson was just 23. Initially, he had approached Tom Waits, Brian Eno and Holger Czukay as possible producers, even spending a week in New York discussing the project with Waits over pool. Though keen, Waits was too busy but suggested that Johnson self-produce with a good engineer. Enter Livesey and Mosimann, later successful producers in their own right.

Despite the album's political edge and sleazy, often jagged arrangements, the recording sessions were anything but po-faced. "We spent a lot of time chasing around the control room with cream cakes and soda siphons," says Johnson. He also recalls that his duet with Neneh Cherry on Slow Train To Dawn came about after he got her "so drunk on vodka that she almost fell down the stairs". Heartland, featuring Steve Hogarth's gorgeous honky-tonk piano, has aged particularly well. Thanks to the now unshocking line "piss-stinking shopping centre", however, it fell foul of the censors when released as a single. Against the political backdrop of a US attack on Libya, Sweet Bird Of Truth's lyrics were also deemed unsuitable for daytime radio. To complicate matters, the title track was misconstrued as a reference to AIDS.

Shortly after its release, *Infected* gained a much-needed profile boost when Tim Pope and Peter Christopherson's promotional film of the entire album scored two Channel 4 screenings in quick succession. It had been filmed at considerable expense in Peru and Bolivia, with Johnson writing the storyboards for Heartland, Infected and The Mercy Beat. The album went on to sell around one million copies worldwide, but for Johnson, the highest accolade came years later: "I was at a party when this young, black American fighter pilot came up to me. He told me that he'd quit his job after listening to Sweet Bird Of Truth."

Record label:
Epic

Produced
by Matt Johnson, Warne Livesey, Gary Langan and Roli Mosimann.

Recorded
at Air Studios, Oxford Circus; Livingstone, North London; The Garden, Shoreditch, London; 1984–86.

Released:
November 1986

Chart peaks:
14 (UK) 89 (US)

Personnel:
Matt Johnson (v, g, k); David Palmer (d); Dan Brown (b); Jeff Cline (acoustic b); Steve Hogarth (p); Judd Lander (hm); Neneh Cherry (v)

Track listing:
Infected (S); Out Of The Blue (Into The Fire); Heartland (S); Angels Of Deception; Sweet Bird Of Truth (S); Slow Train To Dawn (S); Twilight Of A Champion; The Mercy Beat

Running time:
41.10

Current CD:
4886112

Further listening:
Soul Mining (1983)

Further reading:
www.thethe.com

Jane Siberry
The Walking

*A singular vision explodes across an expansive canvas;
Canada's secret is delivered to the world.*

No one says Jane Siberry is crazy – unlike fellow Canadian Mary Margaret O'Hara; eccentric, perhaps. Her early works, this album included, all evoked a sense of vulnerability – but despite the glittering, woozy dreamscapes, Siberry wasn't soft; the experimentalism she prized was subtly focused, and she was tough enough to fight for it in dealings with the music industry. From a non-musical family, Siberry was writing songs before her feet could touch the ground from the piano stool; she would later revisit this juvenilia on *Teenager*, singing songs of innocence with the voice of experience.

As a student of microbiology in Ontario, she financed her debut, *Jane Siberry* (1981), with tips from a waitressing job, and in 1984 signed to a small Canadian label which joined with A&M/Wyndham Hill to release *No Borders Here*. *The Speckless Sky* (1985), went gold in Canada; her vision grew bigger still on this, her fourth album, described by Siberry as "a series of successive clearings and cinematic landscapes, each expanding into the next." While the making of 1993's *When I Was A Boy* was a three-year ordeal, *The Walking*, though profoundly introspective, was completed smartly. As a major label debut, it was a radical thing: no track less than five minutes, and two – the opener and closer – over ten. The dreamlike quality of the songs is enhanced by an array of non-musical effects and snatches of intimate dialogue; on the shiversome *tour de force* for spurned lover and Greek chorus, The Lobby, Siberry duets with a multi-tracked choir of her own voice (Chorus: 'This is your darkest hour'/Siberry: 'This is my finest moment'). What makes it spark is a mix of the seductive, intellectual and humorous, the lush meshes of swooping sound and sudden mood changes, and Siberry's clear, multi-octave voice. The sassy Red High Heels and rapturous The Walking will always be amongst her best work – so will the broken, post-relationship Goodbye: "I want a table/No just for one/But I know you do/I can see some from here/OK then say for two/But there's only one." Epic in scope, with huge emotional punch, the album is freebase poetry of an instantly accessible kind. Reviews were adoring. Siberry has said, "The saving grace for me is that record companies have never considered anything I do a 'hit'." Nevertheless, there was a certain pressure, and in 1996 she left Warner Brothers to start her own label, Sheeba.

Record label:
Reprise

Produced
by Jane Siberry and John Switzer.

Recorded
at Manta Sound Company, Toronto, Canada; Spring–Summer 1987.

Released:
January 1987

Chart peaks:
None (UK) None (US)

Personnel:
Jane Siberry (v, g, k); Anne Bourne (k); John Switzer (b); Ken Myhr (g); Al Cross (d)

Track listing:
The White Tent The Raft; Red High Heels; Goodbye; Ingrid (And The Footman); Lena Is A White Table; The Walking (And Constantly); The Lobby; The Bird In The Gravel

Running time:
54.00

Current CD:
DSBD 31040

Further listening:
Bound By The Beauty bowls along, sometimes hymnal (The Valley), sometimes genially flaky (Everything Reminds Me Of My Dog); Summer In The Yukon collects highlights from her career up until When I Was A Boy (1993), her second masterpiece. Best of the output on her own label, Sheeba, is probably the sparse and lovely Teenager (1996) in which she revisits her earliest songs, originally recorded in her room with the sound of truck gears changing outside.

Further reading:
Try the website www.sheeba.ca to obtain One Room Schoolhouse, Siberry's engaging little book about her thoughts, computers and God.

U2
The Joshua Tree

Irish band imagines a mythic America of frontier spirit and spiritual quest.

U2 had only just finished touring their previous album when they set to work on their next. They had no new songs written at the time; rather, they simply got together at Adam Clayton's house at Danesmoate, and waited to see what happened. "Myself and Edge would be up at six o'clock in the morning, then Adam'd drop in, just writing songs and playing records," Bono explained, while engineer Steve Rainford told author Carter Alan, "at the beginning of [each] session, [there] was a band rehearsal. It's really the essence of how they do it – they bang around till they make it the way they like and then they record it."

Broadening the elemental nature of 1984's *The Unforgettable Fire*, *The Joshua Tree* encapsulated the band's grandiose vision of a mythic America. The videos which accompanied the singles – a Beatles-esque rooftop performance, an impromptu miming session on the streets of Las Vegas – and the ragged frontier innocence which overhangs the album reinforced *The Joshua Tree* became U2's biggest-selling album ever; it wasn't hard to see why.

"We wanted to try and capture a place as well as a mood," Mullen said. "We wanted to give each song a sense of location." From the forlorn ghost-ridden shacks of Red Hill Mining Town to the joyous apocalypse-hoedown of Trip Through Your Wires; from the killer's eye-view of Exit to the CIA training ground of Bullet The Blue Sky, *The Joshua Tree* was a panorama, the Edge said, of "the America of the great R&B and country performers, [of] civil rights people like Martin Luther King and Bobby Kennedy; [of] the new journalism of people like Truman Capote and Norman Mailer, the way they were able to bring you to a place was almost cinematic. We tried to do that on the album."

And the title? "There are many reasons for it," Bono revealed. "But it's almost impossible for me to explain that seriously, for me to take myself as seriously as that. Inevitably we're going to lie a lot." But he did admit, "Larry was too embarrassed to tell his girlfriend that we were going to call the LP after this clump of prickles in the desert."

Record Label:
Island

Produced
by Daniel Lanois and Brian Eno.

Recorded
at Danesmoate, early 1986; Windmill Lane Studios, Dublin; Spring 1986, August 1986–January 1987.

Released:
March 9, 1987

Chart peaks:
1 (UK) 1 (US)

Personnel:
Bono (v); The Edge (g, k, v); Adam Clayton (b); Larry Mullen Jr (d); Daniel Lanois (tambourine, omnichord, g, v); Brian Eno (DX7 programmes, k); Arklow Silver Band. Where The Streets Have No Name; With Or Without You; Bullet The Blue Sky and Red Hill Mining Town remixed by Steve Lillywhite.

Track Listing:
Where The Streets Have No Name (S); I Still Haven't Found What I'm Looking For (S); With Or Without You (S); Bullet The Blue Sky; Running To Stand Still; In God's Country (S); Trip Through Your Wires; One Tree Hill; Exit; Mother Of The Disappeared

Running time:
50.15

Current CD:
U2 6

Further listening:
The Unforgettable Fire (1984); Rattle And Hum (1988)

Further reading:
Outside Is America (Carter Alan, 1992)

Prince
Sign O' The Times

Prince's eighth album was a self-made Technicolor sprawl that netted three US Top 10 singles

Coming off the sales shrinkage of his previous albums *Parade* and *Around The World In A Day*, *Sign O' The Times* was nothing if not a calculated risk. Deeply entrenched in jazz legend Miles Davis' corpus at the time, Prince buffed his new material with tricked-out, high-sheen arrangements that pushed his New Power Soul to new heights. One only needed to check out the neo-fusion changes in Play In The Sunshine and the knotty horn chart in Slow Love to realise something new and wonderful was afoot.

But *Sign O' The Times* seemed to be trouble-plagued from the start. Prince had been bursting with ideas, he'd planned an album by his feminine alter-ego Camille, a double set to be made with sidekicks Wendy & Lisa and a triple album called *Crystal Ball* — all of these ideas were rejected by Warner Brothers as uncommercial. Then there were teething problems with his swanky new facility, Paisley Park.

"Prince hired a guy named Frank Demedi to install one of these state-of-the-art consoles in Paisley Park," recalled the album's engineer Susan Rogers. "One night he dreamt a song, which turned out to be The Ballad Of Dorothy Parker, and insisted on recording it immediately." Despite the console's total absence of high end, Prince laid it down and mixed the song that night.

"Technically it's a total mistake," says Rogers, "but he likes good mistakes if they work." The album which emerged was characterised by many happy accidents. Housequake, the album's funkiest jam, was inspired by a late-night recording session with 80's LA pop queens The Bangles, while a nocturnal studio visit from Scottish *chanteuse* Sheena Easton resulted in U Got The Look.

"Sheena came into the studio unannounced, 'cos she wanted Prince to produce her next album," says Rogers. "U Got The Look had gone through a million changes, and he was really struggling with it. It was originally a mid-tempo thing, but he had sped it up at the last minute and asked her to sing on it. I think she was a little taken aback by the sexual nature of it at first, but he convinced her to get into it, and it worked perfectly."

In the first months at Paisley Park he cut over 300

Record label:
Warner Brothers

Produced
by Prince.

Recorded
at Paisley Park, Chanhassen, Minnesota; Sunset Sound, Los Angeles, and Dierks Studio Mobile Tracks; summer and autum 1986.

Released:
March 1987

Chart peaks:
4 (UK) 6 (US)

Personnel:
Prince (g, d, b, k, v); Eric Leeds (s); Atlanta Bliss (t); Sheena Easton (v); Susan Rogers, Coke Johnson, Prince (e)

Track listing:
Sign O' The Times (S); Play In The Sunshine; Housequake; The Ballad Of Dorothy Parker; It; Starfish and Coffee; Slow Love; Hot Thing; Forever In My Life; U Got The Look (S); If I Was Your Girlfriend (S); Strange Relationship; I Could Never Take The Place Of Your Man (S); The Cross; It's Gonna Be A Beautiful Night; Adore

Running time:
79.59

Current CD:
7599255772

Further listening:
Prince And The Revolution, Purple Rain (1984); Around The World In A Day (1985); Parade (1986)

Further reading:
www.npgonlineltd.com/
http://users.ids.net/~dmsr/dmsr.html — an online archive of Prince history

songs, many of them entirely by himself. Less ornate than pre-decessor *Parade* songs such as The Cross and the sparse but riveting title cut, nevertheless reverberated with an intense, soulful energy that would be missing from subsequent albums. In fact, *Sign O' The Times* was the last great Prince album. A few one-offs aside, little of his subsequent work had this much impact. A prolonged legal battle with his label Warner Brothers and a severe case of monomania sidetracked him in the '90s, and for many of his fans he has yet to reclaim his creative and commercial juice.

Butthole Surfers

Locust Abortion Technician

Psychedelia and punk in a pre-grunge union.

The Butthole Surfers were the Merry Pranksters of '80s US indie rock. Emerging at a time when orthodox hardcore (Black Flag, Bad Brains) still reigned, they belonged to a nonconformist tradition that seemed in danger of extinction. Instead, with Big Black and Sonic Youth, they formed an influential triumvirate that reacquainted rock with an earthy dissonance, a noise that eventually went overground with grunge. Like The Grateful Dead, the Buttholes made music that existed less for itself than as the public expression of a way of life. The Dead epitomised wild drugs and communality; the Buttholes wilder drugs and a conviviality born of boredom.

There was nothing unusual in the band's formation – two high-achieving students, Gibby Haynes and Paul Leary, met at college in 1981 – but there convention ended. As the band's name suggests, Haynes, the son of a Texan children's television host, revelled in ludicrous outrage. His comic-dystopian visions spilled over into live appearances, which would often resemble freak shows, with nude dancers and films depicting all manner of depravity. "The world would be a sad place if we became a monster group," confessed drummer King Coffey. The Buttholes never quite became "monster", but after a handful of records that owed little to rock'n'roll convention, they came of age in 1986 with *Rembrant Pussyhorse*. The record was well-received and paved the way for a successful European tour, where Haynes' debuted his "Gibbytronix", a digital delay box that enabled his voice to match the group's increasingly mangled music. The Gibbytronix was all over *Locust Abortion Technician*, the Buttholes' first record for influential UK indie Blast First, and a definitive statement of rock'n'roll grotesquery. According to Leary, the group reverted back to an 8-track for the sessions (like most things in the Buttholes' history, remain shrouded in mystery) which took place at a studio equipped with one microphone and an archaic tape-machine that weighed around 800 pounds. Disparate styles – psych, punk, electronic, ethnic, even a Black Sabbath pastiche (Sweet Loaf) – sounded strangely compatible after receiving the Buttholes treatment. Sewer blues (Pittsburg To Lebanon), queasy basslines (22 Going On 23), fuzz-guitar overload (Graveyard, USSA), even something approaching a conventional avant-rock song (Human Cannonball).

Record label:
Blast First

Producer not listed

Recorded
winter 1986.

Released:
March 1987

Chart peaks:
None (UK) None (US)

Personnel:
Gibby Haynes (v); Paul Leary (g); King Coffey (d); Theresa Taylor (d); Jeff Pinkus (b)

Track listing:
Sweat Loaf; Graveyard; Pittsburg To Lebanon; Weber; Hay; Human Cannonball; USSA; The O-Men; Kuntz; Graveyard; 22 Going On 23

Running time:
32.42

Current CD:
LBV05

Further listening:
Hairway To Steven (1988) refined the formula – and with a greater acoustic presence, too.

Further reading:
www.buttholesurfers.com/

Slayer
Reign In Blood

Third album by devil-bothering LA thrash metal squad sends moral majority into a tizzy.

When maverick producer Rick Rubin signed Slayer to Def Jam back in late '85 there were those who questioned his judgement. Quite what a Satanic metal band from LA had in common with the rap world was anyone's guess. "To me it made perfect sense. When I heard Slayer I just thought that I had to sign them because they were just as extreme and relevant as, say, Public Enemy," explains Rubin.

As if to introduce the band to the Def Jam family, Rubin also persuaded guitarist Kerry King to lay down the guitar tracks on the Beastie Boys keg-party anthem Fight For Your Right (To Party) on the rap brats' chart-topping *Licensed To Ill* debut. In truth it did little to prepare the world for Slayer's forthcoming album.

Reign In Blood was a short, sharp shocker, causing an immediate storm of controversy thanks to opening track, Angel Of Death. The song's principal protagonist was notorious Nazi death-camp doctor, Joseph Mengele. The band were immediately accused of being Nazi-sympathisers.

"We've had a lot of flak about that, but we are not Nazis," stated frontman Tom Araya, at the time. "The song is very graphic, but it's an observation. No more, no less. People make films about this kind of stuff so why can't you write a song about it?"

Despite the band's attempts to clear the air, Def Jam's distributors, CBS, in a knee-jerk reaction, refused to release the album in the US and Geffen stepped in to distribute the record. In the UK, however, Warner Brothers (Geffen's distributor) felt the album featured "unsuitable content" and pulled the plug. When *Reign In Blood* finally emerged on London Records in the UK, it had already attained legendary status among an audience hungry for taboo thrills.

While Angel Of Death had caused most of the brouhaha, the rest of the subject matter was no less gruesome, tracks like Piece By Piece, Necrophobic and Criminally Insane boasted all the subtle allure of The Texas Chainsaw Massacre, the graphic lyrical imagery matched by clinically savage playing. Slayer had delivered the most brutal metal album of the late '80s.

Record label:
American Recordings

Produced
by Rick Rubin and Slayer.

Recorded
'in LA'; mid-1986.

Released:
April 1987

Chart peaks:
46 (UK) 94 (US)

Personnel:
Kerry King (g); Jeff Hanneman (g); Tom Araya (v, b); Dave Lombardo (d); Andy Wallace (e)

Track listing:
Angel Of Death; Piece By Piece; Necrophobic; Altar Of Sacrifice; Jesus Saves; Criminally Insane (S); Reborn; Epidemic; Post-mortem; Raining Blood

Running time:
29.03

Current CD:
4917982

Further listening:
Hell Awaits (1985); South Of Heaven (1988)

Further reading:
www.diabolus.net

The Replacements
Pleased To Meet Me

Fifth album from the dishevelled, influential alternative rockers, now reduced to a trio.

In the early '80s, Minneapolis, as well as being home to the artist then known only as Prince, was the epicentre of American post-punk rock: Hüsker Dü, Soul Asylum and, wildest of the lot, The Replacements, formed in 1979 after Paul Westerberg joined brothers Bob and Tommy Stinson's and Chris Mars' garage band. Their early Twin/Tone albums were a jumble of styles – country, folk, heavy rock, blues – delivered with a punk spirit and a bar-room swagger like a ragged, budget-version Rolling Stones. By 1985 their garage-punk roots were starting to grow out, and Seymour Stein signed them to his Warner Brothers offshoot label Sire. Suddenly they were label-mates with Madonna.

"We were really young, jaded and nonchalant about the whole thing," said Tommy Stinson about the change in their fortunes. "We weren't thinking, Wow, we're on a major label, we're going to make lots of money, we were just, Who cares? We just had a real Fuck The System attitude about it all."

Though major label debut *Tim* continued their shift towards more evocative, mature material, this musical progress was offset by increasingly fraught relationships within the group, largely thanks to their self-destructive lifestyles. And as the band prepared to record their second Sire album *Pleased To Meet Me*, guitarist Bob Stinson was sacked. (Eight years later, in 1995, he would be found dead in his apartment of a suspected drug over-dose.)

Despite the loss of their guitar player, they hunkered down in Memphis with producer Jim Dickinson, chosen for his Big Star connection – Alex Chilton was Westerberg's idol; his presence is felt elsewhere on the album in the tribute track named after him and in his guest appearance on closer I Can Hardly Wait. Westerberg's growth as a songwriter is highlighted on the bittersweet Never Mind, the acoustic Skyway and the harrowing suicide anthem The Ledge. Ironically, his mellowing approach split the band in 1990 following the mid-tempo melancholia of *All Shook Down*, a Replacements album widely viewed as the frontman's first solo effort. *Pleased To Meet Me*, however, insured that The Replacements' legacy was consider-able, with the likes of Kurt Cobain and The Black Crowes claiming it as a key influence.

Record label:
Sire

Produced
by Jim Dickinson.

Recorded
at Ardent Studios, Studio B, Memphis; 1987.

Released:
May 1987

Chart peaks:
38 (UK) 131 (US)

Personnel:
Paul Westerberg (v, g); Tommy Stintson (b); Chris Mars (d); East Memphis Slim (k); Teenage Steve Douglas (bass flute, bs); Price Gabe (s); Andrew Love (ts); Ben Jr (tp); Alex Chilton (g); John Hampton, Joe Hardy (e)

Track listing:
IOU; Alex Chilton (S); I Don't Know; Nightclub Jitters; The Ledge (S); Never Mind; Valentine; Shooting Dirty Pool; Red Red Wine; Skyway; I Can Hardly Wait (S)

Running time:
33.32

Current CD:
925 557 2

Further listening:
Tim (1985); All Shook Down (1990); Paul Westerberg 14 Songs (1993); Suicaine Gratification (1999)

Further reading:
Student Matt Tomich's Skyway fan site is packed with photos and regular updates on all Replacements activity past and present: www.theskyway.com

LL Cool J
Bigger & Deffer

Ladies' man breaks rap wide open while manager Sean "Puffy" Combes takes notes in the wings.

A in't nothing like the old skool, as Tupac Shakur noted, and there are few modern rappers and hip-hoppers who don't owe something to the original B-boy, the man who styled himself Ladies Love Cool James.

Just 18 years old when this dynamite album was released, James Todd Smith had already established himself as a bare-chested, gold-chained pin-up who could rap alongside the best of them. The first artist to release a single on Def Jam, he'd starred in Krush Groove and his boastful, ladykilling style made him a star of the genre's first big US tour, on which he stole the show night after night from the likes of Run DMC and Grandmaster Flash. Writer Nelson George described LL as "larger than life, almost a cartoon, a rapper as arena rock star".

Debut album *Radio* had borne the influence of Def Jam's resident hard-rock freak Rick Rubin, who had littered it with heavy metal samples in much the same way as he would with Run DMC and the Beastie Boys. But on *Bigger And Deffer*, LL emerged from Rubin's shadow, using the far funkier yet sparse electro scratching and astute sampling of Earl "Bobcat" Erving and his LA Posse colleagues Darry Pierce and Dwayne Simon. Matched with their eclectic choice of samples, from the Shaft theme on Get Down to James Brown on Kanday and Chuck Berry on Go Cut Creator Go, LL's boastful and dynamic raps and charismatic persona helped shoehorn rap into the commercial mainstream, offering an authentic alternative to the whiny white-boy posturing of the genre's other titans, the Beastie Boys.

"*Bigger & Deffer* is a concept album, and the concept is LL's ego," wrote Vibe magazine's Sia Michel. "Self-mythology is the aim of any rapper, but no one else has ever come close to such put-me-in-the-pantheon ego-tripping." The key to the album's appeal lies in his tag – ladies really did love James, particularly when he revealed his sensitive side on the landmark I Need Love, the first true love song of rap and his first UK Top 10 hit. Against the delicate and soulful bedrock of samples, LL serenades a romantic infatuation which teeters on the edge of, but never spills over into, lasciviousness. That was reserved for the ensuing Def Jam tour, when he used I Need Love as an excuse to dry-hump an onstage sofa, sparking charges of public lewdness in Columbus, Ohio.

Record label:
Def Jam

Produced
by LL Cool J and the LA Posse.

Recorded
at the Chung King House Of Metal, NYC

Released:
June 1987

Chart peaks:
54 (UK) 3 (US)

Personnel:
LL Cool J (v); Bobcat Erving (scratches); The LA Posse (samples, programming); Russell Simmons (production supervisor)

Track listing:
I'm Bad (S); Kanday; Get Down; The Bristol Hotel; My Rhyme Ain't Done; .357 – Break It On Down; Go Cut Creator Go; The Breakthrough; I Need Love (S); Aah Let's Get Ill; The Do Wop; On The Ill Tip

Running time:
45.19

Current CD:
527353-2

Further listening:
Kool Moe Dee, How Ya Like Me Now (1988); Run DMC, Raising Hell (1986); Sean "Puffy" Combes, No Way Out (1997)

Further reading:
The Vibe History Of Hip Hop (1999)

Def Leppard
Hysteria

Multi-platinum soft-metal Brummies dodge the worst luck of their career to produce their best album.

While Def Leppard's third album *Pyromania* established the band as a world-beating hard rock outfit, no one would argue that its successor was a triumph over desperate circumstances.

With the release of *Pyromania* in March 1983, Leppard had become the biggest-selling British hard-rock band of the '80s with sales of the album topping the eight-million mark. As the band regrouped in Ireland in early '84 with Mutt Lange to start work on *Hysteria*, the producer announced that he was suffering from exhaustion, having worked on *Pyromania*, Foreigner's *4* and The Cars' *Heartbreak City* in quick succession. Unable to wait for Lange, Leppard enlisted the services of Meat Loaf producer Jim Steinman and elected to start recording in Wisseloord, Holland. The results were nigh-on disastrous, leading to Steinman's departure.

Then, as the band took a Christmas break, drummer Rick Allen's Chevrolet Corvette Stingray spun off the road between Sheffield and his parents' home in Dronfield, severing his left arm in the process. Allen and his girlfriend Mirium Barendsen were rushed to the Royal Hallamshire Hospital, where Allen's arm was sewn back on, only for infection to set in. Three days later it had to be amputated.

In a show of solidarity, Leppard refused to contemplate life without their friend and insisted that they would wait for him.

"We intend to have Rick back on stage and participating if at all possible," stated manager Peter Mensch at the time, leading to speculation that two drummers might be involved. Instead, Leppard soldiered on with Lange back on board and started work on *Hysteria*, programming the drums on a Fairlight computer while Allen began his rehabilitation and began to develop a unique keypad drum system which would allow him to rejoin the band onstage.

After an intense period of speculation *Hysteria* emerged in the summer of '87 and astounded the critics (who'd always resented down-to-earth Leppard's success). Lange's production sounded immense, setting standards for the next generation of stadium-rock bands. A stronger record than *Pyromania*, *Hysteria* matched muscle (on tracks such as Armageddon It!, Animal,

Record label:
Bludgeon Riffola

Produced
by Robert "Mutt" Lange.

Recorded
at Wisseloord Studios, Holland; summer 1984—summer 1985.

Released:
August 1987

Chart peaks:
2 (UK) 1 (US)

Personnel:
Steve Clark (g); Phil Collen (g); Rick Savage (b); Joe Elliott (v); Rick Allen (d); The Bankrupt Brothers (bv); Mike Shipley, Nigel Green (m)

Track listing:
Women (S); Rocket (S); Animal (S); Love Bites (S); Pour Some Sugar On Me (S); Armageddon It! (S); Gods Of War; Don't Shoot Shotgun; Run Riot; Hysteria (S); Excitable; Love And Affection

Running time:
62.40

Current CD:
830 675

Further listening:
Pyromania (1983); Slang (1996)

Further reading:
Def Leppard: Animal Instinct (David Fricke, 1985);
www.webnl.com/senff/leppard.html

Gods Of War) with melody (on the likes of Love Bites, Love And Affection and the title track) with a stadium-sized sense of fun. Even the cheesy Pour Some Sugar On Me, Rocket and Boston-esque opener Women are delivered with a certain tongue-in-cheek charm. While Leppard continued to sell albums by the truckload, however, their on-the-road habits were starting to take their toll, most notably on guitarist Steve Clark. Following a late-night drinking session, Clark was found dead in his Chelsea apartment on January 8, 1991. For Leppard things would never be the same again.

Guns N' Roses
Appetite For Destruction

Full-length debut by LA guttersnipes blends the spirit of the Stones, vintage Aerosmith and the Pistols.

"**I** want this to be the biggest-selling debut album from a rock act ever!" was W Axl Rose's characteristically immoderate cry when Geffen released *Appetite For Destruction*. And so it was, arguably, with 15 million worldwide sales chalked up in the four years before the follow-up dual release of *Use Your Illusion I* and *II* – from baseless fantasy to self-mythologising to fact.

None of them were native Californians – Slash was born in Stoke-on-Trent, England – Guns N' Roses came together in mid-'80s Los Angeles with a common urge to make a new noise out of their mutual interest in hard rock and punk. Their enthusiasm for drink and drugs meant they could never put an exact date to the band's formation, but Geffen's talent scouts discovered them living in vile shared accommodation off Sunset Boulevard in 1985. However, it took A&R woman Teresa Ensenat some time to fix them up with a producer because, she said, "People were very afraid of this band."

Eventually, Mike Clink, a quiet young man who had engineered for Heart and Eddie Money, agreed to take on the general misbehaviour and in particular Rose's posturing, or by some accounts, manic-depressive mood swings.

But, behind all the racket, the band had written a collection of songs fundamentally true to their collective character and, on the right day, they could play them to savage effect. A lot of their writing candidly confessed their bad habits. For example, Nightrain is a tribute to the cheap wine of that name ("It would fuck you up for a dollar. Five dollars and you'd be gone!" Rose crowed nostalgically). The scathing My Michelle refers to one of the singer's girlfriends who "led a crazy life doing drugs" and Mr Brownstone is a cautionary tale of heroin addiction. Yet Rose's commercial boast was fulfilled because they had, unwittingly it seemed, also come up with some far less abrasive material in the radio-friendly Paradise City and Sweet Child O' Mine.

Even so, Rose's voice wasn't the sweetest noise on radio and *Appetite For Destruction* took 12 months of constant touring to reach Number 1 in the US. At which, predictably enough, able to satisfy said appetite at whim, the band began to fall apart. There were endless fights: between themselves, with audience members, with policemen. And there was genuine tragedy

Record label:
Geffen

Produced
by Mike Clink.

Recorded
at Rumbo Recorders, Canoga Park, Los Angeles; August 1986.

Released:
August 1987

Chart peaks:
5 (UK) 1 (US)

Personnel:
W Axl Rose (v, syn, pc); Slash (g); Izzy Stradlin (g); Duff "Rose" McKagan (b); Steven Adler (d)

Track listing:
Welcome To The Jungle (S); It's So Easy (S); Nightrain (S); Out Ta Get Me; Mr Brownstone; Paradise City (S); My Michelle; Think About You; Sweet Child O' Mine (S); You're Crazy; Anything Goes; Rocket Queen

Running time:
53.50

Current CD:
GED 24148

Further listening:
Live @*?! Like A Suicide (1987)

Further reading:
Over The Top: The True Story Of Guns N' Roses (Mark Putterford, 1993)

in the death of two fans trampled to death at the 1988 Castle Donnington festival. Come 2000, with only three more albums behind them, Rose still claimed that Guns N' Roses existed – but that he was the only member.

"It was the success that screwed us up," Slash once lamented before adding with some pride, "but *Appetite* was an album we made because that's what we were about. It wasn't dictated by industry policy or business decisions, it was an honest record."

The Smiths
Strangeways Here We Come

The Smiths' swansong brimmed with images of death.

"I don't think this album is what we're about to most people," says Johnny Marr. "They've decided that *The Queen Is Dead* is the better album and I don't agree. All the songs are better, it's produced better and it's got a better atmosphere. I might be wrong but I don't think I am."

By 1987, The Smiths appeared to have come full circle. Marr, having almost lost his life in a car crash, was eager to enter the studio but his priorities were changing. Andy Rourke had overcome his heroin addiction and was playing well alongside Mike Joyce. Morrissey, as ever, was being enigmatic and unpredictable, but seemed up for another album. Contrary to popular myth, the sessions were relatively stress-free. Drink flowed during the early stages and Marr appeared determined to take the group in a new direction, away from their image as indie jingle-jangle kings. As Andy Rourke observed: "A Rush And A Push And The Land Is Ours stands out because it didn't have any guitars on it at all. I thought that was a first." Other surprises included Morrissey's debut on piano on Death Of A Disco Dancer, a gloomy freeform affair that sounded like a cross between Pink Floyd and late-period Beatles. Morrissey was at his most characteristically maudlin and no less than seven songs were death-related, including the single Girlfriend In A Coma and Death At One's Elbow.

"My favourite memory of making *Strangeways* was putting the strings on Last Night I Dreamt That Somebody Loved Me," says Johnny, "and doing the guitars on Stop Me . . . a load of amps and a load of guitars all turned up full and I was dropping this steel knife onto the guitars and they were making these godawful huge kerrangs, so I enjoyed doing that."

If there was a problem it lay in the background, with Marr insisting on retaining his manager against Morrissey's wishes. There were also changes in attitude about what The Smiths represented. Morrissey voiced a desire to make records and go home, rather than conquer the world. Marr was also getting into dance music, which took him even further away from Morrissey's worldview.

"Sometimes it came down to Sly Stone versus Herman's Hermits," Johnny quipped afterwards, "and I knew which side I was on."

By the following summer the unthinkable had happened.

Record label:
Rough Trade

Produced
by Johnny Marr, Morrissey and Stephen Street.

Recorded
at Wool Hall, Bath; spring 1987.

Released:
September 1987

Chart peaks:
2 (UK) 55 (US)

Personnel:
Morrissey (v); Johnny Marr (g, p); Andy Rourke (b); Mike Joyce (d); Steve Williams (ae)

Track listing:
A Rush And A Push And The Land Is Ours; I Started Something I Couldn't Finish (S); Death Of A Disco Dancer; Girlfriend In A Coma (S); Stop Me If You Think You've Heard This One Before (S/US); Last Night I Dreamt That Somebody Loved Me (S); Unhappy Birthday; Paint A Vulgar Picture; Death At One's Elbow; I Won't Share You

Running time:
36.09

Current CD:
4509918992

Further listening:
Meat Is Murder (1985); The Queen Is Dead (1986)

Further reading:
Morrissey & Marr: The Severed Alliance (1992)

Marr announced his decision to quit. The dream was over.

"It's the one Smiths record I've actually sat down and listened to since the break-up," says Johnny now. "That was about two years ago, when I was producing Marion. I'd been in the studio quite a long time and I came home and I felt that my critical faculties were well and truly *up*. It was about 2am and I thought, OK then, smartarse, put your incredible insight to the test. It really was the first time in 12 years that I'd listened to a Smiths record voluntarily. I found that I knew and remembered every single note. I remembered *being* every single note, and I really, really enjoyed it and thought it was a great record."

Depeche Mode
Music For The Masses

The most subversive pop group of the age finally tire of pop.

They'd begun as defiantly feeble electro-popsters under the guidance of Vince Clarke. When he departed to form, consecutively, The Assembly, Yazoo and Erasure, it seemed that they were doomed, but it turned out that they had another visionary in their midst, bubble-haired changeling Martin Gore, who took control and began to steer them down an ever-darkening path. In terms of credibility, Depeche Mode's sixth album caught them on the cusp. Their precious powder-puff origins had been outgrown; their new role as proto-industrial *Übermensch* not quite established. In America the group were allied with The Cure and The Smiths and fêted accordingly, they were also being checked by emergent house DJs and rated alongside Kraftwerk. At home, on the other hand, they were still twinned with A Flock Of Seagulls, and damned in the same breath. But if the dichotomy worried them, they never said.

Last time out, on *Black Celebration*, the landscape had been bleak, the vision austere, and they'd recorded in Berlin with Daniel Miller. This time around, they went to Paris with Tears For Fears' engineer, and insisted the mood would be "optimistic". And by songwriter Martin Gore's recent standards ("I don't want to start any blasphemous rumours . . .") it probably was. Just Can't Get Enough was a long way off now, and it was about to get pushed back even further.

Amid soaring pinnacles of synthi-symphonic grandeur, *Music For The Masses* emerged as an album of tight corners, dark rooms and deeply private ruminations, voiced through some of Gore's most oblique lyrics yet. New York's Village Voice condemned the militaristic lope of Never Let Me Down Again as "a metaphor for drugs or gay sex" (but omitted mention of the coy tribute to Soft Cell's Torch in the song's coda); others saw the fragile Little 15 as an open endorsement of paedophilia. The Things You Said spat betrayal through sharp, broken teeth; and the understated Behind The Wheel traced its text down similar corridors to the earlier Master And Servant – but without the whiplash smile. Gore, it appeared, was no stranger to the *demimonde* of S&M imagery and fatal attractions.

If Gore's lyrics were left wide open to interpretation, however, in the studio there was no room for manoeuvre. Even his bandmates were simply handed his demos and, according to

Record label:
Mute

Produced
by Depeche Mode and David Bascombe

Recorded
at Studio Guillauhme Tell, Paris; Konk, London; spring 1987

Release date:
October, 1987

Chart peaks:
10 (UK) 35 (US)

Personnel:
Andrew Fletcher (k), Martin Gore (k), Alan Wilder (k), David Gahan (v)

Track listing:
Never Let Me Down Again (S); The Things You Said, Strangelove (S); Sacred; Little 15 (S); Behind The Wheel (S); I Want You Now; To Have And To Hold; Nothing; Pimpf.

Running time:
44.32

Current CD:
STUMM 47 adds: Agent Orange, Never Let Me Down Again (Aggro Mix), Spanish Taster, Pleasure Little Treasure

Further listening:
Black Celebration (1986), Violator (1990)

Further reading:
Depeche Mode: A Biography (Steve Malins 1999)

Andy Fletcher, instructed simply to "Copy what he'd done." Only in the search for sounds and samples did Gore permit the others to contribute, and *Music For The Masses* overflows with the delirium of that freedom, a pantechnicon of clattering kitchenware, tinkling toys and somewhere, what Alan Wilder described as "a pygmy doing his wail . . . turned into something that sounds nothing like a pygmy". The first time *Music For The Masses* fell onto the turntable, that just about summed up Depeche Mode as well.

It would not be lost on them that the darker they became the more success they achieved. Indeed that proved to be a disastrous equation for them on a personal level. But by the time of *Violator*, another helping of oddly upbeat nihilism, they were one of the very biggest pop groups in the world, and the saccharine jingles of their early days were unimaginable.

Bruce Springsteen
Tunnel Of Love

Springsteen veers from stadium-size music and socio-political context to sing of men and women, love and fear.

Since 1984, Springsteen had been through the mill. A huge world tour. Rival American presidential contenders claiming Born In The USA as personal endorsement. Chrysler trying to buy him – or, rather, *that* song again – for $12 million. Rejecting these advances, he had nonetheless succumbed to a degree of hubris when compiling a five-LP live set. On the other hand, he had tackled one declared problem – emotional isolation – by marrying actress Julianne Phillips on May 13, 1985. About two years on, in his home studio, within three weeks he wrote and recorded most of *Tunnel Of Love* (bar One Step Up and a few E Street Band member overdubs).

He told an interviewer he wanted to write romantic songs that "took in the different types of emotional experiences in any relationship where you are really engaging with that other person and not involved in a romantic fantasy or intoxication". His themes – explicitly in Two Faces and Brilliant Disguise – were "the twin issues of love and identity", set against an urgent sense of "the passage of time". Everything about the record reflected an awareness, unusual among artists of any sort, that his audience was "moving on as I was", rather than demanding endless remakes of *Born To Run*.

This produced a luminous honesty. He regularly had to deny that the songs were "literally autobiographical", but their essence plainly came from the bone marrow of his marriage. The Rambo figure of the *Born In The USA* tour metamorphosed into a stoic assailed by fundamental doubts. In One Step Up ("and two steps back") he just doesn't know how to resolve his "dirty little war" of a relationship; in Cautious Man he leaves the marriage bed in the middle of the night, sees "nothing but road" ahead and slips back while his wife still sleeps; in Tougher Than The Rest, despite everything, he swears he will go the real-life distance "if you're rough and ready for love"; in All That Heaven Will Allow and Valentine's Day he simply offers love in hope. *Tunnel Of Love* is one of rock's most profoundly felt albums. Every quiet, sparsely elegant song reaches to the soul of common experience.

Springsteen toured *Tunnel Of Love* with The E Street Band, then broke it up. Within a year of the album's release, he was divorced and beginning another dark night of confusion not

Record label:
CBS

Produced
by Bruce Springsteen, Jon Landau and Chuck Plotkin.

Recorded
at Springsteen's home, Rumson, New Jersey (except One Step Up, recorded at A&M Studios, Los Angeles); January–February and April 1987.

Released:
October 1987

Chart peaks:
1 (UK) 1 (US)

Personnel:
Bruce Springsteen (v, g); Max Weinberg (d, pc); Danny Federici (o); Garry Tallent (b); Nils Lofgren (g, bv); Roy Bittan (syn); Patti Scialfa, Clarence Clemons (bv); James Wood (hm); Toby Scott (e)

Track listing:
Ain't Got You; Tougher Than The Rest; All That Heaven Will Allow; Spare Parts (S); Cautious Man; Walk Like A Man; Tunnel Of Love (S); Two Faces; Brilliant Disguise; One Step Up (S); When You're Alone; Valentine's Day

Running time:
46.28

Current CD:
4602702

Further listening:
The Ghost Of Tom Joad (1995) – the next time he found his voice for a whole album. Darkness On The Edge Of Town (1978) and Born In The USA (1984)

Further reading:

MOJO 17, 62; Songs by Bruce Springsteen (1998); Born In The USA: Bruce Springsteen And The American Tradition (Jim Cullen, 1997); It Ain't No Sin To be Glad You're Alive: The Promise Of Bruce Springsteen (Eric Alterman, 1999); www.backstreets.com.

resolved until he settled down with backing singer Patti Scialfa and, perhaps, accepted his share in "the beauty of God's fallen light" so carefully depicted by Cautious Man.

George Michael
Faith

Former teen idol comes good on his solo debut, in a welter of lust and pained remorse.

George Michael is a bit of a depressive, or he was in the early '80s. The Wham! years had been rampant but not stress-free, and "I had to get away from the whole up-up-up thing because I felt so down." He and Andrew Ridgeley shook hands amicably enough but Michael remained too low to move forward, and hid out in LA getting wrecked on booze and ecstasy. It was only when Ridgeley paid a visit and, during an alcohol-soaked session, Michael poured out his woes, that he began to regroup. "I changed my mind about carrying on, about playing the game. I decided I'd do it all over again, but this time, on my terms."

Two painstaking years went into writing and producing *Faith*, which was to be seen as a turning point, replacing the image of the grinning pop idiot with that of a sophisticated adult. The chosen look was hoodlum chic: designer stubble, torn jeans and a leather jacket (on the sleeve, George has his nose stuck under his arm as if staggered by the reek of pheromones). Said Ridgeley, "I never understood why he wanted to portray that image – the brooding, macho guy. That's not him."

The music was an even bigger surprise. Michael had released two solo singles, heart-on-the-sleeve ballads Careless Whisper and A Different Corner. I Want Your Sex, *Faith's* first single, discussed a different anatomical location. Pumping along on a testosterone-fuelled riff and punctuated by grunts, it was banned by the BBC and hammered for recklessness in the age of AIDS. There was, however, a moral logic.

Michael: "Sex in rock'n'roll is always sex with a stranger, it's the idea that there is nothing erotic at all about your boyfriend or girlfriend." I Want Your Sex was about "fucking within a relationship with someone you know and want to be with, yet you can't keep your hands off them."

The theme of swooning, mature commitment continued with the likes of Father Figure and One More Try. For anxious publisher Dick Leahy, reassurance that his boy knew what he was about came when he heard what would be the second single. "George had just a bit of an intro, the intro to the track Faith. I told him, in the '50s, all we did was: you go into a guitar lick, you go back to the bridge, and then intro the chorus. Two and a half minutes. So why not make a '50s record? Next day I went to the studio and he played me Faith. He said, 'You mean like that?' Cheeky sod."

Record label:
Epic

Produced
by George Michael.

Recorded
at Sarm West and Puk Studios, 1986.

Released:
November 14, 1987

Chart peaks:
1 (UK) 1 (US)

Personnel:
George Michael (v, b, k); Deon Estus (b); Ian Thomas (d); Lee Fothergill (g); Hugh Burns (g); Robert Ahwai (g); Danny Schogger (k); Chris Cameron (p); Shirley Lewis (bv); John Altman, Mark Chandler, Steve Waterman, Malcolm Griffiths, Jamie Talbot, Steve Sidwell, Rick Taylor (horns); Chris Porter (e)

Track listing:
Faith (S); Father Figure (S); I Want Your Sex (S); One More Try (S); Hard Day; Hand To Mouth; Look At Your Hands; Monkey (S); Kissing A Fool (S)

Running time:
58.09

Current CD:
4600002

Further listening:
Older (1996) is an assured and wistful take on personal pain. In the light of George's 1998 outing it can be seen as a landmark record about ageing, AIDS bereavement, and the friction between public and private personae. Ladies And Gentlemen (1998) gives you 30 of George's best, including collaborations with Astrud Gilberto, Elton John and Mary J Blige.

Further reading:
Bare (Tony Parsons, 1991) is thorough but, inevitably, misses out on the bereavements that inform Older, and the 1998 outing.

Leonard Cohen
I'm Your Man

Comeback which redefined the erstwhile king of the bedsit bards as a careworn, comic observer of modern mores.

By his own admission, Leonard Cohen had "lost his voice" sometime in the '70s, started to regain it on 1985's *Various Positions*, but was only really restored to full artistic vigour three years later with *I'm Your Man*, the ninth and finest album of his long and distinguished career. Apologising for his slow workrate (he took two years to write the previous album's highlight Hallelujah, for instance), he explained, "It just seems to take me a long time to bring things to completion. I generally do a book between albums."

Reflecting his peripatetic bohemian lifestyle, the album was recorded in various studios in Paris, Montreal, New York and Los Angeles, and featured the newly computer-literate songwriter's most successful forays into new music technology, with synthesizer and drum-machine replacing the acoustic guitar of earlier albums. The songs, too, seemed to reflect a new sense of resolution and self-confidence, from the opening intellectual battle-cry of First We Take Manhattan to the Zen-like equanimity of the closing Tower Of Song, one of the finest pieces ever written about the lonely predicament of the writer's existence. Throughout, Cohen's wry wit found its perfect medium in his dry, slightly sinister baritone, itself the cue for one of the album's more amusing lines, when he acknowledges sardonically that he was "born with the gift of a golden voice".

"A lot of us don't know how to sing according to certain standards," he told Q magazine, "but there is a whole tradition of music where you just want to hear the man telling a story as accurately and as authentically as you can. That's why people like me can get away with making records. There are certain times when I feel that my voice is absolutely appropriate for the song, like in Tower Of Song."

And, he might have added, in the title track, as devotedly romantic a song as this legendary ladies' man has ever written. Ultimately, the secret to *I'm Your Man*'s success may be the authentically personal ring to the material, which evokes the singer's character in a more multi-dimensional manner than before. "When [a song's] really personal, everybody understands it," Cohen explained. "There's a middle ground which is just unzipping and self-indulgence, but when you really tell the truth people immediately perceive that. Like when I wrote I Can't

Record label:
CBS

Produced
by Leonard Cohen with Roscoe Beck, Michel Robidoux and Jean-Michel Reusser.

Recorded
at Studio Tempo, Montreal; DMS Studios, Montreal; Studio Montmartre, Paris; Soundworks, New York; Stagg Street Studio, Los Angeles; Rock Steady, Los Angeles; Studio 55, Los Angeles, 1987.

Released:
February 1988

Chart peaks:
48 (UK) None (US)

Personnel:
Leonard Cohen (v, k); Jeff Fisher (k); Larry Cohen (k); Michel Robidoux (k, d); Peter Kisilenko (b); Vinnie Colaiuta (d); Tom Brechtlein (d); Lenny Castro (pc); Bob Stanley (g); John Bilezikjian (oud); Raffi Hakopian (vn); Sneaky Pete Kleinow (ps); Jennifer Warnes (v); Anjani (v); Jude Johnstone (v); Ian Terry (e); Roger Guerin (e); Leanne Ungar (e)

Track listing:
First We Take Manhattan (S); Ain't No Cure For Love (S); Everybody Knows; I'm Your Man; Take This Waltz; Jazz Police; I Can't Forget; Tower Of Song

Running time:
41.02

Current CD:
460642 2

Further listening:
Cohen's reputation was founded on his
first three albums Songs Of Leonard
Cohen (1968), Songs From A Room
(1969) and Songs Of Love And Hate
(1971), which remain paradigms of
singer-songwriter soul-mining. Cohen's
revived stock continued to grow with
the mordant The Future (1992), and a
live album (Live,1994) drawing heavily
on his more recent work.

Further reading:
Leonard Cohen: A Life In Art (Ira Nadel,
1994); www.leonardcohen.com

Forget, it started off as a kind of hymn, and I ended up sitting
at this kitchen table thinking, Where am I really? What can I
really tell anyone about anything? So I wrote, 'I stumbled out of
bed / Got ready for the struggle ...'"

Tracy Chapman
Tracy Chapman

An '80s one-off, the black female folk singer whose intimate style went global.

"I just think that people need to understand that if the person next door doesn't have enough food or is about to lose their home, that affects everyone else." This classically simple and sincere protest singer's credo was the improbable basis of Tracy Chapman's (barely six-month) ascent from coffeehouse obscurity in Massachusetts to selling millions of her self-titled debut album. All it took to convert pure intentions into unpredicted commercial bonanza was two spots on the Nelson Mandela tribute concert at Wembley Stadium, the second a lucky accident when she was pushed back on because thieves had whipped some of Stevie Wonder's keyboard programmes.

But for all the industry hand-rubbing at the time, the album remains a pristine realisation of everything burning in a young artist's heart and soul. Born in 1964, she was raised by a single mother in a Cleveland, Ohio ghetto during the latter part of the civil-rights-campaign era, the background to Across The Lines. If that forged her, she then found her musical outlets in a completely different setting. At 16, she was awarded a scholarship to a private school in Connecticut, and subsequently graduated to Tufts University in Medford, Massachusetts. There she studied anthropology and found a home for her songs on the New England coffeehouse circuit. Later, fame sometimes brought graceless questions implying she had somehow invaded a white musical neighbourhood. Naturally, she answered pithily that music had no colour bars: "Folk music comes from an Anglo and Afro tradition. People forget that blacks in this country have a folk music and a history."

Spotted busking on the street, she was quickly signed to Elektra Records and Elliot Roberts' management (he had handled Neil Young, Bob Dylan and Joni Mitchell, whose then husband Larry Klein played bass on *Tracy Chapman*).

Experienced and versatile producer David Kershenbaum accepted the integrity of a very enclosed young artist and so let the songs do the work, from the contained anger of protest and social obervation in Talkin' 'Bout A Revolution and Fast Car to the achingly restrained love song For My Lover and the pained delicacy of Behind The Wall, which concerned child abuse. As Kershenbaum said at the time, "What was difficult was holding back from adding things. What Tracy wanted was to keep the songs earthy and rootsy. I don't think many people have made a record this naked."

Record label:
Elektra

Produced
by David Kershenbaum.

Recorded
at Powertrax, Hollywood, California; 1987.

Released:
April 1988

Chart peaks:
I (UK) I (US)

Personnel:
Tracy Chapman (v, g, pc); David LaFlamme (vn); Ed Black (sg); Paulinho Da Costa (pc); Danny Fongheiser (pc); Jack Holder (o, dobro, dulcimer, sitar, p, g); Larry Klein (b); Bob Marlette (k); Steve Kaplan (k, hm)

Track listing:
Talkin' 'Bout A Revolution (S); Fast Car (S); Across The Lines; Behind The Wall; Baby Can I Hold You (S); Mountains O'Things; She's Got Her Ticket; Why?; For My Lover; If Not Now . . .; For You

Running time:
35.51

Current CD:
60774-2

Further listening:
Crossroads (1989)

Further reading:
www.elektra.com/retro/chapman/index.html

The Go-Betweens

16 Lovers Lane

UK-resident Australians return home to finally make the feelgood pop album they've threatened throughout their ten-year career.

A favourite of English undergraduates; they dropped references to Plath, Genet and Joyce in their lyrics; and one of their two frontmen wore dresses on stage. None of these things are in themselves surprising, of course. It's just that when Brisbane teenagers Robert Forster and Grant MacLennan formed The Go-Betweens, they wanted to be pop stars. "Whenever I think of The Monkees," wrote Forster on the sleeve of their 1978 debut, "it's a sunny morning, Last Train To Clarksville has been written, and we are left with our own imperfection." This didn't stop them trying to emulate it. For most of the '80s, no music press critics' poll was complete without that year's Go-Betweens offering. Fans (among them Morrissey and R.E.M.) seemed perplexed at the commercial failure of claustrophobic, lovelorn classics like Tallulah and Before Hollywood. A move to London opened a seam of emotionally tangled lit-pop (and enough interpersonnel intrigue to rival Fleetwood Mac) but it was only when Forster and MacLennan returned to Australia that they relaxed enough to write that quintessential pop album.

"There was definitely a sense of it being a big party," says MacLennan. "We were back in Australia, away from the rain of London. We'd made so much of our best music in London but we hadn't been happy. I suppose that people think great albums should come from pain and misery but this was the opposite." No Go-Betweens record illustrates better than *16 Lovers Lane* how healthy competition between two songwriters can be. Both Forster and MacLennan had fallen in love and didn't care who knew it. "I don't want to let you onto your flight/The fortune teller might have been right," sighed MacLennan on The Devil's Eye, strumming a battered $25 acoustic. Not to be outdone, Forster crooned, "I'm ten feet underwater/Standing in a sunken canoe. But still the sun it finds/A place to light me" (Love Is A Sign). In producer Mark Wallis, the eccentric Forster had found his match. Wallis demanded that he sing the mournful Dive For Your Memory on the roof of the studio building. Drummer Lindy Morrison hated Wallis, mainly because he replaced her with a machine on five songs. In fairness though, his decision works well with the

Record label:
Beggars Banquet

Produced
by Mark Wallis.

Recorded
at Studios 301, Sydney, Australia;
May 1988.

Released:
August 1988

Chart peaks:
81 (UK) None (US)

Personnel:
Robert Forster (v, g, hm); Grant MacLennan (v, g); Lindy Morrison (d); Amanda Brown (vn, oboe, g, v); John Willsteed (b, g, Hammond organ, p)

Track listing:
Love Goes On!; Quiet Heart; Love Is A Sign; You Can't Say No Forever; The Devil's Eye; Streets Of Your Town (S); Clouds; Was There Anything I Could Do? (S); I'm Allright; Dive For Your Memory

Running time:
37.05

Current CD:
BBL 2006 CD

Further listening:
Liberty Belle And The Black Diamond Express (1986); Tallulah (1987); Go-Betweens 1978–1990 (1990); Robert Forster, Danger In The Past (1990)

Further reading:
The Go-Betweens (David Nichols, 1997); www.users.dircon.co.uk/~jturner/gbroot.htm

should've-been summer hit Streets Of Your Town. After touring *16 Lovers Lane* for a year, The Go-Betweens inked a new deal with Capitol, but on reflection there was nowhere to go. They'd finally completed an album full of the sort of songs they'd aspired to as teenagers.

"Stylistically," mused Forster, "that's the only way we could end. Normally when a band splits up and it's two song-writers you assume that it's the two songwriters who broke up, but it was Grant and I breaking away from the rest of the band. We'd just had enough of everyone else."

An embittered Lindy Morrison summed up their legacy in disparaging terms. "The only people we appealed to were a fistful of wanky journalists and some university students." She had a point, but when Forster and MacLennan reconvened in 2000 for a new Go-Betweens album, she wasn't invited.

Talk Talk
Spirit Of Eden

For their fourth album a London-based pop band travel to previously uncharted territory.

Few could have been prepared for the exquisite and extra-ordinary design of this music. Most listeners of the day thought of Talk Talk as purveyors of yearning synth-pop: It's My Life, Today and the piano-powered groove of Life's What You Make It. But there were one or two clues of what was about to happen for anyone who was paying attention: that latter single's skeletal B-side, It's Getting Late In The Evening and the diaph-onous April 5th or spare Chameleon Day on their hit album *Colour Of Spring* (1986). Following that album's success, Talk Talk frontman Mark Hollis decided he'd tired of pop music and sought a totally new way of working. Under the influence of producer and collaborator Tim Friese-Greene — who had devel-oped his interest in composers like Messiaen, Stockhausen and Cage — Hollis explored the form's outer limits. But it took time to get there. The album was almost complete when Hollis decided it was too much like a rock record and opted to erase the whole thing. With the slate clean, they edged towards the new sound they'd imagined. "Working with space, the idea of the geography of sound was important," says Hollis, "and deciding that we'd treat one side of the album as one whole piece."

Focussing on subtlety and restraint, they constructed new, transparent basic tracks and invited guest musicians to embellish them. One was violin prodigy Nigel Kennedy who found it hard to break out of his virtuoso noodling. Friese-Greene made him play less by gaffer-taping together the fingers on his left hand. On another occasion that has entered into studio lore, the team spent a long and expensive day recording a large brass section and kept only the sound of a trumpeter clearing spit from his mouthpiece.

When all the guests were recorded, the tracks were montaged and sculpted for weeks until the final songs emerged. There were suggestions of Stockhausen in the fragmentary arrangements and echoes of John Lee Hooker in the expressive, percussive guitar, but overall there was a jazz ambience, some-thing akin to Miles Davis' In A Silent Way, a palpable sense of musicians in a room, of instruments resonating against one another, of air being pushed around. The cavernous live-room at Wessex studios — a former church — was the perfect environ-

Record label:
Parlophone

Produced
by Tim Friese-Greene.

Recorded
at Wessex Studios, London; June 1987–August 1988.

Released:
September 1988

Chart peaks:
19 (UK) None (US)

Personnel:
Mark Hollis (v, p, o, g); Lee Harris (d); Paul Webb (b); Tim Friese-Greene (harmonium, p, o, g); Martin Ditcham (pc); Robbie McIntosh (dobro, 12-string g); Mark Feltham (hm); Simon Edwards (Mexican bass); Danny Thompson (db); Henry Lowther (t); Nigel Kennedy (v); Hugh Davies (shozygs); Andrew Stowell (bassoon); Michael Jeans (oboe); Andrew Marriner (clarinet); Christopher Hooker (cor anglais); The choir of Chelmsford Cathedral; Phill Brown (e).

Track listing:
The Rainbow/Eden/Desire; Inheritance; I Believe In You; Wealth

Running time:
41.24

Current CD:
RETALK103

Further listening:
The Colour Of Spring is a magnificent pop record and a dry run for this sound, if a little more typically '80s. Laughing Stock (1991) took the experi-ment even further out. By the time of solo album Mark Hollis (1997), Hollis' work was entirely acoustic. Apparently, he has given up making records to learn the clarinet.

Further reading:
MOJO 51

ment, and Hollis credits engineer Phill Brown, a veteran who'd worked under Hendrix/Yes maestro Eddie Kramer, with capturing its ambience. Brown had approached them after hearing *Colour Of Spring* and maintains that making *Spirit Of Eden* was one of the most intense experiences of his career, also recalling how they customised the control room for maximum atmospheric effect.

"It was very psychedelic," he remembers. "We had candles and oil wheels, strobes going, sometimes just total darkness in the studio. You'd get totally disorientated, no daylight, no time frame. I lost a year of my life to that record, but what a record!"

Mary Margaret O'Hara

Miss America

First — and, to date, final — album of idiosyncratic avant-torch songs from a thoroughly singular artist.

Mary Margaret O'Hara appeared to have been doing fine ploughing her own low-key furrow until she put this out, and came face to face with criticism of the cruellest, most personal sort. Born in Toronto, she joined rock band Songship in 1976, later renaming them Go Deo Chorus. As lead singer, she wrote many of the songs that would appear on *Miss America*, and developed a wild stage manner of scat-style ad-libbing while flapping one arm like a flag, the other limp at her side. She quit Go Deo in '83, but a demo tape drew Virgin's attention, and she was signed in '84. She went into the studio that November, with XTC's Andy Partridge producing; he left after a day. Guitarist Rusty McCarthy explains what may have thrown him: "She might have her rhythm section switching beats, bass playing backwards or bass in 3/4 time and drums in 4/4." Only four tracks (all ballads) were accepted by Virgin, who insisted on something more marketable. There followed a lengthy stand-off, during which O'Hara wrote more, but nothing that pleased the label. Then, in October 1987, experimental guitarist and composer Michael Brook saw her live and offered to help mix and produce. The result was an album of sensuous singing, unorthodox arrangements and a brave emotional range – from the quivering nerves of Year In Song, whose broken and repeated phrases suggest a mind about to fracture, to the yearning To Cry About and the consoling lullaby You Will Be Loved Again. With elements of jazz and country, and the "troubled AOR" of Not Be Alright and Body In Trouble, the album seemed to have realised all that O'Hara intended; she chose the title "because I thought the record was so much unlike what those two words together said."

But Virgin wasn't happy. Though UK reviews were glowing, the album failed to chart. American critics, however, took badly to its audacity: one called her "Annie Hall with a lobotomy", commenting on her anxious live performance, another said "Dementia's not something a crowd expects of a singer-songwriter." Virgin gave the album little support and let it die. (It was repackaged and reissued by Koch in 1996.) Apart from a handful of guest spots, the fragile Miss O'Hara – a force of nature who can deliver with accomplishment – has tragically, but understandably, kept her distance from the record industry ever since.

Record label:
Virgin

Produced
by Mary Margaret O'Hara and Michael Brook.

Recorded
at Rockfield Studios, Monmouth, Wales; Phase One Studios, Toronto, Canada; Comfort Sound, Toronto, Canada.

Released:
October 1988

Chart peaks:
None (UK) None (US)

Personnel:
Mary Margaret O'Hara (v); Rusty McCarthy (g); Michael Brook (infinite g); Don Rooke (s); Hugh March (vn); David Piltch, Hendrik Riik (b)

Track listing:
To Cry About; Year in Song; Body's In Trouble; Dear Darling; A New Day; When You Know Why You're Happy; My Friends Have; Help Me Lift You Up; Keeping You in Mind; Not Be Alright; You Will Be Loved Again

Running time:
46.00

Current CD:
CDV2559

Further listening:
The Christmas EP (three covers, one original) came out on Virgin in 1991, and has also been reissued by Koch (KOC-CD 7935). She appears frustratingly low in the mix on Morrissey's single November Spawned A Monster (May 1990). Other than her floating membership of Toronto's The Henrys – seek out Chasing Grace (1996) and Desert Cure (1998) – and occasional contributions to soundtracks and compilations, that's it.

Further reading:
www.google.com

Keith Richards
Talk Is Cheap

Stone going it alone makes best Stones album in ages.

K eith Richards had never thought of making a solo album until Mick Jagger announced that he didn't want to tour *Dirty Work*, going off instead to cut his own second solo project, *Primitive Cool*, Keith killed time by producing a rip-snorting version of Jumpin' Jack Flash for Aretha Franklin and acting as chief instigator and bandleader on the superb Chuck Berry movie Hail! Hail! Rock and Roll! Richards' accomplice on these ventures was a dreadlocked New York drummer in the David Letterman house band, Steve Jordan. Richards and Jordan began hanging out in New York, jamming and writing in a little studio on Broadway.

"That's where Steve and I became real tight," says Richards. "When you write with someone, you really get to know them. I'd only ever written with Mick before – apart from a few other things, like with Gram Parsons – and suddenly Steve and I had some songs. And then the idea came, y'know: let's make a record." As the writing progressed, the "cute pink room" at Studio 900 became a kind of clubhouse, and a band, the X-Pensive Winos, began to coalesce around Richards and Jordan. Waddy Wachtel was a veteran LA guitarist and bandleader with whom Keith and Steve had long wanted to work. Charley Drayton was a brilliant young bass player who'd been involved with Jordan in a band called Raging Hormones. And keyboard player Ivan Neville was a scion of the illustrious New Orleans music family. "Almost without realising it, we'd put together this incredible machine, this band that was so hot nobody could believe it," says Keith. "After the first night, we looked at each other and it was like we'd been playing together ten years. And then I was hooked."

The ideas came thick and fast – the funk riffs of Big Enough and It Means A Lot, the slow soul of Make No Mistake and Locked Away, the dragging, booze-loosened bar-band rock of Take It So Hard – but they took a while to become songs. "The trouble with me is I leave songs in a sort of half-finished state till somebody grabs it and says, Yeah!" admits Richards. "I have to wait for somebody to react to something that's coming out of me. If I get enthusiasm, then that turns me on and I think, well, maybe I ain't stupid after all."

"My job up to that point had been writing songs for Mick to sing," says Richards. "I'd been confining songwriting to

Record label:
Virgin

Produced
by Keith Richards, Steve Jordan

Recorded
at Air, Montserrat; Le Studio, Montreal.

Chart Peaks:
37 (UK) 24 (US)

Release date:
autumn 1988

Personnel:
Keith Richards (v, g), Steve Jordan (d, bv), Waddy Wachtel (g), Charley Drayton (b, bv), Ivan Neville (k), Sarah Dash (v, bv). Bootsy Collins (b), Bernie Worrell (o, Clavinet), Bobby Keys (s), Maceo Parker (as), Chuck Leavell (o), The Memphis Horns (horns), Stanley "Buckwheat" Dural (accordion), Patti Scialfa (bv), Sam Butler (bv), Michael Doucet (vn), Johnnie Johnson (p), Joey Stampinato (b), Mick Taylor (g)

Track listing:
Big Enough; Take It So Hard; Struggle; Could Have Stood You Up; Make No Mistake; You Don't Move Me; How I Wish; Rockawhile; Whip It Up; Locked Away; It Means A Lot

Running time:
47.06

Current CD:
Virgin CDV2554

Further listening:
Live At The Hollywood Palladium (1991); Keef and his Winos on the get-out-of-jail free tour.

Further reading:
Keith (Stanley Booth, Bob Gruen 1996)

that point of view. So I guess really what *Talk Is Cheap* did for me was that suddenly I could take them in my direction. Most of the songs Mick could have sung, but they wouldn't have taken such funny, quirky leaps, because I just sing differently and I hear different melodies." The album sounded to many ears like the best Stones album the Stones never made. Yes, there was filler on it — Struggle, How I Wish and Whip It Up — but the rest was the pure, unadulterated Keith many of us had longed to hear, free of Jagger's posturings. As for the extraordinary *J'accuse* of You Don't Move Me, as acerbic as Lennon's anti-Macca How Do You Sleep? it may have been, but it was also full of genuine pain at what the Stones had allowed to leak away over the decades. ("Mick's never mentioned it to me, but Bernard Fowler told me that when he was on tour in Australia he'd walk out of the room every time someone put the album on. And hey, I've got a couple of others in reserve if he wants more!")

"For everyone involved in *Talk Is Cheap*, I think there was a sense of release," says Richards. "Everybody was doing something they wanted to do. There was a sense that we'd all been let out of school or something. In fact, I felt like I'd just got out of jail."

My Bloody Valentine
Isn't Anything

FX-laden noiseniks torch the late '80s UK independent scene.

B etween 1984 and 1987, My Bloody Valentine tried everything. Having uprooted from their native Dublin, guitarist/songwriter Kevin Shields and drummer Colm O'Ciosoig, with original vocalist Dave Conway, ventured to Holland, then Berlin, where they flaunted some Birthday Party-inspired art/noise garage rock.By 1985, they were in London, and increasingly coming under the spell of the shambly, jangly class of 1986 like Primal Scream, The Shop Assistants and, more crucially, The Jesus And Mary Chain. By the time of the 1986 EP, The New Record By My Bloody Valentine, the band – now with bassist Debbie Goodge – had fashioned a bubblegum-like wall of fuzz sound with bowl-cut haircuts to match. Only the words "Turn treble and volume up" on the sleeve hinted at future developments. A couple of singles and the *Ecstasy* mini-LP, issued on The Primitives' Lazy label during 1987, hardly suggested much had changed except, perhaps, acquiring a mild thirst for recognition. The limp vocals and folk-rock-style guitar tended to undercut Shields' assertions that MBV remained subversive – though in concert, he said, "We always made sure that the guitar would hurt people's ears." And those early records? "None of us really liked them," he later claimed. "They always came out clinical and dull."

The band's fortunes were turned around by two events. In the summer of 1987, Bilinda Butcher replaced the outgoing Conway, bringing with her a delicate singing style and an untrained but ambitious guitar technique. And Creation Records, home of contemporary retro-pop, offered them plenty of studio time to develop their ideas. The first fruit of this new liaison was the startling You Made Me Realise 12-inch, which had all the thrills of tough American avant-rockers like Sonic Youth and Dinosaur Jr., plus a willingness to mess with the textures of sound. This was achieved to even greater effect on *Isn't Anything*, a remarkable exercise in sonic disorientation where soothing voices lay deep in the mix, and guitars became disfigured by distortion, sampling and effects. Sensual yet dangerous, robust but ethereal, physical and cerebral, the album – recorded by two women and two men – made opposites collide spectacularly. Whether it was the epic romance (No More Sorry), ocean-bed punk rock (Feed Me With Your Kiss) or

Record label:
Creation

Produced
by My Bloody Valentine.

Recorded
at Foel Studios, Wales, Time Square Studios, The Greenhouse.

Released:
November 1988

Chart peaks:
None (UK) None (US)

Personnel:
Kevin Shields (g, v); Bilinda Butcher (g, v); Colm O'Ciosoig (d); Deb Goodge (b); Dave Anderson (e); Steve Nunn (e); Alex Russell (e)

Track listing:
Soft As Snow (But Warm Inside); Lose My Breath; Cupid Come; (When You Wake) You're Still In A Dream; No More Sorry; All I Need; Feed Me With Your Kiss (S); Sueisfine; Several Girls Galore; You Never Should; Nothing Much To Lose; I Can See It (But I Can't Feel It)

Running time:
37.59

Current CD:
CRECD040

Further listening:
Loveless (1991)

Further reading:
www.expectdelay.com/mbv

alien soundscapes (All I Need), MBV could at last justify Shields' public utterances. "We want to go as far as possible," he said. And they did. The follow-up, *Loveless*, was astonishing – richer, stranger, even more oblique. Extraordinarily, the two singles that preceded it – Soon; the Tremolo EP – gave the band their first taste of chart success. But *Loveless* had cost a fortune to record and didn't sell well enough for Creation to fund a third album.

They signed to Island Records but Shields' obsessive working methods proved too much for the rest of the band who drifted away as the decade wore on. Tales emerged of weeks spent in the studio overdubbing feedback and engineers fleeing the sessions in fear of their hearing. In 1998 Shields reportedly delivered a series of stunning instrumentals but without Bilinda to complete them the music missed a vital component. No follow-up to *Loveless* has ever appeared. In 1999 Shields surfaced at last to work with Primal Scream, appearing on their *Exterminator* album, ironically the final release on Creation Records.

Steve Earle
Copperhead Road

Gravel-throated country singer hits paydirt with his least country record.

E arle's biggest-selling album marked his move from MCA's Nashville division to its LA pop branch – a transfer predicated by his deeper move into rock on 1987's *Exit O*. On this record, with its skull-and-crossbones and army camouflage sleeve, country music – other than the pedal steel and mandolin on the title track and the rootsy rebel rock song Devil's Right Hand, still one of Earle's most popular – often seems only a subtext. A diverse, substantial and unpretentious rock album populated with the kind of small-town characters that made debut *Guitar Town* so compelling – from moonshining white trash to the dope-growing Vietnam vet – *Copperhead Road* includes a track with a drum machine (You Belong To Me), another with The Pogues (Johnny Come Lately), a Christmas single (Nothing But A Child) written to raise money for a children's charity and guest appearances by Telluride, Neil MacColl and ex-Lone Justice singer Maria McKee.

Seven of the 10 songs were recorded with backing band The Dukes in Memphis; Nashville, Earle said, didn't have engineers who could make rock records. The Pogues collaboration was done in London on St Patrick's Day – Earle, who had written the song for the band after befriending them on an earlier UK tour, flew over to join them (along with Joe Strummer and The Specials' horn section) for the encore at a show at London's Town And Country Club before moving the party on to Livingston Studios at the other end of the tube line.

"I wanted to make a record that rocked a lot harder than I'd been able to before, something that was a little closer to the way we sounded live," said Earle, "because I think the first two records are a little tamer than I'd have liked. *Copperhead* is almost two records – it's one of the last records where I was really thinking in terms of vinyl and having two distinct sides, that have a different tone. For that reason, and because I did several things on that record that were outside the norm, *Copperhead* is less cohesive to me as an album and I'm less proud of it and the way it hangs together than almost any other album that I've made." Three million record-buyers, however, disagreed.

Record label:
MCA

Produced
by Steve Earle and Tony Brown.

Recorded
at Ardent Studios, Memphis, Tennessee; Livingstone Studios, London.

Released:
December 1988

Chart peaks:
None (UK) 45 (US)

Personnel:
Steve Earle (v, g, hm, 6-string bass, mandolin); Donny Roberts (g, b); Bill Lloyd (g); Bucky Baxter (ps, ls, dobro); Ken Moore (k); John Jarvis (p); Kelly Looney (b); Custer (d); Neil MacColl (mandolin); Maria McKee; John Cowan; Radney Foster (bv); Telluride and The Pogues (various); Joe Harvey (e)

Track listing:
Copperhead Road; Snake Oil; Back To The Wall; The Devil's Right Hand; Johnny Come Lately; Even When I'm Blue; You Belong To Me; Waiting On You; Once You Love; Nothing But A Child

Running time:
43.36

Current CD:
MCLD 19213

Further listening:
Guitar Town (1986); Train A Comin' (1995); The Mountain (1999)

Further reading:
MOJO 79; www.steveearle.net

New Order
Technique

New Order's post-acid house masterpiece revealed the potential of electronic pop to move both the soul and the feet.

The city's music scene had become synonymous with slate-grey miserablism but when Manchester went to Ibiza, strange and wonderful things occurred.

Previous album *Brotherhood* had represented something of an *impasse* and, following a glut of retrospective releases, New Order had begun looking like a spent force. But from late 1987 onwards, they'd been ingesting exciting new sounds at their own Manchester club, The Hacienda. The acid-house/ecstasy explosion they witnessed gave New Order a new lease of life.

"They're one of Europe's biggest dance-pop groups, but New Order never used to fucking dance," claimed label boss Tony Wilson at the time. "They haven't danced for ten years, and now they dance again."

Sessions began in Ibiza, although the recording was hampered by mammoth amounts of partying (with the non-abstemious likes of the Happy Mondays). Working titles for the new album – Balearic Beat, The Disco One, The Happy One – reflected their fascination with the emerging scene. On returning to England and Peter Gabriel's Real World studio, the music began taking form, encompassing equal, seamlessly joined amounts of dance and guitar rock.

"The great thing that happened," confirmed Tony Wilson, "was Alan Meyerson was able to clothe both the dance tracks and the rock tracks in the same ambient world."

From the pure pop rush of Run to the heart-rending intensity of Vanishing Point, the album underlined Sumner as one of Britain's very finest writers of coolly penetrating melody. As usual, the eventual titles were all but unrelated to tracks. Undecided about which track to release as a single, but needing a title for the sleeve production, they simply chose the title Fine Time only fitting it to the song later. Eventually chosen was the song they'd been calling Balearic Beat, its release accompanied by a video featuring a screen full of tumbling computer-generated capsules and a hilarious Top Of The Pops appearance in which Bernard showed the nation the then-unknown Bez dance.

Lyrically, *Technique* was less fun. Bernard had recently separated from wife Sue and lines like "I worked hard to give

Record label:
Factory

Produced
by New Order.

Recorded
at Mediterranean Studios, Ibiza and Real World Studios, Box, Wilts; summer–autumn 1988.

Released:
January 1989

Chart peaks:
1 (UK) 32 (US)

Personnel:
Bernard Sumner (v, g, k); Peter Hook (b, k); Gillian Gilbert (k); Stephen Morris (d, k); Alan Meyerson, Michael Johnson (e)

Track listing:
Fine Time (S); All The Way; Love Less; Round And Round (S); Guilty Partner; Run (S); Mr Disco; Vanishing Point; Dream Attack

Running time:
39.59

Current CD:
8573 81367-2

Further listening:
Low Life (1985); Brotherhood (1986); Substance (1987)

Further reading:
Dreams Never End (Claude Flowers, 1995) http://slashmc.rice.edu/ceremony

you all the things that you need" (from Love Less) have a sharply autobiographical feel far removed from the opaque *ennui* of old. The usually circumspect Sumner even admitted that the lyrical inspiration was, predominantly, "birds".

"*Technique* is held together by being Bernard's *Blood On The Tracks*," Wilson said. "I think it's their finest album to date."

XTC

Oranges And Lemons

Nine albums in and XTC aren't getting any worse.

Artistically and commercially rejuvenated following the cult success of *Skylarking*, XTC were happy to capitalise on their burgeoning Stateside success by returning to the US with a keen young American producer, Paul Fox, who had impressed with his Culture Club and Yes remixes. With a budget that allowed for families to accompany, XTC decamped to Los Angeles for five months.

Having been kept on a short leash during *Skylarking* by Todd Rundgren, Partridge's expansive imagination was given more room by the relatively inexperienced Fox and the sessions dragged on beyond the patience of the musicians' families (who returned to Swindon after two months), not to mention Virgin, who threatened to pull the plug as the album went £30,000 over budget. Also, the band were in dispute with their former manager and Andy was drinking heavily, morbidly dwelling on the pointlessness of future income given the ongoing litigation. Unusually, he relinquished the mix to Fox, flying home to recuperate.

In the end *Oranges And Lemons* was a startling record which, in contrast to the misleading Yellow Submarine cover, fizzes with timeless pop energy and weighty invention. From the eastern metal romp of Garden Of Earthly Delights, the effortless juggling of the baby/penis metaphor on the sly and breezy Pink Thing, the life-giving/destructive evolution of himself as a Miniature Sun to the awe-inspiring Wilson-esque achievement of Chalkhills And Children, it's Partridge's show and he fills it full of showstoppers, though Moulding's solid songs keep their customary cool among impossibly vibrant company; "I won't rock the boat," he sings significantly in One Of The Millions.

Britain, long-since allergic to XTC's vulgar prowess, virtually ignored the album but the States were more receptive, even tempting the stage-wary Partridge out on a radio tour and pre-Unplugged acoustic TV appearances. With Partridge's performing juices flowing again, Tarquin Gotch, XTC's then-manager had one last attempt to get the band on some proper, money-spinning live shows. He fabricated the idea, with Dave and Colin's connivance, of a tour as XTC with Thomas Dolby taking Partridge's place. Andy: "I had actually suggested they

Record label:
Virgin

Produced
by Paul Fox.

Recorded
at Ocean Way and Summa Studios, Los Angeles; May–September 1988.

Release date:
February 27, 1989

Chart peaks:
28 (UK) 44 (US)

Personnel:
Andy Partridge (v, g); Colin Moulding (v, b); Dave Gregory (v, g, p, k); Pat Mastelotto (d); Mark Isham (t); Paul Fox (p)

Track listing:
Garden Of Earthly Delights; The Mayor Of Simpleton; King For A Day; Here Comes President Kill Again; The Loving; Poor Skeleton Steps Out; One Of The Millions; Scarecrow People; Merely A Man; Cynical Days; Across This Antheap; Hold Me My Daddy; Pink Thing; Miniature Sun; Chalkhills And Children

Running time:
60.51

Current CD:
CDV 2581

Further listening:
English Settlement (1981); Skylarking (1986); Apple Venus Volume 1 (1999)

Further reading:
MOJO 64; XTC Song Stories (XTC and Neville Farmer,1998)

tour without me. But when he said, 'Look we'll get someone in who looks a bit like you and who's got a bit of a name,' that really put my nose out of joint. I said, 'Well, perhaps I could come on for a couple of numbers towards the end' and he said, 'Come on for the whole fucking set, you idiot.' Smelt of ruse." Tarquin Gotch retired gracefully, wished XTC well and left them to their cult status.

De La Soul
3 Feet High And Rising

Dazzling debut from three Amityville, NY friends which turned hip hop on its head.

It's no exaggeration to claim that De La Soul's debut casually pulled the rug out from under the established hip hop scene at the time and stamped upon it the hallmark of a whole new genre. Its release marked the dawning of the self-proclaimed D.A.I.S.Y. (Da Inner Sound, Y'all) Age, which replaced the *braggadocio* of big-hitters like LL Cool J and the comedy capers of The Fat Boys with a totally new mood – soulful, downbeat and playful to the point of whimsy. The trio's self-deprecation was reflected not only in their soft-guy stage names (Trugoy invented his by reversing the name of his favourite food – yogurt), but also in the way they dressed – hippyish and bright, as opposed to their peers' suits or gold chains.

Their music was an equally radical kettle of kippers, infusing hip hop's familiar form with soul, psychedelia, pop, jazz, funk, reggae, even big band and television theme sounds, then wrapping the whole in a game-show format, complete with brief skits and pseudo-ads.

"It was us fooling around, acting like assholes when we were supposed to be getting work done," claims Jolicoeur. "Little did we know how important this fooling around would become."

Almost bewilderingly sample-heavy (Steely Dan, Hall & Oates, Funkadelic and Liberace, for starters) at a time when the practice was still in its infancy, the LP soon plunged De La Soul into seriously hot legal water. The Turtles – a sample of whose You Showed Me turns up on Transmitting Live From Mars layered with snippets of a French language lesson – sued the trio for a hefty sum, marking the end of an age of innocence for rap; no crew would ever use an uncleared sample again.

The success of *3 Feet High . . .* (it made Number One in the American R&B chart) encouraged the three to form a loose collective – The Native Tongues Posse – with like-minded souls A Tribe Called Quest, Queen Latifah, Jungle Brothers, Monie Love and Black Sheep. They went on to release three more albums before the end of the century, but none scaled the vertiginous heights of their debut, 1993's *Buhloone Mind State* marking a particularly disastrous attempt to reclaim earlier groundbreaking territory. This year saw them release a brand-new, goodtime, neo-Daisy-age album, *Art Official Intelligence: Mosaic Thump* allegedly part of a trilogy, but De La Soul's place in hip hop history has been secure since the last millennium.

Record label:
Tommy Boy

Produced
by Prince Paul.

Recorded
at Calliope, New York; 1988.

Released:
March 1989

Chart peaks:
26 (UK) 24 (US)

Personnel:
Posdnuos aka Kelvin Mercer, Trugoy the Dove aka David Jolicoeur, P.A. Pasemaster Mace aka Vincent Mason (v); The Jungle Brothers with Q-Tip (guest v); Al "Game Show" Watts (m, e)

Track listing:
Intro; The Magic Number (S); Change In Speak; Cool Breeze On The Rocks; Can U Keep A Secret; Jenifa Taught Me (Derwin's Revenge); Ghetto Thang; Transmitting Live From Mars; Eye Know (S); Take It Off; A Little Bit Of Soap; Tread Water; Say No Go (S); Do As De La Does; Plug Tunin' (Last Chance To Comprehend); De La Orgee; Buddy; Description; Me, Myself And I; This Is A Recording 4 Living In A Full Time Era (L.I.F.E.); I Can Do Anything (Delacratic); D.A.I.S.Y. Age; Plug Tunin' (original 12" version); Potholes In My Lawn

Running time:
67.25

Current CD:
TBCD1019

Further listening:
De La Soul Is Dead (1991), Art Official Intelligence: Mosaic Thump (2000)

Further reading:
http://multsanta.madvision.co.uk/dela and www.tommyboy.com

Bonnie Raitt
Nick Of Time

Perennial promotion contender belatedly makes it into the big league with smooth, modern blues collection.

Bonnie Raitt was respected as one of the finest slide guitarists of her generation, and possessed of one hell of a blues-rock voice to boot.

Nonetheless, she had never really fulfilled her potential, perhaps because of well-publicised drink and drug problems. After 18 years of paying dues and producing albums of varying quality for Warners, Raitt went straight, signed to Capitol and threw in her lot with producer Don Was.

"In many ways it was like a first album. It was for a new label, and it was my first sober album," Raitt recalls, "It was really refreshing for me to play a lot of guitar and go back to a stripped-down production".

Was's sympathetic, roomy treatment manages to apply a loving pop polish to this strong, varied collection of songs while still packing a bottom-end punch. But ultimately it's Bonnie's performances which make *Nick Of Time* special.

The title track is a self-penned slice of smooth but affecting pop-soul, which acknowledges both the ticking of the female biological clock and Raitt's own narrow escape from artistic and emotional oblivion. Her rendition of John Hiatt's Thing Called Love marries sassy vocals to her even sassier slide: a gritty shimmer of sound that comes from the core of the blues ("I don't just put on an electric guitar – I know how to ride it"). And her lustful tones on the slow-burning funk of Love Letter are hotter than Georgia asphalt. She closes with two marvellously contrasting tracks. On the emotive jazz ballad I Ain't Gonna Let You Break My Heart Again, Herbie Hancock's piano provides beautiful (and sole) accompaniment; The Fabulous Thunderbirds back Raitt's own old-fashioned R&B stomper, The Road's My Middle Name.

Raitt was as surprised as anyone by *Nick Of Time*'s four Grammy successes.

"I figured I might win Rock-Female as a sort of career

Record label:
Capitol

Produced
by Don Was.

Recorded
at Oceanway, Los Angeles; Capitol and Hollywood Sound, Hollywood and The Record Plant, Los Angeles. 1988

Released:
April 1989

Chart peaks:
51 (UK) 1 (US)

Personnel:
Bonnie Raitt (g, v, p); Michael Landau (g); Jerry Lee Schell (g); Arthur Adams (g); John Jorgensen (g); JD Maness (ps); Hutch Hutchinson (b); Chuck Domanico (b); Preston Hubbard (b); Herbie Hancock (p); Scott Thurston (k); Michael Ruff (k); Don Was (k); Ricky Fataar (d, pc); Tony Braunagel (d, pc); Paulinho da Costa (pc); Fran Christina (d); Sir Harry Bowens, Sweet Pea Atkinson, Arnold McCuller, David Crosby, Graham Nash (bv); Marty Grebb(s); Kim Wilson (hm); The Heart Attack Horns: Bill Bergman, Dennis Farias, Greg Smith and John Berry Jr (horns); Ed Cherney (e)

Track listing:
Nick Of Time (S); Thing Called Love (S/UK); Love Letter; Cry On My Shoulder; Real Man; Nobody's Girl; Have A Heart (S, US only); Too Soon To Tell; I Will Not Be Denied; I Ain't Gonna Let You Break My Heart Again; The Road's My Middle Name

Running time:
42.57

Current CD:
CDEST 2095

Further listening:
Give It Up (1972); Green Light (1982);
Luck Of The Draw (1991)

Further reading:
Bonnie Raitt: Just In The Nick Of Time
(Mark Bego, 1995) www.bonnieraitt.com

nod – 'All right Bonnie, you got your shit together.' But best album? Ella Fitzgerald was reading my name! I'll never get over it as long as I live. And if I do, you can shoot me!"

The Stone Roses

The Stone Roses

The album that heralded the start of the 1990s: old-fash-ioned psychedelia meets a newly fashionable drug — ecstasy.

"Proper good times," recalls Ian Brown. "We were in London, recording at night. We'd get a taxi back at seven in the morning and we all shared a house in Kensal Rise. They'd give us £10 a day for food, which was a load for us." The Stone Roses had signed to the nascent Silvertone label in April 1988, telling the company — according to Brown — that they had "30 or 40" songs, when in fact their repertoire contained no more than a large handful. The onus was clearly on Brown and John Squire to get writing, and in the slipstream of the deal, they frenziedly augmented older songs such as I Wanna Be Adored and Made Of Stone with the likes of Bye Bye Badman and Shoot You Down. The rush hardly impaired the quality of the material — a fact not lost on producer John Leckie, hired thanks to the Roses' admiration for his work on the XTC side-project The Dukes Of Stratosphear. "I couldn't wait to get them in the studio," he said, given that the Roses had never experienced a long recording project before, he could reasonably expect them to work with goggle-eyed enthusiasm. As evidenced by footage of the sessions (available on Silvertone's Special Edition of the album), they did just that.

Their joie de vivre also manifested itself in experimen-talism: Don't Stop, Brown's favourite track on the LP, was created by running the demo of Waterfall backwards and embel-lishing the results in real-time; the thrilling coda of I Am The Resurrection was built piece-by-piece, and the song's trebly acoustic guitar — reminiscent of Street Fighting Man — was recorded on a Philips ghetto-blaster. Recording was interrupted for the best part of four months by the release of Made Of Stone as a single and the attendant touring and promotion. After stints at Rockfield and Konk, the Roses and Leckie finally called time on the album in early 1989: "When we'd finished," Brown recalls, "Leckie says, 'This is really good. You're going to make it.' And I remember thinking, I know."

His belief was justified. Though its initial chart-placing was fairly low, the album sold well off the back a series of increasingly successful singles and rapidly became a generational touchstone. With the Happy Mondays, the Roses signalled the first significant "alternative" music crossover since The Smiths; moreover, *après* Madchester (as the movement of similarly amiably blokeish bands came to be known) came the New Lad *deluge*.

Record label:
Silvertone

Produced
by John Leckie.

Recorded
at Battery Studios, North London; June—August 1988; Rockfield Studios, Wales and Konk Studios, London; January 1989.

Released:
April 1989

Chart peaks:
19 (UK) 86 (US)

Personnel:
Alan "Reni" Wren (d, bv); Gary "Mani" Mounfield (b); John Squire (g); Ian Brown (v); Paul Schroeder (e)

Track listing:
I Wanna Be Adored (S); She Bangs The Drums (S); Waterfall (S); Don't Stop; Bye Bye Badman; Elizabeth My Dear; (Song For My) Sugar Spun Sister; Made Of Stone (S); Shoot You Down; This Is The One; I Am The Resurrection (S)

Running time:
48.58

Current CD:
ORE CD 502

Further listening:
Non-LP cuts on Turns Into Stone (1992) and The Complete Stone Roses (1995); pre-LP tracks on Garage Flower (1996)

Further reading:
The Stone Roses And The Resurrection Of British Pop (John Robb, 1997)

Tom Petty
Full Moon Fever

His first solo outing featured a stellar cast — and a couple of Heartbreakers.

When Tom Petty first presented *Full Moon Fever* to MCA, they rejected it. No singles, apparently. Fortunately, Plan B involved a prestigious stint with a neat little combo called The Travelling Wilburys. His blues duly chased, Petty returned to *Fever* a year later, augmenting the tracklisting with Love Is A Long Road, All Right For Now and a note-for-note cover of Gene Clark's Feel A Whole Lot Better. In the interim, there had been staff changes at MCA, so it seemed logical to play the album to the new regime. "They loved it," said Petty at the time. "Go figure."

Though billed as Petty's first "official" solo record, *Fever* featured Heartbreakers Campbell and Tench, and all of The Wilburys bar Dylan. Sadly, Roy Orbison died before the record's release: on its sleeve, Petty thanks him for "advice and support during this LP". The record's guitars are taut and muscular, its drums are Ringo-esque, and six of the songs clock-in under three minutes. As Face In The Crowd and Free Fallin' ably demonstrate, Petty's the master of a writing process akin to musical *haiku*.

Much of the record was recorded at Mike Campbell's home studio, and at "lightning speed". Day one yielded Free Fallin', day two Yer So Bad. As ever, Petty and his co-producer Lynne (who also co-wrote half the record) are up-front about their sources. Apartment Song does a cut 'n' paste job on the drum riff from Holly's Peggy Sue; Petty references Del Shannon's Runaway on Runnin' Down A Dream, then gets Del to appear on the record (he's credited with "farmyard noises"). "The album is a chance for Petty to explore, play and maybe fall on his face without having much at stake," suggested Rolling Stone's review, mindful of the new Heartbreakers album Petty was already working on. In the end *Fever* triumphed in its own right, going triple-platinum and winning him an ASCAP award for Free Fallin'. On the accompanying tour, Petty threatened to pull a New Jersey concert if the authorities didn't allow Greenpeace lobby-access, and I Won't Back Down took on a new resonance. He stood firm; they relented.

Record label:
MCA

Produced
by Jeff Lynne, Tom Petty and Mike Campbell.

Recorded
at MC (Mike Campbell's) Studios, Rumbo Studios, Sunset Sound, Devonshire Studios, Conway Studios, Sound City Studios, Los Angeles; May & November 1988

Released:
June 1989

Chart peaks:
8 (UK) 3 (US)

Personnel:
Tom Petty (v, g, k); Mike Campbell (g, sg, b, k, mandolin); Jeff Lynne (b, g, k, bv); Phil Jones, Jim Keltner (d, pc); Benmont Tench (p); George Harrison (g, bv); Roy Orbison, Howie Epstein (bv); Del Shannon ("farmyard noises")

Track listing:
Free Fallin' (S); I Won't Back Down (S); Love Is A Long Road; A Face In The Crowd; Runnin' Down A Dream (S); Feel A Whole Lot Better; Yer So Bad; Depending On You; The Apartment Song; Alright For Now; A Mind With A Heart Of Its Own; Zombie Zoo

Running time:
39.32

Current CD:
MCD 06034

Further listening:
Wildflowers (1994)

Further reading:
www.tompetty.com

NWA
Straight Outta Compton

Album that took gangsta rap out of the underground and onto the front pages after attracting attention from the FBI.

Hard to believe that at one time Eazy-E, Dr Dre and Ice Cube all fought for the spotlight in one powerhouse aggregation. With MC Ren and DJ Yella, Niggaz With Attitude etched the blueprint for West Coast Gangsta Rap with *Straight Outta Compton*. The album – which appeared three years before the LA riots broke out – was shocking in its graphic depiction of South Central LA street life and unrelenting in its young, African-American male perspective. Without the global consciousness of Public Enemy, their closest competitors, NWA played with explicit and sexist language (courtesy of Ice Cube) and freely-borrowed samples (courtesy of Dre) on songs set to some unusually hard, loud beats, that raged at the reality of death, crime and loss of racial pride. *Straight Outta Compton* connected with a large segment of disenfranchised youth and issued a no-apologies wake-up call to the portion of society detached from the reality of ghetto life.

From the opening, title-cut manifesto, through the "built to last" jam Gangsta Gangsta, NWA delivered the goods from the frontlines with keen reporters' eyes. Sirens screeched, gunshots rat-a-tat-tatted and cop radios interfered, adding to the documentary style. Though Express Yourself (which sampled Charles Wright & The Watts 103rd Street Rhythm Band) and Something 2 Dance 2 (cutting together Planet Rock and Dance To The Music) lightened things up, this was a record which begged to be heard at top volume. And that's how it was in the summer of '89 when it blazed from car stereos and boom boxes.

But the group had its detractors. Ruthless anthem Fuck Tha Police, which outlined police brutality in South Central Los Angeles, found attention in all the wrong places. The Parents' Music Resource Center (PMRC) – the US organisation headed by Senator Al Gore's wife Tipper that campaigned to "sticker" albums whose material they considered questionable – declared it a danger to minors, while the FBI sent the group and record retailers a written warning. Meanwhile, the band members – former drug dealer (now deceased) Eazy-E, a hot-tempered Dre and an unrepentant Cube – were not doing much to sweeten their public image. The controversy helped them notch up sales of three quarters of a million albums before they'd even set foot

Record label:
Ruthless

Produced
by Dr Dre and Yella, executive producer, Eazy-E.

Recorded
and mixed at Audio Achievements, Torrance, CA; 1989.

Released:
August 1989

Chart peaks:
47 (UK) 37 (US)

Personnel:
Dr Dre (m); DJ Yella (DJ); Ice Cube (v); Eazy-E (v); MC Ren (v)

Track listing:
Straight Outta Compton; Fuck Tha Police; Gangsta Gangsta (S); If It Ain't Ruff; Parental Discretion Iz Advised; 8 Ball (Remix); Something Like That; Express Yourself (S); Compton's In The House (Remix); I Ain't Tha 1; Dopeman (Remix); Quiet On Tha Set; Something 2 Dance 2

Running time:
60.24

Current CD:
CDL57102

Further listening:
AmeriKKKa's Most Wanted, Ice Cube (1990); The Chronic, Dr Dre (1993).

on tour, cracking the Top 40 in the US and almost managing the same feat in the UK. Follow-up *Efil4zaggin* went further still, topping the US charts. In Britain its release was delayed after being impounded by the Metropolitan Police's Obscene Publications Squad. The ensuing court case, with Geoffrey Robinson QC of the Oz trial fame defending, was found in the band's favour, their barrister successfully arguing that it was "street journalism" and "the black equivalent of our rugby songs." NWA also found supporters in the rock press, who likened *Straight Outta Compton* to The MC5's and Sex Pistols' watershed, revolutionary battle-cries.

Aerosmith
Pump

A textbook study on how to follow the rock comeback of the decade.

The sleeve shot says it all: two trucks, great hunks of road-worn metal, reared up and fucking. "I was in an elevator one day that had a seat and mirrors", said Steven Tyler of Love In An Elevator, the first of the album's five US hit singles. "It's the greatest place in the world to do it. Plus you might get caught so you come even quicker." The major advantage of their newly cleaned-up, healthy lives, according to Tyler, was that time and energy previously spent chasing the dragon could now be more carnally employed. The other advantage, of course, was an end to the drug-fuelled arguments that almost broke up the band and a new focus on their career that resulted in the unimagined success of their first substance-free album *Permanent Vacation*. Sticking with the winning formula, *Pump* found the band back in Vancouver with producer Bruce Fairbairn and song doctors Jim Vallance (Bryan Adams) and Desmond Child (Bon Jovi), who had helped co-write some of that last album's most memorable tracks. But where on the last album you could at times feel the firm hand of a record company steering the has-been rock stars in the desired commercial direction, this time the energised stars were fully in control.

"There was a lot less of other people," said Joe Perry, "and a lot more of us." With the confidence that comes with mega-platinum success, the band knew what was wanted this time. First they would cut the space between songs. "We thought, let's butt the songs up close together so there's no dead time, no air, just go right into the next song like, 'They're bored! Next song – hurry!'" said Tyler.

Next they fancied branching out a little musically, experimenting with different instruments – "Joe came in and said 'Tuba? Not on my record!'" but the Mexican horns and dulcimers stayed – and with songs like the atmospheric Janie's Got A Gun, so did the lyrics – here, about child abuse. But it was the vigorous, horny Aerosmith of the old days that dominated, as the opening track Young Lust attested – no matter that the frontman would soon celebrate his 40th birthday.

Record label:
Geffen

Produced
by Bruce Fairbairn.

Recorded
at Little Mountain Sound Studios, Vancouver, Canada; 1989.

Released:
September 1989

Chart peaks:
3 (UK) 5 (US)

Personnel:
Steven Tyler (v); Joe Perry (g); Brad Whitford (g); Tom Hamilton (b); Joey Kramer (d); Mike Fraser (e)

Track listing:
Young Lust; F.I.N.E; Going Down; Love In An Elevator (S); Monkey On My Back; Water Song; Janie's Got A Gun; Dulcimer Stomp; The Other Side; My Girl; Don't Get Mad Get Even; Hoodoo; Voodoo Medicine Man; What It Takes

Running time:
47.44

Current CD:
GFLD19255

Further listening:
Rocks (1976); Get A Grip (1993); Nine Lives (1997)

Further reading:
Toys In The Attic: The Rise, Fall And Rise Of Aerosmith (Martom Huxley)
www.aerosmith.com

The Blue Nile

Hats

Enigmatic masters of Glaswegian film noir *finally deliver a masterpiece.*

I Love This Life, a lone single on the RSO label in 1981, announced the arrival of a Scottish trio making minimal but evocative music using, as leader Paul Buchanan remembers, just "a bass, a borrowed drum machine, one guitar, a Farfisa organ and a little one-note synthesizer."

Two years later, on their marvellous debut album, *A Walk Across The Rooftops*, the band's ability to paint vivid pictures from such a basic palette was abundantly evident. Buchanan: "Somewhere there we'd started to think, 'If we put that sound with this other rhythm track it makes you think about a mountain or a little city' and we got very interested in that – the visual aspect – using the instruments to represent the context of the song. For example, Robert's bass part on [the title track] sounded vertical to us, [as if] it was going down in a zigzag like a fire escape would. The guitar on Tinseltown In The Rain we thought sounded like traffic, a general background hubbub outside your window. We avoided anything that the listener would think was just a guy playing a solo on a Gibson or Telecaster." On *Hats* they perfected this technique, creating a glistening cityscape, the songs like long camera pans across its vista of chimneypots, neon lights and rain-washed streets where disenchanted lovers walk at night, wondering what tomorrow will bring. It was introspective, intimate, sentimental and often profoundly sad. Its apparently effortless grace was hard won, however. In the six years since their debut, The Blue Nile had cut and discarded an entire album.

"It just wasn't a true record," says Buchanan of this lost work. "It seemed like a record we made because we'd been booked into a studio to make a record. We fell back on tricks – put more reverb on that, put overdub on that. On our days off, we started to work on other things that seemed to have an authenticity about them that the [album] didn't have. It would've probably fooled everybody for about six weeks, it sounded stupendous, but there was nothing there." Legend says the band held an informal playback for this second album and wiped the tapes as they went through the machine. Buchanan doesn't recall it that way, but confirms the music was erased. "If you're struggling with something and it's just not shaping up, to erase the tape is quite liberating."

Record label:
Linn

Produced
by The Blue Nile and Calum Malcolm.

Recorded
at Castle Sound, Pencaitland 1985–89

Released:
October 1989

Chart peaks:
12 (UK) None (US)

Personnel:
Paul Buchanan (v, k); Robert Bell (b); Paul "PJ" Moore (g); Calum Malcolm (e)

Track listing:
Over The Hillside; The Downtown Lights (S); Let's Go Out Tonight; Headlights On the Parade (S); From A Late Night Train; Seven AM; Saturday Night (S)

Running time:
38.47

Current CD:
LKHCD2

Further listening:
A Walk Across The Rooftops (1983); the purposefully rumpled and, therefore, patchy Peace At Last (1996) which manages at least four great songs.

Further reading:
MOJO 32

Management problems kept The Blue Nile out of the studio for almost a year; when they finally resumed work they cut much of *Hats* in the first five days. The new songs – all credited to Buchanan – concerned the bittersweetness of a life which was falling down around the band's ears, long-term relationships coming to an end, close family passing away. "It was a desperately bad time for us," Buchanan recalls. "Fundamental shifts took place in our personal lives during *Hats*. And so I'd say that record's about reassurance. That's why 'It's all right!' crops up in the lyrics so often. It's patently about someone whose circumstances are far from all right."

The Jungle Brothers
Done By The Forces Of Nature

A less bracing, more embracing companion for Public Enemy's Fear Of A Black Planet.

Melle Mel's immortal line, "It's like a jungle/Sometimes it makes me wonder how I keep from going under," had become part of the rap vernacular, but no one took this metaphor further than The Jungle Brothers. Hip hop rarely sounded funkier than this full-flowering of the Native Tongues' psychedelicised, Afrocentric vision. *Done By The Forces Of Nature*, with its bountifully inclusive rhymes and lushly organic samples, is a virtual concept album in which the ghetto is TransAfrikanExpressed into a fertile black Arcadia.

With their low-budget debut *Straight Out The Jungle* (released in 1988 on the minuscule Warlock label), they set out the bones of their liberal, anti-materialist, autonomous agenda, keying hip hop into the black bohemian tradition of their native Harlem. Now, with a much-expanded sound palete, they fluently and resoundingly filled in the gaps. Acknowledge Your Own History speaks proudly of their African heritage; Black Woman offers a sensual corrective to rap's burgeoning misogyny; the storming pow-wow of Doin' Our Own Dang reunited the Native Tongues collective, an idealised community of like-minded New York rappers De La Soul and A Tribe Called Quest (plus female UK rapper Monie Love) created by Afrika in the image of his namesake's Zulu Nation. Bambaataa senior later returned the compliment claiming, "The Jungle Brothers are taking music in a new direction, and now they're influencing *me.*"

Musically, the entire inheritance of black music – from African guitar textures to the P-Funk snare snap – was thrown into the pot. Rolling Stone was moved to comment that "DJ Sammy B trades in mechanical beats for soulful, funky, often downright African grooves making for some of the most musical rap around." Despite its influential status, the album sold only a moderately respectable 250,000 copies thanks to Warners' half-hearted promotional efforts. After two years touring to boost sales further, the JBs ventured further into avant territory with 1993's frequently astonishing *J Beez Wit The Remedy*. But by then the Native Tongues had fragmented and no one was listening. The late '90s saw them returning as a much-reduced post-big-beat novelty act. Today, their masterpiece *Done By The Forces Of Nature* can be seen as hip hop's premier return to the source.

Record label:
Warner Brothers

Produced
by The Jungle Brothers.

Recorded
at Calliope Studios, New York; spring 1989.

Released:
November 1989

Chart peaks:
41 (UK) None (US)

Personnel:
Mike G (v); Afrika Baby Bambaataa (v); DJ Sammy B (samples); Dr Shane Faber (k, e); Red Alert, Greg Curry, Gregg Mann (e)

Track listing:
Doin' Our Own Dang (S); Beyond This World; Feelin' Alright; Sunshine; What U Waitin' 4? (S); U Make Me Sweat; Acknowledge Your Own History; Belly Dancin' Dina; Good Newz Comin'; Done By The Forces Of Nature; Beeds On A String; Tribe Vibes; J. Beez Comin' Through; Black Woman; In Days 2 Come; Kool According 2 A Jungle Broth

Running time:
59.48

Current CD:
7599-26364-2

Further listening:
Straight Out The Jungle (1988); J Beez Wit The Remedy (1993)

Further reading:
The Vibe History Of Hip Hop (1999); The Hip Hop Years: A History Of Rap (Alex Ogg with David Upshall, 1999); www.junglebrothers.com

Virgo
Virgo

Rare, mysterious and unfeasibly beautiful deep house.

For anyone conversant with black music's history, the story of the early Chicago house scene makes depressingly familiar reading: innovative young black artists change music forever while being comprehensively ripped off by wily businessmen. Early house artists gained neither money nor US fame from their genre-defining records. Those smart enough to cross the Atlantic and forge DJing careers on the burgeoning British rave scene survived, the rest vanished into wounded obscurity.

Such was the case with Merwyn Saunders and Eric Lewis, two Chicago producers who recorded for the legendary Trax label – home to Summer Of Love classics like Marshall Jefferson's House Music Anthem (Move Your Body), Mr Fingers' Can U Feel It? and Jamie Principle's Baby Wants To Ride. Trax was owned by Larry Sherman, who controlled Chicago's only pressing plant, Musical Products, and indulged in some highly dubious business practices, including dispensing entirely with the troublesome matter of contracts or paperwork, pressing records onto old LPs and second-hand vinyl (most original Trax releases are virtually unlistenable for this reason), and, according to Marshall Jefferson, charging aspiring producers for the pleasure of having their records released.

Whether Saunders and Lewis paid for the privilege is unknown, but the duo recorded two remarkable 12" EPs for Trax in 1988: Do You Know Who You Are under the name Virgo 4 and Ride as M.E. The music contained on them was as strange and evocative as the track titles – School Hall, In A Vision, Going Thru Life. At a time when most house music celebrated the primal, sexual urgency of the dancefloor, Saunders and Lewis' tracks sounded wistful and desperately sad. Mournful synth melodies and scattered snatches of guitar echo through the mix, simple piano lines endlessly repeat, drenched in reverb. It was thoughtful, contemplative music in an era of instant-fix, ecstasy-friendly anthems. It was, quite literally, deep house.

In the UK, the two EPs were collected onto this album, released on a short-lived offshoot of the Streetsounds label in a sleeve that looked like a cheap bootleg, and incorrectly credited to Virgo. Despite the sleeve credits, most assumed the album was the work of Marshall Jefferson who had, confusingly, recorded under the Virgo moniker. The record sold in minuscule quantities: even if it hadn't, it's doubtful whether Saunders or Lewis would have ever seen a cent.

Record label:
Radical

Produced
by Merwyn Saunders and Eric Lewis.

Recorded
in Chicago, 1988.

Release date:
1989

Chart peaks:
None (UK) None (US)

Personnel:
Merwyn Saunders (k); Eric Lewis (k)

Track listing:
Do You Know Who You Are (S); In A Vision; Going Thru Life; Take Me Higher; Ride (S); School Hall; Never Want to Lose You; All The Time

Running time:
44.27

Currently unavailable on CD

Further listening:
Various Artists The House That Trax Built (1997)

Further reading:
Altered State (Matthew Collin, 1996); Last Night A DJ Saved My Life (Bill Brewster and Frank Broughton, 1999)